T0180768

Lecture Notes in Computer Science　12939

More information about this subseries at http://www.springer.com/series/7407

Zhe Liu · Fan Wu · Sajal K. Das (Eds.)

Wireless Algorithms, Systems, and Applications

16th International Conference, WASA 2021
Nanjing, China, June 25–27, 2021
Proceedings, Part III

 Springer

Editors
Zhe Liu
Nanjing University of Aeronautics
and Astronautics
Nanjing, China

Fan Wu
Shanghai Jiao Tong University
Shanghai, China

Sajal K. Das
Missouri University of Science
and Technology
Rolla, MO, USA

ISSN 0302-9743 ISSN 1611-3349 (electronic)
Lecture Notes in Computer Science
ISBN 978-3-030-86136-0 ISBN 978-3-030-86137-7 (eBook)
https://doi.org/10.1007/978-3-030-86137-7

LNCS Sublibrary: SL1 – Theoretical Computer Science and General Issues

This Springer imprint is published by the registered company Springer Nature Switzerland AG
The registered company address is: Gewerbestrasse 11, 6330 Cham, Switzerland

Preface

The 16th International Conference on Wireless Algorithms, Systems, and Applications WASA 2021 and its workshops was held in Nanjing Dongjiao State Guest House during June 25–27, 2021. The conference was hosted by the Nanjing University of Aeronautics and Astronautics and co-organized by the Beijing University of Posts and Telecommunications, Tsinghua University, Southeast University, Nanjing University, Hohai University, Shandong University, and the Collaborative Innovation Center of Novel Software Technology and Industrialization. WASA is an international conference on algorithms, systems, and applications of wireless networks. WASA is designed to be a forum for theoreticians, system and application designers, protocol developers, and practitioners to discuss and express their views on the current trends, challenges, and state-of-the-art solutions related to various issues in wireless networks. Topics of interests include, but are not limited to, effective and efficient state-of-the-art algorithm design and analysis, reliable and secure system development and implementations, experimental study and testbed validation, and new application exploration in wireless networks.

The conference received 315 submissions. Each submission was reviewed by at least three Program Committee members or external reviewers. The Program Committee accepted 97 full papers and 63 workshop papers which were included in the conference program. The Program Committee also selected the three best papers: "Deep Reinforcement Learning Based Intelligent Job Batching in Industrial Internet of Things" by Chengling Jiang, Zihui Luo, Liang Liu, and Xiaolong Zheng, "A Robust IoT Device Identification Method with Unknown Traffic Detection" by Xiao Hu, Hong Li, Zhiqiang Shi, Nan Yu, Hongsong Zhu, and Limin Sun, and "TS-Net: Device-free Action Recognition with Cross-modal Learning" by Biyun Sheng, Linqing Gui, and Fu Xiao.

We thank the Program Committee members and the external reviewers for their hard work in reviewing the submissions. We thank the Organizing Committee and all volunteers from the Nanjing University of Aeronautics and Astronautics for their time and effort dedicated to arranging the conference.

July 2021

Zhe Liu
Fan Wu
Sajal K. Das

Organization

General Co-chairs

Bing Chen   Nanjing University of Aeronautics and Astronautics, China

Huadong Ma   Beijing University of Posts and Telecommunications, China

Junzhou Luo   Southeast University, China

Ke Xu   Tsinghua University, China

Program Co-chairs

Zhe Liu   Nanjing University of Aeronautics and Astronautics, China

Fan Wu   Shanghai Jiao Tong University, China

Sajal K. Das   Missouri University of Science and Technology, USA

Local Co-chairs

Baoliu Ye   Nanjing University, China

Fu Xiao   Nanjing University of Posts and Telecommunications, China

Shuai Wang   Southeast University, China

Kun Zhu   Nanjing University of Aeronautics and Astronautics, China

Web Co-chairs

Yanchao Zhao   Nanjing University of Aeronautics and Astronautics, China

Bin Tang   Hohai University, China

Organizing Co-chairs

Lei Xie   Nanjing University, China

Liming Fang   Nanjing University of Aeronautics and Astronautics, China

Publicity Co-chairs

Haipeng Dai   Nanjing University, China

Chi (Harold) Liu   Beijing Institute of Technology, China

| Zhibo Wang | Zhejiang University, China |
| Chenren Xu | Peking University, China |

Publication Co-chairs

| Weizhi Meng | Technical University of Denmark, Denmark |
| Junlong Zhou | Nanjing University of Science and Technology, China |

Steering Committee

Xiuzhen Cheng	American University of Sharjah, UAE
Zhipeng Cai	Georgia State University, USA
Jiannong Cao	Hong Kong Polytechnic University, Hong Kong, China
Ness Shroff	Ohio State University, USA
Wei Zhao	University of Macau, China
PengJun Wan	Illinois Institute of Technology, USA
Ty Znati	University of Pittsburgh, USA
Xinbing Wang	Shanghai Jiao Tong University, China

Technical Program Committee

Ran Bi	Dalian University of Technology, China
Edoardo Biagioni	University of Hawaii at Manoa, USA
Salim Bitam	University of Biskra, Algeria
Azzedine Boukerche	University of Ottawa, Canada
Zhipeng Cai	Georgia State University, USA
Srinivas Chakravarthi Thandu	Amazon, USA
Sriram Chellappan	University of South Florida, USA
Quan Chen	Guangdong University of Technology, China
Xianfu Chen	VTT Technical Research Centre of Finland, Finland
Xu Chen	Sun Yat-sen University, China
Songqing Chen	George Mason University, USA
Soufiene Djahel	Manchester Metropolitan University, UK
Yingfei Dong	University of Hawaii, USA
Zhuojun Duan	James Madison University, USA
Luca Foschini	University of Bologna, Italy
Jing Gao	Dalian University of Technology, China
Xiaofeng Gao	Shanghai Jiao Tong University, China
Jidong Ge	Nanjing University, China
Chunpeng Ge	Nanjing University of Aeronautics and Astronautics, China
Daniel Graham	University of Virginia, USA
Ning Gu	Fudan University, China
Deke Guo	National University of Defense Technology, China
Bin Guo	Northwestern Polytechnical University, China

Meng Han	Kennesaw State University, USA
Suining He	University of Connecticut, USA
Zaobo He	Miami University, USA
Pengfei Hu	Shandong University, China
Yan Huang	Kennesaw State University, USA
Yan Huo	Beijing Jiaotong University, China
Holger Karl	University of Paderborn, Germany
Donghyun Kim	Kennesaw State University, USA
Hwangnam Kim	Korea University, South Korea
Bharath Kumar Samanthula	Montclair State University, USA
Abderrahmane Lakas	UAE University, UAE
Sanghwan Lee	Kookmin University, South Korea
Feng Li	Shandong University, China
Feng Li	Indiana University-Purdue University Indianapolis, USA
Ruinian Li	Bowling Green State University, USA
Wei Li	Georgia State University, USA
Zhenhua Li	Tsinghua University, China
Zhetao Li	Xiangtan University, China
Peng Li	University of Aizu, Japan
Qi Li	Tsinghua University, China
Yaguang Lin	Shaanxi Normal University, China
Zhen Ling	Southeast University, China
Weimo Liu	George Washington University, USA
Jia Liu	Nanjing University, China
Fangming Liu	Huazhong University of Science and Technology, China
Liang Liu	Beijing University of Posts and Telecommunications, China
Hongbin Luo	Beihang University, China
Jun Luo	Nanyang Technological University, Singapore
Liran Ma	Texas Christian University, USA
Jian Mao	Beihang University, China
Bo Mei	Texas Christian University, USA
Hung Nguyen	Carnegie Mellon University, USA
Pasquale Pace	University of Calabria, Italy
Claudio Palazzi	University of Padova, Italy
Junjie Pang	Qingdao University, China
Javier Parra-Arnau	University of Ottawa, Canada
Tie Qiu	Tianjin University, China
Ruben Rios	University of Malaga, Spain
Kazuya Sakai	Tokyo Metropolitan University, Japan
Omar Sami Oubbati	University of Laghouat, Algeria
Kewei Sha	University of Houston - Clear Lake, USA
Hao Sheng	Beihang University, China
Bo Sheng	University of Massachusetts Boston, USA

Tuo Shi	Harbin Institute of Technology, China
Sukhpal Singh Gill	Queen Mary University of London, UK
Junggab Son	Kennesaw State University, USA
Riccardo Spolaor	Shandong University, China
Chunhua Su	University of Aizu, Japan
Violet Syrotiuk	Arizona State University, USA
Guoming Tang	National University of Defense Technology, China
Bin Tang	Hohai University, China
Xiaohua Tian	Shanghai Jiaotong University, China
Luis Urquiza	Universitat Politècnica de Catalunya, Spain
Tian Wang	Huaqiao University, China
Yawei Wang	George Washington University, USA
Yingjie Wang	Yantai University, China
Zhibo Wang	Wuhan University, China
Leye Wang	Peking University, China
Wei Wei	Xi'an University of Technology, China
Alexander Wijesinha	Towson University, USA
Mike Wittie	Montana State University, USA
Kaishun Wu	Shenzhen University, China
Xiaobing Wu	University of Canterbury, New Zealand
Wei Xi	Xi'an Jiaotong University, China
Yang Xiao	University of Alabama, USA
Kun Xie	Hunan University, China
Kaiqi Xiong	University of South Florida, USA
Kuai Xu	Arizona State University, USA
Wen Xu	Texas Woman's University, USA
Lei Yang	The Hong Kong Polytechnic University, China
Panlong Yang	University of Science and Technology of China, China
Changyan Yi	Nanjing University of Aeronautics and Astronautics, China
Wei Yu	Towson University, USA
Dongxiao Yu	Shandong University, China
Sherali Zeadally	University of Kentucky, USA
Deze Zeng	China University of Geosciences, China
Bowu Zhang	Marist College, USA
Yong Zhang	Shenzhen Institutes of Advanced Technology, China
Yang Zhang	Nanjing University of Aeronautics and Astronautics, China
Cheng Zhang	George Washington University, USA
Xu Zheng	University of Science and Technology of China, China
Yanwei Zheng	Shandong University, China
Lu Zhou	Nanjing University of Aeronautics and Astronautics, China
Jindan Zhu	Amazon Web Service, USA
Tongxin Zhu	Harbin Institute of Technology, China
Yifei Zou	University of Hong Kong, China

Contents – Part III

Workshops

Workshops

Event-Based American Sign Language Recognition Using Dynamic Vision Sensor

Yong Wang[1], Xian Zhang[1], Yanxiang Wang[1,2,3], Hongbin Wang[1],
Chanying Huang[2], and Yiran Shen[3(✉)]

[1] College of Computer Science and Technology, Harbin Engineering University,
Harbin, China
{wangyongcs,zhangxian,wanghongbin}@hrbeu.edu.cn
[2] School of Computer Science and Engineering, Nanjing University of Science
and Technology, Nanjing, China
hcy@njust.edu.cn
[3] School of Software, Shandong University, Jinan, China
yiran.shen@sdu.edu.cn

Abstract. American Sign language (ASL) is one of the most effective communication tools for people with hearing difficulties. However, most of people do not understand ASL. To bridge this gap, we propose EV-ASL, an automatic ASL interpretation system based on dynamic vision sensor (DVS). Compared to the traditional RGB-based approach, DVS consumes significantly less resources (energy, computation, bandwidth) and it outputs the moving objects only without the need of background subtraction due to its event-based nature. At last, because of its wide dynamic response range, it enables the EV-ASL to work under a variety of lighting conditions. EV-ASL proposes novel representation of event streams and facilitates deep convolutional neural network for sign recognition. In order to evaluate the performance of EV-ASL, we recruited 10 participants and collected 11,200 samples from 56 different ASL words. The evaluation shows that EV-ASL achieves a recognition accuracy of 93.25%.

Keywords: American Sign Language · Convolutional neural networks · Dynamic vision sensor

1 Introduction

According to the statistics of World Health Organization, around 466 million people worldwide have disabling hearing loss, and it is estimated that by 2050 the number will increase to 900 million. American Sign Language (ASL) is the most adopted approach of communication between people with hearing loss. ASL is convenient and effective. Its signs are represented by hands movements, facial expressions and postures of the body. However, few people with normal hearing ability have sufficient knowledge on ASL, which creates an undeniable communication barrier for people with hearing loss adapting into communities. In order

Z. Liu et al. (Eds.): WASA 2021, LNCS 12939, pp. 3–10, 2021.
https://doi.org/10.1007/978-3-030-86137-7_1

to break the obstacle, we present an automatic ASL recognition approach based on dynamic vision sensor (DVS), EV-ASL. ASL recognition has been intensively studied on conventional RGB cameras [5,6,13]. Different from RGB camera, the pixels of DVS work independently and produce asynchronous event stream only when intensity changes are detected. A number of characteristics make EV-ASL superior to RGB-based approaches. First, DVS only detects intensity changes, the hands movement can be conveniently extracted without operating computationally intensive background subtraction. It consumes significantly less resources (energy, computation, bandwidth) than RGB-based approach which enables more pervasive implementation on resource-constrained devices and minimal impact on battery life. Second, DVS sensor has high dynamic range so that EV-ASL can be used smoothly under challenging lighting conditions while RGB-based approaches usually require good or dedicated lighting. At last, DVS sensor has high sampling rate therefore the system performance will not be influenced by shutter effect when the movement is fast.

In this paper, we investigate the possibility of using DVS sensor as a new sensing modality for ASL recognition. The contributions of this paper are as follows,

– To the best of our knowledge, this is the first work considering DVS as a new sensing modality for ASL translation and its unique characteristics including low resources consumption, high dynamic range and high sampling rate, make it preferable than RGB-camera for ASL recognition task.
– We propose EV-ASL, a CNN-based deep learning approach for ASL translation and design a novel input representation for the deep network to better facilitate the asynchronous event streams.
– We recruit 10 subjects and collect a dataset consisting of 11,200 word samples from 56 words using DVS. According to the evaluation on the dataset, EV-ASL achieves 93.25% accuracy on ASL words translation. We will release the dataset as open source to inspire future research in this area.

2   Related Work

We review the related work of using DVS sensors in recognition or classification tasks. Spiking neural networks (SNNs) [10,12] were one of the deep architecture for processing event streams. But the activation functions of spiking neurons are not differentiable, making it difficult to train in an efficient way. In [2], the authors applied a TrueNorth neurosynaptic processor with CNN to recognize hand gestures. Zhu et al. [18] introduced a four-channel representation with the same resolution as the neuromorphic vision sensor to convert the event-streams to image-like representation so that CNN architecture could be directly applied for training and inference. Lagorce at el. [9] employed a new approach, called time-surface, to extract spatio-temporal features from the event-streams and then the time-surfaces could be used as inputs for classification tasks with different machine learning models. Then the event-streams could be also regarded as point cloud [15], and the PointNet [14] was leveraged to capture the spatio-temproal structure of event-streams. The event-streams can also be converted into graph representation. Bin et al. [3] first introduced graph-based CNN to deal with the object recognition then it was extended to address action recognition [4] where a Graph2Grid block was used as feature extractor and 3DCNN was used as temporal feature learning module, modeling coarse temporal dependencies over multiple graphs efficiently. Wang et al. first adopted the event-streams to image-like representation and used a deep neural network as classifier for the task of gait recognition [16]. Then the following work [17] deployed Graph-based Convolutional Network to further improve the gait recognition accuracy.

3   Event-Based ASL Recognition

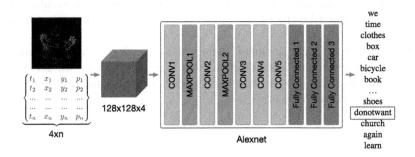

Fig. 1. Flowchart of EV-ASL

In this section, we describe the system design of EV-ASL as shown in the Fig. 1.

3.1   Dynamic Vision Sensor and Asynchronous Events

In this work, we employ DVS128 [11] as our vision sensing platform for collecting event-streams generated by users performing ASL hands movement in front of the camera. Different from RGB cameras, DVS128 has no fixed frame rate. Its pixels are independent from each other and quantified the local intensity change continuously. When the change in log brightness of a pixel exceeds the threshold, i.e., when

$$|\log(I_{\text{now}}) - \log(I_{\text{previous}})| > \theta \qquad (1)$$

the pixel at location (x, y) will emit a negative or positive event according to the polarity of the change where I_{now} is the current intensity of pixel (x,y), $I_{previous}$ is its previous intensity when the last event was generated. The threshold determines the sensitivity of the camera. The event can be denoted as a quadruplet e(t, x, y, p) containing the timestamp t, location of the pixel (x, y), and polarity of intensity change (p = 1 or p = -1).

3.2   Event Representation

Since the output of the event camera is an asynchronous event-stream, it cannot be directly fed into the existing CNN-based networks. Therefore, we need to convert the event-streams into new representation to fit in the structure of CNN. In this paper, we propose a new representation of accumulated event stream by considering both the spatial distribution and local lifetime of the events. The event-streams are converted to image-like representation with four channels and are termed as event images. The size of each channel is 128×128 which is the same as the resolution of DVS128 we use.

In the first two channels of the event image, we adopt the existing representation which has been successfully applied in a number of different approaches [1,19]. These two channels describe the distribution of the counts of positive and negative events over different pixels. The positive (or negative) events occurred at each pixel are counted and the number of events are recorded to form the first two channels. The distribution of the counts of events at each pixel is able to describe the overall trend and intensity of the motion to some extent.

We then propose a new design of representation for the rest of two channels to describe the event stream in temporal domain. The new representation considers the event lifetime of a pixel relative to its neighbors. Specifically, the recorded ratio at pixel (i,j) can be expressed as,

$$r_{i,j} = \frac{t_{i,j}^l - t_{i,j}^f}{t_{i,j}^{max} - t_{i,j}^{min}} \tag{2}$$

where $t_{i,j}^l$ is the timestamp of the last positive (or negative) event at pixel (i,j), $t_{i,j}^f$ is the timestamp of the first event at the same location; $t_{i,j}^{max}$ and $t_{i,j}^{min}$ are the timestamps of the last and first event of the 8 neighboring pixels and itself respectively. Our proposed method is the first attempt to include the local temporal information in the representation of event streams for CNN-based networks and according to our evaluations, EV-ASL with this new design achieves high recognition accuracy.

3.3   Network Architecture

To achieve accurate ASL recognition, EV-ASL employs a Alexnet-like [8] deep neural network structure. It consists of multiple convolution layers with max pooling layers for feature extraction. Fully-connected layers are followed for classification. The alexnet [8] is one of the classic CNN-based networks for classification or recognition. It demonstrates excellent performance in the image classification tasks.

The detailed design of the network is shown on the right hand side of Fig. 1. When a new event-stream E is acquired by DVS sensor, it is first transformed to the event image I as the input to the network. The event image is passed through five convolutional layers and the first two layers are stacked with max pooling layers to alleviate the problem of over-fitting. Then three fully-connected layers are stacked on top of the convoluational layers. At last softmax functions are adopted as the tail of the network to compute the probabilities for all words considered. The word (or class) associate with maximum probability will be the final recognition result. Other parameters of the network are: the relu activation function is used between two consecutive layers except for the last fully-connected; cross entropy and Adam [7] are adopted as the loss function and the optimizer of the network respectively. The flow of the network can be expressed as computing the conditional probability of any word $Q_j = (q_1, ...)$ given a tensor $I \in I_{1 \leq i \leq N}$.

$$p(Q_j|I_i) = p(q_1, ...q_i|I_1...I_i) \tag{3}$$

4 Evaluation on Dataset

4.1 Data Collection

To evaluate the recognition accuracy of EV-ASL, we collected a dataset consisting of event-streams when different users are performing ASL words in front of DVS camera. 56 words (26 one-hand words and 30 two-hand words) are included in the dataset. The words are frequent verbs, nouns, adjectives and pronouns, which are commonly used in our daily life. Table 1 shows the details of all 56 words. When collecting the dataset, we recruited 10 participants (4 females, 6 males) to perform hands movement corresponding to each of the selected ASL word. Due to the constraints of Human IRB, all the participants have normal hearing ability. They learn the movement according to the ASL words by watching online learning videos for two hours. When doing the experiments, we did not strictly control the environment and other conditions so that the collected data could be more practical. For example, as different participants have different preference on seating height and distance to the DVS sensors. We need to reset the focal length of the camera and the height of the adjustable chairs for each participant, this also brought new challenges for EV-ASL to achieve high recognition accuracy. During each experiment session, the participants perform the hands movement of each word for 20 times, so that we collected a total of 11,200 ($= 10 \times 56 \times 20$) samples.

4.2 Experiment Settings

We implemented EV-ASL network described in Sect. 3.3 using Tensorflow framework. The model was trained on a high performance desktop with two 12GB 1080Ti GPUs. We set the learning rate as $3e-6$ while the batch size as 64. During the training stage, we found that the loss of the model tended to be stable after about 20,000 epochs.

Table 1. Words list

Category	Words
One hand	I, woman, you, what, my, your, other, man, drink, yes, up, thank you, come, beautiful, blue, orange, black, green, white, angry, bad, sorry, tuesday, please, shower, need
Two hands	we, time, clothes, box, car, bicycle, book, shoes, year, church, again, learn, don't want, english, help, meet, play, can, big, small, cold, with, without, nice, sad, many, sunday, more, but, gray

4.3   Evaluation Results

When evaluating EV-ASL, We selected the first 80% samples of each word from each participant to form the training dataset and the remaining 20% as the test dataset, i.e., 16 samples from each participant for each word as training and 4 samples as testing. We evaluated the recognition accuracy of EV-ASL on three different categories, i.e., accuracy of recognizing one-hand words, two-hands word and all together. Confusion matrices are used to show the details of the performance on different classes (words).

Figure 2(a) presents the confusion matrix generated from recognizing the 26 one-hand ASL words. The y-axis is the labels of the ground truth classes and the y-axis is the predicted labels. The color depth corresponds to the percentage of recognizing an ASL word (ground truth) to a predicted class. Therefore, the boxes on diagonal accounts for the correct recognition. From the confusion matrix, we can observe, the EV-ASL can achieve 100% recognition accuracy for one-hand ASL words only.

We also evaluated the accuracy of EV-ASL on recognizing the 30 two-hands only words. The confusion matrix is shown in Fig. 2(b). Again, the EV-ASL demonstrates perfect performance on recognition accuracy, all testing samples are predicted into the right classes.

Then we mixed up all samples from both one-hand and two-hand ASL words to evaluate EV-ASL on more challenging circumstance. We again used the first 80% of samples from each word to form training set and the rest 20% samples as test set. We first present its performance using confusion matrix shown in Fig. 2(c). By observing the results in the figure, we can find that for most of words, EV-ASL is able to achieve significantly high accuracy, while some of the words are partially predicted into wrong class. For examples, **Don't want, green** and **sorry**. By investigating the raw data samples, we observe that the movement corresponding to these words are quite subtle, the event camera may not be able to capture sufficient details, which brought confusion and difficulty for ASL words recognition.

At last, we evaluated the recognition accuracy of EV-ASL on all 56 ASL words with different sizes of training set. We gradually change the number of

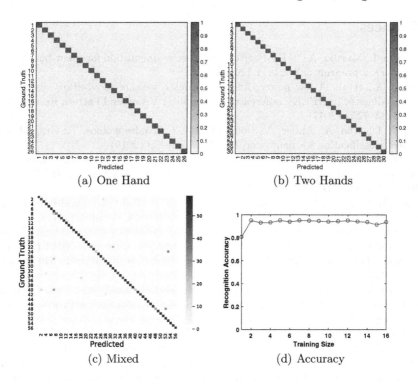

Fig. 2. Evaluation results

training samples x from each participant for each word ($56 \times x \times 10$ in total), i.e., from $x = 1$ to $x = 16$, and hold the size of the test set as the same. As the results shown in Fig. 2(d), we can find when $x = 1$, i.e., only one training sample from each participant for each word is provided to form the training set, the recognition accuracy is less than 80%. When the training samples grows to $x = 3$, the recognition accuracy improves significantly to over 95%. However, with further growth of the number of training samples, the recognition accuracy only fluctuates slightly without noticeable improvement. These results indicate that only few training samples are sufficient for EV-ASL to capture the key characteristics of distinguishing the actions corresponding to different ASL words.

5   Conclusion

In this paper, we propose EV-ASL, a new approach based on Alexnet for ASL words recognition using DVS sensors. Compared with conventional RGB cameras, DVS sensor is preferable as its unique characteristics of low resources cost, high dynamic range and high sampling rate. According to our evaluation on collected dataset with 56 ASL words, EV-ASL achieves up to 93.25% recognition accuracy with few training samples.

References

1. Alonso, I., Murillo, A.C.: EV-SegNet: semantic segmentation for event-based cameras. arXiv preprint arXiv:1811.12039 (2018)
2. Amir, A., et al.: A low power, fully event-based gesture recognition system. In: Proceedings of the IEEE Conference on Computer Vision and Pattern Recognition, pp. 7243–7252 (2017)
3. Bi, Y., Chadha, A., Abbas, A., Bourtsoulatze, E., Andreopoulos, Y.: Graph-based object classification for neuromorphic vision sensing (2019)
4. Bi, Y., Chadha, A., Abbas, A., Bourtsoulatze, E., Andreopoulos, Y.: Graph-based spatio-temporal feature learning for neuromorphic vision sensing. IEEE Trans. Image Process. **29**, 9084–9098 (2020)
5. Camgöz, N.C., Hadfield, S., Koller, O., Bowden, R.: SubUNets: end-to-end hand shape and continuous sign language recognition. In: ICCV, vol. 1 (2017)
6. Huang, J., Zhou, W., Zhang, Q., Li, H., Li, W.: Video-based sign language recognition without temporal segmentation. arXiv preprint arXiv:1801.10111 (2018)
7. Kingma, D.P., Ba, J.: Adam: a method for stochastic optimization. arXiv preprint arXiv:1412.6980 (2014)
8. Krizhevsky, A., Sutskever, I., Hinton, G.E.: ImageNet classification with deep convolutional neural networks. In: Advances in Neural Information Processing Systems, pp. 1097–1105 (2012)
9. Lagorce, X., Orchard, G., Galluppi, F., Shi, B.E., Benosman, R.B.: HOTS: a hierarchy of event-based time-surfaces for pattern recognition. IEEE Trans. Pattern Anal. Mach. Intell. **39**(7), 1346–1359 (2016)
10. Lee, J.H., Delbruck, T., Pfeiffer, M.: Training deep spiking neural networks using backpropagation. Front. Neurosci. **10**, 508 (2016)
11. Lichtsteiner, P., Posch, C., Delbruck, T.: A 128×128 120 db 15μ s latency asynchronous temporal contrast vision sensor. IEEE J. Solid-State Circ. **43**(2), 566–576 (2008)
12. Diehl, P.U., Cook, M.: Unsupervised learning of digit recognition using spike-timing-dependent plasticity. Front. Comput. Neurosci. **9**, 99 (2015)
13. Pigou, L., Dieleman, S., Kindermans, P.-J., Schrauwen, B.: Sign language recognition using convolutional neural networks. In: Agapito, L., Bronstein, M.M., Rother, C. (eds.) ECCV 2014. LNCS, vol. 8925, pp. 572–578. Springer, Cham (2015). https://doi.org/10.1007/978-3-319-16178-5_40
14. Qi, C.R., Su, H., Mo, K., Guibas, L.J.: PointNet: deep learning on point sets for 3D classification and segmentation (2017)
15. Wang, Q., Zhang, Y., Yuan, J., Lu, Y.: Space-time event clouds for gesture recognition: from RGB cameras to event cameras. In: 2019 IEEE Winter Conference on Applications of Computer Vision (WACV) (2019)
16. Wang, Y., et al.: EV-Gait: event-based robust gait recognition using dynamic vision sensors. In: Proceedings of the IEEE/CVF Conference on Computer Vision and Pattern Recognition, pp. 6358–6367 (2019)
17. Wang, Y., et al.: Event-stream representation for human gaits identification using deep neural networks. IEEE Trans. Pattern Anal. Mach. Intell. (2021)
18. Zhu, A.Z., Yuan, L., Chaney, K., Daniilidis, K.: EV-FlowNet: self-supervised optical flow estimation for event-based cameras (2018)
19. Zhu, A.Z., Yuan, L., Chaney, K., Daniilidis, K.: EV-FlowNet: self-supervised optical flow estimation for event-based cameras. arXiv preprint arXiv:1802.06898 (2018)

Multi-step Domain Adaption Image Classification Network via Attention Mechanism and Multi-level Feature Alignment

Yaoci Xiang[1], Chong Zhao[2(✉)], Xing Wei[1], Yang Lu[1], and Shaofan Liu[1]

[1] School of Computer Science and Information Engineering,
HeFei University of Technology, Hefei, China
[2] Engineering Quality Education Center of Undergraduate School,
Hefei University of Technology, Hefei, China
zhaochong@mail.hfut.edu.cn

Abstract. Domain adaption image classification uses source domain task knowledge to enhance the classification effect of target domain tasks. It can reduce the work of data labeling in the target domain and significantly improve the network's adaptive ability. However, the existing methods can not deal well with the performance degradation in large differences in data distribution between the source domain and the target domain. Therefore, based on the idea of reverse gradient layer, a multi-step domain adaptive image classification network with an attention mechanism aligned with multi-level features is proposed in this paper. Specifically, firstly, the attention mechanism is used to combine the source domain and target domain data to generate an intermediate domain. Secondly, several feature alignment strategies are proposed to align the source domain and the target domain from the pixel and global levels.

Keywords: Domain adaption · Attention mechanism · Feature alignment

1 Introduction

In recent years, the task of image classification based on deep learning has been widely discussed and studied. As we all know, the effectiveness of image classification depth network is attributed to two basic assumptions: one is that training samples and test samples come from common data sets or different data sets with similar distribution; the other is that there are a large number of labeled samples in the training stage. First of all, because the domain shift [1] mainly comes from the background difference between the source domain and the target domain, the classification model trained in the source domain will be difficult to generalize to the target domain. Secondly, it will cost much workforce or even can not

© Springer Nature Switzerland AG 2021
Z. Liu et al. (Eds.): WASA 2021, LNCS 12939, pp. 11–19, 2021.
https://doi.org/10.1007/978-3-030-86137-7_2

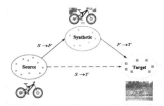

Fig. 1. As shown $S \to T$ in the figure, we use an intermediate composite domain to divide the domain adaptation into two independent subtasks, as shown by $S \to F$ and $F \to T$ in the figure.

be realized, and due to the lack of a unified standard for manual labeling, the human deviation will inevitably be introduced. Previous mainstream algorithms used domain adaptive methods to deal with data scarcity in the target domain and the difference in data distribution between the source domain and the target domain. However, the classification accuracy of conventional domain adaption methods will decrease sharply or even fail when faced with large domain differences. Besides, in training, the convolution neural network may pay too much attention to the most distinguishing small region of the input image rather than the whole image region. Data augmentation techniques can be used to prevent possible overfitting, but how to use data enhancement technology to create new training data to improve the robustness and accuracy of the model is also a problem worth considering.

We propose a multi-step domain adaption image classification model based on attention mechanism and multi-level feature alignment. The whole network model is divided into three steps. The second step is to carry out the domain adaptation process. In the process of feature extraction, the low-order feature graph and the high-order feature graph are respectively sent to the pixel-level domain discriminator and the global-level domain discriminator to train the discriminator, and the classifier model is saved after the training is completed. The third step is the domain adaptive learning process from the intermediate domain to the target domain. The primary step is the same as the second step, only need to inherit the classifier model generated in the second step (Fig. 1).

To sum up, the main contributions of this paper are summarized as follows:

- The intermediate synthetic domain generated by the joint source domain and target domain is introduced to improve the model's generalization ability.
- Attention mechanism combined with class activation graph is proposed to generate intermediate domain pictures.
- In this paper, we use a multi-level feature alignment module, and domain discriminators are added to different network levels to learn domain invariant features against training.

2   Related Work

After the reverse gradient layer was proposed, there are many domain adaptive methods based on adversarial learning [3,5]. In the research of these methods, the idea of generating adversarial network (GAN) is used to minimize the difference between the source domain and target domain, and domain invariant features are learned by adding domain discriminator. The adversarial discriminative domain adaptation (ADDA) proposed by Tzeng et al. [2] trains the feature extractor on the source domain and then trains a different feature extractor on the target domain to send the features generated by two different extractors into the discriminator at the same time. Xu M. et al. [3] proposed that the discriminator use soft scores for evaluation, which improved the model's robustness.

The attention mechanism based on the recurrent neural network was first applied to machine translation and natural language processing. The introduction of an attention mechanism into computer vision was first proposed by the Google DeepMind team in [6]. The attention mechanism of the channel domain proposed by Hu J. et al. [7] learns the weight of each channel through the attention module, thus generating the channel domain's attention. Combined with the above two ideas, Wang F. et al. proposes a residual attention mechanism in the hybrid domain [4]. This method applies the idea of the residual network to the attention mechanism.

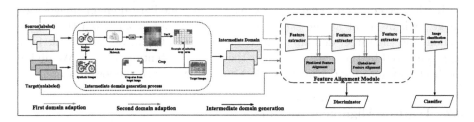

Fig. 2. The paper's overall framework is divided into three parts. First of all, the intermediate domain data is generated by combining the source domain and target domain data, and then the domain adaption process is carried out. In image feature extraction, different levels of feature graphs are used to train the two discriminators. After feature extraction, the image is sent to the image classification network to train the classifier. The process of domain adaptation is divided into two steps: the first step is to train the source domain to the generated intermediate domain, as shown by the blue arrow in the figure, and the second step is to train the intermediate domain to the target domain, as shown by the red arrow in the picture. Furthermore, let the second step of training inherit the classifier generated by the first step of training. (Color figure online)

3   Network Model

3.1   Domain Adaption

The process of image generation in the intermediate domain is divided into two steps (Fig. 2). The first step is to train all source domain images directly using a residual attention network [4]. Each attention module of the residual attention network is divided into two branches: the mask branch and the trunk branch. The output of the attention module can maintain the excellent quality of the original feature.

The second step of the intermediate domain picture generation only retains the residual attention module in the network. It loads the model generated by the first step of the training at the beginning of the training but no longer trains the input picture and replaces the network's last layer's full connection layer output with the class activation mapping (CAM) method. For the input dimensional feature graph, the global average pool is done for each feature graph A to calculate the result as the feature graph's weight λ. After generating the weight λ of all the feature graphs, the weighted feature graph is the heat map generated by the attention mechanism. The weighted process formula is as follows:

$$L_{CAM} = \sum_{i=1}^{n} \lambda_i A_i \qquad (1)$$

In the second step, when generating the intermediate domain image, two images will be input at the same time, the two images come from the source domain and the target domain respectively. Through CAM, we can get the heat map generated by the first image after the residual attention module. We divide the heat map into $n * n$ grids and select the N parts with the lowest score.

3.2   Feature Alignment Module

In the mainstream process of domain adaptation, only one domain discriminator pays attention to the global information of the input image. We use a two-level domain discriminator, which is aligned on two different feature sizes. The discriminator used in the low-level feature map pays attention to the pixel-level content in the picture. It classifies the domain to which each point on the feature map belongs and pays attention to the image's local features. The discriminator used in the high-level feature map has the same function as the discriminator added in the traditional domain adaptation, which mainly focuses on the image's global features, so we classify the whole feature map of the input image.

We use the same adversarial training method as DANN to achieve domain adaptive alignment. For the pixel-level feature alignment module, input low-order features I_s and I_t through the GRL layer and send them to pixel-level domain discriminator D_p, which is a full convolution network with convolution kernel size 1. We use the square difference loss function to train the discriminator

D_p, and the loss function is as follows:

$$L_p^s = \frac{1}{n_s HW} \sum_{i=0}^{n_s} \sum_{h=0}^{H} \sum_{w=0}^{W} (D_p(I_{s_i})_{hw})^2 \tag{2}$$

$$L_p^t = \frac{1}{n_t HW} \sum_{i=0}^{n_t} \sum_{h=0}^{H} \sum_{w=0}^{W} ((1 - D_p(I_{t_i}))_{hw}{}^2) \tag{3}$$

I_s and I_t represent the feature map generated by the convolution layer in the source domain and the target domain, respectively, in which the width of the feature graph is W, and the height is H. We assume that the source domain image's domain label is 0 and the domain label of the target domain image is 1.

The global feature alignment module consists of a GRL layer and a global domain discriminator D_g, consisting of a convolution layer with a step size of 2 and a convolution core size of 3, an average pooling layer, and a full connection layer. The convolution feature map's size is halved each time, and the confidence of the feature map belonging to the source domain or target domain is output by the full connection layer. The loss function is as follows:

$$L_g^s = -\frac{1}{n_s} \sum_{i=0}^{n_s} (D_g(I_{s_i}))^\gamma \log(1 - D_g(I_{s_i})) \tag{4}$$

$$L_g^t = -\frac{1}{n_t} \sum_{i=0}^{n_t} (1 - D_g(I_{t_i}))^\gamma \log(D_g(I_{t_i})) \tag{5}$$

We use the Focal Loss function [8] to optimize the network to control the balance of the number of positive and negative samples. In the experiment, the parameter γ is equal to 2, using the same setting as in [8].

Finally, we add the above loss functions according to formula (4) and (5) to get the total domain classification loss:

$$L_C = \frac{1}{2}(L_p^s + L_p^t + L_g^s + L_g^t) \tag{6}$$

3.3   Training Method

During the training, After sending feature maps f_s and f_t into the domain discriminator, we can get the domain classification results y_s and y_t of the image predicted by the network, assuming that the domain label y_{label_s} of the source domain image is 0 and the domain label y_{label_t} of the target domain is 1. Therefore, the loss function of the source domain image and the target domain image needs to be calculated separately, and the loss function L of the source domain image in the domain discriminator L_{dom_s} and L_{dom_t} we use the cross-entropy loss function.

Finally, by adding the above loss functions, we can get:

$$L = L_{cls} + \lambda L_{dom} \tag{7}$$

Among them, the parameter λ is used to control the proportion of loss in the total loss function.

The network training process is shown in Algorithm 1.

4   Experimental Results and Analysis

This section tests the effectiveness of our model across multiple data sets and domains. It compares it with other unsupervised domain adaptations in experiments, including classical unsupervised algorithms such as DANN [12], ADDA [2], and some latest algorithms.

Algorithm 1. Training flow of multi-step domain adaptive classification network model based on attention mechanism and multi-level feature alignment

---

Input: Source domain data set X_s, Target domain data set X_t; residual attention network F, generated picture network F', domain adaptive classification network C_1/C_2, domain discriminator D_1/D_2;
Output: Model parameters $\theta = (\theta_C, \theta_D)$;
 1: Initialize the parameter θ_F of F randomly;
 2: **for** epoch **do**
 3:     Train F with mini-batch from the training set X_s;
 4: **end for**
 5: Get the trained model M_0 and save it to F' ($F'=M_0$);
 6: Get intermediate domain training set X'_s from X_s, X_t and F';
 7: **for** N **do**
 8:     Train C_1, D_1 with mini-batch from the source set X_s;
 9:     Train C_1, D_1 with mini-batch from the target set X'_s;
10: **end for**
11: Get the trained model M_1 and save C_1 to C_2;
12: **for** N **do**
13:     Train C_2, D_2 with mini-batch from the source set X'_s;
14:     Train C_2, D_2 with mini-batch from the source set X_t;
15: **end for**
16: Get trained model M_2;
17: **return**

4.1   Experimental Setup

In the two training processes of residual attention model training and domain adaption training, we use the weight of ResNet-50 [11], which has been trained on ImageNet, and then use the data of source domain and target domain for fine-tuning training. For experimental parameters, we use the same scheme as [4] in residual attention model training and the same scheme as [12] in domain adaption training. Before the image is sent to the feature extraction network, the image is scaled down to $224 * 224$ pixels, and the input image is randomly flipped horizontally. In each iteration, 32 images of the source domain and target domain are sent into the network training. We train each data set for 20 cycles with the initial learning rate of $lr_{init} = 0.01$ on GTX1080TI.

4.2   Experimental Results

The whole part of the experiment is divided into three times, and the three stages use a step-by-step comparison. Through the data in the table, we can find that the accuracy rate is significantly increased after adding the intermediate domain data, and the accuracy rate is the best after adding the feature alignment module, which proves the effectiveness of our algorithm. The experimental results on OFFICE-31 [9] described in Table 1. The data in Table 1 shows that the experimental results obtained by adding the intermediate domain data are significantly better than the original model. We can find that each algorithm's accuracy is low in the two tasks W→A and D→A because there is a significant difference between the source domain and the target domain in these two tasks. Moreover, the difference in the number of data sets leads to great difficulty in domain adaptation. Table 2 describes the experimental results on OFFICE-HOME [10]. The difference between the four areas of the data set is pronounced. After adding

Table 1. The classification accuracy (%) of unsupervised domain adaptation using ResNet50 on Office-31 [9] data set. Origin represents the experimental results of adapting the source domain to the target domain directly without adding any modules. The ID represents the experimental results of joining the intermediate domain picture, and FAM represents the experimental results after adding the feature alignment module.

Methods	A → W	D → W	W → D	A → D	D → A	W → A	AVG.
RESNET-50 [11]	68.4	96.7	99.3	68.9	62.5	60.7	76.1
DANN [12]	82.6	96.6	99.3	81.5	68.4	67.5	82.7
ADDA [2]	86.2	96.2	98.4	77.8	69.5	68.9	82.9
MCD [15]	88.6	98.5	100.0	92.2	69.5	69.7	86.5
CDAN+E [16]	94.3	98.6	100.0	92.9	71.0	69.3	87.7
Origin	87.8	97.8	99.6	83.7	72.7	73.0	85.8
Origin+ID	90.4	98.0	100.0	85.2	73.1	74.3	86.8
Origin+ID+FAM	92.3	98.6	100.0	87.6	73.7	74.8	87.9

Table 2. The classification accuracy (%) of unsupervised domain adaptation using ResNet50 on Office-Home[10] data set.

Methods	AR → CL	AR → PR	AR → RW	CL → AR	CL → PR	CL → RW	PR → AR	PR → CL	PR → RW	RW → AR	RW → CL	RW → PR	AVG.
RESNET-50 [11]	34.9	50.0	58.0	37.4	41.9	46.2	38.5	31.2	60.4	53.9	41.2	59.9	46.1
DANN [12]	45.6	59.3	70.1	47.0	58.5	60.9	46.1	43.7	68.5	63.2	51.8	76.8	57.6
JAN [14]	45.9	61.2	68.9	50.4	59.7	61.0	45.8	43.4	70.3	63.9	52.4	76.8	58.3
CDAN [16]	50.7	70.6	76.0	57.6	70.0	70.0	57.4	50.9	77.3	70.9	56.7	81.6	65.8
DWT-MEC [13]	50.3	72.1	77.0	59.6	69.3	70.0	58.3	48.1	77.3	69.3	53.6	82.0	65.6
Origin	49.1	61.3	71.4	52.8	64.2	64.0	53.1	49.4	71.3	64.2	54.7	77.9	61.1
Origin+ID	50.6	62.3	72.7	54.6	65.8	66.9	53.9	52.7	77.8	68.6	58.2	78.4	63.5
Origin+ID+FAM	52.4	63.5	73.4	57.2	67.4	69.8	57.5	55.3	79.6	71.2	60.8	81.6	65.8

the intermediate domain data and feature alignment module, our experimental results show strong competitiveness in average accuracy.

5   Conclusion

This paper proposes a domain adaptive classification network based on attention mechanism and multi-level feature alignment. We combine the intermediate domains generated by the source domain and the target domain, and perform multi-step domain adaptation. It enables the classification network trained in the source domain to learn the knowledge of the most discriminative part of the source domain and the background part of the target domain simultaneously. We also propose adding a feature alignment module in the process of domain adaptation to promote the alignment between the source domain and the target domain from the two dimensions of local features and global features. The method we propose is not complicated but effective.

Acknowledgment. This work was supported by Joint Fund of Natural Science Foundation of Anhui Province in 2020 (2008085UD08), Intelligent Networking and New Energy Vehicle Special Project of Intelligent Manufacturing Institute of HFUT (IMIWL2019003) and Anhui Provincial Key R&D Program (202004a05020004, 201904d08020008).

References

1. Gretton, A., Smola, A., Huang, J., Schmittfull, M., Borgwardt, K.: Covariate shift by kernel mean matching. Schölkopf BJDsiml **3**(4), 5 (2009)
2. Tzeng, E., Hoffman, J., Saenko, K., Darrell, T.: Adversarial discriminative domain adaptation. In: Proceedings of the IEEE Conference on Computer Vision and Pattern Recognition (2017)
3. Xu, M., Zhang, J., Ni, B., Li, T., Wang, C., Tian, Q., et al.: Adversarial domain adaptation with domain mixup. In: Proceedings of the AAAI Conference on Artificial Intelligence (2020)
4. Wang, F., Jiang, M., Qian, C., Yang, S., Li, C., Zhang, H., et al.: Residual attention network for image classification. In: Proceedings of the IEEE Conference on Computer Vision and Pattern Recognition (2017)
5. Wang, H., Shen, T., Zhang, W., Duan, L.-Y., Mei, T.: Classes matter: a fine-grained adversarial approach to cross-domain semantic segmentation. In: Vedaldi, A., Bischof, H., Brox, T., Frahm, J.-M. (eds.) ECCV 2020. LNCS, vol. 12359, pp. 642–659. Springer, Cham (2020). https://doi.org/10.1007/978-3-030-58568-6_38
6. Mnih, V., Heess, N.: Recurrent models of visual attention. Graves AJAinips. **27**, 2204–2212 (2014)
7. Hu, J., Shen, L., Sun, G.: Squeeze-and-excitation networks. In: Proceedings of the IEEE Conference on Computer Vision and Pattern Recognition (2018)
8. Lin, T.-Y., Goyal, P., Girshick, R., He, K., Dollár, P.: Focal loss for dense object detection. In: Proceedings of the IEEE International Conference on Computer Vision (2017)

9. Saenko, K., Kulis, B., Fritz, M., Darrell, T.: Adapting visual category models to new domains. In: Daniilidis, K., Maragos, P., Paragios, N. (eds.) ECCV 2010. LNCS, vol. 6314, pp. 213–226. Springer, Heidelberg (2010). https://doi.org/10.1007/978-3-642-15561-1_16
10. Venkateswara, H., Eusebio, J., Chakraborty, S., Panchanathan, S.: Deep hashing network for unsupervised domain adaptation. In: Proceedings of the IEEE Conference on Computer Vision and Pattern Recognition (2017)
11. He, K., Zhang, X., Ren, S., Sun, J.: Deep residual learning for image recognition. In: Proceedings of the IEEE Conference on Computer Vision and Pattern Recognition (2016)
12. Ganin, Y., Ustinova, E., Ajakan, H., Germain, P., Larochelle, H., Laviolette, F., et al.: Domain-adversarial training of neural networks. J. Mach. Lear. Res. **17**(1), 2096–2130 (2016)
13. Roy, S., Siarohin, A., Sangineto, E., Bulo, S.R., Sebe, N., Ricci, E.: Unsupervised domain adaptation using feature-whitening and consensus loss. In: Proceedings of the IEEE Conference on Computer Vision and Pattern Recognition (2019)
14. Long, M., Zhu, H., Wang, J., Jordan, M.I.: Deep transfer learning with joint adaptation networks. In: International Conference on Machine Learning (2017). PMLR
15. Saito, K., Watanabe, K., Ushiku, Y., Harada, T.: Maximum classifier discrepancy for unsupervised domain adaptation. In: Proceedings of the IEEE Conference on Computer Vision and Pattern Recognition (2018)
16. Long, M., Cao, Z., Wang, J., Jordan, M.I.: Conditional adversarial domain adaptation. In: Advances in Neural Information Processing Systems (2018)

Automated Honey Document Generation Using Genetic Algorithm

Yun Feng[1,2], Baoxu Liu[1,2], Yue Zhang[1,2(✉)], Jinli Zhang[1,2], Chaoge Liu[1,2], and Qixu Liu[1,2]

[1] Institute of Information Engineering, Chinese Academy of Sciences, Beijing, China
{fengyun,liubaoxu,zhangyue,zhangjinli,liuchaoge,liuqixu}@iie.ac.cn
[2] School of Cyber Security, University of Chinese Academy of Sciences, Beijing, China

Abstract. Sensitive data exfiltration attack is one of predominant threats to cybersecurity. The honey document is a type of cyber deception technology to address this issue. Most existing works focus on the honey document deployment or bait design, ignoring the importance of the document contents. Believable and enticing honey contents are the foundation for achieving attacker deception, attack discovery, and sensitive data protection. This paper presents a method for automating the generation of honey document contents by measuring believability and enticement. We use real documents as materials, replace sensitive information with insensitive parts of other documents to generate honey contents. A genetic algorithm (GA) is deployed to achieve automatic multiobjective optimization of the generation process. Our method allows generating a set of diverse honey documents from one origin. The attackers have to wade through plenty of documents with the same topics and similar contents in detail to distinguish them, thus hindering the exfiltration attack. We conducted numerical and manual experiments with both Chinese and English documents, where the results validate the effectiveness.

Keywords: Honey document · Genetic algorithm · Exfiltration attack · Cyber deception

1 Introduction

Sensitive data exfiltration is one of the main targets of cyber-attacks, making it urgent to protect intellectual property and sensitive documents. To better deal with the problem, cyber deception technology has received more attention, especially honey documents. Honey documents are documents with enticing but fake titles or contents. They are created and deployed into real systems or honeypots to deceive and misguide attackers. The attackers believe the honey documents are real, or they consume time to distinguish them; both do well for defenders to discover attacks and protect sensitive documents. Honey documents may

© Springer Nature Switzerland AG 2021
Z. Liu et al. (Eds.): WASA 2021, LNCS 12939, pp. 20–28, 2021.
https://doi.org/10.1007/978-3-030-86137-7_3

have attractive titles only but empty contents, or have authentic but insensitive contents. Evidently, the latter is more effective because attackers can easily perceive the former's anomaly. Therefore, we focus on honey document contents generation in this paper.

Ben Salem proposed eight properties to guide the generation and deployment of honey documents [1], where believability and enticement are the most critical indicators for document contents generation. In this paper, we regard the two properties as the primary basis in the implementation and evaluation of our method.

To generate believable and enticing honey document contents, we use real documents (i.e., documents written by human beings) as materials, remove sensitive information from them, and replace it with insensitive parts of other documents to generate honey contents. Besides, we perform batch honey document generation on multiple real document origin at the same time to realize higher efficiency. A genetic algorithm (GA) is employed to achieve automatic optimization of the multiobjective generation process. Our main contributions are described as follows,

- A method is proposed to generate believable and enticing honey document contents from real documents materials.
- An algorithm is designed to carry out multiobjective optimization and achieve automated and batched generation of honey document contents.
- We perform validation experiments and evaluations on our method to prove its effectiveness.

The rest of the paper is organized as follows. Section 2 describes the related work. In Sect. 3, we describe the application scenario of our method. The detailed algorithm for honey document contents generation is described in Sect. 4. We conducted experiments and evaluations in Sect. 5. Finally, we end up with the conclusions and future work in Sect. 6.

2   Related Work

The honey document is one of a vital cyber deception methods, especially for attacks that target sensitive documents. Many works focus on bait generation, document attributes generation or documents deployment [2–4]. To better attract and confuse attackers, the honey document contents are worth attention.

Wang [5] implemented a system that filters keywords from the input data source based on replacement rules. However, this method is not flexible and relies on manual labor. Whitham [6] proposed a method that uses real documents as templates by replacing words with part-of-speech tags while retaining the original punctuation, numbers and symbols. Then the tags are replaced with words drawn from a word bucket to generate honey content. This method has the defect that the retained numbers are possible to leak sensitive information, and cannot achieve syntactically correctness. Chakraborty [7] suggested replacing some concepts in a document with other concepts which have similar semantics, but did not consider syntax issues. Karuna [8,9] presented to generate hard-to-comprehend honey document contents. However, the hard-to-comprehend content increases the honey document's irrationality. Voris [10] attempted to deceive attackers by translating existing documents into a foreign language, but it is likely to retain sensitive information of the original documents.

3 Scenario

The scenario developed for this research is that the system owners place honey documents in honeypots or ordinary computers. When an attacker tries to steal sensitive documents, multiple different documents with the same topic confuse the attacker as they cannot easily distinguish the real documents from the honey ones. They must spend time to read and comprehend the contents to decide if it contains valuable information, which they do not want. Once the attackers failed to pick out the real one, their operation on honey documents, such as file opening and transferring, will be monitored and tracked through baits or watermarks embedded in honey documents.

Our method is universal for all kinds of languages. We implemented experiments on both Chinese and English documents.

4 Content Generation

First, the sensitive sentences of real documents are removed and document templates are generated by leaving the positions of deleted sentences blank and marked. The document templates and the rest sentences are used in the honey contents generation. We employ GA to automatically generate a set of different honey contents by replacing blanks using insensitive sentences.

GA [11] uses the principles of natural selection and the genetic mechanism of Darwin's biological evolution theory, keeps a group of better candidate individuals in each iteration, and then the population of individuals reaches the approximate optimal solution after several generations of iterative evolution. The essence of our document contents generation method is to seek the optimal solution in a finite space. Solving such problems is the advantage of GA. Generally, GA includes three steps: initial population generation, fitness function calculation, and genetic operation. The processing flow is illustrated in Fig. 1.

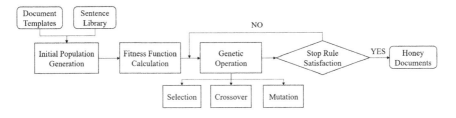

Fig. 1. Flow of honey contents generation through GA.

Initial Population Generation. The generation algorithm begins with a set of initial documents. Document templates and insensitive sentence library are used to generate the initial population. First, a population size is defined, representing the number of honey documents for every real document of each generation. For each document, we extract sentences from the sentence library to fill blanks. Each sentence corresponds to one blank. This operation is totally random to expand the solution space to find the optimal solution as soon as possible. We perform the algorithm on multiple documents at the same time, so the initial population is a collection of the population of each document, and achieve macroevolution as well as microevolution by manipulating the sub-process.

Fitness Function Design. The fitness function is used to measure the degree of fitness of individuals in a population. Specifically, it measures whether the honey contents are believable and enticing enough or not. It affects the possibility of whether the individual can be inherited by the next generation. Two factors are used to measure the fitness, that is, semantic similarity and semantic coherence.

Semantic similarity is the similarity between the original document contents and the new sentences selected to fill the blanks. The more similar they are, the more difficult it is for an attacker to distinguish the documents' realness. Semantic coherence measures whether the new sentences are coherent with the sentences before and after them. It is necessary that the new sentences are coherent with their context to looks more authentic. We calculate the similarity between sentences with the context to obtain the semantic coherence value. While the semantic similarity measures the overall believability and enticement of honey document contents, the semantic coherence evaluates the local.

Due to there are two factors that need to be optimized, simply filling in sentences with higher semantic similarity will not work well, while GA takes both factors into account and is capable of achieving multiobjective optimization.

Sentences and documents consist of words, so the sentences and documents can be converted into vectors through the Word2Vec model that is trained using the simplified Chinese corpus and English corpus of Wikipedia. The similarity between them is measured by cosine similarity. For every offspring of one document population, we note the semantic similarity score as $Score_1$, and the semantic coherence as $Score_2$. Regarding $Score_1$, the similarity between new sentences and the original document contents is calculated as Eq. 1.

$$Score_1 = 2^{Sim(V_{ss}, V_d)} \tag{1}$$

where V_d indicates the vector of the original document, and V_{ss} indicates the vector of the splicing of new sentences. To make the score difference more significant, we use the exponential function, taking the cosine similarity as an index. Regarding $Score_2$, the similarity between new sentences and their context is calculated as follows:

$$Score_2 = \Sigma_{ss} \begin{cases} Sim(V_s, V_{s\_before}) + Sim(V_s, V_{s\_after}) \\ 2 \times Sim(V_s, V_{s\_before}), \quad if \ no \ s\_after \\ 2 \times Sim(V_s, V_{s\_after}), \quad if \ no \ s\_before \end{cases} \quad (2)$$

where V_s indicates the vector of one new sentence, and V_{s_before} and V_{s_after} indicate the vectors of sentences before and after the new sentence, respectively. We add the two similarity values. If there is no sentence before or after the new one, we take twice the other value as the score. As there may be multiple new sentences, we take the sum of each sentence's similarity value per document as $Score_2$.

And $Score$ equals to the sum of $Score_1$ and $Score_2$.

We denote the total fitness of the population of each generation as F. Because every generation is a collection of the population of each document, we take the sum of $Score$ of each document as the fitness value.

$$F = \Sigma_D Score_d \quad (3)$$

where D represents the collection of the corpus of documents, and $Score_d$ represents the score of each document.

Genetic Operation. Genetic Operation includes three operations: selection, crossover, and mutation.

Selection. The selection operation selects individuals from the group who are more suitable according to the fitness values of the individuals. We employ a combination of the roulette's wheel and elitism to select individuals. For elitism, we keep the optimal individual with the highest fitness value F in each generation, as the first child of the next generation. Moreover, because each generation is a collection of multiple documents, we take one best child for each document, which has the highest score value $Score$, and group the best children of all documents into a new collection as the second child of the next generation. In this way, an optimal solution generated in any generation can survive until the end, according to the principle of survival of the fittest. After retaining two elite offspring through elitism, the roulette's wheel is adopted to complete the remaining individuals' selection.

Crossover. The crossover operation is utilized to take two individuals from the population as parents and merge parts of them to produce a new child. It simulates the exchange of partial genes between two chromosomes. The crossover operation is performed in two documents with the same origin from two individuals. We use two random values to perform the operation. The first determines how many documents are taken crossover operation. The second random value determines the sentences in which position will be exchanged. The principle of exchange is allele exchange.

Mutation. The mutation operation is used to change the value of one or some gene bits in an individual according to a certain probability. The probability is typically set to a low value because mutation should be a rare phenomenon. We use two values to perform the operation. The first is the mutation probability. The second value is random, which determines how many gene bits will mutate. If one gene bit meets the condition of mutation, a new sentence is randomly selected from the insensitive sentence library to replace the old one.

Through the three genetic operations, a new generation of population is generated. Depending on the ending rule, the population participates in the next iteration or is output as the final result. After the algorithm terminates, we can obtain multiple honey document contents for each original real document, where the number equals the population size.

5   Experiment and Evaluation

In this section, we implemented experiments and evaluations to demonstrate the results of our method and verify its effectiveness.

5.1   Experiment Setup

We selected 12 Chinese and 12 English documents with topics covering finance, projects, and so on as real document materials, and carried out four groups of experiments on materials in the two kinds of languages, respectively. We set different population sizes and numbers of iterations for each group, the details are shown in Table 1. The generation number act as the termination condition. The mutation probability was set to 0.1.

Table 1. Parameter settings.

	Chinese				English			
Group number	1	2	3	4	5	6	7	8
Population size	50	50	50	100	50	50	50	100
Generation	100	100	200	100	100	100	200	100

5.2   Experiment Results

First, we validated whether the fitness value increases with the progress of the algorithm to achieve population evolution. We recorded the sum of the fitness values of all the offspring in each generation and plotted them in a line chart (see Fig. 2 and Fig. 3). Because Group 4's and Group 8's population sizes were twice of others, we took half of their values. It is obvious that the fitness values show an upward trend with iteration. This shows that the semantic similarity and semantic coherence are increasing. It should be noted that due to the randomness in GA, the fluctuation in the fitness is normal. Moreover, due to the limitation of the solution space, the growth of values slows down in the later period. If we work with a larger corpus, the increasing tendency will be more obvious.

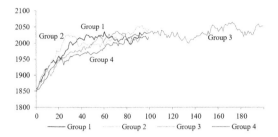

Fig. 2. Fitness of each generation of Chinese experiment.

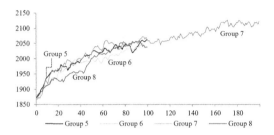

Fig. 3. Fitness of each generation of English experiment.

5.3 Evaluation

Because the aim of honey documents is to attract and deceive attackers, we performed manual verification on Chinese and English documents separately.

We randomly selected 50 documents and divided them into 10 groups. We invited 10 volunteers; each group was evaluated by two volunteers to improve the credibility, which also means every volunteer evaluated two different groups of samples. Volunteers were asked to identify whether the document content was real or fake, and record the time they expended to make a decision. The number of samples and the results are shown in Table 2.

For the Chinese honey document verification, only 22.86% of honey documents were correctly identified. For the English honey document verification, the recall rate is 19.70%. The results show that most honey documents are incorrectly regarded as real. Furthermore, the time expended before correctly identifying honey documents (see Table 3) indicates that it takes approximately one to two minutes or even more time to make a correct identification, which may be too much effort for attackers, thus presenting an obstacle to the attack. Note that our volunteers are all at least postgraduate and have a certain English level but still not native speakers, which may be the reason for lower recall rate and longer time-consuming. In summary, these results indicate that applying our method to honey document contents generation has a positive impact.

Table 2. Number of samples and results of manual verification.

Language	Real	Honey	TP	FP	TN	FN	Accuracy	Recall
Chinese	15×2	35×2	16	1	29	54	45%	22.86%
English	17×2	33×2	13	1	33	53	46%	19.70%

Table 3. Time expended before correctly identifying honey documents.

Times (s)		≤ 30	$30\sim60$	$60\sim90$	$90\sim120$	≥ 120
Count	Chinese	1	5	7	2	1
	English	0	2	3	6	2

6   Conclusions

In this paper, we proposed a method for generating believable and enticing honey document contents. We deployed genetic algorithm to generate honey document contents automatically. Through the algorithm, we could obtain a batch of honey documents from one real document. The method is universal to all languages. An experiment on Chinese and English was implemented to verify the effectiveness regarding improving the believability and enticement of honey document contents. We conducted manual verification, which proved that the honey documents were able to attract and deceive attackers. Future work includes achieving precise sensitive sentence identification by analyzing the semantic meaning. In addition, instant and targeted generation and deployment of honey documents when a data theft attack is detected are also required to be studied.

References

1. Ben Salem, M., Stolfo, S.J.: Decoy document deployment for effective masquerade attack detection. In: Holz, T., Bos, H. (eds.) DIMVA 2011. LNCS, vol. 6739, pp. 35–54. Springer, Heidelberg (2011). https://doi.org/10.1007/978-3-642-22424-9_3
2. Yuill, J., Zappe, M., Denning, D., Feer, F.: Honeyfiles: deceptive files for intrusion detection. In: 2004 Proceedings from the Fifth Annual IEEE SMC Information Assurance Workshop, pp. 116–122. IEEE (2004)
3. Whitham, B.: Automating the generation of fake documents to detect network intruders. Int. J. Cyber-Secur. Digit. Forensics (IJCSDF) **2**(1), 103–118 (2013)
4. Bowen, B.M., Hershkop, S., Keromytis, A.D., Stolfo, S.J.: Baiting inside attackers using decoy documents. In: Chen, Y., Dimitriou, T.D., Zhou, J. (eds.) SecureComm 2009. LNICST, vol. 19, pp. 51–70. Springer, Heidelberg (2009). https://doi.org/10.1007/978-3-642-05284-2_4
5. Wang, L., Li, C., Tan, Q.F., Wang, X.B.: Generation and distribution of decoy document system. In: Yuan, Y., Wu, X., Lu, Y. (eds.) ISCTCS 2013. CCIS, vol. 426, pp. 123–129. Springer, Heidelberg (2014). https://doi.org/10.1007/978-3-662-43908-1_16

6. Whitham, B.: Automating the generation of enticing text content for high-interaction honeyfiles. In: Proceedings of the 50th Hawaii International Conference on System Sciences (2017)
7. Chakraborty, T., Jajodia, S., Katz, J., Picariello, A., Sperli, G., Subrahmanian, V.: A fake online repository generation engine for cyber deception. IEEE Trans. Dependable Secure Comput. **18**, 518–533 (2019)
8. Karuna, P., Purohit, H., Ganesan, R., Jajodia, S.: Generating hard to comprehend fake documents for defensive cyber deception. IEEE Intell. Syst. **33**(5), 16–25 (2018)
9. Karuna, P., Purohit, H., Jajodia, S., Ganesan, R., Uzuner, O.: Fake document generation for cyber deception by manipulating text comprehensibility. IEEE Syst. J. **15**, 835–845 (2020)
10. Voris, J., Boggs, N., Stolfo, S.J.: Lost in translation: improving decoy documents via automated translation. In: 2012 IEEE Symposium on Security and Privacy Workshops, pp. 129–133. IEEE (2012)
11. Holland, J.H., et al.: Adaptation in natural and artificial systems: an introductory analysis with applications to biology, control, and artificial intelligence. MIT Press, Cambridge (1992)

Image Encryption for Wireless Sensor Networks with Modified Logistic Map and New Hash Algorithm

Han Li$^{(\boxtimes)}$ (ID), Bin Ge$^{(\boxtimes)}$ (ID), Chenxing Xia (ID), and Ting Wang (ID)

School of Computer Science and Engineering, Anhui University of Science and Technology, Huainan 232001, China
bge@aust.edu.cn

Abstract. Aiming at the limitations of nodes in wireless sensor networks in terms of energy consumption and communication, this paper proposes a symmetric image encryption algorithm with an improved Logistic map. First, the image is scrambled at the bit level to destroy the interference between adjacent pixels, then use non-linear diffusion operations to complete the image encryption; This paper applies the public key cryptosystem and completes the security identity authentication by constructing a new Hash function. Experiments have proved that the proposed image algorithm can effectively resist typical attacks and increase the reliability of sending information between nodes.

Keywords: Wireless sensor network · Logistic map · Image encryption · Public key cryptosystem · Secure identity authentication

1 Introduction

With the development of Internet technology, wireless sensors have become closer to people's lives from the direction they were originally used for target positioning and tracking in the military field, which involve people's privacy data. Therefore, its safety is concerned by the majority of users. However, due to the limited energy, poor distribution environment and limited communication capabilities, wireless sensor networks have different requirements for security design from traditional wireless networks [1].

Concerning the features of a large amount of information and high redundancy, the traditional encryption algorithms [2], not suitable for encryption of image data transmitted between nodes. Recently, the development of chaotic random sequence has aroused the interest of scholars with the study of chaotic encryption algorithms [10,12].

For image encryption algorithms, the widely used structure is still a cryptosystem base on scrambling and diffusion as demonstrated in [9]; However,

Supported by the National Natural Science Foundation (NO. 51874003) (NO. 61703005) and Natural Science Foundation of Anhui Province (NO. 1808085MG221).

© Springer Nature Switzerland AG 2021
Z. Liu et al. (Eds.): WASA 2021, LNCS 12939, pp. 29–37, 2021.
https://doi.org/10.1007/978-3-030-86137-7_4

some found that the bit-level scrambling operation can change the original pixel value and achieve the purpose of resisting statistical attacks [5–7, 10–12]. In the diffusion stage, most scholars perform XOR operation between the scrambled image and the chaotic random sequence directly or repeated the algorithm with R times [9–11].

For a secure transmission framework, the transmission of data is also the focus of research; Shakiba used a public key cryptosystem to complete the generation of the keys of the shared communication parties [14].

The remaining parts are arranged as follows: in Sect. 2, the improved logistic map with good performance will be stated together with a new Hash algorithm; Sect. 3 will give the secure identity authentication of the communicating parties; In Sect. 4, the proposed encryption algorithm will be introduced; In Sect. 5, the experiments and security analysis will highlight the advantages of the algorithm.

2   Preliminaries

2.1   Chaotic Map

Logistic Map. The 1-D Logistic Map is given as:

$$x_{k+1} = \mu \cdot x_k \cdot (1 - x_k) \tag{1}$$

By introducing the exponential term e^k with the step size of μ is 10^{-3}, the Logistic map has been improved, the improved Logistic Map, which called EL Map given as follows:

$$x_{k+1} = 1 - e^{\mu \cdot x_k \cdot (1 - x_k)} \tag{2}$$

Where $\mu \in (1, 4]$, is the parameter; x_k is the initial value of the iteration; Set the initial value x_0 as 0.52.

From Fig. 1, it can be observed that the chaotic range of EL Map become wider. To eliminate the transient effect, the chaotic system is iterated $N_0 + L$ times, then the last L chaotic sequence values are token to from the key sequence, where $L = M \times N$, M is the row of the pixel matrix, and N is the columns of the pixel matrix.

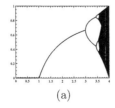
(a)
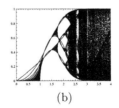
(b)

Fig. 1. Chaotic map bifurcation: a original logistic map; b improved logistic map.

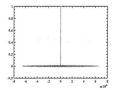

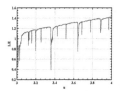

Fig. 2. Cross-correlation   **Fig. 3.** Lyapunov exponent

Autocorrelation Analysis. The autocorrelation considered in this paper refers to the dependence of the value of one step and the value of the other step in the iterative process of a chaotic system with a step length of d and a sequence length of L. The equation can be expressed as:

$$R_{ac} = \int_{n=1}^{N-d} x(n) \cdot x(n+d)\, dn \qquad (3)$$

Analyze the chaotic random sequence $X1$ obtained by inputting the initial value x_0 to the EL Map, Fig. 2 shows that the correlation coefficient is close to 0 with only one highest peak in the detention interval.

Lyapunov Exponent. The Lyapunov exponent is an important numerical feature for identifying chaotic motion. And $LE > 0$ can be used as the basis for judging chaotic behavior.

$$LE = \lim_{n \to \infty} \frac{1}{n} \sum_{k=0}^{n-1} \ln |f(x_k)| \qquad (4)$$

It can be observed from Fig. 3 that the Lyapunov exponents of the improved map are all above the $x-$axis, indicating that it has good chaotic characteristics, which is higher than the improved Logistic map proposed in [5].

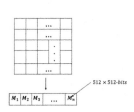

Fig. 4. Divide message into sub-blocks   **Fig. 5.** Non-sequential diffusion

2.2   SHA-C

Constant Initialization. Take a_0 as the initial value, after 3000 iterations of the improved chaotic map:

STEP1: 8 initial hashes
        The first 32 bits of the decimal part of the square root of the 3001 $\sim$ 3008th value are taken to obtain the initial hashes;
STEP2: 32 (256)constants
        The 32 (256)constants take the first 32 bits of the decimal part of the cube root of the 3001 $\sim$ 3032th (3001 $\sim$ 3256th)value;

Pre-processing. By preprocessing the information, add the necessary information after the message:

STEP1: Additional stuffing bits
        Fill the information so that $m \bmod 512 = 448$ and $n \bmod 512 = 448$, m and n are the length and width of the image, the filling method is 100...000;
STEP2: Additional length value
        Use 64-bit data to represent the length information of the original information and append it to the padded information.

Non-linear Logic Operation. The logical operations in the loop operation in SHA-C are the same as the operations in the SHA-256 algorithm.

Calculate the Message Digest. The message is decomposed into 512×512-*bits* blocks, as shown in Fig. 4. If the message can be decomposed into n blocks, the algorithm needs to be iterated n times, and the final result is a 256-bit hash value.

In the first iteration, the initial value of the map H_0 is 8 initial hash values, $H_0 = h_0, h_1, ..., h_7$, each iteration is expressed as $Map(H_{i-1}) = H_i$.

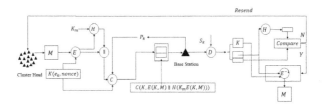

Fig. 6. Secure transmission flowchart

3   Establish a Secure Transmission Mechanism

A secure transmission mechanism is proposed to realize the secure transmission and security authentication between the nodes in WSNs, the flowchart of secure transmission is shown in Fig. 6.

STEP1: **Base Station:** Generate a large prime number p, and randomly select a large positive integer $x \in Z_p$ as the initial value, and an S_k as the private key;

STEP2: **Base Station:** Calculate $t = T_{S_k}(x) \bmod p$ and $u = U_{S_k}(x) \bmod p$, and publish the public key $P_k = (p, x, t, u)$ to Cluster Head;

STEP3: **Cluster Head:** randomly select a large integer e_k and a random number *nonce* as the temporary key to encrypt the image information;

STEP4: **Cluster Head:** Enter a large integer x into SHA-C to obtain the initial value of the key K_0 of the message authentication code;

STEP5: **Cluster Head:** Use an improved chaotic map to generate a key K_m with good key performance after 50 iterations of K_0;

STEP6: **Cluster Head:** Use the key K_m to generate a message verification code for the encrypted image and attach it to the encrypted image;

STEP7: **Cluster Head:** Use the public key $P_k = (p, x, t, u)$issued by the Base Station to encrypt the encrypted image (with message authentication code), e_k and *nonce* and send it to the Base station;

STEP8: **Base Station:** Use the private key S_k to decrypt the message sent by the Cluster Head to obtain the encrypted image (with message authentication code), e_k and *nonce*;

STEP9: **Base Station:** After splitting the encrypted image and the message authentication code, use x to obtain the message digest of the encrypted image and compare it with the information digest attached to the encrypted image: if it is the same, it is a trusted message; Then use e_k and *nonce* to perform the image decryption to obtain the image data; Otherwise, discard the message and request the Cluster Head to resend.

4   Encryption and Decryption Algorithm

4.1   Encryption Algorithm

Bit-Level Scrambling

STEP1: Random sequence generation
e_k is used as the initial value of EL map with $N_0 + 8L$ iterations, and the generated chaotic sequence is combined into a sequence $e = e_1, e_2, e_3, \ldots, e_{8l}$;

STEP2: After transposing the original image P into a one-dimensional pixel array, convert each pixel value into an 8-*bit* binary form $P = p_1, p_2, p_3, \ldots, p_{8l}$;

STEP3: Sort the chaotic sequence $e = e_1, e_2, e_3, \ldots, e_{8l}$ in ascending order to obtain the ordered sequence e' and a index array C, the elements in the sequence P are scrambled into a new sequence A according to the index array C.

Non-sequential Diffusion. In the diffusion stage, this article introduces the plaintext pixel value in the bit XOR operation process, so that the encryption algorithm is related to the plaintext; This paper adopts the non-serialized diffusion method, as shown in the Fig. 5.

Select the pixel value A_{e_k} from the plaintext pixel sequence, and select $A_{e_{k+1}}$ to be added to the chaotic sequence generated with *nonce* as the initial value and generate the chaotic sequence S_1, so that the length of the chaotic sequence is $L + 1$; Use the Eq. 5 to balance the range of the chaotic sequence.

$$S'_i = \mod \left((|S_i| - floor\,|S_i|) \times 10^4, 255 \right) \tag{5}$$

When $l = 1$,

$$\begin{cases} B1 = \mod (A(1) + S_1(2), 256) \\ D1(1) = B1 \oplus \mod (S_1(1) + A_0, 256) \end{cases} \tag{6}$$

When $1 < l \leq L$,

$$\begin{cases} B1 = \mod (A(l) + S_1(l+1), 256) \\ D1(l) = B1 \oplus \mod (S_1(l) + D1(l-1), 256) \end{cases} \tag{7}$$

The final encrypted image was given as $D1$.

4.2   Decryption Algorithm

The decryption algorithm is the reverse operation of the encryption algorithm, and the key used in the decryption process is the same as the key used in the encryption process.

5   Security Analysis

5.1   Encryption and Decryption Results

The encryption algorithm has completely changed the original characteristics of the image, achieving the purpose of image secure transmission as shown in Fig. 7.

(a) (b)

Fig. 7. Encryption result: a Lena; b Encrypted Lena.

5.2 Anti-statistical Attack Analysis

For an image with real meaning, there must be a strong correlation between adjacent pixels. Therefore, an image encryption system that meets the security requirements should resist statistical analysis attacks.

Correlation Analysis. The correlation between adjacent pixels of the original image is destroyed by scrambling the position of the pixels of the original image. Selected **5000** pairs of pixels randomly from the plain image and encrypted image respectively from the three directions of the horizontal, vertical, and diagonal of the pixel for the experiment. It can be observed from Fig. 8 that the correlation is almost to 0 after encryption.

Histogram Analysis. It can be discovered from the histogram of the original image in Fig. 9 that the attacker can achieve the purpose of statistical attack by statistically analyzing the pixel values of the plain image; But the distribution of each pixel in the histogram of the encrypted image becomes uniform, which meets the requirements of resisting statistical attacks.

Information Entropy. Information entropy is a measure of the uncertainty of the information source, which is expressed by Eq. 8. And the ideal value of the information entropy of the encrypted image is 8, the information entropy of the encrypted image proposed is 7.9973, and it is not easy for a third party to obtain the information contained in the image.

$$H\left(S\right) = \sum_{i=0}^{N-1} P\left(S_i\right) \log P\left(S_i\right) \tag{8}$$

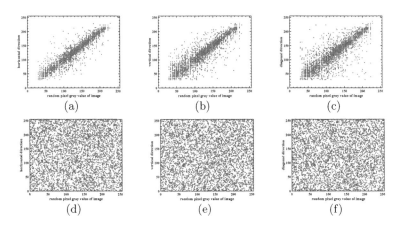

Fig. 8. Correlation analysis: a-c the correlation of adjacent pixels in the horizontal, vertical, and diagonal directions of the original image; d-f the correlation of adjacent pixels in the horizontal, vertical and diagonal directions of the encrypted image

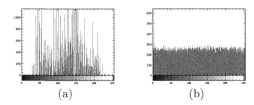

Fig. 9. Histogram analysis: a the histogram of Lena; b the histogram of the encrypted image.

5.3   Anti-noise Attack Analysis

The performance of an encryption algorithm is also reflected in whether the basic outline of the decrypted image can still be observed after the encrypted image is subjected to noise interference. In Fig. 10, 0.1 salt-pepper noise was added to the encrypted Lena image; It can be observed that most of the original image information can be restored from the decrypted image. Therefore, the algorithm can effectively resist noise interference.

Fig. 10. Anti-noise attack: a encrypted image; b decrypted image

6 Conclusion

The image encryption algorithm provided a secure communication model for wireless sensor networks with a good encryption algorithm, and by constructing a new chaotic hash function, the secure identity authentication of the communication parties is completed, which is the novelty of the paper. Due to the resource constraints in WSNs, we would add speed and space as criteria for algorithm feasibility in the future research.

References

1. Ramasamy, J., Kumaresan, J.S.: Image encryption and cluster based framework for secured image transmission in wireless sensor networks. Wireless Pers. Commun. **112**(3), 1355–1368 (2020). https://doi.org/10.1007/s11277-020-07106-7
2. Biham, E., Shamir, A.: Differential cryptanalysis of DES-like cryptosystems. J. Cryptol. **4**(1), 3–72 (1991). https://doi.org/10.1007/BF00630563
3. May, R.: Simple mathematical models with very complicated dynamics. Nature **261**(5560), 459–467 (1976)
4. Yu, S.-S., Zhou, N.-R., Gong, L.-H., Nie, Z.: Optical image encryption algorithm based on phase-truncated short-time fractional Fourier transform and hyperchaotic system. Opt. Lasers Eng. **124**, 105816 (2020)
5. Han, C.: An image encryption algorithm based on modified logistic chaotic map. Optik **181**, 779–785 (2019)
6. Mansouri, A., Wang, X.: A novel one-dimensional sine powered chaotic map and its application in a new image encryption scheme. Inf. Sci. **520**, 46–62 (2020)
7. Artiles, J.A.P., Chaves, D.P.B., Pimentel, C.: Image encryption using block cipher and chaotic sequences. Signal Process. Image Commun. **79**, 24–31 (2019)
8. Luo, H., Ge, B.: Image encryption based on Henon chaotic system with nonlinear term. Multimedia Tools Appl. **78**(24), 34323–34352 (2019). https://doi.org/10.1007/s11042-019-08072-4
9. Zhang, Y.: The unified image encryption algorithm based on chaos and cubic S-Box. Inf. Sci. **450**, 361–377 (2018)
10. Wang, P., Qiu, J.: An adaptive image encryption scheme based on bit-level permutation. In: Artificial Intelligence, Information Processing and Cloud Computing (2019)
11. Shahna, K.U., Mohamed, A.: A novel image encryption scheme using both pixel level and bit level permutation with chaotic map. Appl. Soft Comput. J. **90**, 106162 (2020)
12. Ma, Y., Li, C., Ou, B.: Cryptanalysis of an image block encryption algorithm based on chaotic maps. J. Inf. Secur. Appl. **54**, 102566 (2020)
13. Patro, K.A.K., Acharya, B.: An efficient colour image encryption scheme based on 1-D chaotic maps. J. Inf. Secur. Appl. **46**, 23–41 (2019)
14. Zhang, Y.-Q., Wang, X.-Y.: A symmetric image encryption algorithm based on mixed linear–nonlinear coupled map lattice. Inf. Sci. **273**, 329–351 (2014)

Design and Implementation of a Real-Time Distributed Precise Point Positioning Platform

Jian Ding[1,2(✉)], Dingcheng Wu[2], Xueyong Xu[2], Hongli Xu[1],
and Liusheng Huang[1(✉)]

[1] Department of Computer Science and Technology,
University of Science and Technology of China, Hefei, China
niigdj@sina.com, lshuang@ustc.edu.cn
[2] North Information Control Research Academy Group CO., LTD., Nanjing, China

Abstract. For Global Navigation Satellite System (GNSS) data processing, voluminous real-time Continuously Operating Reference Stations (CORS) data processing is a challenging problem. There are many methods have been proposed for regional network processing, such as parallel computing. However, they are mainly used for post-processing or near real-time processing. Due to the magnitude-increased and epoch-related of large geographic area CORS data processing, it brings huge challenges for real-time reception and efficient processing. Therefore, a real-time distributed Precise Point Positioning (PPP) platform is designed based on the idea of distributed computing and message queue to solve voluminous real-time CORS data processing, and it decomposed the real-time data processing into three processes: Input/output (I/O) multiplexing for real-time stream data acquisition, parallel PPP computing, and Weight Round Robin task scheduling. The real-time data of 5 International GNSS Service (IGS) stations is processed, the results show that it generally takes 30 min to achieve accuracy within centimeter. When the platform is applied for 1414 CORS real-time data processing in China, it can perform PPP calculations with stability and high precision. Application of the real-time Precipitable Water Vapor (PWV) monitoring is also provided.

Keywords: GNSS · Precise Point Positioning · Distributed computing · PWV

1 Introduction

The development of Global Navigation Satellite System (GNSS) technology has significantly promoted the development of location service and the researches of earth sciences over the years. The development of GNSS positioning technology has experienced three stages: Difference-GNSS (DGNSS), Real-Time Kinematic (RTK), and Precise Point Positioning (PPP), and now is heading towards PPP-RTK [1]. Whether it is DGNSS technology, RTK technology or PPP-RTK technology, data generated by a network covering a larger geographic area should be provided. Therefore, a certain number of data source is the key to providing high-precision services.

© Springer Nature Switzerland AG 2021
Z. Liu et al. (Eds.): WASA 2021, LNCS 12939, pp. 38–45, 2021.
https://doi.org/10.1007/978-3-030-86137-7_5

Over the years, GNSS network data processing strategy has been widely studied. Previous researches mainly focus on the algorithm of normal equation and its high-performance matrix operations [2], or parallel computation method by using message passing interface [3]. Recently, Cui et al., developed a service-oriented parallel computing strategy in high-speed local area network environments [4]. Those researches are of great significance for the improvement of GNSS positioning accuracy and calculation efficiency. However, there is still no better method for real-time computation for voluminous CORS network data, especially with an increasing number of stations and the requirement of fast and high precision positioning service.

The task of GNSS real-time data calculation involves the receiving, decoding, and calculating of real-time data streams. GNSS raw data is usually encoded in the format of Radio Technical Commission for Maritime Services (RTCM) [5] and transferred to the analysis center via various protocols, such as Transmission Control Protocol (TCP), User Datagram Protocol (UDP), or Networked Transport of RTCM via Internet Protocol (NTRIP). Some open sources real-time GNSS processing software, for instance, The BKG NTRIP Client (BNC) [6], based on thread and Qt signals-slots, which can only support less than 100 stations on personal workstation, is not suitable for massive CORS stations real-time processing. And there few software or platforms focusing on massive real-time CORS stations processing.

At present, there are many applications of distributed computing or cloud computing in the Internet field. The implementation of distributed computing programs includes pure HTTP, Remote Procedure Call (RPC) like connectors, and message queues [7]. These ideas of distributed computing have not been applied to the field of CORS data processing. The CORS data processing, from a new epoch data observation, transmission, and computation, is more likely a task generation and resolution process. So, the idea of the distribution computing can be introduced into CORS data processing.

Since 2014, the National ground-based BDS Augmentation System (BDGBAS) has been constructed by the China North Industries Group. The BDGBAS is consists of 150 reference stations and thousands of regional Continuously Operating Reference Stations. How to make better use of these data and establish a distributed computing system that can be dynamically expanded to deal with growing number of stations' data management and computation, and provide high-precision BDS positioning service, is worthy of further study.

In this paper, the details real-time distributed PPP platform will be presented, including voluminous real-time CORS streams acquisition, task-driven parallel PPP computation node, and task scheduling. Then, real-time CORS data is to evaluate the feasibility and efficiency of the platform for the parallel PPP computation. Finally, conclusions and discussions of the platform will be briefly stated.

2 Platform Design

The platform is designed according to the stages of real-time processing. In Fig. 1 the architecture of real-time distributed PPP platform is demonstrated, which is mainly consists of three parts, Stream Acquisition Nodes (SAN), Task Scheduling (TS) and PPP Computing Nodes (PCN). SAN controls I/O tasks, and PCN is responsible for computation, and TS is in charge of load balancing.

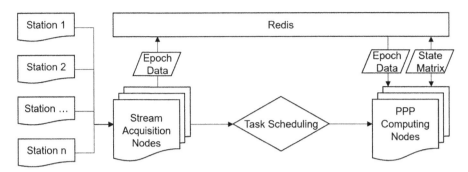

Fig. 1. Architecture of real-time distributed PPP platform

Firstly, raw real-time stream data is read by SAN by using I/O multiplexing via TCP, UDP, NTRIP or serial protocols. The number of SANs can be dynamically deployed to cope with increasing stations. In the SAN, raw data is parsed and serialized thus can be stored in Redis for every epoch as a task, then task is sent to TS for job distribution. Once a PCN is established, its computing performance will be delivered to TS. When task is received by PCN from TS, PCN gets the serialized epoch data from Redis as well as epoch-related state matrix and starts PPP computing. The number of PCN can be also dynamically deployed according to the computation capacity. The role of Redis a high-performance, distributed, in-memory, key-value database, is to exchange stream of bytes that represents the decoded GNSS observation data and state matrix for PPP solution. Protocol Buffers (Protobuf), developed by Google, useful in developing programs to communicate with each other over a network or for storing data, is used for structure data serialization.

2.1 I/O Multiplexing for Real-Time GNSS Data Streams Acquisition

In computing, I/O multiplexing is referred to as the concept of processing multiple input/output events from a single event loop, with system calls like poll, select, and epoll. I/O multiplexing is typically used in networking applications, especially in the scenario: a server handles multiple services and perhaps multiple protocols. In computer resources, creating threads to receive data is resource-cost and limited by computing resources. Also, thread switching will bring a lot of overhead. For data receiving, it is an I/O operation and the speed of I/O is much slower than the speed of CPU. In this situation, the CPU consumption is small, and most of the task is waiting. Since real-time stream data is encoded in RTCM3 format, and it is sent to the analysis center via TCP, UDP, NTRIP, or serial protocol. I/O multiplexing is introduced for real-time GNSS data streams to handle thousands of stream data receiving for various transmission protocols.

Firstly, we use epoll for raw real-time data receiving, and the raw data is parsed according to the RTCM3 format into program structure data by using a thread pool. After that, the parsed structure data is serialized for storing in the Redis cluster. The key of the serialized data in Redis works as a task is sent to TS. To verify the performance of SAN, the experiment is conducted on the personal workstation with 16 GB RAM and 8 cores of Intel Xeon E3-1231 3.40 GHz. Task per second (TPS) is measured including the four stages: raw data reading, decoding, serializing, storing in Redis, and task reporting to TS. The Fig. 2a illustrates the performance of SAN. For 100 1 Hz sampling streams, the median TPS (Task Per Seconds) is about 20 μs. The more streams are processed, the larger TPS is costed. When processing 2000 streams, the median TPS is about 300 μs, and 95% of TPS reaches over 500 μs.

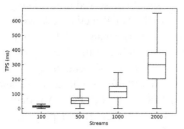
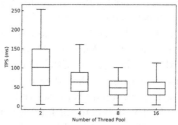

(a) TPS of SAN under different stations.　　　(b) TPS of PCN under different threads.

Fig. 2. TPS of data processing. The limits of the boxplot represent 5% and 95%, respectively. The box and its center line stand for quartile and median, respectively.

2.2 Parallel PPP Computation Node

In this section, the designing of parallel PPP computation node is only introduced, the model and parameter estimation of PPP will be illustrated in Sect. 3.1. To make full use of the resources of the computing node, a parallel strategy based on thread pool is applied for processing single-epoch PPP computation. Once a PCN starts, it establishes a thread pool based on the number of CPU cores, usually, the number of the thread pool is 2 times of CPU cores. Then its thread pool number, as well as its working thread number will be sent to TS via UDP intermittently as a heartbeat message. The TS receives the heartbeat message and distributes the task to the PCN according to its working status.

100 1 Hz real-time CORS data parallel PPP computation experiment is carried out on different number of threads. This experiment is performed to show the relationship between the efficiency of parallel PPP computation and the number of threads. The result is displayed in Fig. 2b. Here TPS is measured from when the task is sent to the task finished message received by the TS. From this figure, we can see that, with increasing thread counts, the TPS decreases dramatically. However, when the number of threads is larger than 8, there is no significant improvement in TPS. Under the 8 thread counts, 100 1 Hz real-time CORS data computation job costs about 50 μs. By using this design, 100 real-time CORS data with 1 Hz sampling PPP processing can be solved easily with only 2 threads. Compared with BNC, it is a significant improvement.

2.3 Weight Round Robin Task Scheduling

Task scheduling is an important research problem in the field of distributed computing. And it is responsible for matching user tasks to appropriate computing resources. The quality of the algorithm of task scheduling will directly affect the computing resource utilization and system service performance. There are serval classical task scheduling methods, for example, Round Robin (RR), Weighted Round Robin (WRR), First Come, First Served (FCFS), and so on. RR scheduling is a polling scheduling algorithm to assign the job to each computation resource in turn. Furtherly, WRR scheduling is developed based on RR for considering weights of computation resources [8].

The GNSS real-time calculation task in real-time should be solved immediately, and the PCN is based on the cores of the CPU. Therefore, the WRR method can well meet the needs of this platform's task scheduling when the performance of PCN is taking into consideration. When a PCN is starting service, its number of the thread pool is set according to the cores of CPU and it is used as the weight for task scheduling.

1414 real-time CORS data processed by using this platform with 2 SANs and 2 PCNs. The thread number is set 16 for PCN A, and 128 for PCN B. PCN A is deployed on the PC1 with 8 cores of Intel Xeon E3-1231 3.40 GHz, PCN B is deployed on the PC2 with 55 cores of Intel Xeon Gold 6132 2.60 GHz. The data sampling is 1 Hz, and the statistics of Table 1 are obtained by an hour of continuous processing.

Table 1. PPP computation statistics of Task scheduling by using WRR method

PCN	TPS (ms)	Thread usage	Task allocation
PCN A	17	16.7%	11.1%
PCN B	43	42.8%	88.9%

From Table 1, PCN B with a large thread number processed 88.9% of the whole tasks, which is equal to their thread numbers percentage. The thread usage is 16.7% and 42.8% for PCN A and PCN B, respectively. The more tasks are processed, the slower the TPS is, for PCN B, its TPS is 43 μs, while PCN A is 17 μs. The WRR methods proved to be suitable for task scheduling in this platform.

3   Applications of the Platform

In this section, the multi-GNSS PPP experiment is carried out for showing the convergence time and positioning accuracy of the real-time distributed PPP platform. Then it is applied to 1 Hz real-time PPP computations for over 1400 stations, as well as PWV monitoring.

3.1   Multi-GNSS PPP

The ionosphere-free combination is applied in the PPP data processing, which is generally expressed as [9]

$$P_{IF} = \frac{f_1^2}{f_1^2 - f_2^2}P_1 - \frac{f_2^2}{f_1^2 - f_2^2}P_2 \tag{1}$$

$$\phi_{IF} = \frac{f_1^2}{f_1^2 - f_2^2}\phi_1 - \frac{f_2^2}{f_1^2 - f_2^2}\phi_2 \tag{2}$$

where P, ϕ are pseudo-range and carrier phase from satellite to receiver, respectively; f is the frequency of the carrier phase observation. This model eliminates the effect of low-order ionospheric delay through dual-frequency combination. The data processing strategy and error models is list in the Table 2. The extend Kalman filter algorithm is applied for parameter estimation. The state of the previous epoch will be used when the Kalman filter is applied, as well as cycle slip detection, the state matrix should be considered when distributed parallel PPP computation is used. So, it is serialized and saved in Redis. When a PCN receives a task, it acquires structure observation data as well as its state matrix from Redis.

Table 2. Strategy for PPP computation.

Observation	Observation	GPS L1/L2 BDS B1I/B3I
	Sampling interval	1 Hz
	Observation weight	$p = 1(e > 30°)$, $\sin^2 e(e \leq 30°)$
Error corrections	Wind phase	Corrected
	Atmospheric loading	Not corrected
	Tides	The earth tides, pole tides and ocean tides
	Relativistic effect	Corrected
Parameter estimation	Satellite orbit and clock	SSRA00CNE0
	Tropospheric random model	5 min piecewise constant estimation
	Receiver clock bias	White noise

We selected 5 IGS stations to verify the feasibility of platform (Fig. 3a), and analyzed their convergence time and positioning accuracy. It turned out that based on this design idea, the continuity of PPP calculation can be ensured. According to the Fig. 3b, the convergence time is about 30 min, and the positioning accuracy can reach the decimeter level after convergence.

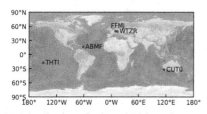

(a) Distribution of selected IGS stations

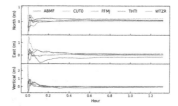

(b) North, east and vertical position errors

Fig. 3. IGS stations and PPP errors

3.2   Real-Time CORS Data Processing

The BDGBAS Reference Stations and CORS of serval of provinces, about 1414 stations, are used for 1Hz parallel PPP computation in this platform. 2 SANs and 2 PCNs are deployed. When all CORS positioning accuracy reach the 10 cm, statistics of 6 h of processing are obtained for the solution ratio, positioning root mean square errors (RMS) of every CORS stations. For the efficiency of PPP computation, the solution ratios of the station for 6 h reach more than 99.5% for almost all the stations, apart from a few stations with data disconnected (Fig. 4a). The average of horizontal and vertical RMS of PPP for the stations are 7.7 cm and 11.4 cm, respectively (Fig. 4b). These results prove that the platform we proposed can perform PPP calculations with stability and high precision.

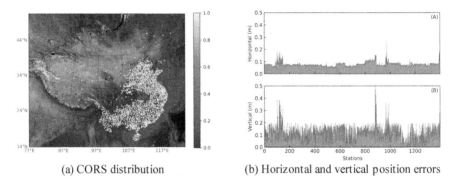

(a) CORS distribution   (b) Horizontal and vertical position errors

Fig. 4. CORS distribution and position errors

Also, the application for the tropospheric monitor is listed (Fig. 5). The PWV is calculated based on the tropospheric wet delay obtained by PPP and Global Pressure and Temperature (GPT) model [10]. Scatters in Fig. 5 stand for PWV of stations. From these four times, there shows a slowly increasing and decreasing from 00:00 to 03:00, at 02:00, the PWV reach the maximums. Compared with 5 min time resolution and 215 stations results of Zhang et al. [11], it has a significant improvement in time resolution and number of stations.

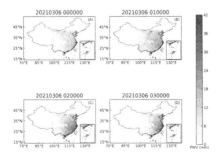

Fig. 5. PWV Monitoring from 00:00:00 to 03:00:00 on March 6th, 2021 (UTC)

4 Conclusions and Discussions

This study focuses on the design and implementation of a real-time distribution platform by using I/O multiplexing, message queue, and parallel computation technologies. This provides a new idea for massive real-time CORS data processing and has qualitatively improved the scale of CORS data processing. Moreover, this platform can be dynamically expanded to cope with the challenges brought by the increasing CORS stations.

The real-time stream data of IGS and BDGBAS are processed in our platform, the positioning accuracy reaches centimeter level. It can be used for thousands of CORS station real-time processing. The PPP computation is a typical application for proving the feasibility of this platform design. And it can also be applied in CORS data management, GNSS data quality monitor, and GNSS positioning service.

1. References

1. Teunissen, P.J.G., Khodabandeh, A.: Review and principles of PPP-RTK methods. J. Geodesy **89**(3), 217–240 (2014). https://doi.org/10.1007/s00190-014-0771-3
2. Gong, X., Gu, S., Lou, Y., Zheng, F., Ge, M., Liu, J.: An efficient solution of real-time data processing for multi-GNSS network. J. Geodesy **92**(7), 797–809 (2017). https://doi.org/10.1007/s00190-017-1095-x
3. Jiang, C., Xu, T., Du, Y., Sun, Z., Xu, G.: A parallel equivalence algorithm based on MPI for GNSS data processing. J. Spat. Sci. 1–20 (2019)
4. Cui, Y., Chen, Z., Li, L., Zhang, Q., Luo, S., Lu, Z.: An efficient parallel computing strategy for the processing of large GNSS network datasets. GPS Solutions **25**(2), 1–11 (2021). https://doi.org/10.1007/s10291-020-01069-9
5. Stansell, T.A., Jr.: RTCM sc-104 recommended pseudolite signal specification. Navigation **33**(1), 42–59 (1986)
6. Weber, G., Mervart, L., Stürze, A., Rülke, A., Stöcker, D.: BKG Ntrip Client (BNC): Version 2.12. No. Band 49 in Mitteilungen des Bundesamtes für Kartographie und Geodäsie, Verlag des Bundesamtes für Kartographie und Geodäsie, Frankfurt am Main (2016)
7. Magnoni, L.: Modern messaging for distributed systems. J. Phys. Conf. Ser. **608**, 012038 (2015)
8. Katevenis, M., Sidiropoulos, S., Courcoubetis, C.: Weighted round-robin cell multiplexing in a general-purpose ATM switch chip. IEEE J. Sel. Areas Commun. **9**(8), 1265–1279 (1991)
9. Zumberge, J.F., Heflin, M.B., Jefferson, D.C., Watkins, M.M., Webb, F.H.: Precise point positioning for the efficient and robust analysis of GPS data from large networks. J. Geophys. Res. Solid Earth **102**(B3), 5005–5017 (1997)
10. Boehm, J., Heinkelmann, R., Schuh, H.: Short Note: A global model of pressure and temperature for geodetic applications. J. Geodesy **81**(10), 679–683 (2007)
11. Zhang, H., Yuan, Y., Li, W., Zhang, B.: A real-time precipitable water vapor monitoring system using the national GNSS network of china: Method and preliminary results. IEEE J. Sel. Top. Appl. Earth Obs. Remote Sens. **12**(5), 1587–1598 (2019)

Deployment of UAV-BS for Congestion Alleviation in Cellular Networks

Xiaojie Liu[1], Xingwei Wang[1(✉)], Jie Jia[1], Novella Bartolini[2], and Yue Sun[1]

[1] College of Computer Science and Engineering, Northeastern University,
Shenyang 110169, China
wangxw@mail.neu.edu.cn
[2] College of Computer Science and Technology, Sapienza University of Rome,
00159 Rome, Italy

Abstract. Due to advantages of moving feasibility and placing flexibility, Unmanned Aerial Vehicle (UAV) mounted Base Stations (UAV-BSs) have been widely utilized to assist congested cellular networks in several scenarios. In this paper, we study the deployment of UAV-BSs to alleviate traffic congestion in cellular networks. We formulate the network model for a UAV-assisted cellular network and formulate the deployment problem. In order to solve this problem, we propose a UAV deployment algorithm to deploy a number of UAV-BSs providing wireless communication services for ground user devices. The algorithm first initializes the service connection between UDs and SBSs. Secondly, UAV-BSs are deployed to ensure that all ground user devices are covered with a minimum number of UAV-BSS. Finally, UAV-BSs' altitudes are adjusted to minimize the coverage range and reduce energy consumption. Furthermore, numerical results demonstrate the efficiency of our proposed algorithm.

Keywords: UAV-BS deployment · Cellular networks · Traffic congestion

1 Introduction

With the boost of ground user devices (UDs), how to provide ubiquitous wireless communication services for all User Devices (UDs) is becoming a significant challenge, which is also a challenge for 5G and beyond 5G (B5G) cellular networks [1]. For example, in scenarios where a group of people gathered temporarily (a football match, an annual concert in a remote area, etc.), wireless communication services provided by Stationary Base Stations (SBSs) are far from enough. Therefore, it is of great significance to provide assisted communication service in congested cellular networks.

Unmanned Aerial Vehicle (UAV) mounted Base Stations (UAV-BSs) have been widely utilized to assist various wireless communication systems [2,3]. For example, UAV-BSs have been used in cellular networks to mitigate traffic congestion in some scenarios, such as temporary gatherings [4]. However, utilizing

© Springer Nature Switzerland AG 2021
Z. Liu et al. (Eds.): WASA 2021, LNCS 12939, pp. 46–55, 2021.
https://doi.org/10.1007/978-3-030-86137-7_6

UAV-BSs bring a number of technical challenges, including constrained battery capacity and radio frequency interference. Both of these two challenges are influenced by the deployment of UAV-BSs. Therefore, it is of great significance to solve the UAV-BS deployment problem.

Recently, the problem of UAV deployment providing wireless communication services has attracted much attention. Some researchers formulate the UAV deployment problem as a circle placing problem [5–7] and solve this problem by improving the coverage area. In [5], Trotta et al. formulated a constrained coverage and persistence aerial network deployment (CCPANP) problem and proposed two approaches, a centralized optimal approach, and a distributed game theory based approach. In [6], Liu et al. proposed a distributed algorithm to deploy mobile robotic agents like UAVs. This algorithm can not only improve the coverage area by placing each agent to candidate position with a larger local coverage area but also save energy consumption by turn redundant agents to idle. In [7], Ruan proposed a multi-UAV coverage model based on energy-efficient communication and presented an energy-efficient coverage deployment algorithm based on spatial adaptive play (MUECD-SAP) to deploy multiple agents to maximize the covered area and achieve power control. However, when the network is congested that a UAV can not offer enough wireless services for all UDs in its coverage range (circle range), these approaches fail by enhancing the coverage area.

In order to provide enough wireless services to ensure that all UDs are covered with good quality of service, some researchers presented on-demand coverage algorithms. In [8], Savkin et al. studied the problem of UAV-BSs deployment to serve users during occasional events and improve network performance. They proposed a constrained optimization model to minimize the average UAV-UD distance while keeping the UAV-BSs connected to SBSs, followed by a distributed locally optimal algorithm to solve this problem. In [9], Zhao et al. proposed two algorithms for deploying UAVs, that is, a centralized algorithm and a distributed algorithm, providing on-demand wireless services for ground UDs. In [10], Wang et al. proposed a hybrid algorithm to deploy UAVs for minimizing the number of UAVs and maximizing the load balance among them. In [9] and [10], service connections are build according to the degrees of UDs to BSs (SBSs or UAV-BSs), however, the UD degrees are too high to build good service connections in congested cellular networks.

Therefore, in this paper, we focus on the problem of UAV deployment to assist congested cellular networks in providing enough wireless communication coverage for all ground UDs with good quality of services. The rest of this paper is organized as follows. In Sect. 2, we present the network model and formulate the UAV-BS deployment problem. In Sect. 3, we propose the UAV deployment algorithm to solve the formulated problem. Numerical results are given in Sect. 4. We conclude this paper in Sect. 5.

2 Network Model and Problem Formulation

2.1 Scenario Model

We consider a UAV-assisted cellular network model with three components: UD, SBS, and UAV-BS, as shown in Fig. 1. Suppose that all UAVs are equipped with omni-directional antennas so that they can communicate with other BSs and UDs in mobile environment.

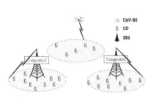 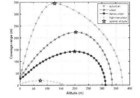 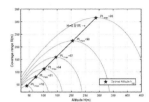

Fig. 1. A scenario of UAV-assistant cellular network.

Fig. 2. Coverage range vs. altitude of UAV curve in different urban environments.

Fig. 3. Coverage radius vs. altitude curve with different maximum path loss in an urban environment.

Let $* \in \{s, u, v\}$ and $\triangle \in \{s, v\}$ denote the component type and the BS type indicators respectively, where s, u and v indicate that the component is an SBS, a UD, and a UAV-BS respectively. Let $\boldsymbol{N}_* = \{N_i^* \langle P_i^* \rangle | i = 1, 2, \ldots, n_* \}$ denote the set of $*$, where n_* is the number of component $*$ and $P_i^* = (x_i^*, y_i^*, h_i^*)$ is the position of the ith $*$. Particularly, (x_i^*, y_i^*) and h_i^* are the horizontal position and the vertical altitude of component N_i^* respectively. Suppose that all UDs are on the ground, i.e., $h_i^u = 0 (i = 1, 2, \ldots, n_u)$, and all SBSs are at the same altitude h_s, i.e., $h_i^s = h_s (i = 1, 2, \ldots, n_s)$. The horizontal and 3D distance between component N_i^* and BS $N_j^\triangle$ is denoted by $r_{ij}^{*\triangle}$ and $d_{ij}^{*\triangle}$ respectively.

2.2 BS-to-UD Communication Channel Model

The BS-to-UD communication channel is modelled as an air-to-ground (A2G) communication link. Herein, the A2G communication channel introduced in [11] is used for its generality. That is, the path loss between a UD N_i^u and a BS $N_j^\triangle$ is composed of Line of Sight (LoS) and Non-LoS (NLoS) communication channels, which can be expressed as a function related to both BS altitude $h_j^\triangle$ and horizontal distance $r_{ij}^{u\triangle}$ [6]:

$$PL_{ij}(h_j^\triangle, r_{ij}^{u\triangle}) = \frac{\eta_{LoS} - \eta_{NLoS}}{1 + \alpha \, e^{-\beta(\frac{180}{\pi} \arctan \frac{h_j^\triangle}{r_{ij}^{u\triangle}} - \alpha)}} + 10\log\left((r_{ij}^{u\triangle})^2 + (h_j^\triangle)^2\right) + 20\log\frac{4\pi f_a}{c} + \eta_{LoS}$$

$$(1)$$

where α and β are environmental constants, f_a is the carrier frequency of A2G channel, c is the speed of light, η_{LoS} and η_{NLoS} are the average additional path loss for LoS and NLoS respectively, and θ_{ij}^{Δ} is the elevation angle (in radian) of BS N_j^{Δ} with respect to UD N_i^u, and $\theta_{ij}^{\Delta} = \arctan \frac{h_j^{\Delta}}{r_{ij}^{u\Delta}} (h_i^u = 0)$.

With the maximum transmission power of BSs $p_{\Delta}^{t,max}$ and the minimum allowed receiving power of UDs $p_u^{r,min}$, the maximum allowed path loss between a UD and a BS is

$$PL_{max}^{\Delta} = p_{\Delta}^{t,max} - p_u^{r,min} \tag{2}$$

In other words, UD N_i^u is covered by BS N_j^{Δ} if its link experiences a path loss less than or equal to this maximum allowed path loss PL_{max}, i.e. $PL_{ij}(h_j^{\Delta}, r_{ij}^{u\Delta}) \leq PL_{max}$. Therefore, the radius of BS coverage range can be defined as $R_{cv}^{\Delta} = r_{ij}^{u\Delta} \big|_{PL_{ij}(h_j^{\Delta}, r_{ij}^{u\Delta}) = PL_{max}}$. With the radio frequency propagation parameters of the different environments in [12], the maximum allowable path loss $PL_{max} = 90\,\mathrm{dB}$, and the carrier frequency of A2G channel $f = 2\,\mathrm{GHz}$, we can obtain the coverage range vs. altitude of UAV curve according to Eq. (1), which is illustrated in Fig. 2. As shown in Fig. 2, for a UAV in a particular environment, its coverage range first increases then decreases with the increase of its altitude, i.e. there is the only optimal altitude denoted by h_{opt} providing the maximum coverage range.

2.3 Problem Formulation

Suppose that Orthogonal Frequency-Division Multiplexing (OFDM) is adopted in this paper. Therefore, a BS Δ can provide communication service for UDs that are within its maximal coverage range R_{cv}^{Δ}. To better describe the UAV-assisted network deployment problem, we give definitions in advance, followed with the problem formulation.

Definition 1 (Service Indicator): Service indicator is used to record whether UD N_i^u is served by BS N_j^{Δ}. Let matrix $\boldsymbol{B}^{\Delta} = [b_{ij}^{\Delta}]_{n_u \times n_{\Delta}}$ denote the service indicator of BSs for UDs, where $b_{ij}^{\Delta} \in \{0,1\}$ is the service indicator for UD N_i^u served by BS N_j^{Δ}. Specifically, $b_{ij}^{\Delta} = 1$ indicates that UD N_i^u is served by BS N_j^{Δ} and $b_{ij}^{\Delta} = 0$ indicates the otherwise.

The maximum number of UDs that can be served by a particular BS is denoted by $n_{max}^{\Delta} = \left\lfloor \frac{C_{\Delta}}{r_u} \right\rfloor$, where r_u is the average spectral efficiency of the UD, $C_{\Delta} = B_{\Delta} \times r_{\Delta}$ is the capacity of BS Δ with B_{Δ} and r_{Δ} as the maximum bandwidth and the average spectral efficiency of BS Δ respectively. To guarantee the quality of service (QoS), the number of UDs served by a BS Δ, is supposed to be smaller than n_{max}^{Δ}, i.e., $\sum_{i=1}^{n_u} b_{ij}^{\Delta} \leq n_{max}^{\Delta}$ (quality constraint). Furthermore, to ensure that all UDs are covered (full coverage constraint), $\sum_{j=1}^{n_v} b_{ij}^v + \sum_{j=1}^{n_s} b_{ij}^s = 1$ should be satisfied.

As mentioned above, the UAV-BS deployment problem discussed in this paper is how to deploy UAV-BSs to assist cellular network providing communication services for n_u ground UDs, to simultaneously (1) ensure that all the UDs are served. (2) provide communication services for UDs with high QoS, and (3) minimize the number of UAV-BSs, Therefore, the above mentioned problem can be formulated as follows:

$$\min_{x_j^v, y_j^v, h_j^v} n_v \tag{3}$$

s.t.:

$$n_v \in \{0, 1, 2, ..., n_u\} \tag{4}$$

$$x_{min} \leqslant x_j^v \leqslant x_{max} \tag{5}$$

$$y_{min} \leqslant x_j^v \leqslant y_{max} \tag{6}$$

$$h_{min} \leqslant x_j^v \leqslant h_{max} \tag{7}$$

$$b_{ij}^\triangle \in \{0, 1\} \tag{8}$$

$$\sum_{j=1}^{n_v} b_{ij}^v + \sum_{j=1}^{n_s} b_{ij}^s = 1 \tag{9}$$

$$\sum_{i=1}^{n_u} b_{ij}^\triangle \leqslant n_{max}^\triangle \tag{10}$$

where $i \in \{1, 2, \ldots, n_u\}$, $j \in \{1, 2, \ldots, n_v\}$, $k \in \{1, 2, ..., n_s\}$, $* \in \{s, u, v\}$, $\triangle \in \{s, v\}$. Formula (4) is the constraint for the number of UAV-BSs required to provide communication services for all UDs. Formulae (5)–(7) are UAV-BS position constraints. Formulae (8) is constraint for UD-to-BS service connection. Formulae (9)–(10) are full coverage and quality constraints respectively. Furthermore, it is a significant factor to reduce energy consumption for UAV deployment, which will be considered in our proposed deployment algorithm.

3   UAV-BS Deployment

To address the aforementioned UAV-BS deployment problem which is 3-dimensional, we propose a UAV-BS deployment algorithm to deploy UAV-BSs in congested cellular networks. There are four steps in our proposed algorithm: (1) initialize UD-to-SBS connections, (2) add a UAV (3) adjust UAV position, and (4) adjust UAV altitudes.

3.1 Initialize UD-to-SBS Connections

In the step of initializing UD-to-SBS connections, connections between UDs and SBSs are build according to the following principles:

1) Each UD is connected with its nearest uncongested SBS.
2) Each UD is connected with no more than one SBS, i.e., $\sum_{j=1}^{n_s} b_{ij}^s \leqslant 1, \forall N_i^u \in N_u$.
3) Each SBS is connected with no more than n_{max}^s UDs, i.e., $\sum_{i=1}^{n_u} b_{ij}^s \leqslant n_{max}^{\Delta}, \forall N_j^s \in N_s$.

Firstly, we initialize the service indicators as a zero matrix. The set of uncovered UDs and the set of uncongested SBSs are denoted by U and S respectively. Secondly, we initialize the horizontal distances between any UD and any SBS and record these distances. Thirdly, we find the shortest horizontal distance between UD N_i^u and SBS N_j^s and compare it with SBSs' coverage range. If this horizontal distance is larger than SBSs' coverage range, we stop initialization. Otherwise, we build the service connection $b_{ij}^s = 1$, delete UD N_i^u from the set of uncovered UDs U. Besides, if SBS N_j^s is congested after building this service connection, it is deleted from the set of uncongested SBSs S. Particularly, the third phase will be repeated and it will not stop until the set of uncovered UDs or the set of uncongested SBSs is empty.

3.2 Add a UAV

In the step of adding a UAV, we add UAVs to serve uncovered UDs. Each added UAV position is located with the horizontal position of an uncovered UD (x_i^u, y_i^u) and the optimal altitude h_{opt}. Firstly, we obtain the set of uncovered UDs U. Secondly, we check whether the set of uncovered UDs is empty. Thirdly, if it is not empty ($U \neq \emptyset$), we select an uncovered UD N_i^u and add a UAV N_k^v.

Definition 2 (UD Density): UD density describes the density of UDs, denoted by $\rho = [\rho_i]_{n_u \times 1}$, is defined as follows:

$$\rho_i = \frac{n_i}{n_u} \tag{11}$$

where n_i is the number of UDs within a close distance d_r of UD N_i^u.

There are two ways to select an uncovered UD: one is based on UD density, and the other is based on UD-to-UAV distance: 1) Based on UD density: the uncovered UD with the minimum UD density is selected. 2) Based on distance: the uncovered UD with the shortest distance to existing UAV-BSs is selected. If the set of UAV-BSs is empty, the former one is performed. Otherwise, the latter one is utilized. Then, we place the added UAV according to the selected uncovered UD, and build service connection between UD N_i^u and UAV-BS N_k^v. Finally, add the novel UAV into the set of UAV-BSs.

3.3   Adjust UAV Position

As initialized in Sect. 3.1, the In the step of adjusting UAV position, we adjust the position of UAV N_k^v (added in step two) to serve as many uncovered UDs as possible. Firstly, the set of uncovered UDs is obtained. Secondly, we select an uncovered UD N_i^u with the shortest distance to UAV N_k^v. Thirdly, compare the shortest distance r_{ik}^{uv} with UAVs' coverage range. If this horizontal distance is larger than UAVs' coverage range, stop this adjustment. Otherwise, i.e., $r_{ij}^{us} \leqslant R_{cv}^v$, build the service connection between UD N_i^u and UAV N_k^v, delete UD N_i^u from the set of uncovered UDs U, update the set of UDs covered by UAV N_k^v, which is denoted by U', calculate the kth UAV's candidate position P', and obtain the maximum horizontal distance r' between its candidate position and its covered UDs. If the maximum horizontal distance is nor larger than UAVs' coverage range, i.e., $r' \leqslant R_v^{max}$, change its position to the candidate position. Particularly, the candidate position is calculated as the minimum circumcircle centered at P' with radius of r' that can encircle all the covered UDs. Moreover, phases two and three will be repeated until there is no uncovered UDs or UAV N_k^v is congested.

3.4   Adjust UAV Altitudes

In the step of adjusting UAV altitudes, the altitude of each UAV is adjusted according to its required coverage range. By adjusting UAV altitudes, maximum coverage range decreases, so the minimum transmit power reduces, which saves energy consumption. The relationship between BS altitude $h_j^\triangle$ and coverage range $r_{ij}^{u\triangle}$ with different maximum path loss in an urban environment, obtained according to Eq. (1), can be expressed as a function:

$$H_{opt} = 0.91 R_{max} \tag{12}$$

The above relationship is illustrated in Fig. 3. Herein, we adjust UAV altitudes according to their minimum required coverage range. For each UAV, its minimum required coverage range is defined as the maximum distance between this UAV and its covered UDs.

4   Simulation Performance

4.1   Simulation Settings

In this section, all the simulation experiments are conducted on a computer with Intel(R) Core(TM) i5-7200U CPU processor and 8.00G RAM. In the simulation, hovering at the optimal altitudes, a number of UAVs are deployed above a target area sized 800 m × 800 m in an urban environment. Other main parameter are set as follows: $x_{max} = 800$ m, $y_{max} = 800$ m, $PL_{max}^v = 90$ dB, $PL_{max}^s = 93$ dB, $f = 2$ GHz, $h_{opt} = 204$ m, $h_s = 200$ m, $R_{cv}^v = 224$ m, $R_{cv}^s = 285$ m, $n_{max}^v = 20$, and $n_{max}^s = 40$. Particularly, all the UDs are scattered in the target area in

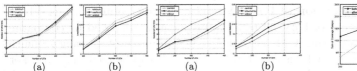

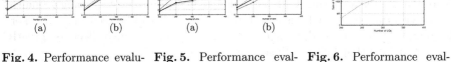

   (a)   (b)   (a)   (b)

Fig. 4. Performance evaluation of UAV adding mechanism.

Fig. 5. Performance evaluation of UAV position adjustment.

Fig. 6. Performance evaluation of UAV altitudes adjustment.

this simulation (clustered and hybrid UD distribution are omitted due to space limitation).

To evaluate the performance of our proposed deployment algorithm, some comparisons are given. Firstly, the minimum UD density UAV adding approach is compared with random and maximum UD density adding approaches. Secondly, the mean UAV position adjustment mechanism is compared with the minimum circumcircle adjustment method. At last, performance with and without UAV altitudes adjustment are compared. All of the algorithms are performed 30 times to obtain the average results.

4.2   Performance Evaluation

Performance Evaluation of UAV Adding Mechanism. In this subsection, different UAV adding mechanisms (based on minimum UD distribution, maximum UD distribution, and random selection respectively), are performed with different numbers of UDs ranging from 200 to 400. The number of deployed UAVs and load balance change along with the number of UDs are illustrated in Fig. 4. As shown in Fig. 4, it can be seen that the UAV adding mechanism based on minimum UD distribution requires fewer UAVs and has a better load balance. Therefore, UAV adding mechanism based on minimum UD distribution performs better than the other two UAV adding mechanisms.

Performance Evaluation of UAV Position Adjustment. In this subsection, different UAV position adjustment mechanisms (centroid and circumcircle) and without UAV position adjustment are performed with different numbers of UDs ranging from 200 to 400. The number of deployed UAVs and load balance change along with the number of UDs are illustrated in Fig. 5. As shown in Fig. 5, it can be seen that UAV position adjustment to the centroid position requires fewer UAVs and has better load balance. Therefore, UAV position adjustment to the centroid position performs better than that to the circumcircle. Besides, the algorithm without UAV position adjustment mechanism has the worst performance.

Performance Evaluation of UAV Altitudes Adjustment. In this subsection, the performance of UAV altitudes adjustment is evaluated by comparing before and after adjusting UAV altitudes. The Sum of coverage ranges change along with the number UDs is illustrated in Fig. 6. It can be seen that after performing UAV altitudes adjustment, the sum of coverage ranges decrease greatly compared with that before adjustment.

5   Conclusion

In this paper, we present a UAV deployment algorithm to provide wireless communication services for all UDs to assist congested cellular networks while minimizing the number of deployed UAVs. The algorithm decouples the deployment problem in the vertical dimension from the horizontal dimension to simplify the problem. Firstly, the algorithm initializes the service connection between UDs and SBSs. Secondly, the algorithm deploys a minimum number of UAVs to cover all UDs and build service connections between UDs and UAV-BSs. Finally, the algorithm adjusts UAV altitudes to minimize UAV transmission power to reduce energy consumption. Moreover, performance evaluations demonstrate the proposed algorithm can minimize the deployed UAVs while providing communication service for all UDs with good quality of services.

Acknowledgments. This work is supported by the National Natural Science Foundation of China under Grant No. 61872073 and the LiaoNing Revitalization Talents Program under Grant No. XLYC1902010.

References

1. Sekander, S., Tabassum, H., Hossain, E.: Multi-tier drone architecture for 5G/B5G cellular networks: challenges, trends, and prospects. IEEE Commun. Mag. **56**(3), 96–103 (2018)
2. Mozaffari, M., Kasgari, A.T.Z., Saad, W., Bennis, M.: Beyond 5G with UAVs: foundations of a 3D wireless cellular network. IEEE Trans. Wireless Commun. **18**(1), 357–372 (2018)
3. Azari, M.M., Geraci, G., Garcia-Rodriguez, A., Pollin, S.: UAV-to-UAV communications in cellular networks. IEEE Trans. Wireless Commun. **19**(9), 6130–6144 (2020)
4. Bin, L., Fei, Z., Zhang, Y.: UAV communications for 5G and beyond: recent advances and future trends. IEEE Internet Things J. **6**(2), 2241–2263 (2018)
5. Trotta, A., Felice, M.D., Montori, F., Chowdhury, K.R., Bononi, L.: Joint coverage, connectivity, and charging strategies for distributed UAV networks. IEEE Trans. Rob. **34**(4), 883–900 (2018)
6. Liu, X., Wang, X., Jia, J., Huang, M.: A distributed deployment algorithm for communication coverage in wireless robotic networks. J. Netw. Comput. Appl. **180**, 103019 (2021)
7. Ruan, L., et al.: Energy-efficient multi-UAV coverage deployment in UAV networks: a game-theoretic framework. China Commun. **15**(10), 194–209 (2018)

8. Savkin, A.V., Huang, H.: Deployment of unmanned aerial vehicle base stations for optimal quality of coverage. IEEE Wireless Commun. Lett. **8**(1), 321–324 (2019)
9. Zhao, H., Wang, H., Wu, W., Wei, J.: Deployment algorithms for UAV airborne networks toward on-demand coverage. IEEE J. Sel. Areas Commun. **36**(9), 2015–2031 (2018)
10. Wang, H., Zhao, H., Wu, W., Xiong, J., Ma, D., Wei, J.: Deployment algorithms of flying base stations: 5G and beyond with UAVs. IEEE Internet Things J. **6**(6), 10009–10027 (2019)
11. Al-Hourani, A., Kandeepan, S., Lardner, S.: Optimal LAP altitude for maximum coverage. IEEE Wireless Commun. Lett. **3**(6), 569–572 (2014)
12. Bor-Yaliniz, R.I., El-Keyi, A., Yanikomeroglu, H.: Efficient 3-D placement of an aerial base station in next generation cellular networks. In: IEEE International Conference on Communications (ICC), Malaysia, pp. 1–5 (2016)

Robust Estimator for NLOS Error Mitigation in TOA-Based Localization

Jing Dong[1(✉)], Xiaoqing Luo[2], and Jian Guan[3]

[1] College of Electrical Engineering and Control Science,
Nanjing Tech University, Nanjing, China
`jingdong@njtech.edu.cn`
[2] School of Artificial Intelligence and Computer Science,
Jiangnan University, Wuxi, China
[3] College of Computer Science and Technology,
Harbin Engineering University, Harbin, China

Abstract. Localization based on range measurements may suffer from non-line-of-sight (NLOS) bias, which can significantly degrade the accuracy of localization. In this paper, the time-of-arrival (TOA) based localization problem in NLOS environments is addressed. In particular, we approximately model the hybrid noise formed by measurement noise and NLOS bias errors with a Gaussian distribution, and develop a robust estimator based on maximum likelihood (ML) which can mitigate the NLOS bias errors while estimating the location of the source. The Lagrange programming neural network (LPNN) is then applied to address the obtained nonlinear constrained optimization problem. Furthermore, a weighted version of the proposed algorithm is developed by incorporating the distances as weight factors in the formulation. Simulation results show that the proposed algorithms can provide better results as compared with several the state-of-the-art methods.

Keywords: Time-of-arrival (TOA) · Non-line-of-sight (NLOS) · Maximum likelihood (ML) estimation · Lagrange programming neural network (LPNN)

1 Introduction

Source localization is a fundamental requirement in many areas including radar, sonar, communications and multimedia [18]. A common approach to estimating the coordinates of the source is based on time-of-arrival (TOA) measurements, i.e., arrival times of an emitted signal from a mobile source to receivers [2,15,22]. The principle of the TOA-based localization is that the actual distance between a

This work was supported by the National Natural Science Foundation of China (61906087), the Natural Science Foundation of Jiangsu Province of China (BK20180692), the National Natural Science Foundation of China (61772237), and the Six Talent Climax Foundation of Jiangsu (XYDXX-030).

Z. Liu et al. (Eds.): WASA 2021, LNCS 12939, pp. 56–67, 2021.
https://doi.org/10.1007/978-3-030-86137-7_7

source and a receiver can be measured by calculating the product of the TOA of the signal at the receiver and the signal transmission speed, and then the position of the source can be estimated using the areas spanned from a couple of receivers with the distances. For example, in a 2-dimensional localization scenario, the distances between the receivers and the source define circles centered at the receivers, and the position of the source can be estimated as the intersection point of at least three circles.

However, in real applications, the distances measured based on TOA are usually contaminated by various noises, and thus the actual distances between the source and the receivers need to be estimated from the measured distances. A typical kind of noise is measurement noise, which can be formulated as additive white Gaussian noise. Considering this noise, under line-of-sight (LOS) transmission conditions, the maximum likelihood (ML) based cost function for estimating the source position is usually constructed using the TOA measurements [2,15,22].

Another key challenge in TOA-based localization is non-line-of-sight (NLOS) propagation which is commonly encountered in urban areas or indoor scenarios. Under the NLOS conditions, there are obstacles, e.g., buildings, trees, and indoor facilities, in the direct transmission paths from the source to the receivers, and wireless waves might travel longer than in LOS scenarios due to the existence of obstacles. NLOS propagation will result in unreliable range measurements and seriously degrade the localization accuracy if its effect is not taken into account [4,8]. The effect of NLOS propagation can be formulated as NLOS bias which also contaminates range measurements. In NLOS scenarios, the model of TOA measurements contains two kinds of noise, i.e., Gaussian measurement noise, and NLOS bias errors, which makes it challenging to use traditional ML based methods to estimate the source location. In fact, the probability density function of the combined Gaussian measurement noise and NLOS bias errors can be formulated exactly and an ML estimator can be obtained based on the probability density function [6,8]. However, this ML estimator is quite complicated and it requires prior discriminating information of NLOS and LOS measurements which is usually not available.

To simplify the model of TOA measurements in NLOS scenarios, some localization approaches omit the Gaussian measurement noise and only consider NLOS bias by assuming that the NLOS bias errors are much larger than the Gaussian measurement errors [5,8,9,13]. However, when the level of Gaussian measurement noise is comparable to the NLOS bias error, ignoring the Gaussian noise will degrade the localization accuracy significantly. To address this problem, many approaches have been proposed to mitigate the NLOS effect in TOA-based localization. One intuitive way is to identify the NLOS paths based on ML-detection [16,17], or residual test [3], and then localize the source using only LOS measurements [3,16,17]. Common problems of this kind of methods are misidentification and missed detection of NLOS connections, which may degrade the localization performance.

In the absence of a prior information that which connections are NLOS, robust estimators have been proposed to mitigate NLOS errors in localization

[1,19]. In [19], Huber M-estimator has been used for NLOS mitigation by employing a robust Huber function to capture the effects of NLOS bias error. This estimator is severely nonlinear and nonconvex, and appropriate initialization is required to obtain the solution. The least-median-of-squares (LMS) estimator [1] is also a robust estimator that has been employed for NLOS localization, but its performance degrades when more than half of the connections are NLOS. Another category of methods for NLOS mitigation is to use relaxation techniques [20]. Vaghefi et al. [20] formulates the TOA-based localization task in NLOS scenarios as an semidefinite programming (SDP) optimization problem by squaring both sides of the measurement model and ignoring the quadratic term related to the Gaussian measurement noise. However, this method may lead to a trivial semidefinite problem caused by irregular positions or inappropriate initialization of the solver [7]. A summary of NLOS mitigation techniques in TOA-based localization can be found in [8]. It should be noted that the existing TOA-based localization methods under NLOS conditions cannot directly capture the real features of the hybrid noise formed by Gaussian measurement errors and NLOS bias errors. This motivates us to inspect the hybrid noise in terms of distribution and develop localization methods that are not sensitive to NLOS bias.

In this paper, the Gaussian measurement noise and NLOS bias errors are considered simultaneously by formulating an approximate probability density function for the hybrid noise, and then an approximate ML based algorithm is proposed to estimate the location of the source. Furthermore, by re-weighting the effect of the NLOS bias errors according to the distances between the source and anchors, a weighted version of the algorithm is proposed. As the proposed localization frameworks lead to highly nonlinear minimization problems, optimization methods based on Lagrange programming neural networks (LPNN) are explored to solve the problems. Simulation results with fixed and random sources show that the proposed algorithms have effective performance as compared to the state-of-the-art algorithms.

The rest of the paper is organized as follows. Section 2 presents the background including the NLOS localization problem and the LPNN method used to address the proposed formulations. The two proposed algorithms for mitigating NLOS effects are introduced in Sect. 3. Experimental results are given in Sect. 4, and conclusions are drawn in Sect. 5.

2   Background

2.1   NLOS Localization

In TOA-based localization, the location of the source is estimated from noisy and probably biased distance measurements extracted from the propagation delay between a source and known sensors. In 2-dimensional situations, let $c = [c_1, c_2]^T$ and $u_i = [u_{i,1}, u_{i,2}]^T, i = 1, 2, ..., N$ denote the coordinates of the source and the ith sensor, respectively. The number of sensors is N. The measured distance r_i

between the source and the ith sensor can be modeled as [8, 19, 21]

$$r_i = \|\boldsymbol{c} - \boldsymbol{u}_i\|_2 + n_i + b_i, \ i = 1, \cdots, N, \tag{1}$$

where n_i is a zero-mean Gaussian measurement error with variance σ_i^2, i.e., $n_i \backsim \mathcal{N}(0, \sigma_i^2)$, and b_i is a positive bias error caused by NLOS propagation. The statistical characteristics of the bias error b_i can be modeled using various distributions, e.g., exponential [12], uniform [14], and Gaussian distributions. We assume that the NLOS bias error b_i follows the exponential distribution with mean μ_i and variance μ_i^2, i.e., $b_i \backsim \mathcal{E}(1/\mu_i)$.

2.2   Lagrange Programming Neural Network

Consider the following nonlinear optimization problem with equality constraints

$$\min_{\boldsymbol{x}} f(\boldsymbol{x}), \quad \text{s.t.} \quad \boldsymbol{h}(\boldsymbol{x}) = \boldsymbol{0}, \tag{2}$$

where $\boldsymbol{x} \in \mathbb{R}^N$ is the variable vector and $f : \mathbb{R}^N \rightarrow \mathbb{R}$ is a nonlinear objective function. The function $\boldsymbol{h} : \mathbb{R}^N \rightarrow \mathbb{R}^M (M < N)$ denotes the M equality constraints, and $\boldsymbol{0}$ represents the $M \times 1$ zero vector. The objective function f and the constraints $\boldsymbol{h}$ are assumed to be twice differentiable.

The Lagrangian function of this nonlinear optimization problem can be formulated as

$$\mathcal{L}(\boldsymbol{x}, \boldsymbol{\lambda}) = f(\boldsymbol{x}) + \boldsymbol{\lambda}^T \boldsymbol{h}(\boldsymbol{x}), \tag{3}$$

where $\boldsymbol{\lambda} = [\lambda_1, \cdots, \lambda_M]^T$ denotes the Lagrangian multiplier vector. Based on the results from optimization theory, the first-order necessary optimality condition of problem (2) can be expressed as a stationary point $(\boldsymbol{x}^\star, \boldsymbol{\lambda}^\star)$ of $\mathcal{L}(\boldsymbol{x}, \boldsymbol{\lambda})$, i.e.,

$$\begin{aligned} \nabla_x \mathcal{L}(\boldsymbol{x}^\star, \boldsymbol{\lambda}^\star) = \nabla f(\boldsymbol{x}^\star) + \boldsymbol{\lambda}^\star \nabla h(\boldsymbol{x}^\star) = 0 \\ \nabla_\lambda \mathcal{L}(\boldsymbol{x}^\star, \boldsymbol{\lambda}^\star) = h(\boldsymbol{x}^\star) = 0. \end{aligned} \tag{4}$$

The LPNN approach [23] develops a neural network that settles down to an equilibrium point satisfying the first-order optimality condition (4), and finds the solution to the original problem by searching the equilibrium point iteratively.

Specifically, in LPNN two types of neurons, i.e., variable neurons and Lagrangian neurons, are used to hold the state variables $\boldsymbol{x}$ and $\boldsymbol{\lambda}$, respectively. The equilibrium point satisfying (4) can be obtained iteratively based on the dynamics of $\boldsymbol{x}$ and $\boldsymbol{\lambda}$, that are given by

$$\frac{1}{\tau} \frac{d\boldsymbol{x}}{dt} = -\nabla_x \mathcal{L}(\boldsymbol{x}, \boldsymbol{\lambda}) \tag{5}$$

$$\frac{1}{\tau} \frac{d\boldsymbol{\lambda}}{dt} = \nabla_\lambda \mathcal{L}(\boldsymbol{x}, \boldsymbol{\lambda}). \tag{6}$$

τ denotes the time constant of the circuit, which depends on the resistance and capacitance of the analog circuit. Without loss of generality, τ can be set as 1.

The dynamic of the variable neurons (5) is used for minimizing the Lagrangian function, while the dynamic of the Lagrange neurons (6) aims to constrain the variables $\boldsymbol{x}$ in the feasible region of the original problem (2). The equilibrium point of the network can be determined by solving the differential equations (5) and (6) iteratively, and thus the solution to the problem (2) can be obtained.

3   Algorithm Development

In this section, we consider the hybrid of the Gaussian measurement noise and the NLOS bias errors in TOA-based localization, which commonly arises in localization in indoor or highly urbanized areas, e.g., in Hong Kong and Tokyo when the global position system is used [10,11]. Two ML based algorithms are proposed by exploring and relaxing the distribution information of the hybrid noise.

3.1   Hybrid Approximate ML (Hybrid AML)

Considering the measurements are contaminated by Gaussian noise $n_i \sim \mathcal{N}(0, \sigma_i^2)$ and the NLOS exponential bias errors $b_i \sim \mathcal{E}(1/\mu_i)$ simultaneously, and the exact probability density function of the hybrid errors $n_i + b_i$ can be written as [6]

$$P(x) = \exp\left[-(x - \sigma_i^2/2\mu_i)/\mu_i\right] Q(\sigma_i/\mu_i - x/\sigma_i)/\mu_i, \tag{7}$$

where $Q(\alpha) = \frac{1}{\sqrt{2\pi}} \int_\alpha^\infty \exp(-x^2/2)\mathrm{d}x$. Based on this distribution, and the ML solution to the localization problem is [6]

$$\hat{\boldsymbol{x}} = \arg\ \min_{\boldsymbol{x}} \left\{ \sum_{i=1}^{N_{NL}} (e_i - \sigma_i^2/2\mu_i)/\mu_i \right.$$
$$\left. - \sum_{i=1}^{N_{NL}} \log\left[Q\left(\sigma_i/\mu_i - \frac{e_i}{\sigma_i}\right)\right] + \sum_{i=N_{NL}+1}^{N} \frac{e_i^2}{2\sigma_i^2} \right\}, \tag{8}$$

where N_{NL} is the number of NLOS measurements and $e_i = r_i - \|\boldsymbol{c} - \boldsymbol{u}_i\|_2$. As shown in (8), the ML solution is quite complicated. In addition, to obtain the exact ML solution, NLOS measurements need to be identified from all of the obtained measurements. However, the NLOS connections are usually not available in practice and it is challenging to identify them accurately.

To consider the measurement noise and the NLOS bias errors simultaneously without identifying the NLOS measurements, we approximate the statistics of the hybrid errors with a colored-Gaussian distribution. In particular, the hybrid error $n_i + b_i$ in the ith measurement is assumed to follow a Gaussian distribution with mean μ_i and variance $\sigma_i^2 + \mu_i^2$. Based on this approximation, the propagation model (1) can be relaxed as

$$r_i = \|\boldsymbol{c} - \boldsymbol{u}_i\|_2 + \gamma_i, i = 1, \cdots, N, \tag{9}$$

with $\gamma_i \sim \mathcal{N}(\mu_i, \sigma_i^2 + \mu_i^2)$.

Assuming that $\mu_1 = \mu_2 = \cdots = \mu_N = \mu$ and $\sigma_1^2 = \sigma_2^2 = \cdots = \sigma_N^2 = \sigma^2$, the ML estimation based on (9) can be then naturally formulated as

$$
\begin{aligned}
\arg\min_{c,g} &\sum_{i=1}^{N}(r_i - g_i - \mu)^2 \\
s.t.\ &g_i^2 = \|c - u_i\|_2^2,\ i = 1,\cdots,N, \\
&g_i \geq 0,\ i = 1,\cdots,N.
\end{aligned}
\tag{10}
$$

As this formulation is developed based on the approximate distribution of the hybrid noise, it can mitigate NLOS bias while estimating the source position. The proposed algorithm based on this formulation is referred to as Hybrid approximated maximum likelihood (Hybrid AML).

Notice that the inequality constraints $g_i \geq 0, i = 1, ..., N$ can be surrogated by equality constraints $g_i = y_i^2, i = 1, ..., N$ using auxiliary variables $y_i, i = 1, ..., N$, and thus (10) can be equivalently written as the following problem

$$
\begin{aligned}
\arg\min_{c,g,y} &\sum_{i=1}^{N}(r_i - g_i - \mu)^2 \\
s.t.\ &g_i^2 = \|c - u_i\|_2^2,\ i = 1,\cdots,N, \\
&g_i = y_i^2,\ i = 1,\cdots,N.
\end{aligned}
\tag{11}
$$

However, it should be noted that it is not trivial to solve this problem as both of the objective function and the constraints are highly nonlinear. In this paper, the LPNN approach is utilized to address this optimization problem.

To employ the LPNN approach, we first construct the Lagrangian function of (11), that is

$$
\mathcal{L}(x,\lambda) = \sum_{i=1}^{N}(r_i - g_i - \mu)^2 + \sum_{i=1}^{N}\alpha_i(g_i^2 - \|c - u_i\|_2^2) + \sum_{i=1}^{N}\eta_i(g_i - y_i^2), \tag{12}
$$

where $\lambda = [\alpha_1,\cdots,\alpha_N,\eta_1,\cdots,\eta_N]^T$ denotes the Lagrangian multipliers corresponding to the constraints and $x = [c^T, g^T, y^T]^T$ represents the variables to be optimized.

To improve the convexity of the problem and the global stability of the LPNN algorithm, the augmented term

$$
\frac{C_0}{2}\left[\sum_{i=1}^{N}(g_i^2 - \|c - u_i\|_2^2)^2 + \sum_{i=1}^{N}(g_i - y_i^2)^2\right]
\tag{13}
$$

is added to the Lagrangian function [23], where C_0 is a positive constant. As a result, the augmented Lagrangian function extended from (12) is

$$
\begin{aligned}
\mathcal{L}(x,\lambda) =\ &\sum_{i=1}^{N}(r_i - g_i - \mu)^2 + \sum_{i=1}^{N}\alpha_i(g_i^2 - \|c - u_i\|_2^2) + \sum_{i=1}^{N}\eta_i(g_i - y_i^2) \\
&+ \frac{C_0}{2}\left[\sum_{i=1}^{N}(g_i^2 - \|c - u_i\|_2^2)^2 + \sum_{i=1}^{N}(g_i - y_i^2)^2\right].
\end{aligned}
\tag{14}
$$

Based on Eqs. (5) and (6), the dynamics of the variable neurons $\boldsymbol{x}$ and the Lagrangian neurons $\boldsymbol{\lambda}$ in the LPNN corresponding to (14) can be obtained, i.e.,

$$\frac{d\boldsymbol{c}}{dt} = -\frac{\partial \mathcal{L}(\boldsymbol{x}, \boldsymbol{\lambda})}{\partial \boldsymbol{c}}$$

$$= 2C_0 \sum_{i=1}^{N}(g_i^2 - \|\boldsymbol{c} - \boldsymbol{u}_i\|_2^2)(\boldsymbol{c} - \boldsymbol{u}_i) + 2\sum_{i=1}^{N}\alpha_i(\boldsymbol{c} - \boldsymbol{u}_i),$$

$$\frac{dg_i}{dt} = -\frac{\partial \mathcal{L}(\boldsymbol{x}, \boldsymbol{\lambda})}{\partial g_i}$$

$$= 2(r_i - g_i - \mu) - 2C_0(g_i^2 - \|\boldsymbol{c} - \boldsymbol{u}_i\|_2^2)g_i \tag{15}$$
$$-2\alpha_i g_i - \eta_i - C_0(g_i - y_i^2),$$

$$\frac{dy_i}{dt} = -\frac{\partial \mathcal{L}(\boldsymbol{x}, \boldsymbol{\lambda})}{\partial y_i} = 2\eta_i y_i + 2C_0(g_i - y_i^2)y_i, \tag{16}$$

$$\frac{d\alpha_i}{dt} = \frac{\partial \mathcal{L}(\boldsymbol{x}, \boldsymbol{\lambda})}{\partial \alpha_i} = g_i^2 - \|\boldsymbol{c} - \boldsymbol{u}_i\|_2^2, \tag{17}$$

$$\frac{d\eta_i}{dt} = \frac{\partial \mathcal{L}(\boldsymbol{x}, \boldsymbol{\lambda})}{\partial \eta_i} = g_i - y_i^2. \tag{18}$$

The solution to (11), i.e., the equilibrium point of the LPNN, can be obtained by solving the above differential equations (15)–(19) iteratively.

3.2   Hybrid and Weighted Approximate ML (Hybrid WAML)

Generally, in localization, sensors that are farther from the source are less important than those closer to the source, as longer distances between the source and the sensors usually lead to less reliable measurements. This motivates us to consider the influence of the distances between the source and the sensors in the formulation of localization.

In particular, the accuracy of the measured distances is assumed to be proportional to the magnitude of the distances $g_i = \|\boldsymbol{c} - \boldsymbol{u}_i\|_2$, $i = 1, 2, \cdots, N$ between the source and the sensors. By incorporating the distances g_i, $i = 1, 2, \cdots, N$ as weighting factors, a weighted version of the Hybrid AML formulation (11) can be developed, that is

$$\arg\min_{\boldsymbol{c}, \boldsymbol{g}, \boldsymbol{y}} \sum_{i=1}^{N}\frac{1}{g_i}(r_i - g_i - \mu)^2$$

$$s.t. : g_i^2 = \|\boldsymbol{c} - \boldsymbol{u}_i\|_2^2, \ i = 1, \cdots, N, \tag{19}$$
$$g_i = y_i^2, \ i = 1, \cdots, N.$$

The physical meaning of this formulation is that the reliability of the i-th measurement is inversely proportional to the actual distance between the source and the i-th sensor. Due to the introduction of the weights, this formulation is able to further mitigate NLOS bias errors. Since the true distances $g_i, i = 1, ..., N$ are not available, we relax it with the measured distance $r_i, i = 1, ..., N$ for simplicity. Therefore, (19) can be relaxed as

$$\arg\min_{c,g,y} \sum_{i=1}^{N} \frac{1}{r_i}(r_i - g_i - \mu)^2$$

$$s.t. : g_i^2 = \|c - u_i\|_2^2, \quad i = 1, \cdots, N,$$

$$g_i = y_i^2, \quad i = 1, \cdots, N.$$

(20)

Similar to (11), problem (20) can also be addressed effectively via LPNN. As the only difference between (11) and (20) is the weight $\frac{1}{r_i}$ in the objective function, which has influence on the update of g_i, the dynamics corresponding to (20) are the same as those of (11) except for g_i. In particular, the dynamics of g_i in (20) is

$$\frac{dg_i}{dt} = -\frac{\partial \mathcal{L}(x, \lambda)}{\partial g_i}$$

$$= 2(r_i - g_i - \mu)/r_i - 2C_0(g_i^2 - \|c - u_i\|^2)g_i$$

$$- 2\alpha_i g_i - \eta_i - C_0(g_i - y_i^2).$$

(21)

This proposed algorithm based on the weighted formulation (20) is referred to as Hybrid and weighted approximate maximum likelihood (Hybrid WAML).

4   Experimental Results

In this section, several experiments are performed to evaluate the performance of the two proposed algorithms, i.e., Hybrid AML and Hybrid WAML. Four state-of-the-art algorithms: LMS [1], Huber [19], SDP [20], and AML [9] are used as comparison benchmarks.

Two kinds of configurations of the sensors are tested, as shown in Fig. 1. In the first configuration, 4 sensors at coordinates $[10, 0]^T$, $[0, 10]^T$, $[-10, 0]^T$ and $[0, -10]^T$ are used. In the second configuration, 6 sensors at coordinates $[10, 0]^T$, $[5, 8.66]^T$, $[-5, 8.66]^T$, $[-10, 0]^T$, $[-5, -8.66]^T$ and $[5, -8.66]^T$ are used. The sources locate at fixed positions or uniformly distribute within the circular area centered at the origin with radius 15, i.e., the blue area in Fig. 1. For each experiment, 1, 000 independent trails are performed, and the average mean-squared-error (MSE) is calculated for each case.

4.1   Experiments with Various Levels of NLOS Bias Errors

In this subsection, the effect of the level of NLOS bias errors on the performance of the proposed algorithms are investigated in the cases of fixed and random source positions, respectively. In particular, the variance of the zero-mean Gaussian measurement noise is fixed as $\sigma^2 = 0.1$, and the mean μ of NLOS bias error varies from 0.5 to 5.

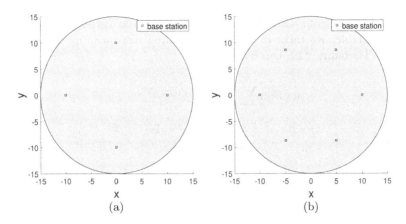

Fig. 1. The configurations of sensors. (a) Four receivers ($N = 4$). (b) Six receivers ($N = 6$).

Figure 2 shows the MSE results versus the mean μ of the NLOS bias error with the source at $[4, 2]$, in the case of 4 receivers and 6 receivers respectively. From Fig. 2(a), it can be seen that, when 4 receivers are used, the proposed Hybrid AML and Hybrid WAML algorithms perform better than the other algorithms. When the number of receivers increases to 6, the performance of the algorithms all improves as shown in Fig. 2(b). In this case, the Hybrid AML algorithm outperforms AML, LMS and Huber for the full range of NLOS bias errors, and outperforms SDP only for relatively small NLOS bias errors. The Hybrid WAML algorithm outperforms Hybrid AML and obtains the best results in all cases with both $N = 4$ and $N = 6$. This verifies the effect of the weights introduced to the objective function of Hybrid WAML.

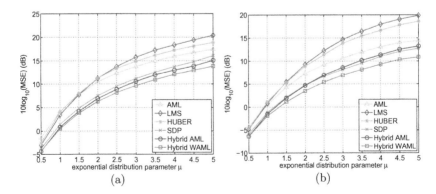

Fig. 2. Source locates at $[4, 2]$ with variance $\sigma^2 = 0.1$ and $\mu \in [0.5, 5]$. (a) $N = 4$. (b) $N = 6$.

Besides the experiments with sources at fixed positions, the scenario where the source uniformly distributes within the circular area centered at the origin with radius 15 is also tested. The MSE results with the number of receivers $N = 4$ and $N = 6$ are present in Fig. 3. When 4 receivers are used, from Fig. 3(a) we can see the proposed algorithms perform better than the benchmarks, which is consistent with the results with sources at fixed positions. When the number of receivers increase to 6, the proposed Hybrid AML algorithm outperforms LMS, HUBER and AML, and the Hybrid WAML outperforms all the benchmarks.

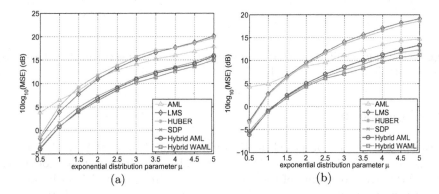

Fig. 3. The source uniformly distributes within the circular area centered at the origin with radius 15, $\sigma^2 = 0.1$, and $\mu \in [0.5, 5]$. (a) $N = 4$. (b) $N = 6$.

4.2 Experiments with Various Levels of Gaussian Measurement Noise

We also investigate the performance of the algorithms with various variances of Gaussian measurement noise. Specifically, the mean of the NLOS bias error is fixed as $\mu = 2$, and the variance of Gaussian measurement noise, i.e., σ^2, varies in the range of $[10^{-2}, 10^1]$. The location of the source is also uniformly distributed within the circle centered at the origin with radius 15. The MSE results with 4 sensors and 6 sensors are present in Fig. 4.

From Fig. 4, we can see that the proposed algorithms achieve much lower MSE's than the other methods when σ^2 is less than 1. However, the performance of the proposed algorithms degrades with the increase of σ^2. In particular, when $\sigma^2 = 10^{0.5}$, the proposed algorithms achieve comparable results with the SDP method, whereas when the variance continues increasing, the results of the proposed algorithms get worse than the benchmark algorithms. This indicates that the proposed methods are not suitable for the cases when the variance of the Gaussian measurement noise is very large. However, it should be noted that in practice measurements with very large Gaussian measurement variances seldom exists. This extreme setting is considered in the experiment to illustrate the robustness of the proposed algorithms with the varying of σ^2.

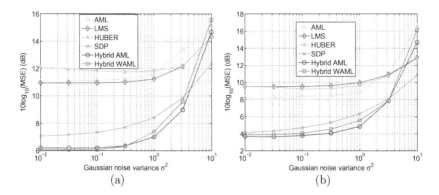

Fig. 4. The source uniformly distributes within the circular area centered at the origin with radius 15, $\mu = 2$, and $\sigma^2 \in \left[10^{-2}, 10^1\right]$. (a) $N = 4$. (b) $N = 6$.

5   Conclusion

In this paper, we have proposed the Hybrid AML and Hybrid WAML algorithms to mitigate NLOS bias errors in TOA-based localization. In these two algorithms, the hybrid error consisting of the measurement noise and the NLOS bias error is considered and it is approximately modeled using a Gaussian distribution. Specifically, Hybrid AML formulates the localization problem based on the ML estimation, and Hybrid WAML further improves this formulation by taking the distances between the source and the sensors into account. To obtain the solution to the proposed formulations, the LPNN approach is employed. Experimental results have shown that the proposed algorithms can provide more accurate results as compared with several existing state-of-the-art methods, especially when fewer sensors are used.

References

1. Casas, R., Marco, A., Guerrero, J., Falco, J.: Robust estimator for non-line-of-sight error mitigation in indoor localization. EURASIP J. Adv. Signal Process. **2006**(1), 1–8 (2006)
2. Chan, Y.T., Hang, H.Y.C., Ching, P.: Exact and approximate maximum likelihood localization algorithms. IEEE Trans. Veh. Technol. **55**(1), 10–16 (2006)
3. Chan, Y.T., Tsui, W.Y., So, H.C., Ching, P.C.: Time-of-arrival based localization under NLOS conditions. IEEE Trans. Veh. Technol. **55**(1), 17–24 (2006)
4. Chen, H., Wang, G., Wang, Z., So, H.C., Poor, H.V.: Non-line-of-sight node localization based on semi-definite programming in wireless sensor networks. IEEE Trans. Wireless Commun. **11**(1), 108–116 (2012)
5. Cheung, K.W., So, H.C., Ma, W., Chan, Y.T.: Least squares algorithms for time-of-arrival-based mobile location. IEEE Trans. Signal Process. **52**(4), 1121–1130 (2004). https://doi.org/10.1109/TSP.2004.823465
6. Gezici, S., Sahinoglu, Z.: UWB geolocation techniques for IEEE 802.15.4a personal area networks. MERL Technical report (2004)

7. Grant, M., Boyd, S.: CVX: Matlab software for disciplined convex programming (2008)
8. Guvenc, I., Chong, C.C.: A survey on TOA based wireless localization and NLOS mitigation techniques. IEEE Commun. Surv. Tutor. **11**(3), 107–124 (2009)
9. Han, Z.-F., Leung, C.-S., So, H.C., Sum, J., Constantinides, A.G.: Non-line-of-sight mitigation via Lagrange programming neural networks in TOA-based localization. In: Arik, S., Huang, T., Lai, W.K., Liu, Q. (eds.) ICONIP 2015. LNCS, vol. 9491, pp. 190–197. Springer, Cham (2015). https://doi.org/10.1007/978-3-319-26555-1_22
10. Hsu, L.-T.: Analysis and modeling GPS NLOS effect in highly urbanized area. GPS Solutions **22**(1), 1–12 (2017). https://doi.org/10.1007/s10291-017-0667-9
11. Hsu, L.-T., Jan, S.-S., Groves, P.D., Kubo, N.: Multipath mitigation and NLOS detection using vector tracking in urban environments. GPS Solutions **19**(2), 249–262 (2014). https://doi.org/10.1007/s10291-014-0384-6
12. Li, J., Wu, S.: Non-parametric non-line-of-sight identification and estimation for wireless location. In: 2012 International Conference on Computer Science & Service System (CSSS), pp. 81–84. IEEE (2012)
13. Li, Z., Trappe, W., Zhang, Y., Nath, B.: Robust statistical methods for securing wireless localization in sensor networks. In: IPSN 2005. Fourth International Symposium on Information Processing in Sensor Networks 2005, pp. 91–98, April 2005. https://doi.org/10.1109/IPSN.2005.1440903
14. Liu, N., Xu, Z., Sadler, B.M.: Geolocation performance with biased range measurements. IEEE Trans. Signal Process. **60**(5), 2315–2329 (2012)
15. Ma, Z., Ho, K.C.: TOA localization in the presence of random sensor position errors. In: 2011 IEEE International Conference on Acoustics, Speech and Signal Processing (ICASSP), pp. 2468–2471, May 2011. https://doi.org/10.1109/ICASSP.2011.5946984
16. Qi, Y., Kobayashi, H., Suda, H.: Analysis of wireless geolocation in a non-line-of-sight environment. IEEE Trans. Wireless Commun. **5**(3), 672–681 (2006)
17. Riba, J., Urruela, A.: A non-line-of-sight mitigation technique based on ML-detection. In: IEEE International Conference on Acoustics, Speech, and Signal Processing 2004. Proceedings, vol. 2, pp. ii–153-6 (2004)
18. So, H.C.: Source localization: algorithms and analysis. In: Handbook of Position Location: Theory, Practice, and Advances, pp. 25–66 (2011)
19. Sun, G.L., Guo, W.: Bootstrapping M-estimators for reducing errors due to non-line-of-sight (NLOS) propagation. IEEE Commun. Lett. **8**(8), 509–510 (2004)
20. Vaghefi, R.M., Schloemann, J., Buehrer, R.M.: NLOS mitigation in TOA-based localization using semidefinite programming. In: 10th Workshop on Positioning, Navigation and Communication (WPNC), pp. 1–6, March 2013
21. Wang, G., So, A.M.C., Li, Y.: Robust convex approximation methods for TDOA-based localization under NLOS conditions. IEEE Trans. Signal Process. **64**(13), 3281–3296 (2016)
22. Xu, E., Ding, Z., Dasgupta, S.: Source localization in wireless sensor networks from signal time-of-arrival measurements. IEEE Trans. Signal Process. **59**(6), 2887–2897 (2011). https://doi.org/10.1109/TSP.2011.2116012
23. Zhang, S., Constantinides, A.: Lagrange programming neural networks. IEEE Trans. Circuits Syst. II Analog Digital Signal Process. **39**(7), 441–452 (1992)

Effectiveness Analysis of UAV Offensive Strategy with Unknown Adverse Trajectory

Hao Yan, Heng Zhang$^{(\boxtimes)}$, Jianwei Sun, Tao Tian, Hongbin Wang,
Dandan Zhang, Weiwei Xu, Jian Zhang, Hongran Li, and Dongqing Yuan

School of Science, Jiangsu Ocean University, Lianyungang, China
`zhangheng@jou.edu.cn`

Abstract. In this paper, we consider a scene of UAV confrontation, which has the same altitude, given channel width W and attack depth L. For the unknown adverse trajectory, we design an optimal interception strategy based on the UAV straight line breakthrough, and propose an effective breakout strategy for UAV clusters to break through its defending line. To verify the effectiveness of the breakout strategy, we provide a simulation example for UAV confrontation in a dynamic confrontation environment. The breakout region has reached 99% of all regions battlefield through simulation, which proves the effectiveness of the proposed breakout strategy.

Keywords: UAV · Cooperative confrontation · Trajectory planning · Offensive strategies

1 Introduction

With artificial intelligence and autonomous technology development, collaboration technology of UAV cluster evolves into popular applications. Collaborative work of UAV clusters overcomes the disadvantages of a single UAV, such as insufficient execution ability, limited load capacity, lightweight load and other shortcomings [1,2]. Through multiple UAV reconnaissance, detection, tracking, attack, interception, etc., complex combat missions can be completed together. It plays an important role in the field of application of urban rescue, environmental detection, etc. [3,4].

A lot of efforts have been made in the research of UAV cluster collaboration technology [5–7]. In [5], aiming at the problem of multi-UAV cooperative

The work was partially supported by the National Natural Science Foundation of China under Grant 61873106, Nature Science Foundation of Jiangsu Province for Distinguished Young Scholars under Grant BK20200049, Jiangsu Provincial Innovation and Entrepreneurship Training Program Key Project under Grant 20200419.

Z. Liu et al. (Eds.): WASA 2021, LNCS 12939, pp. 68–76, 2021.
https://doi.org/10.1007/978-3-030-86137-7_8

search and tracking of multi-moving targets in the region, a multi-UAV cooperative search and tracking strategy based on vertical search is proposed. [6] applies the ant colony algorithm to solve the problem of multi-UAV systems in the coordinated reconnaissance of complex target groups. [7] proposes the task allocation and trajectory optimization algorithm for multi-target attacks. In addition, [8–10] use a data-driven method to control the robot. Although these studies are accurate for UAV flight control, they have the disadvantages of exponential increase in calculation, long convergence time and insecurity, etc. Regarding the safety issue, [11–14] have made a detailed study on it.

The key to UAV cluster confrontation is selecting the two sides battle strategy, so choosing the method of decision-making has an important impact on the fight result. In [15], the Bezier curve is introduced for multi-aircraft coordinated trajectory planning. [16] puts forward a three-stage consensus saturation attack strategy under the coordinated control of UAVs, and designs corresponding improved consensus algorithms according to the mission characteristics of different stages. However, the current UAV clustering algorithms tend to be complex, computationally intensive, expensive to demonstrate, resulting in no clustering algorithms can demonstrate synergistic confrontation and verification on the actual UAV cluster.

To address the issue of complexity, we propose a novel model of six-tuple for the confrontation of UAV. According to the application requirements of UAV planning and control in a dynamic confrontation environment, we establish the iterative model of the defender UAV and the deceptive model of the breakout UAVs. For verifying the effectiveness of the breakout strategy, the design and implementation of the UAV cluster cooperative countermeasure system is accomplished.Motivated by the above observations, the contributions of this paper are provided in the following twofold.

1) To solve the problem of exponential growth in calculation, we design a trajectory planning algorithm based on real-time location, and a cooperative confrontation strategy of UAV is established.
2) Based on the trajectory representation method of six-tuple , the iterative real-time position of the UAVs can be realized through the optimization of the heading angle and the minimum turning radius parameters.

The remainder of this paper is organized as follows. Section 2 analyzes the original problem and transformed the problem. Section 3 proposes a solution to the problem, including the UAV breakthrough strategy and interception strategy. Section 4 gives the simulation results and analysis of UAV cooperative countermeasures. Section 5 concludes this paper.

2   Problem Statement

For simplicity, we mark the breakout UAVs (offensive side) as blue and the intercepted UAV cluster as red. Then we consider the problem of confrontation, where the red and blue UAVs are maneuvering at the same altitude.

As the offensive side, the blue UAV hopes to break through the interception of the red UAV cluster and successfully reach the destination to carry out military operations. As the intercepted side, the red UAV cluster hope to complete the interception of the blue UAV in a given area.

The confrontation area Map is agreed to be the rectangular area $ABCD$ shown in Fig. 1. The depth of the attack L is the distance between BC. The channel bandwidth W is the distance between the two sides. The blue UAV has an advantage in maneuvering speed, and the defender side considers the coordination of multiple UAV, which is to make up for the disadvantages in performance through the number of advantages and improve its own counter-measures.

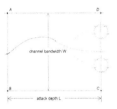
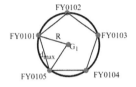

Fig. 1. The background of UAV confrontation (Color figure online)

Fig. 2. Red UAV cluster formation (Color figure online)

Fig. 3. Interception region (Color figure online)

When the blue UAV is in the confrontation region, the red UAV cluster intercepts it. Meanwhile, the blue UAV needs to adopt a suitable strategy to avoid the interception of the red UAV cluster and achieve a successful pene-tration. The UAV cluster confrontation problem can be described as a six-tuple $<M, R_U, B_U, \pi, J, U>$, where M means the given confrontation environment, R_U delegates the red UAV cluster, B_U represents the blue target collection, π is the red UAV cluster coordination strategy, J stands for the blue UAV break-through strategy, and the U is the evaluation of the effectiveness of the blue UAV breakthrough. Each factor in the six-tuple is described as follows.

The red UAV cluster contains multiple UAV. Each UAV is a collection of some states, which can be expressed as a tuple $<ID, P, V_C, K, T_P>$, where ID means the unique identifier of the UAV in the R_U, P is the current position of the UAV, Vc represents the current speed of the UAV, T_P stands for the mission target selected by the UAV, K delegates the flight operation constraint in the current state of the UAV. This constraint is described as $K(\alpha, R)$, where α represents the heading angle of the UAV in the current state, and R means the turning radius of the UAV in the current state.

The R_U coordination strategy consists of the trajectory planning of each UAV cluster $Path(i)$ and the interception strategy $e(i)$ adopted by each UAV cluster. It can be derived as $J = \{e(i), path(i)\}$. The utility evaluation of the blue UAV breakthrough can be expressed as $U = \frac{S_B}{S_M}$, where S_B delegates the area with the blue UAV being able to achieve a successful penetration, S_M represents the total area of the confrontation area. According to the introduction of the above six-tuple, the optimization problem can be described as:

$$\max_{x_j, y_j, R, \alpha, \theta} U \tag{1a}$$

$$0 \leq x_j \leq L, 0 \leq y_j \leq W \tag{1b}$$

$$|\alpha| \leq \pi, |\theta| \leq \theta_{\max}, R \geq R_{\min}, \tag{1c}$$

where the variable L is the depth of attack, W means the width of the channel, α delegates the heading angle, θ represents the deflection angle, θ_{max} is on behalf of the deflection angle when the turning radius is the smallest, R stands for the turning radius, R_{min} evinces the minimum turning radius, (X_j, Y_j) is the real-time position of the blue UAV.

3   Problem Solution

In this part, we first take B as the origin, BC as the X axis, and BA as the Y axis to establish a rectangular coordinate system. The defense then launches five UAVs from the $FY01$ and $FY02$ carriers to form two UAVs clusters for interception missions. Because of communication and collision avoidance, the UAV should not be less than d_{min} or greater than d_{max}.

For the red UAV cluster formation, we adopt a circular formation. The positions of 5 UAVs are approximately distributed on a circle, as shown in Fig. 2. The distance between any two adjacent UAVs is d_{max}, the circle centers of the two red UAV clusters are located at G_1 and G_2, and the circle radius is $\frac{d_{max}}{2 sin \frac{\pi}{5}}$.

When the distance between the blue UAV and at least two red UAVs is less than the interception distance r, the red side is considered to intercept success. The blue UAV must cross the boundary within Ts, otherwise it will be regarded as failure to penetration. The interception region is the area surrounded by circles with five UAVs in the red UAV cluster as the center and the interception distance r as the radius, as shown in Fig. 3.

The interception model can be described as

$$\begin{cases} \sum_{i=1}^{5} \varepsilon \left\{ r^2 - [(X_r - X_b)^2 + (Y_r - Y_b)^2] \right\} < 2 \\ t \leq T, \end{cases} \tag{2}$$

$$\sum_{i=1}^{5} \varepsilon \left\{ r^2 - [(X_r - X_b)^2 + (Y_r - Y_b)^2] \right\} \geq 2 \; or \; t > T \; , \begin{cases} \varepsilon(x) = 1 & x \geq 0 \\ \varepsilon(x) = 0 & x < 0 \end{cases}, \tag{3}$$

where X_r, Y_r are the coordinates of five UAVs in the red UAV cluster, and X_b, Y_b are the coordinates of the blue UAV. Whether red or blue UAVs are subject to its heading angle and minimum turning radius, the location that the UAV can reach at the next moment is limited. We design a model of its future position.

We give the red UAV's horizontal heading angle to the left. The location that the UAV can reach at the next moment is limited. We develop a model of its future position. The coordinates of the point expression on the curve E is obtained as

$$Q(X_G - Rsin(\frac{V_p}{R}), Y_G + Rcos(\frac{V_p}{R}) - Y) , \qquad (4)$$

$$H(X_G - Rsin(\frac{V_p}{R}), Y_G + Rcos(\frac{V_p}{R}) + Y) , \qquad (5)$$

where the UAV speed is V_p, R is the turning radius, Q is the point on the curve $E_{11} \sim E_{21}$, and H is the point on the curve $E_{21} \sim E_{31}$. Therefore, curve E only needs to be represented by three points Q, E_{21}, and H.

For a UAV with any heading angle, we can determine its position set by its heading angle relative to the horizontal. The following theorem provides the change of UAV position at different angles of deflection

$$x_0 = (x - rx_0)cos(\alpha) - (y - ry_0)sin(\alpha) + rx_0 , \qquad (6)$$

$$y_0 = (x - rx_0)sin(\alpha) + (y - ry_0)cos(\alpha) + ry_0 , \qquad (7)$$

$$\alpha_t = \alpha_{t-1} + \theta_{t-1} , \qquad (8)$$

where (x, y) is an arbitrary point coordinate axis, and the new coordinate after rotating (rx_0, ry_0) counterclockwise by an angle of α is (x_0, y_0). θ represents the angle at which the UAV will deflect in the next second, and the rotation angle α is the heading angle. The above introduces the movement of the red UAV cluster, the movement of the blue UAV is the same as the method of the red UAV cluster mentioned above, so here will not be introduced.

Both UAVs are equipped with detection devices and data links, which can accurately detect the real-time location of the other UAV and the own UAV. Therefore, we use the position of the blue UAV to determine the target position and heading angle of the red UAV cluster at the next moment. The target position of the red UAV cluster is Iterated to form a red UAV cluster interception strategy.

Algorithm 1. Intercepting decision

1: **Initialize:** the location(x_r^l, y_r^l), rotation(z_r^l, w_r^l), velocity V and maximum turning radius R of R_U, the location(x_b^l, y_b^l) and rotation(z_b^l, w_b^l) of B_U,

2: Solve the ideal location(x_{ib}, y_{ib}) and rotation(z_{ib}, w_{ib}) of B_U with formula **(1)**. The ideal situation is $(x_r, y_r, z_r, w_r) = (0, 0, 1, 0)$

3: **if** $|\frac{y_{ib}}{x_{ib}}| < \frac{1 - cos(\frac{V}{R})}{sin(\frac{V}{R})}$, we can obtain (x_{ir}, y_{ir}) by solving **(P1)**.

4.**else**

5: $k \leftarrow sign(\frac{y_{ib}}{x_{ib}})$, $(x_{ir}, y_{ir}) \leftarrow (R * sin(\frac{V}{R}), k * (R - R * cos(\frac{V}{R})))$

6.**endif**

7.Solve the rotated location increment(dx_r^{l+1}, dy_r^{l+1}) and last rotation(z_r^{l+1}, w_r^{l+1}) of R_U with formula **(1)**, $(x_r^{l+1}, y_r^{l+1}) = (dx_r^{l+1}, dy_r^{l+1}) + (x_r^l, y_r^l)$

Determination of the target position: we set the blue UAV position B_{t-1} as (X_{b-1}, Y_{b-1}) and the position mapped to the boundary CD B'_{t-1} as (X'_{b-1}, Y'_{b-1}), then the target of the red UAV cluster is $\{B_{t-1}, B'_{t-1}\}$.

We connect the position of the center G of the red UAV cluster with the position of the blue UAV to obtain the line segment RB connecting the two points. The red curve E is the point that the UAV may reach within the radius of rotation. The target point of the red UAV cluster is determined by RB which is shown in Fig. 5. When the next target point of the red UAV cluster is obtained, the corresponding heading angle can be calculated. For example, if E_1 is the next target point of the red UAV cluster, the heading angle is the tangent direction of E_1 and circle O_1. Next, we map the position of the blue UAV to the boundary CD (the horizontal coordinate of the blue UAV is fixed to L). The mapped the position of blue UAV B' and the position of red UAV cluster center G are connected as RB'. At this time, the target point of the red UAV cluster is determined by RB'.

For the selection of the target position, we introduce the red critical distance λ and propose decision model. When $|Y_G - Y_b| \geq \lambda$, RB' decide the position of red UAV cluster at the next moment. When $|Y_G - Y_b| < \lambda$, its position is decided by the RB. The intercepting decision is shown in Algorithm 1. For the red two UAV clusters, $\pi(1)$ and $Path(1)$ represent the operating strategy and trajectory planning of G_1. $\pi(2)$ and $Path(2)$ represent the operating strategy and trajectory planning of G_2.

There are two types of blue UAV breakout strategies, including straight-line flight and deceptive breakout flight. Straight flight $e(1)$: The blue UAV flys straight for saving time. Deceptive breakout strategy $e(2)$: In our model, the blue UAV approaches the midpoint of G_1 and G_2 for deceiving the two red UAV clusters to approach each other, thereby weakening the defensive capabilities of both sides. When the distance between the blue UAV and one of the red UAV clusters reach the critical distance ε, the deceptive strategy ends. Next, the blue UAV judges the distance between CG_1 and DG_2, selects the side with the larger distance (solves $max\{CG_1, CG_2\}$), and attacks the boundary point on the larger side. When $X_b > X_G$, the blue UAV takes a straight flight. The deceptive decision is expressed in Algorithm 2.

Algorithm 2. Deceptive decision

1: **Initialize:** the location(x_{G1}, y_{G1}) of G1, the location(x_{G2}, y_{G2}) of G2, the location(x_b, y_b) of B_U, the location(x_C, y_C) of C, the location(x_D, y_D) of D, minimum distance ϵ

2: **if** $min(|x_b - x_{G1}|), |x_b - x_{G1}|) < \epsilon$, $(x_{aim}, y_{aim}) \leftarrow \frac{(x_{G1}, y_{G1}) + (x_{G2}, y_{G2})}{2}$

3: **elseif** $|(x_C, y_C) - (x_{G1}, y_{G1})| > |(x_D, y_D) - (x_{G2}, y_{G2})|$

4: $(x_{aim}, y_{aim}) \leftarrow (x_C, y_C)$

5: **else**

6: $(x_{aim}, y_{aim}) \leftarrow (x_C, y_C)$

7: **endif**

The blue critical distance ε is $|X_b - X_G|$. When ε is less than the critical distance, the blue UAV may fail to bypass the red UAV cluster. On the contrary, the red UAV cluster can reach the position in advance where the blue UAV is about to arrive, hence there will be an optimal distance or distance range.

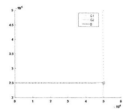 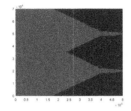 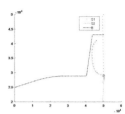

Fig. 4. Red UAV cluster intercepting motion trajectory simulation (Color figure online)

Fig. 5. Red UAV cluster interception area simulation (Color figure online)

Fig. 6. Blue UAV deceptive breakthrough simulation results (Color figure online)

4   Simulation Example

The initial position x, y of the blue UAV is randomly generated in the confrontation area M. The confrontation area and UAV performance parameters are set as: attack depth $L = 50$ km, channel bandwidth $W = 70$ km, the speed of the blue UAV $V_E = 250$ m/s, the minimum turning radius of blue UAV $R_E = 500$ m, the speed of the red UAV cluster $V_P = 250$ m/s, the minimum turning radius of the red UAV cluster $R_P = 500$ m, Maximum spacing $d_{max} = 200$ m, interception distance $R = 300$ m, time limit $T = 360$ s, red square critical distance $\lambda = 10000$ m, blue square critical distance $\varepsilon = 10000$ m.

We made the blue UAV adopt a straight-line strategy. The trajectory of the opposing parties is shown in Fig. 4, and the interception area is shown in Fig. 5. The red area represents the successful interception region. The blue area means the successful breakthrough region. It can be seen from Fig. 5 that the interception strategy of the red UAV cluster can effectively intercept most of the confrontation areas, and the breakout utility of the blue UAV can be calculated $U = 0.36$.

In the experiment, the blue UAV adopts a deceptive breakthrough strategy, and the red UAV cluster intercept it. The trajectory of red and blue UAVs are shown in Fig. 6, and the interception area is shown in Fig. 7. The breakout strategy of blue UAV can effectively breakthrough most of the confrontation areas, and the breakout utility of the blue UAV can be calculated $U = 0.86$.

In Fig. 7, we can see that the deceptive breakout strategy of blue UAV is more ideal than the effect of straight-line flight. But in some cases, it's the other way around. When the blue UAV is located in different positions, different breakout strategies should be adopted. The simulation result of the final breakout region

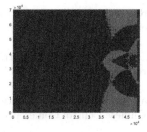

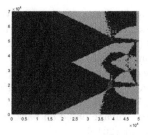

Fig. 7. Blue UAV breakthrough area simulation (Color figure online)

Fig. 8. Blue UAV final breakout area simulation (Color figure online)

is shown in Fig. 8. At this time, the breakout utility of the blue UAV is $U = 0.99$. The green area is on behalf of the region where the blue UAV can successfully reaches the destination. The blue area represents the region where the blue UAV can break the line through optimal strategies, and the red area delegates the region where the blue UAV cannot break through no matter which strategy it adopts.

5   Conclusion

This paper has proposed a novel model with six-tuple based on UAV cooperative confrontation. According to this model, the interception strategy of intercepting UAV and the deceptive breakout strategy of breaking UAV are established respectively, which realizes the simulation of UAV cooperative confrontation in a dynamic confrontation environment. Through the traversal method, we have obtained the UAV breakthrough region based on the maximum utility evaluation.

References

1. Crowther, T.W.: The emergence of trait-based approaches in fungal ecology. Fungal Ecol. **46**, 100946 (2020)
2. AL-Madani, B., Elkhider, S.M., El-Ferik, S.: DDS-based containment control of multiple UAV systems. Appl. Sci. **10**(13), 4572 (2020)
3. Weiwei, X., Zhang, H., Cao, X., Deng, R., Li, H., Zhang, J.: Securing wireless relaying communication for dual unmanned aerial vehicles with unknown eavesdropper. Inf. Sci. **546**, 871–882 (2021)
4. Sun, J., et al.: Improving security performance of dual UAVs system with unknown eavesdropper location. In: Proceedings of the International Conference on Internet-of-Things Design and Implementation, pp. 257–258 (2021)
5. Wang, H., Tian, J., Wei, L., Zhuang, Y.: Multi-UAV collaborative search and tracking strategy for multiple moving targets. Control Theory Appl. **38**(7), 971–978 (2021)

6. Liang, F., Yang, Y., Liu, G., Wan, B., Gao, W.: Research on collaborative reconnaissance planning algorithm for multi-UAV systems. Aerosp. Defense **4**(1), 103–108 (2021)
7. Zhang, Y., Lin, D., Zheng, D., Cheng, Z., Tang, P.: Task allocation and trajectory optimization of multi-target space-time synchronized coordinated attack UAV. Acta Armamentarii **7**, 1–14 (2021)
8. Xu, W., Li, H., Zhang, J., Zhu, Y., Zhang, H.: Trajectory tracking for underwater rescue salvage based on backstepping control. In: Chinese Control Conference, pp. 422–427 (2019)
9. Xu, W., Xiao, Y., Li, H., Zhang, J., Zhang, H.: Trajectory tracking for autonomous underwater vehicle based on model-free predictive control. In: IEEE 20th International Conference on High Performance Switching and Routing, pp. 1–6 (2019)
10. Li, H., Weiwei, X., Zhang, H., Zhang, J., Liu, Y.: Polynomial regressors based data-driven control for autonomous underwater vehicles. Peer-to-Peer Netw. Appl. **13**(5), 1767–1775 (2020). https://doi.org/10.1007/s12083-020-00878-6
11. Weiwei, X., et al.: Iterative trajectory optimization for dual-UAV secure communications. In: IEEE/ACM Fifth International Conference on Internet-of-Things Design and Implementation, pp. 260–261 (2020)
12. Yang, W., Li, D., Zhang, H., Tang, Y., Zheng, W.X.: An encoding mechanism for secrecy of remote state estimation. Automatica **120**, 109116 (2020)
13. Gan, R., Shao, J., Xiao, Y., Zhang, H., Zheng, W.X.: Optimizing attack schedules based on energy dispatch over two-Hop relay networks. IEEE Trans. Autom. Control **65**(9), 3832–3846 (2020)
14. Wang, L., Cao, X., Sun, B., Zhang, H., Sun, C.: Optimal schedule of secure transmissions for remote state estimation against eavesdropping. IEEE Trans. Industr. Inf. **17**(3), 1987–1997 (2020)
15. Askari, A., Mortazavi, M., Talebi, H.A., Motamedi, A.: A new approach in UAV path planning using Bezier-Dubins continuous curvature path. Proc. Inst. Mech. Eng. Part G J. Aerosp. Eng. **230**(6), 1103–1113 (2016)
16. Lu, X., Pu, H., Zhen, Z., Chen, P.: UAV swarm saturation attack based on improved consensus algorithm. Electro-Opt. Control 1–6 (2021)

Delivery Optimization for Unmanned Aerial Vehicles Based on Minimum Cost Maximum Flow with Limited Battery Capacity

Rui Wang$^{(\boxtimes)}$, Xiangping Bryce Zhai, Yunlong Zhao, and Xuedong Zhao

Nanjing University of Aeronautics and Astronautics, Nanjing, China
{wrtamara,blueicezhaixp,zhaoyunlong}@nuaa.edu.cn

Abstract. The significance of unmanned aerial vehicles (UAVs) for delivery services is increasing nowadays. Due to the energy capacity limitations, long-distance distribution is still a challenging problem in the UAV logistics market. In this paper, allowing UAVs to be charged in UAV stations, we studied the long-distance delivery of single UAV. We planed the route in advance with the cloud computing platform and send it to the designated UAV. First, an optimization algorithm is proposed based on the minimum cost maximum flow theory, which divides locations and UAV stations into several takeoff UAV station-locations-landing UAV station (SLS) sets. Then a sequence of SLSs is determined by comparing the total energy consumption to minimize the consumption of the UAV under the energy capacity limitation. Finally, experiments verify the effectiveness of the proposed methods.

Keywords: UAVs delivery · Tasks allocation · Long-distance distribution · Energy capacity constraints

1 Introduction

In the transportation industry, compared with traditional trucks, Unmanned aerial vehicles (UAVs) can automatically execute the planned routes to reduce labor costs. The working area of UAV is in the air, which can effectively avoid various problems caused by ground transportation. Moreover, for areas with poor road conditions such as remote mountainous areas, UAV delivery is an effective solution for difficult distribution.

With the development of e-commerce, many companies have pay much attention to transport small packages with UAVs [1]. However, there are still many

This work was supported in part by National Natural Science Foundation of China (No. 61802181, No. 61701231), and the Foundation of Key Laboratory of Safety-Critical Software (Nanjing University of Aeronautics and Astronautics), Ministry of Industry and Information Technology (No. NJ2020022).

Z. Liu et al. (Eds.): WASA 2021, LNCS 12939, pp. 77–85, 2021.
https://doi.org/10.1007/978-3-030-86137-7_9

technologies need to be overcome. Besides the limited carrying capacity, the energy capacity is also a main concern, leading to the limited operating range of UAVs without energy supplementation. W. Chen et al. [2] proposed that UAVs unable to perform heavy computation tasks during the complicated disaster recovery process. Therefore, the unmanned ground vehicles perform the computation tasks offloaded from UAVs, and they developed a stable matching algorithm to realize the collaboration. However, if UAVs can be allowed to stop at UAV stations in the mission area and replenish energy, just like intelligent cars [3], the range of activities and tasks completion rate of UAVs will be greatly improved.

In response to this logistical problem, some papers have studied the transportation problem of allowing UAVs to supplement power during flight. [4] developed a two-stage route-based modeling approach and a hybrid heuristic integrating nearest neighbor and cost saving strategies to solve the problem of collaborative distribution of trucks and UAVs. The authors of [5] proposed the drone delivery problems that minimize cost or delivery time while considering battery weight, payload weight, and drone reuse. They implemented the problem as mixed integer linear programs and raised a string-based simulated annealing algorithm.

In this paper, we study a UAV delivery problem (UDP) for minimizing energy consumption with limited energy capacity, which allows the UAV to park at any UAV station to charge. We focus on two challenges: 1) how to allocate the takeoff and landing UAV stations and delivery tasks of each flight mission; and 2) how to ensure that the total flight distance of each flight mission is less than the longest flying distance of the UAV. UDP is similar to the few-participants-more-tasks (FPMT) problem in [6], which not only includes the combinational optimization problem of locations and UAV stations, but also includes the shortest path problem. We convert UDP to be a minimum cost maximum flow (MCMF) problem and use the cloud computing platform to plan routes in advance.

2   System Model

The mission area consists of N locations and M UAV stations, and the UAV denoted as U can be recharged at any UAV station. Without loss of generality, we make two assumptions to simplify the problem: one is that the UAV will not encounter obstacles, the other is to ignore the energy consumption of UAV caused by takeoff, landing and natural factors. To formulate the problem mathematically, a list of key symbols used hereafter is provided in Table 1. Note that a location l_n will not be included by $\mathcal{L}$ when l_n is too far away from the nearest UAV station s_m of l_n, which means the energy of U cannot support it to takeoff from s_m and return to s_m.

Our objective is to minimize the total energy consumption of U while completing all locations. Without considering natural factors, the flying distance can be used to approximate energy consumption. Therefore, our objective can

Table 1. Symbol definitions

Symbol	Definition
$\mathcal{S}=[s_1,s_2,\ldots,s_M]$	A set of M UAV stations
$\mathcal{L}=[l_1,l_2,\ldots,l_N]$	A set of N locations, and each location is a delivery task that only need to be executed once
$\mathcal{LU}_k=[l_{k1},l_{k2}\ldots]$	A set of locations that waiting to be performed in a takeoff and landing process
$\mathcal{SU}_k=[s_{k1},s_{k2}]$	A UAV station set containing takeoff UAV station s_{k1} and landing UAV station s_{k2} of U in a takeoff and landing process
$\mathcal{LS}_k=[\mathcal{LU}_k,\mathcal{SU}_k]$	A SLS that represents a takeoff and landing process of U
$\mathcal{I}=[i_1,i_2\ldots]$	A set of SLSs selected by the initial path $\mathcal{I}$
$\mathcal{CLS}=[c_1,c_2\ldots]$	A set of SLSs not selected by the initial path $\mathcal{I}$
$\mathcal{F}=[\,f_1,f_2\ldots]$	A set of SLSs in the final path $\mathcal{F}$, which can be executed sequentially

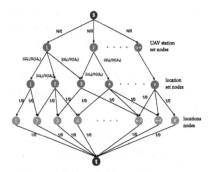

Fig. 1. MCMF model of UDP. (Color figure online)

Fig. 2. Formation of initial path $\mathcal{I}$.

be converted to minimize the total flight distance. Then, the problem can be formulated as follow:

$$
\begin{aligned}
\text{minimize } & D(\mathcal{F}) \\
\text{subject to } & D\left(f_r\right) \leqslant \bar{d}\left(0 \leqslant r \leqslant |\mathcal{F}|\right),
\end{aligned}
\tag{1}
$$

where $D(\mathcal{F})$ and $D\left(f_r\right)$ is the total flight distance of U to complete all locations in $\mathcal{F}$ and f_r, $\bar{d}$ is the longest flight distance of U with full charge and r represents the number of SLS in the final path $\mathcal{F}$.

The purpose of the MCMF model is to find a group of optimal paths with minimum cost and maximum flow. Hence, the authors of [6] transformed FPMT into the MCMF problem. Different from FPMT, we require that every location should be executed and each location can only be delivered once. Therefore, we construct a new constrained MCMF model according to UDP, that obtains the optimal solution of the combination optimization problem [6]. As shown in Fig. 1, the flow network of the MCMF model is a directed graph, where each edge has capacity, flow and cost. The capacity and cost of an edge respectively represent the maximum amount of flow that can be accommodated by the edge and the cost of each flow passing through the edge. We use the total flight distance to represent the cost, and the total number of accomplished locations is modeled as the flow.

We adding the first-level nodes (blue nodes) to the flow network to represent the UAV station sets. Each UAV station set contains two UAV stations, which represent takeoff UAV station and landing UAV station respectively. And the two UAV stations may be same or different. Therefore, there are altogether $C_M^2 + M$ UAV station sets. Then, adding the second-level nodes (green nodes) to represent the location sets. For any UAV station set $\mathcal{SU}_k$, it can form a completely undirected graph G_{SU_k} with all locations in $\mathcal{L}$, and the weight of each edge is represented by the distance between two points. Moreover, all the paths from s_{k1} to s_{k2} in G_{SU_k} and the flight distance of these paths can be calculated by using the Depth-first algorithm [7,8]. Considering the energy limitation of UAV, we eliminate all paths with a distance greater than $\bar{d}$. In addition, some paths may execute the same locations in a different order of execution, so we only leave the shortest distance among these paths. Hence, the remaining paths are the feasible paths of $\mathcal{SU}_k$. A path can be transformed into a SLS, and all locations in this path can form a location set. Assuming that the total number of feasible paths for all UAV station set is P, then the number of location set nodes is P. Finally, we add the third-level nodes (yellow nodes) to the flow network to represent locations, and the number of location nodes is N.

The cost of each edge between UAV station set nodes and location set nodes represents the flight distance of the corresponding SLS $\mathcal{LS}_k$, which is calculated by the Depth-first algorithm and denoted by $D(\mathcal{LS}_k)$. Except for these edges, the cost of other edges is 0, because the other edges represent a corresponding relationship with no movement distance. In addition, we use different capacities of edges to represent different requirements. Because it is possible that the UAV will takeoff and land at the same UAV station every time, the maximum capacity of each edge between the source node and blue nodes is N.

As we know, a UAV station set may correspond to multiple feasible paths, which means that it may correspond to multiple location sets. Moreover, a UAV station node $\mathcal{SU}_k$ is only connected to its corresponding location set node $\mathcal{LU}_k$, and the capacity of the edge between them is the number of locations which can be denoted as $|\mathcal{LU}_k|$ in $\mathcal{LU}_k$. Notice that the flow on the edge between green node and blue node is either 0 or $|\mathcal{LU}_k|$, which cannot be adjusted incrementally. Furthermore, the capacity of each edge between the sink node and yellow nodes is set as one, which means that each location can only be executed once. Hence, the maximum flow from the source node to the sink node is the total number of locations. On the basis of the previous assumptions, we can construct the flow network $G = (V, E, \$, W)$, where W is the capacity of each edge, and $\$$ is the total cost.

3   Tasks Allocation of UDP

According to the analysis of UDP, we realize that the UAV needs to takeoff and land repeatedly to complete all locations. Therefore, we need to divide the locations and the UAV stations into several SLSs, which can be expressed as $\mathcal{LS} = [\mathcal{LS}_1, \mathcal{LS}_2 \ldots]$, and the locations in these SLSs should not be repeated. We transform this division problem into the MCMF problem and propose the division of locations and UAV stations algorithm (DLSA) to solve it.

Algorithm 1. The division of locations and UAV stations algorithm (DLSA)

Input: the UAV U, the location set $\mathcal{L}$, the UAV station set S
Output: a selected SLS set $\mathcal{LS}$
1: construct the flow network $G = (V, E, \$, W)$ of the MCMF model
2: **function** F_COST(a flow f)
3:     **while** there exists an augmenting path in the residual network G_f **do**
4:         select the augmenting path p^* with minimum cost and no conflict with f
5:         augment flow f along with p^*
6:     **end while**
7:     **return** f and the total cost of the f
8: **end function**
9: initialize flow f to $|LU_k|$ along with the path including LS_k of the minimum cost
10: $Cost_{min} \leftarrow$ F_Cost(f)
11: **for** the minimum cost to maximum cost of $\mathcal{LS}_k$ **do**
12:     **if** there is no conflict between $\mathcal{LS}_k$ and f **then**
13:         augment flow f along with the path with $\mathcal{LS}_k$
14:     **else**
15:         $f_{LS_k} \leftarrow f$
16:         release all combinations of location set node and UAV station set node that contain same locations with $\mathcal{LS}_k$ in f_{LS_k} and augment flow f_{LS_k} along with the path of $\mathcal{LS}_k$
17:         $(f_{LS_k}, Cost_{\mathcal{LS}_k}) \leftarrow$ F_Cost(f_{LS_k})
18:         **if** $Cost_{\mathcal{LS}_k} < Cost_{min}$ **then**
19:             $f \leftarrow$ flows in f_{LS_k} whose cost is not greater than $\mathcal{LS}_k$
20:         **end if**
21:     **end if**
22: **end for**
23: **output** a selected SLS set $\mathcal{LS}$ in f

DLSA algorithm mainly includes two parts: one is to find the total cost of flow f in residual network G_f (lines 2–8), and the other is to find the optimal solution in flow network G (lines 9–23). During DLSA, the combinations of location sets and UAV station sets in f are continuously adjusted based on the idea of retracement in the MCMF theory. The time complexity of DLSA is $O\left(M^2N^2\right) + O\left(PNM^2\left(M+N+P\right)\right)$. $O\left(M^2N^2\right)$ denotes the complexity of calculating all feasible combinations by the Depth-first algorithm, and

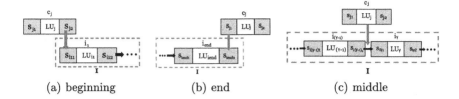

Fig. 3. Potential insert positions in $\mathcal{I}$ where a candidate SLS can be inserted.

$O\left(PNM^2\left(M+N+P\right)\right)$ is the complexity of the MCMF model to find the optimal solution in the flow network.

We need to connect those selected SLSs into a continuous path. Thus, we construct an initial path $\mathcal{I}$ for those SLSs that can be performed sequentially in advance, and then insert the remaining SLSs into $\mathcal{I}$ one by one. Firstly, we initialize $\mathcal{I}$ be empty and assume the initial stop UAV station s_{start}. Before the following steps, it is necessary to confirm whether the takeoff UAV stations and the landing UAV stations of all SLSs in $\mathcal{LS}$ are not s_{start}. If neither of them is s_{start}, s_{start} is used to replace the takeoff or landing UAV station of a SLS which including the location closest to s_{start}. For each $\mathcal{LS}_k$ in $\mathcal{LS}$, if $s_{k1} = s_{k2} = s_{start}$, insert it into $\mathcal{I}$. If no one meets the condition, look for the one with $s_{k1} = s_{start}$ (or $s_{k2} = s_{start}$) and insert it into the end of $\mathcal{I}$ and set $s_{start} = s_{k2}$ (or $s_{start} = s_{k1}$). Repeat the above operations until no SLSs can be inserted into $\mathcal{I}$. As shown in Fig. 2, take UAV station s_1 as the initial stop UAV station, and we will get an initial path $\mathcal{I}=[\mathcal{LS}_1,\overline{\mathcal{LS}_3}]$. In Fig. 2, $\overline{\mathcal{LU}_3}$ and $\overline{\mathcal{LS}_3}$ indicate that the order of $\mathcal{LU}_3$ and $\mathcal{LS}_3$ are reversed. Therefore, it is easy to know that $D\left(\mathcal{I}\right) = D\left(\mathcal{LS}_1\right) + D\left(\overline{\mathcal{LS}_3}\right)$, where $D\left(\mathcal{I}\right)$, $D\left(\mathcal{LS}_1\right)$ and $D\left(\overline{\mathcal{LS}_3}\right)$ represent the total flight distance of $\mathcal{I}$, $\mathcal{LS}_1$ and $\overline{\mathcal{LS}_3}$. Moreover, those SLSs not included in $\mathcal{I}$ will become candidate SLSs and can be defined as $\mathcal{CLS}=[c_1,c_2 \ldots]$. For example, $\mathcal{CLS}=[\mathcal{LS}_2]$ in Fig. 2.

Next, we process a scheme of inserting candidate SLSs into $\mathcal{I}$ in three different situations, and we can find the best insert point (BIP) for each candidate SLS by comparing the total cost after inserting candidate SLS into a specified point. As we can see in Fig. 3, a candidate SLS can be inserted at the beginning and end of $\mathcal{I}$ and between two adjacent SLSs in $\mathcal{I}$. Therefore, assuming that the number of SLSs in $\mathcal{I}$ is N_i, the number of potential insertion positions N_{cls} for candidate SLSs can be defined as $N_{cls} = N_i + 1$. For a candidate SLS c_j, its takeoff UAV station and landing UAV station are represented as s_{j1} and s_{j2} respectively. The total flight distance of $\mathcal{I}$ after inserting c_j at position p can be defined as $D\left(\mathcal{I} \vee_p c_j\right) = D\left(\mathcal{I}\right)+\varDelta$, where $D\left(\mathcal{I} \vee_p c_j\right)$ indicates the total flight distance after inserting c_j into the position p in $\mathcal{I}$, $\varDelta$ represents the adjusted amount of $\mathcal{I}$ after inserting c_j and $\varDelta$ will be different in different situations. The specific strategy is as follows:

Insert into the Beginning of $\mathcal{I}$: We use s_z to denote the first takeoff UAV station of $\mathcal{I}$ in Fig. 3(a), and $s_z = s_{i11}$. If $s_{j1} = s_{j2} = s_z$, then c_j must have already been included in the $\mathcal{I}$. If $s_{j1} = s_z$ and $s_{j1} \neq s_{j2}$, then s_{j1} will be taken as the takeoff UAV station. Obviously, the flight distance from s_{j2} to the first location of $\mathcal{LU}_{i1}$ must be less than the flight distance from s_{j2} to s_z and to the first location of $\mathcal{LU}_{i1}$. For a SLS A, if one of its UAV stations s_a is replaced by another UAV station s_b, the new flight distance of A can be defined as $D^{s_a}(A, s_b)$. Hence, $\Delta = D(c_j) - D(i_1) + D^{s_z}(i_1, s_{j2})$, where $D(c_j)$ and $D(i_1)$ represent the flight distance of c_j and i_1 respectively, and $D^{s_z}(i_1, s_{j2})$ denotes the total flight distance calculated by *Christofides* [6] of i_1 after replacing s_z with s_{j2}. It is the same when $s_{j2} = s_z$ and $s_{j1} \neq s_{j2}$, we take s_{j2} as the takeoff UAV station and the order of all locations in $\mathcal{LU}_j$ needs to be reversed. If $s_{j1} \neq s_z$, $s_{j2} \neq s_z$, where s_{j1} and s_{j2} may or may not be equal. In this case, it is necessary to calculate the total flight distance for replacing s_{j1} with s_z and replacing s_{j2} with s_z respectively. Consequently, $\Delta = min\{\Delta_{s_{j1}}, \Delta_{s_{j2}}\}$, and $\Delta_{s_{j1}} = D^{s_{j1}}(c_j, s_z) - D(i_1) + D^{s_z}(i_1, s_{j2})$ and $\Delta_{s_{j2}} = D^{s_{j2}}(c_j, s_z) - D(i_1) + D^{s_z}(i_1, s_{j1})$, where $\Delta_{s_{j1}}$ and $\Delta_{s_{j2}}$ denote the adjusted amount after inserting c_j which stations s_{j1} and s_{j2} are replaced with s_z respectively into the position p.

Insert into the end of $\mathcal{I}$: The landing UAV station of the last SLS of $\mathcal{I}$ is represented by s_z in Fig. 3(b), and $s_z = s_{iend2}$. If $s_{j1} = s_z$ and $s_{j2} \neq s_z$, then take s_{j1} as the takeoff UAV station of c_j and insert c_j at the end of $\mathcal{I}$. Therefore, $\Delta = D(c_j)$. It is the same when $s_{j2} = s_z$ and $s_{j1} \neq s_z$, we take s_{j2} as the takeoff UAV station. If $s_{j1} \neq s_z$ and $s_{j2} \neq s_z$, where s_{j1} and s_{j2} may or may not be equal. To determine whether replaces s_{j1} or s_{j2} with s_z, we have $\Delta = min\{\Delta_{s_{j1}}, \Delta_{s_{j2}}\}$, where $\Delta_{s_{j1}} = D^{s_{j1}}(c_j, s_z)$ and $\Delta_{s_{j2}} = D^{s_{j2}}(c_j, s_z)$.

Insert into the middle of the two adjacent SLSs : Use s_z to represent the landing UAV station of the previous SLS and the takeoff UAV station of the next SLS at p in Fig. 3(c). Thus, $s_{i(\gamma-1)2} = s_z = s_{i\gamma1}$. If $s_{j1} = s_{j2} = s_z$, c_j can be inserted directly, so $\Delta = D(c_j)$. If $s_{j1} = s_z$ and $s_{j2} \neq s_z$, then take s_{j1} as the takeoff UAV station of c_j and insert c_j. Meanwhile, $s_{i\gamma1}$ should be replaced with s_{j2}. Hence, we can know that $\Delta = D(c_j) - D(i_\gamma) + D^{s_z}(i_\gamma, s_{j2})$. It is the same when $s_{j2} = s_z$ and $s_{j1} \neq s_z$. If $s_{j1} \neq s_z$ and $s_{j2} \neq s_z$, where s_{j1} and s_{j2} may or may not be equal. The method of calculating the total flight distance is similar to insert into the beginning of $\mathcal{I}$ under the same conditions. Finally, after calculating the $D(\mathcal{I} \vee_p c_j)$ of c_j at each position p in $\mathcal{I}$, we utilize (2) to obtain BIP with the minimum flying distance $D(\mathcal{I} \vee c_j)$:

$$D(\mathcal{I} \vee c_j) = \min_{p=1}^{N_{cls}}\{D(\mathcal{I} \vee_p c_j)\}. \tag{2}$$

4 Evaluation

In this section, we first demonstrate the final results obtained from the DLSA algorithm, and then numerically verify the feasibility and effectiveness. We assumed that U stops at the UAV station s_1 at the beginning. Consider there are 8 locations and 3 UAV stations in the mission area of 900×900 units. In addition, the longest flight distance $\bar{d}$ of U with full charge is 1400 m.

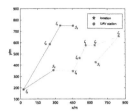
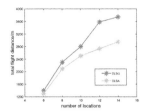

Fig. 4. Flight trajectory using DLSA.

Fig. 5. Comparison of DLSA and DLSG.

As shown in Fig. 4, the flight trajectory obtained by DLSA algorithm can be represented by s_1-l_5-l_7-l_1-l_6-l_8-s_2-l_2-l_4-l_3-s_3. The divide locations and the UAV stations by greedy algorithm (DLSG) proposes that it is necessary to calculate the sum Q of the distance from the current position p_{now} to the unimplemented location l_{next} closest to p_{now} and the distance from l_{next} to the nearest UAV station s_{next} of l_{next} in advance. If Q is greater than the distance the UAV can fly with the remaining energy, then the UAV is allowed to fly toward l_{next}. Otherwise, the UAV is required to fly to s_{next} for charging when p_{now} is a location, and required to fly to the UAV station closest to l_{next} when p_{now} is a UAV station.

We assume that there are 3 UAV stations in the mission area, and compare DLSA and DLSG with different number of locations. DLSG is the greedy algorithm that can obtain a local optimal solution in a short time as shown in Fig. 5. We can see that the total flight distance increases with the increasing number of locations. Moreover, we find the gap between DLSA and DLSG is gradually increasing and the performance of DLSG is getting worse as shown in Fig. 5.

5   Conclusion

In this paper, an optimization problem for minimizing energy consumption was proposed for delivery tasks allocation of a UAV with energy capacity constraints. Due to this constraint, the UAV cannot complete all delivery tasks at once. Hence, the UAV is allowed to be recharged at UAV stations. We applied the MCMF model and proposed DLSA algorithms to select SLSs which have the smallest total energy consumption among all feasible combinations. In addition, we proposed connect methods to connect these selected SLSs into a sequential path with the least energy consumption.

References

1. Wen, J.: JD built the world's first unmanned drone operation dispatch center (2017)
2. Chen, W., Su, Z., et al.: VFC-based cooperative UAV computation task offloading for post-disaster rescue. In: IEEE INFOCOM, pp. 228–236 (2020)

3. Arslan, O., Yildiz, B., Karasan, O.E.: Minimum cost path problem for plug-in hybrid electric vehicles. Transp. Res. Part E: Logistics Transp. Rev. **80**, 2109–2121 (2015)
4. Liu, Y., Liu, Z., Shi, J., Wu, G., Pedrycz, W.: Two-echelon routing problem for parcel delivery by cooperated truck and drone. IEEE Trans. Syst. Man Cybern. Syst., 1–16 (2020)
5. Dorling, K., Heinrichs, J., Messier, G.G., et al.: Vehicle routing problems for drone delivery. IEEE Trans. Syst. Man Cybern. Syst. **47**(1), 70–85 (2016)
6. Liu, Y., Guo, B., Wang, Y., et al.: TaskMe: multi-task allocation in mobile crowd sensing. In: ACM International Joint Conference on Pervasive and Ubiquitous Computing, pp. 403–414 (2016)
7. Tarjan, R.: Depth-first search and linear graph algorithms. SIAM J. Comput. **1**, 146–160 (1972)
8. Cui, L., et al.: A novel artificial bee colony algorithm with depth-first search framework and elite-guided search equation. Inf. Sci. **367**, 1012–1044 (2016)

Optimized Segment Routing Traffic Engineering with Multiple Segments

Sichen Cui, Lailong Luo$^{(\boxtimes)}$, Deke Guo, Bangbang Ren, Chao Chen, and Tao Chen

Science and Technology on Information Systems Engineering Laboratory, National University of Defense Technology, Changsha 410073, Hunan, People's Republic of China
luolailong09@nudt.edu.cn

Abstract. Network traffic balancing plays a key role in improving network performance. Recently, a new source routing technology, segment routing (SR), has been proposed to increase the network programming ability. SR expresses an end-to-end logical path as a sequence of segments, each of which represents the shortest path between its upstream node and downstream node. This new routing mechanism calls for a new traffic engineering method, i.e., Segment Routing Traffic Engineering (SRTE). In this paper, we devote ourselves to leveraging SRv6 to steer multiple flows in the network with the goal of minimizing the bandwidth utilization of the most congested link. Different from existing methods, we do not limit the number of available segments. We formulate this problem as an integer programming model. After proving the NP-hardness of this problem, we propose an efficient algorithm based on restricted widest paths. Comprehensive experimental results show that our method realizes similar routing performance as the optimal method while reducing the computation time by orders of magnitude.

Keywords: Segment routing · Traffic engineering · Widest path · Optimization

1 Introduction

A recent report from Cisco forecasts that global IP traffic will reach an annual run rate of 4.8 zettabytes per year by 2022 [1]. It is not sufficient to support such a huge volume of traffic only through expanding network capacity. Leveraging existed network infrastructure efficiently is also a potential solution. As we all know, network congestion is a major reason for network performance degradation [2]. To relieve the congestion, traffic engineering which targets analyzing, predicting, and regulating network traffics, has been proposed twenty years ago [3]. Multi-Protocol Label Switching (MPLS) [4] and Openflow-based Software Defined Networking (SDN) [5,6] are two typical traffic engineering methods. However, these methods can only be applied to specific networks like

© Springer Nature Switzerland AG 2021
Z. Liu et al. (Eds.): WASA 2021, LNCS 12939, pp. 86–98, 2021.
https://doi.org/10.1007/978-3-030-86137-7_10

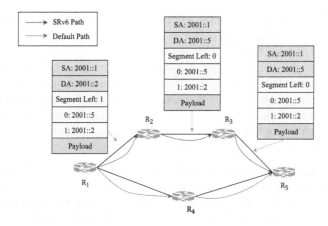

Fig. 1. An illustrative example of SRv6 routing. The IPv6 addresses of the five routers range from 2001::1 to 2001::5.

sub-networks of an ISP or datacenter networks due to their complexity in config-uration and management [7]. Besides, the trend of application-driven networks hopes possess the end-to-end control ability that could cross multiple networks including wireless sensor networks, mobile access networks, and core networks [8]. In this case, segment routing, a new source routing mechanism that can simplify the configuration of traffic engineering strategies, has been proposed. The core idea of SR is to divide a routing path into multiple segments which are expressed as a series of instructions in the packet header [9]. Both MPLS and IPv6 can be used as data planes of SR.[1]

Figure 1 illustrates a toy example of SRv6 (Segment Routing with IPv6) where a flow needs to be transmitted from router R_1 to R_5. Based on traditional routing protocols, e.g., OSPF, the default shortest path is (R_1, R_4, R_5) from router R_1 to R_5. If we hope to change the default routing path for the sake of congestion control, we have to update the link weight and wait until the routing protocol converges, which is complicated and time-consuming. By contrast, SRv6 can change the routing path more easily. In SRv6, R_1 will add a segment routing header (SRH) into the packet header. The SRH is composed of two parts, i.e., *segment left* indicator and *segment lists*. The destination address is the copy of the current activated segment which is indexed by the value of *segment left* in the *segment list*. In R_1, it will steer the flow to R_2 along the default path, i.e., (R_1, R_2). When R_2 receives the packet, it decreases the value of the *segment left* part and activates the corresponding segment, i.e., setting the current destination

---

[1] According to the different data planes, SR could be classified with SR-MPLS and SRv6. SR-MPLS describes the path by a label stack, and SRv6 uses SRH embed-ded in IPv6 packets to steer flows [9]. From the SRTE view, they have the same abstraction model. Without loss of generality, we select SRv6 as our basic routing model.

address as 2001::5. Then the packet will traverse along the shortest path between R_2 and R_5, i.e., (R_2, R_3, R_5).

Though SRv6 provides a flexible mechanism to steer flows in the data plane, it still faces two main challenges: i) how to plan routing paths for multiple flows in a sharing network; ii) how to use the SRv6 segments to encode the planned paths. The existing methods for Segment Routing Traffic Engineering (SRTE) lack generality since they only consider the cases where two or three segments are involved (refer to details in Sect. 2). In this paper, aiming to solve the optimal SRTE problem, we make the following contributions:

– We generalize the SRTE model with n segments, where $n \geq 2$. We first model this problem as an integer programming problem and prove its NP-hardness.
– We propose an efficient algorithm based on the widest paths between the sources and destinations. After searching out the widest path for a flow, the relay nodes are selected within the path with joint consideration of the shortest path in the network. By doing so, our algorithm bypasses the most congested link with the best effort.
– We quantify the performance of our algorithm under different parameter settings. Extensive experiments based on both real-world and synthetic network topologies highlight that our algorithm achieves comparable performance as the optimal 2-segment solution with much less time-consumption.

2   Related Work

Though SR-MPLS and SRv6 have different strengths in network management, they have the same abstraction model from the traffic engineering view. The SRTE problem is first proposed in literature [10] where the authors devoted to minimizing the maximum link utilization (MLU) with a given network and traffic matrix. In literature [11], the authors studied the SRTE problem with the bounded stretch to limit the length of the shortest path between segments to avoid long paths. In [12], the authors propose a two layer architecture DEFO (Declarative and Expressive Forwarding Optimizer), which combined constrained programming model and local search algorithm together to find middle point routing solutions. All the above works only permit at most two segments in their routing paths.

To explore the potentiality of more available segments in traffic engineering, literature [13–15] researched how to optimize the traffic engineering goal, i.e., minimize the MLU, with at most three segments. From their works, we can easily find that more segments can optimize the goal further. This fact motivates us to study how to give a general model for SRTE without limiting the number of available segments.

3   System Model and Problem Formulation

We model the network as an undirected graph $G = (V, E, W, C)$, where V represents the set of network routers, E denotes the physical links among the

Table 1. Table of symbols

Symbols	Description
V, E	Set of nodes and links
W, C	Weight and capacity of links
e_{uv}	Link between node u and v
$c(e_{uv})$	Capacity of link e_{uv}
s_i, d_i, λ_i	Source node, destination node, and the size of flow f_i
n	The maximal number of segments
p_{ij}	The j-th alternative SR path of flow f_i
t_i	The number of alternative SR paths of flow f_i
x_{ij}	A binary variable; 1 if flow f_i is routed by path p_{ij}, and 0 otherwise.
$g_{ij}(e_{uv})$	The ratio of traffic carried by link e_{uv} in path p_{ij}
θ	The maximum link utilization

routers, W represents IGP weights configured on the links and C denotes the link capacities. Table 1 lists the mathematical symbols used in this paper. We use $\{f_1, f_2, ..., f_m\}$ to denote m flows. Flow f_i is represented by a tuple with three attributes, i.e., $\{s_i, d_i, \lambda_i\}$, where s_i is the source node, d_i denotes the destination node, and λ_i is the size of the flow. To ease the description, we first give the definition of n-segment routing:

Definition 1. n-segment routing (n-SR): *each flow f_i in the network G could be routed along a SR path $p_i = \{\phi_0(s_i) \to \phi_1 \to, ..., \to \phi_{n-1} \to \phi_n(d_i)\}$, where ϕ_0 and ϕ_n represent source node and destination node. Each subpath in p_i is the shortest path in G between its upstream node and downstream node. There are at most n segments, i.e., subpaths, in a SR path.*

For a flow f_i, let t_i represent the number of possible n-SR paths between s_i and d_i, then we have

$$t_i = \sum_{h=0}^{n-1} A_{|V|-2}^h \tag{1}$$

where $A_{|V|-2}^h$ means the number of permutations of h distinct nodes taken from set $V - s_i - d_i$ which have $|V| - 2$ nodes at a time. Without loss of generality, we denote these t_i flows as $P_i = \{p_{i1}, p_{i2}, ..., p_{it_i}\}$.

Note that, if there are multiple shortest paths between a pair of nodes, the flow is distributed evenly among these paths which is powered by ECMP to enable load balancing [10]. Since the candidate path p_{ij} only restricts the must-go intermediate nodes, there will be multiple shortest paths in each subpath of p_{ij}. When p_{ij} is selected, we can calculate the ratio of traffic carried by link e_{uv} as follows:

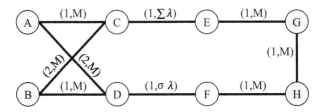

Fig. 2. An example to show that the 2-SR problem is NP-hard.

$$g_{ij}(e_{uv}) = \sum_{k=0}^{n-1} \frac{\#e_{uv}^{\phi_k\phi_{k+1}}}{|SP(\phi_k,\phi_{k+1})|} \tag{2}$$

where $SP(\phi_k,\phi_{k+1})$ represents all the shortest paths between node ϕ_k and node ϕ_{k+1}. And $\#e_{uv}^{\phi_k\phi_{k+1}}$ denotes the total frequency of link e_{uv} in $SP(\phi_k,\phi_{k+1})$.

Let binary variable x_{ij} denote whether f_i is routed by path p_{ij}, $c(e_{uv})$ be the capacity of link e_{uv}, and θ be the maximum link utilization (MLU) in the network. Then the ***n-SRTE*** problem could be modeled as:

$$n - SRTE: \qquad \min \quad \theta$$

$$\text{s.t.} \qquad \sum_{j=1}^{t_i} x_{ij} = 1 \qquad\qquad \forall i \tag{3}$$

$$\sum_{i=1}^{m}\sum_{j=1}^{t_i} g_{ij}(e_{uv})x_{ij}\lambda_i \leq \theta c(e_{uv}) \qquad \forall e_{uv} \in E \tag{4}$$

$$x_{ij} \in \{0,1\} \tag{5}$$

Constraint (3) ensures that all the traffic is routed in the network and each flow is only routed by a single n-SR path. In constraint (4), if flow f_i is routed by path p_{ij}, $g_{ij}(e_{uv})x_{ij}\lambda_i$ represents the amount of traffic that belongs to f_i in e_{uv}. Constraint (4) indicates that the link utilization of each link should be less than the maximum link utilization. From constraint (3) to (5), the n-SRTE model introduces $O(m \times |V|^n)$ variables and constraints. In a network with 104 nodes, our experimental results show that it takes over 6 h to solve the 3-SR model for 400 flows. The following theorem gives the complexity of the n-SRTE problem.

Theorem 1. *The n-SRTE problem is NP-hard.*

Proof. Before proving Theorem 1, we first prove that the n-SRTE problem is NP-hard in a special case where $n = 2$. We construct an example network in Fig. 2. Assume that there are l flows with size $\{\lambda_1, \lambda_2, \cdots, \lambda_l\}$ from A to G and $m - l$ flows with size $\{\lambda_{l+1}, \lambda_{l+2}, \cdots, \lambda_m\}$ from B to H. The attributes on each link represent its weight and capacity where $M >> \sum_{i=1}^{m} \lambda_i$. It is obvious that the most congested link will be e_{CE} or e_{DF}. To minimize the network MLU, we need to divide flows into two parts. These two parts have an equal amount of traffic. One part passes e_{CE}, e.g., path $A \rightarrow G$ and $B \rightarrow C \rightarrow H$, the other part passes e_{DF}, e.g., path $B \rightarrow H$ and $A \rightarrow D \rightarrow G$. If we could solve the 2-SR problem, then we can know whether the number set $\{\lambda_1, \lambda_2, ..., \lambda_m\}$ could be divided into two subsets where the sum of each subset are equal. However, this subset sum problem is a classical NP-hard problem [16]. Therefore, the 2-SRTE problem is proved to be NP-hard problem. The n-SRTE problem is also NP-hard because the 2-SRTE problem is the sub-problem of the n-SRTE problem.

4   Algorithm Design

Since Theorem 1 has proved that our n-SRTE problem is NP-hard, we cannot solve it quickly by commercial solvers especially when the size of topology and the number of flows increase. Hence, we propose a heuristic algorithm, based on the restricted widest path (RWP).

4.1   Restricted Widest Path

In RWP algorithm, we first rank flows in a descending order and then find the n-SR path for each flow one by one. RWP firstly finds the widest path (WP) in step 1 and then encodes the path with a series of segments in step 2. To satisfy the limitation of the maximal number of segments, RWP further refines the encoded SR paths in step 3. Before introducing the RWP algorithm in detail, we first give the definition of *the widest path*. We use W' to represent the link utilization of all links. Let $w'_{uv} \in W'$ denote the link utilization of link e_{uv}.

Definition 2. *The widest path:* *For any flow f_i, let $Q_i = \{q_{i1}, q_{i2}, ..., q_{ia}\}$ denote all the paths between s_i and d_i. For each path q_{ij}, we define the path utilization as the MLU among links, i.e., $\max(\{w'_{uv}|e_{uv} \in q_{ij}\})$. Then the widest path between s_i and d_i is q_{ik} where $k = \arg\min\limits_j \max(\{w'_{uv}|e_{uv} \in q_{ij}\})$.*

With the above definition, then we can introduce the RWP algorithm with the following three steps.

Step 1: Searching for the Widest Path. The widest path for f_i can be found iteratively by the *Widestpath* function in Algorithm 1. We set a visited list S and an unvisited list S'. Let $B_{ij}(t)$ denote the path utilization of the path from s_i and $v_j \in V$ in the tth iteration. Initially, $S = \{s_i\}$, $v_k = s_i$, $S' = V - \{s_i\}$, and $\{B_{ij}(0) = +\infty | v_j \in S'\}$. In each iteration, we update path utilization from source node s_i to other nodes v_j using $B_{ij}(t) = \min\{B_{ij}(t-1), \max\{B_{ik}(t-1), w'_{kj}\}\}$, where node $v_j \in V - \{s_i\}$ and node v_k is added in the $(t-1)^{th}$ iteration. Particularly, we set $B_{ik}(0) = B_{ii}(0) = 0$. Then we find $v_k \in S'$ which has the minimal value of $B_{ik}(t)$ and move node v_k from S' to S. When S' becomes empty, we will find the widest paths from s_i to any node v_j through backtracking $B_{ij}(t)$.

Algorithm 1. The Algorithm based on **R**estricted **W**idest **P**ath (RWP)

Require: $G = (V, E, W, C)$, multiple flows $\{f_1, f_2, ..., f_m\}$, the maximal number of segments n.

Ensure: segment routing paths $\{p_1^r, p_2^r, ..., p_m^r\}$

1: $W' = \{w'_{uv} = 0 | e_{uv} \in E\}$
2: **for all** $f_i \in \{f_1, f_2, ..., f_m\}$ **do**
3:     $p_i^r = \textbf{Encodepath}(G, p_i^w, f_i)$
4:     $p_i^r = \textbf{Refinepath}(G, p_i^w, p_i^r, f_i, n)$
5:     update W' with occupying the bandwidth for f_i along p_i^r
6: return $\{p_1^r, p_2^r, ..., p_m^r\}$

$p_i^w = \textbf{Widestpath}(G, W', s_i, d_i)$

1: Initialize $S = \{s_i\}$, $S' = V - \{s_i\}$, $v_k = s_i$, $t = 0$ and $\{B_{ij}(0) = +\infty | v_j \in S'\}$
2: **while** $S' \neq \emptyset$ **do**
3:     $t = t + 1$
4:     **for all** $v_j \in V - \{s_i\}$ **do**
5:         $B_{ij}(t) = \min\{B_{ij}(t-1), \max\{B_{ik}(t-1), w'_{kj}\}\}$
6:     find $v_k \in S'$ that has the minimal value of $B_{ik}(t)$
7:     move v_k from S' to S
8: Get p_i^w through backtracking $B_{s_i d_i}$.

$p_i^r = \textbf{Encodepath}(G, p_i^w, f_i)$

1: $p_i^w = \{a_0 = s_i, a_1, a_2, ..., a_{l-1}, a_l = d_i\}$
2: $j = 0$, $k = 1$, $p_i^r = [s_i]$
3: **while** $k \neq l$ **do**
4:     **if** $p_i^w[j, k] = p_i^s(j, k)$ **then**
5:         $k = k + 1$
6:     **else**
7:         $j = k - 1$, $p_i^r = [p_i^r \to a_j]$

$p_i^r = \textbf{Refinepath}(G, p_i^w, p_i^r, f_i, n)$

1: Find the value of π for each segment by observing p_i^w and p_i^r
2: Delete the segment with the minimal π value until p_i^r has no more than n segments.

Step 2: Path Encoding. After finding the widest path for f_i, we represent it as a combination of segments with the *Encodepath* function as shown in Algorithm 1. The key idea is to simplify subpath including the shortest path in the widest path p_i^w. Without loss of generality, let $p_i^w = \{a_0, a_1, ..., a_{l-1}, a_l\}$ denote the widest path for f_i where $a_0 = s_i$ and $a_l = d_i$. Let $p_i^w[j, k]$ and $p_i^s(j, k)$ be the subpath of path p_i^w and the shortest path between a_j and a_k. If $p_i^w[j, k] = p_i^s(j, k)$, which means the subpath from a_j to a_k is exactly the shortest path, then we move on and check the next node, i.e., a_{k+1}. Otherwise, we add node a_{k-1} to the SR path p_i^r then initialize $p_i^w[j = k-1, k]$ and $p_i^s(j = k-1, k)$. The final combination of segments p_i^r can be searched out until node a_k reaches destination node d_i.

Step 3: Refinement of the Encoded Paths. The above steps specify p_i^r which may violate the constraint of the maximal number of segments. To solve the problem, we assign each non-destination segment an attribute π that records the number of hops for the SP path between it and its upstream segment in p_i^r. Then we remove the segment with the lowest value of π until the constraint of the maximal number of segments is satisfied. The reason is that these segments contribute the least upon steering the flow bypass the congested links. An example is given to illustrate this problem. Suppose the widest path $p_i^w = \{s_i, a, b, c, e, f, g, h, d_i\}$ is represented as $p_r = \{s_i \rightarrow c \rightarrow e \rightarrow g \rightarrow d_i\}$, wherein $\pi(c) = 3$, $\pi(e) = 1$, $\pi(g) = 2$. When the maximal number of segments $n = 3$, we will remove node e with the minimal π value from the path p_i^r. The RWP path of flow f_i is represented as $p_r = \{s_i \rightarrow c \rightarrow g \rightarrow d_i\}$.

4.2   Time Complexity Analysis

In Step 1, we have $|V|$ iterations and each iteration needs to execute $O(|V|)$ comparisons, thus its time complexity is $O(|V|^2)$. In Step 2, the algorithm only compares the widest path and the shortest paths $O(|V|)$ times since the length of the widest path cannot be larger than $|V|$. In Step 3, the algorithm sorts all the π values where the time-complexity cannot be more than $O(|V|^2)$. Thus, the time-complexity of one iteration is $O(|V|^2)$. Since we have m flows, the total time complexity of the RWP algorithm is bounded as $O(m \times |V|^2)$.

5   Experimental Results

In this section, we first introduce the experiment design and then evaluate the performance of the algorithm. Our evaluations quantify the performance of our algorithm in terms of MLU, time-consumption, and transmission cost.

5.1   Experiment Design

Topologies and Flows. We run experiments in six network topologies including five synthetic networks and a real network. Topology rand50 and rf1221 are provided by DEFO [12]. Topology rand20, rand30, rand40, and rand80 are synthetic networks with an average degree of 3. Topology rf1221 is a real network with an average degree of 6. We use real flow traces from DEFO in rand50 and rf1221, while feeding other networks with synthetic flows generated by the gravity model [17]. Details of the dataset are summarized in Table 2.

Experiment Settings. Our experiments are conducted on a typical PC with an Intel(R) Core(TM) i7-7700HQ 2.80 GHz CPU with 16 GB of RAM. We compare our algorithm with other four methods: the shortest path (SP), DEFO, H2 [13], and results generated by solving the n-SRTE model with CPLEX. The main metrics of our experiments include the overall network MLU and the time-consumption. To this end, we vary the maximal number of segments, the network size, and the number of flows in the network. We randomly choose flows from the flow dataset for 10 runs and report the average value and standard deviation results. Additionally, we compare the number of hops and cost between RWP's solutions and SP's solutions.

Table 2. Dataset summary

Type	ID	# nodes	# links	# flows
Synthetic	rand20	20	30	600
Synthetic	rand30	30	45	900
Synthetic	rand40	40	60	1600
Synthetic	rand50	50	150	2449
Synthetic	rand80	80	120	6400
Real	rf1221	104	302	11663

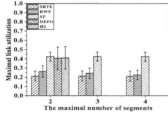 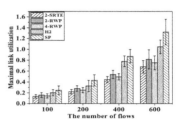

(a) The impacts of different values (b) The impacts of different values of n in topology rand20 ($m = 400$). of m in topology rf1221.

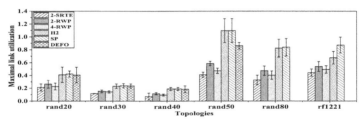

(c) The comparisons of these methods in networks with different sizes ($m = 400$).

Fig. 3. Different experiment results in terms of the value of MLU among n-SRTE(CPLEX), RWP, SP, H2, and DEFO.

5.2   The Comparisons of Algorithm Performance in MLU

In this subsection, we evaluate the MLU of different methods. Figure 3(a) depicts the impacts of the maximal number of segments. It is noted that both DEFO and H2 only support at most two segments, thus, we do not present their results in $n > 2$ cases. We can see that both n-SRTE (CPLEX) and RWP perform better than SP. RWP can realize about 40% MLU reduction against SP. The MLU of n-SRTE does not decrease as the number of segments increases. This phenomenon may result from that two segments are enough to optimize the rand20 network. However, we can find that RWP performs better as the number of segments increases. And the gaps between the results of the RWP algorithm and the theoretical results (n-SRTE) decrease when more segments are allowed.

Next, we increase the number of flows to compare the performance of SP, 2-SRTE, H2, and RWP in topology rf1221. As shown in Fig. 3(b), with more flows, the MLU of all methods increases. 2-SRTE and RWP achieve better performance than the SP. To be specific, 2-SRTE outperforms others and achieves the lowest MLU. By contrast, SP always has the highest MLU. Our RWP algorithm has almost the same MLU as 2-SRTE. In the case of 600 flows, link congestion occurs in SP where the MLU could reach as high as 130%, while the other two methods are below 80%. This phenomenon shows that RWP can efficiently reduce the maximal link utilization and realize similar routing performance as the optimal solution of the 2-SRTE model.

We also evaluate the performance of these methods in networks of different sizes. Because the open-source code of DEFO [18] only supports networks at most 50 nodes, the results of DEFO are not shown in rand80 and rf1221. Compared with DEFO and H2, RWP can always find better solutions. In the three small networks (rand20, rand30, rand40) with low network load, the RWP method outperforms the SP method. By contrast, H2 and DEFO fail to achieve such a significant performance improvement. We further evaluate the other three networks with high network load. In rand50, DEFO and RWP can reduce the MLU below 100%, while H2 fails to do this. In rand80 and rf1221, when the MLU of SP is over 80%, 2-SRTE and RWP can reduce the MLU below 50%. These experiments highlight that our RWP certainly performs better than DEFO and H2, and can achieve comparable performance as the optimal 2-SRTE solution.

Table 3. The average execution time of different methods when $m = 400$.

topology	SP	2-SRTE	3-SRTE	4-SRTE	2-RWP	4-RWP	H2	DEFO
rand20	0.03 s	2.67 s	122.13 s	2.5 h	0.70 s	1.10 s	0.05 s	0.08 s
rand30	0.09 s	10.74 s	812.39 s	>6 h	0.80 s	1.10 s	0.16 s	0.11 s
rand40	0.18 s	18.87 s	1.6 h	>6 h	1.13 s	1.41 s	0.39 s	0.11 s
rand50	0.32 s	22.69 s	>6 h	>6 h	1.72 s	2.82 s	0.69 s	1.45 s
rand80	1.35 s	165.24 s	>6 h	>6 h	3.62 s	5.81 s	2.66 s	–
rf1221	2.80 s	488.31 s	>6 h	>6 h	5.28 s	8.14 s	5.78 s	–

5.3 The Comparisons of Algorithm Performance in Time Consumption

Table 3 reports the average execution time of the five methods (SP, n-SRTE, RWP, H2, and DEFO) in six different networks. It is clear that our RWP algorithm outperforms the n-SRTE method significantly. As we can see, when the network scale increases, the 2-SRTE spends more and more time (from 2.67 s to

488.31 s) to search for the best path. 3-SRTE and 4-SRTE models even cannot
be solved in 6 h. By contrast, the time consumption of our RWP algorithm only
increases from about 1 s to 8 s. The reason is that the n-SRTE model is NP-hard
and the number of variables increases severely as the scales increase, while the
time complexity of our RWP is $O(m \times |V|^2)$.

We further compare the time consumption of RWP and the other three
heuristic methods (SP, H2, and DEFO). Generally speaking, more time consumption will produce better network performance. Though RWP takes some
extra time against DEFO and H2, it can reduce the MLU by 30% averagely as
shown in Fig. 3(b).

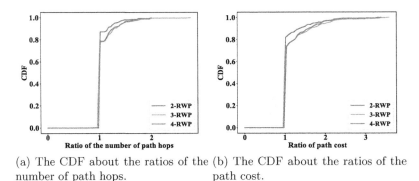

(a) The CDF about the ratios of the
number of path hops.

(b) The CDF about the ratios of the
path cost.

Fig. 4. The comparisons of transmission cost between SP and RWP when $m = 400$.

5.4   The Comparisons of Algorithm Performance in Transmission Cost

In addition to evaluating the performance of our RWP algorithm in MLU, we also
want to know how it performs from latency view, i.e., the number of path hops
and the path cost. To achieve this goal, we compare RWP and SP in rf1221. We
set the related metrics of SP as baselines and calculate the ratios between RWP's
and SP's metrics. Figure 4 presents the CDFs of the two ratios. To minimize the
MLU, RWP will route flows in a longer path to balance the traffic. And using
more segments will produce much longer paths. To be specific, as shown in
Fig. 4(a), there are only 14% flows (ratio>1) in 2-RWP that have longer paths,
while the percentages in 3-RWP and 4-RWP could be as high as 25%. Figure 4(b)
presents similar results. As the maximal number of segments n increases, the
paths produced by n-RWP paths have higher path cost. Specifically, more than
17% of paths in 2-RWP and 25% of paths in 3-RWP and 4-RWP have higher
path cost. This phenomenon agrees with the results in Fig. 4(a). From Fig. 4,
we can conclude that SRTE can distribute the flows in the network more evenly
with more segments by steering them along free links.

6 Conclusion

Segment routing, as a new source routing mechanism, has brought profound changes to traffic engineering. However, existing methods of segment routing traffic engineering (SRTE) usually limit the maximal number of available segments. Though this limitation simplifies the computation, it meanwhile restricts the potentiality of SRTE. In this paper, we extended the existing 2-SRTE or 3-SRTE model to a more general case, i.e., n-SRTE, where $n \geq 2$. We formulated the n-SRTE problem as an integer programming model and proved the NP-hardness of this problem. Next, we proposed an efficient algorithm based on restricted widest paths which have three specific steps. With extensive experimental evaluations, we disclosed that our method can provide comparable MLU as an optimal 2-segment solution with reducing the computation time by orders of magnitude.

Acknowledgment. This work is partially supported by the National Key Research and Development Program of China under Grant No. 2018YFE0207600, and the National Natural Science Foundation of China under Grant No. U19B2024 and No. 62002378.

References

1. Barnett Jr, T., Jain, S., Andra, U., Khhurana, T.: Cisco Visual Networking Index (VNI) Complete Forecast Update, 2017–2022
2. Al-Bahadili, H.: Simulation in computer network design and modeling: Use and analysis. IGI Global (2012)
3. Awduche, D., Chiu, A., Elwalid, A., Widjaja, I., Xiao, X.: Overview and Principles of Internet Traffic Engineering. RFC 3272 (2002)
4. Foteinos, V., Tsagkaris, K., Peloso, P., Ciavaglia, L., Demestichas, P.: Operator-friendly traffic engineering in IP/MPLS core networks. IEEE Trans. Network Service Manage. **11**, 333–349 (2014)
5. Guo, Y., Wang, Z., Yin, X., Shi, X., Wu, J.: Traffic engineering in hybrid SDN networks with multiple traffic matrices. Computer Networks, pp. 187–199 (2017)
6. Cheng, H., Liu, J., Mao, J., Wang, M., Chen, J.: OSCO: an open security-enhanced compatible OpenFlow platform. In: Proceedings of WASA, pp. 66–77 (2018)
7. Luo, L., et al.: Vlccube: a vlc enabled hybrid network structure for data centers. IEEE Trans. Parallel Distributed Syst., 2088–2102 (2017)
8. Ren, B., Guo, D., Tang, G., Wang, W., Luo, L., Fu, X.: SRUF, low-latency path routing with srv6 underlay federation in wide area network. Accepted to appear at in Proc. of IEEE ICDCS (2021)
9. Filsfils, C., Camarillo, P., Leddy, J., Voyer, D., Matsushima, S., Li, Z.: Segment Routing over IPv6 (SRv6) Network Programming. RFC 8986 (2021)
10. Bhatia, R., Hao, F., Kodialam, M., Lakshman, T.V.: Optimized network traffic engineering using segment routing. In: Proceedings of IEEE INFOCOM, pp. 657–665 (2015)
11. Settawatcharawanit, T., Suppakitpaisarn, V., Yamada, S., Ji, Y.: Segment routed traffic engineering with bounded stretch in software-defined networks. In: Proceedings of IEEE Conference on Local Computer Networks, pp. 477–480 (2018)

12. Hartert, R., et al.: A declarative and expressive approach to control forwarding paths in carrier-grade networks. In: Proceedings of ACM SIGCOMM, pp. 15–28 (2015)
13. Eduardo, M., Alejandra, B., Filippo, C.: Traffic engineering in segment routing networks. Computer Networks, pp. 23–31 (2017)
14. Schüller, T., et al.: Traffic engineering using segment routing and considering requirements of a carrier IP network. In: IEEE/ACM TON, pp. 1851–1864 (2018)
15. Pereira, V., Rocha, M., Sousa, P.: Traffic engineering with three- segments routing. In: IEEE TNSM, pp. 1896–1909 (2020)
16. Subset sum is np-complete. http://www.cs.cornell.edu/courses/cs4820/2018fa/lectures/subsetsum.pdf
17. Roughan, M.: Simplifying the synthesis of internet traffic matrices. In: Proceedings of ACM SIGCOMM, pp. 93–96, October 2005
18. Declarative and expressive forwarding optimizer. http://sites.uclouvain.be/defo/

Robust and Efficient Mechanism Design for Heterogeneous Task Crowdsensing

Qiangqiang He, Yu Qiao, Shang Yang, and Chongjun Wang[(✉)]

State Key Laboratory for Novel Software Technology,
Nanjing University, Nanjing 210046, China
{qqhe,yuqiao,yangshang}@smail.nju.edu.cn
chjwang@nju.edu.cn

Abstract. Crowdsensing is a novel concept that divides tasks between participants in order to get an accumulated result. To make the crowdsensing system work well and get better quality, it is indispensable to set up incentive mechanisms to get more workers involved. As far as the bidding of heterogeneous combinations is concerned, combinatorial auctions are the natural choice for workers to bid. Truthfulness and efficiency can be guaranteed based on the properties of VCG mechanism which will result in the higher bid price and high overpayment. To overcome this potential shortcoming of the VCG mechanism, we propose the core-selecting mechanism for the heterogeneous task auction under the crowdsensing market. Two payment rules are applied to the core-selecting auction based on linear programming and quadratic programming techniques to minimize the bidders' incentives which deviate from their truthful-telling. After extensive simulation experiments, it is proved that our model can decrease the cost significantly.

Keywords: Core-selecting · VCG-mechanism · Game theory

1 Introduction

In the past decade, the prosperity of online social networking sites has changed the way of hiring labor and created a market for a new form of labor market called crowdsensing market [1]. A successful attempt at crowdsensing is inseparable from a good incentive design. To make the crowdsensing system work well and get better quality, it is essential to set up an incentive mechanism to get more workers involved. From the view of the crowdsourcers, too high task pricing will lead to too low output. Furthermore, too low task pricing will disincentivize the workers who participate in the task. The trade-off between the overhead of the crowdsourcers and workers' motivation makes the pricing decisions complicated in crowdsensing markets. Therefore, we desperately require novel algorithms which can consider both the self-interest of workers and the financial goal of the crowdsourcers [2].

Q. He and Y. Qiao—Contribute equally to this work.

© Springer Nature Switzerland AG 2021
Z. Liu et al. (Eds.): WASA 2021, LNCS 12939, pp. 99–107, 2021.
https://doi.org/10.1007/978-3-030-86137-7_11

The previous work of the crowdsensing auctions is mainly focusing on the homogeneous tasks, in which it assumes that each unit of the tasks is the same in the crowdsensing. When it comes to the heterogeneous tasks auctions where each task group has no relationship with others, the famous VCG mechanism is the main research direction [3]. The VCG mechanism has been proven to be the unique mechanism that can ensure truthfulness and efficiency. The mechanism is truthful if the workers have no incentive to misreport their true cost and the mechanism is efficient.

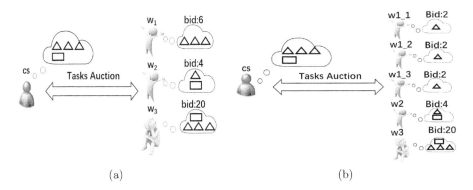

(a)   (b)

Fig. 1. An example of task auction: cs means crowdsourcer and w_1, w_2, w_3 are workers. Different shapes represent different kinds of tasks.

However, two economic problems of VCG prevent its application in practice. The first one is the VCG mechanism will have an overpayment to the workers. For example, in Fig. 1(a), there are three workers $\{w_1, w_2, w_3\}$ bidding for two types of tasks $\{t1, t2\}$. Three t1 and one t2 tasks are auctioned. The workers bid for $\{3 * t1\}$, $\{t1, t2\}$, $\{3 * t1, t2\}$, respectively, the cost of workers is 6, 4, 20. In order to ensure that all tasks are completed, the VCG will allocate tasks to w_1 and w_2 and pay 16, 14 to w_1, w_2. Thus, the overpayment factor is nearly 3 times compared to the true cost 10.

The false-name cheating is the second problem of VCG. In the VCG mechanism, one worker can create multiple accounts to bid for tasks and get higher payments for tasks with the same number of tasks than a single account. For example, in Fig. 1(b), the worker w_1 uses three fake accounts, and submits separately three bids 2 for one t1. Then, his benefit will increase from 16 to 36 by obtaining from the three fake account. From the above cases, we know that the overpayment of VCG is high and it could suffer from the false-name bidding. To tackle the aforementioned problems, we propose a core-selecting crowdsensing mechanism. We show it avoids the false-name cheating and pay less than VCG auction. The contributions of our paper are as follows.

– We introduce the core-selecting framework to the crowdsensing market with heterogeneous tasks, and analyze its properties.

- We propose CCG algorithms to reduce the complexity of the core-selecting algorithm.
- We perform a lot of numerical simulations to demonstrate our proposal is better than the famous VCG auction.

2 Related Work

The term "crowdsensing" was coined by Jeff Howe in 2006 [4]. After that, crowd-sensing systems are used everywhere in our lives [5]. Unfortunately, not everyone is willing to participate in sensing tasks and provides high-quality information [6]. We urgently require a efficient incentive mechanism. Not only can it improve the quality of tasks, but it can also control the cost of crowdsensing and reduce edge costs for service subscriber. Vickery et al. designed a general method to construct a real mechanism, namely the VCG mechanism [7]. Liu et al. proved that the performance of VCG is far from optimal in some cases and proposed a mechanism that is always within a constant factor of optimal [8]. In order to improve the dynamic task allocation performance of multiple unmanned aerial vehicles, X. Duan et al. proposed a hybrid "two-stage" auction algorithm based on hierarchical decision-making mechanism and improved objective function [9].

On the other hand, we want to prevent fraud. L et al. showed that in VCG mechanism, only when valuations are additive can the incentives to shill and merge simultaneously disappear. Zhu et al. proposed an incentive mechanism that focuses on reverse auctions [10]. Yu et al. proposed a core-selecting multi cast routing mechanism based on the VCG mechanism to overcome false-name bidding [11].

3 Preliminaries

In this part, we will transform our problems into mathematical language and discuss the weakness of the prevailing methods.

3.1 Problem Formulation

The crowdsensing system is made up of a *service subscriber* (SS) and a set of *service providers* (SPs) which are denoted as $\mathcal{N} = \{1, 2, ..., n\}$. The task set $\mathcal{T}$ of the SS publicized includes a set of heterogeneous tasks $\Pi = \{\pi_1, \pi_2, ..., \pi_T\}$. $\pi_k \in N^+$ denotes the number of k-th tasks to be completed. For each bundle of tasks $\mathcal{S} = \{t_1, t_2, ..., t_T\}, t_k \leq \pi_k$, where t_k represent the number of task k that SP i wants to finish. Let $\mathcal{B}_i$ be the set of SP i's all bundles of tasks. We use $\mathcal{S}(k)$ to index the number of the type k task in the bundle $\mathcal{S}$. $c_i(\mathcal{S})$ represents SP i's cost of bundle $\mathcal{S}$. And $b_i(\mathcal{S})$ represents SP i's bid of bundle $\mathcal{S}$. In this system, a SP can submit as many bids as it needs, but it can win only one bid. Let payment profile $p = (p_1, p_2, ..., p_N)$. *How do we design a mechanism which can hire workers to finish all tasks in the set with the least cost?*

We formulate the winner determination question (WDP) as follows:

$$\mathcal{W}(\mathcal{N}) = \min \sum_{i \in \mathcal{N}} \sum_{\mathcal{S} \in \mathcal{B}} x_i(\mathcal{S})c_i(\mathcal{S}))$$

$$\text{subject to} \sum_{\mathcal{S} \in \mathcal{B}_i} x_i(\mathcal{S}) \leq 1 \quad \forall i \in \mathcal{N}$$

$$\sum_{\mathcal{S} \in \mathcal{W}(\mathcal{N})} \mathcal{S}(k) \geq \pi_k \quad \forall 1 \leq k \leq T \tag{1}$$

$$x_i(\mathcal{B}) \in \{0,1\} \quad \forall i \in \mathcal{N}$$

Although WDP has NP-hardness, it can be solved in few seconds on the order of a thousand variables and constraints on today's general computer. The WDP will return the minimized task payment in the crowdsensing market.

In addition, the following four attributes are required by our mechanism:

- Individual Rationality. Only when the utility is non-negative, can a mechanism be accepted and participated by bidders.
- Computational Efficiency. If we can calculate distribution and payment in polynomial time, the mechanism is computationally efficient.
- Efficiency. The minimum task payment is obtained by the results of the auction, and that means the mechanism requires to determine the bidders who are on the minimum spanning tree as the winners.
- Group-strategy-proof. Renegotiation of mutual benefit can not be formed between every coalition (subset of all bidders).

3.2 The *VCG* Mechanism for Heterogeneous Task Crowdsensing

The *VCG* payment to bidder i can be computed as follow,

$$p_{VCG,i} = u_{VCG,i} + b_i = \mathcal{W}(\mathcal{N}^+) - \mathcal{W}(\mathcal{N}^+ - \{i\}) + b_i \tag{2}$$

where $\mathcal{N}^+ = \mathcal{N} \cup \{i_0\}$ and $\mathcal{W}(\mathcal{N}^+ - \{i\})$ is the social welfare if bidder i's bid is ignored.

The *VCG* mechanism is dominant strategy truthful, but suffers from high payment and vulnerability to shill bidding which make the VCG mechanism rarely used in practice.

4   Core-selecting Mechanism for Crowdsensing

At first, we define the core in the crowdsensing auction. A group of players in the cooperative game is $\mathcal{N}^+ = \mathcal{N} \cup \{i_0\}$, and that covers all the SPs and the SS $\{i_0\}$. The value function for coalition $\mathcal{C} \subseteq \mathcal{N}^+$ is $\mathcal{W}(\mathcal{C})$, where $\mathcal{W}(\mathcal{C})$ is the task payment on the basis of allocation scheme formed by $\mathcal{C}$. For every coalition $\mathcal{C}$, the value function $\mathcal{W}(\mathcal{C})$ is *zero* when $\mathcal{C}$ does not contain the SS i_0. A core result has two attributes. First of all, $\mathcal{W}(\mathcal{N}^+)$ represents the total utility of $\mathcal{N}^+$. Secondly, the total utility of each coalition $\mathcal{C}$ has to be no less than the minimum value $\mathcal{W}(\mathcal{C})$.

Definition 1. (Core outcome.) Allocation and payment is a core outcome of crowdsensing auction so as to make the utility profile $\mathbf{u} = (u_1, ..., u_n)$ satisfies:.

$$\Phi_1 : \mathcal{W}(\mathcal{N}^+) = \sum_{i \in \mathcal{N}^+} u_i \qquad \Phi_2 : \mathcal{W}(\mathcal{C}) \leq \sum_{i \in \mathcal{C}} u_i \quad \forall \mathcal{C} \subseteq \mathcal{N}^+ \tag{3}$$

The first core constraint Φ_1 will ensure that the $\mathcal{W}(\mathcal{N}^+)$ is assuredly selected, since the total utility of $\mathcal{N}^+$ and $\mathcal{W}(\mathcal{N}^+)$ are equal. As for the effect of the second core constraint Φ_2, it is used to constrain the total utility of C not to be less than the value it can obtain. It is necessary to note that the core can not be empty.

4.1 Payment Maximization Rule

In this and next section we present *VCG*-nearest pricing rule for our mechanism, which is proven to provide incentives for bidders to bid truthfully. The idea is to find core payments that maximize the total payment and are as close to the *VCG* payments as possible.

After solving WDP, we denote the set of winning bundles as $\{\mathcal{S}_i\}_{i \in \mathcal{N}}$, and get an alternative formulation:

$$\sum_{i \in \mathcal{C}} u_i = u_{i_0} + \sum_{i \in \mathcal{C} \cap \mathcal{W}} u_i + \sum_{i \in \mathcal{C} \setminus \mathcal{W}} u_i = - \sum_{i \in \mathcal{W} \setminus \mathcal{C} \cap \mathcal{W}} p_i - \sum_{i \in \mathcal{C} \cap \mathcal{W}} b_i(\mathcal{S}_i) \geq \mathcal{W}(\mathcal{C}) \quad \forall \mathcal{C} \subseteq \mathcal{N}^+ \tag{4}$$

where $\mathcal{W}$ is the set of winning workers. Let $\tilde{\mathcal{C}} = \mathcal{C} \cap \mathcal{W}$, then we have $\mathcal{W}(\mathcal{C}) \geq \mathcal{W}(\tilde{\mathcal{C}} \cup (\mathcal{N}^+ \setminus \mathcal{W}))$, since $\mathcal{C} \subseteq \tilde{\mathcal{C}} \cup (\mathcal{N}^+ \setminus \mathcal{W})$. (4) is equal to

$$\sum_{i \in \mathcal{W} \setminus \tilde{\mathcal{C}}} p_i \leq -\mathcal{W}(\tilde{\mathcal{C}} \cup (\mathcal{N}^+ \setminus \mathcal{W})) - \sum_{i \in \tilde{\mathcal{C}}} b_i(\mathcal{S}_i) \tag{5}$$

We use $\beta_{\tilde{\mathcal{C}}}$ to denote $-\mathcal{W}(\tilde{\mathcal{C}} \cup (\mathcal{N}^+ \setminus \mathcal{W})) - \sum_{i \in \tilde{\mathcal{C}}} c_i(\mathcal{S}_i)$. Let the vector of all $\beta_{\mathcal{C}}$ values as $\boldsymbol{\beta}$. Then the Eq. (5) can be rewritten as

$$A\boldsymbol{p} \leq \boldsymbol{\beta} \tag{6}$$

where A is a $2^{|\mathcal{W}|-1} \times |\mathcal{W}|$ matrix and $|\mathcal{W}|$ is the number of winners in $\mathcal{W}$. If bidder i is selected in the jth subset, A_{ij} is equal to 1, otherwise equal to 0. After that, we can employ the following linear program to find the maximum payment result σ:

$$\sigma = \max \boldsymbol{p} \cdot \mathbf{1}$$
$$\text{subject to } A\boldsymbol{p} \leq \boldsymbol{\beta} \tag{7}$$
$$\boldsymbol{p} \geq \boldsymbol{c}$$

Lemma 1. We can solve the linear program (7) in polynomial time to compute the maximum core payment β.

4.2   *VCG*-Nearest Rule

In the second step, a point reference rule is introduced and it always results in a unique payout vector. One more constraint is added to Eq. (7) that the maximum total payment should have the same value as the total payment, that is, $\boldsymbol{p} \cdot \boldsymbol{1} = \sigma$. Therefore, we could obtain the nearest *VCG* payment vector p by the following quadratic program:

$$\min \ (\boldsymbol{p} - \boldsymbol{p}_{VCG})^T (\boldsymbol{p} - \boldsymbol{p}_{VCG})$$
$$\text{subject to } \boldsymbol{Ap} \leq \boldsymbol{\beta}$$
$$\boldsymbol{p} \geq \boldsymbol{c} \tag{8}$$
$$\boldsymbol{p} \cdot \boldsymbol{1} = \sigma$$

In order to optimize the quadratic programming, we use Karush-Kuhn-Tucker (KKT) condition [12]. KKT conditions show that $\boldsymbol{p}^*$ is an optimal solution to quadratic program iff there exists a vector $\boldsymbol{\lambda} \geq 0$, a vector $\boldsymbol{\omega} \geq 0$, and a scalar $\varphi \geq 0$, such that

$$\boldsymbol{p}^* - \boldsymbol{p}_{VCG} + A^T \boldsymbol{\lambda} + \boldsymbol{I}_p \boldsymbol{\omega} + \boldsymbol{1}\varphi = 0 \tag{9}$$

in which $\boldsymbol{I}_p$ is the identity matrix. Therefore, we can decompose $\boldsymbol{p}^*$ for each bidder, as shown below:

$$p_i^* = p_{(VCG,i)} - \sum_{\tilde{C} \in \mathcal{W} \backslash \{i\}} \lambda_{\tilde{C}} - \omega_i - \varphi \tag{10}$$

We can remove the constraint $\boldsymbol{c} \leq \boldsymbol{p}$, which is proved redundant under the VCG-Nearest rule by using the KKT condition.

Theorem 1. The Vickrey-nearest core-selecting mechanism minimizes the maximum regret for bidders across all core-selecting heterogeneous task crowdsensing mechanisms. Due to the space limitation, we omit the proof.

4.3   Payment Generation Algorithm

There are thousands of workers (SPs) in the crowdsensing platform. Therefore, the number of core constraints is too large in practice, because the number of core constraints is an exponential multiple of k. Nevertheless, the complexity can be reduced by using the core constraint generation program, as shown in Algorithm 1. Instead of considering the possibilities of all constraints, the payment of the most valuable constraints are increased to effectively block coalitions, thus we can reduce the complexity. The in-core payment vector under other rules can also be easily solved by this algorithm.

The algorithm is an iterative algorithm. By continuously reducing the payment of the winning bidder, until there is no violating coalition in the auction and the core outcome is reached, then the iteration is stopped. The pseudo code of the algorithm is shown in Algorithm 1.

Algorithm 1 VCG-Nearest In-Core Payment Generation

1: Set $t := 0$, payment vector $\boldsymbol{p}^t = \boldsymbol{p}_{VCG}$, coefficient matrix $\boldsymbol{A}^t := \emptyset$, and vector $\boldsymbol{\beta}^t := \emptyset$;

2: **while** True **do**

3:　　$t = t + 1$;

4:　　**for** bidder $i \in \mathcal{N}$ **do**

5:　　　**for** bundle $\mathcal{S}$ bid by i **do**

6:　　　　$b_i(\mathcal{S})^t := b_i(\mathcal{S}) - (b_i(\mathcal{S}_i) - p_i^{t-1})$;

7:　　　**end for**

8:　　**end for**

9:　　Calculate $\mathcal{W}^t(\mathcal{N}^+)$ with b^t, with the set of winning SPs $\mathcal{C}^t$ be the first violated coalition in WDP;

10:　　**if** $-\mathcal{W}(\mathcal{N}^+) \leq 1 \cdot p^{t-1}$ **then**

11:　　　break;

11:　　**end if**

12:　　$\tilde{\mathcal{C}}^t := \mathcal{C}^t \cap \mathcal{W}$

13:　　$\beta_{\tilde{\mathcal{C}}^t} := -\mathcal{W}^t(\tilde{\mathcal{C}}^t \cup (\mathcal{N}^+ \setminus \mathcal{W})) - \sum_{i \in \tilde{\mathcal{C}}^t} b_i^t(\mathcal{S}_i)$;

14:　　Append the corresponding row $a_{\tilde{\mathcal{C}}^t}$ and new entry $\beta_{\tilde{\mathcal{C}}^t}$ to A^{t-1} and β^{t-1} to form A^t and β^t respectively;

15:　　Solve the linear programming (7) with $\boldsymbol{A}^t$ and $\boldsymbol{\beta}^t$, obtaining σ^t;

16:　　Solve the quadratic programming (8) with $\boldsymbol{A}^t$, $\boldsymbol{\beta}^t$ and σ^t, obtaining $\boldsymbol{p}^t$;

17: **end while**

18: $\boldsymbol{p}^* := \boldsymbol{p}^{t-1}$ is the final payment vector.

Theorem 2. The in-core payment is always the payment vector computed by Algorithm 1. Due to the space limitation, we omit the proof.

5　Simulation Results

5.1　Simulation Environment

There are twelve heterogeneous tasks $\Pi = \{\pi_1, \pi_2, ..., \pi_{12}\}$ to be considered. Among the twelve heterogeneous tasks, the revenue and difficulties of completing the tasks decrease in turn. The default number of tasks of each type is $T = \{10, 20, 30, ..., 120\}$. In other cases, the number of tasks varies from 0.5T to 5T. When simulating the auction of six types of tasks, we choose the tasks with odd numbers in Π. The number of bids submitted by each SP is unified within the range of [1].

Two performance standards is used.

– Task payment, calculated by the sum of the task rewards of all winning SPs.
– Task redundancy rate, refers to the ratio of the sum of all tasks assigned minus all the original tasks to all the original tasks.

5.2　Allocation Results

The auction settings are indicated by x-yT, where x represents the number of types of tasks bundles and y represents that y*T tasks are available. (T represents the default setting of each tasks, it appears in the Sect. 5.1).

In Fig. 2(a), the relative task payment under CTA can be kept lower than VCG by more than 8%. In addition, we can see other interesting conclusions, that is, the task payment of 6-1T-CTA is always lower than 12-1T-CTA, this is because in the former case, the 6 types of tasks are more refined than the 12 types of task configuration, so a large number of task bundles can be constructed for auction, thereby reducing task overhead.

Figure 2(b) shows that when using our auction mechanism and assigning tasks, the task redundancy rate has slightly changed, among which the redundancy rate of our CTA is about 3% lower than that of VCG. We can find that

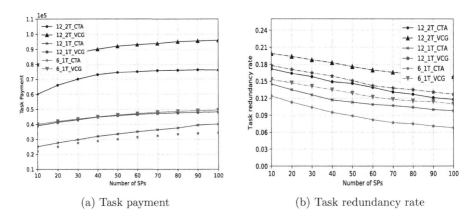

(a) Task payment   (b) Task redundancy rate

Fig. 2. Simulation results

the task redundancy rate is inversely correlated with SP and task types, and positively correlated with task scale, which reminds us that the more task types, the more complex the combination of tasks, the more likely it is to produce a better combination.

6   Conclusion

As an emerging combinatorial auction mechanism, the core-selecting has a unique effect in allocating bundled tasks. It ensures efficiency while reducing the overhead of SS. This work is the first work for heterogeneous task auction in the crowdsensing market, which can avoid false-name bidding and help SS pay less to obtain close output. After simulation, we prove that our proposal is better than the famous VCG in task payment and task redundancy rate, thus promote the development of crowdsensing task auctions mechanism.

Acknowledgements. This paper is supported by the National Key Research and Development Program of China (Grant No. 2018YFB1403400), the National Natural Science Foundation of China (Grant No. 61876080), the Key Research and Development Program of Jiangsu (Grant No. BE2019105), the Collaborative Innovation Center of Novel Software Technology and Industrialization at Nanjing University.

References

1. Gunti, R.K., Yi, F., Len, H.: Mobile crowdsensing: current state and future challenges. IEEE Commun. Mag. **49**, 32–39 (2011)
2. Goal, G., Nekzad, A., Singea, A.: Allocating tasks to workers with matching constraints: truthful mechanisms for crowdsensing markets. In: Proceedings of WWW, 2014, pp. 279–280 (2014)
3. Holmtrom, B.: Groves scheme on restricted domains. The Econometric Society, pp. 1137–1144, September 1979

4. Yuan, M.-C., Kang, I., Laung, K.-S.: A survey of crowdsensing systems. In: Proceedings of IEEE 3rd International Conference on Social Computing, Boston, MA, USA, pp. 766–773, October 2011

5. Yung, X., Wung, T., Ran, X., Yu, W.: Copula-based multidimensional crowd428 sourced data synthesis and release with local privacy. In: 2017 IEEE Global Communications Conference, GLOBECOM 2017, Singapore, pp. 1–6, December 2017

6. Zhe, X., An, J., Yung, M., Xiang, L., Yung, Q., Gui, X.: A fair incentive mechanism for crowdsensing in crowd sensing. IEEE Internet Things J **3**, 1364–1372 (2016)

7. Nise, N., Ronen, A.: Computationally feasible VCG mechanisms. In: Proceedings of the 2nd ACM Conference on Electronic Commerce ACM, New York (2000)

8. Karlen, A.U., Kempe, D., Beyond, V.C.G.: Frugality of truthful mechanisms. In: IEEE Symposium on Foundations of Computer Science, pp. 615–624 (2005)

9. Duan, X., Liu, H., Tang, H., Cai, Q., Zhang, F., Han, X.: A novel hybrid auction algorithm for multi-UAVs dynamic task assignment. IEEE Access **8**, 86207–86222 (2020). https://doi.org/10.1109/ACCESS.2019.2959327

10. Zhe, X., An, J., Yung, M., Xiang, L., Yang, Q., Gui, X.: A fair incentive mechanism for crowdsensing in crowd sensing. IEEE Internet Things J. **3**, 1364–1372 (2016)

11. Qiao, Y., Song, Y., Wang, N., Wu, J., Zhang, L., Wang, C.: A false-name-proof protocol for multicast routing auctions. In: IEEE International Conference 2018, pp. 72–79 (2018)

12. Day, R., Cramton, J.: The quadratic core-selecting payment rule for combinatorial auctions. Oper. Res. **60**(3), 588–603 (2012)

Lightweight Threshold Private Set Intersection via Oblivious Transfer

Shengnan Zhao[1,2], Ming Ma[1,2], Xiangfu Song[1,2], Han Jiang[1,2(✉)], Yunxue Yan[1,2], and Qiuliang Xu[1,2(✉)]

[1] School of Software, Shandong University, Jinan 250101, People's Republic of China
{jianghan,xql}@sdu.edu.cn
[2] Key Laboratory of Shandong Province for Software Engineering, Jinan 250101, People's Republic of China

Abstract. As a significant basis for privacy-preserving applications of Secure Multiparty Computation (MPC), Private Set Intersection (PSI) has long been a question of great interest in a wide range of field, such as ad conversion rates and private contact tracing. Threshold PSI (t-PSI), a variant of PSI, allows two parties to learn the intersection of two sets only if the cardinality of intersection is larger (or lesser) than a threshold t. In this paper, we give a generic t-PSI construction that relies heavily on Oblivious Transfer (OT). Without resorting to the relatively expensive homomorphic calculation approaches from public-key mechanism, two kinds of t-PSI protocols could be efficiently implemented based on our proposed construction, *i.e.*, $t^{\leq}$PSI and $t^{>}$-PSI. Specially, we construct two efficient protocols named secret-sharing private equality test ^{ss}PEQT and membership text ^{ss}PMT, which enable PSI to scale to a wide range of practical applications. The experimental simulation results show that our protocols are efficient and computation friendly.

Keywords: Secure Multiparty Computation · Private Set Intersection (PSI) · Threshold PSI · Private Membership Test

1 Introduction

Originating from Yao's millionaire's problem [1] in 1982, Secure Multiparty Computation (MPC) has witnessed notable achievement as a research area and in experimental performance, though we are still in the early steps of deploying MPC solutions to real problems [2].

Two-party Private Set Intersection (PSI) allows two parties, denoted by Alice and Bob with their respective sets X and Y, to compute the intersection $X \cap Y$ without revealing anything else about the two sets. Oblivious Transfer (OT) is currently one of the most popular methods for investigating how to construct efficient PSI protocol [3–5] and its variants in different settings [6–8] and adversary models [9,10].

© Springer Nature Switzerland AG 2021
Z. Liu et al. (Eds.): WASA 2021, LNCS 12939, pp. 108–116, 2021.
https://doi.org/10.1007/978-3-030-86137-7_12

Threshold PSI (t-PSI) enables the parties to learn the intersection only if the number of their common items is sufficiently large (or small), *i.e.*, a threshold t. Take over-threshold PSI protocol ($t^{\leq}$PSI) as an example, the protocol $t^{\leq}$PSI outputs the intersection only when $t \leq$ PSI^{CA}, where PSI^{CA} represents PSI *cardinality* that restricts the output of PSI and reveals only the intersection size and nothing else. Without resorting to generic MPC methods or public-key based PSI^{CA} protocols, however, designing an efficient and generic t-PSI protocol is not an easy task [11,12]. Recent developments in the field of PSI have led to a renewed interest in practical threshold PSI [13,14]. Most studies in the field of t-PSI have only focused on communication cost and rely on expensive public-key operations [11–13], such as additive homomorphic encryption (HE), oblivious polynomial evaluation and fully homomorphic encryption. Such approaches, however, have failed to address the situation where participants have computation limitations. Constructing t-PSI based on lightweight techniques with better efficiency is non-trivial.

We are interested in balanced PSI, where $|X| = |Y| = n$ and the output should be received by the party who does not hold the threshold t, to whom we refer as a receiver $\mathcal{R}$. We provide comparisons to prior classical protocols in Table 1. Main contributions of this work are summarized as follows:

- We give a secret-shared Private Equality Test functionality $\mathcal{F}_{\mathrm{PEQT}}^{\mathrm{ss},q}$, and construct an efficient protocol ^{ss}PEQT that is based on OT and proves secure under semi-honest model.
- We propose a secret-shared Private Membership Test functionality $\mathcal{F}_{\mathrm{PMT}}^{\mathrm{ss},q}$, and introduce an efficient protocol ^{ss}PMT which is a basis for PSI^{CA} and t-PSI.
- Based on $\mathcal{F}_{\mathrm{PMT}}^{\mathrm{ss},q}$, we give a generic t-PSI protocol framework where two kinds of t-PSI could be efficiently implemented, *i.e.*, $t^{\leq}$PSI and $t^{>}$-PSI.

Table 1. Threshold PSI protocol comparisons

Protocol	Public-key computation	Communication	Leakage	Functionality	Main cryptographic tools
[11]	$O(n^2)$	$O(ln + \kappa n)$	$|X \cap Y|$	$t^{\leq}$PSI	HE, OT
[12]	$O(n)$	$O(ln + \kappa n)$	–	$t^{\leq}$PSI & $t^{>}$-PSI	HE
[13]	$O(nl)$	$O(t^2)$	–	$t^{\leq}$PSI	HE
Ours	$O(\kappa + l)$	$O(ln \log n)$	–	$t^{\leq}$PSI & $t^{>}$-PSI	OT

Note: The complexity in [11,12] refers to PSI^{CA} phase. 'Threshold' t in [13] is used to measure the number of different items instead of common ones. κ denotes the computational security parameters.

2 Preliminaries

2.1 Notation

In this work, we denote the computational and statistical security parameters by κ, μ, respectively. $r \in_R \mathbb{Z}_q$ denotes that r is chosen uniformly at random from $\mathbb{Z}_q$. $x := y$ denote assigning the value of y to x.

2.2 Cryptographic Notions

Oblivious Transfer. OT is fast becoming a significant primitive in secure computation. Functionality $\mathcal{F}_{\mathrm{OT}}^n$ gives the receiver $\mathcal{R}$ the exact one among n messages sent by the sender $\mathcal{S}$, who learns nothing in the whole process.

Secret Sharing. A secret sharing scheme allows a secret s to be divided into several pieces held by different individuals, a certain coalition of which would recover the original secret value s, or does not real anything about s. We use the sharing over both $\mathbb{Z}_q$ and $\mathbb{Z}_2$, and refer them as *arithmetic* and *boolean* sharing, respectively.

Security Definition. Goldreich [15] proposed the formal security definition of secure multiparty protocols by comparing two output distributions, which comes from an ideal world and a real world, respectively. We write $X \stackrel{c}{\equiv} Y$ if two distribution probability ensembles X and Y are computationally indistinguishable.

3 Secret-Shared Private Equality Test (^{ss}PEQT)

3.1 Functionality $\mathcal{F}_{\mathrm{PEQT}}^{\mathrm{ss},q}$

In Fig. 1, we give the ideal definition of a secret-shared PEQT functionality $\mathcal{F}_{\mathrm{PEQT}}^{\mathrm{ss},q}$, which enables two parties $\mathcal{S}$ and $\mathcal{R}$ learn whether two strings are equal in

---

Functionality $\mathcal{F}_{\mathrm{PEQT}}^{\mathrm{ss},q}$

PARAMETERS: *sender $\mathcal{S}$, receiver $\mathcal{R}$, public integer q.*
FUNCTIONALITY:

- Wait for input $x = \{0,1\}^*$ from $\mathcal{S}$.
- Wait for input $y = \{0,1\}^*$ from $\mathcal{R}$.
- Give the *sender $\mathcal{S}$* output $r \in_R \mathbb{Z}_q$.
- Give the *receiver $\mathcal{R}$* output r', where
    - $r' = -r + 1$, if $x = y$;
    - $r' = -r$, otherwise.

Fig. 1. Secret-shared private equality test $\mathcal{F}_{\mathrm{PEQT}}^{\mathrm{ss},q}$

a secret-sharing way. We define a public parameter q in $\mathcal{F}_{\text{PEQT}}^{\text{ss},q}$ so as to indicate the outputs type of $[\![z]\!]_P$, i.e., Boolean sharing (when $q = 2$) or Arithmetic sharing.

3.2 Protocol ^{ss}PEQT

The core idea of the ^{ss}PEQT is to reduce the comparison procedure between two long input strings to two smaller arithmetic shares, which are obtained by sharing the Hamming Distance of the two long binary strings. The notation $d_{\text{H}}(x, y)$ denotes the Hamming Distance between two binary strings (vectors) x and y, here $x, y \in \{0,1\}^l$ and $l = 2^k$.

PARAMETERS:

- Two parties: Sender $\mathcal{S}$ and Receiver $\mathcal{R}$.
- Security parameters κ and μ.
- Public integer q.
- Ideal functionality $\mathcal{F}_{\text{OT}}^n$.

INPUT OF $\mathcal{S}$: $x \in \{0,1\}^l$.
INPUT OF $\mathcal{R}$: $y \in \{0,1\}^l$.
PROTOCOL:

1. Set $p := l + 1, x_{\text{IN}} := x, y_{\text{IN}} := y$.
2. For each bit of the x_{IN}, denoted by x_i, $\mathcal{S}$ chooses $r_i \in_R \mathbb{Z}_p$.
   - (1) $\mathcal{S}$ sets $m_0 = r_i + x_i$, $m_1 = r_i + (x_i \oplus 1)$.
   - (2) $\mathcal{R}$ sets selection bit $b = y_i$.
   - (3) $\mathcal{S}$ and $\mathcal{R}$ invoke 1-out-of-2 OT functionality, i.e., $\mathcal{F}_{\text{OT}}^n$.
3. $\mathcal{R}$ receives m_{y_i} and computes $y_{\text{OUT}} = \sum_{i=1}^{l} m_{y_i} \mod p$
4. $\mathcal{S}$ computes $x_{\text{OUT}} = \sum_{i=1}^{l} r_i \mod p$.
5. Compute $l' = \lceil \log p \rceil$. If $l' > 2$, then reset $p := l' + 1, x_{\text{IN}} := x_{\text{OUT}}, y_{\text{IN}} := y_{\text{OUT}}$ and go to step 2.
6. $\mathcal{S}$ and $\mathcal{R}$ get $x_{\text{OUT}}, y_{\text{OUT}} \in \mathbb{Z}_4$.
7. $\mathcal{S}$ randomly chooses $r \in_R \mathbb{Z}_q$ and sets $m_{x_{\text{OUT}}} = -r + 1$ and $m_j = -r$, here $j = i + x_{\text{OUT}} \mod 4$ for $i = 1, 2, 3$. Four messages $\{m_i | i = 0, 1, 2, 3\}$ serve as inputs in 1-out-of-4 OT next step.
8. $\mathcal{R}$ prepares y_{OUT} as selection input. After invoking 1-out-of-4 OT with $\mathcal{S}$, $\mathcal{R}$ gets $r' = m_{y_{\text{OUT}}}$.
9. $\mathcal{S}$ outputs r and $\mathcal{R}$ outputs r'.

Fig. 2. Secret-shared private equality test protocol ^{ss}PEQT

Theorem 1. *The ^{ss}PEQT protocol in Fig. 2 securely computes the functionality $\mathcal{F}_{PEQT}^{\text{ss},q}$ (Fig. 1) in semi-honest setting, as described, given the functionality $\mathcal{F}_{OT}^n$.*

Due to the page limit, the proof of Theorem 1 is given in our supplementary materials [16].

3.3   Secret-Shared Private Membership Test

Given functionality $\mathcal{F}_{\text{PEQT}}^{\text{ss},q}$, it is trivial to construct secret-shared PMT protocol $^{\text{ss}}\text{PMT}$ (see Fig. 3) that securely realizes functionality $\mathcal{F}_{\text{PMT}}^{\text{ss},q}$ where a sender $\mathcal{S}$ holding a set X and a receiver $\mathcal{R}$ hold an element y share a bit z indicating whether $y \in X$ or not. The correctness of $^{\text{ss}}\text{PMT}$ is obvious and the security boils down to the functionality $\mathcal{F}_{\text{PEQT}}^{\text{ss},q}$.

PARAMETERS:

- Two parties: *Sender* $\mathcal{S}$ and *Receiver* $\mathcal{R}$.
- Public integer q.
- Ideal functionality $\mathcal{F}_{\text{PEQT}}^{\text{ss},q}$ in Fig. 1.

INPUT OF $\mathcal{S}$: $X = \{x_1, \cdots, x_n\}$.
INPUT OF $\mathcal{R}$: $Y = \{y\}$.
PROTOCOL:

1. For each $i \in [n]$, $\mathcal{S}$ and $\mathcal{R}$ invoke functionality $\mathcal{F}_{\text{PEQT}}^{\text{ss},q}$ where:
    - $\mathcal{S}$ acts as sender in $\mathcal{F}_{\text{PEQT}}^{\text{ss},q}$ and obtains r_i
    - $\mathcal{R}$ acts as receiver in $\mathcal{F}_{\text{PEQT}}^{\text{ss},q}$ and obtains r_i'.
2. $\mathcal{S}$ outputs a share $[r]_{\mathcal{S}} = \sum_{i=1}^{n} r_i \mod q$.
3. $\mathcal{R}$ outputs a share $[r]_{\mathcal{R}} = \sum_{i=1}^{n} r_i' \mod q$.

Fig. 3. Secret-shared Private Membership Test protocol $^{\text{ss}}\text{PMT}$

4   Generic Threshold PSI Protocol ($t^{\leq}$PSI and $t^{>}$-PSI)

We start by giving the functionality of over-threshold PSI ($t^{\leq}$PSI), which gives $\mathcal{R}$ the intersection $X \cap Y$ only when $t \leq \text{PSI}^{\text{CA}}$. On the one hand, we would not give the $t^{>}$-PSI functionality in this paper due to the page limit and its similarity with $t^{\leq}$PSI. On the other hand, we would explain that our $t^{\leq}$PSI protocol is generic, and it is very easy to execute $t^{>}$-PSI without any extra communication or computation, which benefits from the flexibility of our t-PSI framework.

4.1   Over-Threshold PSI Protocol: $t^{\leq}$PSI

Our over-threshold PSI protocol $t^{\leq}$PSI benefits from hashing the item of the input set to bins, and executing $^{\text{ss}}\text{PMT}$ protocol separately on each bin where functionality $\mathcal{F}_{\mathrm{PEQT}}^{\mathrm{ss},q}$ features a useful linearity property. Based on $^{\mathrm{ss}}\mathsf{PMT}$, two parties could get shares of $\mathsf{PSI}^{\mathsf{CA}}$ by adding their local $^{\mathrm{ss}}\mathsf{PMT}$ outputs. The protocol $t^{\leq}\mathsf{PSI}$ would output the intersection $X \cap Y$ when $t \leq \mathsf{PSI}^{\mathsf{CA}}$.

PARAMETERS:

- Two parties: *Sender* $\mathcal{S}$ and *Receiver* $\mathcal{R}$.
- Security parameters κ and μ.
- Public integer q and $\beta = O(n)$.
- Ideal functionality $\mathcal{F}_{\mathrm{PMT}}^{\mathrm{ss},q}$ and $\mathcal{F}_{\gtrless(y_0,x,y_1)}$.

INPUT OF $\mathcal{S}$: $X = \{x_1, \cdots, x_n\}$, a threshold t.
INPUT OF $\mathcal{R}$: $Y = \{y_1, \cdots, y_n\}$.
PROTOCOL:

1. $\mathcal{S}$ randomly chooses functions $h_1, h_2, h_3 : \{0,1\}^l \rightarrow [\beta]$ and assigns each item of X into bins under chosen hash functions. Let $\mathcal{B}_{\mathcal{S}}[b]$ denote the set of items in the sender's bth bin.
2. $\mathcal{R}$ maps all items Y to β bins using Cuckoo hashing. Let $\mathcal{B}_{\mathcal{R}}[b]$ denote the item in the receiver's bth bin.
3. For each bin $b \in [\beta]$, $\mathcal{S}$ and $\mathcal{R}$ invoke $\mathcal{F}_{\mathrm{PMT}}^{\mathrm{ss},q}$:
   (1) $\mathcal{S}$ acts as *sender* with input $\{\mathcal{B}_{\mathcal{S}}[b]\}$
   (2) $\mathcal{R}$ acts as *receiver* with input $\{\mathcal{B}_{\mathcal{R}}[b]\}$
   (3) $\mathcal{S}$ obtains r_b and $\mathcal{R}$ obtains r'_b.
4. $\mathcal{S}$ prepares $I := r_1||r_2|| \cdots ||r_\beta$ and computes $c_0 = -\sum_{b=1}^{\beta} r_b \mod q$. $\mathcal{R}$ computes $c_1 = \sum_{b=1}^{\beta} r'_b \mod q$. $\mathcal{S}$ and $\mathcal{R}$ invoke $\mathcal{F}_{\gtrless(c_0,t,c_1)}$ in Figure ??, from which $\mathcal{R}$ gets output z.
5. $\mathcal{S}$ and $\mathcal{R}$ invokes OT functionality $\mathcal{F}_{\mathrm{OT}}^n$:
   (1) $\mathcal{S}$ acts as *sender* with pair-input $\{0, I\}$
   (2) $\mathcal{R}$ acts as *receiver* with bit input $\sigma = z$
   (3) $\mathcal{R}$ obtains the output $I' = \hat{r}_1||\hat{r}_2|| \cdots ||\hat{r}_\beta$.
6. $\mathcal{R}$ outputs $\{\mathcal{B}_{\mathcal{R}}[i] \mid i \in [\beta]$ and $r_i + \hat{r}_i = 1\}$.

Fig. 4. Over-Threshold PSI protocol $t^{\leq}\mathsf{PSI}$

It is trivial to compare the threshold t and intersection cardinality $\mathsf{PSI}^{\mathsf{CA}}$, although $\mathsf{PSI}^{\mathsf{CA}}$ is secret-shared between two parties. We give an ideal comparison functionality $\mathcal{F}_{\gtrless(y_0,x,y_1)}$ with three inputs that outputs a bit z indicating whether $t < \mathsf{PSI}^{\mathsf{CA}}$ or not. Different secure comparison implementation could be realized. We leverage the capability of garbled circuit to give a lightweight solution for this task. It is very efficient to deploy a comparison circuit for short inputs, where $\mathcal{S}$ encodes c_0 and t and $\mathcal{R}$ encodes c_1 for corresponding input wires.

In semi-honest model, the security of $t^{\leq}\mathsf{PSI}$ in Fig. 4 boils down to the functionality $\mathcal{F}_{\mathrm{PMT}}$ and $\mathcal{F}_{\gtrless(y_0,x,y_1)}$. Here we omit proof details for the page limit.

Below-Threshold PSI Protocol ($t^>$-PSI). The protocol $t^>$-PSI outputs the intersection to $\mathcal{R}$ when $t > \mathsf{PSI}^{\mathsf{CA}}$. According to Step 4. in Fig. 4, it is very easy to execute $t^>$-PSI by setting chosen bit $\sigma := 1 - z$ when $\mathcal{F}_{\geqslant(y_0,x,y_1)}$ gives $\mathcal{R}$ the comparison result z.

5   Implementation

In this section, we test the performance of $^{\mathsf{ss}}\mathsf{PEQT}$. The experiments were performed on Ubuntu version 20.10 equipped with 2.90 GHz Intel Core i7-10700 CPU and 16 GB RAM. Our tests refer to the implement on Github: https://github.com/encryptogroup/OTExtension. We simulate the protocol $^{\mathsf{ss}}\mathsf{PEQT}$ on a single machine.

The repeated experiments results in Fig. 5a shows that, on average, it takes no more than 300 ms to finish one simulation, in which we choose to simulate 10^4 instances of OT_2^1 in every $^{\mathsf{ss}}\mathsf{PEQT}$. We claim that $^{\mathsf{ss}}\mathsf{PEQT}$ could be instantiated directly by OT_n^1. As a comparison, we also test several OT_n^1 instances in Fig. 5b. This means that, when the length of (x,y) to be compared is long, it would not be an efficient way to invoke OT_n^1 directly due to time increase.

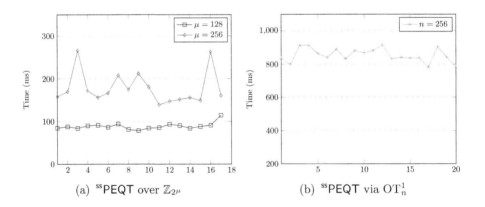

(a) $^{\mathsf{ss}}\mathsf{PEQT}$ over $\mathbb{Z}_{2^\mu}$ (b) $^{\mathsf{ss}}\mathsf{PEQT}$ via OT_n^1

Fig. 5. Running time of $^{\mathsf{ss}}\mathsf{PEQT}$

6   Conclusions and Future Work

We propose a generic t-PSI construction via Oblivious Transfer without resorting to the relatively expensive calculation. We believe $^{\mathsf{ss}}\mathsf{PEQT}$ and $^{\mathsf{ss}}\mathsf{PMT}$ would be important building blocks in PSI applications. In future work, we are going to focus on multiparty t-PSI scenarios and secure constructions under malicious models.

Acknowledgements. We thank the anonymous reviewers. This work was supported by the National Natural Science Foundation of China under Grant 61632020, and the Special Project of Science and Technology Innovation Base of Key Laboratory of Software Engineering of Shandong Province under Grant 11480004042015.

References

1. Yao, A.C.: Protocols for secure computations. In: 23rd Annual Symposium on Foundations of Computer Science (SFCS 1982), pp. 160–164. IEEE (1982)
2. Zhao, C., et al.: Secure multi-party computation: theory, practice and applications. Inf. Sci. **476**, 357–372 (2019)
3. Kolesnikov, V., Kumaresan, R., Rosulek, M., Trieu, N.: Efficient batched oblivious PRF with applications to private set intersection. In: Proceedings of the 2016 ACM SIGSAC Conference on Computer and Communications Security, pp. 818–829 (2016)
4. Chase, M., Miao, P.: Private set intersection in the internet setting from lightweight oblivious PRF. In: Micciancio, D., Ristenpart, T. (eds.) CRYPTO 2020. LNCS, vol. 12172, pp. 34–63. Springer, Cham (2020). https://doi.org/10.1007/978-3-030-56877-1_2
5. Song, X., Gai, M., Zhao, S., Jiang, H.: Privacy-preserving statistics protocol for set-based computation. J. Comput. Res. Dev. **57**(10), 2221 (2020). (in Chinese)
6. Zhao, C., Jiang, H., Wei, X., Xu, Q., Zhao, M.: Cut-and-choose bilateral oblivious transfer and its application. In: 2015 IEEE Trustcom/BigDataSE/ISPA, vol. 1, pp. 384–391. IEEE (2015)
7. Kolesnikov, V., Matania, N., Pinkas, B., Rosulek, M., Trieu, N.: Practical multi-party private set intersection from symmetric-key techniques. In: Proceedings of the 2017 ACM SIGSAC Conference on Computer and Communications Security, pp. 1257–1272 (2017)
8. Kolesnikov, V., Rosulek, M., Trieu, N., Wang, X.: Scalable private set union from symmetric-key techniques. In: Galbraith, S.D., Moriai, S. (eds.) ASIACRYPT 2019. LNCS, vol. 11922, pp. 636–666. Springer, Cham (2019). https://doi.org/10.1007/978-3-030-34621-8_23
9. Pinkas, B., Schneider, T., Tkachenko, O., Yanai, A.: Efficient circuit-based PSI with linear communication. In: Ishai, Y., Rijmen, V. (eds.) EUROCRYPT 2019. LNCS, vol. 11478, pp. 122–153. Springer, Cham (2019). https://doi.org/10.1007/978-3-030-17659-4_5
10. Karakoç, F., Küpçü, A.: Linear complexity private set intersection for secure two-party protocols. Cryptology ePrint Archive, Report 2020/864 (2020). https://eprint.iacr.org/2020/864
11. Zhao, Y., Chow, S.S.M.: Are you the one to share? Secret transfer with access structure. In: Proceedings on Privacy Enhancing Technologies 2017, no. 1, pp. 149–169 (2017)
12. Zhao, Y., Chow, S.S.M.: Can you find the one for me? In: Proceedings of the 2018 Workshop on Privacy in the Electronic Society, pp. 54–65 (2018)
13. Ghosh, S., Simkin, M.: The communication complexity of threshold private set intersection. In: Boldyreva, A., Micciancio, D. (eds.) CRYPTO 2019. LNCS, vol. 11693, pp. 3–29. Springer, Cham (2019). https://doi.org/10.1007/978-3-030-26951-7_1

14. Badrinarayanan, S., Miao, P., Rindal, P.: Multi-party threshold private set inter-section with sublinear communication. IACR Cryptology ePrint Archive 2020:600 (2020)
15. Goldreich, O.: Foundations of Cryptography: Volume 2, Basic Applications. Cambridge University Press, Cambridge (2009)
16. http://note.youdao.com/s/RXCVwsI1

Person Re-identification Algorithm Based on Spatial Attention Network

Shaoqi Hou[1], Chunhui Liu[1], Kangning Yin[1,2], and Guangqiang Yin[2(✉)]

[1] School of Information and Communication Engineering,
University of Electronic Science and Technology of China, Chengdu, China
{sqhou,chliu,knyin}@std.uestc.edu.cn
[2] School of Information and Software Engineering,
University of Electronic Science and Technology of China, Chengdu, China
yingq@uestc.edu.cn

Abstract. Person Re-identification (Re-ID) aims to solve the matching problem of the same pedestrian at a different time and in different places. Due to the cross-device condition, the appearance of different pedestrians may have a high degree of similarity, at this time, using the global features of pedestrians to match often cannot achieve good results. In order to solve these problems, we designed a Spatial Attention Network (SAN), which introduces attribute features as auxiliary information. Different from the previous approach of simply adding a branch of attribute binary classification network, our SAN is mainly divided into two connecting steps. First, we generate Attribute Attention Heat map (AAH) through Grad-CAM algorithm to accurately locate fine-grained attribute areas of pedestrians. Then, the Attribute Spatial Attention Module (ASAM) is constructed according to the AHH which is taken as the prior knowledge, and introduced into the Re-ID network to assist in the discrimination of the Re-ID task. In particular, our SAN network can integrate the local attribute information and global ID information of pedestrians, which has good adaptability. The test results on Market1501 and DukeMTMC-reID show that our SAN can achieve good results, which is obviously competitive compared with most Re-ID algorithms.

Keywords: Person Re-identification · Attribute information · Spatial attention

1 Introduction

As a hot field in computer vision, person Re-ID makes up for the deficiency of face recognition technology in cross-camera surveillance images, and has a wide application prospect in intelligent video surveillance fields such as airports and supermarkets. However, due to the differences between different cameras and the characteristics of both rigid and flexible pedestrians, its appearance is easily affected by clothing, scale, occlusion, posture and perspective, which makes person Re-ID become a hot topic with both research value and challenges in the field of computer vision.

Z. Liu et al. (Eds.): WASA 2021, LNCS 12939, pp. 117–124, 2021.
https://doi.org/10.1007/978-3-030-86137-7_13

In order to solve the above problems, scholars at home and abroad have made many explorations over these years. The traditional Re-ID algorithms relies on some manual features such as color and texture, and measures the correlation by calculating the feature distance [1–3]. Due to the complexity of calculation and poor representational ability, these algorithms based on manual features are gradually phased out. With the development of convolutional neural network (CNN), since 2014, scholars began to use deep learning models to solve the problem of person Re-ID [4, 5].

At present, person Re-ID algorithms based on deep learning are mainly divided into two categories: metric learning and representation learning. metric learning restricts feature space by designing a distance measurement function, so that intra-class spacing of pedestrian features is decreased and inter-class features are increased. Classical methods such as Triplet loss [6], Quadruple loss [7] and Group consistent similarity learning [8], the key of such methods lies in sample selection, especially the mining of difficult samples.

Different from metric learning, representational learning takes person Re-ID as a classification task and focuses on designing robust and reliable pedestrian feature representation. At present, scholars generally adopt the method of obtaining global features to solve the Re-ID problem, that is, only the pedestrian ID label is used and the loss function constraint is adopted to make the network automatically learn the features that are more discriminative for different pedestrian IDs from the entire pedestrian images [9]. In order to enhance the adaptability of the model under the scenes of scale, occlusion and blur, some scholars [10–12] introduced the attention mechanism into the Re-ID task, so as to improve the models' attention to the salient information in the global features of pedestrians, while suppressing irrelevant noises. However, since different pedestrians may have similar appearance and the same pedestrian varies greatly in different environments, they cannot be correctly matched from the perspective of global appearance alone. Studies show that [13], as a kind of prior knowledge, the attributes of pedestrians contain rich semantic information and can provide key discriminant information for Re-ID. However, in addition to the pedestrian attribute labels marked by DukeMTMC-reID [14] and Market1501 [15], the current Re-ID datasets do not mark the related areas of pedestrian attributes.

In order to solve these problems, we propose a SAN network, which combines pedestrian attribute and attention mechanism for auxiliary discrimination without additional attribute region labeling. The main contributions are summarized as follows:

(1) In the pedestrian attribute classification network, the attribute labels are used to guide and the Grad-CAM algorithm [16] is combined to generate AAH;
(2) In the person Re-ID network, feature maps of different locations and sizes are selected, and combined with the corresponding size of attention heat maps generated by the attribute classification network, ASAM is constructed to assist the discrimination of Re-ID task.

2   Related Work

Person Re-ID based on attribute classification can accurately and quickly mark the target pedestrians in the pedestrian database according to the predicted attribute labels.

In 2017, Lin et al. [13] proposed an Attribute Person Recognition (APR) joint recognition network in order to improve the overall accuracy of person Re-ID network. The essence of the attention mechanism is to imitate the human visual signal processing mechanism, in order to selectively observe the area of interest. Inspired by this, Liu et al. [17] proposed a classic network model HydraPlus-Net with advantages in fine-grained feature recognition based on attention neural network in 2017.

3 Method

3.1 Spatial Attention Network (SAN)

In order to introduce the local features of pedestrian salience into the Re-ID task without adding additional regional annotation, we design SAN, as shown in Fig. 1. As a dual-trace network, SAN consists of two branches: pedestrian attribute classification network and Re-ID network. Each branch is based on the pre-trained ResNet50 [18], in which the attribute classification task provides attribute prior information to assist the discrimination of the Re-ID task.

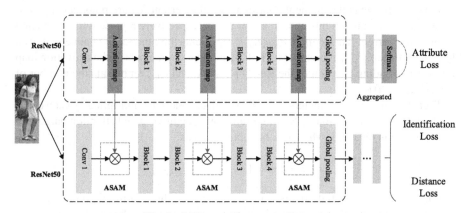

Fig. 1. SAN overall structure diagram.

The general process is as follows:

Firstly, the attribute classification network extracts features in the gradient forward propagation process, and the extracted features are aggregated to connect attribute classification losses;

Then, the activation map output from Softmax layer (in the Aggregated module) calculates the AAH on the activation map of different positions and sizes in the backbone network through the Grad-CAM algorithm, so as to locate the key area of the attribute;

Finally, in order to enhance the ability of the re-identification network to extract salient attribute information, the generated AAH is combined with the activation map of the corresponding position in the re-identification network to construct the ASAM. At the same time, the re-identification network is optimized after further training.

3.2 Attribute Spatial Attention Module (ASAM)

The ASAM introduces the attribute prior knowledge into the Re-ID network to assist the discrimination. In order to reduce network complexity and computation consumption, ASAM keeps the structure and size of the activation maps in the Re-ID network unchanged. In particular, in each ASAM, the first half of the channel features of the activation map that keeps the corresponding location of the Re-ID network are kept unchanged in order to maintain a certain amount of global information and avoid information loss that may be caused by the attention mechanism. In addition, the first half of the channel features in the activation map were used to learn channel attention, because the contributions of different attributes to the Re-ID task are generally different.

Firstly, the attention parameter β_c of each channel of AHH is calculated, as shown in Eq. (1). In order to avoid additional parameters, we use channel block average pooling and global average pooling when we calculate β_c.

$$\beta_c = Sigmoid\left(\frac{1}{hw}\sum_{k=1}^{c_{activ}/c_{attr}}\sum_{j=1}^{w}\sum_{i=1}^{h}x_{ijk}^c\right) \tag{1}$$

where (i, j) represents the element coordinate on the current feature map, and x_{ijk}^c represents the pixel value on this coordinate; w and h respectively represent the width and height of the current feature map, c_{activ}/c_{attr} represents the number of channels of each block feature map, c_{activ} represents half of the number of channels of the activation map in the corresponding position of the Re-ID network, and c_{attr} represents the number of channels for AAH;

Then, the attention parameters $(1 * 1 * c)$ of all channels are multiplied by each channel of AHH. After activation by Sigmoid function, weighted spatial attention parameter α_c $(h * w * c)$ is obtained, which can be represented as:

$$\alpha_c = Sigmoid\left(\beta_c \otimes L_{Grad-CAM}^k\right) \tag{2}$$

Finally, after the spatial attention parameter passes through the Sigmoid function again, the spatial attention parameter is dotted with the last half channel features of the corresponding location activation maps of the Re-ID network in blocks to get the final spatial attention (i.e. the feature map contains salient attribute information).

4 Experiment

4.1 The Experimental Details

(1) Dataset

DukeMTMC-reID: DukeMTMC-reID is a person Re-ID subset of DukeMTMC dataset and provides manually annotated bounding boxes. DukeMTMC-reID contains 16,522 training images of 702 of these pedestrian IDs, 2,228 query images from another 702 pedestrian IDs, and 17,661 images' gallery of 702 pedestrian IDs.

Market1501: It was captured on the campus of Tsinghua University in the summer with 6 cameras. The dataset contains a total of 32,688 images with 1,501 pedestrian IDs.

Among them, the training set contains 12,936 images of 751 pedestrian IDs, the query set contains 3,368 images of 750 pedestrians, and the test set includes 16,384 images of 750 pedestrians, all of whom have appeared in at least two cameras.

We adopt the Rank-1 and the mean Average Precision (mAP) as the evaluation indicators to test the performance of different Re-ID methods on these datasets.

(2) Loss function

We set both attribute loss and identification loss to Cross-entropy loss (in our code, it is the combination of Softmax function and Cross-entropy function), and distance loss as Triplet loss.

(3) Training details

In order to ensure the consistency of the experimental results, the experimental process is carried out in the same software and hardware environment. The experimental platform is based on 64-bit Ubuntu18.04 operating system, the device memory is 32G, the CPU is Intel® Xeon E5-2678V3 CPU @2.5 GHz, and the training is conducted on the NVIDIA GTX1080TI single GPU platform, the CUDA version is 10.2, and the experimental framework is based on the PyTorch 1.6.0 version.

4.2 Ablation Experiments

In order to fully verify the effectiveness of our proposed module and method, we conduct two ablation experiments on Market1501 and DukeMTMC-reID. The specific experimental contents are as follows: firstly, only the pedestrian global ID information is used to train the Re-ID network as the baseline; on the basis of the above steps, the ASAM is introduced to form the final design scheme. The experimental results are shown in Table 1.

As shown in Table 1, the Rank-1 and mAP values of ID_only method on the Market1501 dataset are 92.6% and 81.3%, and the Rank-1 and mAP values on the DukeMTMC-reID dataset are 82.3% and 72.2%. It can be seen that using global features alone bring a limited effectiveness to the Re-ID task. After introducing our attribute attention mechanism on the basis of ID_only method, the improvement is significant, especially the mAP is improved by 2.3% on Market1501 and the Rank-1 is improved by 3.2% on the DukeMTMC-reID, which fully proves the effectiveness of our scheme.

Table 1. Comparison of ablation performance.

Methods	Market1501		DukeMTMC-reID	
	Rank-1 (%)	mAP (%)	Rank-1 (%)	mAP (%)
ID_only (Baseline)	92.6	81.3	82.3	72.2
ID + Attr_attention (**Our SAN**)	**94.0**	**83.6**	**85.5**	**73.8**

4.3 Comparison of Algorithms

We select some representative Re-ID algorithms for comparison. As shown in Table 2, our SAN algorithm outperforms most of the algorithms on Market1501 and DukeMTMC-reID datasets. Among all the algorithms listed, compared with PAN in 2018 TCSVT, the Rank-1 and mAP of our SAN on Market1501 are improved by 11.8% and 20.2%, respectively, and the Rank-1 and mAP of our SAN on DukeMTMC-reID are improved by 13.9% and 22.3%, respectively. Compared with the VPM in 2019, SAN is 2.8% higher than its mAP on Market1501. However, compared with BFE, there is still a 1.3% gap in Rank-1 on Market1501. In particular, our SAN does not add any feature enhancement module or special training technique other than the introduction of a specific attribute attention mechanism. Therefore, our SAN is an algorithm with both performance and potential.

Table 2. Performance comparison between our SAN and other classic Re-ID methods

Methods	Market1501		DukeMTMC-reID	
	Rank-1 (%)	mAP (%)	Rank-1 (%)	mAP (%)
PAN (TCSVT18) [19]	82.2	63.4	71.6	51.5
PCB (ECCV18) [20]	92.3	77.4	81.8	66.1
VPM (CVPR19) [21]	93.0	80.8	83.6	72.6
IANet (CVPR19) [22]	94.4	83.1	87.1	73.4
SAN (Ours)	**94.0**	**83.6**	**85.5**	**73.8**
BFE (ICCV19) [23]	95.3	86.2	88.9	75.9

5   Conclusion

In order to overcome the limitation of global pedestrian features in cross-device scenarios, we proposed SAN. Firstly, by generating AAH, we can accurately locate the fine-grained attributes of pedestrians. Then, on the basis of AAH, ASAM is constructed to integrate the global ID information and local attribute information to enhance the discrimination. In particular, our "dual-trace" network does not need additional attribute region annotation on the dataset, so it has better flexibility. By testing on Market1501 and DukeMTMC-reID datasets, the effectiveness and superiority of our scheme design are proved.

Acknowledgements. The authors would like to thank Center for Public Security Information and Equipment Integration Technology, UESTC for providing computation platform.

Conflict of Interest. The authors declare that they have no conflict of interest.

References

1. Zheng, W.S., Gong, S., Xiang, T.: Reidentification by relative distance comparison. IEEE Trans. Pattern Anal. Mach. Intell. **35**(3), 653–668 (2012)
2. Dalal, N., Triggs, B.: Histograms of oriented gradients for human detection. In: 2005 IEEE Computer Society Conference on Computer Vision and Pattern Recognition (CVPR 2005), vol. 1, pp. 886–893. IEEE (2005)
3. Lowe, D.G.: Object recognition from local scale-invariant features. In: Proceedings of the Seventh IEEE International Conference on Computer Vision, vol. 2, pp. 1150–1157. IEEE (1999)
4. Yi, D., Lei, Z., Liao, S., et al.: Deep metric learning for person re-identification. In: 2014 22nd International Conference on Pattern Recognition, pp. 34–39. IEEE (2014)
5. Li, W., Zhao, R., Xiao, T., et al.: DeepReID: deep filter pairing neural network for person re-identification. In: Proceedings of the IEEE Conference on Computer Vision and Pattern Recognition, pp. 152–159 (2014)
6. Hermans, A., Beyer, L., Leibe, B.: In defense of the triplet loss for person re-identification. arXiv preprint arXiv:1703.07737 (2017)
7. Chen, W., Chen, X., Zhang, J., et al.: Beyond triplet loss: a deep quadruplet network for person re-identification. In: Proceedings of the IEEE Conference on Computer Vision and Pattern Recognition, pp. 403–412 (2017)
8. Chen, D., Xu, D., Li, H., et al.: Group consistent similarity learning via deep CRF for person re-identification. In: Proceedings of the IEEE Conference on Computer Vision and Pattern Recognition, pp. 8649–8658 (2018)
9. Geng, M., Wang, Y., Xiang, T., et al.: Deep transfer learning for person re-identification. arXiv preprint arXiv:1611.05244 (2016)
10. Fang, P., Zhou, J., Roy, S.K., et al.: Bilinear attention networks for person retrieval. In: Proceedings of the IEEE/CVF International Conference on Computer Vision, pp. 8030–8039 (2019)
11. Fu, Y., Wang, X., Wei, Y., et al.: STA: spatial-temporal attention for large-scale video-based person re-identification. In: Proceedings of the AAAI Conference on Artificial Intelligence, vol. 33, no. 01, pp. 8287–8294 (2019)
12. Li, S., Bak, S., Carr, P., et al.: Diversity regularized spatiotemporal attention for video-based person re-identification. In: Proceedings of the IEEE Conference on Computer Vision and Pattern Recognition, pp. 369–378 (2018)
13. Lin, Y., Zheng, L., Zheng, Z., et al.: Improving person re-identification by attribute and identity learning. Pattern Recogn. **95**, 151–161 (2019)
14. Zheng, Z., Zheng, L., Yang, Y.: Unlabeled samples generated by GAN improve the person re-identification baseline in vitro. In: 2017 IEEE International Conference on Computer Vision (ICCV), pp. 3774–3782 (2017). https://doi.org/10.1109/ICCV.2017.405
15. Zheng, L., Shen, L., Tian, L., Wang, S., Wang, J., Tian, Q.: Scalable person re-identification: a benchmark. In: 2015 IEEE International Conference on Computer Vision (ICCV), pp. 1116–1124 (2015). https://doi.org/10.1109/ICCV.2015.133
16. Selvaraju, R.R., Cogswell, M., Das, A., et al.: Grad-CAM: visual explanations from deep networks via gradient-based localization. In: Proceedings of the IEEE International Conference on Computer Vision, pp. 618–626 (2017)
17. Liu, X., Zhao, H., Tian, M., et al.: HydraPlus-Net: attentive deep features for pedestrian analysis. In: Proceedings of the IEEE International Conference on Computer Vision, pp. 350–359 (2017)
18. He, K., Zhang, X., Ren, S., et al.: Deep residual learning for image recognition. In: Proceedings of the IEEE Conference on Computer Vision and Pattern Recognition, pp. 770–778 (2016)

19. Zheng, Z., Zheng, L., Yang, Y.: Pedestrian alignment network for large-scale person re-identification. IEEE Trans. Circuits Syst. Video Technol. **29**(10), 3037–3045 (2018)
20. Sun, Y., Zheng, L., Yang, Y., Tian, Q., Wang, S.: Beyond part models: person retrieval with refined part pooling (and A strong convolutional baseline). In: Ferrari, V., Hebert, M., Sminchisescu, C., Weiss, Y. (eds.) ECCV 2018. LNCS, vol. 11208, pp. 501–518. Springer, Cham (2018). https://doi.org/10.1007/978-3-030-01225-0_30
21. Tay, C.P., Roy, S., Yap, K.H.: AANet: attribute attention network for person re-identifications. In: Proceedings of the IEEE/CVF Conference on Computer Vision and Pattern Recognition, pp. 7134–7143 (2019)
22. Hou, R., Ma, B., Chang, H., et al.: Interaction-and-aggregation network for person re-identification. In: Proceedings of the IEEE/CVF Conference on Computer Vision and Pattern Recognition, pp. 9317–9326 (2019)
23. Dai, Z., Chen, M., Gu, X., et al.: Batch dropblock network for person re-identification and beyond. In: Proceedings of the IEEE/CVF International Conference on Computer Vision, pp. 3691–3701 (2019)

OFDMA-Based Asymmetric Full-Duplex Media Access Control for the Next Generation WLANs

Jianjun Lei[1]([✉]) [iD], Sipei Zhang[1] [iD], Ying Wang[1] [iD], Xunwei Zhao[2] [iD], and Ping Gai[2] [iD]

[1] School of Computer Science and Technology, Chongqing University of Posts and Telecommunications, Chongqing 400065, China
leijj@cqupt.edu.cn
[2] State Grid Information and Telecommunication Group CO., LTD., Beijing 102211, China
{zhaoxunwei,gaiping}@sgitg.sgcc.com.cn

Abstract. Along with physical layer advancements, the introduction of in-band full-duplex (IBFD) into the next generation wireless local area networks (WLANs) has become feasible. This paper presents AO-FDMAC, a novel OFDMA-based full-duplex media access control (MAC) that alleviates the inter-STA interference problem and supports uplink and downlink transmission of asymmetric lengths traffic in full-duplex scenarios. Meanwhile, access point (AP) maintains a global interference graph based on the power information collected by STAs for the proposed greedy sub-channel allocation algorithm, which governs the transmission of uplink data for multiple STAs during a single downlink transmission in one sub-channel. Simulation results show that compared with the legacy IEEE 802.11ax protocol and a centralized full-duplex MAC protocol, our proposed protocol achieves higher performance in terms of throughput and transmission delay.

Keywords: WLANs · OFDMA · MAC · IBFD · Asymmetric transmission · Channel interference

1 Introduction

To improve the efficiency in dense user scenario, OFDMA under upcoming standard IEEE 802.11ax is considered as one of the promising solutions [1]. OFDMA enables multiple wireless nodes to access sub-channels for data transmission simultaneously by dividing the whole channel into several sub-channels. At the same time, IBFD communication is regarded as an emerging technology, which allows wireless nodes to simultaneously send and receive frames on the same wireless channel. In case of IBFD in WLANs, inter-STA interference is a crucial problem, which is caused by the transmission of an uplink (UL) STA to the reception at a downlink (DL) STA. On the other hand, the DL traffic load from the AP to the STA is usually much higher than the UL traffic load, which results in an inevitable traffic asymmetry between the UL and DL traffic loads [2].

Z. Liu et al. (Eds.): WASA 2021, LNCS 12939, pp. 125–132, 2021.
https://doi.org/10.1007/978-3-030-86137-7_14

Recent literatures [3–6] develop some MAC protocols and analytical models to attempt to solve the problem of ISI. Meanwhile, a few researches [7–12] have been conducted to address the asymmetric traffic in designing MAC protocols for IBFD wireless communications. In addition, some authors combine the full-duplex MAC solution with OFDMA technology. For example, an OFDMA two-symbol coordination MAC protocol called full-duplex WLAN (02-MAC) is proposed in [13]. The authors in [14] proposed to use subchannels to effectively coordinate full-duplex TXs in the frequency domain. In [15], considering the multi-user scenario in the FD network, it uses centralized scheduling of uplink and downlink transmissions. [16] based on the research in [15], proposed a multi-user FD MAC protocol using power control. However, none of the above-mentioned are not compatible with the existing IEEE 802.11ax protocol. To successfully achieve the advantages of IBFD wireless communication in IEEE 802.11ax, we need to design a suitable MAC protocol.

This paper proposes a novel FD-MAC protocol named AO-FDMAC, which aims to alleviate the problem of ISI and support asymmetrical traffic length of the UL and DL, especially by multiuser FD technology with OFDMA. In AO-FDMAC, STAs contend for channel resources through randomly selected sub-channel transmission buffer status report (BSR) packets within the contention period dynamically adjusted by the AP. Then, AP can send a Probe frame to ask STAs that have successfully contended to transmit their collected power information, so as to calculate the inter-STA interference information and maintain an interference graph. Finally, the global interference graph can be used to complete the channel allocation of UL and DL STAs. Since spectrum resource allocation is a difficult NP problem, we introduce a novel greedy scheduling algorithm, which allows multiple uplink STAs and the best single downlink STA to be allocated to different sub-channels. Our simulation results also verify that the AO-FDMAC not only alleviates the ISI problem, but also makes full use of the idle UL time in the full-duplex asymmetric scenario.

The remainder of the paper is organized as follows. In Sect. 2, the design details of proposed AO-FDMAC are described. Performance evaluation of AO-FDMAC is presented in Sect. 3. This paper is summarized in Sect. 4.

2 Proposed AO-FDMAC Protocol

2.1 System Model

We consider a WLAN consisted of one AP and n STAs within the range of the AP. It is assumed that the AP and each STA have full-duplex capability. Therefore, FD communications are categorized in this paper in two ways, i.e., bi-directional FD and three-node FD communications. During bi-directional FD communication, the AP and one STA simultaneously transmit packets to each other, while in the three-node FD communication, one STA sends packets to the AP, and the AP sends packets to another STA at the same time. The total bandwidth is divided into m sub-channels, which may also be called resource units (RUs). Each STA can only transmit on one RU at a time, but the AP can transmit data packets to different STAs on different RUs. Three phases are defined to explain AO-FDMAC in detail: multiple stages for random access (MSRA) phase, information collection (IC) phase, and data transmission (DT) phase. Figure 1 shows the process of AO-FDMAC protocol.

Initially, the AP sends a random-access trigger frame (TF-R) after the entire channel has been idle for distributed interframe space (DIFS) to start the MSRA phase. During MSRA phase, multiple rounds of UL transmission contention are conducted until the TF-R frame or multi-STAs block acknowledgement (M-BA) frame sent by the AP indicates the end of the MSRA phase. Then in the IC phase, the AP broadcasts a Probe frame to collect the power of other STAs overheard by the successful STAs. After the IC phase is completed, the AP sends the trigger frame (TF) to broadcast the allocation result to start the DT phase, in which the UL STAs transmits data packets on the fixed sub-channel according to the instructions in the TF, while the DL STAs receives data packets on the fixed sub-channels.

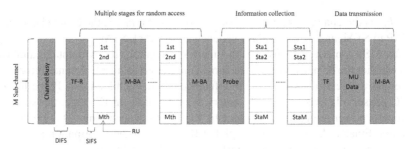

Fig. 1. The procedure of AO-FDMAC protocol.

2.2 Multiple Stages for Random Access Phase

In this phase, the number of rounds k used for competition is uncertain. AP can make dynamic adjustments based on two parameters: the count of STAs that currently compete successfully N_{suc}, and the historical UL/DL traffic load ratio r. There are four cases for AP to determine whether it should enable a new round of competition:

1) If $n < m/r$ and $N_{suc} < n$, it indicates a new round of competition.
2) If $n < m/r$ and $N_{suc} = n$, it indicates the end of the competition.
3) If $n \geq m/r$ and $N_{suc} < m/r$, it indicates a new round of competition.
4) If $n \geq m/r$ and $N_{suc} \geq m/r$, it indicates the end of competition.

After each round of competition, AP replies a M-BA to announce the STAs that have successfully competed in this round, and indicates in the M-BA whether to commence a new round of competition. When the STA with data in the buffer and unsuccessful competition hears the indication in TF-R or M-BA, it adopts OFDMA back-off (OBO) mechanism to compete for the channel. If the STA current back-off counter is less than the number of available RUs, a buffer status report (BSR) packet can be sent to compete for the channel. In our method, the number of STAs acquiring channels is greater than the number of subchannels. Therefore, multiple STAs are allowed to transmit their UL data packets to the AP in the same subchannel, and the AP transmits DL data packets to a single STA simultaneously, which is used to support asymmetric traffic scenarios.

2.3 Information Collection Phase

AO-FDMAC uses SINR to quantize interference information between STAs as in [4]. To calculate the SINR value, we need the signal strength from the AP and the interference strength from neighbors. In the MSRA phase, when a STA uploads a BSR packet, its neighbors can overhear the signal strength of the packet, so they can record the power information from the STA to itself. Meanwhile, STA utilizes any data packet from the AP to calculate the signal strength from the AP to itself.

Let $P_{o,i}$ and $P_{j,i}$ be the powers used for transmission from the AP to STAi and from STAj to the STAi, respectively. Thus, the SINR at DL STAi is given by

$$SINR_{j,i} = \frac{P_{0,i}|h_{0,i}|^2}{\sigma_i^2 + P_{j,i}|h_{j,i}|^2} \tag{1}$$

Where $h_{j,i}$ is the channel coefficient from STAj to STAi, $h_{0,i}$ is the channel coefficient from AP to STAi, and σ_i^2 is the noise variance at downlink STAi.

After MSRA phase, AP observes the interference graph (IG) it maintains and determines whether the IC phase needs to be turned on. If there is no interference information between the successful STAs in the interference graph, AP broadcasts Probe frame to start IC phase, otherwise it directly enters the DT phase. In IC stage, the successful STA reports power information at a specific RU and time according to the Probe frame indication. Finally, AP improves the global IG based on the information reported by STAs. The construction process of interference graph is as follows:

1) AP quantifies the interference information between STAs through Eq. (1).
2) AP judges whether the calculated SINR exists in the interference graph. If it exists, replace it with a new value; otherwise, fill in the SINR information.
3) After all power information is used for calculation, if there is no SINR among STAs that successfully compete in this super-frame, set their SINR to 0.

2.4 Data Transmission Phase

After GSA phase, a contention free DT phase is scheduled. Using the global IG, AP performs RUs and transmission opportunity (TXOP) allocation on UL and DL STAs. The optimal channel allocation can be achieved by exhaustive search, however it has a high computational complexity especially when the count of STAs increases. Therefore, we propose a simple sub-channel allocation algorithm using greedy strategy.

UL sub-channel allocation (Algorithm 1): AP attempts to sequentially put UL STAs into a certain sub-channel. Whenever the total BSR of STAs in this sub-channel exceeds the amount of data that can be sent in TXOP, AP puts the next STA into the next sub-channel until all STAs are allocated. It may happen that some STAs cannot send the expected data in the remaining TXOP. At this time, these STAs are only allowed to send data packets with the remaining TXOP time in the scheduling table.

DL sub-channel allocation (Algorithm 2): AP traverses STAs in the order of DL buffer queue. According to the IG, AP determines whether there is interference between the currently traversed STA and all UL STAs in a certain sub-channel. If there is no interference, the STA is placed in this sub-channel. AP performs this process until all subchannels are filled. It may appear that there is no matching DL STA in a sub-channel, then this channel adopts half-duplex transmission with only UL.

Algorithm 1: UL sub-channel allocation algorithm

Inputs: BSR_i: BSR for successful STAi; IG: Global interference graph
Output: ST_{UL}: UL scheduling allocation table
1: **Start** UL sub-channel allocation
2: $TXOP_{limit} \leftarrow$ The limit of TXOP; $n_{UL} \leftarrow$ The number of UL STAs
3: $A = \{STA1, ..., STAn_{UL}\}$; $Total\_UL_1, ..., Total\_UL_m = 0$; $Order\_UL_1, ..., Order\_UL_m = \emptyset$
4: **for** $j = 1$ to m **do**
5:   **for** $i = 1$ to n_{UL} **do**
6:     **if** STAi $\in A$ **then**
7:       **if** $Total\_UL_j + BSR_i \leq TXOP_{limit}$ **then**
8:         $Order\_UL_j \leftarrow$ Insert BSR_i of the STAi; $Total\_UL_j = Total\_UL_j + BSR_i$; $A = A \setminus STAi$
9:       **else**
10:        $y \leftarrow (TXOP_{limit} - Total\_UL_j)$
11:        **if** $y > 0$ **then**
12:          $Order\_UL_j \leftarrow$ Insert y as the BSR_i of the STAi; $A = A \setminus STAi$
13:        **end if**
14:      **end if**
15:    **end if**
16: **end for**
17: $ST_{UL} \leftarrow$ add the $Order\_UL_j$
18: **end for**
19: **END** UL sub-channel allocation

Algorithm 2: DL sub-channel allocation algorithm

Inputs: ST_{UL}: UL scheduling allocation table; IG: Global interference graph
Output: ST_{DL}: DL scheduling allocation table
1: **Start** DL sub-channel allocation
2: $n_{DL} \leftarrow$ The number of DL STAs; $\beta \leftarrow$ ISI threshold
3: $B = \{STA1, ..., STAn_{DL}\}$; $\{Order\_DL_1, ..., Order\_DL_m\} = \emptyset$
4: **for** $j = 1$ to m **do**
5:   **for** $k = 1$ to n_{DL} **do**
6:     **if** STAk $\in B$ **then**
7:       **if** $Order\_UL_j \neq \emptyset$ **then**
8:         $p = 0$; $l \leftarrow$ length of $Order\_UL_j$
9:         **for** $i = 1$ to l **do**
10:          **if** $SINR_{i,k} \geq \beta$ **then**
11:            $p = p + 1$
12:          **end if**
13:        **end for**
14:        **if** $p \geq l$ **then**
15:          $Order\_DL_j \leftarrow$ Insert STAk; $B = B \setminus STAk$; $ST_{DL} \leftarrow$ add the $Order\_DL_j$
16:          **break**
17:        **end if**
18:      **else**
19:        $Order\_DL_j \leftarrow$ Insert STAk; $B = B \setminus STAk$; $ST_{DL} \leftarrow$ add the $Order\_DL_j$
20:        **break**
21:      **end if**
22:    **end if**
23: **end for**
24: **end for**
25: **END** DL sub-channel allocation channel

3 Simulation Results

3.1 The Simulation Settings

In this section, we use MATLAB simulation to compare the performance of AO-FDMAC with the legacy IEEE 802.11ax and a centralized MAC protocol MU-FuPlex [15] in terms of network throughput and packet delay. Meanwhile, we investigate the impact of asymmetric traffic and inter-STA interference on our proposed MAC protocol. All simulations are run under saturation conditions, that is, each STA always has data frames sent to the AP, and the AP always has data frames sent to each STA. In addition, to ensure the fairness of the evaluation without loss of generality, we test 50 rounds each time, and the test time of one round is set to 200 ms. The parameters used in the simulation are shown in Table 1.

Table 1. Simulation parameters

Parameters	Value	Parameters	Value
Channel bandwidth	80 MHz	STA number	40
Sub-channel number	8	CW_{min}	32
Physical rate	175.5 Mbps	CW_{max}	1023
TF length	110 Bytes	Slot time	9 us
BSR length	22 Bytes	DIFS	34 us
M-BA length	60 Bytes	SIFS	16 us
Probe length	80 Bytes	TXOP	4 ms
PI length	52 Bytes	Non-interference rate α	0.3
TF-R length	38 Bytes	SINR threshold β	13 dB
Packet length	1500 Bytes	UL/DL traffic ratio r	1/3

3.2 Throughput

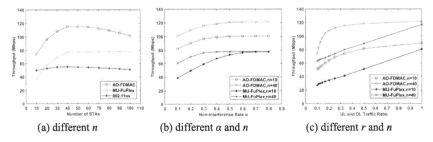

(a) different n (b) different α and n (c) different r and n

Fig. 2. Throughput performance of the three MAC protocols under different parameters.

Through the simulation, we can find that AO-FAMAC outperforms the other two methods. As shown in Fig. 2(a), when there are 40 STAs in the network, AO-FDMAC improves throughput by approximately 120% and 45% compared with 802.11ax and MU-FuPlex, respectively. There are two main reasons for this: (1) As the amount of STAs in the network increases, full-duplex communication opportunities increase; (2) For asymmetric traffic scenarios, multiple UL STAs can reuse the same sub-channel, which greatly improves UL channel utilization. In Fig. 2(a), when the non-interference rate increases, the throughput gradually increases. This is mainly due to the establishment of more full-duplex communication pairs. In addition, as the UL/DL traffic ratio increases, the AP will control to reduce the number of UL STAs competing, so the duration of the MSRA phase will be greatly reduced, and the channel can be fully utilized without matching many full-duplex pairs. The result is shown as the curve in Fig. 2(c).

3.3 Delay

In the simulation, considering that the delay time will be the cost of collecting interference information and the average time to access the channel, we define the delay as the sum of the average completion time of all STAs sending 0.1M files to the AP and receiving 0.1M files from the AP minus the ideal state time required. Figure 3(a) shows that our proposed protocol has the shortest average delay time, which is mainly due to the parallelism between the transmission processes in AO-FDMAC. And the delay is basically kept below 0.2 s in both the higher and the lower number of STAs. This shows that with the growth of the network scale, AO-FDMAC shows good scalability. Meanwhile, as shown in Fig. 3(b) and 3(c), no matter we change the non-interference rate or the UL and DL traffic ratio, AO-FDMAC has a lower and smooth delay, which fully shows that the AO-FDMAC has stable performance.

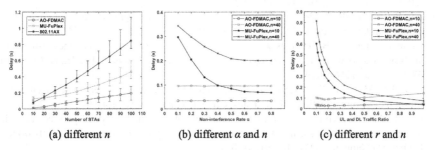

(a) different n (b) different α and n (c) different r and n

Fig. 3. Delay performance of the three MAC protocols under different parameters.

4   Conclusion

In this paper, we propose a full-duplex AO-FDMAC protocol based on OFDMA, which can be utilized in WLANs infrastructure based on 802.11ax. At the same time, by employing a greedy sub-channel resource allocation algorithm, the AO-FDMAC can well support the asymmetric service of uplink and downlink communication, and solve the problem of interference between STAs. And the experimental results show that AO-FDMAC improves network performance in terms of throughput and delay with other methods.

References

1. Khorov, E., Kiryanov, A., Lyakhov, A., Bianchi, G.: A Tutorial on IEEE 802.11ax high efficiency WLANs. IEEE Commun. Surv. Tutor. **21**(1), 197–216 (2019)
2. Zhang, Z., et al.: Full-duplex wireless communications: challenges, solutions, and future research directions. Proc. IEEE **104**(7), 1369–1409 (2016)
3. Liu, S., Fu, S., Xie, W.: Hidden-node problem in full-duplex enabled CSMA networks. IEEE Trans. Mob. Comput. **19**(2), 347–361 (2020)
4. Chen, S., et al.: Probabilistic medium access control for full-duplex networks with half-duplex clients. IEEE Trans. Wireless Commun. **16**(4), 2627–2640 (2017)
5. Chen, Y., Sun, Y., Zuo, H., Li, S., Lu, N., Wang, Y.: Rate selection based medium access control for full-duplex asymmetric transmission. Wireless Netw. **25**(8), 4873–4885 (2018). https://doi.org/10.1007/s11276-018-1771-7
6. Kai, C., et al.: Energy saving and interference cancellation in the WLAN with a full-duplex access point. In: 2019 IEEE International Conference on Communications, ICC, Shanghai, pp. 1–6. IEEE (2019)
7. Ahn, H., Suh, Y.J.: Full-duplex MAC Protocol using buffer status reports during unused uplink periods in WLAN. Ad Hoc Netw. **94**, 101950 (2019)
8. Malik, H., Ghoraishi, M., Tafazolli, R.: Cross-layer approach for asymmetric traffic accommodation in full-duplex wireless network. In: 2015 European Conference on Networks and Communications, EuCNC, Paris, pp. 265–269. IEEE (2015)
9. Alim, M.A., Saruwatari, S., Watanabe, T.: Asym-FDMAC: in-band full-duplex medium access control protocol for asymmetric traffic in wireless LAN. Wireless Netw. **26**(2), 807–822 (2018). https://doi.org/10.1007/s11276-018-1827-8
10. Liu, S., Han, B., Peng, W.: A polling-based traffic-aware MAC protocol for centralized full-duplex wireless networks. IEEE Access **6**, 28225–28238 (2018)
11. Kiran, R., Mehta, N.B., Thomas, J.: Design and network topology-specific renewal-theoretic analysis of a MAC protocol for asymmetric full-duplex WLANs. IEEE Trans. Commun. **67**(12), 8532–8544 (2019)
12. Hirzallah, M., Afifi, W., Krunz, M.: Provisioning QoS in Wi-Fi systems with asymmetric full-duplex communications. IEEE Trans. Cogn. Commun. Netw. **4**(4), 942–953 (2018)
13. Lee, J., Ahn, H., Kim, C.: An OFDMA two-symbol coordination MAC protocol for full-duplex wireless networks. In: 2017 International Conference on Information Networking, ICOIN, Da Nang, pp. 344–348. IEEE (2017)
14. Ahn, H., et al.: Frequency domain coordination MAC protocol for full-duplex wireless networks. IEEE Commun. Lett. **23**(3), 518–521 (2019)
15. Qu, Q., et al.: MU-FuPlex: a multiuser full-duplex MAC protocol for the next generation wireless networks. In: 2017 IEEE Wireless Communications and Networking Conference, WCNC, San Francisco, pp. 1–6. IEEE (2017)
16. Qu, Q., Li, B., Yang, M., Yan, Z.: Power control based multiuser full-duplex MAC protocol for the next generation wireless networks. Mobile Netw. Appl. **23**(4), 1008–1019 (2017). https://doi.org/10.1007/s11036-017-0966-y

Equitable Valuation of Crowdsensing for Machine Learning via Game Theory

Qiangqiang He, Yu Qiao, Shang Yang, and Chongjun Wang[✉]

State Key Laboratory for Novel Software Technology, Nanjing University,
Nanjing 210046, China
{qqhe,yuqiao,yangshang}@smail.nju.edu.cn, chjwang@nju.edu.cn

Abstract. In the era of mobile Internet, it has became easier to obtain personal data through crowdsensing platforms, which promotes the development of data-driven machine learning. A fundamental challenge is how to quantify the value of data provided by each worker. In this paper, we use the powerful tool of game theory called Shapely value to solve this challenge. Shapley value is a classic concept in game theory and can satisfy the equitable valuation of data. However, the calculation of Shapley value is exponentially related to the number of workers. Worse still, in the deep learning model, the time cost of retraining the model and evaluating the contribution of each worker's data to the model is unacceptable. Therefore, we propose two algorithms based on Monte Carlo and batch gradient descent to approximate Shapley value in machine learning and deep learning. We take K-fold validation as the benchmark, and prove that our proposed algorithms can reduce the time overhead while ensuring lower error in the experiment. Finally, we find that it can provide better insight into the labor value of each worker in specific learning tasks.

Keywords: Game theory · Shapley value · Data valuation

1 Introduction

With data becoming the oil to promote the development of machine learning, it has become a common practice to obtain data from different individuals on crowdsensing platform. For example, companies collect data from different users to improve model performance, increase user stickiness, and finally help them make money (Fig. 1). Due to the uneven quality of data between different individuals, therefore, a key problem encountered by data collection companies is how to equitably allocate the budget to each worker.

The current research mainly focuses on the valuation of a single data point, without considering the dependence between the data provided by the same worker, and the valuation of each worker mostly depends on the amount of data provided by the worker. We use Shapley method to model each worker as an alliance player in game theory and take the performance contribution of data

© Springer Nature Switzerland AG 2021
Z. Liu et al. (Eds.): WASA 2021, LNCS 12939, pp. 133–141, 2021.
https://doi.org/10.1007/978-3-030-86137-7_15

provided by each worker to the machine learning model as the valuation of the worker's data. The Shapley value is a classic method in game theory, which can reasonably distribute the total revenue generated by all players in the alliance. It has been successfully applied to counter-terrorism [1], environmental science [2], machine learning [3], etc. Its fairness, reasonability, group rationality and other characteristics are the main reasons for its application.

Although Shapley value has many advantages above, the calculation function is exponentially related to the number of workers. In the past, it was feasible to use Shapley value to evaluate data value in the scenario where few workers could be hired and the data set was small. However, in the crowdsensing scenario, it was common to hire tens of thousands of geographically isolated workers to provide data, which made the time cost of using Shapley value to evaluate data value unaffordable. Worse still, with the development of deep learning, the time required to retrain the model and evaluate the performance of the model by using the learning algorithm is already quite expensive. In this paper, we try to find an approximation algorithm, which can greatly reduce the time cost and approximate the real Shapley value.

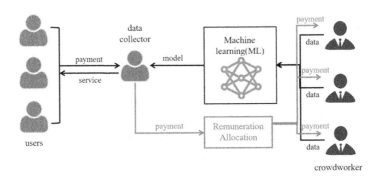

Fig. 1. Overview of the data valuation of Crowdsensing.

K-fold validation (KFV) is a common method to evaluate the importance of data, that is, to compare the performance of predictor when training a complete data set with that of a predictor when a subset is subtracted from a complete data set [4], so that the performance increment brought by the subset is taken as the value of the subset. KFV measures how the predictor changes when the weight of a subset changes slightly [5]. However, KFV does not meet our expectation of equitable data evaluation. For example, there are two workers who provide the same data, and our learning algorithm is the nearest neighbor, that is, for each data, the label of the data closest to it is assigned to it. Then, even if we delete the data of one of the workers, the label assigned will not be changed because of the existence of the data of another worker. This example shows that KFV can't capture the dependence and interaction between data subsets, but our methods take this relationship into account precisely and give more meaningful estimates.

Our Contribution: First of all, we take each worker as the basic unit and consider the contribution of data provided by each worker to the machine learning model for the first time. Secondly, due to the high computational complexity of Shapley value, and it is unacceptable to retrain the model in deep learning to evaluate the contribution of each worker' data, we propose two approximate algorithms, which can effectively reduce the time cost and approach the true Shapley value. Finally, we get some other characteristics of Shapley value calculated by our algorithms through experiments: 1) Compared with KFV, it can provide more accurate insights into the importance of each worker's data. 2) It can identify the noise in the data and give appropriate evaluation. 3) It can tell us how to make a trade-off between the quantity of data and the quality of the data.

2   Related Work

The Shapley value was proposed by Shapley and had been tried to apply to machine learning. Kononenko [6] began to qualify the importance of features, that is, for a fixed prediction, he tried to calculate the impact score of each feature on the model output. Lundberg [7] further quantifies which features have the greatest impact on a particular model. There are some studies focused on the use of Monte Carlo methods to approximate the Shapley value.

Some scholars have begun to consider the valuation of data points, taking the valuation of data points as the importance of data points and ranking them, so as to understand the behavior of the model, check the error of the data set, etc. Koh et al. use the concepts of leverage and impact to measure how the perturbations at each point affect the model parameters and the model's predictions about other data [8]. Amirata proposed to use SV to quantify the value of a single sample in machine learning [9]. David et al. given the error range of the Shapley value in a stable learning environment [10]. However, their evaluation is not suitable for crowdsensing scenarios, and especially cannot meet our evaluation requirements for a set of data provided by each crowdsensing worker in the deep neural network.

3   Problem Formulation

In a crowdsensing task, the training set D consists of n data points, which provided by k workers, that is, $D = \{w_i\}_1^k = \{(x_j, y_j)\}_1^n$, in which w_i represents the i-th worker, (x_j, y_j) represents the j-th point in the D. x_j are the features, and y_j is the label of the classification or the real number of regression. We don't make any assumption about the distribution of data and allow the data of different workers to have dependencies. The amount of data provided by each worker is not necessarily equal. We use $|w_i|$ to represent the number of data provided by the i-th worker. $\mathcal{A}$ is a learning algorithm, and a predictor is obtained from the training data set through the algorithm $\mathcal{A}$. What we are interested in is the predictor trained on the $S \subset D$. The performance score V is a black box that takes the predictor as input and outputs the performance score of the predictor. We use $V(S, \mathcal{A})$ to represent the predictor score that we trained on subset S by using algorithm $\mathcal{A}$. Our goal is to calculate the value of the data $\Phi_i(D, \mathcal{A}, V) \in \mathbb{R}$ provided by i-th worker, as a function of D, $\mathcal{A}$ and V to quantify the value of each worker. For the sake of convenience, we sometimes abbreviate w_i as i, and abbreviate $\Phi_i(D, \mathcal{A}, V)$ as Φ_i. We take the data provided by each worker as the basic unit instead of the single data as the basic unit.

In machine learning settings, we let $V = - \sum_{t \in testset} l_t$ where l_t is the loss of the predictor on the t-th test point. We can define $V_t = -l_t$ to be the predictor performance on the t-th test point. The negative sign is added to give a higher score to lower loss. Similarly, $\Phi_i(V_t)$ quantifies the value of the i-th worker's data to the t-th test point. The Shapley value uniquely has the following properties:

1. **Group Rationality:** The value of the entire training set is fully allocated to the workers who make up the training set.
2. **Fairness:** The contributions of two workers are the same, iff their data is added to any subset of the training set can have the same effect.
3. **Additivity:** Additivity shows that when the overall predictor score is the sum of t independent predictions, the value of the data set is the sum of its value for each prediction.

Proposition 1. *The following formula must be satisfied for any data evaluation meeting the above 1–3 properties:*

$$\Phi_i = C \sum_{S \subseteq D - \{i\}} \frac{V(S \cup \{i\}) - V(S)}{\binom{n-1}{|S|}} \tag{1}$$

Where S is the subset of D that do not contain i. It should be noted that since we take each worker as the basic unit, so $|S|$ represents the number of workers in the S rather than the number of the data in the S. C can be set arbitrarily, which is a fixed constant and will not affect the experimental results and analysis. Φ_i is the Shapley value of the i-th worker's data. Due to the limitation of space, the proof here is omitted.

4   Approximation of Data Shapley

Although the Shapley value defined in Eq. 1 can provide the equitable data valuation for each worker, to obtain such a valuation, we need to calculate all possible marginal distributions, which is exponentially related to the number of workers. In addition, it takes a lot of time to generate a predictor for each subset S of D in deep learning. There are often thousands of workers on crowdsensing platforms, which causes this calculation is unacceptable. We use approximation algorithms to estimate Shapley value.

4.1   The Necessity of Data Grouping

In this section, we will explain the necessity of data grouping. In our setting, we group the training set, and take the data contributed by the same worker as a group, thus obtaining k groups of data. There are three advantages to doing so:

1. **Expand data scale:** When the data scale is large, even if the approximation algorithm is used, the time overhead required to calculate the valuation of each data point is still unbearable.
2. **Consider data dependencies:** By grouping, we can directly consider the impact of the dependencies of a group of data on the model performance, thus obtaining the valuation of this group of data.
3. **Increase data differences:** In the scenario of large-scale data, the value of a single data point is negligible that it can be ignored. By grouping the data, the value difference between groups can be increased, and a more effective valuation can be obtained.

4.2   Approximation Algorithms

Monte Carlo-Based Approach: Let Π be the uniform distribution over all $k!$ permutations of workers, then we get the following formula.

$$\Phi_i = \mathbb{E}_{\pi \sim \Pi} \left[V \left(S_\pi^i \cup \{i\} \right) - V \left(S_\pi^i \right) \right] \tag{2}$$

In the above equation, S_π^i represents the set of workers before i in the permutation π (excluding the i-th worker). When i is the first worker in the permutation π, then $S_\pi^i = \emptyset$.

We obtain a random permutation π of k workers, and then start to scan π from the first worker to the last worker and calculate the marginal distribution of each worker. Repeat the process in multiple Monte Carlo processes, and finally get the average value of all edge contributions for each worker is taken as the SV. The following theorem gives the influence of sampling times on accuracy.

Theorem 1. *If we want to get $\hat{v} \in \mathbb{R}^N$ which satisfies $P \left[\|\hat{v}_i - v_i\|_p \leq \epsilon \right] \geq 1 - \delta$ with respect to l_p-norm, then the number of permutation we need is $T = 2r^2 k/\varepsilon^2 \log(2k/\delta)$, where r is the performance score range, that is, the range of $V(S)$ and k is the number of workers.*

Proof.

$$P \left[\max_{i=1,\cdots,N} |\hat{v}_i - v_i| \geq \epsilon \right] = P \left[\cup_{i=1,\cdots,N} \{|\hat{v}_i - v_i| \geq \epsilon\} \right]$$

$$\leq \sum_{i=1}^N P \left[|\hat{v}_i - v_i| \geq \epsilon \right] \leq 2N \exp \left(-\frac{2T\epsilon^2}{4r^2} \right)$$

The first inequality follows from the union bound and the second one is due to Hoeffding's inequality. Since $\|\hat{v} - v\|_2 \leq \sqrt{k}\|\hat{v} - v\|_\infty$, we have

$$P\left[\|\hat{v} - v\|_2 \geq \epsilon \leq P\left[\|\hat{v} - v\|_\infty \geq \epsilon/\sqrt{k}\right] \leq 2k\exp\left(-\frac{2T\epsilon^2}{4kr^2}\right)\right.$$

Setting $2k\exp\left(-\frac{T\epsilon^2}{2kr^2}\right) \leq \delta$ yield, then

$$T \geq \frac{2r^2 k}{\epsilon^2}\log\frac{2k}{\delta}$$

In the experiment, $T = 3k$ can make the SV converge. For lower error, we set $T = 5k$. We set a threshold, and when the performance change obtained by adding a single worker data is lower than this threshold, we set the SV of the worker and the workers behind it to zero. It has no obvious impact on the accuracy and can save time. See algorithm one for more details.

Group Batch Gradient Descent Approach: When the training model is a complex deep learning model instead of a simple regression or Bayesian model, it is expensive to train the model on each S. In the case of k workers, we need to train $5k^2$ models, and this time overhead is beyond our reach (We need to get $5k$ permutations, and every permutation we need to train k models). For the deep learning model, we use randomly selected batches to update the weights of the model. Algorithm $\mathcal{A}$ involves a random gradient change. In our experiment, we take workers as the smallest unit. In order to calculate the Shapley value of a group of data at the same time, for a permutation of workers, we can set the batch size to the size of S_π^i and use S_π^i to perform a batch gradient descent on the model, thus obtaining the performance score of the model on the test set. This setting can be well adapted to our framework with group as the smallest unit. In order to find the best performance that can be obtained by training the model with only one batch gradient descent, we use super-parameter search for the learning algorithm, which leads to our learning rate being higher than that of multiple epoch models.

Algorithm 1. Group Truncated Monte Carlo Shapley

1: **Input:** Training set $D = \{w_i\}_1^k = \{(x_j, y_j)\}_1^n$, learning algorithm $\mathcal{A}$, performance score V, the number of Permutations T
2: **Output:** SV of workers: $\Phi_1, \Phi_2, \ldots, \Phi_k$
3: Initialize $\Phi_i = 0$ for $i = 1, \ldots, k$ and $t = 0$
4: **while** $t<T$ **do**
5:    $t \leftarrow t + 1$;
6:    π_t : Random permutation of workers
7:    $v_0^t \leftarrow V(\emptyset, \mathcal{A})$
8:    **for** $j \in \{1, \ldots, k\}$ **do**
9:      **if** $\left|V(D) - v_{j-1}^t\right| <$Performance Threshold **then**
     $v_j^t = v_j^{t-1}$
10:      **else**
     $v_j^t \leftarrow V\left(\{\pi^t[1], \ldots, \pi^t[j]\}, \mathcal{A}\right)$
11:      **end if**
     $\phi_{\pi^t[j]} \leftarrow \frac{t-1}{t}\phi_{\pi^{t-1}[j]} + \frac{1}{t}\left(v_j^t - v_{j-1}^t\right)$
12:    **end for**
13: **end while**

Algorithm 2. Group Batch Gradient-Shapley

1: **Input:** Training set $D = \{w_i\}_1^k = \{(x_j, y_j)\}_1^n$, learning algorithm $\mathcal{A}$, performance score V, the number of Permutations T, loss function $\mathscr{L}(.; \theta)$, learning rate α

2: **Output:** SV of workers $\Phi_1, \Phi_2, \ldots, \Phi_k$

3: Initialize $\Phi_i = 0$ for $i = 1, \ldots, k$

4: **for** $i \in \{1, \ldots, T\}$ **do**

5:   θ_0^i: The parameters of a model trained on the entire training set

6:   π_i : Random permutation of train data groups

7:   $v_0^t \leftarrow V(\theta_0^i, \mathcal{A})$

8:   **for** $j \in \{1, \ldots, k\}$ **do**

9:     S_π^j : A subset of the first $j - 1$ workers in the π_i

10:     $\theta_j^t \leftarrow \theta_{j-1}^t - \alpha \frac{1}{|S_\pi^j|} \sum_{d_p \in S_\pi^j} \nabla_\theta \mathscr{L}(d_p; \theta_{j-1})$

11:     $v_j^i \leftarrow V(\theta_j^i)$

12:     $\Phi_{\pi^i[j]} \leftarrow \frac{i-1}{i} \Phi_{\pi^{i-1}[j]} + \frac{1}{i}(v_j^i - v_{j-1}^i)$

13:   **end for**

14: **end for**

---

5 Experiments and Application

In this section, we conduct experiments based on real-world data to demonstrate SV estimation and application. We find that a small number of data groups with high SV is dominant for the model and most data groups have little effect on model performance. In addition, we also perform two experiments. The first experiment compares the error of SV calculated by different algorithms. The second experiment tells us how to make a trade-off between the quality of data and the quantity of data.

Our convergence standard for GTM-Shapley and GBG-Shapley is: $\frac{1}{k} \sum_{i=1}^k \frac{|\Phi_i^t - \Phi_i^{t-100}|}{|\Phi_i^t|} < 0.03$. In all experiments, we group the data to simulate crowdsensing scenarios. Assuming that the size of the D is n, the number of our groups is $\sqrt{n}$ and the number of data provided by each worker follows a normal distribution. This setting can reduce the number of data groups while keeping the number of data in each group at a reasonable level.

5.1 Error Comparison

In this part, we will compare the error between the SV calculated by GTM-Shapley, GBG-Shapley and KFV and the real SV. Since SV time overhead is exponentially related to the amount of data, we use heart disease with a smaller dataset which contains 303 samples and aims to check whether the user has heart disease and the severity of the heart disease. For the sake of simplicity, we do not consider the severity of heart disease, and simply mark the heart disease as 1, but not the 0. We use 250 points as the training set and 50 points as the validation set. We train a three-layer neural network for classification and sort the 25 groups according to SV from low to high. Figure 2(a) shows the estimates by the three methods and the real SV. Figure 2(b) shows the error changes of GTM-Shapley and GBG-Shapley under different groups. Due to the small amount of data, the errors of the three methods are relatively large, but the error of most groups of GTM-Shapley is the smallest, followed by KFV, and the GBG-Shapley has the highest error.

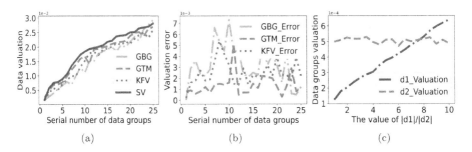

Fig. 2. Experimental results of experiment 5.1 and experiment 5.2.

5.2   Trade-Off Between Quality and Quantity

In machine learning scenarios, we always tend to get more data to prevent the model from overfitting. This is because massive data can make the model more robust. In reality, however, more data is not always better. In this part, we design the experiment to show what kind of scale ordinary data should achieve in order to have the same effect on the performance of the model as high quality data. Using the film review dataset, we take each data point as a group, and calculate the value of each group by GBG-Shapley. Then, we sort the data points according to their SV from low to high and obtain the sorted data set $\hat{D}$. $D1$ is composed of the middle forty percent data points of $\hat{D}$ and $D2$ is composed of the last ten percent data points of $\hat{D}$. We obtain new data sets $d1$ and $d2$ by sampling from $D1$ and $D2$, and find out the size of ordinary data set to achieve the effect of high SV data sets by designing the value of $\frac{|d1|}{|d2|}$. In order to achieve more accurate results, we perform multiple sampling for each value of $\frac{|d1|}{|d2|}$. The size of $d2$ is fixed to 10. Figure 2(c) shows the valuation of the two data sets for different $\frac{|d1|}{|d2|}$. It can be found that when the size of the ordinary data set is 7.5 times the size of the high SV dataset, the two can have the same effect on the model, which reminds us that when obtaining data from crowdsensing workers, we should pay more attention to the quality of the data instead of the quantity of the data, which can help reduce costs while guaranteeing the performance of the model.

6   Conclusion

We have discussed the SV method in the crowdsensing scenario, and our research shows that the SV method can be applied to estimation of the data provided by the crowdsensing workers. As machine learning opens up opportunities to solve problems, how to effectively calculate the SV on large-scale dataset has become an urgent problem to be solved. Our proposed algorithms can effectively reduce the time cost and ensure the relatively small error. They are not only suitable for ordinary machine learning models, but also for deep learning models with huge computational costs, especially models with stable characteristics.

For future work, we hope to continue to clarify the role game theory can play in machine learning and to study other effective evaluation methods. The concept of cooperative alliance in game theory also plays a vital role in data estimation. Last but not least, we hope to apply it to actual scenarios to improve the way of data collection and distribution.

Acknowledgements. This paper is supported by the National Key Research and Development Program of China (Grant No. 2018YFB1403400), the National Natural Science Foundation of China (Grant No. 61876080), the Key Research and Development Program of Jiangsu (Grant No. BE2019105), the Collaborative Innovation Center of Novel Software Technology and Industrialization at Nanjing University.

References

1. Lindelauf, R., Hamers, H., Husslage, B.: Cooperative game theoretic centrality analysis of terrorist networks: The cases of jemaah islamiyah and al qaeda. Eur. J. Oper. Res. **229**(1), 230–238 (2013)
2. Petrosjan, L., Zaccour, G.: Time-consistent shapley value allocation of pollution cost reduction. J. Econ. Dyn. Control **27**(3), 381–398 (2003)
3. Cohen, S., Ruppin, E., Dror, G.: Feature selection based on the shapley value. In other words, 1:98Eqr (2005)
4. Cook, R.D.: Detection of influential observation in linear regression. Technometrics **19**(1), 15–18 (1977)
5. Cook, R.D., Weisberg, S.: Residuals and Influence in Regression. Chapman and Hall, New York (1982)
6. Lundberg, S.M., Lee, S.-I.: A unified approach to interpreting model predictions. In: Advances in Neural Information Processing Systems, pp. 4765–4774 (2017)
7. Lundberg, S.M., Erion, G.G., Lee, S.-I.: Consistent individualized feature attribution for tree ensembles. arXiv preprint arXiv:1802.03888 (2018)
8. Koh, P.W., Liang, P.: Understanding black-box predictions via influence functions. arXiv preprint arXiv:1703.04730 (2017)
9. Ghorbani, A., Zou, J.: Data shapley: equitable valuation of data for machine learning. arXiv preprint arXiv:1904.02868 (2019)
10. Jia, R., et al.: Towards efficient data valuation based on the shapley value. arXiv preprint arXiv:1902.10275 (2019)

AERM: An Attribute-Aware Economic Robust Spectrum Auction Mechanism

Zhuoming Zhu[1], Shengling Wang[1], Rongfang Bie[1(✉)], and Xiuzhen Cheng[2]

[1] School of Artificial Intelligence, Beijing Normal University, Beijing, China
rfbie@bnu.edu.cn
[2] Department of Computer Science, The George Washington University, Washington D.C. 20052, USA

Abstract. The lack of radio spectrum resources and low resource utilization have always been existing problems. Current researchers usually use spectrum auctions to improve the utilization of radio spectrum. The existing auction mechanisms rarely consider the attributes of the radio frequency spectrums, which is likely to cause problems that it cannot meet user needs. Based on the double auction mechanism, we propose an auction mechanism perceiving spectrum attributes to solve this problem. This mechanism can improve the satisfaction of secondary users, provide a certain incentive for high-quality service providers, and at the same time reuse spectrums. The economic robustness of the auction mechanism is of great importance. The auction mechanism proposed in this paper satisfies the three economic properties of truthfulness, individual rationality, and ex-post budget balance, so it is economically robust.

Keywords: Spectrum auction · Economically robust · Heterogeneous spectrum

1 Introduction

With the rapid development of information technology, the shortage of radio communication spectrum resources has become increasingly serious. The contradiction between the ever-increasing demand for radio users and limited spectrum resources has become increasingly prominent. Currently used static spectrum allocation based on spectrum authorization is mainly authorized by the government to use by primary users (PU), such as mobile communication operators, broadcasting, television, military and security departments, etc. However, the primary user does not always occupy its channel, which causes a waste of spectrum resources and makes the scarce spectrum resources inefficient use.

In November 2002, the Federal Communication Commission (FCC) issued a report [1] showing that some frequency bands are idle most of the time (90%), while some frequency bands (such as the frequency band where mobile phone networks are located) are overloaded. This shows that spectrum utilization is a more important issue than spectrum scarcity. The measurement of Berkeley Wireless Research Center in the United States [2] also confirmed this point of view.

© Springer Nature Switzerland AG 2021
Z. Liu et al. (Eds.): WASA 2021, LNCS 12939, pp. 142–153, 2021.
https://doi.org/10.1007/978-3-030-86137-7_16

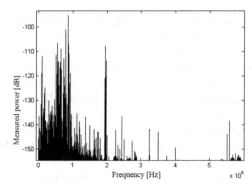

Fig. 1. Spectrum utilization status of different frequency bands.

Most researchers believe that the use of scarce resources such as radio frequency spectrum is more effective to be allocated by auction [3, 4]. This is because auction theory is a theoretical branch of game theory in non-cooperative games. It has the advantages of fairness, effectiveness, and independence of valuation [5]. These advantages fit the characteristics of cognitive radio networks. The spectrum auction is not only feasible in theory but also adopted by FCC in reality[1].

However, the existing auction mechanism is not suitable for auctions that consider spectrum attributes. On the one hand, the main purpose of most existing auction mechanisms is to maximize social welfare or auction revenue, and their transaction matching results may reduce the satisfaction of secondary users (SU) with services; on the other hand, the existing auction mechanisms are not suitable for attribute-based differential pricing in the heterogeneous secondary spectrum market.

Based on the problems existing on spectrum auctions, we propose an attribute-aware economic robust auction mechanism (AERM), which improves the service satisfaction of secondary users and achieves trustfulness, while improving the utility of the winning primary and secondary users. Such a mechanism can effectively encourage primary users and secondary users to participate in auctions, and improve the sustainable development of the spectrum market. The main contributions of this article are as follows:

- We proposed AERM that perceives the properties of the spectrum to complete the auction while maximizing the satisfaction of secondary users with the spectrum.
- We proposed a spectrum differential pricing method based on user satisfaction, which effectively encourages primary and secondary users to participate in auctions
- We proved the economic robustness of AERM theoretically

2 Related Work

The existing auction mechanism mainly considers the trustfulness of the bid price and can be divided into VCG type or McAfee type according to the pricing strategy. To support spatial reuse, TRUST [8], SMALL [9], TAHES [10], DOTA [11] and others [12, 13]. The

---

[1] https://www.fcc.gov/auctions-summary.

recently proposed auction mechanism first does not consider buyers' bids, but groups buyers based on interference graphs and then apply McAfee style to determine winning bids and pricing. These auction models have economic robustness, but they lose their trustfulness when extended to heterogeneous multiunit bids [9]. Fan Wu and Nitin Vaidya [9] believe that channel requirement is closely related to trustfulness. Therefore, a remedy is to delete channel requirements to ensure trustfulness. Mahmoud AlAyyoub, Yuefei Zhu, and others [14–18] studied the one-way real auction based on VCG. VERITAS [14] is the first one-way trustful auction based on the VCG pricing policy under the traditional auction setting. [13–16] are trustful auctions based on Myerson's Optimal Mechanism (MOM) [19].

The difference between them is that the algorithms/heuristics used to determine the winner and its channel have different computational complexity. DISTRICTD [13] studied MOM-based double auctions, which use discriminatory pricing strategies, which are economically robust. When P. Xu [20, 21], L. Deek [22], T. Jing [23], and others studied the VCG-style online one-way real auction, they considered the spectrum reuse in the spatial domain. TODA [24] is an economically robust McAfee-style double auction mechanism that does not consider spatial reuse.

Analyzing the existing auction mechanism, we found that the current research largely ignores the role of auction spectrum attributes, and rarely discusses the effect of auction results and the market on user satisfaction.

3 Preliminaries and Problem Formulation

3.1 Problem Formulation

The spectrum auction problem can be summarized as follows: there are M primary users who sell their idle spectrum and N secondary users who want to buy a certain amount of spectrum. Idle spectrum has multiple attributes, such as channel bandwidth, available time, coverage, etc. Secondary users have certain preferences for the attributes of the spectrum, such as the available time is long enough, the channel bandwidth is large enough, and so on. In the auction, the primary users and the secondary users each give their bids B_i^s and $B_j^b (i = 1, \cdots, M, j = 1, \cdots, N)$.

We need to determine the matching between secondary users and primary users and determine buyers' and sellers' reasonable auction prices.

Most of the current research regards the auctioned spectrum as a homogeneous product, that is, it does not consider the difference in the properties of the spectrum itself, and only considers the bids of buyers and sellers. This can easily lead to the fact that the spectrum purchased by buyers cannot meet their own needs. The auction loses interest. Therefore, we also need to maximize the satisfaction of secondary users.

The allocation of spectrums must meet economic robustness, otherwise, it will lead to fraudulent behaviors that are not conducive to the virtuous cycle of auction activities, such as fake bids. Therefore, the auction mechanism also needs to be economically robust.

3.2 Economic Robustness

Economic robustness is extremely important for spectrum auctions [6]. Economic robustness consists of three properties: trustfulness, individual rationality, and ex-post budget balance. The formal definitions of these three properties are given below.

We use PU_i to denote the ith primary user. B_i^s is the selling price. V_i^s is the estimated price of the spectrum. P_i^s is the final selling transaction price of the spectrum, and $U_i^s = P_i^s - V_i^s$ to be the utility of the main user. When this spectrum is not successfully sold, $U_i^s = 0$. We use SU_j to represent the jth secondary user, B_j^b to indicate the purchase bid, V_j^b to indicate the estimated value of the spectrum that this user expects to buy, P_j^b to indicate the purchase transaction price, $U_j^s = V_j^b - P_j^b$ is called the utility of this secondary user. When the secondary user fails to purchase spectrum this time, $U_j^b = 0$.

Truthfulness. If no matter how other people bid, buyers or sellers cannot increase their effectiveness through untrue quotes ($B_m^s \neq V_m^s$ or $B_n^b \neq V_n^b$), it is said that this kind of auction has truthfulness.

Individual Rationality. If the transaction price of all the winning sellers is not lower than the quoted price, and the transaction price of all the winning buyers is not higher than the quoted price, it is said that the auction has individual rationality. That means the auction need to meet:

$$\forall PU_m \forall SU_n, P_m^s \geq B_m^s, P_n^b \leq B_n^b$$

Ex-Post Budget Balance. If the auctioneer's revenue $\Phi \geq 0$, the auction is said to have an ex-post budget balance. Therefore, the auction needs to satisfy this inequality:

$$\Phi = \sum_{n=1}^{N} P_n^b - \sum_{m=1}^{M} P_m^s \geq 0$$

If the auction mechanism satisfies these three economic properties, we believe that the auction method is economically robust.

4 Details About AERM

AERM takes the user's bids, the preference scheme of the secondary user, and the interference graph of the spectrum as input, and matches the primary and secondary users together based on the spectrum attributes and the satisfaction of the secondary users. The final differential pricing is concerning users' satisfaction. Spatial reuse of spectrums is realized based on the interference graph, and the transaction plan is finally output. The overall framework is as follows: first, determine the set of winning PUs and SUs, then conduct preference-based transaction matching, and finally implement attribute-based differential pricing.

4.1 Determining the Winning PUs and SUs

In this stage, AERM determines several primary users and secondary users as auction winners among the multiple PUs and SUs participating in the auction according to certain rules. It should be noted that a PU may own multiple spectrums for sale at the same time, and a SU may also want to purchase multiple spectrums. By setting virtual PUs and SUs for this situation, we can only discuss that a PU only sells one spectrum, and a SU only buys one spectrum.

The mechanism sorts the selling prices of all PUs in non-decreasing order and sorts the purchase prices of all SUs in non-increasing order.

$$B_1^s \leq B_2^s \leq \cdots \leq B_M^s \tag{1}$$

$$B_1^b \geq B_2^b \geq \cdots \geq B_N^b \tag{2}$$

To determine the number of winners and maintain the budget balance of the auction, we select the buying and selling boundary pair according to the following rules:

$$k^* = \mathrm{argmax}_k B_k^s \leq B_k^b \tag{3}$$

According to the obtained boundary pairs (PU_{k^*}, SU_{k^*}), the top $(k^* - 1)$ PUs and the top $(k^* - 1)$ SUs are regarded as winners.

4.2 Matching

After determining the set of auction winners, a solution is needed to match each PU with the SU. There are differences in spectrum attributes between the various spectrums. To satisfy the secondary users as much as possible, we adopt transaction matching based on preferences. The supply and demand transaction pairing is determined according to the satisfaction of the secondary users. This matching process includes four steps: quantifying secondary users' preference, matching to maximize the preference value, spectrum reusing, and differential pricing.

Quantify the Preference. AERM mainly adopts the analytic hierarchy process (AHP) [7] to quantify the user's spectrum preference. First, build a hierarchical structure model based on the attributes of the spectrum. Users compare the spectrum attributes in pairs, and give the importance of the spectrum attributes according to their subjective preference, and obtain a pairwise comparison matrix. Finally, the weight vectors of these pairwise comparison matrices are solved. The final combined weight vector is a vector composed of the user's preference values for each spectrum, and these preference values can describe the user's degree of satisfaction. Readers can learn more details about AHP in [7].

Matching to Maximize the Preference. After obtaining the preference values of the secondary users for each frequency spectrum, using the preference values as the weights, we can construct a complete bipartite weighted graph describing the preference relationship of the secondary users to each frequency spectrum.

Our goal is to provide a matching scheme between secondary users and primary users, while maximizing the sum of the preference values of all secondary users, thereby maximizing the satisfaction of secondary users. This problem can be formalized as the following 0–1 programming problem:

$$\max \sum_{i=1}^{k-1} \sum_{j=1}^{k-1} w(PU_i, SU_j)\delta_{ij} \tag{4}$$

$$\text{s.t.} \sum_{i=1}^{k-1} \delta_{ij} \leq 1, \forall PU_j \in M$$

$$\sum_{j=1}^{k-1} \delta_{ij} \leq 1, \forall SU_i \in N$$

$$\delta_{ij} \in \{0, 1\}$$

$$e(PU_i, SU_j) \in E$$

M is the set of PUs, N is the set of SUs and E is the edges set of the bipartite graph constructed before. $e(PU_i, SU_j)$ represents the edge linking PU_i to SU_j. We denote the preference value by $w(PU_i, SU_j)$. If there exists an edge linking PU_i to SU_j, $\delta_{ij} = 1$, otherwise $\delta_{ij} = 0$.

AERM applies the Kuhn-Munkres algorithm to solve this problem and obtains the matching scheme between the primary user and the secondary user. This matching scheme is a scheme that makes the secondary user satisfy as much as possible.

Algorithm 1: Kuhn-Munkres

Input: Bipartite Graph $G = (N, M, E)$
Output: $Match$ of G which maximize the satisfaction of SUs
1 $Match = \phi$;
2 **foreach** $SU \in N, PU \in M$ **do**
3 $\quad$ $l(SU) = \max_{PU \in M}\{w(SU, PU)\}$;
4 $\quad$ $l(PU) = 0$;
5 **end**
6 **while** $Match$ *is not a perfect matching* **do**
7 $\quad$ select a vertex $SU \in N$ which has not been matched;
8 $\quad$ $S = \{SU\}, T = \phi$;
9 $\quad$ **while** *True* **do**
10 $\quad\quad$ **if** $N_l(S) \neq T$ **then**
11 $\quad\quad\quad$ select $PU \in N_l(S) - T$;
12 $\quad\quad\quad$ **if** *PU has not been matched* **then**
13 $\quad\quad\quad\quad$ inverse the augmenting path adding path to $Match$;
14 $\quad\quad\quad\quad$ break;
15 $\quad\quad\quad$ **else**
16 $\quad\quad\quad\quad$ $S = S \cup \{SU\}, T = T \cup \{PU\}$ if PU matches SU;
17 $\quad\quad\quad$ **end**
18 $\quad\quad$ **else**
19 $\quad\quad\quad$ $alpha_l = \min_{SU \in S, PU \notin T}\{l(SU) + l(PU) - w(SU, PU)\}$;
20 $\quad\quad\quad$ **if** $v \in S$ **then**
21 $\quad\quad\quad\quad$ $l(v) = l(v) - \alpha_l$;
22 $\quad\quad\quad$ **end**
23 $\quad\quad\quad$ **if** $v \in T$ **then**
24 $\quad\quad\quad\quad$ $l(v) = l(v) + \alpha_l$;
25 $\quad\quad\quad$ **end**
26 $\quad\quad$ **end**
27 $\quad$ **end**
28 **end**
29 **return** $Match$;

Spectrum Reuse. If multiple SUs do not conflict with the time and space requirements of the same spectrum, and this spectrum is what they want most, the kuhn-munkres algorithm will allocate different spectrums for these users, which leads to unnecessary satisfaction loss. At this stage, AERM fine-tunes the matching scheme based on the interference graph, allowing multiple SUs that do not conflict to match the same spectrum, which improves the reusability of the radio spectrum.

Algorithm 2: Reuse Algorithm

Input: Bipartite Graph $G = (N, M, E)$, Interference
Graph$G' = (N, E')$, $Match$
Output: G's improved matching $Match'$

1   $Match' = Match$;
2   **foreach** $SU \in N$ **do**
3      $currentEdge = (SU, PU) \in Match$;
4      $currentPref = w(currentEdge)$;
5      $E_{SU} = \{(SU, PU) \in E : w(SU, PU) > currentPref\}$;
6   **foreach** $e \in E_{SU}$ **do**
7   **if** $e \notin E'$ **and** $w(e) > currentPref$ **then**
8            $currentPref = w(e)$;
9            $Match' = Match' - currentEdge$;
10           $currentEdge = e$;
11           $Match' = Match' + e$;
12   **end**
13   **end**
14 **end**
15 **return** $Match'$;

Pricing. After determining the transaction matching plan, we will determine the final price of spectrum transactions between buyers and sellers, not only to maximize the utility of primary users and secondary users, but also to meet the economic robustness required by the auction, and to incentivize the provision of high-quality services.

Assuming that PU_i and SU_j match, their selling and buying prices are B_i^s and B_j^b respectively. The price that the auctioneer needs to pay the seller PU_i. is:

$$P_i^s = \alpha_j \frac{B_k^s + B_k^b}{2} + (1 - \alpha_j) B_k^s \tag{5}$$

The final price that the auctioneer charges the buyer SU_j is:

$$P_j^b = (1 - \alpha_j) \frac{B_k^b + B_k^s}{2} + \alpha_j B_k^b \tag{6}$$

Where α_j is SU_j's preference value for PU_i.

5   Proof of Economic Robustness

Theorem 1. AERM is trustful.

Proof: According to whether the secondary user can win, it can be divided into the following four situations as what Table 1 shows:

In cases 2 and 3, the secondary user cannot win when making an unreal bid. At this time, the utility is 0. When they make a real bid, the utility is not less than 0. These two situations are trivial.

Table 1. Four situations when bidding truthfully and untruthfully.

Case	1	2	3	4
The SU bids truthfully	Not win	Win	Not win	Win
The SU bids untruthfully	Not win	Not win	Win	Win

In case 1, assuming that the real bid of SU_i is $B_b^i = V_b^i$, the bids of the buying and selling boundary pair are B_s^{k*} and B_b^{k*}. Because the SU cannot win, it must satisfy $V_b^i \leq B_b^k$. The utility of SU_i is 0 now. If the SU wins after making an unreal bid $B_{i'}^b \neq V_i^b$, there must be an inequality $B_{i'}^b > B_k^b \geq V_i^b$. The utility of SU_i is $U_{i'}^b = V_i^b - B_k^b \leq 0$. As a result, SU cannot improve its utility through unreal bids in this case.

In case 4, assuming that the real bid of SU_I is $B_b^i = V_b^i$, the bids of the buying and selling boundary pair are B_s^{k*} and B_b^{k*}. If the SU can still win when he makes an unreal bid $B_{i'}^b \neq V_i^b$, then we know $B_{i'}^b \geq B_k^b$. The bids of the buying and selling boundary pair are still B_s^{k*} and B_b^{k*}. SU cannot improve its utility through unreal bids. A similar discussion about PU bids untruthfully is omitted. It can be proved that PU cannot improve its utility through unreal bids.

∎

Theorem 2. AERM is individually rational.

Proof: Because $k^* = \text{argmax}_k B_k^b \geq B_k^s, \alpha_j \in [0, 1]$ and the pricing formula above, we can show that $P_i^s \geq B_k^s$. When AERM sorted the selling prices of all PUs in non-decreasing order, we have $P_i^s \geq B_i^s$. For the same reason, we can prove $P_j^b \leq B_j^b$. This complete the proof.

∎

Theorem 3. AERM is ex-post budget balanced.

Proof:

$$\Phi = \sum_{j=1}^{k^*-1} P_j^b - \sum_{i=1}^{k^*-1} P_i^s$$

$$\Phi = \sum_{j=1}^{k^*-1} \left[\frac{B_{k*}^b + B_{k*}^s}{2} + \alpha_j \frac{B_{k*}^b - B_{k*}^s}{2} \right] - \sum_{i=1}^{k^*-1} \left[\alpha_j \frac{B_{k*}^s + B_{k*}^b}{2} + (1 - \alpha_j) B_{k*}^s \right]$$

Because $k^* = \text{argmax } B_k^b \geq B_k^s$, we have $B_{k*}^b \geq B_{k*}^s$ and $B_{k*}^s \leq \frac{B_{k*}^s + B_{k*}^b}{2}$. Then we have

$$\Phi \geq \sum_{j=1}^{k^*-1} \frac{B_{k*}^s + B_{k*}^b}{2} - \sum_{i=1}^{k^*-1} \frac{B_{k*}^s + B_{k*}^b}{2} = 0$$

∎

6   Experiments

We use C++ language to implement the prototype of the auction mechanism proposed in this article, and the code is hosted under the GitHub repository[2]. To verify that this auction mechanism can effectively improve the satisfaction of secondary users, improve the utility of primary users and secondary users, and explore the performance of the algorithm, we used a computer equipped with Intel(R) Core™ i5-4200H CPU in Windows 10 operating system to make a simulation experiment.

Because our auction mechanism performs primary-secondary users matching based on spectrum attributes, other auction mechanisms that do not consider spectrum attributes are no different from random matching under this framework. We set the number of spectrum attributes to 100 and compared them with different numbers of primary users and secondary users. The results show that our auction mechanism helps to improve the satisfaction of secondary users. We also conducted comparative experiments with McAfee-style pricing to verify that this mechanism has an incentive effect on the provision of the excellent spectrum. We also evaluated the performance of the algorithm in the case of a large number of spectrum attributes: even if there are 80 primary users and 80 secondary users participating in the auction at the same time when there are as many as 150 spectrum attributes, our auction mechanism can still achieve 15 The auction scheme can be obtained within seconds.

We compare matching randomly and using Kuhn-Munkres Algorithm to match in the matching stage. The number of primary users ranges from 20 to 60 and the number of secondary users ranges from 20 to 80. We observed the sum of preference values which represent the satisfaction of secondary users. The results show that our methods reach a higher satisfaction level than those mechanisms not considering spectrum attributes. We compare the utility using our pricing plan and using the McAfee pricing plan. The results show that our mechanism has an incentive effect on the provision of excellent spectrum by increasing users' utility.

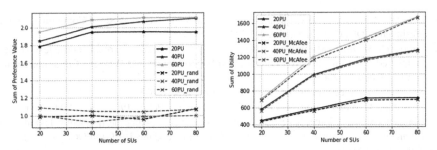

Fig. 2. The mechanism helps to improve satisfaction (Left). The mechanism has an incentive effect on the provision of excellent spectrum by increasing users' utility (Right).

---

[2] https://github.com/PiggerZZM/SpectrumAuction.

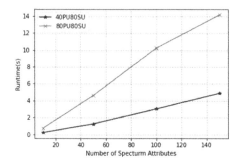

Fig. 3. The runtime of this auction mechanism.

7 Conclusion

This paper proposes AERM to solve the contradiction between the increasing demand for wireless communication and the scarcity of radio spectrum resources. AERM matches transactions between the two parties according to the spectrum attributes and the preference of the secondary users, which can improve the satisfaction of the secondary users with the transaction results. AERM also achieves an incentive effect for those who provide high-quality services through a differential pricing method based on preferences. We analyze the economic robustness of AERM and prove that AERM is economically robust.

Acknowledgments. This research was sponsored by the National Natural Science Foundation of China (No. 6217020594, 61571049).

References

1. Kolodzy, P., Interference Avoidance: Spectrum policy task force. Federal Commun. Comm., Washington, DC, Rep. ET Docket, 40(4):147–158 (2002)
2. Čabrić, D., Mishra, S.M., Willkomm, D., et al.: A cognitive radio approach for usage of virtual unlicensed spectrum. In: Proceedings of 14th IST Mobile and Wireless Communications Summit. Citeseer (2005)
3. Klemperer, P.: Spectrum on the block. Wall Street J. **5**, 8 (2000)
4. McMillan, J.: Why auction the spectrum? Telecommun. Policy **19**(3), 191–199 (1995)
5. Dong, M., Sun, G., Wang, X., et al.: Combinatorial auction with time-frequency flexibility in cognitive radio networks. In: Proceedings of 2012 Proceedings IEEE INFOCOM, pp. 2282–2290. IEEE (2012)
6. Klemperer, P.: What really matters in auction design. J. Econ. Perspect. **16**(1), 169–189 (2002)
7. Saaty, T.L.: Decision Making for Leaders: The Analytical Hierarchy Process for Decisions in a Complex World (1982). Belmont, California: Wadsworth. ISBN 0-534-97959-9; Paperback, Pittsburgh: RWS. ISBN 0-9620317-0-4. Focuses on practical application of the AHP; briefly covers theory
8. Zhou, X., Zheng, H.: TRUST: a general framework for truthful double spectrum auctions. In: Proceedings of IEEE INFOCOM 2009, pp. 999–1007. IEEE (2009)

9. Wu, F., Vaidya, N.: SMALL: a strategy-proof mechanism for radio spectrum allocation. In: Proceedings of 2011 Proceedings IEEE INFOCOM, pp. 81–85. IEEE (2011)
10. Feng, X., Chen, Y., Zhang, J., et al.: TAHES: truthful double auction for heterogeneous spectrums. In: Proceedings of 2012 Proceedings IEEE INFOCOM, pp. 3076–3080. IEEE (2012)
11. Wang, Q., Ye, B., Xu, T., et al.: DOTA: a double truthful auction for spectrum allocation in dynamic spectrum access. In: Proceedings of 2012 IEEE Wireless Communications and Networking Conference (WCNC), pp. 1490–1495. IEEE (2012)
12. Jing, T., Zhao, C., Xing, X., et al.: A multiunit truthful double auction framework for secondary market. In: Proceedings of 2013 IEEE International Conference on Communications (ICC), pp. 2817–2822. IEEE (2013)
13. Wang, W., Liang, B., Li, B.: Designing truthful spectrum double auctions with local markets. IEEE Trans. Mob. Comput. **13**(1), 75–88 (2012)
14. Zhou, X., Gandhi, S., Suri, S., et al.: eBay in the sky: strategy-proof wireless spectrum auctions. In: Proceedings of the 14th ACM International Conference on Mobile Computing and Networking, pp. 2–13 (2008)
15. AlAyyoub, M., Gupta, H.: Truthful spectrum auctions with approximate revenue. In: Proceedings of 2011 Proceedings IEEE INFOCOM, pp. 2813–2821. IEEE (2011)
16. Jia, J., Zhang, Q., Zhang, Q., et al.: Revenue generation for truthful spectrum auction in dynamic spectrum access. In: Proceedings of the tenth ACM International Symposium on Mobile Ad Hoc Networking and Computing, pp. 3–12 (2009)
17. Gopinathan, A., Li, Z., Wu, C.: Strategy-proof auctions for balancing social welfare and fairness in secondary spectrum markets. In: Proceedings of 2011 Proceedings IEEE INFOCOM, pp. 3020–3028. IEEE (2011)
18. Zhu, Y., Li, B., Li, Z.: Truthful spectrum auction design for secondary networks. In: Proceedings of 2012 Proceedings IEEE INFOCOM, pp. 873–881. IEEE (2012)
19. Myerson, R.B.: Optimal auction design . Math. Oper. Res. **6**(1), 58–73 (1981)
20. Xu, P., Li, X.-Y.: Online market driven spectrum scheduling and auction. In: Proceedings of Proceedings of the 2009 ACM Workshop on Cognitive Radio Networks, pp. 49–54 (2009)
21. Ping, X., Wang, S., Li, X.-Y.: SALSA: Strategy-proof online spectrum admissions for wireless networks. IEEE Trans. Comput. **59**(12), 1691–1702 (2010)
22. Deek, L., Zhou, X., Almeroth, K., et al.: To preempt or not: tackling bid and timebased cheating in online spectrum auctions. In: Proceedings of 2011 Proceedings IEEE INFOCOM, pp. 2219–2227. IEEE (2011)
23. Jing, T., Zhang, F., Ma, L., Li, W., Chen, X., Huo, Y.: Truthful online reverse auction with flexible preemption for access permission transaction in macro-femtocell networks. In: Ren, K., Liu, X., Liang, W., Xu, M., Jia, X., Xing, K. (eds.) WASA 2013. LNCS, vol. 7992, pp. 512–523. Springer, Heidelberg (2013). https://doi.org/10.1007/978-3-642-39701-1_42
24. Wang, S., Xu, P., Xu, X., et al.: TODA: truthful online double auction for spectrum allocation in wireless networks. In: Proceedings of 2010 IEEE Symposium on New Frontiers in Dynamic Spectrum (DySPAN), pp. 1–10. IEEE (2010)

Application of Matrix-NMS in Face Detection and Autonomous Driving

Xin Zhao[1]⬤, Yang Peng[2](✉), and Jing Yang[1](✉)

[1] Beijing University of Posts and Telecommunications, Beijing 100876, China
2019110238@bupt.cn, yangjing21@baidu.com
[2] Baidu ADT, Beijing, China
pengy@urplus.cn

Abstract. Matrix-NMS is derived from the SOLO network, an instance segmentation network. Matrix-NMS was transplanted to the target detection network YOLO to improve the detection accuracy and recall rate of the actual application scenario of "similar objects closed to each other or have a certain occlusion relationship". The model used in this article is based on YOLOv3.ResNet18 and ResNet50 were studied as pre-trained networks to compare the accuracy and recall rate of using Matrix-NMS or not. The results show that the model using Matrix-NMS not only has a certain degree of improvement in accuracy and recall rate, but also has the similar inference time. The accuracy and recall rate of the model have been improved to a certain extent. The study in this article could be applied to face detection, sign detection within complex road conditions for autonomous driving or for focus detection in medical imaging. In addition to Matrix-NMS, the convolution layer with DropBlock, the pre-trained networks ResNet50, and ResNet18 with Deformable Convolutional Networks have also been studied.

Keywords: Matrix-NMS · Face detection · Autonomous driving

1 Introduction

1.1 Related Work

In the task of target detection, there is generally such a scene, that is, the recognition or detection of similar objects that are close to each other or have a certain occlusion relationship. For example, there might be a large number of faces in large-scale exhibitions or parades, they are very close, and some have a certain degree of occlusion; in the field of autonomous driving, a certain number of traffic signs will be gathered in the complex scenes of signage scenes such as intersections and high-speed toll stations; in medical images, the field of X-ray film detection and recognition, human organs or lesions are mutually obscuring.

Supported by Baidu ADT.

In the above situations, Hard-NMS used in traditional object detection could affect the accuracy and recall rate of target detection, while the Matrix-NMS in the instance segmentation network SOLO for target detection could improve the accuracy and recall rate. Under the premise of using the same pre-trained network, the accuracy and recall rate of the network using Matrix-NMS are 0.3%–7.5% higher than those of the network using Hard-NMS.

Face Detection. Face detection is a classic problem in the field of computer vision. The face detection algorithms must solve the following core problems: the position of the face in the image is not fixed; the multi-scale problem of the face, and the face might have different expressions; the partial occlusion might in the pose and face.

The development process of face detection algorithms can be divided into 3 stages, namely traditional algorithms, AdaBoost frameworks, and Convolutional Neural Networks (CNN). Traditional algorithms use template matching technology, that is, use a pre-prepared face template to compare each position in the original image, and use indicators such as normalized correlation coefficients to determine whether there is a face at the current position. Compared with CNN, although this method does not require a lot of data, it is less robust and sensitive to changes in factors such as light and face angle, and it will use sliding windows when matching the template with the original image. Window sampling results in very slow processing speed. The idea of the AdaBoost frameworks is to cascade multiple simple weak classifiers. Viloa et al. [1] designed a face detection algorithm that uses simple Harr-like features and levels. The combined AdaBoost classifier constructs the detector, which not only maintains a good accuracy, but also improves the detection speed by 2 orders of magnitude compared with the previous algorithm. CNN were soon used in face detection problems after their success in image classification. Compared with the previous models, the method of CNN for face detection has greatly improved the accuracy and inference time. The HR [2] model detects small targets by fusing multiple information such as multi-scale, resolution, and context; the highlight of SSH [3] lies in the irrelevance of scales. The input of the network is just a picture, and different layers of the network structure's feature map is processed to realize multi-scale detection.

Non-Maximum Suppression. Non-Maximum Suppression is widely used in computer vision models and is a very important part of the model. The traditional Hard-NMS is not suitable in the detection of similar objects with occlusion. Later Soft-NMS [4], Adaptive NMS [5], etc., compared the traditional accuracy or processing time, the NMS was improved. Soft-NMS does not remove duplicate detection frames based on thresholds like traditional NMS, it reduces their confidence scores according to the degree of overlap between these boxes and higher-scoring prediction boxes. Adaptive-NMS uses a dynamic suppression threshold method in each instance to improve the accuracy rate, which has a very good effect in pedestrian detection in a crowd. Fast-NMS [6] can decide whether to keep or remove the test results in parallel, but it improves the detection speed at the expense of the detection effect. Matrix-NMS in SOLOv2 [7] addresses the issues of hard removal and sequential operations at the same time.

2   Our Method: Application of Matrix-NMS Based on YOLOv3

2.1   Matrix-NMS

The Matrix-NMS used in this article comes from the SOLOv2 network [7], which is an instance segmentation network. The inference time of the lightweight version of SOLOv2 on the COCO dataset is 31.3 FPS and 37.1% AP, which becoming a new baseline in the recognition task at the instance segmentation level.

Matrix-NMS is motivated by Soft-NMS. Soft-NMS decays the other detection scores as a monotonic decreasing function of their overlaps, higher IoU will be eliminated with a minimum score threshold. However, such process is sequential like traditional Greedy NMS and could not be implemented in parallel.

Matrix-NMS views this process from another perspective by considering how a predicted prediction p_j being suppressed. For p_j, its decay factor is affected by:(a) The penalty of each prediction p_i on $p_j(s_i > s_j)$, where s_i and s_j are the confidence scores; and (b) the probability of p_i being suppressed. For (a), the penalty of each prediction p_i on p_j could be easily computed by $f(iou._{,i})$. For (b), the probability of p_i being suppressed is not easy to calculate. However, the probability usually has correlation with the IoUs. So it can directly approximate the probability by the most overlapped prediction on p_i as

$$f(iou._{,i}) = \min_{\forall s_k > s_i} f(iou_{k,i}) \tag{1}$$

To this end, the final decay factor becomes

$$decay_j = \min_{\forall s_i > s_j} \frac{f(iou_{i,j})}{f(iou._{,j})} \tag{2}$$

and the updated score is computed by $s_j = s_j \cdot decay_j$. Considering two most simple decremented functions, denoted as linear $f(iou_{i,j}) = 1 - iou_{i,j}$, and Gaussian $f(iou_{i,j}) = exp(-\frac{iou_{i,j}^2}{\sigma})$.

Matrix-NMS calculates the IoU between any two boxes through a matrix parallel operation. When calculating the suppression coefficient of prediction A, firstly calculate all other predictions with a score higher than A and the IoU of A, and then based on these IoU and the probability of suppression of the prediction with a score higher than A to estimate the suppression coefficient of A.

2.2   DropBlock

The use of Dropout [8] in the fully connected layer can improve the generalization ability of the network, but its ability in the convolutional layer is not obvious. The reason is that the features of the convolutional layer are spatially related. If Dropout is used in the convolutional layer, it only works in this layer, and the information removed in this layer can still exist in the next layer and propagate backward. Therefore, Golnaz Ghiasi et al. proposed DropBlock [9], which is a structural form of Dropout in which an adjacent region in the feature map is dropped. The basic principle of this method is to inject noise into the network so that the network does not overfitting the data, thereby enhancing the generalization ability of the network.

Dropblock has two main parameters, block_size and γ. block_size is the size of the feature block to be dropped. This parameter is shared throughout the network and does not change due to the size of the feature map; γ is the number of activation units to be dropped. In addition, keep_prob is reserved for each probability of each unit, feat_size is the size of the feature such as, γ can be expressed as

$$\gamma = \frac{1 - keep\_prob}{block\_size^2} \cdot \frac{feat\_size^2}{(feat\_size - block\_size + 1)^2} \tag{3}$$

2.3 Deformable Convolutional Networks

Traditional CNN can only rely on some simple methods to adapt to the deformation of the object, such as max pooling. There are two common methods. The first is to use a large amount of data for training, using flips, distortions and other methods to amplify the training set, thinking that it simulates the deformation that may occur in the actual task. The second is to design special operators to adapt to the deformation, such as SIFT [10]. However, due to the limits of data and the complexity of object features, the network has not always had a good solution to the deformation of objects. Jifeng Dai et al. [11] proposed DCN, a deformable convolution structure, which adds an offset to each point on the receptive field. The size of the offset is obtained through learning. The receptive field is no longer a square, but matches the actual shape of the object, which makes the convolutional area always cover the shape of the object no matter what kind of deformation of the object occurs.

In this article, the pre-trained networks ResNet18 and ResNet50 were improved by the Deformable Convolutional Networks.

3 Experiments

In order to evaluate the performance of Matrix-NMS in similar objects that are close to each other or have a certain occlusion relationship, we conducted comparative experiments. The basic network structure is YOLOv3, and the pre-trained networks are ResNet18 and ResNet50. Experiments were carried out on the Wider Face dataset and the TT100K dataset.

The network is trained with Momentum and over 2 GPUs with a total of 12 images per mini-batch. All models are trained for 20 epochs with an initial learning rate of 0.0004, which is then divided by 10 at 15th and again 17th epoch. We use scale resize where the image side is randomly resized from 320 to 800 pixels.

3.1 Main Results

Taking Matrix-NMS as the control variable, take ResNet50_dcn networks as pre-trained networks. The accuracy and recall rates of the model with Wider Face are shown in Table 1 and Table 2 below. ResNet18_dcn was also studied as a pre-trained network. The performance comparison is shown in Table 3 and Table 4 below.

Table 1. Comparison of inference time and accuracy of models using Hard-NMS and Matrix-NMS (use ResNet50_dcn as pre-trained network)

Method	Times (fps)	AP	AP_{50}	AP_{75}
Hard-NMS	**2.89**	34.6	**63.1**	34.6
Matrix-NMS	2.86	**34.9**	62.9	**35.4**

Table 2. Comparison of the recall rate of models using Hard-NMS and Matrix-NMS (use ResNet50_dcn as pre-trained network)

Method	AR_{all}	AR_s	AR_m	AR_l
Hard-NMS	40.3	29.9	66.1	72.9
Matrix-NMS	**42.8**	**31.2**	**71.7**	**80.4**

The test results of the model in the Wider Face and TT100K are shown from Fig. 1, 2, 3, 4, 5, 6. Representative pictures were selected and the comparison of the effects is as follows, the left picture is studied by Hard-NMS, the right picture is studied by Matrix-NMS.

Fig. 1. Part of the faces is obscured, Matrix-NMS gets all targets while Hard-NMS misses some of them.

Fig. 2. Hard-NMS misses the man while Matrix-NMS detects both of them.

Fig. 3. Hard-NMS misses all faces on the right of the picture.

Fig. 4. Hard-NMS misses targets randomly while Matrix-NMS has good performance

Table 3. Comparison of inference time and accuracy of models using Hard-NMS and Matrix-NMS(use ResNet18_dcn as pre-trained network)

Method	Times (fps)	AP	AP_{50}	AP_{75}
Hard-NMS	6.83	29.9	**57.7**	28.7
Matrix-NMS	**7.83**	**30.3**	57.5	**29.3**

The model with the same configuration is used for training on the TT100K, and the comparison of inference time, accuracy and recall of the models using ResNet50_dcn is shown in Table 5, 6.

Table 4. Comparison of recall of models using Hard-NMS and Matrix-NMS (use ResNet18_dcn as pre-trained network)

Method	AR_{all}	AR_s	AR_m	AR_l
Hard-NMS	36.0	25.7	61.5	69.3
Matrix-NMS	**38.2**	**26.6**	**66.5**	**75.7**

Table 5. Comparison of inference time and accuracy of models using Hard-NMS and Matrix-NMS (use ResNet50_dcn as pre-trained network)

Method	Times (fps)	AP	AP_{50}	AP_{75}
Hard-NMS	2.89	**54.7**	**84.0**	63.2
Matrix-NMS	**2.92**	54.5	83.3	**63.8**

Fig. 5. In the situation of targets which have occlusion relationship, Matrix-NMS's performance is better than Hard-NMS.

Table 6. Comparison of recall of models using Hard-NMS and Matrix-NMS (use ResNet50_dcn as pre-trained network)

Method	AR_{all}	AR_s	AR_m	AR_l
Hard-NMS	60.9	**45.5**	67.7	75.9
Matrix-NMS	**63.6**	44.5	**72.3**	**80.3**

Fig. 6. In the situation of targets which have small distance between each other, Matrix-NMS's performance is better than Hard-NMS.

4   Discussion

In this work, we apply Matrix-NMS and DropBlock to YOLOv3. The results show that the accuracy and recall rate of the model using Matrix-NMS in the scene of "the same object with occlusion or close distance" are better than those of Hard-NMS models are 0.3%–7.5% higher.

The model using Hard-NMS is model_1, and the model using Matrix-NMS is model_2.

In the test of the Wider Face, ResNet50_dcn is used as the pre-trained network. From Table 1, it can be seen that the accuracy of model_2's AP and AP_{75} are higher than the results of model_1 when the inference time is almost the same; As can be seen from Table 2, the recall rate of Model_2 is significantly improved compared to Model_1.

In addition, comparing the use of ResNet50 and ResNet18 as the model of the pre-trained network, it can be seen from Table 1 and Table 3 that the latter's inference speed has increased by about 2.3 times, and the accuracy rate has dropped by 4 to 6% points. It can be seen that in scenarios that require high inference speed such as security monitoring, ResNet18 can be used as a pre-trained model; in automatic driving, the production of high-precision maps has high requirements for accuracy and recall so ResNet50 could be used as a pre-trained model to help improve the performance of the model.

The scene of "similar objects that are close to each other or have a certain occlusion relationship" is common in daily life, such as face detection and recognition for security surveillance in exhibitions, parades, sports meets, and large conferences, etc. Scenes such as sign detection in the field of autonomous driving. The use of Matrix-NMS can improve the detection accuracy and recall rate in these scenarios, and the inference time is almost unchanged compared with Hard-NMS.

References

1. Li, S.Z., Zhu, L., Zhang, Z.Q., Blake, A., Zhang, H.J., Shum, H.: Statistical learning of multi-view face detection. In: Heyden, A., Sparr, G., Nielsen, M., Johansen, P. (eds.) ECCV 2002. LNCS, vol. 2353, pp. 67–81. Springer, Heidelberg (2002). https://doi.org/10.1007/3-540-47979-1_5
2. Hu, P., Ramanan, D.: Finding tiny faces. In: Proceedings of the IEEE Conference on Computer Vision and Pattern Recognition, pp. 951–959 (2017)
3. Najibi, M., Samangouei, P., Chellappa, R., Davis, L.S.: SSH: single stage headless face detector. In: Proceedings of the IEEE International Conference on Computer Vision, pp. 4875–4884 (2017)
4. Bodla, N., Singh, B., Chellappa, R., Davis, L.S.: Soft-NMS-improving object detection with one line of code. In: Proceedings of the IEEE International Conference on Computer Vision, pp. 5561–5569 (2017)
5. Liu, S., Huang, D., Wang,Y.: Adaptive NMS: refining pedestrian detection in a crowd. In: Proceedings of the IEEE/CVF Conference on Computer Vision and Pattern Recognition, pp. 6459–6468 (2019)
6. Bolya, D., Zhou, C., Xiao, F., Jae Lee, Y.: YOLACT: real-time instance segmentation. In: Proceedings of the IEEE/CVF International Conference on Computer Vision, pp. 9157–9166 (2019)
7. Wang, X., Zhang, R., Kong, T., Li, L., Shen, C.: SOLOv2: dynamic, faster and stronger. arXiv preprint arXiv:2003.10152 (2020)
8. Srivastava, N., Hinton, G., Krizhevsky, A., Sutskever, I., Salakhutdinov, R.: Dropout: a simple way to prevent neural networks from overfitting. J. Mach. Learn. Res. 15(1), 1929–1958 (2014)
9. Ghiasi, G., Lin, T.-Y., Le, Q.V.: DropBlock: a regularization method for convolutional networks. arXiv preprint arXiv:1810.12890 (2018)
10. Lowe, D.G.: Object recognition from local scale-invariant features. In: Proceedings of the Seventh IEEE International Conference on Computer Vision, vol. 2, pp. 1150–1157. IEEE (1999)
11. Dai, J., et al.: Deformable convolutional networks. In: Proceedings of the IEEE International Conference on Computer Vision, pp. 764–773 (2017)

Blockchain-Based Verifiable DSSE with Forward Security in Multi-server Environments

Chang Xu[1], Lan Yu[2], Liehuang Zhu[1(✉)], and Can Zhang[2]

[1] School of Cyberspace Science and Technology, Beijing Institute of Technology,
Beijing 100081, China
{xuchang,liehuangz}@bit.edu.cn
[2] School of Computer Science and Technology, Beijing Institute of Technology,
Beijing 100081, China
{yu_lan,canzhang}@bit.edu.cn

Abstract. With big data and cloud computing development, data own-ers begin to outsource their large-volume data to remote servers to reduce local storage costs. Researchers have currently proposed some Dynamic Searchable Symmetric Encryption (DSSE) schemes that support efficient keyword searches on encrypted data with dynamic update operations. Unfortunately, most of them are constructed based on a single server architecture, which means that they cannot be used directly when mul-tiple servers participate in the search process. Some schemes assume that the server is honest-but-curious, which cannot be guaranteed, espe-cially in the multi-server scenario. This paper proposes a Blockchain-based Verifiable DSSE scheme with forwarding security in Multi-server environments. In the scheme, the data owner encrypts the partitioned files and randomly stores them in different servers from which a sin-gle server cannot recover any complete file. The use of blockchain and smart contracts to achieve reliable and verifiable search can detect mali-cious servers' improper behaviors. Experimental evaluation show that the scheme achieves verifiable search, forward privacy with less leakage, and high search efficiency.

Keywords: Dynamic searchable symmetric encryption · Verifiability · Multiple servers · Blockchain · Forward security · Malicious servers

1 Introduction

We are entering the era of big data, local storage and computing resources can no longer meet data owners' needs. They begin to outsource data to remote servers, however, this brings new problems, such as data privacy, since data may contain sensitive information. The leakage of sensitive information may result in the disclosure of privacy [1,2]. To protect data privacy while maintaining searchability, Searchable Symmetric Encryption (SSE) has been leveraged [3,4]. However, traditional SSE schemes do not support dynamic updates.

© Springer Nature Switzerland AG 2021
Z. Liu et al. (Eds.): WASA 2021, LNCS 12939, pp. 163–171, 2021.
https://doi.org/10.1007/978-3-030-86137-7_18

To support dynamic updates, researchers have proposed Dynamic Searchable Symmetric Encryption (DSSE) schemes [5,6]. Kamara et al. [7] proposed the first DSSE scheme, which is designed to support efficient data addition and deletion. Zhang et al. [8] proposed the file injection attack with which attackers can inject a few new files into an encrypted database to infer the user's query. To resist the attack, a new security requirement is proposed namely forward security [9,10]. Stefanov et al. [11] proposed a Path ORAM-based solution, which not only guarantees forward privacy but also minimizes information leakage.

The existing DSSE schemes can be categorized into two types: single-server architecture and two-server architecture (including a proxy server)[12]. However, a single server cannot undertake the tasks to store heavy data. Therefore, the data owner needs to allocate data storage to multiple servers, each containing only a part of the file and related metadata.

Most DSSE schemes assume that the server is "honest-but-curious" [13,14]. However, malicious servers may return incomplete or incorrect results to users. To solve the problems, some verifiable SSE schemes [15,16] have been proposed, in which the integrity of the result can be verified. Based on the blockchain's programmable nature [17,18], smart contracts mainly package various scripts, protocols, and calculations. Hu et al. [19] used a carefully-designed smart contract to replace the central server. Li et al. [20] utilized blockchain to resist the attacks from the malicious servers.

Our main contributions can be summarized as follows:

1. We propose a blockchain-based DSSE scheme in a multi-server scenario, which utilizes smart contracts to achieve the reliability of program execution process, correctness of search results, and can resist attacks from malicious servers.
2. We construct a verifiable query mechanism under multiple servers to achieve verifiability of SSE query files. The mechanism utilizes lightweight cryptographic primitives to achieve verification of files' integrity.
3. We achieve forward privacy based on trapdoor permutation and have implemented our scheme by experiment simulation in terms of the index size and the search time.

The remaining structure of this paper is as follows: Sect. 2 describes system model, threat model, and design goals. After that, in Sects. 3, we develop a Blockchain-based verifiable DSSE scheme. Section 4 gives the experimental performance. In the last section, we present the conclusion of this paper.

2 Problem Formalization

2.1 System Model

There are five roles in the system model: (1) m servers, $\mathbf{S} = \{S_1, ..., S_m\}$, which store the encrypted file set. (2) un users, denoted as $\mathbf{U} = \{U_1, ..., U_{un}\}$, U_i issues a search operation request and generates a search token. (3) The smart contract, which stores the encrypted index. (4) Data owner O, provides file set and generates a local index. (5) TA, a trustworthy organization, is responsible for the keys generation and distribution.

TA generates and distributes a set of key $\mathbf{K}$ through a secure channel for the data owner and users. At the same time, it generates a public and private key pair (pk_i^u, sk_i^u) for each user that can be used for identity verification and a key pair (pk^o, sk^o) to the data owner. The data owner generates an encrypted index table locally, uploads it to the chain and the encrypted block file to the corresponding server. The user generates a search token according to the keyword to be searched and sends a search request. The smart contract performs a query in the index table and returns the query result to the user. If the data owner wants to add/delete files, it will generate an add/delete token to update the encrypted index table and process the server's content.

2.2 Threat Model and Design Goals

Three types of threats are considered in our scheme: (1) A malicious server may return incomplete or incorrect files; (2) The data on the blockchain is transparent, so anyone, including the attacker, can analyze the data to obtain information; (3) Unauthorized users may illegally call the smart contract during the process of searching. The scheme should satisfy the following requirements:

Reliability. The stored index and data cannot be tampered with, and the server's malicious behavior and illegal smart contract calls can be detected.

Verifiability. The users can verify the completeness and correctness of the files and determine which server is malicious.

Forward security. Forward security refers to the ability to resist file injection attacks. It ensures that the newly added file set's keyword information is not leaked due to the old search token.

3 Blockchain-Based Verifiable DSSE Scheme

3.1 Notations

To help the readers understand the following algorithms and the scheme, we list the symbols used in the paper in Table 1.

Table 1. A list of symbols.

Symbol	Description	Symbol	Description
n	Number of files	$\mathbf{c}$	Encrypted block file set
m	Number of servers	ST	Search token generated by a user
id_{S_s}	The s-th server identifier	STS	Search verification token
un	Number of users	t	Search token generation time
U_j	The j-th user	pk	Public key generated by TA
W	Keyword set	h	Hash value for the block file
$\mathbf{F}$	File set	$\mathbf{DB}(w)$	Identifiers whose files contain w
id_{F_i}	The i-th file identifier	t_1	Preset time limit
h_f	Number of blocks the file needs to be divided into	$id_{f_{i,j}}$	The identifier of the j-th block of the i-th file
λ	Security parameter	$\mathbf{K}$	Secret key set
$\mathbf{A}$	Encrypted index	$pkList$	List of public keys for users
DT	Delete token generated by the data owner	$\mathbf{DB}$	$(w_i,$ file identifiers containing $w_i)$ set

3.2 Algorithms of the Scheme

In this section, we will introduce the Key generation, Index generation, Search token generation, Search, File deletion procedures by providing KeyGen, Index-Gen, SearchTokenGen, Search, and FileDel algorithms.

Key Generation: Algorithm 1 generates all keys used in the scheme, where k refers to the master key used to generate search tokens and identifier encryption keys, K_e is used to encrypt and decrypt block files. $\mathbf{K} = \{k, K_e\}$ is distributed through secure channels and shared by users and the data owner. Besides, TA distributes the corresponding key-pair to the data owner and each user.

Algorithm 1. KeyGen

Input: Security parameter λ.
Output: $\mathbf{K} = \{k, K_e\}$, un key pairs for users, a key pair (pk^o, sk^o) for data owner O.
1: $k \xleftarrow{\$} \{0,1\}^\lambda$, $K_e \leftarrow SKE.GEN(1^\lambda)$; Set $\mathbf{K} = \{k, K_e\}$.
2: Generate (pk^o, sk^o) for data owner O and send (pk^o, sk^o) to data owner O.
3: **for** $i = 1$ **to** un **do**
4:     Generate (pk_i^u, sk_i^u) for user U_i and send (pk_i^u, sk_i^u) to user U_i.
5: **end for**

Index Generation: Algorithm 2 divides each file F_i into h_f blocks, which are encrypted and randomly allocated to any server. For a keyword w, if op is a setup operation, the data owner uses PRF to create an obfuscated keyword α and an identifier encryption key β. For each item of each file containing the keyword w, Algorithm 2 uses β to encrypt the items of T, adds the encrypted item $p_{f_{i,j}}$ to $\mathbf{t}_{S_s}$ and processes all files containing the keyword w. If op is an add operation, the data owner uses trapdoor permutation to ensure forward privacy. A trapdoor is used to make the search token previously unable to establish contact with the newly added files. Algorithm 2 uses trapdoor permutation $\gamma_{w\_(c+1)} = \pi_{sk^o}^{-1}(\gamma_{w\_c})$, where γ_{w_0} is a randomly chosen integer. To adapt to the deletion of files, we treat file identifiers as keywords and generate corresponding α' and β'. In Algorithm 2, the PRF is a pseudo-random function, which is used to generate encoding keys, and defined as: $PRF : \{0,1\}^{\lambda} \times \{0,1\}^{*} \rightarrow \{0,1\}^{\lambda}$. $s \xleftarrow{R} [m]$, it means to randomly select a value s from the set m, where we denote $\{1, 2, ..., m\}$ as $[m]$.

Algorithm 2. IndexGen

Input: $(\mathbf{DB}, op, \mathbf{F}, \mathbf{S}, \mathbf{K}, \mathbf{WK})$, a server set $\mathbf{S}$, a dictionary $\mathbf{WK}$, op is an operation.
Output: $(\mathbf{A}, \mathbf{c})$, a set of encrypted index table $\mathbf{A}$ and an encrypted file set $\mathbf{c}$.
1: Initialize a temporary index table T and $\mathbf{c}$.
2: **for** $i = 1$ to n **do**
3:     $F_i = \{f_{i,1}||1, f_{i,2}||2, ..., f_{i,h_f}||h_f\}$.
4:     **for** $j = 1$ to h_f **do**
5:         $s \xleftarrow{R} [m]$, $h = H(f_{i,j}||j)$, set $T[id_{F_i}, j] = (id_{F_i}, id_{f_{i,j}}, id_{S_s}, h)$.
6:         $c_{f_{i,j}} \leftarrow SKE.Enc(K_e, f_{i,j}||j)$, set $\mathbf{c}[id_{F_i}, j] = c_{f_{i,j}}$.
7:     **end for**
8: **end for**
9: Initialize empty index tables $\mathbf{A} = (AS_1, ..., AS_m)$ and set a counter $str = 1$.
10: **for** each $w \in W_F$ **do**
11:     **if** $op = Set+$ **then**
12:         $\alpha \leftarrow PRF(k, 1||w)$, $\beta \leftarrow PRF(k, 2||w)$.
13:     **else if** $op = Doc+$ **then**
14:         $(\gamma_{w\_c}, c) = \mathbf{WK}[w]$, $\gamma_{w\_(c+1)} = \pi_{sk^o}^{-1}(\gamma_{w\_c})$, $\mathbf{WK}[w] = (\gamma_{w\_(c+1)}, c+1)$;
15:         $\alpha \leftarrow PRF(k, 1||w||\gamma_{w\_(c+1)})$, $\beta \leftarrow PRF(k, 2||w)$.
16:     **end if**
17:     Initialize empty lists $\mathbf{t}_{S_1}, ..., \mathbf{t}_{S_m}$.
18:     **for** each $id_{F_i} \in \mathbf{DB}(w)$ **do**
19:         **for** $j = 1$ to h_f **do**
20:             $s \xleftarrow{R} [m]$, $p_{f_{i,j}} \leftarrow SKE.Enc(\beta, T[id_{F_i}, j])$; Add $p_{f_{i,j}}$ to $\mathbf{t}_{S_s}$.
21:         **end for**
22:     **end for**
23:     **for** $s = 1$ to m **do**
24:         $AS_s[PRF(\alpha, id_{S_s})] = \mathbf{t}_{S_s}$.
25:     **end for**
26:     $str++$.
27: **end for**
28: Initialize temporary empty lists $\mathbf{a}_{S_1}, ...\mathbf{a}_{S_m}$.
29: **for** each id_{F_i} in T **do**
30:     $\alpha' \leftarrow PRF(k, 1||id_{F_i})$, $\beta' \leftarrow PRF(k, 2||id_{F_i})$.
31:     **for** $j = 1$ to h_f **do**
32:         $s \xleftarrow{R} [m]$, add $SKE.Enc(\beta', T[id_{F_i}, j])$ to $\mathbf{a}_{S_s}$.
33:     **end for**
34:     **for** $s = 1$ to m **do**
35:         $AS_s[PRF(\alpha', id_{S_s})] = \mathbf{a}_{S_s}$.
36:     **end for**
37: **end for**
38: Permute entries in each AS_s to mix entries of keyword and file identifiers.
39: **for** each $cm \in \mathbf{c}$ **do**
40:     Send $\mathbf{c}[id_{F_i}, j]$ to S_s based on $T[id_{F_i}, j]$.
41: **end for**
42: Send $\mathbf{A}$ to the smart contract.

Search Token Generation: If a user wants to search a keyword, he generates his search token ST and identifier encryption key β. The timestamp t is used to determine whether the search token is obsoleted. The public key pk is used to authenticate the user. The signature algorithm $Sign_{sk}(h')$ is utilized to detect the search token's integrity.

Algorithm 3. SearchTokenGen

Input: $(\mathbf{K}, w, (pk, sk), \mathbf{S}, \mathbf{WK})$, a search keyword w, and the user's key pair (pk, sk).
Output: A search verification token STS.
1: $\alpha \leftarrow F(k, 1||w)$, $\beta \leftarrow F(k, 2||w)$, $(\gamma_{w\_c}, c) = \mathbf{WK}[w]$.
2: Initialize two empty lists TK, $ST = (ST_1, ..., ST_m)$ and add α to TK.
3: **for** $i = c$ **to** 1 **do**
4:     $\alpha' \leftarrow F(k, 1||w||\gamma_{w\_i})$, add α' to TK, set $\gamma_{w\_(i-1)} = \pi_{pk \circ}(\gamma_{w\_i})$.
5: **end for**
6: **for** $s = 1$ **to** m **do**
7:     **for** each $tk \in TK$ **do**
8:         $l_{w,s} \leftarrow PRF(tk, id_{S_s})$, add $l_{w,s}$ to ST_s.
9:     **end for**
10: **end for**
11: Get current time t; $h' = H(ST||pk||t)$, $Sh = Sign_{sk}(h')$, sign with private key sk.
12: Send $STS = (Sh, ST, pk, t)$ to the smart contract.

Search: The smart contract gets the current timestamp t'. If the search token is not obsolete and is verified to be legal/correct, the smart contract uses ST to get the encrypted entry in the encrypted index table. The servers return their respective query block file results which are merged by the user and the file is finally restored.

Algorithm 4. Search

Input: $(STS, \mathbf{A})$, a search verification token STS, a set of encrypted index table $\mathbf{A}$.
Output: $(\mathbf{st}_{S_1}, ..., \mathbf{st}_{S_m})$, lists of identifiers.
1: Get current time t'.
2: **if** $|t - t'| \leq t_1$ **and** $pk \in pkList$ **and** $Ver_{pk}(H(ST||pk||t)) = 1$ **then**
3:     Initialize empty lists $\mathbf{st}_{S_1}, ..., \mathbf{st}_{S_m}$.
4:     **for** $s = 1$ **to** m **do**
5:         **for** each $st \in ST_s$ **do**
6:             Set $\mathbf{p}_{w,s} = \mathbf{A}_s[st]$, add $\mathbf{p}_{w,s}$ to $\mathbf{st}_{S_s}$.
7:         **end for**
8:     **end for**
9:     Send $(\mathbf{st}_{S_1}, ..., \mathbf{st}_{S_m})$ to the user.
10: **end if**

File Deletion: Algorithm 5 generates α' associated with the file identifier, extracts the corresponding items in the encrypted index table, and deletes these related items in the index. Based on the extracted corresponding items, the data owner uses the identifier encryption key β' to decrypt the identifier tuple information and uses these identifiers to delete the encrypted block in the servers.

Algorithm 5. FileDel

Input: $(\mathbf{K}, Doc-, id_{F_x}, \mathbf{A}, \mathbf{S})$, a file identifier id_{F_x} that needs to be deleted, the deleting operation identifier $Doc-$.
Output: $\mathbf{A}$, a set of updated encrypted index table.
1: $\alpha' \leftarrow F(k, 1||id_{F_x})$, $\beta' \leftarrow F(k, 2||id_{F_x})$; Initialize an empty list DT.
2: **for** $s = 1$ **to** m **do**
3:     $dl_s \leftarrow PRF(\alpha', id_{S_s})$, add dl_s to DT.
4: **end for**
5: Send DT to the smart contract.

6: Initialize an empty list PD.
7: **for** each $dt \in DT$ **do**
8:     $\mathbf{p}_{F_{x,s}} = \mathbf{A}_s[dt]$.
9:     **if** $\mathbf{p}_{F_{x,s}} \neq \perp$ **then**
10:         Add $\mathbf{p}_{F_{x,s}}$ to PD, delete $\mathbf{p}_{F_{x,s}}$ in $\mathbf{A}_s$.
11:     **end if**
12: **end for**
13: Return PD to the data owner.

4   Performance Evaluation

This scheme is implemented based on a blockchain framework fabric with 16GB RAM, 6 Intel core i7-8700k, and running ubuntu 14.4. The data points for all drawings below represent the average of 30 executions. The dataset used in the experiment comes from NSF Research Award Abstracts 1990–2003 Data Set.

Figure 1(a) gives that the index's size depends on the total number of files n and h_f. When the total number of files n is fixed, it can be observed that the size of the index increases linearly with h_f. And when h_f is fixed, the larger the total number of files n, the more files that contain keywords. Therefore, if the items added to the index increase, the index size also becomes larger.

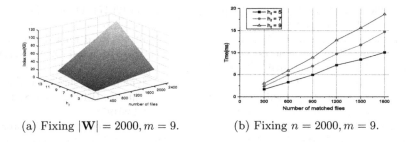

(a) Fixing $|\mathbf{W}| = 2000, m = 9$.   (b) Fixing $n = 2000, m = 9$.

Fig. 1. (a) index size of different h_f and n; (b) the search time under different number of matched files and h_f.

Figure 1(b) shows the relationship between the search time and the number of search matching files and h_f. The search time(including the execution time of Algorithm 4 and the time of decryption of file blocks and merging) will increase as the number of matching files increases, is linearly correlated. When the number of matching files is fixed, the search time increases with the increase of h_f.

5   Conclusion

This paper proposes a novel blockchain-based DSSE scheme that can be used in multi-server environments. The file is encrypted and divided into multiple block files, which are randomly assigned to various servers to reduce the leakages, thereby preventing the server from recovering a complete file. Besides, we also use a trapdoor permutation mechanism to ensure the forward security of the scheme. Based on blockchain technology and smart contracts, the scheme can guarantee the search results' reliability. Also, users can easily verify the search file results' completeness and correctness and find malicious servers' misbehavior. In the future, we will focus on backward privacy, because it is important secure properties that aim to enhance security in DSSE schemes.

Acknowledgments. This research is supported by the National Key Research and Development Program of China (Grant No. 2020YFB1006101) and the National Natural Science Foundation of China (Grant Nos. 61972037, 61872041, U1836212).

References

1. Zhang, C., Zhu, L., Xu, C., Zhang, C., Sharif, K., Wu, H., Westermann, H.: BSFP: blockchain-enabled smart parking with fairness, reliability and privacy protection. IEEE Trans. Veh. Technol. **69**(6), 6578–6591 (2020)
2. Zhang, C., Zhu, L., Xu, C., Liu, X., Sharif, K.: Reliable and privacy-preserving truth discovery for mobile crowdsensing systems. IEEE Trans. Dependable Secure Comput. (2019). https://doi.org/10.1109/TDSC.2019.2919517
3. Poh, G.S., Mohamad, M.S., Chin, J.-J.: Searchable symmetric encryption over multiple servers. Cryptogr. Commun. **10**(1), 139–158 (2017). https://doi.org/10.1007/s12095-017-0232-y
4. Zarezadeh, M., Mala, H., Ashouri-Talouki, M.: Multi-keyword ranked searchable encryption scheme with access control for cloud storage. Peer-to-Peer Networking Appl. **13**(1), 207–218 (2019). https://doi.org/10.1007/s12083-019-00736-0
5. Ti, Y., Wu, C., Yu, C., Kuo, S.: Benchmarking dynamic searchable symmetric encryption scheme for cloud-internet of things applications. IEEE Access **8**, 1715–1732 (2020). https://doi.org/10.1109/ACCESS.2019.2961971
6. Hiemenz, B., Krämer, M.: Dynamic searchable symmetric encryption for storing geospatial data in the cloud. Int. J. Inf. Secur. **18**(3), 333–354 (2018). https://doi.org/10.1007/s10207-018-0414-4
7. Kamara, S., Papamanthou, C., Roeder, T.: Dynamic searchable symmetric encryption. IACR Cryptol. ePrint Arch. **2012**, 530 (2012)
8. Zhang, Y., Katz, J., Papamanthou, C.: All your queries are belong to us: the power of file-injection attacks on searchable encryption. IACR Cryptol. ePrint Arch. **2016**, 172 (2016)
9. Zuo, C., Sun, S., Liu, J.K., Shao, J., Pieprzyk, J., Xu, L.: Forward and backward private DSSE for range queries. IACR Cryptol. ePrint Arch. **2019**, 1240 (2019)
10. Patranabis, S., Mukhopadhyay, D.: Forward and backward private conjunctive searchable symmetric encryption. IACR Cryptol. ePrint Arch. **2020**, 1342 (2020)
11. Stefanov, E., Papamanthou, C., Shi, E.: Practical dynamic searchable encryption with small leakage. In: 21st Annual Network and Distributed System Security Symposium, NDSS. The Internet Society (2014)
12. Orencik, C., Selcuk, A., Savas, E., Kantarcioglu, M.: Multi-Keyword search over encrypted data with scoring and search pattern obfuscation. Int. J. Inf. Secur. **15**(3), 251–269 (2015). https://doi.org/10.1007/s10207-015-0294-9

13. Zhang, C., Fu, S., Ao, W.: A blockchain based searchable encryption scheme for multiple cloud storage. In: Vaidya, J., Zhang, X., Li, J. (eds.) CSS 2019. LNCS, vol. 11982, pp. 585–600. Springer, Cham (2019). https://doi.org/10.1007/978-3-030-37337-5_48

14. He, K., Chen, J., Zhou, Q., Du, R., Xiang, Y.: Secure dynamic searchable symmetric encryption with constant client storage cost. IEEE Trans. Inf. Forensics Secur. **16**, 1538–1549 (2021). https://doi.org/10.1109/TIFS.2020.3033412

15. Zhang, Z., Wang, J., Wang, Y., Su, Y., Chen, X.: Towards efficient verifiable forward secure searchable symmetric encryption. In: Sako, K., Schneider, S., Ryan, P.Y.A. (eds.) ESORICS 2019. LNCS, vol. 11736, pp. 304–321. Springer, Cham (2019). https://doi.org/10.1007/978-3-030-29962-0_15

16. Wang, K., Dong, X., Shen, J., Cao, Z.: An effective verifiable symmetric searchable encryption scheme in cloud computing, pp. 98–102. ACM (2019). https://doi.org/10.1145/3377170.3377251

17. Chen, B., Wu, L., Wang, H., Zhou, L., He, D.: A blockchain-based searchable public-key encryption with forward and backward privacy for cloud-assisted vehicular social networks. IEEE Trans. Veh. Technol. **69**(6), 5813–5825 (2020). https://doi.org/10.1109/TVT.2019.2959383

18. Yan, X., Yuan, X., Ye, Q., Tang, Y.: Blockchain-based searchable encryption scheme with fair payment. IEEE Access **8**, 109687–109706 (2020). https://doi.org/10.1109/ACCESS.2020.3002264

19. Hu, S., Cai, C., Wang, Q., Wang, C., Luo, X., Ren, K.: Searching an encrypted cloud meets blockchain: a decentralized, reliable and fair realization, pp. 792–800. IEEE (2018). https://doi.org/10.1109/INFOCOM.2018.8485890

20. Li, H., Tian, H., Zhang, F.: Block chain based searchable symmetric encryption. IACR Cryptol. ePrint Arch. **2017**, 447 (2017)

GGCAD: A Novel Method of Adversarial Detection by Guided Grad-CAM

Zhun Zhang[✉], Qihe Liu, and Shijie Zhou

School of Information and Software Engineering, University of Electronic Science
and Technology of China, Chengdu 610054, China
201822090417@std.uestc.edu.cn, {qiheliu,sjzhou}@uestc.edu.cn

Abstract. The emergence of adversarial examples has seriously threat-
ened the security of deep learning models, and how to effectively detect
them has become an issue. Most of the existing detection methods have
low detection accuracy in the face of strong attacks such as C&W.
Inspired by the visualization techniques of the model, this paper proposes a Guided-Grade-Cam based method to detect adversarial examples, which mainly consists of two parts. The first part is to extract the
Guided Grad-CAM of the samples based on the model of resnet50. In
the second part, we construct a classifier to detect the adversarial examples by the differences of the Guided Grad-CAM. This method is the
first to introduce the model interpretation method into the detection
of adversarial examples. Through experimental observation, it is found
that there is a difference between the normal samples and the adversarial examples in Guided Grad-CAM, that is, the outlines information
is masked after the adversarial perturbations are added to the normal
samples. Experimental results on ImageNet based on the ResNet50 show
that our method achieves an average success rate of 99.2% in the face of
C&W attacks, which is superior to other methods.

Keywords: Adversarial examples detection · Deep learning · Class
activate mapping

1 Introduction

Deep learning algorithms have been widely used in various fields and achieved
excellent results [8]. However, deep learning algorithms also show extreme vulnerability to face the adversarial examples. By adding the small perturbations
to generate adversarial examples, which make the model misclassify with high
confidence. The emergence of adversarial examples poses a serious threat to the
security of deep learning models, and how to effectively defend against them
becomes an issue. Current defense strategies can be roughly divided into two

This work was supported in part by the Sichuan Science and Technology Program
under Grant No. 2020YFG0472.

categories: reinforcement of models and detection of adversarial examples [12]. This paper focuses on the detection of adversarial examples.

At present, the methods of adversarial examples detection can be roughly divided into weak attack detection and strong attack detection. And the adversarial perturbations added by strong attack are smaller than those by weak attacks, so it is difficult to detect strong attack. In terms of weak attack detection, Hendrycks and Gimpel [3,11] proposed three detection methods: Reconstruction, PCA and Softmax. However, these methods can only detect FGSM [2] and BIM [4]. Metzen et al. [6] proposed the Adversary Detector Network (ADN), which can realize the classification of adversarial examples by extending the binary detector network into a pre-trained neural network. ADN can effectively detect FGSM, DeepFool [7] and BIM, but it cannot detect strong attacks such as C&W [5]. Gong et al. [1] improved ADN, however, the improved method was still unable to detect C&W on the CIFAR10 dataset [12].

In terms of strong attack detection, Xu et al. [13] believed that the excessive dimension of input features was the reason for the emergence of adversarial examples. According to this principle, they proposed a detection method based on Feature squeezing (FS), which realized the detection by comparing the predicted results between squeezed and unsqueezed inputs.

Inspired by the model visualization method [9], we propose a novel method of adversarial examples detection by Guided Grad-CAM (GGCAD) to detect strong attacks such as C&W. The GGCAD includes a Resnet50-Guided Grade-CAM model for generating the Guided Grad-CAM (GGCAM) [9] and a binary classifier for the classification of adversarial examples. In this paper, the methods of model interpretation are used for the first time in adversarial examples detection. Through experimental observation, we find that the GGCAM of normal samples has very clear outlines, while the outlines information is masked after the adversarial perturbation is added. The proposed method protects the data input of the protected model in an additional form, without any modification of the protected model. Experimental results show that on ImageNet datasets our method can detect C&W attacks with an average accuracy of 99.2%, which is better than other detection methods. The main contributions of this paper are as follows:

(1) The methods of model interpretability are introduced into the adversarial example detection for the first time. By applying the model interpretability methods to analyze the feature of adversarial examples, it is found that there is a difference between normal samples and adversarial examples from the GGCAM. Due to the addition of adversarial perturbation, the outline information of the normal sample is masked.

(2) Based on the findings of (1), we propose a novel method of GGCAD to detect strong attacks. In this method, a Guided Grade-CAM model based on Resnet50 is constructed to generate GGCAM, and a classifier is constructed to detect the adversarial examples. The average accuracy can obtain 99.2%.

2   The Proposed Method of GGCAD

2.1   Feature Analysis of Adversarial Examples

Existing studies [14] have shown that the techniques of model interpretability likes Class Activate Mapping (CAM) [15] can explain why the adversarial examples are misclassified, as shown in Fig. 1. The first row is the normal sample and its corresponding CAM. The second row is the adversarial example and its corresponding CAM. Through observation, it can be found that the CAM of the adversarial sample is more scattered and disordered than that of the normal sample. It is because of the adversarial perturbation that the area of concern of the model changes, which leads to the result of misclassification.

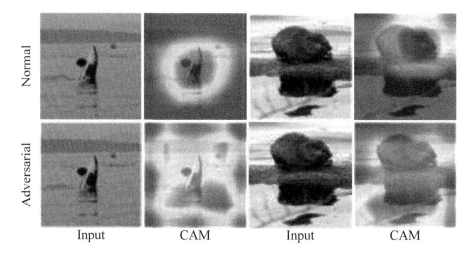

Fig. 1. Normal samples and adversarial examples and their corresponding CAM [14]. CAM in normal samples focuses on the animal itself, while CAM in adversarial examples focuses on a more diffuse area.

Inspired by this phenomenon, we introduce the method of model visualization into adversarial examples detection. In order to take into account the impact of fine-grained classification, experiments are carried out on the public ImageNet dataset and the widely used resnet50 model. The results are shown in Fig. 2. Among them, CAM, Guided-Backpropagation [10] (G-BP) and Guided Grad-CAM (GGCAM) are selected for feature observation. The first line is the interpretation feature map of normal samples, and the second line is the interpretation feature map of adversarial examples.

Through observation, we can find that the CAM are less differentiating (such as elephant), which is not suitable for sample detection. However, for other interpretation feature map, the addition of adversarial perturbation makes the contour of samples change greatly. The results show that the GGCAM and G-BP of the normal samples and the adversarial samples are obviously different.

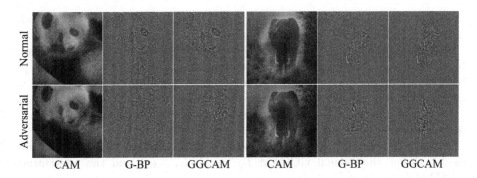

Fig. 2. Explanation feature map of normal sample and adversarial sample.

GGCAM is the result of G-CAM dot product by G-BP, which ignores part of the clutter information and is more conducive to detection. Therefore, based on this observation phenomenon, we design an adversarial examples detection method based on GGCAM.

2.2 Methodology Framework

The proposed GGCAD method is mainly divided into two parts. The first part is to generate GGCAM based on the model of resnet50, and the second part is the construction of the adversarial examples detection classifier. The overall framework is shown in Fig. 3.

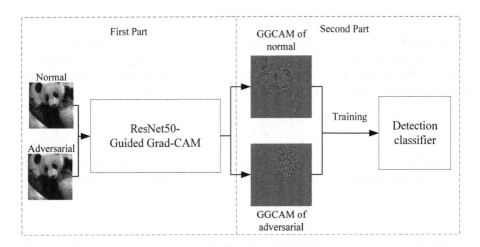

Fig. 3. The framework of adversarial example detection method based on GGCAM.

The first part is to generate GGCAM, such as Step 1 to Step 3. The second part is to use the GGCAM to train the detection classifier, such as Step 4 to Step 6. Step 7 is the detection stage.

Step1: Normalize the dateset $X = \{x_1, x_2, ..., x_n\}$ and resize the pictures into 299×299, where x_i is the sample and n is the number of samples;

Step2: Convert the samples in the dataset X to the adversarial examples by the method of C&W, and get the adversarial dataset $X' = \{x'_1, x'_2, ..., x'_m\}$, because not all samples can generate adversarial examples, so there may be a $m \neq n$, and m is the number of adversarial examples;

Step3: Construct the model T by based on ResNet50, which is mainly used to generate the GGCAM;

Step4: Respectively input the dataset X and adversarial dataset X' to the model T, get the normal GGCAM $L_n = \{l_1, l_2, ..., l_n\}$ and the adversarial GGCAM $L'_m = \{l'_1, l'_2, ..., l'_m\}$;

Step5: A classifier D is constructed to realize the classification of adversarial examples;

Step6: L_n and L'_m were input into the classifier D as the training data labeled as normal and adversarial respectively, and the trained binary classifier D_{dec} was obtained;

Step7: In the test stage, input the test data X_{te} to the model T, to get the GGCAM L_{te}, and input the L_{te} into the trained classifier D_{dec}, to realize the detection of adversarial examples.

Next, we will introduce the combination model of ResNet50-Guided-Grad-CAM and the construction of classifier model in details.

2.3 The Combination Model of ResNet50-Guided-Grad-CAM

This part mainly includes G-BP and Gard-CAM, where the Gard-CAM is a simple improvement of CAM. The specific steps are as follows:

Step1: Calculate the gradient of the classification score y^c of the class c with respect to the feature a^k of the convolution layer, that is $\frac{\partial y^c}{\partial A^k}$. Set backpropagation gradient to global average, to get the weight of feature map α_k^c. It is shown in the following formula, Where Z is the size of feature A^k.

$$\alpha_k^c = \frac{1}{Z} \sum_i \sum_j \frac{\partial y^c}{\partial A_{ij}^k} \tag{1}$$

Step2: After obtaining the weight α_k^c of the feature map, the feature map is weighted and combined to obtain the activation mapping L^c, as shown in the following formula.

$$L^c = \sum_k \alpha_k^c A^k \tag{2}$$

Step3: Since only the features that have a positive impact on class c are of interest, and the negative pixels may belong to other classes, $ReLU$ is used to calculate L^c to obtain the class activation mapping $L_{Gard-CAM}^c$, as shown in the following equation.

$$L_{Gard-CAM}^c = ReLU(\sum_k \alpha_k^c A^k) \tag{3}$$

Step4: The main difference between backpropagation and DeconvNet is the non-linear way in which they are handled through $ReLU$. The forward transfer operation at $ReLU$ is shown in Eq. (4), where f_I^l is the input to the $ReLU$ layer. The threshold value selected by the backpropagation method during the operation of $ReLU$ is the feature value of forwarding transmission, as shown in Eq. (5), where f^{out} is the output of the hidden layer. While DeconvNet uses the gradient value as the threshold, as shown in Eq. (6). G-BP combines backpropagation with DeconvNet and is able to well visualize features learned at higher levels of the neural network, as shown in Eq. (7).

$$f_i^{l+1} = ReLU(f_i^l) = max(f_i^l, 0) \tag{4}$$

$$R_i^l = R_i^{l+1} \cdot (f_i^l > 0), R_i^{l+1} = \frac{\partial f^{out}}{\partial f_i^{l+1}} \tag{5}$$

$$R_i^l = R_i^{l+1} \cdot (R_i^{l+1} > 0) \tag{6}$$

$$R_i^l = R_i^{l+1} \cdot (R_i^{l+1} > 0) \cdot (f_i^l) \tag{7}$$

Step5: The class activation mapping obtained by Grad-CAM method is extended by linear interpolation using interpolation functions of two variables, and the size of the class activation mapping after upsampling is the same as that of the input sample. Then the dot product of G-BP and Grad-CAM is calculated. As shown in Eq. (8), B represents the bilinear interpolation operation. Finally, the GGCAM is obtained.

$$L_{GuidedGrad-CAM}^c = R_i^l \cdot B(L_{Grad-CAM}^c) \tag{8}$$

2.4 Classifier

The classifier constructed in this paper consists of four continuous Convolution, ResNet, Pooling, plus a full connection layer and Softmax classifier. The training process of this classification model is as follows:

Step1: The normal dataset $X = \{x_1, x_2, ..., x_n\}$ and the adversarial dataset $X' = \{x_1', x_2', ..., x_m'\}$ marked as normal and adversarial two classes respectively are entered into the model together.

Step2: The samples are respectively passed through four modules composed of Convolution layer, ResNet layer and the Pooling layer. Finally, enter the Dense layer and Softmax, in which the gradient descent formula of the ResNet layer is:

$$\frac{\partial X_L}{\partial X_l} = \frac{\partial X_l + F(X_L, W_L, b_L)}{\partial X_l} = 1 + \frac{F(X_L, W_L, b_l)}{\partial X_l} \tag{9}$$

where, $F(X_L, W_L, B_L)$ represents the loss function.

Step3: The trained adversarial examples detection model T is obtained.

3   Experiment

3.1   Dataset

Due to the large amount of ImageNet, only its verification set (50000 images) is taken as the dataset of this experiment. In the part of adversarial example generation, 50000 normal samples are transformed into adversarial samples through C&W method, and the data processing is shown in Table 1.

Table 1. Adversarial examples generation

Data	Class	Number	Success rate	Sum
50000	Normal	50000	55.13%	77563
	Adversarial	27563		

In order to fully test the detection effect of the experiment, this paper adopts random division in the partition of the dataset, and takes about 30% of the dataset as the verification set for the experiment. The data partition is shown in Table 2.

Table 2. The division of dataset

Type	Class	Number	Sum
Training set	Normal	35000	54294
	Adversarial	19294	
Validation set	Normal	15000	23269
	Adversarial	8269	

3.2   The Result of Experiment

Among them, the validation sets (A1, A2, A3) of each experiment are different, consisting of about 30% of the normal samples and about 30% of the adversarial examples randomly selected. The training set is about 70% of the remaining data. The validation set consisted of 15,000 normal samples and 8269 adversarial examples.

Feature Sprawling (FS), the most effective adversarial examples detection method now, is chosen as the contrast experiment of this experiment. Among them, there are 15000 normal samples and 8269 adversarial examples in the verification set. Experiments are in the same environment, the results are shown in Table 4.

Table 3. Three experiments of GGCAD with different validation set

Experiment	Class	Number	Recall	Precision	Accuracy
A1	Normal	15000	0.995	0.994	0.993
	Adversarial	8269	0.989	0.991	
A2	Normal	15000	0.994	0.994	0.992
	Adversarial	8269	0.990	0.989	
A3	Normal	15000	0.994	0.993	0.992
	Adversarial	8269	0.987	0.990	

Table 4. Comparative experiments

Method	Adversarial examples	TP	FP	TN	FN	Recall	Precision	Accuracy
FS	8269	7640	2129	12871	629	0.924	0.782	0.881
GGCAD	8269	8184	72	14928	85	0.989	0.991	0.993

3.3 Discussion

The experimental results shows:

(1) The average accuracy of the proposed method in detecting C&W attacks is 99.2%, which means the proposed method is effective in the detection of adversarial examples by the methods of model interpretable.

As is shown in Table 3, the results of the three experiments were almost identical. The recall and the precision have obtained about 99% in the result of each experiment, indicating that it is feasible to apply the methods of model interpretable to the detection of adversarial examples. Through observation data, it is found that the classification success rate of adversarial examples is slightly lower than that of the normal samples, which may be due to the small number of adversarial examples.

(2) Table 4 show that our method is better than FS which is the most effective detection method now.

It is found in Table 4 that the FP of FS is too high, that is, a large number of normal samples are classified as adversarial examples, which leads to low precision. The comparative experiment proves that our method has superior performance in the classification of both normal samples and adversarial examples.

(3) At the same time, we observe that a very small number of normal sample will also disperse the focus of the model, and a very small number of adversarial examples will also keep the focus of the model consistent.

In the first experiment, 73 of the normal samples were misclassified, and 86 of the adversarial examples were misclassified.

In the misclassified normal samples (Fig. 4, truly labeled as normal samples, but classified as adversarial examples), except for the clear outline of the first one, the rest of the contours are fuzzy, similar to the antagonized samples in this

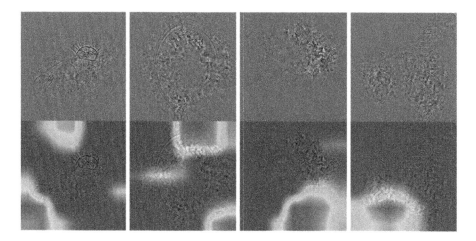

Fig. 4. Normal samples that have been misclassified

experiment. The outline of the first column of images is so clear that the shape of a baby can be seen by the eyes, but the CAM results show that the model is focusing on other scattered places rather than the baby. Therefore, a normal sample without adding any perturbation will also make the position of concern of the model deviate and lead to misjudgment. The contour of the second, third and fourth column images is not very clear, especially the third and fourth columns, because the contour information is not completely extracted in the gradient extraction of the model, so they are misjudged as adversarial examples by the classifier.

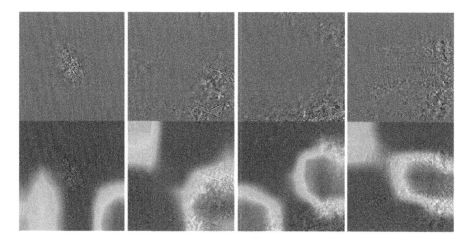

Fig. 5. Adversarial examples that have been misclassified

In the misclassified adversarial examples (Fig. 5, real labels for the adversarial examples, but were classified as normal samples), can be divided into two classes. The first class is column 1 and column 3. The contours almost disappear due to the addition of adversarial perturbation. It can also be seen from CAM that the region concerned by the model is not in the region with the largest gradient change. The second class is column 2 and column 4. Although the adversarial perturbation is added, their outline is still relatively clear. In the first class, the region concerned by the model is relatively scattered through the addition of adversarial perturbation, and it is all in the position where the gradient change is not obvious. In the second class, benches and letter plates can be distinguished, and the CAM shows that the area the model focuses on is the area with a clear outline, so the adversarial examples are identified as the normal samples.

4   Conclusion

The Guided Grad-Cam method proposed by us can effectively implement the detection of adversarial examples. Compared with other adversarial examples detection methods, this method is simpler and can be used to detect strong attacks such as C&W, with a success rate of 99.2%. Experiments show the superiority of our method. From the experiment results, normal samples with a clear outline are recognized as adversarial examples in column 1 (as shown in Fig. 4). And adversarial examples with a fuzzy outline are recognized as normal examples (as shown in Fig. 5 first, three columns). Therefore, model visualization technology does not bring trust to the model, it can only represent the area of concern of the model. What features the model learns in the deeper position of the pixel still needs to be further studied, which is also the focus of the next research.

References

1. Gong, Z., Wang, W., Ku, W.S.: Adversarial and clean data are not twins (2017)
2. Goodfellow, I.J., Shlens, J., Szegedy, C.: Explaining and harnessing adversarial examples. Computer Science (2014)
3. Hendrycks, D., Gimpel, K.: Visible progress on adversarial images and a new saliency map. CoRR, abs/1608.00530 (2016)
4. Kurakin, A., Goodfellow, I., Bengio, S.: Adversarial machine learning at scale. arXiv (2016)
5. Liu, M., Shi, J., Li, Z., Li, C., Zhu, J., Liu, S.: Towards better analysis of deep convolutional neural networks. IEEE Trans. Visualization Comput. Graph. **18**, 1 (2016)
6. Metzen, J.H., Genewein, T., Fischer, V., Bischoff, B.: On detecting adversarial perturbations. arXiv preprint arXiv:1702.04267 (2017)
7. Moosavi-Dezfooli, S.M., Fawzi, A., Frossard, P.: Deepfool: a simple and accurate method to fool deep neural networks (2016)
8. Qiu, S., Liu, Q., Zhou, S., Wu, C.: Review of artificial intelligence adversarial attack and defense technologies. Appl. Sci. **9**(5), 909 (2019)

9. Selvaraju, R.R., Cogswell, M., Das, A., Vedantam, R., Parikh, D., Batra, D.: Grad-cam: visual explanations from deep networks via gradient-based localization. Int. J. Comput. Vision **128**(2), 336–359 (2020)
10. Springenberg, J., Dosovitskiy, A., Brox, T., Riedmiller, M.: Striving for simplicity: The all convolutional net. eprint arxiv (2014)
11. Tanay, T., Griffin, L.: A boundary tilting persepective on the phenomenon of adversarial examples (2016)
12. Wiyatno, R.R., Xu, A., Dia, O., Berker, A.D.: Adversarial examples in modern machine learning: a review (2019)
13. Xu, W., Evans, D., Qi, Y.: Feature squeezing: detecting adversarial examples in deep neural networks. In: Network and Distributed System Security Symposium (2017)
14. Zhang, X., Wang, N., Shen, H., Ji, S., Luo, X., Wang, T.: Interpretable deep learning under fire. In: 29th {USENIX} Security Symposium ({USENIX} Security 20) (2020)
15. Zhou, B., Khosla, A., Lapedriza, A., Oliva, A., Torralba, A.: Learning deep features for discriminative localization. In: CVPR (2016)

Online Task Scheduling for DNN-Based Applications over Cloud, Edge and End Devices

Lixiang Zhong, Jiugen Shi, Lei Shi$^{(\boxtimes)}$, Juan Xu, Yuqi Fan, and Zhigang Xu

School of Computer Science and Information Engineering,
Hefei University of Technology, Hefei 230009, China
shilei@hfut.edu.cn

Abstract. As a combination of artificial intelligence (AI) and edge computing, edge intelligence has made great contributions in pushing AI applications to the edge of the network, especially in reducing delay, saving energy and improving privacy. However, most of researchers only considered the computation approach of end device to edge server and ignored the scheduling of multi-task. In this paper, we study DNN model partition and online task scheduling over cloud, edge and devices for deadline-aware DNN inference tasks. We first establish our mathematical model and find the model can not be solved directly because the solution space is too large. Therefore, we propose the partition point filtering algorithm to reduce the solution space. Then by jointly considering management of the networking bandwidth and computing resources, we propose our online scheduling algorithm to meet the maximum number of deadlines. Experiments and simulations show that our online algorithm reduces deadline miss ratio by up to 51% compared with other four typical computation approaches.

Keywords: Edge computing · Edge intelligence · Model partition · Task scheduling

1 Introduction

In recent years, machine learning, especially deep learning, has attracted significant attention from both industry and academia. As the key component of deep learning, Deep Neural Networks (DNNs) is widely used in various fields, such as natural language [1], computer vision [2], speech recognition [3] and so on. With the growth of the number of Internet of Things (IoT) devices, the traditional cloud-centric computating approach will inevitably lead to network congestion, high transmission delay and privacy disclosure [4–6]. Therefore, it is a trend to offload the computation to the end device. However, Internet of Things devices with limited energy and computing resources cannot afford computing-intensive tasks.

Z. Xu—Supported by the National Natural Science Foundation of China (Grant No. 61806067), the Anhui Provincial Key R&D Program of China (202004a05020040).

© Springer Nature Switzerland AG 2021
Z. Liu et al. (Eds.): WASA 2021, LNCS 12939, pp. 183–191, 2021.
https://doi.org/10.1007/978-3-030-86137-7_20

Edge computing (EC) is proposed as a promising computing model for solving these problems by deploying servers at the network edge close to the end devices [7]. In [8], authors define a query processing problem in an Edge Assisted IoT Data Monitoring System which aims to deriving a distributed query plan with the minimum query response latency. In [9,10], the authors studied task scheduling and resource allocation in edge computing environment for different scenarios, and the experimental results have been significantly improved. In [11], authors set the weighted value of the delay sensitivity of the task, and optimized the offloading strategy of the task with the goal of minimizing the total weighted corresponding time of all tasks. In addition, edge computing has great potential in smart cities [12] and smart homes [13].

Indeed, the combination of artificial intelligence and edge computing has given rise to a new research area, namely edge intelligence, which was proposed in [14]. Instead of entirely relying on the cloud, edge intelligence makes the most of the widespread edge resources to perform tasks such as DNN inference. On this basis, offloading for DNN-based applications in EC has been broadly studied. In [15], authors proposed the DeepWear model, which uses DNN model partition to offload tasks to wearable applications, and achieves a good acceleration effect. In [16], authors realized the task offloading through model partition, and combined with the model early exit technology to further reduce the delay of DNN-based applications. In [17], authors proposed the partition and offloading strategy which can make the optimal tradeoff between performance and privacy for mobile devices. In [18], authors proposed a technique to divide a DNN in multiple partitions that can be processed locally by end devices or offloaded to one or multiple powerful nodes.

Previous work has made some contributions in the field of edge intelligence. However, most of them only considered the computation approach of end device to edge server and ignored the scheduling of multi-task. In this paper, for deadline-aware DNN inference tasks, we study DNN model partition and online task scheduling over cloud, edge and devices. We first establish our mathematical model, which can hybridly exploit all the available resources from the cloud, the edge and the devices to unleash all the full power of the deep learning networks therein. Since the model contains a large number of variables, which make the model can not be solved directly because the solution space is too large, we propose the partition point filtering algorithm to reduce the solution space. Then by jointly considering management of the networking bandwidth and computing resources, we propose our online scheduling algorithm to meet the maximum number of deadlines. Experiments and simulations show that our online algorithm achieves better performance than other typical computing approaches.

The rest of this paper is organized as follows: In Sect. 2, we introduce our system model and define our problem. In Sect. 3, we give the model partition filtering algorithm and online scheduling algorithm respectively. In Sect. 4, we give the simulation results and analyze them. In Sect. 5, we summarize this paper.

2   System Model and Problem Definition

2.1   DNN Model Partition and Network

Consider a two-dimensional network consists of n servers, m end devices and one cloud center. Denote C as the could center, s_j $(s_j \in S, j = 0, \ldots n)$ as one of the edge servers and d_i $(d_i \in D, i = 0 \ldots m)$ as one of the end devices. As shown in Fig. 1, we consider that edge servers are heterogeneous and have different computing power, end devices are all of the same specifications and have the same computing power, and cloud center has the strongest computing power.

For the whole task scheduling time T, it is divided into h time slots and each time slot is expressed as t_τ $(\tau = 0 \ldots h)$. The length of t_τ is 1 ms. The task may be generated at any time slot, and the transmission time and calculation time of the task are counted in time slot. For one end device, the next task can only be generated after the current task is completed. Each end device or edge server can only compute one task at a time and there is no waiting queue, while the cloud center can compute multiple tasks at the same time. We denote m_i^τ as one of the task, where i means the task is generated by device d_i, and τ means the task is generated in the τ-th time slot.

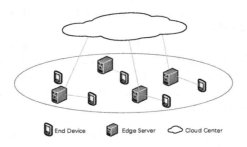

Fig. 1. System model.

We suppose that all tasks are inference tasks of the same DNN model. The model has r layers, and we denote $l_k(k = 0, 1 \ldots r)$ as one of the layer. We denote $G_k(k = 0, 1 \ldots r)$ as output data size of the lay l_k. It is obvious that G_0 means the size of the input data and G_r means the size of the result of the model.

As shown in Fig. 2, each task can be divided into up to three parts, which can be computed in turn on the end device, the edge server, and the cloud center. Therefore, by comprehensively considering all the current tasks, our formulated problem should not only determine the partition point, but also consider the appropriate scheduling of the partitioned DNN inference tasks, so that as many tasks as possible can be completed before the deadline in the scheduling time.

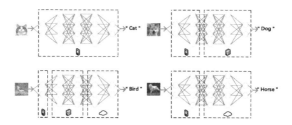

Fig. 2. Four typical DNN partition strategies.

2.2   Problem Formulation

For each task m_i^τ, its total completion time $t(m_i^\tau)$ can be expressed as

$$t(m_i^\tau) = t_d(m_i^\tau) + t_e^\uparrow(m_i^\tau) + t_e(m_i^\tau) + t_c^\uparrow(m_i^\tau) + t_c(m_i^\tau). \tag{1}$$

The total completion time is made up of five parts. The first part $t_d(m_i^\tau)$ is the computing time of the task in the end device. The second part $t_e^\uparrow(m_i^\tau)$ is the transmission time of the intermediate data from the device to the edge server. The third part $t_e(m_i^\tau)$ is the computing time of the task in the edge server. The fourth part $t_c^\uparrow(m_i^\tau)$ is the transmission time of the intermediate data from the edge server to the cloud center, and the fifth part $t_c(m_i^\tau)$ is the computing time of the task in the cloud center.

For the $t_d(m_i^\tau)$, we use binary variable $x_u(m_i^\tau)$ to indicate whether the first partition point is the layer l_u. If the first partition point is the layer l_u, $x_u(m_i^\tau) = 1$, which means after computing layer l_u, the device will upload the intermediate data to the edge server and no longer participates in the computation of the task m_i^τ. Otherwise, $x_u(m_i^\tau) = 0$.

$$x_u(m_i^\tau) = \begin{cases} 1 : & \text{the first partition point is the layer } l_u; \\ 0 : & \text{otherwise.} \end{cases} \tag{2}$$

It satisfies

$$\sum_{u=0}^{r} x_u(m_i^\tau) = 1. \tag{3}$$

We express $t_d(m_i^\tau)$ as the time cost for computation from l_0 to l_u for d_i. It can be calculated by

$$t_d(m_i^\tau) = \sum_{u=0}^{r} \left(x_u(m_i^\tau) \cdot \sum_{k=0}^{u} \alpha_i^k \right), \tag{4}$$

where α_i^k represents the time cost for d_i to compute the lay l_k of DNN model.

For the $t_e^\uparrow(m_i^\tau)$, we use binary variable $y_j(m_i^\tau)$ to indicate whether the task m_i^τ is uploaded to the edge server s_j. If the task is uploaded to the server s_j, $y_j(m_i^\tau) = 1$. Otherwise $y_j(m_i^\tau) = 0$.

$$y_j(m_i^\tau) = \begin{cases} 1 : & \text{the task is uploaded to the edge server } s_j; \\ 0 : & \text{otherwise.} \end{cases} \tag{5}$$

It satisfies

$$\sum_{j=0}^{n} y_j\left(m_i^\tau\right) = 1. \tag{6}$$

Then we express $t_e^\uparrow\left(m_i^\tau\right)$ as the time cost for transmission from d_i to s_j. It can be calculated by

$$t_e^\uparrow\left(m_i^\tau\right) = \sum_{j=0}^{n}\left(y_j\left(m_i^\tau\right) \cdot \sum_{u=0}^{r}\left(x_u\left(m_i^\tau\right) \cdot \frac{G_u}{b_j\left(m_i^\tau\right)}\right)\right), \tag{7}$$

where $b_j\left(m_i^\tau\right)$ represents the bandwidth allocated between d_i and s_j for m_i^τ. The bandwidth $b_j\left(m_i^\tau\right)$ satisfies

$$0 < b_j\left(m_i^\tau\right) \le b, \tag{8}$$

$$\sum_{j=0}^{n} b_j\left(m_i^\tau\right) \le b, \tag{9}$$

where b represents the total bandwidth between all edge servers and devices.

For the $t_e\left(m_i^\tau\right)$, we use binary variable $y_j\left(m_i^\tau\right)$ to indicate whether the second partition point is l_v. If the second partition point is l_v, $z_v\left(m_i^\tau\right) = 1$, which means after computing layer l_v, the edge server will upload the intermediate data to cloud center. Otherwise, $z_v\left(m_i^\tau\right) = 0$.

$$z_v\left(m_i^\tau\right) = \begin{cases} 1: & \text{the second partition point is the layer } l_v; \\ 0: & \text{otherwise.} \end{cases} \tag{10}$$

It satisfies

$$\sum_{v=0}^{r} z_v\left(m_i^\tau\right) = 1. \tag{11}$$

It should be noted that when $v = u$, the edge server does not participate in the computation of the task and uploads the task directly to cloud center. Then we express $t_e\left(m_i^\tau\right)$ as the time cost for computation from l_{u+1} to l_v of DNN model for s_j. It can be calculated by

$$t_s\left(m_i^\tau\right) = \sum_{v=0}^{r}\left(z_v\left(m_i^\tau\right) \cdot \sum_{u=0}^{r}\left(x_u\left(m_i^\tau\right) \cdot \sum_{k=u+1}^{v} \beta_i^k\right)\right), \tag{12}$$

where β_i^k represents the time cost for s_j to compute the lay l_k of DNN model.

For the $t_c^\uparrow\left(m_i^\tau\right)$, we express it as the time cost for transmission from s_j to C. It can be calculated by

$$t_c^\uparrow\left(m_i^\tau\right) = \sum_{v=0}^{r}\left(z_v\left(m_i^\tau\right) \cdot \frac{G_v}{b_c}\right), \tag{13}$$

where b_c represents the bandwidth between edge servers and cloud center.

For the $t_c(m_i^\tau)$, we express it as the time cost for computation from l_{v+1} to l_r of DNN model for cloud center. It can be calculated by

$$t_c(m_i^\tau) = \sum_{v=0}^{r} \left(z_v(m_i^\tau) \cdot \sum_{k=v+1}^{r} \gamma_i^k \right), \tag{14}$$

where γ_i^k represents the time cost for C to compute the lay l_k of DNN model.

For each task m_i^τ, there is a deadline $D(m_i^\tau)$. If $t(m_i^\tau) > D(m_i^\tau)$, the task misses its deadline. We denote N as the total number of tasks generated during the scheduling time and N_{miss} as the total number of tasks that missed deadline. Then the deadline miss rate for tasks is

$$\eta_{miss} = \frac{N_{miss}}{N}. \tag{15}$$

Our problem can be formulated as

$$\begin{aligned} &\min \quad \eta_{miss} \\ &\text{s.t. } (3)(4)(6)(7)(8)(9)(11)(12)(13)(14)(15). \end{aligned} \tag{16}$$

In (16), α_i^k, G_u, b, β_i^k, b_c, γ_i^k are are all constants or determined values for specific network. $x_u(m_i^\tau)$, $y_j(m_i^\tau)$, $b_j(m_i^\tau)$ and $b_j(m_i^\tau)$ are variables. However, these variables appear in almost different forms in all formulas, which makes the original problem model complex and difficult to solve directly. Therefore, for the problem to be solved in polynomial time, we need to make further analysis and find some ways to reduce the complexity of the original problem.

3   Algorithm

In this section, we introduce the algorithm to solve the optimization problem. In the optimization problem, the variables are $x_u(m_i^\tau)$, $y_j(m_i^\tau)$, $b_j(m_i^\tau)$ and $z_v(m_i^\tau)$, which are not independent but restrict each other. The variables $z_v(m_i^\tau)$ and $z_v(m_i^\tau)$ which control the partition point will influence the variables $y_j(m_i^\tau)$ and $b_j(m_i^\tau)$ which correspond to the scheduling strategy. In order to solve this problem, we propose online scheduling algorithm for multi-task computation.

3.1   Partition Point Filtering

As we all know, the layered structure of the neural network determines it can be divided at any layer. However, through the analysis of the structural characteristics and the number of parameters of each layer, we find that some neural network layers have no potential to become partition point. Therefore, we propose a DNN partition point filtering algorithm, which can effectively help us to get a suitable set of partition points κ. We first calculate the corresponding total delay for different partition points. Then we give a delay baseline L and take the partition point where the total delay is less than the baseline as the optional partition point. Since the number of parameters in each layer in the DNN model is structural characteristics, these partition points will perform well on heterogeneous edge servers. At the same time, due to the great reduction of the number of optional partition points, the solution space of the later algorithm can be further reduced.

3.2   Online Strategy

For the online strategy, we propose a scheduling solution for multi-task. We dynamically allocate the bandwidth of the end device and the edge server, and try to calculate the total task time under the hybrid computing approach. While minimizing the deadline miss rate, we choose the computation strategy with the minimum total time. We schedule tasks when there is no idle server, and try to maximize the computing resources of edge servers by means of preemption.

We first determine the number of tasks n_τ generated by the current time slot, the deadline of the task, and the status s_{sta}^j of each edge server. When s_j is working, $s_{sta}^j = 1$. Othwewise $s_{sta}^j = 0$. We denote b_τ as the total bandwidth that can be allocated for the τ-th time slot and n_b^τ as the number of servers that need to allocate bandwidth. We determine the bandwidth between device and server based on the deadline. We select the optimal partition strategy with the minimum total computing time, and calculate the time t_j^{up} for the task to be uploaded to the edge server. When all the partition strategies fail to meet the deadline requirements of the task, we will upload the task to S_0, where S_0 does not participate in the computation of the task.

It should be noted that after the end device completes the computation, the edge server starts to compute at time t_j^{up}. The computing resources of the edge server are available during this period of time. When all edge servers are scheduled but there are still tasks, we first try to use the partition strategy to schedule these tasks. If there is no edge server that meets the requirements, we let the task compute on the edge server as much as possible and choose the partition strategy with the minimum total time. If the task still cannot be completed by the deadline, we upload the task to S_0.

4   Simulation and Experiment

In this section, we present experiments to demonstrate the performance of our algorithms. The DNN model in experiments is VGG16 and the input data is a set of RGB images with each of the size is $320 \times 320 \times 3$. All tasks in our system are inference task and the programming backend is pytorch. The devices are HP notebook computers with Inter Core i5-6200U 2.3 GHz quad core CPU. The edge servers are computers with different processors. The cloud center is the Google Cloud Platform with NVIDIA Ampere A100 GPU.

We first get the values of α_i^k, β_i^k, γ_i^k and G_k and then calculate the total computing time under different partition points and get the optional partition point set κ. We deploy several end devices, 8 edge servers, and a cloud center in the network. The total bandwidth b is set to $800\,Mbps$, where $s_0 = 100\,Mbps$, $b_c = 35\,Mbps$. h is set to 1000. We get the deadline miss rate η_{miss} under five different approaches and the result of each approach is the average of 20 repeated experiments. According to the analysis of the structural characteristics of VGG16, we find that there are five points have the smallest amount of intermediate data. Therefore, we believe that whether these five partition points can perform well in any case.

In 1000 time slots, for a different number of tasks, we get the deadline miss rate η_{miss} under five different computation approaches. The result is shown in Fig. 3.

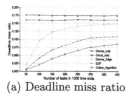
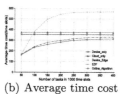

(a) Deadline miss ratio   (b) Average time cost

Fig. 3. Simulation result. (a) Deadline miss ratio under different number of tasks. (b) Average time cost under different number of tasks

As shown in the Fig. 3(a), when the number of tasks increases gradually, the performance online scheduling algorithm is obviously better. In Fig. 3(b), we show the average completion time of a task. Obviously, our online algorithm has an advantage in any number of tasks.

5   Conclusion

In this paper, we study DNN model partition and online task scheduling over cloud, edge and devices for deadline-aware DNN inference tasks. We first establish our mathematical model and find that the model contains a large number of variables. Therefore, we propose the partition point filtering algorithm to reduce the solution space. Then we propose our online scheduling algorithm to meet the maximum number of deadlines. Experiments and simulations show that our online algorithm reduces deadline miss ratio by up to 51% compared with other four typical computation approaches.

References

1. Li, H.: Deep learning for natural language processing: advantages and challenges. Nat. Sci. Rev. **5**, 24–26 (2018)
2. Parkhi, O.M., Vedaldi, A., Zisserman, A.: Deep face recognition, pp. 41.1–41.12. BMVA Press (2015)

3. Nassif, A.B., Shahin, I., Attili, I.B., Azzeh, M., Shaalan, K.: Speech recognition using deep neural networks: a systematic review. IEEE Access **7**, 19143–19165 (2019)
4. Li, S., Xu, L., Zhao, S.: The internet of things: a survey. Inf. Syst. Front. **17**, 243–259 (2015)
5. Chettri, L., Bera, R.: A comprehensive survey on internet of things (iot) toward 5G wireless systems. IEEE Internet Things J. **7**, 16–32 (2020)
6. Cai, Z., Zheng, X.: A private and efficient mechanism for data uploading in smart cyber-physical systems. IEEE Trans. Netw. Sci. Eng. **7**, 766–775 (2020)
7. Shi, W., Cao, J., Zhang, Q., Li, Y., Xu, L.: Edge computing: vision and challenges. IEEE Internet Things J. **3**, 637–646 (2016)
8. Cai, Z., Shi, T.: Distributed query processing in the edge assisted IoT data monitoring system. IEEE Internet Things J. **8**, 12679–12693 (2020)
9. Zhu, T., Shi, T., Li, J., Cai, Z., Zhou, X.: Task scheduling in deadline-aware mobile edge computing systems. IEEE Internet Things J. **6**, 4854–4866 (2019)
10. Duan, Z., Li, W., Cai, Z.: Distributed auctions for task assignment and scheduling in mobile crowdsensing systems. In: 2017 IEEE 37th International Conference on Distributed Computing Systems (ICDCS), pp. 635–644 (2017)
11. Han, Z., Tan, H., Li, X., Jiang, S.H., Li, Y., Lau, F.C.M.: Ondisc: online latency-sensitive job dispatching and scheduling in heterogeneous edge-clouds. IEEE/ACM Trans. Netw. **27**, 2472–2485 (2019)
12. Khan, L.U., Yaqoob, I., Tran, N.H., Kazmi, S.M.A., Tri, N.D., Hong, C.: Edge-computing-enabled smart cities: a comprehensive survey. IEEE Internet Things J. **7**, 10200–10232 (2020)
13. Alam, M.R., Reaz, M., Ali, M.A.: A review of smart homes: past, present, and future. IEEE Trans. Syst. Man Cybern. Part C Appl. Rev. **42**, 1190–1203 (2012)
14. Zhou, Z., Chen, X., Li, E., Zeng, L., Luo, K., Zhang, J.: Edge intelligence: paving the last mile of artificial intelligence with edge computing. Proc. IEEE **107**, 1738–1762 (2019)
15. Xu, M., Qian, F., Zhu, M., Huang, F., Pushp, S., Liu, X.: Deepwear: adaptive local offloading for on-wearable deep learning. IEEE Trans. Mobile Comput. **19**, 314–330 (2020)
16. Li, E., Zeng, L., Zhou, Z., Chen, X.: Edge AI: on-demand accelerating deep neural network inference via edge computing. IEEE Trans. Wirel. Commun. **19**, 447–457 (2020)
17. Shi, C., Chen, L., Shen, C., Song, L., Xu, J.: Privacy-aware edge computing based on adaptive DNN partitioning. In: 2019 IEEE Global Communications Conference (GLOBECOM), pp. 1–6 (2019)
18. Mohammed, T., Joe-Wong, C., Babbar, R., Francesco, M.D.: Distributed inference acceleration with adaptive DNN partitioning and offloading. In: IEEE INFOCOM 2020 - IEEE Conference on Computer Communications, pp. 854–863 (2020)

An SDN-Based Self-adaptive Resource Allocation Mechanism for Service Customization

Zhaoyang Dai[1], Xingwei Wang[1(✉)], Bo Yi[1], Min Huang[2], and Zhengyu Li[1]

[1] College of Computer Science and Engineering, Northeastern University,
Shenyang 110169, China
wangxw@mail.neu.edu.cn
[2] College of Information Science and Engineering, Northeastern University,
Shenyang 110819, China

Abstract. With the emergence of tremendous novel network applications, the user demand on service quality becomes not only higher, but also more diverse. To address these challenges, the Quality of Experience (QoE) and Quality of Service (QoS) should both be improved. In this regard, we intend to offer a fine-grained and customized service model for users with the objective of minimizing the overall cost. In this model, the idea of Software Defined Networking (SDN) is introduced to implement a self-adaptive resource allocation mechanism. Specifically, the proposed mechanism consists of four parts which are the topology management, the resource monitoring, the service customization and the routing management. In particular, the first two parts are used to support service customization and routing, while the third part is used to compose services and the last part is used to achieve the self-adaptive resource allocation. Experimental results show that the proposed mechanism can achieve better performance in terms of the network resource utilization and the average packet loss rate.

Keywords: Resource allocation mechanism · Service customization · SDN · Ant colony algorithm

1 Introduction

With the emergence of novel network applications, traditional network uses best-effort service which means all applications should compete for limited network resources fairly. However, some types of applications are sensitive to delay and bandwidth, which need to be treated differently from other applications.

In previous research, great effort has been paid on service customization and network resource allocation. SDN has global visibility, which has been widely used in resource allocation [1]. SDN and NFV are combined for service customization [2–4], which use the knowledge obtained by SDN controller. The work presented in [4–8] achieve consistent quality of service supply for multiple

Z. Liu et al. (Eds.): WASA 2021, LNCS 12939, pp. 192–199, 2021.
https://doi.org/10.1007/978-3-030-86137-7_21

service level network slices. The work presented in [9–11] used machine learning to dynamically allocate real-time service flow in SDN network. The work presented in [9,10,12] proposed the ant colony optimization algorithm to solve the routing problem. Besides, the genetic optimization algorithm was proposed to solve the problem of slow convergence speed [13,14].

In this paper, we design a self-adaptive resource allocation mechanism based on SDN and propose a self-adaptive resource allocation (SARA) algorithm to customize the personalized service for the diverse user demands. The contributions of our research are summarized as follows:

- We propose the service customized self-adaptive resource allocation mechanism based on SDN, which can select the corresponding resources and dynamically route according to the service types and levels selected by users.
- In order to improve the speed of response, we propose SARA algorithm based on ant colony algorithm to calculate the optimal path for the application.
- The experimental results show that the proposed mechanism can achieve better performance, which is superior to the existing solutions.

The rest of the paper is organized as follows. Section 2, 3 and 4 introduces the proposed mechanism and algorithm in detail. Section 5 explains the experimental results. Section 6 emphasizes conclusions and discuss plans for future.

2   System Framework

Figure 1 shows the overall system framework of the proposed mechanism. The system consists of four parts which are the topology management, the resource monitoring, the service customization and the routing management.

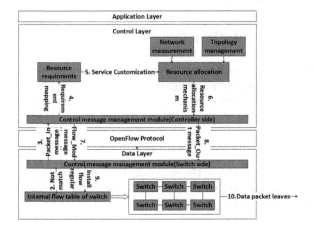

Fig. 1. System framework.

2.1   The Topology Management

SDN controller extracts Packet-In message from switches to obtain global view.

2.2   The Resource Monitoring

SDN controller regularly collect data, which can not only obtain network resources information, but also measure the flow statistics information of devices.

2.3   The Service Customization

Mapping different types of applications to corresponding QoS levels, which is shown in Table 1.

Table 1. QoS level mapping

QoS level	Application type
Expedited forwarding	Video chat, real-time game, voice call, etc.
Assured forwarding	Multimedia, web browsing, transaction processing, etc.
Best effort	Email, static images, etc.

2.4   The Routing Management

The proposed SARA algorithm is used to select the optimal path. If the link in the optimal path fails or congests, the corresponding request message is sent to the controller. Then the controller will select the sub-optimal path from the redundant paths and send flow rules to switches.

3   Problem Formulation

In order to satisfy the various service requirements, we consider computing QoS routing for the application under multiple constraints and balancing the different factors that affect the quality of service. We formulate the routing problem as a fine-grained customized service model, which is shown in Eq. (1).

$$minf(i,j) = min(\alpha \times Delay_{i,j} + \beta \times Jitter_{i,j} + \gamma \times LossRate_{i,j}) \quad (1)$$

i and j are two adjacent nodes in the network. $Delay_{i,j}$, $Jitter_{i,j}$ and $LossRate_{i,j}$ refer to the delay, jitter and packet loss rate of the link between node i and j respectively. α, β, γ are weights, and $\alpha + \beta + \gamma = 1$.

4   Algorithm Design

Figure 2 describes the workflow of the system.

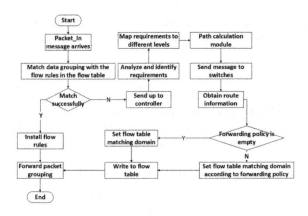

Fig. 2. System workflow.

4.1 Service Customization

Service customization part is divided into the following two steps:

1) Obtain user demand: When the user demand arrives, SDN controller will obtain related information.

2) Service customization: We define different routing schemes in advance and distribute flow tables to switches. Switches will forward packets by matching data and flow regular. Controller will map applications to QoS levels if match fails.

4.2 Self-adaptive Resource Allocation Algorithm

We propose SARA algorithm to realize resource allocation. SARA algorithm is a combination of improved ant colony algorithm and Dijkstra algorithm. The amount of pheromone on the path (i, j) at $t + 1$ time can be calculated by

$$T_{i,j}(t + 1) = \mu T_{i,j}(t) + \sum_{n=1}^{N} \Delta T_{i,j} \tag{2}$$

where $\mu \in [0, 1]$ represents the evaporation rate of pheromone. $\Delta T_{i,j}$ evaluates the pheromone on the path. E is the quantity of predefined pheromone. $link_n$ is the length of the nth path. $S_{i,j}$ represents the probability of selecting adjacent nodes. γ represents a collection of available adjacent nodes. $\xi_{i,j} = \frac{1}{\omega_{i,j}}$, $\omega_{i,j}$ represents the used bandwidth on the path (i, j).

$$\Delta T_{i,j} = \begin{cases} \frac{E}{link_n}, & on\ the\ link\ (i, j). \\ 0, & otherwise. \end{cases} \tag{3}$$

$$S_{i,j} = \begin{cases} \frac{T_{i,j}^{\alpha} \xi_{i,j}^{\beta}}{\sum_{k \in \gamma} T_{i,k}^{\alpha} \xi_{i,k}^{\beta}}, & if\ j \in \gamma \\ 0, & otherwise. \end{cases} \tag{4}$$

We use Dijkstra algorithm to calculate the shortest path with the lowest total link cost, which can be calculated by Eq. (5). $C_{v_i v_j}$ represents the link cost.

$$C(p) = \sum_{v_i v_j \in E} C_{v_i v_j} \tag{5}$$

If the calculated path meets the delay requirement of the user, the path will be returned. Otherwise, aggregation cost of routing will be calculated by Eq. (6), (7), (8) and (9). $C_\lambda(p)$ represents aggregation cost of routing.

$$p^* = min\{C(p) \mid D(p) \le \delta_{delay}\}, p \in Pst \tag{6}$$

$$\lambda = \frac{c(p_c) - c(p_d)}{d(p_d) - d(p_c)} \tag{7}$$

$$C_{v_i v_j}(\lambda) = C_{v_i v_j} + \lambda \times D_{v_i v_j} \tag{8}$$

$$C_\lambda(p) = \sum_{v_i v_j \in E} C_{v_i v_j}(\lambda) \tag{9}$$

The pheromone on new path is updated by Eq. (10). $\beta_{v_i v_j}$ denotes the link utilization of $v_i v_j$. α is the weight of link utilization.

$$C_{v_i v_j} = \alpha \beta_{v_i v_j} + (1 - \alpha), 0 \le \alpha \le 1, (v_i v_j) \in E. \tag{10}$$

The algorithm is described in Algorithm 1.

Algorithm 1. SARA algorithm

1: Obtain related information from topology management part and resource monitoring part.
2: LARAC(G,s,t,c,d,δ_{delay})
3:       $p_c = Dijkstra(G, s, t, c)$
4:       IF $d(p_c) \le \delta_{delay}$
5:               RETURN p_c
6:       $p_d = Dijkstra(G, s, t, d)$
7:       IF $d(p_d) > \delta_{delay}$
8:               RETURN NULL
9: WHEN TRUE DO
10:         $\lambda = \frac{c(p_c) - c(p_d)}{d(p_d) - d(p_c)}$
11:         $C_{v_i v_j}(\lambda) = C_{v_i v_j} + \lambda \times D_{v_i v_j}$
12:         $p_r = Dijkstra(G, s, t, c_\lambda)$
13:         IF $c_\lambda(p_r) = c_\lambda(p_c)$
14:                 RETURN p_d
15:         ELSE IF $d(p_r) \le \delta_{delay}$
16:                 $p_d = p_r$
17:         ELSE $p_c = p_r$
18:         END IF
19: END WHEN

---

5 Experiments and Evaluation

Comparing Dijkstra algorithm with SARA algorithm, we obtain graphs where Dijkstra and SARA algorithm is denoted by D and S mechanism respectively.

Packet Loss Rate: When network congestion occurs, D mechanism will continue to adopt the shortest path, which will cause more serious packet loss than SARA algorithm. The results are shown in Fig. 3 and Fig. 4.

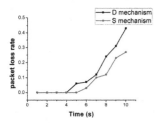

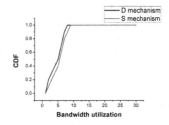

Fig. 3. Experimental results of packet loss rate.

Fig. 4. CDF graph of packet loss rate.

The CDF graph of S mechanism is higher than that of D mechanism in interval [1.5, 8], which reflects S mechanism is superior to D mechanism when the packet loss rate is less than or equal to 8. The standard deviations of D mechanism and S mechanism are 2.28279 and 1.90029 respectively. It reflects that S mechanism is more stable and hardly causes a lot of packet loss.

Bandwidth Utilization: The experimental result graph and CDF graph of bandwidth utilization are shown in Fig. 5 and Fig. 6 respectively. The probability distribution of bandwidth utilization of S and D mechanism is mainly concentrated in the interval of $[11, +\infty]$ and $[2, 8]$ respectively. The bandwidth utilization of S mechanism is higher than D mechanism.

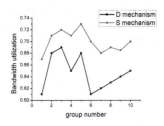

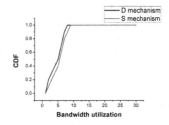

Fig. 5. Experimental results of bandwidth utilization.

Fig. 6. CDF graph of bandwidth utilization.

S mechanism is higher than D mechanism in the mean, median and maximum values, which means overall bandwidth utilization of S mechanism is better than D mechanism. However, the standard deviation of S mechanism is slightly higher than that of D mechanism, which means the stability of S mechanism needs to be strengthened.

Time Cost: The experimental result graph and CDF graph of time cost are shown in Fig. 7 and Fig. 8 respectively. In the CDF graph of time cost, D mechanism is higher than S mechanism in the interval of [5.5, 18], which reflects that S mechanism is not ideal in extreme cases of time cost.

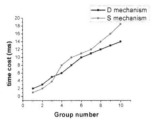 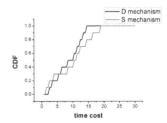

Fig. 7. Experimental results of time cost.

Fig. 8. CDF graph of time cost.

6   Conclusion

In this paper, we present an SDN-based service customized self-adaptive network resource allocation mechanism and SARA algorithm, which combines Dijkstra algorithm with ant colony optimization algorithm. We evaluated the algorithm by simulation experiments. Simulation results demonstrate that our algorithm is effective and has better performance. In future work, we will concentrate on reducing time cost of SARA algorithm.

Acknowledgments. This work is supported by the National Key R&D Program of China under Grant No. 2019YFB1802800; the Major International (Regional) Joint Research Project of NSFC under Grant No. 71620107003; the National Natural Science Foundation of China under Grant No. 61872073 and 62002055; the Fundamental Research Funds for the Central Universities of China under Grant No. N2016012; the Postdoctoral Research Fund of Northeastern University of China under Grant No. 20200103.

References

1. Liu, R., Li, S., Wang, H.: Hierarchical multi-constraint routing algorithm based on software defined networking. In: 2019 IEEE 9th International Conference on Electronics Information and Emergency Communication (ICEIEC), pp. 1–5 (2019)

2. Alex Barakabitze, A., et al.: QoE management of multimedia streaming services in future networks: a tutorial and survey. IEEE Commun. Surv. Tutorials **22**(1), 526–565 (2020)
3. Li, J., Shi, W., Yang, P., Shen, X.: On dynamic mapping and scheduling of service function chains in SDN/NFV-enabled networks. In: 2019 IEEE Global Communications Conference (GLOBECOM), pp. 1–6 (2019)
4. Sun, G., Xiong, K., Boateng, G.O., Ayepah-Mensah, D., Liu, G., Jiang, W.: Autonomous resource provisioning and resource customization for mixed traffics in virtualized radio access network. IEEE Syst. J. **13**, 2454–2465 (2019)
5. Sexton, C., Marchetti, N., DaSilva, L.A.: Customization and trade-offs in 5G RAN slicing. IEEE Commun. Mag. **57**(4), 116–122 (2019)
6. Marquez, C., Gramaglia, M., Fiore, M., Banchs, A., Costa-Pérez, X.: Resource sharing efficiency in network slicing. IEEE Trans. Netw. Serv. Manage. **16**(3), 909–923 (2019)
7. Sun, G., Xiong, K., Owusu Boateng, G., Liu, G., Jiang, W.: Resource slicing and customization in RAN with dueling deep Q-network. J. Netw. Comput. Appl. **157**, 102573 (2020)
8. Qu, K., Zhuang, W., Ye, Q., Shen, X., Li, X., Rao, J.: Traffic engineering for service-oriented 5G networks with SDN-NFV integration. IEEE Netw. **34**(4), 234–241 (2020)
9. Kumar Mondal, P., Aguirre Sanchez, LP., Benedetto, E., Shen, Y., Guo, M.: A dynamic network traffic classifier using supervised ML for a Docker-based SDN network. Connection Sci. **33**, 1–26 (2021)
10. Nassiri, M., Mohammadi, R.: A joint energy- and QoS-aware routing mechanism for WMNs using software-defined networking paradigm. J. Supercomputing **76**(1), 68–86 (2020)
11. Ananthalakshmi Ammal, R., Sajimon P.C., Vinodchandra S.S.: Termite inspired algorithm for traffic engineering in hybrid software defined networks. PeerJ Comput. Sci. **6**, 19 (2020)
12. Balta, M., Özçelik, İ.: A proposal of SDN based VANET architecture for urban intersection management systems. J. Fac. Eng. Archit. Gazi Univ. **34**(3), 1451–1468(2019)
13. Li, H., Lu, H., Fu, X.: An optimal and dynamic elephant flow scheduling for SDN-based data center networks. J. Intell. Fuzzy Syst. **38**(1), 247–255 (2020)
14. Akbar Neghabi, A., Jafari Navimipour, N., Hosseinzadeh, M., Rezaee, A.: Energy-aware dynamic-link load balancing method for a software-defined network using a multi-objective artificial bee colony algorithm and genetic operators. IET Commun. **14**(18), 3284–3293 (2020)

Privacy Risk Assessment for Text Data Based on Semantic Correlation Learning

Ping Xiong[1(✉)], Lin Liang[1], Yunli Zhu[1], and Tianqing Zhu[2]

[1] Zhongnan University of Economics and Law, Wuhan 430073, China
pingxiong@zuel.edu.cn
[2] China University of Geosciences, 388 Lumo Road, Wuhan 430074, China

Abstract. Privacy risk assessment determines the extent to which generalization and obfuscation should be applied to the sensitive data. In this paper, we propose PriTxt for evaluating the privacy risk associated with text data by exploiting the semantic correlation. Using definitions derived from the General Data Protection Regulation (GDPR), PriTxt first defines the private features that related to individual privacy. By using the word2vec algorithm, a word-embedding model is further constructed to identify the quasi-sensitive words. The privacy risk of a given text is finally evaluated by aggregating the weighted risks of the sensitive and the quasi-sensitive words in the text.

Keywords: Privacy risk · Privacy preservation · GDPR

1 Introduction

In the era of big data, privacy risk has become a serious public concern. Most existing works on privacy preservation have tended to focus on structured data [6,10], rather than unstructured data; examples of the latter include text documents, e-mail, video, audio, etc.

For text data, the risk to privacy is caused by sensitive words that disclose the identity or personal characteristics of an individual. An intuitive solution for text privacy risk assessment is to measure the risk with reference to the ratio of the number of sensitive words/characters to the total number of words/characters. However, this straightforward solution has ignored the essential semantic correlations among words: in context, non-sensitive words may potentially reveal information about sensitive words. It is insufficient to consider only sensitive words; words that are non-sensitive but highly correlated to the private features, defined as *quasi-sensitive words* in this paper, should also be involved in risk assessment.

In this paper, we propose a novel privacy risk assessment method, PriTxt, for text data. We introduce a semantic similarity measurement [4] to evaluate the semantic correlation in text. Specifically, we reference the private features defined in GDPR to specify the sensitive words, then use the *word2vec* algorithm

© Springer Nature Switzerland AG 2021
Z. Liu et al. (Eds.): WASA 2021, LNCS 12939, pp. 200–208, 2021.
https://doi.org/10.1007/978-3-030-86137-7_22

to identify the quasi-sensitive words. We also present an approach to measure the risk of each identified word, along with a metric for evaluating the risk associated with specific text by aggregating the risk of all sensitive and quasi-sensitive words. Finally, we apply our PriTxt to real-world text to demonstrate the effectiveness of the proposed method.

2   Related Works

As a *de facto* standard of privacy preservation in practice, the General Data Protection Regulation [9] issued by the European Union (EU) in 2018 clearly defines that personal private data as *any information related to an identified or identifiable natural person*, e.g., a name, an identification number or gender. In this paper, we define private data according to the rules set out in GDPR.

Lots of privacy risk assessment approaches have recently been proposed for specific applications. Roberto et al. [8] proposed a data mining approach for the risk assessment of mobility data, in which classification is used to evaluate the probability that a trajectory may be re-identified from mobility datasets. Roberto et al. [7] also focused on retail data and evaluated the risk associated with published individual purchasing patterns.

While most of the above research has focused on the risk assessment of structured data, few works have addressed unstructured data such as text data. Chen et al. [1] proposed a privacy preservation approach for text data in electronic medical records, the goal of which is to automatically locate the specific private information from the text of electronic medical records in order to conduct de-identification. Recently, Feyisetan et al. [3] proposed a textual analysis method for privacy preservation via word perturbation, making it the existing work that most closely resembles ours. However, this work has a different goal from ours, in that it aims to perturb the target words with minimized utility loss, while our goal is to identify the correlative words of the target words.

3   Proposed Method

3.1   The Workflow of PriTxt

The frameflow of PriTxt consists of three steps, namely *data preparation, model training*, and *risk evaluation.*

Data Preparation. The goal of data preparation is to construct the corpus used to train a word embedding model. Given a particular application scenario, we first define the private features that an individual is unwilling to disclose in this scenario. For text data, the privacy risk stems primarily from the words that reveal information relating to the private features. In PriTxt, these private features are defined according to the rules in GDPR. To construct a corpus given a particular application, we need to collect text data related to the application, then abstract words and label those sensitive words that directly reveal information pertaining to private features (according to the definition of private features provided in advance). The labelled words, as well as the corpus, are used to training the word embedding model in the later stage.

Model Training. The goal of this step is to generate a word embedding model by which the degree of correlation between two words can be measured. First of all, we use the labelled sensitive words and their context words to generate training pairs, which are used as the training data. We then apply the word2vec algorithm with Continuous Bag-of-Words (CBOW) to learn a predictive model, which maps the words in the corpus to an embedding space. Therefore, the correlation between a sensitive word and its semantically close words, referred to as quasi-sensitive words, can be evaluated by their distance in the embedding space.

Risk Evaluation. The goal of this step is to aggregate the risk of all sensitive and quasi-sensitive words and thereby obtain a comprehensive risk assessment. First of all, we specify the sensitive words according to the defined private features. The quasi-sensitive words can then be identified as those that are highly correlated with the private features by using the word embedding model. For each sensitive and quasi-sensitive words, a risk index is specified according to its degree of sensitivity. Finally, the risk degree of the text is obtained by aggregating the risk index of all sensitive and quasi-sensitive words.

Further details about each stage are presented in the following subsections.

3.2   Data Preparation

Private Feature Definition. Private information generally refers to sensitive information that can be used to determine the identity or characteristics of individuals under circumstances in which they are not inclined to disclose such information [2]. In practice, the definition of privacy differs from the specific application scenario.

In this paper, we strictly follow the regulations outlined in GDPR to define privacy features. As shown in Table 1, 19 features, denoted by F_{GDPR}, are defined as the features of private information. Features in a particular application could then be a subset of F_{GDPR}.

Table 1. Features of private information defined in GDPR

I	Name	XI	Bank card number
II	E-mail address	XII	Nationality
III	Mobile phone number	XIII	Political party
IV	Home phone number	XIV	GPS
V	Any address	XV	DNA
VI	Identification number	XVI	Fingerprint
VII	Passport number	XVII	Iris
VIII	License plate number	XVIII	Disease diagnosis
IX	Date of birth	XIX	Others
X	Network data		

For text data, sensitive words are those directly describing information relating to the private features of an individual, while quasi-sensitive words potentially imply some information contained in private features. Thus, the risk of the text data can be measured by determining the amount of information disclosed by sensitive and quasi-sensitive words.

Corpus Construction. To train a word-embedding model, we need to construct the corpus according to the particular application of a given text data analysis project. More specifically, we collect a text dataset, $D = \{doc_1, doc_2, \cdots, doc_m\}$, which consists of sufficient texts related to the given application scenario. For each text doc_i, we remove the stop words from the text (such as *the, is, on*, etc.). We then label the sensitive words according to the private feature set pre-defined in advance. It should be noted that, for each sensitive word in the text, we replace it with its corresponding private feature to convey a more general meaning. After the above preprocessing is complete, we encode every word and obtain the corpus.

3.3 Training Word Embedding Model

PriTxt applies the word2vec algorithm with the CBOW model to generate word embeddings. To improve the training speed and the quality of the word embeddings, Pritxt uses negative sampling (NEG) [5] when training the CBOW model. In NEG, a target word (in this context, a sensitive word) with one of its context words forms a pair, which is used as a positive sample. Negative samples can then be generated by replacing the target word in the pair with another word in the corpus. Let D be a given corpus, C_w be the context words of a target word w, and $N_w \neq \emptyset$ be the negative sample set. For $\forall (C_w, u)$, $u \in \{w\} \bigcup N_w$, the probability of u in the output layer is computed via binary logistic regression:

$$p(u|C_w) = \begin{cases} \delta(x_w^\top v^u), & L^w(u) = 1 \\ 1 - \delta(x_w^\top v^u), & L^w(u) = 0 \end{cases} \quad (1)$$

where x_w is the output value of the hidden layer, v^u is the weight vector when the output target word is u, and $\delta(\cdot)$ is a logistic regression function. $L^w(u)$ is the label of the word u, namely, $L^w(u) = 1$ when u is a positive sample and $L^w(u) = 0$ when u is a negative sample. The likelihood function is then constructed as follows:

$$L = \sum_{w \in D} \{ \lg[\delta(x_w^\top v^w)] + \sum_{u \in N_w} \lg[\delta(-x_w^\top v^u)] \}. \tag{2}$$

The likelihood function is therefore optimized with gradient ascent, as shown in Eqs. 3 and 4.

$$\frac{\partial L}{\partial v^u} = [L^w(u) - \delta(-x_w^\top v^u)] x_w \tag{3}$$

$$\frac{\partial L}{\partial x_w} = [L^w(u) - \delta(-x_w^\top v^u)] v^u \tag{4}$$

Finally, the update formula of the vector v^u is given by Eq. 5, while the update formula of word embedding $V(c), c \in C_w$ is given by Eq. 6:

$$v^u := v^u + \eta[L^w(u) - \delta(-x_w^\top v^u)] x_w \tag{5}$$

$$V(c) := V(c) + \xi \sum_{u \in \{w\} \cup N_w} [L^w(u) - \delta(-x_w^\top v^u)] v^u \tag{6}$$

where, η and ξ are learning rates.

After training the CBOW model, we can obtain the word embedding of each word in the corpus. More specifically, for each word $word_i$, its word embedding is the ith row vector in the weight matrix W.

3.4   Privacy Risk Evaluation

Given a text T to be evaluated, we first identify the sensitive words in T according to the private features, and further divide the words in T into two sets: the sensitive word set W and the candidate word set $W' = T - W$.

For each word w_i in W, the risk index of w_i, I_i, is set to 1.0. For each candidate w_j in W', we compute the cosine similarity between w_j and each private feature f_i in F, denoted as $s(f_i, w_j)$, the risk index of w_j is then set to $I_j = max_{f_i \in F}\{s(f_i, w_j)\}$. Given a pre-defined threshold θ, any word w_j for which $I_j \geq \theta$ is then considered as a quasi-sensitive word.

Finally, We use the average of the risk indices of all words as the privacy risk of the given text T, as shown in Eq. 7:

$$Pri\_Risk = \frac{1}{n} \sum_{i=1}^{n} I_i \tag{7}$$

where n is the number of words in T, while I_i is the risk index of w_i.

4   Experiments

4.1   Experimental Setup

Given a piece of published text data in which the sensitive words in the text have been replaced by '*', the goal of an adversary is to infer the replaced sensitive words by exploring the context. We suppose that the adversary also uses the CBOW method to predict the sensitive words by using the context words. Therefore, the risk of the text under this attack—denoted as AS_Risk—can be simulated by the probability that the sensitive words are successfully inferred, which is calculated as follows:

$$AS\_Risk = \frac{\sum_{i=1}^{k} P_i}{Len^* + 1} \tag{8}$$

where k is the number of sensitive words in the text, P_i is the probability that the ith sensitive word is predicted successfully, Len^* is the normalized text length.

We suppose that the adversary launches white-box attack and the black-box attack. The white-box attack means that the attacker knows the parameter setting of the training word embeddings model in PriTxt. While in black-box attacks, the adversary may try any possible parameter settings.

We suppose an adversary attacks ten pieces of text data using the above models, and rank the risk levels in a ranking sequence S_{base}, which is used as a benchmark. Next, we use PriTxt and the traditional methods (measuring the risk by the ratio of the number of sensitive words/characters to the total number of words/characters, denoted as PriW and PriCh respectively) to evaluate the risk of the ten texts, and obtain the ranking sequences S_{PriTxt}, S_{PriW} and S_{PriCh}. The consistency between these sequences and the benchmark sequence S_{base} are accordingly investigated. We use two metrics—the Mean Absolute Error, denoted as MAE, and the Average Kendall tau distance [11], denoted as AKT—to evaluate the consistency between two rankings sequences.

MAE is calculated according to Eq. 9:

$$MAE(x, y) = \frac{1}{n} \sum_{i=1}^{n} |x_i - y_i| \tag{9}$$

where x and y represent two ranking sequences with the same length n.

Average Kendall tau distance is the normalization of Kendall tau distance, which is calculated by Eq. 10:

$$AKT(x, y) = \frac{\tau(x, y)}{n(n - 1)/2} \tag{10}$$

where $\tau(x, y)$ is the number of inversions between the ranking sequences x and y with length n.

We used three text datasets in our experiments: *Author Information, Sports News* and *Political News*. The *Author Information Dataset* is extracted from the public journal *IEEE Transactions on Information Forensics and Security*, which introduces 1, 200 authors along with their career profile and research directions. The two news datasets consist of text news published by *www.sina.com.cn* from 2005 to 2011.

4.2   Experimental Results

For each experiment, we repeat five times to obtain the average result. The experimental result on the *Author Information* dataset is shown in Fig. 1. It can be observed that the consistency of S_{PriTxt} to S_{Base} is for superior to that of S_{PriW} and S_{PriCh} in terms of both of MAE and AKT. More specifically, under either white-box or black-box attack conditions, PriTxt always has the lowest MAT and AKT, while PriCh has the worst performance among the three methods. We obtained similar experimental results on the three news datasets. Figures 2, 3 present the MAE and AKT on the Sports News Dataset and Political News Dataset.

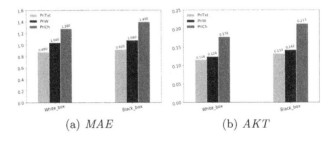

(a) *MAE*   (b) *AKT*

Fig. 1. Experimental results for author information dataset

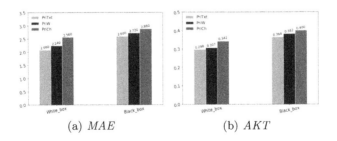

(a) *MAE*   (b) *AKT*

Fig. 2. Experimental results for sports dataset

The experimental results reveal that the proposed PriTxt steadily outperforms the traditional methods in various scenarios. In addition, they imply that the semantics of text are a double-edged sword for both the attacker and defender

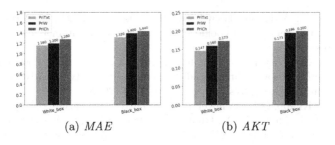

(a) *MAE*   (b) *AKT*

Fig. 3. Experimental results for political dataset

and plays a very important role in this game. An attacker may exploit the semantics of text to infer sensitive information from the text, while a defender can also exploit the text semantics to identify and further protect the quasi-sensitive words in order to preserve the sensitive information in the text. PriCh measures the risk by using only the number of characters of sensitive words that without considering the semantics of text; thus, it has the worst performance among the three methods. Comparatively, while PriW exploits the semantics of text to some extent and achieves better performance than PriCh, PriTxt fully utilizes the semantic correlation to identify the quasi-sensitive words that may potentially disclose sensitive information, and thereby obtains the most accurate risk assessment.

5   Conclusions

Ubiquitous unstructured text data contains huge stores of valuable information. Misuse of these data may pose a great threat to individual privacy.

In this paper, we propose a new method, PriTxt, to accurately evaluate the text privacy risk by aggregating the risk indices of sensitive and quasi-sensitive words. Experimental results on real-world datasets show that semantic correlation plays several crucial roles in privacy evaluation.

Acknowledgment. This work is supported by the Humanities and Social Sciences Planning Project of the China Ministry of Education under Grant No. 19YJAZH099.

References

1. Chen, L., Yang, J., Wang, Q.: Privacy-preserving data publishing for free text Chinese electronic medical records. In: 2012 IEEE 36th Annual Computer Software and Applications Conference, pp. 567–572 (2012)
2. Fang, B., Jia, Y., Aiping, L.I., Jiang, R.: Privacy preservation in big data: a survey. Big Data Res. **5**, 33 (2016)
3. Feyisetan, O., Balle, B., Drake, T., Diethe, T.: Privacy- and Utility-Preserving Textual Analysis via Calibrated Multivariate Perturbations. Association for Computing Machinery, New York (2020)

4. Hu, K., et al.: A domain keyword analysis approach extending term frequency-keyword active index with google word2vec model. Scientometrics **114**(3), 1031–1068 (2018)

5. Mikolov, T., Sutskever, I., Chen, K., Corrado, G.S., Dean, J.: Distributed representations of words and phrases and their compositionality. In: Advances in Neural Information Processing Systems, pp. 3111–3119 (2013)

6. Orooji, M., Knapp, G.M.: A novel microdata privacy disclosure risk measure (2019)

7. Pellungrini, R., Monreale, A., Guidotti, R.: Privacy risk for individual basket patterns. In: ECML PKDD 2018 Workshops, pp. 141–155. Springer International Publishing, Cham (2019)

8. Pellungrini, R., Pappalardo, L., Pratesi, F., Monreale, A.: A data mining approach to assess privacy risk in human mobility data. ACM Trans. Intell. Syst. Technol. **9**(3), 1–27 (2017)

9. Presthus, W., Sørum, H.: Are consumers concerned about privacy? An online survey emphasizing the general data protection regulation. Procedia Comput. Sci. **138**, 603–611 (2018)

10. Torra, V.: Privacy Models and Disclosure Risk Measures, pp. 111–189. Springer, Cham (2017). https://doi.org/10.1007/978-3-319-57358-8_5

11. Yan, Z., Li, G., Liu, J.: Private rank aggregation under local differential privacy. Int. J. Intell. Syst. **35**(10), 1492–1519 (2020)

Multi-dimensional LSTM: A Model of Network Text Classification

Weixin Wu, Xiaotong Liu, Leyi Shi[✉], Yihao Liu, and Yuxiao Song

College of Computer Science and Technology, China University of Petroleum
(East China), Qingdao 266580, China
{20200039,shileyi}@upc.edu.cn

Abstract. Focusing on the diversified opinion expression form and
the explosive growth of information amount in network environment
of big data, we propose a text emotion recognition model based on
multi-dimensional LSTM to improve classification accuracy of network
information by making full use of additional information of text samples. In this paper, we divide the original sample into two parts: the
main information sample and the additional information sample. Then
multi-dimensional LSTM model is used to extract their features vectors.
Finally, according to the results of the two feature vectors, the classification result is carried out by feature fusion and further computation.
The multi-dimensional LSTM model is implemented and tested by TensorFlow. The experimental results show that the emotion recognition
classification accuracy has been greatly improved by taking advantage of
multi-dimensional LSTM in big data environment.

Keywords: Text big data · Emotion analysis · LSTM · Tensorflow ·
Feature fusion

1 Introduction

With the popularization and development of the network, a large amount of text
information is flooding in the network environment, and timely monitoring and
analysis of the emotional trend of network information has a great significance
to grasp the network public opinion. However, in the big data environment,
the accuracy of previous classification techniques is not accurate enough. This
paper proposes a text emotion recognition model based on multi-dimensional
LSTM, which improves the accuracy of classification by making full use of the
additional information of big data text. The main contributions of this paper
are summarized as follows:

1. We design and implement the multi-dimensional LSTM model. Through
   learning the characteristics of different samples, the accuracy of classification is improved on the premise of improving information utilization.

Z. Liu et al. (Eds.): WASA 2021, LNCS 12939, pp. 209–217, 2021.
https://doi.org/10.1007/978-3-030-86137-7_23

2. We improve the preprocessing algorithm of the original sample. The text information of the sample is separated from the emoticons and the emotional characteristics are extracted respectively.
3. A data set suitable for the multi-dimensional LSTM model is established through 8000 modified sample data for training and testing of the model.

The rest of the paper is organized as follows: In Sect. 2 we will overview some related works. Section 3 presents a text emotion recognition model in detail based on multi-dimensional LSTM. The experiments and performance analysis are performed in Sect. 4 and Sect. 5. Finally, we conclude the paper in Sect. 6.

2   Related Work

Hao et al. [1] applied FPGA to neural networks to analyze input data and predict emotion recognition of words and texts, realizing faster and more accurate operations in FPGA devices. NGOC-HUYNH HO et al. [2] proposed a model method using a recurrent neural network and self-to-MultiHead attention mechanism. The model trains the MFCC of the audio signal and the word embedding of the text data, but ignores the chroma, rhythm, etc.

Yao et al. [3] successfully merged the three classifiers of DNN, RNN and CNN into one framework. Experimental results show that the weighted merging method greatly improves the ability of neural networks to focus on the prominent parts of emotion.

Aiming at the problem of document level sentiment classification, Liu et al. [4] used the hierarchical neural network model of dynamic word embedding (HieNN-DWE) to deeply consider the semantic information of polysemous words, and achieved good results on the sentiment classification of words at the document level. Wang et al. [5] proposed a Danmaku sentiment analysis model based on Bi-LSTM, which has a good ability to analyze the complex sentiment features of irregular text.

There are also a lot of works improve the classification accuracy by optimizing LSTM model structure. Wan et al. [6] applied Graph LSTM to short text classification to mine deeper information and achieved good results.

Both the improvement of model structure and the optimization of grammar algorithm are of great importance to the improvement of classification accuracy. However, these methods ignore the use of additional information of the sample itself. In this paper, our contribution is to improve the structure of the classification model so as to make full use of the additional information of the samples for improving the classification accuracy.

3   Model

3.1   Multi-dimensional Models

The current network environment allows people to express their opinions in various forms. There are always some additional information in the web text information, which also plays an important role in the semantic expression, such as emoticons and expression pictures.

Firstly, original samples need to be processed by tokenizer. And original samples also need some operations like clipping to adapt to the input format. Then word embeddings translates words into vectors for calculation. Feature extraction can be achieved by various kinds of deep learning model like RNN. Finally, classifier is used to classify the samples. However, in the whole process of classification, the additional information of the original sample is ignored. This has a negative effect on the expression of the words meaning and the accuracy of the classification of samples.

In order to make full use of the additional information of samples to improve the accuracy of text classification, we design a text categorization model based on multi-dimension LSTM (MD-LSTM). Figure 1 shows the model structure of multi-dimensional LSTM.

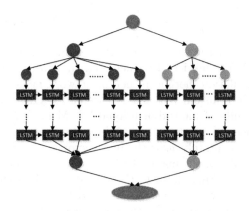

Fig. 1. Model structure of multi-dimensional LSTM

Algorithm 1. MD-LSTM Classification Algorithm Input:dataset of samples(x_1,x_2,x_3...x_n)and its lables(y_1,y_2,y_3...y_n) Output:θ,classification result y_0

1: Initialize the weight matrix W_i, W_f,W_c,W_o,U_i,U_f,U_c,U_o,$V_o$and bias vectors b_i,b_f,$b_c$and setthe parameters:learning rate and batch size etc
2: Preprocess all the samples in dataset
3: Train MD-LSTM model
4: Get new W_i, W_f,W_c,W_o,U_i,U_f,U_c,U_o,$V_o$andb_i,b_f,b_c
5: Compute feature vectors V_w,V_e
6: Compute θ
7: Get the classification result y_0=dis(θ)

Algorithm 1 shows the classification process of MD-LSTM. Based on the data collected in the network, the samples are sorted according to our classification target. Then the multi-dimensional LSTM model is trained with these data sets and the target parameter matrix is obtained. According to the calculation results of target parameter matrix and distance formula, the trained model can be used to classify the samples. Therefore, the cultivation of models is very important to our work.

In multi-dimensional LSTM model, the main information and additional information of the original samples are processed separately. In this paper, additional information mainly refers to the expression pictures. In the data preprocessing stage, original samples are processed into main information samples and additional information samples. Two kinds of samples are obtained through the preprocessing process. They are trained by multi-dimensional LSTM model. We can get the feature vector which behalf of the samples by calculating results.

$$y = softmax(w_x + b) \tag{1}$$

$$\theta = W_w \cdot V_w + W_e \cdot V_e + b_r \tag{2}$$

Both of these two feature vectors are the results of feature extraction, and the classification results need to be calculated by feature fusion. Formula (1) is a traditional calculation method of neural network model. In formula (2), θ is the result of feature fusion. W_w and W_e are two weight matrixes, representing the training results of multi-dimensional LSTM model. V_w and V_e are the feature vector, which represent the main information sample and the additional information sample separately. b_r is the bias vector.

The training results of the main information and additional information are mapped through the Softmax layer to the probability distribution of each value range of (0,1) to form weight matrices W_w and W_e. The weight matrix keeps changing through learning. By fusing the inner product of the weight matrix and the eigenvector, plus the bias vector b_r, we can get the final output result of the multidimensional least squares model.

To verify the effectiveness of the multi-dimensional LSTM fusion method, we evaluated the multi-dimensional LSTM and the traditional LSTM in experiments. According to the calculation results of formula (2), we can compare them with the corresponding sample labels to judge the accuracy and effectiveness of the model classification.

4   Experiment

4.1   Dataset

This paper used the modified IMDB [7] dataset. We selected 8000 samples from the IMDB, and improved these samples by adding the appropriate additional information that is the expression image.

As shown in Table 1, the modified samples are divided into four parts, which are positive training samples, negative training samples, positive test samples and negative test samples, to adaptive model training and model accuracy test.

Table 1. Dataset

	Training samples	Test samples
Negative	2000	2000
Positive	2000	2000
Sum	4000	4000

4.2   The Training of Word Vector

As skip-gram model has more advantages in word vector training, the model adopted in this paper is skip-gram model.

The dataset used for Word2vec model training was the universal dataset Text8. In order to observe the training results intuitively, some trained word vectors were processed with dimension reduction process, and compressed into a two dimensional scatterplot.

As shown in Fig. 2, fig (a) and fig (b) are the local enlarged images. It can be seen from fig (a) and fig (b) that the spatial distance of some words with similar meanings or parts of speech is relatively close. The word vector trained by word2vec model has obvious advantages, which is also of great help and improvement to the semantic expression ability of multi-dimensional LSTM model.

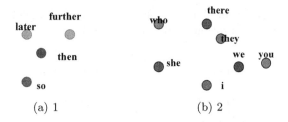

Fig. 2. Training result of word2vec

4.3   Evaluation Criterion

Loss is an important standard to evaluate a model. An important goal in the training process of the model is to minimize the loss. The cost function in this paper we selected is cross entropy. The meaning of cross entropy is the difficulty degree of identifying text with a model, or each word is encoded in several bits on average from a compressed point of view.

Accuracy is a significant index to evaluate the performance of classification system. Training accuracy is the prediction result of training precision in training process. Test accuracy is the test result of the current classification accuracy of the model by using the test data set. In order to achieve the calculation of the accuracy, which should concerned various results of sample classification, we need to define a confusion matrix. It is shown as Table 2.

Table 2. Confusion matrix

Confusion matrix		Predicted categories	
		Positive	Negative
Actual categories	Positive	True positive	False negative
	Negative	False positive	True negative

According to the confusion matrix, the formula of accuracy is defined as:

$$Accuracy = \frac{T_p + T_n}{T_p + F_p + F_n + T_n} \tag{3}$$

T_p, T_n, F_p, F_n respectively represent true positive probability, true negative probability, false positive probability and false negative probability.

5 Results Analysis

We use the dataset to train LSTM model and MD-LSTM model by TensorFlow. Model Parameter configuration is shown in Table 3.

Table 3. Model parameter configuration

Parameter name	Values
Batch size	64
Learning rate	0.1
Decay value of learning rate	0.6
Dictionary	20000
Nested dimension	128
Verification interval	100
Checkpoint interval	1000
Number of categories	2

5.1 Loss Analysis

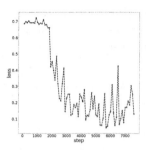

Fig. 3. Line chart of loss change

The data of loss during the training process is drawn into a line chart, which is given as Fig. 3. As can be seen from the figure, when the model training is completed, the loss is optimized, which indicates that the performance of our model is excellent.

5.2 Accuracy Analysis

For the evaluation of model performance, besides the loss, we also need to experiment and analyze the accuracy of the model.

Figure 4(a) shows the change of training accuracy during multilayer MD-LSTM model training process and Fig. 4(b) shows the change of test accuracy in training process of multilayer MD-LSTM model.

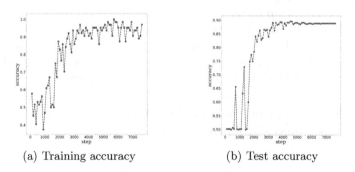

(a) Training accuracy   (b) Test accuracy

Fig. 4. Line chart of accuracy change

We compared and analyzed the text classification accuracy of the two models. As it shown in Table 4, the text classification accuracy of multilayer LSTM model is 80.1%, and the text classification accuracy of multilayer MD-LSTM model is 89.5%. The accuracy of text classification is improved. It is proved that the MD-LSTM model is effective to improve the classification accuracy. It can be seen from the variation curves of loss and accuracy that our model has a good convergence in the training process. Compared with other models, this model is proved to have good classification performance.

Table 4. Accuracies of different models

Hidden layer	Model	Accuracy (%)
Monolayer	LSTM	79.3
	MD-LSTM	88.2
Multilayer	LSTM	80.1
	MD-LSTM	89.5

6   Conclusions

With the massive growth of network data, information explosion has become a major problem facing the current big data network environment, which seriously affects the safety of network public opinion. Instead of spending days calculating logic by hand, we grab a lot of information on each line and use machine learning to find patterns for us. However, due to the complexity and diversity of opinion information, many valuable information is ignored in this process.

In this article, we combined several hot topics such as deep learning and natural language processing. In view of the diversified expression forms and explosive growth of information in network environment, MD-LSTM model was developed to make full use of additional information of text samples to improve the classification accuracy of text samples. MD-LSTM can process massive information quickly, efficiently and accurately. The validity and performance of MD-LSTM model were verified by experiments and tensorflow analysis.

Funding:. This research was funded by the Shandong Provincial Natural Science Foundation under Project ZR2019MF034.

References

1. Hao, F.: Emotion recognition simulation of Japanese text based on FPGA and neural network. Microprocess. Microsyst. (2020)
2. Ho, F., Yang, S.: Multimodal approach of speech emotion recognition using multi-level multi-head fusion attention-based recurrent neural network. IEEE Access **8**, 61672–61686 (2020)
3. Yao, F., Wang, S.: Speech emotion recognition using fusion of three multi-task learning-based classifiers: HSF-DNN, MS-CNN and LLD-RNN. Speech Commun. **120**, 11–19 (2020)
4. Liu, F., Zheng, S.: HieNN-DWE: a hierarchical neural network with dynamic word embeddings for document level sentiment classification. Neurocomputing **403**, 21–32 (2020)
5. Wang, F., Chen, S.: HieNN-DWE: improved Danmaku emotion analysis and its application based on Bi-LSTM model. IEEE Access **8**, 114123–114134 (2020)
6. Wan, Y.: Short-text sentiment classification based on graph-LSTM. In: AIAM, pp. 35–38(2019)
7. Ding, F., Cheng, S.: The power of the "like" button: the impact of social media on box office. Decis. Support Syst. **94**, 77–84 (2017)

Incentive Cooperation with Computation Delay Concerns for Socially-Aware Parked Vehicle Edge Computing

Youcun Li, Ying Li$^{(\boxtimes)}$ ⓘ, Jianbo Li, and Yuxiang Liang

College of Computer Science and Technology, Qingdao University,
Qingdao 266071, China
yingli2016@qdu.edu.cn

Abstract. Massive computing requirements of mobile applications greatly challenge the limited resources in the cloud. It is observed that parked vehicles (PVs) have redundant computing resources for task execution. Hence, we focus on how to efficiently and economically apply PVs for assisting the cloud. An proposed incentive mechanism, initiated by the cloud, motivates PVs to participate in the offloading of cloud's computing tasks. We build the utility to characterize a PV's profits, generated from task execution and socially-aware effects from other PVs. The benefits of the cloud consider many factors, such as computing tasks of mobile users, energy cost, economic compensation for PVs and PVs' computation delay. The interactions among PVs and the cloud formulate a two-stage Stackelberg game to maximize their profits. The performance of the proposed model is investigated by simulations. Numerical results prove its efficiency for enhancing PVs' utilities and cloud's quality of service.

Keywords: Edge · Cloud · Computing resources · Incentive mechanism · Stackelberg game.

1 Introduction

With the rapid development of mobile applications, the demand for computing resources has increased a lot [1,3,8]. The cloud needs to handle large numbers of computing tasks. Due to the limited hardware capabilities, the cloud operator focuses on edge computing to gather computing resources for improving

Supported in part by National Natural Science Foundation of China under Grant No. 61802216, National Key Research and Development Plan Key Special Projects under Grant No. 2018YFB2100303, Shandong Province colleges and universities youth innovation technology plan innovation team project under Grant No. 2020KJN011, Program for Innovative Postdoctoral Talents in Shandong Province under Grant No. 40618030001 and Postdoctoral Science Foundation of China under Grant No. 2018M642613.

© Springer Nature Switzerland AG 2021
Z. Liu et al. (Eds.): WASA 2021, LNCS 12939, pp. 218–225, 2021.
https://doi.org/10.1007/978-3-030-86137-7_24

its Quality of Service (QoS) and profits. As a matter of fact, a huge waste of computing resources exists when PVs are parked in the parking lot. PVs enable the cloud to rent their computing resources on the basis of wireless communication. Therefore, it would be necessary to build an efficient edge-cloud model, especially when the development of mobile devices cannot satisfy the needs of computing resources [11].

The study of how to enhance the performance of the cloud has been discussed in [4,7,9]. As a matter of fact, we need to employ incentive mechanism to improve PVs' willingness to provide computing resources [2,5,6,10]. Li et al. in [2] proposed a three-stage Stackelberg game to jointly consider the benefits of three different kinds of players. Authors in [5] designed a data offloading network to maximize the utilities of two kinds of players. To maximize multi-users' interests, Xu et al. in [6] designed a game-based multi-user computing offloading model. In [10], the authors designed a model using Stackelberg game to simulate the interactions between different users.

We are motivated to propose an efficient model for edge-cloud network, which aids the cloud to obtain enough computing resources for task execution. The efficiency of this model depends on the PVs' willingness to rent their computing resources. Hence, it challenges us to utilize incentive Stackelberg game for maximizing the cloud and the PVs' profits.

2   System Model and Game Formulation

Using the classic edge-cloud computing network, we study interactions between PVs and a cloud through wireless communication. A simple illustration is given (see Fig. 1). We model the interactions between the cloud and PVs as a two-stage Stackelberg game.

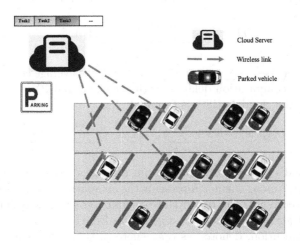

Fig. 1. The system model.

Assume that PVs $\mathcal{N} = \{1, 2, \ldots, N\}$ are parked within the communication range of the cloud. The computing resources owned by PV i are quantified by $y_i, i \in \mathcal{N}$. We denote $\boldsymbol{y} = \{y_1, y_2, \ldots, y_N\}^T$. The computing resources provided by PVs are represented as $\boldsymbol{x} = \{x_1, x_2, \ldots, x_N\}^T$, where x_i quantifies the computing resources from PV i, $i \in \mathcal{N}$. Let $\boldsymbol{x}_{-i}$ denote the computing resources provided by other PVs expect PV i. Then, we define the utility of PV i,

$$U_i(x_i, \boldsymbol{x}_{-i}, p) = px_i - \frac{1}{2}a_i x_i^2 + d_i(y_i - x_i) + \sum_{j \neq i} g_{ij} x_i x_j - c_i y_i. \tag{1}$$

For PV i, its profits can be divided into three parts. The first part $px_i - \frac{1}{2}a_i x_i^2$ is the satisfaction of offloading resources x_i, where p is the price per unit computing resource and resource sensitivity $a_i > 0$. While handling the tasks allocated by the cloud, PV i also deals with its own tasks. The second part $d_i(y_i - x_i)$ represents the benefits generated from the remaining computing resources. The third part, social benefits $\sum_{k \neq i} g_{ij} x_i x_j$, acquires from PV i's social effects. The cost of PV i is $c_i y_i$, incurred by energy consumption.

Depending on PVs' strategies, we then define the cloud's utility. Note that, when the offloading event occurs, the computing tasks at the cloud will be offloaded to PVs. Without loss of generalization, we assume that the arrival of computing tasks at the cloud follows a Poisson distribution with an expected value λ_t during time slot t and the computing workload of each computing task follows an exponential distribution with an expected value of R_t. Assume that D_t represents the computation delay. In order to specifically express the calculation of D_t, we use the queuing theory to simulate the model of the cloud and PVs. We model an $M/M/N_1$ queuing system, in which $N_1 = N + 1$. In the system, the arrival of computing tasks follows a Poisson distribution with $\lambda = \frac{\lambda_t}{N+1}$ during time slot t and the average service rate is $\mu = \frac{s + \sum_{i \in \mathcal{N}} x_i}{NR_t}$. Based on the above definition, the average computation delay is defined as

$$D_t = [\frac{(\lambda/\mu)^N \mu}{(N-1)!(N\mu - \lambda)^2}]P_0 + \frac{1}{\mu}, \tag{2}$$

where $P_0 = [\frac{\mu}{\mu - \lambda} \frac{(N\lambda)^N}{N!\mu^N} + \sum_{n \in N-1} \frac{(N\lambda)^n}{n!\mu^n}]^{-1}$. And, the average computation delay is the expected computation delay at both the cloud and PVs.

Therefore, the cloud's utility is formulated as

$$U_c(p, \boldsymbol{x}) = b(s + \sum_{i \in \mathcal{N}} x_i) - c_0 s - p \sum_{i \in \mathcal{N}} x_i - kD_t. \tag{3}$$

where the cloud's gain mainly comes from the tasks' payments represented by $b(s + \sum_{i \in \mathcal{N}} x_i)$. Among them, s represents the computing resources owned by the cloud, and b represents the benefits of per unit resource. Considering practical factors, we set $b > p$. The cloud's cost generates from three aspects: 1) the energy cost of task execution, denoted as $c_0 s$, where c_0 is the unit energy cost of the cloud; 2) expenses required to allocate tasks to PVs, represented by $p \sum_{i \in \mathcal{N}} x_i$; 3) the computation delay kD_t.

We simulate the interactions between the cloud and PVs as a two-stage Stackelberg Game. The cloud acts as a leader and PVs act as followers. The two types of participants maximize their own benefits by determining their strategies. The cloud decides the unit price to maximize its profits. The definition of the optimization problem is defined as,

$$\max_{p \geqslant 0} U_c(p, \boldsymbol{x}). \tag{4}$$

Given unit price p, PV i determines the computing resources it provides for the cloud to maximize its utility. The optimization problem is denoted as,

$$\max_{x_i \geqslant 0} U_i(x_i, \boldsymbol{x}_{-i}, p), \tag{5a}$$

$$\text{subject to } \underline{x} \leqslant x_i \leqslant \overline{x}, \tag{5b}$$

where $[\underline{x}, \overline{x}]$ defines the minimum and maximum computing resources that PV i provides for the cloud, respectively. Our goal is to find the equilibrium of each sub-problem. The definition of the Nash equilibrium is given as follows.

Definition 1. *Nash equilibrium: Given the price p set by the cloud, and shared resources of other PVs $\boldsymbol{x}_{-i}^*$, the computing resource x_i^* is the Nash equilibrium of the game, if for PV $i \in \mathcal{N}$, $U_i(x_i^*, \boldsymbol{x}_{-i}^*, p) > U_i(x_i, \boldsymbol{x}_{-i}^*, p)$, for all $x_i \in [\underline{x}, \overline{x}]$.*
Given the NE of the strategies of PVs, a strategy profile p^* is the optimal price, if at p^*, the cloud can't further increase its profit by unilaterally changing its strategy, $U_c(p^*, \boldsymbol{x}^*) > U_c(p, \boldsymbol{x}^*), \forall p > 0$.

3   Analysis of the Game

We analyze the interactions between the cloud and PVs as a two-stage Stackelberg Game. The cloud acts as a leader and PVs act as followers. First, we analyze the best strategies of PVs, which achieve the Nash equilibrium in Stage 2. Then, we discuss the cloud server's optimal strategy in Stage 1.

Given an initial price p, PV i determines an optimal computing resource x_i according to (1) in order to maximize its utility. The optimization problem is calculated as (5a and 5b).

Theorem 1. *Given unit price p and other PVs' strategies $\boldsymbol{x}_{-i}$, the best strategy of PV i is calculated as:*

$$x_i^* = \begin{cases} \overline{x} & \text{if } \frac{p - d_i + \sum_{j \neq i} g_{ij} x_j}{a} > \overline{x}, \\ \frac{p - d_i + \sum_{j \neq i} g_{ij} x_j}{a} & \text{if } \underline{x} \leqslant \frac{p - d_i + \sum_{j \neq i} g_{ij} x_j}{a} \leqslant \overline{x}, \\ \underline{x} & \text{if } \frac{p - d_i + \sum_{j \neq i} g_{ij} x_j}{a} < \underline{x}. \end{cases} \tag{6}$$

Given the following condition

$$\sum_{j \neq i} g_{ij} x_j < a_i, \tag{7}$$

PVs' best strategies in (6) can be rewritten into a matrix form,

$$x^* = (H - G)^{-1}(p1 - d),$$ (8)

where d is a vector with $d = (d_i), i \in N$, and 1 is a vector with elements of 1. H and G are matrices, where $H = diag(a_1, \ldots, a_N)$, $G=$

$$\begin{bmatrix} 0 & g_{12} & \cdots & g_{1,N} \\ g_{21} & 0 & \cdots & g_{2,N} \\ \vdots & \vdots & \ddots & \vdots \\ g_{N,1} & g_{N,2} & \cdots & 0 \end{bmatrix}.$$

The Stackelberg Game we proposed achieves a Nash equilibrium by the interactions between the cloud server and PVs. So, these two types of participants are able to optimize the subproblem in their stages. We then discuss the price optimization of the cloud in stage 1.

Substituting x^* in (8) into (3), we get

$$U_c(p, x) = (b - c_0)s + (b - p)1^T K(p1 - d) - kD_t,$$ (9)

Considering D_t is a complex function with respect to μ, we then introduce $C(N, \lambda/\mu) = \frac{\mu(\lambda/\mu)^N}{(N-1)!(N\mu-\lambda)}P_0$ and rewrite $D_t = \frac{C(N,\lambda/\mu)}{N\mu-\lambda} + \frac{1}{\mu}$. We get $\frac{\partial^2 U_c(p,x)}{\partial p^2} < 0$, indicating the concavity of $U_c(p, x)$. So, there exists the unique optimal price p^*. Unfortunately, the non-linearity of $U_c(p, x)$ prevents us to find the optimal price by setting $\frac{\partial U_c(p,x)}{\partial p} = 0$. To this end, we design an algorithm to iteratively approximate the optimal price, $p^{(l+1)} = p^{(l)} + \gamma^{(l)}\frac{\partial U_c(p,x)}{\partial p}\Big|_{p^{(l)}}$, where $\gamma^{(l)}$ is the step size at iteration l. Submitting $\frac{\partial D_t}{\partial p}$ into $\frac{\partial U_c(p,x)}{\partial p}$, we obtain $\frac{\partial U_c(p,x)}{\partial p} = 1^T K(b1 - 2p1 + d) - k(\frac{\frac{\partial C(N,\lambda/\mu)}{\partial \mu}(N\mu-\lambda) - NC(N,\lambda/\mu)}{(N\mu-\lambda)^2} - \frac{1}{\mu^2})\frac{1^T K1}{NR_t}$. After calculating the unique optimal price p^*, we substitute p^* into (8) to obtain the optimal resource allocation x^*.

4   Performance Evaluation

In this chapter, we first introduce the initialization of model parameters. Then, we illustrate the simulation results. The scenario we considered is a cloud server and N parked vehicles. The vehicles' computing resources are idle when parked. We assume that the parameters a_i, c_i, d_i and y_i follow the normal distribution $N(\mu_a, \sigma_a), N(\mu_c, \sigma_c), N(\mu_d, \sigma_d)$ and $N(\mu_b, \sigma_b)$, respectively. As for the social effect g_{ij} in the model, it is assumed to follow a uniform distribution $U(0, 1)$. We here only consider the one-way influence in social relations, such as $g_{ij} = g_{ji}$. We assume that the arrival of computing tasks at the cloud is $\lambda = 500$ per second. The parameter R_t is set to be $R_t = 0.2\,\text{GHz}$, while $k = 10000$. Other parameters are given in Table 1.

Table 1. Parameter initialization in the proposed model.

Parameter	Description	Value
μ_a	Mean of a_i	0.5
μ_b	Mean of a_i	15
μ_c	Mean of a_i	1.5
μ_d	Mean of a_i	3
σ_a, σ_c, σ_d	Variance of a_i, d_i and c_i	1
σ_b	Variance of y_i	2
c_0	Cloud's unit cost	1
s	Cloud's resource	100

We start with studying the computation delay function D_t. From (2), we notice that the computation delay mainly relays on the task arrival rate λ and the average service rate μ. Considering the complexity of function D_t and associations among parameters, we take different parameters into account for observing the computation delay. We see from Fig. 2(a) that the computation delay is stable with the increment of task arrival rate. This is because the average service improves with the increase of task arrival rate. Moreover, the average service are positively related with resources, provided by the cloud and PVs. The cloud thus requires more computing resources to maintain the service intensity. We also observe the impact of task price and number of PVs on computation delay. It is found from Fig. 2(b) that the task price has a positive impact on the computation delay. It indicates that the average service rate improves with a rise in task price. However, the increasing PV number incurs the low average service rate, which leads to the long computation delay in Fig. 2(c). It is easily seen from Fig. 2 that high cloud's resource reduces the computation delay.

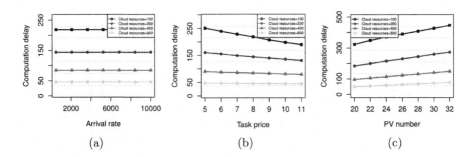

(a)   (b)   (c)

Fig. 2. The effects of model parameters on computation delay.

We are then interested in the impact of task price on the performance of the proposed model. The task price is observed from 5 to 11. From Fig. 3(a),

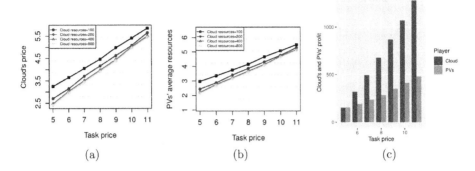

Fig. 3. The effects of task price on model performance.

we see that the cloud's price improves with the incremental task price, but reduces with the increased cloud resources. Figure 3(b) shows PVs increase their average renting resources with a rise in task price. The increase of task price leads to a higher resource pricing from the cloud, which motivates the PVs rent more computing resources to the cloud. PVs' total profits improve due to the high cloud's price and PV's increased renting resources, shown in Fig. 3(c). The benefit of task execution, generated by high task price, is able to completely compensate the cost of renting more PVs' resources. The cloud's profit thus improves with the rise of task price, displayed in Fig. 3(c).

We finally consider the effect of number of PVs on the performance of the proposed model. Figure 4(a) and Fig. 4(b) shows an increasing trend of the cloud's pricing and PVs' renting resources. It implies that the cloud improves the price for obtaining more resources with the increment of PV number. Therefore, as shown in Fig. 4(c), the cloud's profit reduces with the increasing number of PV while the PVs' total profits improves with the increasing number of PVs. The increase of PV number leads to the cloud's high expenditure for the PVs.

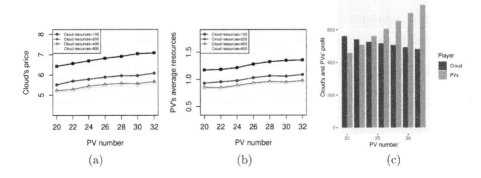

Fig. 4. The effects of number of PVs on model performance.

5   Conclusion

In this paper, we introduce a model to offload tasks from the cloud to PVs. The success of this model mainly depends on the incentive mechanism of the cloud to provide rewards for PVs. In return, PVs rent computing resources for the cloud. To maximize the benefits of the cloud and PVs, we adopt a two-stage Stackelberg game with the consideration of social effect and computation delay. Specifically, the cloud determines the price per unit resource, on which PVs determine the computing resources they rent. Simulation results illustrate that the proposed model can aid to improve QoS and computing resources' utilization.

References

1. Chen, J., Kang, H., Qi, W., Sun, Y., Shi, Z., He, S.: Narrowband internet of things: implementations and applications. IoT J. IEEE **4**(6), 2309–2314 (2017)
2. Li, Y., Li, J., Ahmed, M.: A three-stage incentive formation for optimally pricing social data offloading. J. Netw. Comput. Appl. **172**, 102816 (2020)
3. Lin, C., Pan, J., Lian, Z., Shen, X.: Networked electric vehicles for green intelligent transportation. IEEE Commun. Stan. Mag. **1**(2), 77–83 (2017)
4. Lyu, X., Tian, H., Sengul, C., Zhang, P.: Multiuser joint task offloading and resource optimization in proximate clouds. IEEE Trans. Veh. Technol. **66**, 3435–3447 (2017)
5. Qiao, Y., Li, Y., Li, J.: An economic incentive for D2D assisted offloading using Stackelberg game. IEEE Access **8**, 136684–136696 (2020)
6. Xu, C., Lei, J., Li, W., Fu, X.: Efficient multi-user computation offloading for mobile-edge cloud computing. IEEE/ACM Trans. Netw. **24**(5), 2795–2808 (2016)
7. Yuan, Q., Zhou, H., Li, J., Liu, Z., Yang, F., Shen, X.S.: Toward efficient content delivery for automated driving services: an edge computing solution. IEEE Netw. **32**(1), 80–86 (2018)
8. Yue, L., Kai, S., Lin, C.: Cooperative device-to-device communication with network coding for machine type communication devices. IEEE Trans. Wireless Commun. **17**(1), 296–309 (2017)
9. Zhang, J., et al.: Energy-latency tradeoff for energy-aware offloading in mobile edge computing networks. IEEE IoT J. **5**, 2633–2645 (2017)
10. Zhang, X., Guo, L., Li, M., Fang, Y.: Motivating human-enabled mobile participation for data offloading. IEEE Trans. Mob. Comput. **17**, 1624–1637 (2017)
11. Zhang, Y., Lan, X., Ren, J., Cai, L.: Efficient computing resource sharing for mobile edge-cloud computing networks. IEEE/ACM Trans. Netw. **28**, 1227–1240 (2020)

Complex Task Allocation in Spatial Crowdsourcing: A Task Graph Perspective

Liang Wang[1], Xueqing Wang[1(✉)], Zhiwen Yu[1], Qi Han[2], and Bin Guo[1]

[1] Northwestern Polytechnical University, Xi'an 710129, China
{liangwang,xqwang,zhiwenyu,guob}@nwpu.edu.cn
[2] Colorado School of Mines, 1500 Illinois Street, Golden, CO 80401, USA
qhan@mines.edu

Abstract. In this paper, we study a novel spatial crowdsourcing scenario, where a complex outsourced task is divided into a group of subtasks with dependency relationships. Under this scenario, we investigate a **T**ask **G**raph **A**ssignment problem in **S**patial **C**rowdsourcing (**TGA-SC**), which strives to achieve an optimal task assignment solution, with the goal of minimizing the overall makespan and idle time, simultaneously. We propose two heuristic approaches, namely random walk-based algorithm *RwalkS*, and layered evolutionary algorithm *LayGA* to tackle **TGA-SC** problem. Using two real-world data sets, we implement extensive experiments to show the superiority of our proposed approaches.

Keywords: Spatial Crowdsourcing · Task allocation · Directed Acyclic Graph (DAG)

1 Introduction

The rapid growth of smart mobile devices and the convenient access to wireless network are promoting a novel distributed problem-solving paradigm, namely Spatial Crowdsourcing (SC), which takes advantage of the collaboration of individuals to accomplish spatial tasks [6]. In general, a SC platform outsources location-based tasks to a group of suitable workers by an open call, and the selected workers need to physically move to the specified positions to fulfill the assigned tasks. However, some complex tasks require specific skills to finish, such as car repairing, wall painting.

Prior researches [1,4,5] in SC focus on dividing complex tasks into a series of easier subtasks, and then matching the subtasks requirements with the workers' skill/resource ability. However, in many cases, the divided subtasks are not independent, but highly interdependent. For instance, when we want to hold an orienteering race, we have to arrange a set of checkpoints following a specific order. Since the clue of the next checkpoint should be put in the last checkpoint, the tasks of setting each checkpoint should be conducted following the order.

Z. Liu et al. (Eds.): WASA 2021, LNCS 12939, pp. 226–234, 2021.
https://doi.org/10.1007/978-3-030-86137-7_25

If the previous solutions [1,4,5] are used directly, the dependency among the subtasks will cause the efficiency of the assignment to become very low.

Actually, precedence-constrained tasks are common in the filed of multi-core computing and distributed computing [2,7]. The interdependent tasks are usually characterized with the tool of task graph, i.e., Directed Acyclic Graphs (DAGs). However, as the recruited workers need to physically move to the specified locations, task assignment in DAG-oriented SC needs to additionally consider the geographical distances between the tasks and workers, which have a great impact on workers' traveling distance, tasks' makespan and the overall idle time. Thus, the scenario we studied becomes more difficult and intractable.

In this paper, we investigate a problem of complex SC task assignment, namely **Task Graph Assignment in Spatial Crowdsourcing (TGA-SC)**, where a group of highly interdependent subtasks need to be assigned to suitable workers with the goal of minimizing the overall makespan and idle time, simultaneously. Nevertheless, the **TGA-SC** problem is NP-hard. To tackle it, we propose two effective heuristic approaches, including a random walk-based algorithm (*RwalkS*) and a layered evolutionary algorithm (*LayGA*), which can balance makespan and idle time well. Our main contributions are listed as follows.

- We study and formalize a novel spatial crowdsourcing problem, namely **TGA-SC** problem, where dependencies between divided subtasks of complex SC task are considered.
- We propose two efficient heuristic approaches, namely Random Walk-based aSsignment algorithm (*RwalkS*), and Layered Genetic Assignment (*LayGA*) to tackle our **TGA-SC** problem.
- We conduct extensive experiments on two real-world data sets, and show the effectiveness and efficiency of our proposed approaches.

2   Preliminary and Problem Formulation

2.1   Preliminary

Definition 1 *(Complex SC Task). Generally, a complex task T in SC systems can be divided into several easier subtasks, i.e., $T = \{t_i | 1 \leqslant i \leqslant n\}$, where $\bigcup_{i=1}^{n} t_i = T$ and $t_i \cap t_j = \varnothing, i \neq j$. For each subtask $t_i \in T$, it is denoted as $t_i = (loc_{t_i}, S_{t_i})$, where $loc_{t_i} \in \mathcal{L}$ represents a specified location for t_i, and $S_{t_i} \in \mathcal{S}$ is the set of skills/resources required to accomplish it.*

Here, the subtasks we considered are interdependent, and we adopt Directed Acyclic Graph (DAG) to characterize the dependency relationship.

Definition 2 *(Task Graph). Given a complex task $T = \{t_i | 1 \leqslant i \leqslant n\}$, one task graph $G = (T, E)$ is used to model the dependencies among its included subtasks, in which the node set T represents all the subtasks, and each element in the edge set E reflects the dependency between two related nodes.*

For one edge $t_i \rightarrow t_j$ in G, t_i is regarded as t_j' predecessor node, and t_j is the successor node of t_i. The node without any predecessors is called Entry Node $\mathcal{T}_{\text{Entry}}$, while the node without any successor is named Exit Node $\mathcal{T}_{\text{Exit}}$. Starting from the nodes in $\mathcal{T}_{\text{Entry}}$, tasks are carried out successively. We define node t_i's layer $Ly(t_i)$ as the maximum value of the path from nodes in $\mathcal{T}_{\text{Entry}}$ to t_i.

Definition 3 *(Available Workers). There is a set of available workers $\mathcal{W} = \{w_1, w_2, \ldots, w_m\}$ registered on SC platform to conduct tasks/subtasks. Each worker is denoted as $w_j = (loc_{w_j}, v_j, S_{w_j})$, where (1) spatial location $loc_{w_j} \in \mathcal{L}$ is w_j's current position; (2) v_j denotes the moving speed of w_j; (3) S_{w_j} is the skills/resources owned by the worker w_j.*

Considering a complete set of skills/resources, such as $\mathcal{S} = \{s_1, s_2, \ldots, s_q\}$, one worker w_j's skill/resource could be represented as $S_{w_j} = \{s_{w_j}^1, s_{w_j}^2, \ldots, s_{w_j}^q\}$, where $s_{w_j}^k \in [0,1], 1 \leqslant k \leqslant q$, denotes the level of k-th skill/resource. When we assign $t_i \in \mathcal{T}$ to the worker w_j, the skill/resource set of the worker w_j must fully cover the requirements of subtask t_i. For ease of exposition, the required skill/resources in subtask t_i are also expressed as $S_{t_i} = \{s_{t_i}^1, s_{t_i}^2, \ldots, s_{t_i}^q\}$, where $s_{t_i}^k \in [0,1], 1 \leqslant k \leqslant q$, indicating that the skill/resource s_k is the minimum requirement level for completing t_i. Formally, the valid candidate workers $\mathcal{W}_{t_i}$ for node t_i could be formalized as follows:

$$\mathcal{W}_{t_i} = \{w_j \mid \forall s_{t_i}^k > 0, \exists s_{w_j}^k \geqslant s_{t_i}^k, 1 \leqslant k \leqslant q\}, \tag{1}$$

where $s_{w_j}^k \in S_w$ denotes worker w_j's skill/resource level, and $s_{t_i}^k \in S_t$ denotes subtask t_i's skill/resource requirement, $1 \leqslant k \leqslant q$.

2.2   Problem Formulation

To complete the assigned subtask t_i, the selected worker $w_j \in \mathcal{W}_{t_i}$ needs to physically move to the specified location loc_{t_i}, and utilize his/her own skill/resource to perform it. Thus, the completion time of t_i should take into account both the traveling time and execution time. Assuming that the worker w_j moves with speed v_j, the traveling time can be deduced as below:

$$\theta_m^{t_i, w_j} = dist(loc_{w_j}, loc_{t_i})/v_j, \tag{2}$$

where $dist(loc_{w_j}, loc_{t_i})$ denotes the distance from w_j's current position to t_i's location. In this paper, we adopt Euclidean distance to calculate it. While for execution time, it is directly related to workers' qualification for t_i. According to previous research [3], we use an exponential function to model it as follows:

$$\begin{cases} \theta_e^{t_i, w_j} = \alpha * \sum_{1 \leqslant k \leqslant q} e^{-\beta * \Theta(s_{t_i}^k, s_{w_j}^k)} \\ \Theta(s_{t_i}^k, s_{w_j}^k) = \begin{cases} 1, & s_{t_i}^k \leqslant s_{w_j}^k \wedge s_{t_i}^k > 0 \\ s_{w_j}^k, & s_{t_i}^k > s_{w_j}^k \wedge s_{t_i}^k > 0, \end{cases} \end{cases} \tag{3}$$

where α and β denote constant coefficients.

Furthermore, under the dependency constraint, the completion time of any subtask is also related to the completion time of all its predecessor subtasks. Specifically, t_i's **Process Ready Time** $P_r(t_i)$ is equal to the maximum completion time of all its predecessor nodes', i.e.,

$$P_r(t_i) = Max\{P_f(t_x)|t_x \in \mathcal{T}_{\text{pre}}(t_i)\}, \tag{4}$$

in which $P_f(t_x)$ represents the completion time of one predecessor t_x. Obviously, if the worker's arrival time $P_v(t_i, w_j)$ is later than t_i's process ready time $P_r(t_i)$, t_i can only wait; otherwise, w_j will have to wait for the completion of all t_i's predecessor nodes. Thus, t_i's actual start time $P_s(t_i, w_j)$ and completion time $P_f(t_i, w_j)$ can be calculated as below:

$$\begin{cases} P_s(t_i, w_j) = \begin{cases} P_v(t_i, w_j) \ if \ P_r(t_i) \leqslant P_v(t_i, w_j), \\ P_r(t_i), \qquad\quad Otherwise. \end{cases} \\ P_f(t_i, w_j) = \begin{cases} P_v(t_i, w_j) + \theta_e^{t_i, w_j} \ if \ P_r(t_i) \leqslant P_v(t_i, w_j), \\ P_r(t_i) + \theta_e^{t_i, w_j}, \qquad\quad Otherwise. \end{cases} \end{cases} \tag{5}$$

We define **Idle Time** $IT(t_i, w_j)$ as the difference between t_i's process ready time $P_r(t_i)$ and its executor w_j's arrival time $P_v(t_i, w_j)$, i.e., $IT(t_i, w_j) = |P_r(t_i) - P_v(t_i, w_j)|$. The **Makespan** MS of $\mathcal{T}$ is formalized as $MS(\mathcal{T}) = Max\{P_f(t_{k_1}), P_f(t_{k_2}), \ldots, P_f(t_{k_p})\}$, where $t_{k_i} \in \mathcal{T}_{\text{Exit}}, 1 \leqslant i \leqslant p$, $P_f(t_{k_i})$ denotes the completion time of subtask t_{k_i}. We adopt a matrix structure $\mathcal{X}$ to represent task schedule solution. Specifically, one entry $\mathcal{X}_{i,j}, 1 \leqslant i \leqslant n, 1 \leqslant j \leqslant m$, denote whether subtask t_i has been assigned to worker w_j. If so, the value of $\mathcal{X}_{i,j}$ would be set as 1; otherwise, $\mathcal{X}_{i,j}$ equals 0.

Definition 4 (*Task Graph Assignment in Spatial Crowdsourcing, TGA-SC*). *For a complex SC task $\mathcal{T} = \{t_i | 1 \leqslant i \leqslant n\}$, where each subtask $t_i \in \mathcal{T}$ is denoted by $t_i = (loc_{t_i}, S_{t_i})$ and the dependency between subtasks is represented as a task graph $G = (\mathcal{T}, E)$. Given a set of available workers $\mathcal{W} = \{w_1, w_2, \ldots, w_m\}$, in which $w_j = (loc_{w_j}, v_j, S_{w_j})$, the TGA-SC problem is to obtain an assignment solution $\mathcal{X}$ between $\mathcal{T}$ and $\mathcal{W}$, to minimize the overall makespan and idle time.*

$$\begin{cases} Min : Max\{P_f(t_{k_1}), P_f(t_{k_2}), \ldots, P_f(t_{k_p})\}, \\ Min : \quad \sum_{t_i \in \mathcal{T}} |P_r(t_i) - P_v(t_i, w_j)|, \\ S.t. : \qquad \forall \mathcal{X}_{i,j} \in \mathcal{X}, \mathcal{X}_{i,j} = 1, \end{cases} \tag{6}$$

where $t_i \in \mathcal{T}$, $w_j \in \mathcal{W}$, $t_{k_x} \in \mathcal{T}_{\text{Exit}}$, and $\mathcal{X}_{i,j}$ denotes subtask-worker pair (t_i, w_j).

3 Proposed Approaches

3.1 Random Walk-Based Assignment Algorithm

In this subsection, we propose a **R**andom **walk**-based a**S**signment algorithm, namely *RwalkS algorithm*, to solve our problem. *RwalkS* traverses over graph G and assigns the subtasks to suitable workers in turn. However, during random walk, not all the encountered nodes can be assigned immediately, such as, non-ready subtasks. In fact, if a node is an entry node, or all of its predecessor nodes have already been finished, *RwalkS algorithm* can assign it promptly; otherwise, we temporarily skip it and turn to other nodes.

Initially, we select one entry node to start a random walk. In order to improve the search efficiency, we derive an initial node selecting strategy according to specified probability distribution. Formally, given a set of entry nodes $\mathcal{T}_{\text{Entry}} = \{t_1, \ldots, t_r\}$, for each node t_i in $\mathcal{T}_{\text{Entry}}$, its successor nodes and their associated layer labels are listed as $\mathcal{T}_{\text{suc}}(t_i) = \{(t_1^i, Ly(t_1^i), |\mathcal{T}_{\text{pre}}(t_1^i)|), \ldots, (t_r^i, Ly(t_r^i), |\mathcal{T}_{\text{pre}}(t_r^i)|)\}$, while t_i would be selected as an initial node with probability $p(t_i)$, such that:

$$\begin{cases} p(t_i) = \frac{1}{\Gamma} * \sum_{t_j^i \in \mathcal{T}_{\text{suc}}(t_i)} \frac{1}{Ly(t_j^i)*|\mathcal{T}_{\text{pre}}(t_j^i)|} \\ \Gamma = \sum_{t_i \in \mathcal{T}_{\text{Entry}}} \sum_{t_j^i \in \mathcal{T}_{\text{suc}}(t_i)} \frac{1}{Ly(t_j^i)*|\mathcal{T}_{\text{pre}}(t_j^i)|}, \end{cases} \quad (7)$$

where $|\mathcal{T}_{\text{pre}}(t_j^i)|$ represents the number of t_j^i's predecessor nodes. Essentially, it indicates that one entry node having more successor nodes, and their successor nodes with less preceded nodes are associated with larger selection probability.

To balance these two involved optimal objectives, we construct an integrated utility function as below to measure each candidate worker w_j's utility with respect to subtask t_{i_k},

$$\partial(t_{i_k}, w_j) = \varphi * P_f(t_{i_k}, w_j) + (1 - \varphi) * IT(t_{i_k}, w_j), \quad (8)$$

where the factor φ equals to 0.5. By using the integrated utility function, current node could be assigned by examining each candidate worker's benefit. Once current node has been tackled, *RwalkS algorithm* will walk to the next node to continue the assignment process. A natural choice is its successor nodes. However, its successor nodes might have other unassigned predecessors. Thus, it should activate a *Reverse Walk* upon the lower layer to explore other process ready nodes. If the predecessor during reverse walk is also non-ready task, it will continue until one ready node has been found. Furthermore, in order to improve the efficiency, we introduce a *maximum step of reverse walk* η, to limit the process. In other words, when the reverse walk reaches a maximum walk layer, *RwalkS algorithm* would escape from it, and restarts a new traveling started from one of unassigned nodes in G. The procedure will not quit until all the subtasks have been assigned.

3.2 Layered Evolutionary Assigning Algorithm

From the perspective of worker, assigning each subtask is not independent. When a worker is assigned to one subtask, he/she might lose the chance to undertake another one, due to the constraints of the task graph topology and spatiotemporal requirements. During the incremental scheduling process, each subtask will inevitably focus only on optimizing itself to the greatest extent, ignoring global optimum for the whole task $\mathcal{T}$. Thus, this strategy might narrows down the potential schedule solutions to a very small part of the whole solution space [8].

It is better to build assignment solutions from the whole problem space consisting of all subtasks and workers. Unfortunately, the combination search space is too large to traverse. Actually, even for the heuristic algorithms, the calculation is also difficult to converge to the optimal solution. Thus, we propose a divide-and-conquer heuristic evolutionary algorithm, namely *LayGA algorithm*, to balance the trade-off between optimal performance and efficiency. The basic idea of *LayGA algorithm* is to partition the whole problem space into many sub-spaces, where each sub-space corresponds to one layer in task graph. Concretely, at each layer, say $Ly = K$, all the subtasks contained within it, i.e., $\mathcal{T}_{\#} = \{t_i | Ly(t_i) = K\}$, are grouped as a cluster to be handled together. For subtasks $\mathcal{T}_{\#}$, we utilize a Genetic Algorithm to optimally search its sub-solution $\mathcal{X}_{\mathcal{T}_{\#}}$. After all layers have been processed, the obtained sub-solutions could be merged to generate a complete assignment solution. Obviously, within each layer subspace, *LayGA algorithm* could achieve "approximate global optimization".

At each layer, for the subtask set $\mathcal{T}_{\#}$, an initial population should be firstly generated, in which a specified size of individuals are contained. Based on the set of candidate workers, we construct initial individuals one by one in a stochastic manner, i.e., randomly choose one worker from candidates $\mathcal{W}_t$ for each subtask t. Formally, an individual is encoded with a symbol string with length equals to the size of $\mathcal{T}_{\#}$, i.e., $|\mathcal{T}_{\#}|$, where each symbol indicates the designated worker for relative subtask. And then, we adopt Eq. 8 to represent its fitness value. As graph scheduling is a dynamic process, one simulation process is required to derive its fitness. The simulation is incremental based on the determined sub-solutions for the prior layers, i.e., pairs for subtasks (t_i, w_j), where $t_i \in \{t_i | Ly(t_i) < K\}$.

Next, for each successive generation, the current population will evolves toward better solutions. When conducting one selection operation, we randomly choose a group of individual from the current population, and pick up the one with highest fitness value for the new generation. A crossover and mutation operation is then performed on these new individuals to modify their representation. After the iteration runs out, the best population in the evolution process would be determined as one output. Finally, all the returned results on each layer will be combined as the final complete scheduling solution.

4 Evaluation and Discussion

4.1 Experimental Settings

Data Set: In our experiments, we choose two real-world data sets. The first small-scale data set is StudentLife[1] published by researchers at Dartmouth College. We use the WiFi readings in the data set as workers' initial positions, and 101 Point-of-Interests (POIs). The second large-scale data set is a GPS trajectory data set collected from about 1200 taxicabs in Chengdu city, China. The GPS data points are employed to simulate participant workers' initial positions. And 3000 POIs in Chengdu city are randomly extracted to generated subtasks.

---

[1] http://studentlife.cs.dartmouth.edu/.

Baseline Algorithms: To the best of our knowledge, our work is the first to investigate task assignment in SC platforms that considers task dependency constraints. Consequently, we select three most related methods from DAG task scheduling for comparison, which are listed as follows:

1) *HEFTM Algorithm:* the method is developed by modifying one of the most frequently cited and used DAG task scheduling algorithm, i.e., *HEFT* [2]. Specifically, all subtasks are firstly prioritized based on their average execution time and traveling time. Afterwards, the assignment procedure will handle subtasks according to the determined priority order.
2) *ClustS Algorithm:* this method adopts the clustering heuristics approaches in DAG scheduling. By calculating pairwise similarity between subtasks in the representation space, all the subtasks are clustered into different groups. And the subtasks contained in one cluster are exclusively assigned to the same worker, in order to reduce the traveling cost.
3) *GloGa Algorithm:* this method adopts Genetic Algorithm to search optimal solutions. Based on the population-based evolutionary process, it globally searches a desired solution throughout the whole problem space.

4.2   Experimental Results and Analysis

In this experiment, we generate complex MC tasks, i.e., task graphs, from these two above-mentioned real-world data sets, which contains a total of 80 subtasks and 60 registered workers. With respect to parameter setting, the values of α, β and η (in *RwalkS* algorithm) are set to 1, 0.05, and 3, respectively. And the skill/resource set $\mathcal{S}$ includes 10 different elements. Using these two data sets, we simulate four different experiment scenarios: *E1, E2, E3, E4*, where *E1, E2* are based on StudentLife data set and *E3, E4* are based on Chengdu data set. The corresponding results are reported in Fig. 1(a) and (b), where the results of *ClustS* algorithm are listed separately in Table 1 due to its too large value. In order to fix the performance of all involved scheduling algorithms, we report the average results over 10 repeated trails.

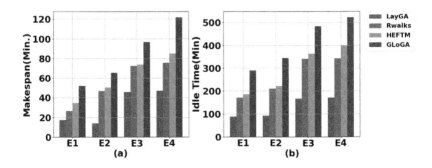

Fig. 1. Experimental results of task assignment.

Table 1. The experimental results of *ClustS* algorithm.

	E1	E2	E3	E4
Makespan (Min.)	152.84	177.36	257.97	272.84
Idle time (Min.)	578.13	607.76	873.19	985.26

Above all, the performance of *E1, E2* are obviously superior to *E3, E4*, due to the fact that *E1, E2* are conducted in campus environment, while *E3, E4* are conducted within a larger city-level scale. As a result, the traveling time cost in *E3, E4* would increase sharply. From the experiments results, it is obvious that the assignment performance of *LayGA* achieve the best performance, followed by *RwalkS*, *HEFTM*, *GloGA* and *ClustS* algorithms. By comparing our *LayGA* with *GloGA* algorithm, the divide-and-conquer strategy can obtain better results. This also verifies that the problem space is too large to be explored globally. Because *RwalkS* adopts a quasi Depth-First-Search mode, the dependence constraints among subtasks hinder its search capabilities.

5   Conclusion

In this work, we focus on task graph assignment in SC paradigm with dependency relationship between the involved tasks. Specifically, a complex outsourced task to be performed is decomposed into one set of highly interdependent subtasks. Our goal is to find an efficient assignment solution between the subtasks and available workers, such that the overall makespan and idle time is minimized simultaneously. We try our best to find an desired solution and propose a random walk-based *RwalkS* algorithm and a layered genetic *LayGA* algorithm. Extensive experiments show the effectiveness of our proposed approaches.

References

1. Gao, D., Tong, Y., et al.: Top-k team recommendation and its variants in spatial crowdsourcing. Data Sci. Eng. **2**(2), 136–150 (2017)
2. Ijaz, S., Munir, E.U.: MOPT: list-based heuristic for scheduling workflows in cloud environment. J. Supercomput. **75**(7), 3740–3768 (2019)
3. Janiak, A., Kovalyov, M.Y.: Job sequencing with exponential functions of processing times. Informatica **17**(1), 13–24 (2006)
4. Li, M., Zheng, Y., et al.: Task assignment for simple tasks with small budget in mobile crowdsourcing. In: 2018 14th International Conference on Mobile Ad-Hoc and Sensor Networks (MSN), pp. 68–73. IEEE (2018)
5. Miao, C., Yu, H., et al.: Balancing quality and budget considerations in mobile crowdsourcing. Decis. Support Syst. **90**, 56–64 (2016)
6. Tong, Y., Chen, L., Shahabi, C.: Spatial crowdsourcing: challenges, techniques, and applications. Proc. VLDB Endow. **10**(12), 1988–1991 (2017)

7. Wang, H., Sinnen, O.: List-scheduling versus cluster-scheduling. IEEE Trans. Parallel Distrib. Syst. **29**(8), 1736–1749 (2018)
8. Xu, Y., Li, K., et al.: A hybrid chemical reaction optimization scheme for task scheduling on heterogeneous computing systems. IEEE Trans. Parallel Distrib. Syst. **26**(12), 3208–3222 (2014)

Jointly Optimizing Throughput and Cost of IoV Based on Coherent Beamforming and Successive Interference Cancellation Technology

Lan Wu[1], Juan Xu[1], Lei Shi[1(✉)], Xiang Bi[1], and Yi Shi[2]

[1] School of Computer Science and Information Engineering, Intelligent
Interconnected Systems Laboratory of Anhui Province,
Hefei University of Technology, Hefei 230009, China
shilei@hfut.edu.cn
[2] Department of ECE, Virginia Tech, Blacksburg, VA 24061, USA

Abstract. The high transmission performance of 5G provides the Internet of Vehicles (IoV) more opportunities for doing tasks which need to handle large amount of data within a small time span. However, 5G base station has a small coverage and a high cost which may restrict its development in the IoV. In this paper, we try to give some feasible solution for this problem. We will use two physical layer techniques, the coherent beamforming (CB) technology and the successive interference cancellation (SIC) technology to increase the total amount of data transmitted by vehicles while reducing network infrastructure costs. We first establish the mathematical model and prove it couldn't be solved directly, and then design two algorithms, the Road and CB-nodes Assignment (RCA) algorithm and the Throughput Optimization of Vehicle Scheduling based on SIC (TOVSS) algorithm. Simulation results show that our method has the advantages of cost saving and throughput improvement.

Keywords: Coherent beamforming · Edge computing · Internet of Vehicles · 5G · Successive interference cancellation

1 Introduction

As an important research and industrial field, the Internet of Vehicles (IoV) has been studied for some years [1,2]. However, since people's pursuit to the quality of experience (QoE) grows constantly, the privacy and efficiency of data processing has always been a concern [3–5], among them, the problem of task unloading in Internet of Vehicles has always been concerned [6,7]. Recently, many researchers focus on the edge computing technique on the IoV, which makes lots of complex computing tasks work on the edge servers to makes it possible to improve the

Supported by the National Natural Science Foundation of China (Grant No. 61806067), the Anhui Provincial Key R&D Program of China (202004a05020040).

Z. Liu et al. (Eds.): WASA 2021, LNCS 12939, pp. 235–243, 2021.
https://doi.org/10.1007/978-3-030-86137-7_26

data throughput [8]. The basic communication of the edge computing framework is built on the 5G network, with the characteristics of high data volume and low latency [9]. However, the base station of 5G has the shortcoming of high cost and small coverage area [10], which may delay the development of the edge computing technique on the IoV.

Fortunately, the coherent beamforming (CB) technology provides us a method to compensate for the 5G's shortcoming. The transmitting node needs to broadcast data to several other idle nodes, which will then help the transmitter's transmitting, thus increasing the transmission distance by increasing the power gain. Many researchers have done their work on CB. In [11], authors developed an improved beamforming scheme which has clutter suppression capability and sensitivity to signal energy. In [12], authors presented a novel space-time waveform design scheme for MIMO radar to meet the beamforming constraints and requirements of waveform orthogonality in time domain. In [13], authors proved that the power gain of N senders and M receivers in coherent beamforming communication can reach N^2M to improve transmission range of the node.

Another useful technology for 5G environment is the successive interference cancellation (SIC). When using the SIC technology, a receiver can receive multiple signals simultaneously from transmitters. The receiver will first decode the strongest signal in the multiple data. After a successful receiving, the strongest signal will be removed from the initial multiple data. The cycle is repeated until all signals are decoded or some signal cannot be decoded. In [14], authors promoted the SIC use in multi-hop wireless network by systematically studying. In [15], authors proposed the use-up-link-capacity iterative (UULC-iterative) algorithm to improve throughput. In [16], authors proposed a new algorithm by combining the SIC technique with the neighbor discovery algorithm to improve the performance of the original neighbor discovery algorithm.

However, no paper considers using SIC and CB to improve the QoE of IoV and makes the use of 5G become reality. In our previous work, we have build a relatively simple model based on CB technology, then optimized the CB-node layout scheme to reduce the cost of network communication [17]. In this paper, we try to study the task unloading problem for multiple vehicles by using CB and SIC under 5G vehicle networking scenario, under the premise of reducing the communication cost while maximizing the unloading data amount.

The paper is organized as the following. In Sect. 2, we analyze the mathematical model of CB and SIC for 5G multi-vehicle network and the mathematical model is reorganized. In Sect. 3, we design two algorithms which we name as RCA and TOVSS. In Sect. 4, we chose two groups of comparative experiments, and obtained the superiority of our algorithms. In Sect. 5, we conclude the whole paper.

2   System Overview

We first describe the system model. Consider a straight multiple-lane road. An edge server is located on the road side and covers a part of the road with length

L. A number of wireless nodes are placed on both sides of the road for helping communicating, vehicles will first broadcast data to its nearby nodes, and then these nodes will collaborate to send data to the edge server by using the CB technique. We call these nodes as CB-nodes. Suppose each vehicle needs to upload at least D_{min} data to the edge server. According to our previous research results, in this paper, we want to present an optimal scheduling scheme to maximize the sum of the total data D_{total} transmitted by all vehicles while reduce the cost of network transmission infrastructure.

2.1 System Model and Problem Formulation

Denote s_i as one of the CB-node. Denote N as the set of all CB-nodes, i.e., $s_i \in N$. Denote n as the number of N. Denote b as the edge server. Denote S_j as the set of fixed CB-nodes required for each vehicle to transmit data. Denote M as the set of all CB-node groups, i.e., $S_j \in M$. Denote m as the number of M. Since the CB-node is a low cost device, we suppose there are enough CB-nodes in each set. **Apparently** $m \ll 2^n - 1$. Denote c_l as one of vehicles. Denote C as the set of all vehicles on that section of the road in time T, i.e., $c_l \in C$. Denote q as the number of C. Suppose the whole schedule time T is divided into h time slots equally, and denote time slot as $t_k(i = 1 \dots h)$. We have $t_1 = \cdots = t_h$. Denote D_l as the amount of data for vehicle c_l's transmitting. Denote D_l^j as c_l's transmitting data to the set S_j, then we have

$$D_{min}^l \le D_l = \sum_{j=1}^{m} D_l^j. \tag{1}$$

One transmission data has two stages. In the first stage, the vehicle broadcasts data to its nearby CB-nodes. In the second stage, CB-nodes transmit data to the edge server by using CB technique. We use $x_{c_l \to S_j}(t_k)$, $x_{S_j \to b}(t_k)$ to indicate the transmission cases of a CB-node or a set at time t_k, i.e., if $x_{c_l \to S_j}(t_k) = 1$ (or $x_{S_j \to b}(t_k) = 1$), it means that S_j (or b) will receive data at time t.

For a set S_j, it cannot transmit or receive simultaneously. We have

$$x_{c_l \to S_j}(t_k) + x_{S_j \to b}(t_k) \le 1 \quad (\forall j, l, k, S_j \in M, c_l \in C, t_k \in T). \tag{2}$$

When using SIC technology, multiple sets of CB-node can transmit data to the edge server at the same time. Suppose there are at most m CB-node sets which can transmit simultaneously, we have

$$\sum_{S_j \in M} x_{S_j \to b}(t_k) \le m. \tag{3}$$

When using the SIC technology, for the first step, the signal-to-noise-ratio $SINR_{c_l \to s_i}(t_k)$ from c_l to the CB-node s_i at time t_k can be expressed as

$$SINR_{c_l \to s_i}(t_k) = \frac{(d_{c_l \to s_i}(t_k))^{-\lambda} P_v \cdot x_{c_l \to S_j}(t_k)}{\sum\limits_{c_g \in C, c_l \ne c_g} (d_{c_g \to s_i(t_k)})^{-\lambda} P_v + N_0} \ge \beta \cdot x_{c_l \to S_j}(t_k), \tag{4}$$

where P_v is the transmission power of each vehicle, N_0 is the noise power, λ is the pass loss index, β is a constant, and $d_{c_l \to s_i}(t_k)$ is the distance between the vehicle c_l and the CB-node s_i at time t_k.

For the second step, denote $SINR_{S_j \to b}(t_k)$ as the sum of SINR from all CB-nodes in the group S_j sending data to the edge server collaboratively at time t_k, we have

$$SINR_{S_j \to b}(t_k) = \frac{(\sum\limits_{s_i \in S_j} \sqrt{d_{s_i \to b}^{-\lambda}})^2 P_s \cdot x_{S_j \to b}(t_k)}{\sum\limits_{\substack{S_l \in G}} (\sum\limits_{\substack{s_l \neq s_i \\ s_l \in S_l}} \sqrt{d_{s_l \to b}^{-\lambda}})^2 P_s \cdot x_{S_l \to b}(t_k) + N_0} \geq \beta \cdot x_{S_j \to b}(t_k), \quad (5)$$

where $d_{s_i \to b}$ is the distance between s_i and the edge server, G is the set for all CB-node sets which satisfy the condition $(\sum\limits_{s_i \in S_l} \sqrt{d_{s_l \to b}^{-\lambda}})^2 P_s < (\sum\limits_{s_i \in S_j} \sqrt{d_{s_i \to b}^{-\lambda}})^2 P_s$, and P_s is the transmission power for each CB-node (suppose all CB-nodes have the same power).

Then we can represent D_l^j and D_l in (1) to (6) and (7). Denote W as the bandwidth, we have,

$$D_l^j = \sum_{k=1}^{h} W \log_2(1 + SINR_{c_l \to S_j}(t_k)) \cdot x_{c_l \to S_j}(t_k), \quad (6)$$

$$D_l = \sum_{j=1}^{m} D_l^j = \sum_{j=1}^{m} \sum_{k=1}^{h} W \log_2(1 + SINR_{c_l \to S_j}(t_k)) \cdot x_{c_l \to S_j}(t_k). \quad (7)$$

Denote D_j as the amount of data received over the entire time period T. Since the amount of data transmitted by the vehicle to the set should be equal to the amount of data transmitted by the set to the edge server, we have

$$D_j = \sum_{k=1}^{h} W \log_2(1 + SINR_{S_j \to b}(t_k)) \cdot x_{S_j \to b}(t_k) \quad (\forall j, S_j \in M) \quad (8)$$

Denote D_{total} as the total of data transmitted by all vehicles pass through the whole road at time T, we have

$$D_{total} = \sum_{l=1}^{q} D_l = \sum_{l=1}^{q} \sum_{j=1}^{m} \sum_{k=1}^{h} W \log_2(1 + SINR_{c_l \to S_j}(t_k)) \cdot x_{c_l \to S_j}(t_k). \quad (9)$$

Based on the above discussions, we can get the final formula,

$$\max D_{total} \atop \text{s.t.} \quad (1), (2) - (9). \quad (10)$$

Notice that in (10), we don't know how many S_j and the number of m may be a very large number. We also notice that we have variable $x_{c_l \to S_j}(t_k)$ in the numerator and the denominator about time t_k. So (10) cannot be solved directly.

2.2   Problem Refinement

In this section, we reformulate the problem of the previous section. Notice that we have two main problems to design the algorithm. First, how to determine the exact number of CB-node sets and the exact number of CB-nodes in each CB-node set. Second, how to determine which time slots for vehicles or CB-node sets communication by calculating the variables of $x_{c_i \to S_j}(t_k)$ and $x_{S_j \to b}(t_k)$.

We now discuss the first problem. Since vehicles usually travel with constant speeds on roads and we assume that the vehicle has a speed v_l in time T. We have $v_l \geq v_{min} = L/T$. We should ensure that each vehicle complete the communication within $\frac{2R_s}{v_{min}}$ time. Assume that the communication range of the CB-nodes in each segment is not intersected with the other segments, we can find that we should at least divide the whole road equally into $h(\geq h_{min} = \frac{L}{2R_s})$ parts. In each path part, denote the length as $l_j (j = 1, 2, ..., h)$, and we will arrange a set S_j for each vehicle transmitting D_l^j data to the edge server. We also notice that when a vehicle entering a path part, the $d_{c_l \to s_i}(t_k)$ in this part will not change too much. So we consider $d_{c_l \to s_i}(t_k)$ as a constant d_{c_l} approximately, and the distance between S_j and the edge server as d_j. We have the following lemmas.

Lemma 1. *If S_j is transmitting data $(x_{S_j \to b}(t_k) = 1)$ to the edge server in time t_k, then we have: If $[\beta(n_l^2 \cdot d_l^{-\lambda} + \frac{N_0}{P_s})]^{-\frac{1}{\lambda}} \leq d_j \leq (\frac{n_l^2 \cdot d_l^{-\lambda}}{\beta} - \frac{N_0}{P_s})^{-\frac{1}{\lambda}}$, then S_l cannot transmits data to edge server during time t_k $(x_{S_j \to b}(t_k) = 1)$, else the remaining S_l may transmit data to the edge server in time t_k. $(n_l^2 \cdot d_l)$ represents the channel gain, d_j represents the distance between the S_j and the edge server, β is a constant, P_s is the CB-node transmission power, λ is the pass loss index [18].*

Lemma 1 has been proved in [18]. According to Lemma 1, we can get $l_j = (\frac{n_j^2 \cdot d_j^{-\lambda}}{\beta} - \frac{N_0}{P_s})^{-\frac{1}{\lambda}} - [\beta(n_j^2 \cdot d_j^{-\lambda} + \frac{N_0}{P_s})]^{-\frac{1}{\lambda}} + \delta$, where δ is a very small number and $x_{S_j \to b}(t_k) = 1$. So, $L = \sum_{j=1}^{h} l_j$.

Denote $(n_j)_{min}$ as the least number of CB-nodes that needed. Denote n_j as the actual number of CB-nodes contained in set, i.e., $n_j \geq (n_j)_{min}$. We have

$$(n_j)_{min} = \lceil \frac{d_j}{R_s} \rceil. \tag{11}$$

Lemma 2. *If the road is divide into h segments, the edge server can receive data simultaneously at most from h CB-node sets when using SIC technology. We can get the number of CB-nodes n_j in each segment l_j through $n_j = $*

$$\sqrt{\frac{\beta \cdot (\sum_{s_l \in G}^{s_l \neq s_i} n_l^2 d_l^{-\lambda} P_s + N_0)}{P_s \cdot d_j^{-\lambda}}}. \textit{ (For space reasons, the proof of Lemma 2 is omitted here.)}$$

In Lemma 2, n_l, d_l and d_j are unknown, but we know $d_h = \frac{L}{2}$ and $d_j = d_l - l_j$, so that we can get n_h, then we can obtain n_{h-1} and d_{n-1}, so we have

$$n_h = \sqrt{\frac{\beta \cdot N_0}{P_s \cdot d_h^{-\lambda}}}, \ldots, n_1 = \sqrt{\frac{\beta \cdot \left(\sum_{S_l=S_2}^{S_h} n_l^2 d_l^{-\lambda} P_s + N_0\right)}{P_s \cdot d_1^{-\lambda}}}. \tag{12}$$

Base on Lemma 1 and Lemma 2, we design the Road and CB-nodes Assignment Algorithm (RCA) for deciding for the number of CB-node sets and the number of CB-nodes in each set.

The second problem is calculating variables $x_{c_l \to S_j}(t_k)$ and $x_{S_j \to b}(t_k)$ in formula (10). $x_{c_l \to S_j}(t_k)$ is about the interference between vehicles and CB-node sets and the data that a particular vehicle transmits to the set S_j. $x_{S_j \to b}(t_k)$ depends on the data received by the edge server and the interference decomposition between the data. We design the Algorithm for Throughput Optimization of Vehicle Scheduling based on SIC (TOVSS) for solving them.

3   Algorithms

In this section, we will introduce algorithms. We will first introduce the RCA algorithm for dividing the road and arranging CB-nodes, and then introduce the TOVSS algorithm for distributing the vehicle's data and get optimal results.

The fist algorithms is RCA algorithm. From Lemma 1 and Lemma 2, we solve the problem of road segmentation and the number of CB-nodes and sets, and can directly get the RCA algorithm, the main steps of the TOVSS algorithm are shown as follows.

Step 1: Initializing l_0, d_0, n_0; initial $j = 1$.
Step 2: Calculate distance between the CB-node set and edge server: $d_j = d_{j-1} - l_j$, and $l_j = \left(\frac{n_{j-1}^2 \cdot d_{j-1}^{-\lambda}}{\beta} - \frac{N_0}{P_s}\right)^{-\frac{1}{\lambda}} - \left[\beta\left(n_{j-1}^2 \cdot d_{j-1}^{-\lambda} + \frac{N_0}{P_s}\right)\right]^{-\frac{1}{\lambda}} + \delta$.
Step 3: We set $f = \sum_{S_l \in G}^{s_l \neq s_i} n_l^2 d_l^{-\lambda} P_s$, then we can get $n_j = \sqrt{\frac{\beta \cdot (f \cdot p + N_0)}{P_s \cdot d_j^{-\lambda}}}$.
Step 4: Output and save a series of data about l_j and n_j.

The second algorithms is TOVSS algorithm. Since the two variables $x_{c_l \to S_j}(t_k)$ and $x_{S_j \to b}(t_k)$ in formula (10) are affected by the time slice, the result of the later time slice will be affected by the result of the previous time slice, we need to design an algorithm to solve it. The main steps of the TOVSS algorithm are shown as follows.

Step 1: Input the data obtained by RCA, L, l_j, d_j, h; Initialize D_l.
Step 2: If several vehicles are in the same segment i, we will select one of them to broadcast data. According to the v_l, the D_l, and the road conditions, the most appropriate vehicle is selected for data transmission.
Step 3: First, we judge whether the i is idle. If no vehicle occupies it, we according to S_j send data to the edge server of interference situations and task emergencies to determine whether it sends the cached data or it receives the data in the current time slice. If no vehicle occupies it to broadcast data and it

hasn't cached data, it will receive broadcast data from vehicle. If the i has been occupied by the vehicle, we do not operate. When the segment i is decided to receive broadcast data of vehicle, the vehicle selected in the previous step can broadcast data to S_j in the current segment i, i.e., $(x_{c_l \to S_j}(t_k) == 1)$.

Step 4: Record the amount of data transmitted by each vehicle, sum it up.

4   Simulation

In this section, we give simulation results. Firstly, we use the RCA algorithm to calculate the number of CB-nodes and the cost under different length of road, and compare it with the cost of the layout scheme of 5G base stations. Then, we use the TOVSS algorithm to calculate results compare them with the scheme only CB technology and the scheme only SIC technology (it covered by 4G base station which transmission rate is 75 Mbps). The straight-line distance between the edge server and the road is $a = 100$ m. The noise power N_0 is 10^{-9} W. The road strength loss factor $\lambda = 3$ and bandwidth $W = 1$ GHz.

4.1   Compare the Cost of Network Infrastructure

In this section, we let L to 800 m, 1000 m, 1200 m 1400 m. The transmission range of 5G base station is 200 m, so if we don't use the CB technique, we may need the number of 5G base stations change from 4 to 7. We let P_s as 0.3 W and 0.4 W. We set the cost of a CB-node at \$15 and a 5G base station at \$30000. According to our algorithms, we can get the total number of CB-nodes and the cost of our scheme is shown in Fig. 1. The blue one represents the cost of the 5G base station layout scheme and the orange one represents using our algorithm.

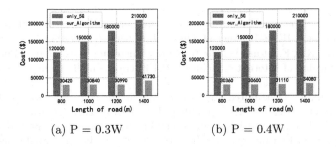

(a) P = 0.3W   (b) P = 0.4W

Fig. 1. The cost of infrastructure under different road lengths (Color figure online)

4.2   Comparison of Data Throughput

In this section, we let L change from 900 m to 1400 m, with the step 100 m, and let q to 2, 4, 6, 8, and let $R_s = 144$ m. Based on these settings, we can obtained a series of results. In Fig. 2, the red lines represent D_{total} obtained by our algorithm, and the green ones represent D_{total} obtained by the scheme of only CB technology, the blue ones represent D_{total} obtained by the scheme of only SIC technology and covered by 4G base station. We can see that D_{total} obtained by our algorithm is always the largest, therefore, we can intuitively conclude that our algorithm has the advantage of improving data throughput.

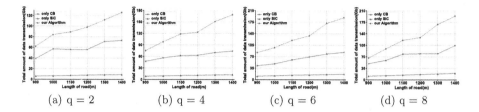

(a) q = 2   (b) q = 4   (c) q = 6   (d) q = 8

Fig. 2. Data throughput with different number of vehicles (q) (Color figure online)

5   Conclusion

In this work, we combine CB and SIC technology for increasing vehicles throughput while reducing the cost of network infrastructure. To address this problem, we develop a general model which cannot be solved directly. Then we propose two algorithms, the RCA algorithm and the TOVSS algorithm. In simulation, we compare our scheme with schemes of only CB and only SIC, and experimental results show that our scheme can save cost and improve throughput respectively.

References

1. Liu, L., Lu, S., et al.: Computing systems for autonomous driving: state-of-the-art and challenges. IEEE Internet of Things J. **8**, 6469–6486 (2020)
2. Wang, W., Xia, F., et al.: Vehicle trajectory clustering based on dynamic representation learning of Internet of Vehicles. IEEE Trans. Intell. Transp. Syst. **22**, 1–10 (2020)
3. Cai, Z., Shi, T.: Distributed query processing in the edge assisted IoT data monitoring system. IEEE Internet of Things J. **8**, 12679–12693 (2020)
4. Duan, Z., Li, W., et al.: Distributed auctions for task assignment and scheduling in mobile crowdsensing systems. In: 2017 IEEE 37th International Conference on Distributed Computing Systems (ICDCS), pp. 635–644 (2017)
5. Cai, Z., Zheng, X.: A private and efficient mechanism for data uploading in smart cyber-physical systems. IEEE Trans. Netw. Sci. Eng. **7**, 766–775 (2020)
6. He, X., Lu, H., et al.: QoE-based task offloading with deep reinforcement learning in edge-enabled Internet of Vehicles. IEEE Trans. Intell. Transp. Syst. **22**, 1–10 (2020)
7. Cao, Y., Chen, Y.: QoE-based node selection strategy for edge computing enabled Internet-of-Vehicles (EC-IoV). In: 2017 IEEE Visual Communications and Image Processing (VCIP), pp. 1–4 (2017)

8. Luo, Q., et al.: Minimizing the delay and cost of computation offloading for vehicular edge computing. IEEE Trans. Serv. Comput. **14**, 1–1 (2021)
9. Shah, S.A.A., Ahmed, E., et al.: 5G for vehicular communications. IEEE Commun. Mag. **56**(1), 111–117 (2018)
10. Cheng, X., Chen, C., et al.: 5G-enabled cooperative intelligent vehicular framework: when Benz meets Marconi. IEEE Intell. Syst. **32**(3), 53–59 (2017)
11. Ozgun, K., Tierney, J., et al.: An adapted coherent flow power doppler beamforming scheme for improved sensitivity towards blood signal energy. In: 2018 IEEE International Ultrasonics Symposium (IUS), pp. 1–4 (2018)
12. Deng, H., Geng, Z., et al.: Mimo radar waveform design for transmit beamforming and orthogonality. IEEE Trans. Aerosp. Electron. Syst. **52**(3), 1421–1433 (2016)
13. Shi, Y., Sagduyu, Y.E.: Coherent communications in self-organizing networks with distributed beamforming. IEEE Trans. Veh. Technol. **69**(1), 760–770 (2020)
14. Jiang, C., Shi, Y., et al.: Cross-layer optimization for multi-hop wireless networks with successive interference cancellation. IEEE Trans. Wireless Commun. **15**(8), 5819–5831 (2016)
15. Shi, L., Li, Z., et al.: Full-duplex multi-hop wireless networks optimization with successive interference cancellation. Sensors (Basel, Switzerland) **18**(12), 4301–4316 (2018)
16. Liang, Y., Wei, Z., et al.: Neighbor discovery algorithm in wireless ad hoc networks based on successive interference cancellation technology. In: 2020 International Conference on Wireless Communications and Signal Processing (WCSP), pp. 1137–1141 (2020)
17. Xu, J., Lan, W., et al.: Research on 5G internet of vehicles facilities based on coherent beamforming. In: The 15th International Conference on Wireless Algorithms, Systems, and Applications (WASA), Qingdao, China, 13–15 September, pp. 68–77 (2020)
18. Shi, L., Han, J., et al.: Maximizing throughput for wireless sensor network with multi-packet reception. Telecommun. Sci. **27**(3), 47–53 (2011)

Deep Reinforcement Learning Based Dynamic Content Placement and Bandwidth Allocation in Internet of Vehicles

Teng Ma[1(✉)], Xin Chen[2], Zhuo Ma[2], and Libo Jiao[2]

[1] School of Automation, Beijing Information Science and Technology University,
Beijing 100192, China
mateng@bistu.edu.cn

[2] School of Computer Science, Beijing Information Science
and Technology University, Beijing 100101, China
{chenxin,mazhuo,jiaolibo}@bistu.edu.cn

Abstract. With the rapid development of Internet of vehicles (IoV), the emerging in-vehicle applications meet people's demand for intelligent experience, while also increasing the cost of network communication. Driven by the fact that a few popular content accounted for most of the traffic load, caching popular content at the wireless edge has become a trend of content delivery. However, the limitation of cache resources and the ever-changing mobile environment bring a severe challenge to content delivery cost optimization. In this paper, we first investigate the joint optimization of content placement and bandwidth allocation (JOCB) in IoV. In order to minimize the long-term system cost in the mobile scenario, we first establish an innovative vehicle mobility model based on the probability distribution. Then we use the Lagrangian multiplier method to solve the bandwidth allocation sub-problem to reduce the algorithm complexity. Considering the high-dimensional continuity of action and state spaces, the original problem is transformed into a Markov Decision Process (MDP), and we propose a Deep reinforcement learning based Dynamic Content Placement (DDCP) algorithm. DDCP algorithm has low algorithm complexity and can handle high-dimensional continuous state and action space. The simulation results show that compare with other three benchmark algorithms, DDCP algorithm can reduce the system cost effectively.

Keywords: Internet of Vehicles · Edge cache · Content placement · Bandwidth allocation · Deep reinforcement learning

---

This work is partly supported by the National Natural Science Foundation of China (Nos. 61872044, 61902029).

Z. Liu et al. (Eds.): WASA 2021, LNCS 12939, pp. 244–253, 2021.
https://doi.org/10.1007/978-3-030-86137-7_27

1 Introduction

With the rapid development and popularization of 5G and mobile edge computing technologies, the IoV has become one of the important research fields [1]. Emerging in-vehicle service programs, such as in-vehicle maps and videos, can meet our needs for smart life [2,3]. These ever-increasing applications generate a lot of data traffic, resulting in increased network pressure and communication cost. Fortunately, mobile edge caching is a promising solution to relieve network pressure and reduce system cost.

Mobile edge caching is designed to cache popular content at the edge of the wireless network so that these contents can be transmitted directly from the edge server instead of the remote cloud. By actively downloading content to edge base stations or users, not only the load on the backhaul link can be greatly reduced, but also the communication cost can be significantly increased. Due to the mobility of users, the wireless channel shows more uncertainty. Therefore, how to design a reasonable caching scheme in mobile scenarios is very important.

At present, there are still some shortcomings in the research of caching strategies in mobile scenarios. On the one hand, most researches consider the optimization of cache cost or transmission cost alone [4–6]. On the other hand, more researches tend to regard the IoV as a static environment in edge caching [7–9]. These researches seldom consider the cache and transmission costs comprehensively, and consider the impact of vehicle mobility on the system. Therefore, it is meaningful to design a system cost optimization strategy in the mobile scene. The main contribution of this paper are as follows:

- We investigate the dynamic JOCB problem in IoV. In the every-changing mobile environment, the system cost for completing all the requested tasks over a period of time is optimized.
- In order to solve the problem of solution complexity and high-dimensional continuous space in JOCB, we apply Lagrange multiplier method to solve the bandwidth allocation sub-problem, and transform the long-term system cost minimization problem into MDP problem. The DDCP algorithm is proposed to deal with the high dimensional continuity of the action and state spaces.
- Considering the actual situation, we evaluate the performance of DDCP algorithm in different conditions, and compared it with A3C, DQN and RCP algorithms, which prove the effectiveness of the DDCP algorithm.

2 System Model

Network Model: As shown in Fig. 1, we consider a heterogeneous vehicle network with edge cache, which consists of one MBS, one cloud service provider (SP), $R = \{1, 2, ..., \mathsf{R}\}$ road side units (RSUs) and $U = \{1, 2, ..., \mathsf{U}\}$ vehicle users. As a content pool, SP contains all the poplar content denoted by $F = \{1, 2, ..., \mathsf{F}\}$. The SP can cache the popular content in RSUs or vehicles, which have certain storage and communication capability in advance. Note that RSUs are communication device established by a third party, which means both the SP and users will pay the corresponding cost to the third party when they use resources of RSUs.

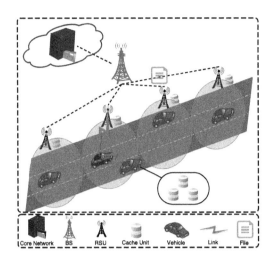

Fig. 1. Schematic diagram of JOCB in vehicular networks.

Task Model: We adopt a time-slotted model denoted $\{1, 2, ..., T\}$, in which each duration of time slot is τ [10]. At the beginning of the time slot t, each user generates a request task $Q_f = \{p_f, z_f\}$, where p_f is the probability that the file f is requested by the users. z_f is the size of the file f, and p_f obeys Zipf distribution [11]. Then, the system makes a content placement and bandwidth allocation decision based on the current network information, and users obtain these data through RSUs. If the user does not get the complete content, the nearest RSU will get the rest from the remote server and deliver it to user through wireless transmission. This situation can incur high communication cost, so the system cost depends on the content placement and bandwidth allocation.

Vehicle Mobility Model: In order to solve the problem of high dynamic communication environment between vehicles caused by vehicle mobility, we propose a vehicle movement model based on probability distribution. Particularly, the communication duration of any vehicle n and vehicle m in the time slot t obeys the exponential distribution with parameter $\mu_{n,m}$, which represents the average value of each communication duration. The non-communication duration of the two vehicles in time slot t (during this time, there is no communication between vehicle n and vehicle m) obeys Poisson distribution with parameter $\xi_{n,m}$. $\xi_{n,m}$ is the arrival rate of communication events, which means that the average communication times of the two vehicles in unit time is $\xi_{n,m}$.

The communication duration and non-communication duration between vehicles are independent of each other, so the communication time between any two vehicles in the time slot t can be modeled as a compound Poisson distribution $X_{n,m}(t) = \sum_{i=1}^{w_{n,m}(t)} x_{n,m}^i$, where $w_{n,m}(t)$ obeys the Poisson distribution with a communication rate of $\xi_{n,m}$, which represents the number of communications between two vehicles in the time slot t. $x_{n,m}^i$ represents the duration of the i-th communication between two vehicles.

In actual scenarios, due to the high-speed mobility of vehicles, each communication duration between vehicles is usually short. When the communication rate $\mu_{n,m}$ is small, the above Poisson distribution can be approximated as a normal distribution with $\xi_{n,m}\mu_{n,m}\tau$ as the mean and $\frac{2\xi_{n,m}\tau}{\mu_{n,m}^2}$ as the variance. Therefore, the communication time of vehicle n and vehicle m in time slot t can be expressed as the following normal distribution,

$$X_{n,m}(t) \sim N(\xi_{n,m}\mu_{n,m}\tau, \frac{2\xi_{n,m}\tau}{\mu_{n,m}^2}). \tag{1}$$

Content Delivery Model: According to Shannon formula, the transmission rate between the service-node i and the user-node j can be given by,

$$R_{i,j} = b_{i,j} \log_2(1 + \frac{P_T d_{i,j}^{-\alpha}}{\sigma^2 + I_{i,j}}), \tag{2}$$

where $b_{i,j}$ is the bandwidth allocated by the service-node i to the user-node j, and P_T is the transmit power of service-node i. $d_{i,j}$ is the distance between two nodes and α is the path loss exponent. σ^2 and $I_{i,j}$ represent the power density of Gaussian noise and the inter-cell interference in the range of service-node i, respectively. In our system scene, the transmission links includes V2R and V2V modes.

We define r_N and n_M as vehicles that served by RSU_r and vehicle n. B is defined as the total bandwidth of the system, the bandwidth allocated to RSU_r by MBS based on the network state is $\varphi_{n_r} \cdot B$, where φ_{n_r} represents the bandwidth allocation variable, and n_r represents the RSU_{n_r} that vehicle n can pass in time slot t. Therefore, the communication bandwidth between vehicle n and RSU_r is denoted as $\varphi_{n_r}B/r_N$, and the inter-vehicle communication reuses the V2R uplink. In order to simplify the model, we ignore the inter-cell interference between vehicles.

Content Placement Model: In our scenario, the vehicle needs to pass several RSUs to obtain the request file in the time slot t. c_i^f means that the c data size of file f is pre-cached in node i. Therefore, the content placement matrix is represented as $\left[\mathbf{C_i^f}\right]$ with size $F \times (n_R + n_M)$.

System Cost Model: In the task, the cost caused by SP occupying RSUs cache resources is expressed as C^{sp}, and the cost caused by vehicle users transmitting data through RSUs is expressed as C^{user}. The system cost C^{system} takes C^{sp} and C^{user} into consideration, which can be expressed as,

$$C_{n,f}^{system}(t) = C_{n,f}^{sp}(t) + C_{n,f}^{user}(t) = \omega_{sp} \sum_{n_r}^{n_R} p_f c_{n_r}^f z_f + \omega_{user}(\sum_{n_r}^{n_R} \frac{p_f c_{n_r}^f z_f}{\mathbb{E}\left[R_{v2r}^{r,n}\right]}$$
$$+ \sum_{n_m}^{n_M} \frac{p_f c_{n_m}^f z_f}{\mathbb{E}\left[R_{v2v}^{n,m}\right]}) + \omega_{back} \sum_{n_r}^{n_R} \sum_{n_m}^{n_M} p_f(1 - c_n^f - c_{n_r}^f - c_{n_m}^f)z_f, \tag{3}$$

where c_n^f, $c_{r_n}^f$, and $c_{n_m}^f$ are the cache variables of file f cached in the target vehicle n, the RSU_{n_r} that the vehicle n can pass through, and the neighboring vehicle m, respectively. $\mathbb{E}\left[R_{v2r}^{r,n}\right]$ and $\mathbb{E}\left[R_{v2v}^{n,m}\right]$ represent the expected wireless communication rate of V2R and V2V links. ω_{sp}, ω_{user}, and ω_{back} represent the price factor of the RSU cache resource, RSU communication resource and the backhaul link data transmission, where $\omega_{back} \gg \omega_{sp}, \omega_{user}$.

3   Problem Formulation

Our aim is to optimize the system cost over a period of time through reasonable caching and bandwidth allocation decisions. The *joint optimization of content placement and bandwidth allocation* (JOCB) problem can be formulated as follows:

$$\textbf{P1:} \quad \min_{\mathbf{c},\varphi} \quad \frac{1}{T}\sum_{t=1}^{T}\frac{1}{N}\sum_{n=1}^{N}\sum_{f=1}^{F}C_{n,f}^{system}(t),$$

$$\text{s.t.} \quad C1: 0 \leqslant c_i^f(t) \leqslant 1, \forall i \in (R+N),$$

$$C2: \sum_{t=1}^{T}\sum_{n=1}^{N}\sum_{f=1}^{F}c_{n_r}^f(t)z_f \leqslant L_{rsu}, \forall n_r \in n_R,$$

$$C3: \sum_{t=1}^{T}\sum_{n=1}^{N}\sum_{f=1}^{F}c_{n,n_m}^f(t)z_f \leqslant L_{veh}, \forall n_m \in N_M, \qquad (4)$$

$$C4: c_{n,m}^f(t)z_f \leqslant \mathbb{E}\left[R_{v2v}^{n,m}\right] \cdot X_{n,n_m}(t), \forall n_m \in n_M,$$

$$C5: \sum_{n=1}^{N}\sum_{n_r=1}^{n_R}\varphi_{n_r} \leq 1,$$

$$C6: \varphi_{n_r} \geq 0, \forall n_r \in n_R,$$

where $C1$ limits the data size of file f cached to any node. $C2$ and $C3$ indicate that the memory occupied by all requested tasks within a period of time cannot exceed the cache capacity of the cache node, L_{rsu} and L_{veh} represent the cache capacity of RSU and vehicle, respectively. $C4$ considers the mobility of the vehicles, and the amount of caching in vehicle m cannot exceed the maximum amount of data that can be transmitted by two vehicles in time slot t. $C5$ and $C6$ are constraints on bandwidth allocation variables.

4   Algorithm Design

The high-dimensional cache variable $\mathbf{c}$ and bandwidth allocation variable φ in **P1** can cause high solution complexity. Since the bandwidth allocation in the current time slot can not affect the decision-making in the next time slot, we transform the bandwidth allocation into a static programming problem by applying Lagrange multiplier method to reduce the complexity of the solution.

4.1 Bandwidth Allocation Sub-problem:

For a given content placement matrix $\left[\mathbf{C}_i^f\right](t)$, the $Cost^{user}$ only varies with the bandwidth allocation variable φ_r, which can be expressed as the optimization of the user's V2R communication cost:

$$\mathbf{P2}: \quad \min_{\{\varphi_{n_r}\}} \quad \omega_{user} \sum_{n_r}^{n_R} \frac{p_f c_{n_r}^f z_f}{\varphi_{n_r} B \cdot \log_2(1 + \frac{P_T d_{n_r,n}^{-\alpha}}{\sigma^2 + I_{n_r,n}})} \tag{5}$$

$$\text{s.t.} \quad C5, C6.$$

P2 is a convex optimization with respect to $\{\varphi_{n_r}\}$, since $\frac{\partial^2 C_{user}^{v2r}(t)}{\partial^2 \varphi_{n_r}} > 0$. The optimal bandwidth allocation is given as Theorem 1, obtained with the Lagrange multiplier method.

Theorem 1. *For a given content placement, the optimal bandwidth allocation can be given by,* $\hat{\varphi_{n_r}} = \frac{\sqrt{c_{r_n}^f}}{\sum_{n=1}^{N}\sum_{j=1}^{n_R}\sqrt{c_i^f}}$.

Proof. For brevity, we omit the proof process which can refer to [12]. ∎

4.2 MDP Based Content Placement Problem

JOCB is a typical dynamic programming problem over a finite T-slot domain. Therefore, we transform it into a MDP problem with a finite time range of T [13], and design an dynamic content placement algorithm base on deep reinforcement learning (DRL) to solve it. We define the MDP 4-tuple $\{S, A, P, R\}$ and describe it in the following section.

State Space: During the current decision-making period, the system agent makes decisions according to the environment state,

$$s(t) = \{\mathbf{F}(t), \mathbf{V}(t), X(t), \mathbf{N}(t), \mathbf{L}(t)\}, \tag{6}$$

where $\mathbf{F}(t)$ represents the file state, including z_f and p_f, $f \in F$. $\mathbf{V}(t)$ represents the vehicle state, including the location i_n and speed v_n, $n \in N$. $X(t)$ represents the communication time distribution between vehicles in time slot t. $\mathbf{N}(t) = \{r_N, n_M, n_R\}$ consists of three sub-sets. $\mathbf{L}(t) = \{l_{rsu}^{rem}, l_{veh}^{rem}\}$ represents the remaining cache capacity of the RSU_r and the vehicle n, $r \in R$ and $n \in N$.

Action Space: By observing the current network environment state $s(t)$, the system agents need to make the following decision,

$$a(t) = \{\mathbf{C}_i^f(t)| i \in (n_R + n_M), f \in F, n \in N\}, \tag{7}$$

and $a(t)$ is given by $C1$ and $C4$ in **P1**.

Reward Function: The reward function $r(t)$ represents the immediate reward after performing action $a(t)$ in state $s(t)$, which is expressed as follows,

$$r(t) = \begin{cases} -\frac{1}{N}\frac{1}{F}\sum\limits_{n=1}^{N}\sum\limits_{f=1}^{F} C_{n,f}(t), & \text{C2 and C3 are satisfied;} \\ -\frac{T}{N}\frac{1}{F}\sum\limits_{n=1}^{N}\sum\limits_{f=1}^{F} C_{n,f}(t), & \text{otherwise,} \end{cases} \tag{8}$$

when $C3$ and $C4$ in **P1** are not satisfied, the size of the content placement can exceed the remaining caching capacity of cache nodes, resulting in caching failure. Therefor, when the constraints are not satisfied, $r(t)$ is set to an extremely small value, $-\frac{1}{N}\frac{1}{F}\sum\limits_{n=1}^{N}\sum\limits_{f=1}^{F} C_{n,f}(t) \gg -\frac{T}{N}\frac{1}{F}\sum\limits_{n=1}^{N}\sum\limits_{f=1}^{F} C_{n,f}(t)$.

4.3 DRL Based Dynamic Content Placement (DDCP) Algorithm

Algorithm 1. DRL Based Dynamic Content Placement (DDCP) Algorithm

---

1: Initialize the primary network parameters: θ^Q and θ^μ;
2: Initialize the target network parameters: $\theta^{Q'} \leftarrow \theta^Q$ and $\theta^{\mu'} \leftarrow \theta^\mu$;
3: Initialize replay memory with a capacity of O;
4: **for** *episode* $= 1$, K **do**
5:    Initialize the 5G IoV environment and the random noise $\vartheta(t)$, get the initial state s_0;
6:    **for** $t = 1$, T **do**
7:       Execute action $a(t)$, calculate the optimal bandwidth allocation with **Theorem 1**, and receive reward $R(s(t), a(t))$ and next state $s(t+1)$;
8:       Store tuple $\{s(t), a(t), R(s(t), a(t)), s(t+1)\}$ into replay memory;
9:       Randomly sample a mini-batch of M experience tuples from replay memory;
10:      Calculate the target value $y(t)$ with $y(t) = r(t) + \gamma Q'(s(t+1), \mu'(s(t+1)|\theta^{\mu'})|\theta^{Q'})$;
11:      Train the primary Critic network by minimizing the loss function with $L(\theta^Q) = \mathbb{E}\left[(Q(s(t), a(t)|\theta^Q) - y(t))^2\right]$;
12:      Train the primary Actor network using the sampled policy gradient with $\nabla_{\theta^\mu} J(\mu) \approx \mathbb{E}\left[\nabla_{a(i)}(Q^\mu(s(i), a(i)|\theta^Q) \nabla_{\theta^\mu} \mu(s(i)|\theta^\mu))\right]$;
13:      Soft update the parameters of target networks with $\theta^{Q'} = \omega\theta^Q + (1-\omega)\theta^{Q'}$ and $\theta^{\mu'} = \omega\theta^\mu + (1-\omega)\theta^{\mu'}$, where $\omega \gg 1$;
14:   **end for**
15: **end for**

In this paper, we use the Deep Deterministic Policy Gradient algorithm (DDPG) that can handle continuous state and action space. For each training episode, before the beginning of each time slot t, the agent makes $a(t)$ according to the current state $s(t)$, and the state transitions to the next state $s(t+1)$. Then, the agent collects the system cost of each task. At the end of time slot t, the agent calculates $r(t)$ based on the average system cost of all tasks. The experience tuple $\{s(t), a(t), R(s(t), a(t)), s(t+1)\}$ is stored in the replay memory, and a mini-batch of samples are randomly selected for the training of Actor network and Critic network. The input of the Actor network is $S(i)$ and output is policy $\mu(s(i)|\theta^\mu)$. For the Critic network, the input is $s(i)$, $a(i)$ and $\mu(s(i)|\theta^\mu)$, the output is action-value function $Q(s(i), a(i)|\theta^Q)$ and $Q^\mu(s(i), \mu(s(i)|\theta^\mu))$. After a period of iteration, the accuracy of DNNs approximation of the value function and policy function is gradually improved. In order to reduce the correlation of data and enhance training stability, the network parameters θ^μ and θ^Q after training are used to update the target network, which has the same structure as the primary network.

5 Performance Evaluation

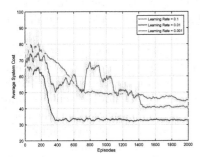

Fig. 2. The impact of learning rate on convergence

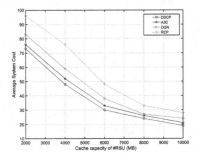

Fig. 3. The impact of RSU cache capacity on average system cost

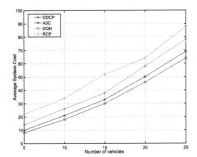

Fig. 4. Average system cost with different numbers of vehicle

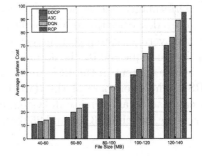

Fig. 5. Average system cost with different file size

5.1 Parameter Analysis

Figure 2 shows the impact of the different learning rates of DDCP algorithm on the system cost. In Fig. 2, we set the learning as 0.1, 0.01 and 0.001, respectively. When the learning rate is 0.01, the convergence speed of the training curve and the optimal value after convergence are better than the other two curves. This is because the learning rate determines the step length of the weight changing in gradient direction. A large step length can make the algorithm easy to fall into a local optimal solution, and a small step length can cause the loss function to update slower, which make the algorithm convergence speed decrease.

5.2 Comparison Experiments

In order to analyze the performance of our DDCP algorithm, we evaluate the average system cost over a period of time from three aspects. And we compare it with other three content placement schemes: Asynchronous Advantage Actor-Critic (A3C) [14], DQN and Random Content Placement (RCP) algorithm. Specifically, the decisions are given discretely and randomly within the constraints in DQN and RCP.

Figure 3 describes the impact of RSU cache capacity on average system cost. We can conclude that for the four algorithm, the average system cost is very high when the RSU cache capacity is insufficient. This is because when the RSU cache capacity is insufficient, the SP must cache more data in the vehicles, and most of the data is sent to the users through the backhaul link, which is the main reason for the high system cost. Note that in different cache capacity limitations, the performance of DDCP is better than the other three algorithms.

Figure 4 describes the impact of vehicles number on average system cost. In Fig. 4, the average system cost can increase as the number of vehicles increases. This is because the task number in each time slot can increase when the vehicle number increase, which can cause more buffering costs and transmission cost. The average system cost optimized by the DDCP is 11.7% and 22.5% higher than the A3C and DQN algorithms on average. The RCP algorithm has the worst performance due to no optimization.

Figure 5 describes the impact of file size on average system cost. As the Fig. 5 show, the average system cost increases as the file size increases. This is because when the file requested by the users is large, the SP occupy more cache resources to cache the content in the RSU, more data is transmitted to the users through the RSU, and even part of the data is sent to the user by backhaul link, all these can lead to an increase in system cost. The DDPC algorithm has the best performance, which is 13.3% and 25.6% higher than A3C and DQN, respectively.

6 Conclusion

In this paper, we investigate the joint optimization of content placement and bandwidth allocation problem in IoV. In order to reduce the complexity of the algorithm and minimize the long-term average system cost, we apply Lagrangian multiplication to solve the bandwidth allocation sub-problem and transform the original problem into an MDP problem. Considering the high-dimensional continuity of the state and action space, we propose a DDCP algorithm based on DRL, which jointly optimizes the cache placement and bandwidth allocation. Experimental results show that compared with conventional DQN, A3C, RCP algorithms, DDCP algorithm can reduce system cost effectively.

References

1. Al Ridhawi, I., Aloqaily, M., Kantarci, B., et al.: A continuous diversified vehicular cloud service availability framework for smart cities. Comput. Netw. **145**, 207–218 (2018)
2. Guevara, L., Auat, C.F.: The role of 5G technologies: challenges in smart cities and intelligent transportation systems. Sustainability **12**(16), 6469 (2020)
3. Zhou, H., Xu, W., Chen, J., et al.: Evolutionary V2X technologies toward the internet of vehicles: challenges and opportunities. Proc. IEEE **108**(2), 308–323 (2020)
4. Song, J., Sheng, M., Quek, T.Q.S., et al.: Learning-based content caching and sharing for wireless networks. IEEE Trans. Commun. **65**(10), 4309–4324 (2017)
5. Alioua, A., Senouci, S.M., Sedjelmaci, H., et al.: Incentive edge caching in software" defined internet of vehicles: a Stackelberg game approach. Int. J. Commun. Syst. **32**(17), e3787 (2019)
6. Zhong, C., Gursoy, M.C., Velipasalar, S.: Deep reinforcement learning-based edge caching in wireless networks. IEEE Trans. Cogn. Commun. Netw. **6**(1), 48–61 (2020)
7. Zhang, Y., Wang, R., Hossain, M.S., et al.: Heterogeneous information network-based content caching in the Internet of Vehicles. IEEE Trans. Veh. Technol. **68**(10), 10216–10226 (2019)
8. Hong, X., Jiao, J., Peng, A., et al.: Cost optimization for on-demand content streaming in IoV networks with two service tiers. IEEE Internet of Things J. **6**(1), 38–49 (2018)
9. Chien, W.C., Weng, H.Y., Lai, C.F.: Q-learning based collaborative cache allocation in mobile edge computing. Future Gener. Comput. Syst. **102**, 603–610 (2020)
10. Zhan, W., Luo, C., Wang, J., et al.: Deep-reinforcement-learning-based offloading scheduling for vehicular edge computing. IEEE Internet of Things J. **7**(6), 5449–5465 (2020)
11. Ma, T., Chen, X., Ma, Z., et al.: Deep reinforcement learning for pre-caching and task allocation in Internet of Vehicles. In: 2020 IEEE International Conference on Smart Internet of Things (SmartIoT), pp. 79–85. IEEE (2020)
12. Zhang, S., He, P., Suto, K., et al.: Cooperative edge caching in user-centric clustered mobile networks. IEEE Trans. Mob. Comput. **17**(8), 1791–1805 (2017)
13. Sutton, R.S., Barto, A.G.: Reinforcement Learning: An Introduction. MIT press (2018)
14. Chen, M., Wang, T., Ota, K., et al.: Intelligent resource allocation management for vehicles network: an A3C learning approach. Comput. Commun. **151**, 485–494 (2020)

A Probabilistic Resilient Routing Scheme for Low-Earth-Orbit Satellite Constellations

Jiahao Liu[1], Ziling Wei[1], Baokang Zhao[1(✉)], Jinshu Su[1], and Qin Xin[2]

[1] School of Computer, National University of Defense Technology, Changsha, China
bkzhao@nudt.edu.cn
[2] Faculty of Science and Technology, University of the Faroe Islands, Torshavn, Faroe Islands, Denmark

Abstract. Many Internet Service Providers (ISPs) are introducing low-earth-orbit satellite networks into Internet these years. A critical challenge in deploying Internet into space is to guarantee the network resilience for satellite mega-constellations in space due to its dynamic topology and complex environment. In this paper, we propose PRE, a Probabilistic REsilient routing scheme for the low-earth-orbit satellite constellations, which can maximize the throughput of constellation and avoid routing congestion which is caused by the link failure. PRE categorizes the whole network into groups. For each group, the probability of failure scenarios is analyzed and modeled, then the minimum bandwidth for each flow can be guaranteed with a given probability. The simulation experiments show that PRE provides the optimal routing resilience and link utilization compared with other state-of-the-art resilient routing schemes.

Keywords: Satellite constellations · Resilient routing · Traffic engineering · Network optimization

1 Introduction

A constellation of Low Earth orbit (LEO) satellites has drawn attention of many countries and major companies. Recently, "SpaceX" has planned to launch more than ten thousand LEO satellites to provide global Internet service with low latency and high capacity. The aggregated downlink bandwidth is estimated to be comparable with current aggregated fiber capacity.

While LEO satellite constellation can be very promising, it is challenging for the constellation to react to link failures quickly due to the following reasons. The first reason is a high level of topology dynamics. It is almost impossible for a satellite to keep stable connections with adjacent nodes. When the topology changes which results from the regular moving of satellites, some satellites that are involved will switch their neighborhoods. The second reason is that irregular link failures in satellite networks are common. The accidental link failure rate can be very high even with laser links. Thirdly, the combination of link failure events causes more complex network failure cases. The number of failure scenarios grows exponentially with the increase of simultaneous link failure events. We define the failure scenario as a fault event where one or more links fail. In a mega-constellation, there may be thousands of possible failure scenarios in total.

In this paper, we design a semi-SDN framework for satellite network management, in which all satellites are divided into groups according to their connectivity. Each group is similar to an AS (Autonomous System). We focus on the routing problem in a group instead of the whole network[1]. We set forth PRE, a resilient routing scheme for LEO satellite constellations. Considering the probability feature of link failure, in this scheme, we construct a probabilistic resilient routing model for LEO satellite constellations. This model computes the traffic assignment policy that satisfies users' specified demands, and guarantees a certain probability of providing specific bandwidth. Our key contributions lie in:

- By demonstrating the deficiency of current routing methods in satellite networks, we reveal the necessity for a resilient routing scheme.
- We propose a novel probabilistic routing scheme dedicated for LEO satellite constellations, which guarantees routing resilience and improves network utilization. In the proposed scheme, the inter-satellite link failure is constructed to a probabilistic model, and then, the traffic loss of all flows is minimized by optimizing conditional Value-at-Risk(cVaR). To the best of our knowledge, this is the first paper to tackle the link failure problem in LEO satellite constellations from the perspective of probability model.
- We implement the PRE scheme and do extensive simulations. Compared with state-of-the-art resilient routing schemes, PRE has higher link utilization and lower rate of routing congestion under the scenario of LEO satellite constellation.

The remainder of this paper is organized as follows. Section 2 gives related work about resilient routing in satellite networks. Section 3 analyzes some important features of LEO mega constellations and describes PRE scheme in detail. In Sect. 4, we evaluate our PRE scheme through extensive experiments. Finally, we conclude our work and do some discussions.

2   Related Work

To guarantee the reliability of satellite networks, many works have focused on network routing protocols in satellite networks [1–3]. Similar to routing on the ground, routing methods for LEO satellite constellations can be roughly divided into two categories: centralized routing and distributed routing.

Centralized routing utilizes the notion of Software-Defined-Networking (SDN) to manage the whole constellation. The network dynamics of LEO satellite constellations should be carefully considered. [2] proposed a software-defined

---

[1] The routing issue between groups can be transformed into an inter-domain routing problem.

satellite network architecture to provide highly efficient network services. It designed a hierarchical network framework, which includes data plane, control plane and management plane. The Geostationary Earth Orbit (GEO) satellites perform as the control media between management plane(the ground control center) and data plane(the satellite constellation).

In distributed routing, each satellite decides forwarding rules independently. [4] proposed a traffic-light based routing method in which each satellite utilizes the periodically shared congestion information about adjacent satellites to update its routing table. Tang [1] proposed NCMCR protocol which combines network coding with multipath routing. Moreover, recent papers presented new routing protocols in satellite networks [5,6]. Nevertheless, these works fail to guarantee minimal bandwidth for network flows with an expected confidence level. When an failure scenario occurs, they are unable to avoid routing oscillation and link congestion.

3   PRE Routing Scheme

The polar-orbit network design is generally adopted by LEO satellite constellations. Take the Iridium as an example. As is shown in Fig. 1, there are six orbit planes in total, with 11 satellites on one plane. Each satellite has four links connected with adjacent nodes, two of which for intra-plane connection and the others for node connection on the same plane. When the satellite moves into polar regions (latitude $\geq$ 66), its connections with the satellites on other orbit planes will be disconnected. Then the network topology will change into another state.

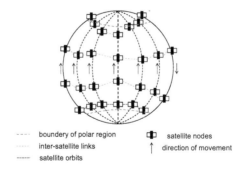

---- boundery of polar region   satellite nodes
---- inter-satellite links   ↑ direction of movement
---- satellite orbits

Fig. 1. The structure of a polar-orbit satellite constellation.

There are two steps in the design of a traffic engineering scheme. The first one is to select paths for network flows. The second step is to control bandwidth allocated to these paths. Online re-calculation of traffic split ratio costs much time which is impractical for such a highly dynamic network. In path selection period, negative effects that result from regular disconnections can be eliminated by periodically computing path selection. For irregular disconnections, it is hard for controller to select a set of paths that avoid all traffic loss for the massive combination of link failures. Thus, we try to mitigate the traffic loss by tuning traffic split ratio for each flow.

We address those challenges mentioned before by firstly categorizing the network topology into three scenarios. While scale of the whole network is large, we divide them into groups. We then formulate the TE and use an optimizer to obtain the optimal traffic allocation scheme for flows in each scenario. Once the topology changes due to regular disconnection or reconnection, the traffic routing and splitting scheme is performed again.

The goal of our method is to relieve congestion that results from link failures. There are at least a certain fraction of traffic transmitted on normal paths whenever link failure happens. Specifically, Given traffic demands of all flows, we select paths for each flow, and allocate bandwidth to each path for the flow. The probability of bandwidth availability is guaranteed at a certain level, i.e., "flow i is guaranteed to be allocated b bandwidth with probability γ".

The whole satellite constellation is described as a graph $G = (V, E)$, where V and E are the set of satellite nodes and links respectively. Before making decisions on satellite routing, all nodes are divided into M groups, with N satellites in each group. Group members are adjacent and constitute a small mesh topology. State of any satellite group can be categorized into three scenarios, which is shown in Fig. 2. The first scenario is that all satellites in the group are outside the polar region. It is a usual state, which accounts for over half of the time. The second is when part of the satellites are in the polar region (Fig. 2 (iii)). The last one is the moment when the satellite group enters or leaves the polar region (Fig. 2 (ii), (iv)). In each scenario, the connection relationship between satellites is different. We make routing policy for these scenarios respectively.

To test a static routing policy on all network topologies, we propose another one-shot routing strategy, in which controllers only need to initialize the routing scheme at first. In this paper, the probability is calculated as in Eq. (1).

$$p'_f = 1 - \left(1 - \frac{t_p}{T}\right) \cdot (1 - p_f) \tag{1}$$

where T denotes the cycle period of a satellite, and t_p is the duration when a satellite is in the polar region. p_f refers to the probability of irregular link failure.

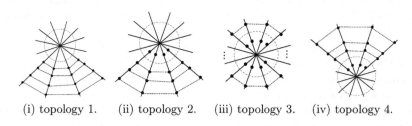

(i) topology 1.   (ii) topology 2.   (iii) topology 3.   (iv) topology 4.

Fig. 2. Satellite topology scenarios.

When link failure happens, all traffic that traverse this link will shift to other paths (tunnels), which may cause congestion if not re-allocated properly. So as to handle link failure scenarios as many as possible, we utilize a probability-based resilient routing algorithm. We translate the routing optimization into a traffic engineering form. The major problem is to optimize a given target (or loss) function. This probability-based idea has been widely utilized in stock field.

Similar with investment, this optimization formulation can also be utilized in satellite routing. SDN controller can manage traffic splitting ratio by this model. For the number of nodes in a group is small, and geological relationship among satellites is stable, information about satellites in a group can be easily collected. Consequently, it is possible for a controller to manage traffic routing in one group.

Suppose that there are n flows in total. y refers to the connectivity states for all links. It is defined as follows:

$$y_{ij} = \begin{cases} 1, & p_1 = p_{ij} \\ 0, & p_0 = 1 - p_{ij}, \end{cases} \tag{2}$$

where p_{ij} is the failure probability of link (i, j). x decides the traffic split ratio on each path. We provide k tunnels for each flow. The paths are calculated by K-shortest Path(KSP). Then, x is defined as:

$$x = \{b_{f,t} \mid \forall f, t \in T_f\} \tag{3}$$

where $b_{f,t}$ is the bandwidth allocated to tunnel t for flow f. We set the loss function in satellite network to minimize the maximum of traffic loss among all flows. It is defined as follows [7].

$$L(x, y) = \max_i \left[1 - \frac{\Sigma_{r \in R_i} x_r y_r}{d_i} \right]^+ \tag{4}$$

where d_i denotes the traffic demand of ith flow. Under certain link state and given flow splitting decision, the loss function varies significantly.

The most significant conception used in our probability-based method is Value-at-Risk(VaR). VaR is an effective measurement of risk in robust optimization [8]. It is highly related with the probabilistic distribution of loss function $L(x, y)$. Our target is to obtain the optimal VaR. To this end, we utilize the CVaR (Conditional VaR) and characteristic function to construct the optimization object. CVaR is the average value of loss under the condition that loss value is over VaR. The characteristic function is proposed to obtain optimal solution indirectly [8].

After optimization, we get the corresponding bandwidth allocation scheme x and CVaR $\hat{c}$, and then VaR $\hat{v}$ is known. It means that for every flow, the maximum traffic loss does not exceed $\hat{v}$ with probability γ. Consequently, we can guarantee b_i bandwidth for ith flow with probability γ, in which $b_i = (1 - \hat{v}) \times d_i$. Moreover, unlike other satellite routing schemes, this resilient routing method provide secured bandwidth for each flow with no network information exchange between satellites.

4   Evaluation

4.1   Experiment Setting

We evaluate our method based on a Iridium-like polar-orbit constellation including 64 satellites in total. We set the number of group members as 16, including four adjacent orbits with four satellites in each orbit.

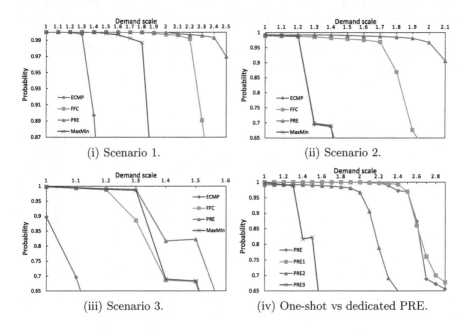

(i) Scenario 1.   (ii) Scenario 2.

(iii) Scenario 3.   (iv) One-shot vs dedicated PRE.

Fig. 3. Guaranteed probabilities across different scenarios.

The failure probabilities of inter-satellite links and intra-satellite links are different. In most cases, links between intra-satellites are stable. However, the links between inter-satellites are cut off regularly. The irregular link failure probability follows WeiBull distribution. We compare our method with three state-of-the-art resilient routing approaches respectively: FFC [9], ECMP and MaxMin. Forward fault correction (FFC) is one of the state-of-the-art resilient routing protocols to solve network faults. ECMP and MaxMin are two popular routing protocols that optimize user traffic.

4.2   Results Analysis

We evaluate the performance of our method by three metrics: the guaranteed probability with the increasing traffic demand, traffic throughput and link utilization.

Resilience. We test the resilience of PRE by measuring its guaranteed probability under different demand scales in the three satellite topology scenarios. We generate 10 traffic demands for each network topology. The scale of traffic demand increases linearly from 1 to 4. Figure 3 shows the traffic satisfaction guaranteed with different demand scales. We discover a similar trend that PRE scheme guarantees higher probability than others in different satellite topologies, especially when demand scale rises up. It should be noted that the tunnel selection of all schemes uses consistent methods and thus alternative paths are always the same. In Fig. 3(iv), PRE is utilized across the whole network period, i.e. the "one shot" method we proposed before. Compared with PRE1 which is for scenario 1, it is slightly less resilient. The robustness of PRE across all satellite topology scenarios performs well in general.

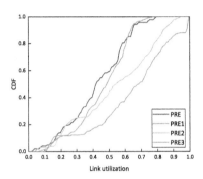

Fig. 4. Link utilization distribution across PREs. (Color figure online)

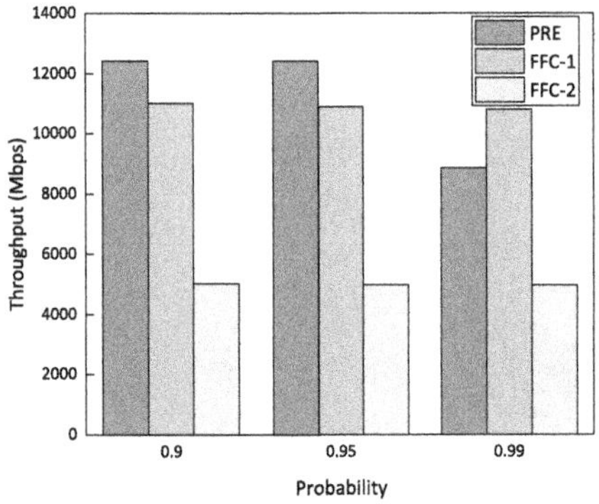

Fig. 5. Throughput under different guaranteed probabilities.

Link Utilization. Figure 4 shows a CDF of the link utilization of the whole network group under PRE schemes in different scenarios. PERs that is dedicated designed for each topology performs better than "one-shot" PRE (the red line). It is due to the fact that the "one-shot" method overestimate the failure probability of some links, thus decreasing the traffic over this links.

Throughput. Figure 5 presents the throughput of the topology under different guaranteed probabilities for PRE and two FFC schemes (with different k values in FFC). The link capacity of each link is set to 2 Gbps. Throughput keeps a high level when possibility is less than 95%. We observe that with the increasing guaranteed probability, the network suffers slight throughput loss compared with FFC. It is the result of guaranteeing higher availability of flow demands that could be omitted.

5   Conclusion

In this paper, we show that existing routing schemes in satellite network cannot realize congestion free traffic routing when link failure happens. To bridge this gap, we present PRE, a probabilistic resilient routing scheme that determines how to split flow traffic resilient to failure scenarios under given probabilities. The insight is to construct a probability model for each network scenario and make flow splitting policy. Emulation results show that PRE is more resilient to regular and irregular link failures than other state-of-the-art routing schemes.

Acknowledgment. This work was supported in part by the National Natural Science Foundation of China (Grant No. 61972412), the National Postdoctoral International Exchange Program Funding for Incoming Postdoctoral Students and the science and technology innovation Program of Hunan Province(2020RC2047).

References

1. Tang, F., Zhang, H., Yang, L.T.: Multipath cooperative routing with efficient acknowledgement for LEO satellite networks. IEEE Trans. Mob. Comput. **18**, 179–192 (2019)
2. Bao, J., Zhao, B., Yu, W., Feng, Z., Wu, C., Gong, Z.: OpenSAN: a software-defined satellite network architecture. In: SIGCOMM (2014)
3. Gu, R., Qin, J., Dong, T., Yin, J., Liu, Z.: Recovery routing based on q-learning for satellite network faults. Complex **2020**, 8829897:1–8829897:13 (2020)
4. Song, G., Chao, M., Yang, B., Zheng, Y.: TLR: a traffic-light-based intelligent routing strategy for NGEO satellite IP networks. IEEE Trans. Wirel. Commun. **13**, 3380–3393 (2014)
5. Bhattacherjee, D., Singla, A.: Network topology design at 27,000 km/hour. In: Proceedings of the 15th International Conference on Emerging Networking Experiments and Technologies (2019)
6. Handley, M.: Using ground relays for low-latency wide-area routing in mega constellations. In: Proceedings of the 18th ACM Workshop on Hot Topics in Networks (2019)
7. Bogle, J., et al.: TEAVAR: striking the right utilization-availability balance in WAN traffic engineering. In: Proceedings of the ACM Special Interest Group on Data Communication (2019)
8. Boginski, V., Commander, C.W., Turko, T.: Polynomial-time identification of robust network flows under uncertain arc failures. Optim. Lett. **3**, 461–473 (2009). https://doi.org/10.1007/s11590-009-0125-x
9. Liu, H., Kandula, S., Mahajan, R., Zhang, M., Gelernter, D.: Traffic engineering with forward fault correction. In: SIGCOMM (2014)

An Efficient Multi-link Concurrent Transmission MAC Protocol for Long-Delay Underwater Acoustic Sensor Networks

Yue Wang, Xiaoqin Song, and Lei Lei[✉]

College of Electronic and Information Engineering,
Nanjing University of Aeronautics and Astronautics, Nanjing 211106, China
leilei@nuaa.edu.cn

Abstract. Underwater acoustic sensor networks (UASNs) are confronted with great challenges on the design of medium access control (MAC) protocol due to its poor reliability, small channel capacity, and large propagation delay. How to optimize the channel access technology and increase the network throughput has become a research hotspot. Aiming at the star topology consisting of the sink node and its one-hop neighboring nodes, this paper proposes a concurrent transmission MLC-MAC protocol based on CSMA. We introduce BCTS frames to broadcast the sending order scheduled by sink node. We further model and analyze the transmission phase of our protocol, and derive the collision and transmission probability to achieve the saturation network throughput. Simulation results prove that our model is validated and our protocol effectively improves the performance of UASNs.

Keywords: Underwater acoustic sensor networks · Medium access control · Concurrent transmission · Markov chain

1 Introduction

Similar to wireless sensor networks (WSNs), the medium access control (MAC) protocol plays a critical role in underwater acoustic sensor networks (UASNs) [1, 2]. An efficient MAC protocol allows multiple nodes to share the channel fairly, without transmission conflicts, thus reducing the energy consumption and propagation delay of the networks. However, MAC protocol designed for UASNs faces many inevitable challenges, since the inherent properties of underwater communication environment like poor reliability, small channel capacity, and large propagation delay [3]. Furthermore, Multipath effect and Doppler effect can lead to serious frequency dispersion and inter-symbol interference. Both electromagnetic and light waves have large attenuation in seawater [4]. However, the rate of sound travelling underwater can only be up to 1500 m/s, five orders of magnitude slower than electromagnetic waves. High conflict probability caused by the large delay, as well as the limited battery energy are the major problems, which results in poor performance of data transmission underwater over long distance.

© Springer Nature Switzerland AG 2021
Z. Liu et al. (Eds.): WASA 2021, LNCS 12939, pp. 262–273, 2021.
https://doi.org/10.1007/978-3-030-86137-7_29

Efforts have been made on studying efficient MAC protocols for UASNs. For competing multiple access strategies, ALOHA protocol [5] is the simplest, but its maximum normalized throughput can only reach 18.4%. The throughput of slotted-ALOHA [6] can be about twice of original ALOHA, however, the conspicuous propagation delay underwater can still make it quickly decline to that of ALOHA. Therefore, Syed A A et al. [7] first come up with the concept of *spatio-temporal uncertainty*, and point out that data transmission duration should be longer than propagation delay. MACA protocol [8] based on RTS/CTS handshake mechanism is of great importance. After receiving RTS from the sending node, sink node broadcast CTS, reminding other nodes to remain silent during this period, in order to avoid conflicts. However, the high latency of UASNs makes the problem of hidden terminal become more serious, the conflict caused by it makes the design of MAC protocol more challenging. Thus, based on FAMA protocol, S-FAMA protocol [9] combines carrier detection and RTS/CTS handshake mechanism, successfully solving the problem of spatio-temporal uncertainty, but its time slot is about maximum propagation delay, resulting in low channel utilization. Then RC-FAMA protocol [10] adds a random competing number, called a C-number, to each RTS control frame, solving the problem of repeatedly retransmitting RTS due to failure of channel contention. However, for the scene of multiple sending and one receiving, the above are not very suitable for the star network topology formed by the sink node and its one-hop neighboring underwater sensor nodes, where the transmission congestion is serious.

Our research in this paper aims at reducing conflicts and increasing the network throughput. In view of the star network topology of shortsea UASNs, this paper designs a Multi-Link Concurrent transmission MAC protocol (MLC-MAC). The research work of this paper focuses on the design and performance analysis of the MLC-MAC protocol. The main contributions consist of two aspects as follows:

1) For the star network topology formed by the sink node and its one-hop neighboring underwater sensor nodes, we design the first two phases, RTS reservation, sink node scheduling and broadcasting BCTS; and later two phases, data transmission and ACK acknowledgement, in order to guarantee the collision-free and efficient transmission as far as possible.
2) Two-dimensional Markov chain modeling and simulation verify the performance improvement of our protocol, effectively reducing the collision probability and increasing saturation network throughput.

The remainder of this paper is organized as follows. The system model and protocol description is detailed in Sect. 2, Sect. 3 proposes the Markov chain modeling, followed by the simulation and performance analysis in Sect. 4. Finally, the paper is concluded in Sect. 5.

2 Proposed MLC-MAC Protocol

In our design, the sink node only needs to receive packets, while the one-hop neighboring nodes of the sink node not only have to send information they acquired to sink node, but also need to converge and forward data from other remote nodes, it is obvious that the closer the nodes are to the sink node, the more data they need to transmit. We call this Funnel effect, which may causes network congestion and traffic collision, thus reduces the network throughput. In view of the high propagation delay in UASNs, problem becomes more serious.

In this section, we describe the details of the transmission strategy for the star network topology formed by the sink node and its one-hop neighboring underwater sensor nodes. As shown in Fig. 1, for the star network topology, non-competing MAC protocols are not very suitable, our proposed MLC-MAC protocol adopts competing access protocol based on carrier sensing to randomly compete the channel reservation.

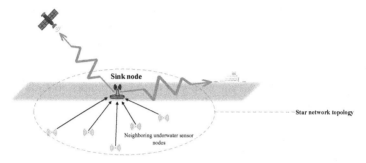

Fig. 1. Typical star network topology formed by the sink node and its one-hop neighboring underwater sensor nodes.

Considering that there are N neighboring nodes in the communication range of the sink node. Each time slot includes four stages, RTS reservation, sink node scheduling, concurrent data transmission and ACK acknowledgement, shown as Fig. 2.

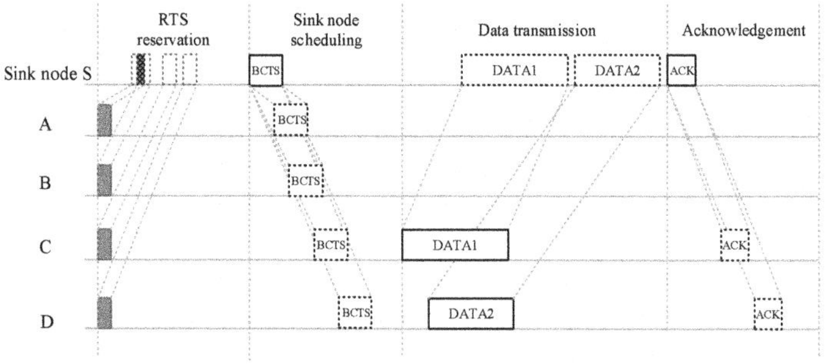

Fig. 2. Operations of MLC-MAC.

In the beginning, if a node has data to send, a random value of backoff counter is selected in the initial competition window. When the backoff value comes to 0, the node reserves the channel at the starting time of the current time slot by sending RTS to the sink node. Due to the different propagation delay of nodes, their RTS frames may collide, or be respectively received successfully.

During the period of sink node scheduling, the sink node S schedules the data transmission order according to the RTS frames correctly received. Firstly, S derives the propagation delay of the node by its RTS reaching time and its sending time carried in the RTS. Assume that there are n RTS frames received successfully in the current time slot, c represents the propagation delay and d represents the data length. S queues the sending order due to their propagation delay with temporary number as $c_1 \leq c_2 \leq \ldots \leq c_n$. To realize non-conflict transmission, when the data of the i_{th} node reaches S, the data of the $(i$-$1)_{th}$ should have already been transmitted over, which we written as

$$t_i + c_i \geq t_{i-1} + d_{i-1} + c_{i-1} \tag{1}$$

We definite δ as the minimum protection interval for continuously receiving data packets, when the i_{th} node and the $(i-1)_{th}$ node send data at the same time, if it satisfies

$$c_i = d_{i-1} + c_{i-1} + \delta \tag{2}$$

Then S could successfully receive the data sent by both two nodes. Similarly, the sending time of the $(i+1)_{th}$ node can be written as

$$t_{i+1} = t_i + d_i + c_i + \delta - c_{i+1} \tag{3}$$

From the above, the scheduled sending time of the nodes is as following:

$$t_i = t_{i-1} + \max\{c_{i-1} + d_{i-1} + \delta - c_i, 0\} \quad i \in [2, n] \tag{4}$$

Hence, S schedules all the data transmission order and their time needed according to (4), and put the *(Node address, Sending time)* information pair into BCTS frames in sequence. Actually, we can know from (4) that the ideal delay for S to receive the data frames is $c_1 + d_1 + d_2 + \ldots + d_n$. Before starting the data transmission period, the sensor nodes examine the arrangement of data sending time, and then begin transmitting in turn.

Each time frame is composed of several fixed time slots. We set the time slot length as $(T_{BCTS} + c_{max})$, where T_{BCTS} is the time for transmitting BCTS frame and c_{max} is the maximum propagation delay among the whole network. Meanwhile, we set RTS/BCTS/ACK can only be sent at the beginning of time slot, so that they can be received within one time slot. If the channel is detected idle in the current time frame, then the node backoff counter value reduce by 1. If it is detected busy, then the node suspends its backoff counter and waiting for the channel become idle. If a node has sent an RTS, but there is none arrangement in BCTS, then the node adopt Binary Exponential Back-off (BEB) mechanism to doubly the window length.

3   Models and Analysis

In the proposed MLC-MAC protocol, the contention window length W_i plays an important role in the network efficiency. If the window length is small, certainly it will shorten the backoff time, but when the number of nodes becomes larger, the collision probability will increase; whereas if the length is too large, although collision can be reduced, the queuing time will increase accordingly, thus reducing the channel utilization rate. Therefore, an appropriate value of W_i has an important effect on achieving the optimal throughput. In this section, we first propose the two-dimensional Markov chain model for MLC-MAC. Next, we analyze the collision and transmission probabilities. Finally, the saturation network throughput is derived.

3.1 Markov Chain Model

In view of UASNs transmission characteristics, the two-dimensional Markov chain model in Fig. 3 is based on the following assumptions: 1) the underwater acoustic channel is ideal, without considering the capture effect; 2) the sending nodes are all saturated, i.e., they always have data to send; 3) the duration time for data transmission is longer than one time slot.

In this model, a discrete and integer time scale is adopted, where t and $t + 1$ correspond to the beginning of two consecutive backoff time slots. The status of any sending nodes during the network operation can be expressed as a two-dimensional random variable $\{s(t), b(t)\}$, their values depend on the previous status. We define the variables as follows,

$s(t)$ – the backoff stage of the node at time t, $s(t) \in [1, n]$;
$b(t)$ – the stochastic process representing the backoff time counter for a given node, $b(t) \in [0, W_i - 1]$;
P_f – Probability of conditional sending failure, i.e., collision probability;
τ – Transmission probability, i.e., probability that the node transmits in a randomly chosen slot time.

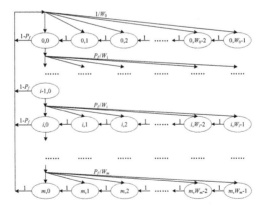

Fig. 3. Markov chain model for MLC-MAC.

According to the operation process of MLC-MAC protocol, the backoff time counter of the node decrements at the beginning of each time slot. When the backoff time counter decreases to 0, the node send RTS at the beginning of the next time slot. If the reservation successes, the node will send data at the scheduled time. Otherwise, it will enter BEB process, i.e., randomly selects a value from $[0, W_i - 1]$ as the initial value of backoff counter, if the channel is idle for one time slot, then minus 1. When the node successfully sends or reaches the maximum retransmission time m, i.e., the maximum backoff level, it will send next data frame.

The non-null one-step state transition probabilities of the model are:

$$
\begin{cases}
P\{i, k|i, k+1\} = 1 & k \in [0, W_i - 2], i \in [0, m] & \text{(a)} \\
P\{0, k|i, 0\} = \frac{1-P_f}{W_0} & k \in [0, W_0 - 1], i \in [0, m-1] & \text{(b)} \\
P\{i, k|i-1, 0\} = \frac{P_f}{W_i} & k \in [0, W_i - 1], i \in [1, m] & \text{(c)} \\
P\{0, k|m, 0\} = \frac{1}{W_0} & k \in [0, W_0 - 1] & \text{(d)}
\end{cases}
\tag{5}
$$

The equations account for the following facts:

1) At the beginning of each slot time, the backoff time of the node decreases by one with probability 1 as given in (5a).
2) Probability that may lead to the end of the current backoff cycle, and the start of a new cycle is expressed in (5b), i.e., a new frame following a successful transmission starts with backoff stage 0, and thus the backoff timer is initially uniformly chosen in the range $(0, W_0 - 1)$.
3) When an unsuccessful transmission occurs at backoff stage $(i - 1)$, the backoff stage increases by 1, and the new initial backoff value is uniformly chosen in the range $(0, W_i)$ as given in (5c).
4) Once the backoff stage reaches the maximum value m, whether the transmission succeeds or not, it will not continue to increase. The node shall start a new backoff stage 0, waiting for transmit a new packet, and the new backoff value is initially uniformly chosen in the range $(0, W_0 - 1)$ as in (5d).

Let $b_{i,k}$ be the stationary distribution of the Markov chain, written as

$$
b_{i,k} = \lim_{t \to \infty} P\{s(t) = i, b(t) = k\} i \in [0, m], k \in [0, W_i - 1]
\tag{6}
$$

Owing to the one-step transition probabilities (5), we can rewrite (6) as

$$
b_{i,k} = \frac{W_i - k}{W_i}
\begin{cases}
(1 - P_f) \sum_{i=0}^{m-1} b_{i,0} + b_{m,0} & i = 0, k \in [0, W_0 - 1] \\
b_{i,0} & i \in [1, m], k \in [0, W_i - 1]
\end{cases}
\tag{7}
$$

Where $\sum_{i=0}^{m} \sum_{k=0}^{W_i-1} b_{i,k} = 1$, there is

$$
\tau = \sum_{i=0}^{m} b_{i,0} = \frac{b_{0,0}(1 - P_f^{m+1})}{1 - P_f} = \frac{2(1 - P_f^{m+1})(1 - 2P_f)}{W(1 - P_f)[1 - (2P_f)^{m+1}] + (1 - P_f^{m+1})(1 - 2P_f)}
\tag{8}
$$

3.2   Concurrent Transmission Probability and Collision Probability

Supposed that a circular region, takes the sink node as circle center, the diameter is R, equals to the maximum propagation range. Four sending nodes randomly distributed, as Fig. 4(a). We assume that r_i is the distance between sending node and sink node, it is easy to obtain the probability density function of the distribution of the sending nodes as $2r_i/R^2$. For convenience, we number the nodes according to their distance to sink node, there is $r_1 \leq r_2 \leq r_3 \leq r_4$. If RTS sent by two nodes can be successfully received by sink node without collision, we can consider that their propagation difference is larger than T_{RTS}, i.e., the difference between their distance to sink node is longer than a. We define the variables as follows,

$p(N_{tr}, N_{suc})$ – Probability of sink node receiving N_{suc} RTS, when there are N_{tr} underwater nodes sending RTS to sink node simultaneously.
P_{con} – Probability that RTS frames not all fail to be received by the sink node when several nodes compete for the channel simultaneously.
T_{RTS} – Transmission delay of RTS frames, $t_i = T_{RTS_i}$ in Fig. 4(b).
v – Propagation speed of acoustic wave underwater.
a – To simplify calculation, we set $a = v \cdot T_{RTS}$.

Fig. 4. Four nodes sending at the same time. (a) Propagation range and distance. (b) Different collision situation.

As shown in Fig. 4(b), we assume $N_{tr} = 4$.

1) $N_{suc} = 4$
All the 4 RTS are successfully received. Easily, there is,

$$p(4,4) = A_4^4 \cdot \int_0^{R-3a} \frac{2r_1}{R^2}dr_1 \int_{r_1+a}^{r_3-a} \frac{2r_2}{R^2}dr_2 \int_{r_1+2a}^{r_4-a} \frac{2r_3}{R^2}dr_3 \int_{r_1+3a}^{R} \frac{2r_4}{R^2}dr_4 \quad (9)$$

2) $N_{suc} = 2$
The sink node successfully receives two RTS, other two RTS conflict with each other. There are 3 possibilities, to simplify the calculation, we set $s_1 = v \cdot t_1$, there is

$$p'(4,2) = A_4^4 \cdot \int_0^a ds_1 \int_0^{R-2a-s_1} \frac{2r_1}{R^2} \cdot \frac{2(r_1+s_1)}{R^2}dr_1 \int_{r_1+s_1+2a}^{R} \frac{2r_3}{R^2}dr_3 \int_{r_1+a+s_1}^{r_3-a} \frac{2r_2}{R^2}dr_2 \quad (10)$$

$$p''(4,2) = A_4^4 \cdot \int_0^a ds_1 \int_0^{R-2a-s_1} \frac{2r_1}{R^2} dr_1 \int_{r_1+s_1+2a}^{R} \frac{2r_3}{R^2} dr_3 \int_{r_1+a}^{r_3-s_1-a} \frac{2r_2}{R^2} \cdot \frac{2(r_2+s_1)}{R^2} dr_2 \quad (11)$$

$$p'''(4,2) = A_4^4 \cdot \int_0^a ds_1 \int_0^{R-2a-s_1} \frac{2r_1}{R^2} dr_1 \int_{r_1+s_1+2a}^{R} \frac{2r_3}{R^2} \cdot \frac{2(r_3-s_1)}{R^2} dr_3 \int_{r_1+a}^{r_3-a-s_1} \frac{2r_2}{R^2} dr_2 \quad (12)$$

$$p(4,2) = p'(4,2) + p''(4,2) + p'''(4,2) \quad (13)$$

3) $N_{suc} = 1$

There is only one RTS being received successfully, and it only can be node 1 or 4.
We set $s_1 = v \cdot t_1$, $s_2 = v \cdot t_2$ as, there is

$$p'(4,1) = A_4^4 \cdot \int_0^a ds_1 \int_0^a ds_2 \int_0^{R-s_1-s_2-a} \frac{2r_1}{R^2} \cdot \frac{2(r_1+s_1)}{R^2} \cdot \frac{2(r_1+s_1+s_2)}{R^2} dr_1 \int_{r_1+a+s_1+s_2}^{R} \frac{2r_2}{R^2} dr_2 \quad (14)$$

$$p''(4,1) = A_4^4 \cdot \int_0^a ds_1 \int_0^a ds_2 \int_{r_1+s_1+s_2+a}^{R} \frac{2r_2}{R^2} \cdot \frac{2(r_2-s_1)}{R^2} \cdot \frac{2(r_2-s_1-s_2)}{R^2} dr_2 \int_0^{R-a-s_1-s_2} \frac{2r_1}{R^2} dr_1 \quad (15)$$

$$p(4,1) = p'(4,1) + p''(4,1) \quad (16)$$

4) $N_{suc} = 0$

The sink node never get any one of the 4 RTS frames. That is, the RTS frames collide
in pairs or end to end. Similarly to the above, we set $s_1 = v \cdot t_1$, $s_2 = v \cdot t_2$, $s_3 = v \cdot t_3$
as, there is

$$p'(4,0) = A_4^4 \cdot \int_0^a ds_1 \int_0^a ds_2 \int_0^a ds_3 \int_0^{R-s_1-s_2-s_3} \frac{2r_1}{R^2} \cdot \frac{2(r_1+s_1)}{R^2} \cdot \frac{2(r_1+s_1+s_2)}{R^2} \cdot \frac{2(r_1+s_1+s_2+s_3)}{R^2} dr_1$$
$$(17)$$

$$p''(4,0) = A_4^4 \cdot \int_0^a ds_1 \int_0^a ds_2 \int_0^{R-s_1-s_2-a} \frac{2r_1}{R^2} \cdot \frac{2(r_1+s_1)}{R^2} dr_1 \int_{r_1+s_1+s_2+a}^{R} \frac{2r_2}{R^2} \cdot \frac{2(r_2-s_2)}{R^2} dr_2 \quad (18)$$

$$p(4,0) = p'(4,0) + p''(4,0) \quad (19)$$

For $N_{tr} > 4$, the collision probability can also be obtained similar to the above.

Therefore, combining with τ and $p(N_{tr}, N_{suc})$ discussed above, we can derive the
value of P_{con} is

$$P_{con} = \sum_{N_{tr}=2}^{N} \sum_{N_{suc}=1}^{N_{tr}-2} C_N^{N_{tr}} \tau^{N_{tr}} (1-\tau)^{N-N_{tr}} p(N_{tr}, N_{suc}) + \sum_{N_{tr}=2}^{N} C_N^{N_{tr}} \tau^{N_{tr}} (1-\tau)^{N-N_{tr}} p(N_{tr}, N_{suc}) \quad (20)$$

While P_f mentioned in Sect. 3.1, depending on the number of nodes in UASNs, the
length of RTS and contention window. We can derive it as

$$P_f = 1 - (1-\tau)^{N-1} - P_{con} \quad (21)$$

3.3 Saturation Network Throughput

Since the data transmission time is longer than one time slot, the time slot length occupied by the node successfully transmitting data frames is

$$T_i = [ceil(\frac{i \cdot L_{data}/V_{rate} + T_i^{delay}}{T_{slot}}) + 3] \cdot T_{slot} \tag{22}$$

Where $ceil()$ means to round up the value to the next highest integer, T_{slot} represents the length of one time slot, L_{data} represents the average length of data frames, V_{rate} means the transmission rate of nodes, i represents the number of data frames successfully transmitted. T_i^{delay} represents the average delay of the first data frame received when the receiving node successfully receives i data frames, written as

$$T_i^{delay} = \frac{A_i^i \cdot \int_0^{R-(i-1)d} r_1 \cdot \frac{2r_1}{R^2} dr_1 \int_{r_1+d}^{r_3-d} \frac{2r_2}{R^2} dr_2 \cdots \int_{r_1+(i-1)d}^{R} \frac{2r_i}{R^2} dr_i}{c} \tag{23}$$

Considering the probability that in any given time slot, at least one node transmits data frames

$$P_t = 1 - (1 - \tau)^N \tag{24}$$

Therefore, the probability that the data frames of at least one node can be successfully received is

$$P_s = \frac{P_{con} + N\tau(1-\tau)^{N-1}}{P_t} \tag{25}$$

For the average time slot length of data frames successfully transmitted, we can get from (20) and (22) that

$$T_s = P_t \cdot \frac{\left(\sum_{i=1}^{N}\sum_{N_{tr}=i+2}^{N} T_i \cdot C_N^{N_{tr}}\tau^{N_{tr}}(1-\tau)^{N-N_{tr}}p_{N_{tr},i} + \sum_{i=1}^{N} T_i \cdot C_N^i\tau^i(1-\tau)^{N-i}p_{i,i}\right)}{P_t} \tag{26}$$

When the sending node compete for channels, if it cannot receive CTS in the next time slot, then the RTS sent this time is considered to collide with the control frames sent by other nodes. Since the RTS/CTS handshake mechanism of MLC-MAC must last two time slots, the sending node collision duration is

$$T_{col} = 2 \cdot T_{slot} \tag{27}$$

For the condition that there is at least one node transmits data frame, the collision probability is

$$P_{col} = (1 - P_s) \cdot P_t \tag{28}$$

Let S be the normalized saturation throughput, defined as the fraction of time the channel is used to successfully transmit payload bits. To compute S, we analyze the conditions that can happen in a randomly chosen slot time:

1) None node competing channel in the current time slot, and the channel remains idle;
2) The sending node competes successfully, occupying the channel and transmitting the data;
3) The sending node fails in the channel competition, collision occurs, and all nodes start to backoff.

Thus, the normalized saturation throughput is calculated by

$$
S = \frac{\frac{L_{data}}{V_{rate}} \cdot \left(\sum_{i=1}^{N} \sum_{N_{tr}=i+2}^{N} i \cdot C_N^{N_{tr}} \tau^{N_{tr}} (1-\tau)^{N-N_{tr}} p_{N_{tr},i} + \sum_{i=1}^{N} i \cdot C_N^i \tau^i (1-\tau)^{N-i} p_{i,i} \right)}{T_s + P_t \cdot (1-P_s) \cdot T_{col} + (1-P_t) \cdot T_{slot}}
$$

(29)

4 Simulation and Performance Analysis

In this section, we show the performance evaluation of our MLC-MAC protocol. Considering that different network topologies have a great impact on the performance of protocol, the simulation results of 50 randomly generated topologies are averaged, and the simulation time of each is 30 min. The values of the main parameters used in simulation are listed in Table 1.

Table 1. Simulation parameters.

Parameter	Value	Parameter	Value
Transmission rate	3 kbps	DATA packet size	3600 bit
Transmission rang	1500 m	RTS size	176 bit
Carrier sensing range	1600 m	BCTS size	320 bit
Transmission power	10 W	ACK size	56 bit
Reception power	80 mW	Backoff time slot	1.1 s
Idle power	80 mW	Retransmission times	2

To validate the rationality and accuracy of the Markov chain model we proposed above, we compare the simulation results obtained through the Exata network simulator with the theoretical values obtained by matlab numerical calculation, then analyze the relationship between the normalized saturation throughput and the number of nodes, as well as the contention window length.

We set 4 underwater nodes sending RTS simultaneously. Figure 5(a) illustrates that the probability derived in Sect. 3.2 matches very well with the simulation, thus proving the accuracy of our model. Figure 5(b) shows the theoretical value of normalized saturation network throughput is very close to the simulation, and their error is no more than 0.05. In addition, when the number of nodes is small, a large contention window will cause a decline of the network throughput, because this will prevent the sink node from receiving more RTS in the reservation phase, thus losing the advantage of scheduling multiple underwater nodes to transmit data concurrently.

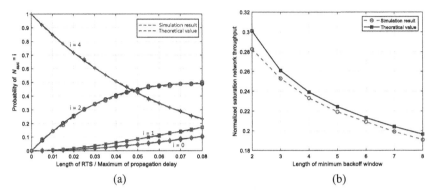

(a)   (b)

Fig. 5. When $N_{tr} = 4$, (a) Probability of the sink node successfully receiving i RTS frames. (b) Normalized saturation network throughput for different contention window length.

Figure 6(a) shows the comparison between our protocol and typical protocols. At first, the network throughput of the three protocols is similar, however, with the number of nodes increasing, the network throughput of RC-FAMA and S-FAMA will rapidly decline after a small lift, while MLC-MAC keeps getting further increase. We can see our protocol improves network throughput by allowing nodes to transmit data concurrently, especially very beneficial for the star topology around sink node. Figure 6(b) reveals that selecting suitable contention window length according to the network scale can maximize the saturation network throughput, and the optimal window length increases with the number of nodes. Meanwhile, we notice that the declining trend of throughput becomes gentle with the increase of the number of nodes.

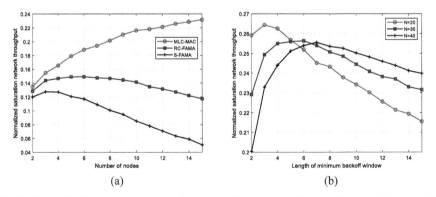

(a)   (b)

Fig. 6. Normalized saturation network throughput (initial contention window length is set as 10) (a) Different protocol under different N. (b) Different N under different contention windows.

5   Conclusions

The research of this paper focuses on propose an efficient MLC-MAC for long-delay USANs. We introduce BCTS frames to broadcast the sending order scheduled by sink node. We use a two-dimensional Markov chain model to derive the network saturation throughput and collision probability. The simulation results show that the model and analysis are accurate. Our future work will focus on further improving the performance of network throughput and average energy consumption, especially through optimizing the concurrent transmission MAC protocols for UASNs.

Background. This work was supported in part by the National Natural Science Foundation of China (No. 61902182), the Natural Science Foundation of Jiangsu Province of China (No. BK20190409), the Aeronautical Science Foundation of China (No. 2016ZC52029), Qing Lan Project of Jiangsu Province of China, China Postdoctoral Science Foundation (No. 2019TQ0153), and the Foundation of CETC Key Laboratory of Aerospace Information Applications of China (No. SXX18629T022).

References

1. Li, S., Qu, W., Liu, C., et al.: Survey on high reliability wireless communication for underwater sensor networks. J. Netw. Comput. Appl. **148**, 102446 (2019)
2. Song, Y.: Underwater acoustic sensor networks with cost efficiency for internet of underwater things. IEEE Trans. Industr. Electron. **68**(2), 1707–1716 (2020)
3. Jiang, S.: State-of-the-art medium access control (MAC) protocols for underwater acoustic networks: a survey based on a MAC reference model. IEEE Commun. Surv. Tutor. **20**(1), 96–131 (2017)
4. Qu, F., Wang, Z., Yang, L., et al.: A journey toward modeling and resolving doppler in underwater acoustic communications. IEEE Commun. Mag. **54**(2), 49–55 (2016)
5. Geethu, K.S., Babu, A.V.: Energy optimal channel attempt rate and packet size for ALOHA based underwater acoustic sensor networks. Telecommun. Syst. **65**(3), 429–442 (2017)
6. Huang, H., Ye, T., Lee, T.T., et al.: Delay and stability analysis of connection-based slotted-Aloha. IEEE/ACM Trans. Netw. **29**, 203–219 (2020)
7. Syed, A.A., Ye, W., Heidemann, J., et al.: Understanding spatio-temporal uncertainty in medium access with ALOHA protocols. In: Proceedings of the Second Workshop on Underwater Networks, pp. 41–48. ACM (2007)
8. Qian, L., Zhang, S., Liu, M., et al.: A MACA-based power control MAC protocol for underwater wireless sensor networks. In: 2016 IEEE/OES China Ocean Acoustics (COA), pp. 1–8. IEEE (2016)
9. Zhang, S., Qian, L., Liu, M., et al.: A slotted-FAMA based MAC protocol for underwater wireless sensor networks with data train. J. Signal Process. Syst. **89**(1), 3–12 (2017)
10. Qian, L., Zhang, S., Liu, M.: A slotted floor acquisition multiple access based MAC protocol for underwater acoustic networks with RTS competition. Front. Inf. Technol. Electron. Eng. **16**(3), 217–226 (2015)

An Advanced Cache Retransmission Mechanism for Wireless Mesh Network

Bing Liu, YiFang Qin, Xu Zhou$^{(\boxtimes)}$, TaiXin Li, WangHong Yang, Zhuo Li, and YongMao Ren

Computer Network Information Center, Chinese Academy of Sciences, Beijing, China
zhouxu@cstnet.cn

Abstract. Wireless Mesh networks (WMN) are widely used in scenarios such as emergency communications, military self-organizing networks, and urban network access based on the capabilities of self-organization, self-configuration, and mesh multi-hop. Nowadays, various areas have increasingly requirements of mobility support, low latency, and quick response for WMN. However, the performance of traditional WMN is affected by frequent interruption and switch when the WMN nodes are moving. Re-establishing the connection will lead to additional time costs, which greatly increases network delay and instability. In addition, the receiving end sends retransmission requests because of packet loss and receive responses via long-distance multi-hop transmission, which leads to obvious relays and uncertainty. As a result, the utilization rate of network resources is dramatically reduced, and this kind of network is unable to cover the needs of dynamic or long-distance scene such as battlefields and emergency communications. Therefore, we innovatively propose a mechanism named Advanced Cache Retransmission Mechanism (ACRM) in this paper. ACRM includes the Cache Retransmission Mechanism (CRM) and the Trend-Jacobson (TJ) algorithm. Besides, the unique message format, interaction logic and relay node caching are used to enhance the WMN system based on UDP protocol transmission. The simulation shows that ACRM can improve the transmission efficiency and stability of WMN networks in dynamic or long-distance multi-hop Scenes.

Keywords: Wireless Mesh Network · Cache · Retransmission · Jacobson

1 Introduction

Wireless Mesh network is a wireless multi-hop mesh topology network, which is generally composed of wireless access points and relay routing nodes [1, 2]. These nodes promote the connection and intercommunication of mobile terminal devices by relaying wireless multi-hop [3]. WMN has self-organization, self-management, and self-healing capabilities, and has compatibility and interoperability with existing wireless networks. At the same time, the deployment of multiple nodes can increase network coverage and network throughput [4].

However, with the rapid development of various industries, people's demand for WMN mobility and low latency is increasing. The movement of traditional WMN nodes

© Springer Nature Switzerland AG 2021
Z. Liu et al. (Eds.): WASA 2021, LNCS 12939, pp. 274–281, 2021.
https://doi.org/10.1007/978-3-030-86137-7_30

will frequently cause network connection interruptions and handovers, and reconnection will cause additional time costs and increase network delays [2, 5].

Therefore, how to make the WMN maintain a stable network environment with high bandwidth and low latency in a diverse and complex environment is one of the key issues that currently concerned by the industry [6]. In order to solve the above problems, there are traditional methods to introduce caching on the WMN transmission node, so that the application of data caching in the wireless network becomes more flexible and effective. Apart from caching on one node, WMN can also be cached on multiple nodes collaboratively [7, 8], reducing the cost of data query and access through resource storage and sharing, and reducing the negative impact of relay multi-hop and node mobility.

Among them, Cohen et al. proposed a square root rule copy caching strategy, which makes the density of content in the network coverage inversely proportional to the square root of the amount of content [9]. However, the application scenarios of the above methods are relatively simple, and the support for the mobility of WMN nodes is not strong, and it is still difficult to meet the network usage requirements in a diverse environment. Therefore, this paper proposes a method to improve the transmission efficiency and stability of the system by using the cache retransmission mechanism in the Wireless Mesh Network, and designs a message format that supports multiple and flexible networking. Based on the UDP protocol in the WMN environment, the introduction of ACRM can achieve efficient data caching, request and response, etc. weaken the negative problems caused by relay multi-hop and mobility, and can play an active role in heterogeneous complex environments.

In addition, the WMN that introduces a cache retransmission mechanism is compatible with traditional wireless networks and does not affect the normal operation of other network node functions while exerting the cache mechanism. As shown in Fig. 1.

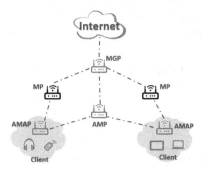

Fig. 1. Brief description: schematic diagram of WMN topology with the introduction of 'cache retransmission mechanism'.

The "cache retransmission mechanism" proposed in this paper will be explained in detail in the first section of Sect. 3. The second section of Sect. 3 will describe in detail a set of timeout request time discrimination algorithms based on trend judgment included in the cache retransmission mechanism, so that the receiving end can adaptively change the frequency of sending request messages according to different environments.

2 Related Work

Although the WMN is widely used [10], there is still a lot of room to transform and improve the performance of the existing network based on the ability of caching [11]. Some caching systems involving hierarchical structures can be found in [12], which are more similar to the WMN architecture. The work in [13] assumes the use of Ad-hoc networks, but they impose a cluster structure on the network. The caching protocols in other multi-hop wireless networks are mainly proposed in ad-hoc networks [14]. In [15], CacheData for caching data and CachePath for caching paths are mentioned, where data and paths are cached on the routing node between the source and the target. However, the characteristics of WMN are different from those of Ad-hoc networks, and different cache designs are required.

The ACRM proposed in this paper can compensate for the current WMN inadequate support for mobility, link instability, and network performance issues brought by relay multi-hop transmission through improved cache retransmission mechanism and time-out discrimination algorithm. At the same time, ACRM has characteristics and effects in heterogeneous and complex environments such as military deployment, emergency response in disaster areas, and urban network access, and has certain utility and reference value in related fields.

3 ACRM Design

3.1 CRM

The 'cache retransmission mechanism' is implemented in the wireless Mesh environment using UDP protocol transmission, allowing the network system itself to ensure stable, flexible, and reliable transmission. For this reason, based on the idea of IP compatibility, a unique message format and application layer protocol are designed. The message format is shown in Tables 1, 2, and 3. ACRM message format is detailed in Table 1.

Table 1. Sending message format.

Sending message			
Package type	Stream ID	Packet sequence number	load
WMN relay node cache message			
Stream ID	Packet sequence number		Is it cached
Receiver cache message format			
Stream ID	Packet sequence number	Delivery time	Receiving time	Delay per packet	Whether to cache	overtime time

As shown in Fig. 2, take 4 WMN devices as an example to describe the 'cache retransmission mechanism'. WMN devices are represented as nodes 3, 2, 1, 0. Node 3 is used as the sender, node 0 is used as the receiver, and nodes 2 and 1 are used as relay devices to cache, forward, and respond to data packets. In fact, this mechanism does not limit the number of WMN devices, and is applicable when the WMN device is at rest or in motion.

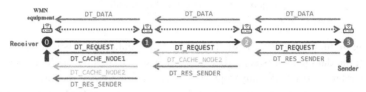

Fig. 2. Schematic diagram of message forwarding with cache retransmission mechanism.

When the sender of node 3 sends the data packet, the 'ReceiverExpireCheck' retransmission mechanism is started, and after each interval of ExpireTime, the receiver will be detected for packet loss. The ExpireTime retransmission interval is calculated by an adaptive algorithm based on the current system time and network delay. ExpireTime = TimeNow + RTO. Among them, TimeNow is the current time of the system, and RTO is calculated by Jacobson, the classic algorithm of adaptive discrimination in TCP/IP.

When node 1 near the receiving end receives a DT_REQUEST message, it checks whether there is a data packet corresponding to the packet sequence number in the local cache, and if so, respond directly from the local, reply to node 0 with the data packet of the corresponding packet sequence number of type DT_CACHE_NODE1, and discard the request message at the same time; if not, forward the request message to other nodes connected later.

However, when the CRM mechanism is simply used, when packet loss occurs at the receiving end and the link quality is good, the receiving end will frequently send request messages, which will cause a large amount of redundancy in the request messages, resulting in network congestion, which actually causes a decrease in network transmission quality. Therefore, the Trend-Jacobson (TJ) algorithm is introduced to reasonably reduce the number of request messages, effectively alleviate network congestion, and further improve network transmission efficiency. The TJ algorithm will be specifically introduced in the next section.

3.2 Trend-Jacobson

A very important point in this process is the configuration of the size of the detected period parameter. However, in the actual network environment, the network quality is not static. Therefore, it is particularly important to design a set of reasonable timeout algorithms for judging time.

The trend judgment is introduced on this basis, it is first judged whether the delay change is in the same trend, and only the third one of the three consecutive increasing or decreasing RTOs is accepted to effectively reduce the number of request messages. Network review and redundancy, to avoid network congestion, and named it Trend Jacobson (TJ) algorithm, as shown in Fig. 3.

$$RTO = EstimateRTT + 4 \cdot DevRTT$$
$$DevRTT = (1 - Beta) \cdot DevRTT + Beta \cdot abs(Dev)$$
$$Dev = SampleRTT - EstimatedRTT$$
$$EstimatedRTT = (1 - Alpha) \cdot EstimatedRTT + Alpha \cdot SampleRTT$$
$$SampleRTT = ReceiveTime - SendTime$$

Fig. 3. Trend Jacobson (TJ) algorithm.

Among them, SampleRTT is the time when each data packet is received minus the time when the data packet is sent, that is, the one-way transmission delay of each data packet. In order to avoid too many requests for packet redundancy, the lower limit of RTO is set as RTO limit during trend judgment. Judge whether the RTO for three consecutive times is increasing or decreasing, if it is increasing or decreasing, accept the third RTO value and update the data three times at the same time, if not, discard the third record result and continue to update the data.

4   Simulation

4.1   Static Test

As shown in Fig. 4, based on the NS3 simulation platform, reference and simulate the sensor data return scenario in the fishing ground or pasture environment. Based on the WMN environment, 4 WMN nodes are set up, among which node 3 is the sender and node 0 is the receiver. The nodes are separated by 1500 m and form a straight line arrangement. The environmental configuration parameters are shown in Table 2.

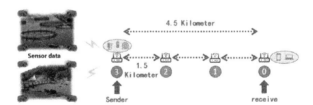

Fig. 4. Schematic diagram of the scene of sensor data return of fishery and pasture.

As shown in Fig. 5, the delay statistics of 1000 data packets. By recording the time of sending and receiving data packets, the transmission delay of each packet is calculated, and the delay of 1000 data packets is accumulated, and then divided by 1000 to obtain the average transmission delay. The average delay of the WMN that does not use the CRM in the static embodiment environment is 1412 ms. In the static transmission embodiment of the WMN using the 'cache retransmission mechanism', the delay statistics of 1000 data packets is 691 ms on average.

The abscissa is the number of statistical data packets, and the ordinate is the one-way delay of each data packet (ns). Experiments show that the introduction of the CRM can reduce the delay by about 51% in the current environment.

Table 2. Environment configuration parameters in static environment embodiment.

Average transmission level	36 dbm	Wireless signal frequency	5.2 GHz	Wireless transmission standard	IEEE 802.11s
Noise level	15.5 dbm	Bandwidth	20 MHz	Threshold	−86 dbm
Transmission gain	1	Transmission loss model	Friis-Loss	Packet Number	1000

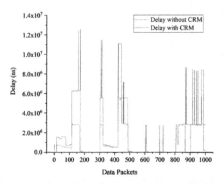

Fig. 5. Whether to apply CRM latency comparison data.

4.2 Dynamic Test

Also based on the NS3 simulation platform to simulate military deployment scenarios. 9 nodes are used as 9 infantry combat units, starting from the same location (0, 0), moving randomly within a 500 m × 500 m matrix area at a constant speed of 20 m/s, and bounce back after hitting the boundary. Node 7 is the sender and sends 100 M files, node 0 is the receiver, and the environment configuration parameters are shown in Table 3.

Table 3. Environmental configuration parameters in a dynamic environment embodiment.

Average transmission level	18 dbm	Wireless signal frequency	5.2 GHz	Wireless transmission standard	IEEE 802.11s
Noise level	15 dbm	Bandwidth	20 MHz	Threshold	−86 dbm
Transmission gain	1	Transmission loss model	Friis-Loss	System loss	11
Transfer file size	100 M bytes	Node moving speed	20 m/s	Routing Protocol	HWMP

The sender sends 39560 data packets with a load of a file with a total size of 100 M. The receiver counts the transmission completion time, and compares the control variables between WMN based on the traditional TCP protocol and WMN based on the UDP protocol and using the Jacobson timeout discrimination algorithm. Compare the WMN of the CRM (CRM). The result is shown in Fig. 6. The abscissa is the transmission time (s), and the ordinate is the size of the transmitted file (bytes).

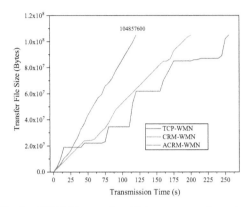

Fig. 6. 100 M file transfer efficiency comparison chart.

Traditional WMN is based on TCP protocol for data transmission. In a mobility environment, the link is complex and changeable when relaying multi-hop transmission, and it is difficult for the network system to maintain stable data transmission. But using the ACRM, data packet can be cached on the WMN relay node, and carried and transmitted. The data of this mechanism does not need to be maintained based on a stable link. In a highly dynamic environment, the sender will send data to other nearby nodes that can be touched, and when the surrounding nodes touch the receiving end, the information it carries will be transmitted. At the same time, after receiving the feedback request, you can also directly obtain the data at the nearest WMN node with the target data packet. Simulation experiments show that the ACRM can increase the transmission efficiency by 216% compared with the traditional TCP protocol in the current dynamic mobile environment.

5   Conclusion

ACRM with the introduction of TJ algorithm can effectively reduce the number of request redundant messages, alleviate network congestion, and further enhance the effect of CRM. Validated by the NS3 simulation platform, compared with the traditional WMN, in the static environment of this paper, ACRM can reduce the end-to-end delay by about 51%, and in the dynamic simulation environment, the transmission efficiency can be increased by about 216%. It can be seen that the ACRM mechanism proposed in this paper can improve the stability, reliability and transmission efficiency of the WMN system itself, while reducing the data transmission delay, and weakening the negative impact of WMN relay multi-hop and mobility on the network system. It has certain reference and application value in WMN. In the follow-up work, WMN multi-channel communication will be added, and WMN characteristics will be fully considered and combined with WMN characteristics to conduct simulation experiments in more realistic scenarios.

Acknowledgment. This Work was supported by Youth Innovation Promotion Association of Chinese Academy of Sciences (2020175).

References

1. Akyildiza, I.F., Wang, X.D., Wang, W.L.: Wireless mesh networks: a survey. Comput. Netw. **47**(4), 445–487 (2005)
2. IEEE Computer Society: Wireless LAN medium access control (MAC) and physical layer (PHY) specifications. ANSI/IEEE Std 802.11, June 2003
3. Camp, J.D., Knightly, E.W., Reed, W.S.: Developing and deploying multihop wireless networks for low-income communities. J. Urban Technol. **13**(129), 1063–1732 (2006)
4. Hara, T.: Effective replica allocation in ad hoc networks for improving data accessibility. In: Proceedings of INFOCOM 2001 (2001)
5. Perkins, C., Bhagwat, P.: Highly dynamic DSDV routing for mobile computers. In: Proceedings of SIGCOMM 1994 (1994)
6. Sampaio, S., Souto, P., Vasques, F.: A review of scalability and topological stability issues in IEEE 802.11s wireless mesh networks deployments. Int. J. Commun. Syst. **29**(4), 671–693 (2016)
7. Nuggehalli, P., Srinivasan, V., Chiasserini, C.: Energy-efficient caching strategies in ad hoc wireless networks. IEEE/ACM Trans. Networking **14**(5), 25–34 (2006)
8. Sailhan, F., Issarny, V.: Cooperative caching in ad hoc networks. In: Chen, M.-S., Chrysanthis, P.K., Sloman, M., Zaslavsky, A. (eds.) MDM 2003. LNCS, vol. 2574, pp. 13–28. Springer, Heidelberg (2003). https://doi.org/10.1007/3-540-36389-0_2
9. Alasaad, A., Gopalakrishnan, S., Leung, V.C.: Peer-to-peer file sharing over wireless mesh networks. In: Proceeding of the IEEE PacRim 2009, Victoria, Canada, pp. 697–702 (2009)
10. BT selects Motorola to deploy wireless cities across the UKs. Government technology news report. http://www.govtech.com/gt/articles/102602
11. Tang, B., Gupta, H., Das, S.: Benefit-based data caching in ad hoc networks. IEEE Trans. Mob. Comput. **7**(3), 289–304 (2008)
12. Breslau, L., Cao, P., Fan, L., Phillips, G., Shenker, S.: Web caching and zipf-like distributions: evidence and implications. In: Proceedings of INFOCOM 1999 (1999)
13. Yin, L., Cao, G.: Supporting cooperative caching in ad hoc networks. IEEE Trans. Mob. Comput. **5**(1), 77–89 (2006)
14. Wu, W., Cao, J., Fan, X.: Overhearing-aided data caching in wireless ad hoc networks. In: 6th IEEE ICDCS International Workshop on Wireless Ad Hoc and Sensor Networks (WWASN 2009), Montreal, Canada, 22–26 June 2009
15. Zhao, J., Zhang, P., Cao, G., Das, C.R.: Cooperative caching in wireless p2p networks: design, implementation, and evaluation. IEEE Trans. Parallel Distrib. Syst. **21**(7), 229–241 (2010)

Efficient Budget-Distance-Aware Influence Maximization in Geo-Social Network

Yue Gu, Xiaopeng Yao, Guangxian Liang, Chonglin Gu, and Hejiao Huang[(✉)]

Harbin Institute of Technology (Shenzhen), Shenzhen 518055, Guangdong, China
huanghejiao@hit.edu.cn

Abstract. With the popularity of location-based information sharing in social networks, more and more businesses are trying to advertise their products online. In reality, users are more likely to choose a shopping location that is affordable in price and near in distance, while businesses hope to maximize the number of potential users through a geo-social network. Here the affordable ability for each user is defined as budget. There is an urgent need to fast find a certain number of influencers, so as to influence as many users as possible, which is called the Budget-Distance-Aware Influence Maximization (BDAIM) problem. To overcome this challenge, we propose a BDAIM model and design four pruning rules that can remove low-influence users to reduce time complexity. Then, we develop an algorithm with a $1-1/e$ approximation ratio to find high-influence users by combining these pruning rules. Finally, extensive experimental results on real-world datasets have demonstrated the efficiency and effectiveness of proposed methods.

Keywords: Influence maximization · Geo-social network · Budget · Distance · Localization

1 Introduction

With the prevalence of social networks, influence maximization problem emerges. It seeks a set of users in a social network to maximize the number of influenced users (called influence spread). The existing studies [6] show that it is more effective than general advertising channels, such as TV. In recent years, it has become increasingly common to share location-based information in social networks, and it is the trend to study the influence maximization problem in geo-social networks, which can be classified into two types:

- *The first type* is the most common case that only considers location. Given a query region, [4] tries to select k seed nodes that influence as many nodes in the region as possible. Besides, [9] take distance into account.

- *The second type* combines geographical location with other aspects such as topic [7], community [5], and the stay time of users [3]. Considering topic preference, [11] tries to block the influence of negative seeds in a given region. [10] maximizes the influence in a dynamic geo-social network.

However, the existing works ignore that users are more likely to choose a shopping location that is affordable in price and near in distance. A shopping location can be any place that involves user purchase behaviors, such as a restaurant, shopping mall, hotel, amusement park, and so on. For example, when a restaurant owner wants to make an advertisement through social networks, he/she will first hire a certain number (defined as k) of influencers to promote the products to their followers, who will then share the information with their friends through "word-of-mouth". Three factors are affecting the probability for a user to eat at the restaurant: the influence from a friend online, geographical distance to the location, and budget. Note that, when a user receives a recommendation from an online friend, he may still eat at the restaurant with a higher probability by increasing the original budget even if it is just a little less than the average consumption price (defined as cost). Therefore, there is an urgent need to fast find k influencers to influence as many users as possible to go to a certain shopping location, taking budget and distance into account, which is defined Budget-Distance-Aware Influence Maximization (BDAIM) problem.

The main challenges of BDAIM problem are: *(1)* The scale of users is enormous in social networks and each user has a budget and a location, which means that it is very time-consuming to calculate and rank the influence of each user to get the largest k influencers. *(2)* The k influencers are selected one by one. When a new influencer is selected, the influence value of all non-influencer users will be reduced if there is any following user influenced by both this node and the influencer. It is because a user can be influenced only once in a recommendation shopping scenario, and it is the influencer that really works if there is any. Therefore, influence updating is a time-consuming process.

To overcome these challenges, we make the following contributions.

• To the best of our knowledge, we are the first to propose a BDAIM model that takes both budget and distance into account.

• We design four bound estimation techniques as pruning rules to quickly find influencers. The first rule is used to find the first influencer, while the other three rules are separately designed to find the remaining influencers. In the first rule, we design an upper bound and lower bound of each user's influence. The other three rules can update the upper bound of influence for each non-influencer user when a new influencer is selected, although with different calculating methods.

• We develop an efficient algorithm (called the Anchor-Min algorithm) that preferentially calculates the influence of the users with large upper bounds obtained by these pruning rules. This algorithm finds k influencers to maximize the number of influenced users with a $1 - 1/e$ approximation ratio.

• Extensive experimental results on real-world datasets have demonstrated the efficiency and effectiveness of proposed methods.

2   Preliminary

Definition 1 (BDAIM Model).   *Given a geo-social network $G = (V, E)$ and a shopping location Q with cost, where each node $v \in V$ has a budget and a location. At timestamp 0, only nodes in seed set S are activated. At timestamp $t + 1$, active nodes who have just been activated at timestamp t are trying to activate their inactive out-neighbors. When no more nodes can be activated, the procedure terminates. The probability of v being activated by u consists of the online influence of u on v and the budget-distance weight of v according to Q.*

Definition 2 (Influence spread).   *The number of nodes that are active at the termination of the procedure is called influence spread.*

Firstly, definitions based on the fact that users are more likely to choose a shopping location that is affordable in price and near in distance are as follows.

Definition 3 (Distance weight). $D(v, Q) = \frac{d_{max} - d_{v,Q}}{d_{max}}$ *[1], where d_{max} is the longest distance in G and $d_{v,Q}$ is a Euclidean distance which represents the distance between node v and Q.*

Definition 4 (Economic weight).   *Given a b_{max}, let b_v represent the budget of v and c_Q is the cost of Q. Then we define economic weight as*
$$B(v, Q) = \begin{cases} 1, & b_v \geq c_Q \\ \frac{b_v}{c_Q}, & b_v < c_Q \end{cases}, \text{ where } 0 < b_v \leq b_{max} \text{ and } 1 \leq c_Q \leq b_{max}.$$

Definition 5 (Budget-distance weight). $g(v, Q) = \alpha D(v, Q) + (1 - \alpha)B(v, Q)$, *where α represents the importance of budget and distance in the willingness of a user v to go to Q ($\alpha \in [0, 1]$).*

Based on the method in [2], we define the online influence of u on v, denoted as $I(u, v)$. Because the maximal influence path $(MIP(u, v))$ shows the largest probability for u to influence v online, u can only influence v online through the maximize influence path which is from u to v.

$$MIP(u, v) = argmax_{p(u,v) \in p_G(u,v)}\{\mathcal{P}(p(u, v))\}$$
$$= argmax_{p(u,v) \in p_G(u,v)}\{\prod_{i=1}^{m-1} \mathcal{P}(w_i, w_{i+1})\}$$

where $p_G(u, v)$ is a set of paths from u to v in G. $\mathcal{P}(p(u, v))$ represents the probability of that u influence v online through a path $p(u, v) = \langle u = w_1, \cdots, w_m = v \rangle$, for each edge $\langle w_i, w_{i+1} \rangle$. Note that we set the condition that $\mathcal{P}(MIP(u, v))$ must satisfy no less than a given threshold θ to remove insignificant paths. Thus, $I(u, v) = \mathcal{P}(MIP(u, v))$ and $\mathcal{P}(MIP(u, v)) \geq \theta$, otherwise, u can not influence v online.

Because the online influence of the set S on v (denoted as $I(S, v)$) cannot simply be counted as $\sum_{u \in S} I(u, v)$. To solve this problem, two trees with v as root and containing all nodes that can influence node v online or nodes that can be influenced by v online are defined in the following equation.

$$In(v)/Out(v) = \cup_{u \in V} MIP(u,v)/MIP(v,u) \tag{1}$$

$$I(S,v) = 1 - \prod_{w \in N(v)} (1 - I(S,w)\mathcal{P}(w,v)) \tag{2}$$

where N_v is neighbors of v in $In(v)$.

The influence of S on v in the BDAIM model is defined as $I_{QB}(S,v)$.

$$I_{QB}(S,v) = I(S,v) \times g(v,Q) \tag{3}$$

It is easy to get $I_{QB}(S) = \sum_{v \in V} I_{QB}(S,v)$. The increment influence of u (denoted as $I_{QB}(u|S)$) is $I_{QB}(u|S) = I_{QB}(\{u\} \cup S) - I_{QB}(S)$.

Definition 6 (BDAIM Problem). *Given a geo-social network $G = (V,E)$ and a shopping location Q with cost c_Q, the BDAIM problem finds a set $S = argmax_{S \in V} I_{QB}(S)$ of k nodes where $I_{QB}(S)$ is the influence spread of S.*

Lemma 1. *The problem of computing BDAIM is NP-hard and $I_{QB}(S)$ is submodular and monotonic in the BDAIM problem.*

3 Pruning Methods

3.1 Find the First Seed

There are infinite locations and costs of Q in G, so it is hard to pre-compute the influence of every node in the offline process. To solve this problem, we use some anchor nodes which denote as q_i to compute the influence of each node in advance. In this subsection, we develop approaches in [9] to find out the relationship between q_i and Q. Let c_{q_i}, $B(v,q_i)$ represent the cost of q_i, and the economic weight of v based on q_i, respectively. Let $I_{q_i B}(u,v)$ and $d_{q_i,Q}$ denote the influence for u to v based on that the shopping location is q_i and Euclidean distance between q_i and Q, respectively. Then we can infer that $B(v,q_i) \geq B(v,Q)$, when $c_{q_i} \leq c_Q$. Based on the above definitions, the first prune rule is proposed.

Rule (i). For the first seed selection, Lemma 2 or Lemma 3 can be used to prune low-influence nodes.

Lemma 2. $I_{QB}(u)^U = I_{q_i B}(u) + \alpha \times \frac{d_{q_i,Q}}{d_{max}} \times I(u)$, *when* $c_{q_i} \leq c_Q$

Lemma 3. $I_{QB}(u)^L = I_{q_i B}(u) - \alpha \times \frac{d_{q_i,Q}}{d_{max}} \times I(u)$, *when* $c_{q_i} > c_Q$

Let l_q represent the location of the anchor node q_i. Each anchor node q_i consists of the location l_q and the cost c_{q_i}. For setting anchor nodes, first, we partition G into $\mathcal{F}$ rows and $\mathcal{W}$ columns equally to get $\mathcal{F} \times \mathcal{W}$ cells, where l_q equals the coordinate of any one of the vertices of each cell. Second, we calculate

$\{c_{q_i} | \frac{c_i}{c_m} \times (b_{max} - 1) + 1, \forall c_i \in 0, 1, \ldots, c_m\}$, where c_m is the number of possible values of c_{q_i}.

For selecting an anchor node (denoted by q), after a business inputs a shopping location Q with price c_Q online, we try to find q which must satisfy: (1) $d_{q_i,Q}$ is minimal, (2) $c_{q_i} \leq c_Q$ and the difference between them is as small as possible, (3) q is used to get $I_{QB}^U(u)/I_{QB}^L(u)$.

3.2   Find Subsequent Seed

The influence of S consists of the influence of the first seed node and the incremental influence of the subsequent seed nodes. In this subsection, different upper bounds of incremental influence by extending approaches in [8] are presented. For the subsequent seed selection, the three pruning rules are as follows:

Rule (ii).   Corollary 1 can be used to prune low increment influence nodes.
Rule (iii).   Corollary 2 can be used to prune low increment influence nodes.
Rule (iv).   Lemma 6 can be used to prune low increment influence nodes.

Lemma 4. $I_{QB}(u|S) \leq I_{QB}(u) - min_{v \in V} I_{QB}(u, v) \times I_{QB}(S)$

Corollary 1. $I_{QB}(u|S) \leq I_{QB}(u) - min_{v \in V}(I_{q_i B}(u, v) - \alpha \times I(u, v)) \times I_{QB}(S)$

Using the above lemma and corollary, it is fast to estimate the upper bound of $I_{QB}(u|S)$ by storing $I_{QB}(u)$, $min_{v \in V}(I_{q_i B}(u, v) - \alpha \times I(u, v))$ and $I_{QB}(S)$ in ahead. However, if there is a $\mathcal{P}(MIP(u, v))$ which smaller than θ for $v \in V$, then $min_{v \in V} I_{QB}(u, v)$ is equal to 0. In this situation, the upper bound of $I_{QB}(u|S)$ is too loose. Then we prompt it as following:

Lemma 5. $I_{QB}(u|S) \leq I_{QB}(u) - min_{v \in Out(u)} I_{QB}(u, v) \times \sum_{v \in Out(u)} I_{QB}(S, v)$

The following result can be directly deduced by **Corollary** 1 and **Lemma** 5.

Corollary 2. $I_{QB}(u|S) \leq I_{QB}(u) - min_O^L \times \sum_{v \in Out(u)} I_{QB}(S, v)$ where min_O^L is $min_{v \in Out(u)}(I_{q_i B}(u, v) - \alpha \times I(u, v))$.

It can be infer that only when $Out(u) = |V|$, $min_{v \in V} I_{QB}(u, v) \times I_{QB}(S) \geq min_{v \in Out(u)} I_{QB}(u, v) \times \sum_{v \in Out(u)} I_{QB}(S, v)$. Hence, most of the time, we use **Lemma** 5 to estimate the nodes. To get a tight bound, we have **Lemma** 6.

Lemma 6. $I_{QB}(u|S) \leq I_{QB}(u) - I_{QB}(u) \times min_{v \in Out(u)} I_{QB}(S, v)$.

According to the above lemmas and corollaries, when $Out(u) = |V|$, we use **Corollary** 1 to estimate $I_{QB}^U(u|S)$. Otherwise, the minimum value of **Corollary** 2 and **Lemma** 6 is a better choice. If $I_{QB}(u)$ has not been calculated, then we use $I_{QB}^U(u)$ instead of $I_{QB}(u)$ to estimate $I_{QB}^U(u|S)$.

Time Complexity. The time complexity of **Rule (i)** and **Rule (ii)** are $O(1)$. Meanwhile, the time complexity of **Rule (iii)** and **Rule (iv)** are $O(|Out(u)|)$.

4   Algorithm

To simplify the input and output of the algorithm, we give these definitions: *(1)* $\mathcal{A}$: the anchor node set, *(2)* $\mathcal{I}$: a hash map with the node id as the key and the $I_{QB}(u)$ as the value, *(3)* $\mathcal{H}$: a max-heap with $I_{QB}(u|S)$ or $I_{QB}(u)$ of each node u, *(4)* $I_{qB}(u)$: the influence of node u when u treats q as the shopping location.

To achieve instant performance in solving a BDAIM problem, we devise an Anchor-Min algorithm and the pseudocode is illustrated in Algorithm 1, which selects k seed nodes as fast as possible to satisfy the approximation ratio of $1 - 1/e$. This algorithm consists of three main components:

  • *offline Processing. (Line 1–2)* We calculate and store $In(u)$ and $Out(u)$ for each node $u \in V$. $\mathcal{A}$ and other variables need to be computed and saved later.

Algorithm 1: Anchor-Min Algorithm. **Input:** G, k, Q, **Output:** S

---

1 Precompute $In(u),Out(u)$ for $u \in V$,$I_{q_iB}(u)$ for $q_i \in \mathcal{A}$;
2 Precompute $min_{v \in V}(I_{q_iB}(\{u\}, v) - \alpha \times I(u,v))$, min_O^L for $u \in V$ and $q_i \in \mathcal{A}$;
3 Find q in $\mathcal{A}$; Build max-heap $\mathcal{H}$ for $u \in V$ with $I_{QB}^U(u)$ by using **Rule (i)**;
4 The state of u for $u \in V$ set to *estimated* in $\mathcal{N}$;
5 Initialize a seed set $S \leftarrow \emptyset$, a hash map $\mathcal{I} \leftarrow \mathcal{H}$;
6 **while** $|S| < k$ **do**
7 $\quad$ **if** $|S| \neq 0$ **then**
8 $\quad\quad$ Initialize a hash map $\mathcal{N} \leftarrow \emptyset$;
9 $\quad$ **while** $\mathcal{H} \neq \emptyset$ **do**
10 $\quad\quad$ $u \leftarrow \mathcal{H}.pop()$;
11 $\quad\quad$ **if** $|S| = 0$ *and estimated* **then**
12 $\quad\quad\quad$ Compute $I_{QB}(u)$; Add $< u, I_{QB}(u) >$ to update $\mathcal{H}$; Add $< u, computed >$ to update $\mathcal{N}$; Change $< u, I_{QB}^U(u) >$ to $< u, I_{QB}(u) >$ in $\mathcal{I}$; continue;
13 $\quad\quad$ **if** $u \notin \mathcal{N}$ *(i.e., outdated)* **then**
14 $\quad\quad\quad$ **if** $Out(u) = |V|$ **then**
15 $\quad\quad\quad\quad$ Compute $I_{QB}^U(u|S)$ by using **Rule (ii)**;
16 $\quad\quad\quad$ **else**
17 $\quad\quad\quad\quad$ Compute $I_{QB}^U(u|S)$ by using **Rule (iii)**;
18 $\quad\quad\quad\quad$ Compute $I_{QB}^{U1}(u|S)$ by using **Rule (iv)**;
19 $\quad\quad\quad\quad$ $I_{QB}^U(u|S) \leftarrow min(I_{QB}^U(u|S), I_{QB}^{U1}(u|S))$;
20 $\quad\quad\quad$ Add $< u, I_{QB}^U(u|S) >$ into $\mathcal{H}$; Add $< u, estimated >$ to update $\mathcal{N}$;
21 $\quad\quad$ **if** $u \in \mathcal{N}$ *and estimated in* $\mathcal{N}$ **then**
22 $\quad\quad\quad$ Compute $I_{QB}(u|S)$; Add $< u, I_{QB}(u|S) >$ into $\mathcal{H}$; Add $< u, computed >$ to update $\mathcal{N}$;
23 $\quad\quad$ **if** $u \in \mathcal{N}$ *and computed in* $\mathcal{N}$ **then**
24 $\quad\quad\quad$ $S \leftarrow S \cup \{u\}$; update();

25 **return** S

- *Initialization. (Line 3-5)* After the business inputs the location and the price of Q, we find the anchor node q. Next we create an empty seed set S, a max-heap H with $I_{qB}^{U}(u)$ by using **Rule (i)**, a map $\mathcal{I}$ whose value is same as H, and status of all nodes are *estimated*.

- *Seeds selection. (Line 6-24)* We find k seeds by continuously fetching the top element u of the $\mathcal{H}$ that matches the following condition. If u is *computed*, the next seed is u. We put u into S. Then we change status of all nodes to *outdated* and call update().

The update() function is used to handle the change of adding a new seed. This function will recalculate $I_{QB}(S)$ and $Out(S)$.

If u is not *computed*, we will do the following operations depending on status of u. *(1)* When u is *outdated*, we estimate the upper bound of increment influence of u by using influence of u or the upper bound of influence of u in $\mathcal{I}$. If $Out(u) = |V|$, we need to use **Rule (ii)**. Otherwise, we use **Rule (iii)**, **Rule (iv)**. We change status of u to *estimated*. *(2)* When u is *estimated* and S is empty, we compute $I_{QB}(u)$, add it into heap $\mathcal{H}$ and $\mathcal{I}$. Then we change status of u to *computed*. *(3)* When u is *estimated* and S is not empty, we compute $I_{QB}(u|S)$, add it into heap $\mathcal{H}$ and change status of u to *computed*.

5 Experiment

This section experimentally evaluates our algorithm and against the state-of-the-art solutions. All experiments are carried out on a machine with an Intel(R) Xeon(R) Gold 2.10 GHz CPU and $125 GiB$ memory, running Ubuntu 20.04.1 LTS. All algorithms are implemented in C_{++} and randomly selecting 100 different Q. There are 500 round simulations for each seed set, the average of all simulation results is the influence spread. The Euclidean distance between two nodes is obtained by converting the latitude and longitude of the two nodes.

5.1 Experiment Setup

Datasets. Real-world geo-social networks (Gowalla and Twitter) where users can share check-ins are used in our experiments. Gowalla consists of $197K$ vertices and $1.9M$ edges and its average degree is 9.67. Twitter consists of $554K$ vertices and $4.29M$ edges and its average degree is 7.75. These two datasets which can be obtained in [4] do not have the budget of each user, so we choose a random number from 0 to b_{max} as the budget of everyone, which means that all users are guaranteed to have as many budgets as possible.

Algorithms. We implemented our proposed methods and compared them with two state-of-the-art algorithms PMIA [2] and DAIM [9]. PMIA is used to calculate $Out(u)$ and $In(u)$ and to obtain the seed set of nodes using a purely greedy algorithm without advance estimation. Compared with PMIA, DAIM only considers the distance between the user and the shopping location, although the influence of a node is estimated first and then calculated. The source code of PMIA is obtained from the authors. In this experiment, we extend PMIA and the first two rules of $DAIM$ to compute the budget-distance-aware spread (Table 1).

5.2   Spread and Efficiency

Figure 1 shows the influence spread and running time of different algorithms.

As we can see, Fig. 1(a)–Fig. 1(d) show the influence spread of three methods in different datasets and models. The smaller the propagation probability is, the smaller the influence spread is. First, PMIA and our algorithm have the same influence spread, which means that our algorithm really prunes only the unimportant nodes to increase the program speed. Secondly, because DAIM only considers geographical distance, its chosen seed set is not ideal when users need to consider both geographical distance and economic disparity. The influence spread of DAIM is only about 70% of the other two algorithms.

Table 1. Parameters setting

Notation	Meaning	Default value
k	The size of seed set	$\{10, 20, 30, 40, 50\}$
α	The weight of geographic distance in the BDAIM model	0.5
b_{max}/c_{max}	The max budget and cost	1000
θ	The value to distinguish valid maximum influence paths	0.001
l_Q	The location of the shopping location	randomly
$\mathcal{W}/\mathcal{F}$	The number of rows/columns in Subsect. 3.1	14
c_m	The number of possible costs of anchor nodes	10
$\mathcal{P}_{WC}$	The propagation probability on the WC model [2]	$\frac{1}{N_v^*}$
$\mathcal{P}_{TC}$	The propagation probability on the TC model [2]	$\{0.1, 0.01, 0.001\}$

*where N_v specifies the number of incoming neighbors of v.

In Fig. 1(e)–Fig. 1(h), the running time of PMIA is much larger than BDAIM and DAIM. The runtimes of our algorithm and DAIM are almost the same,

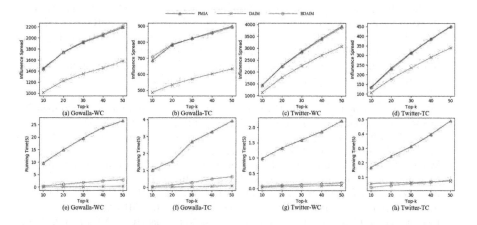

Fig. 1. Influence spread and running time

because they all prune low-influence nodes in advance with prune methods. In addition, the running time of PMIA increases with k. But the runtime of DAIM and BDAIM is almost the same with different k.

6   Conclusion

We propose a budget-distance-aware influence maximization problem and the model. We design four pruning rules for reducing time complexity. The first pruning rule uses the upper bound and the lower bound of influence. The remaining three pruning rules all use the upper bound of the marginal influence. Based on our pruning rules, we develop an algorithm that returns a seed set with a $1 - 1/e$ approximation ratio. Lastly, extensive experimental results have demonstrated the efficiency and effectiveness.

Acknowledgement. This work is financially supported by the National Key R&D Program of China under Grant No.2017YFB0803002 and National Natural Science Foundation of China under Grant No. 61732022.

References

1. Berman, O., Krass, D., Drezner, Z.: The gradual covering decay location problem on a network. Eur. J. Oper. Res. **151**(3), 474–480 (2003)
2. Chen, W., Wang, C., Wang, Y.: Scalable influence maximization for prevalent viral marketing in large-scale social networks. In: Proceedings of the 16th ACM SIGKDD International Conference on Knowledge Discovery and Data Mining, pp. 1029–1038 (2010)
3. Chen, X., Zhao, Y., Liu, G., Sun, R., Zhou, X., Zheng, K.: Efficient similarity-aware influence maximization in geo-social network. IEEE Trans. Knowl. Data Eng. 1 (2020). https://doi.org/10.1109/TKDE.2020.3045783
4. Li, G., Chen, S., Feng, J., Tan, K.l., Li, W.S.: Efficient location-aware influence maximization. In: Proceedings of the 2014 ACM SIGMOD International Conference on Management of Data, pp. 87–98 (2014)
5. Li, X., Cheng, X., Su, S., Sun, C.: Community-based seeds selection algorithm for location aware influence maximization. Neurocomputing **275**, 1601–1613 (2018)
6. Nail, J., Charron, C., Baxter, S.: The consumer advertising backlash. Forrester research and intelliseek market research report 137 (2004)
7. Shi, Q., Wang, C., Chen, J., Feng, Y., Chen, C.: Location driven influence maximization: online spread via offline deployment. Knowl.-Based Syst. **166**, 30–41 (2019)
8. Su, S., Li, X., Cheng, X., Sun, C.: Location-aware targeted influence maximization in social networks. J. Assoc. Inf. Sci. Technol. **69**(2), 229–241 (2018)
9. Wang, X., Zhang, Y., Zhang, W., Lin, X.: Distance-aware influence maximization in geo-social network. In: ICDE, pp. 1–12 (2016)
10. Wang, Y., Li, Y., Fan, J., Tan, K.L.: Location-aware influence maximization over dynamic social streams. ACM Trans. Inf. Syst. **36**(4), 1–35 (2018)
11. Zhu, W., Yang, W., Xuan, S., Man, D., Wang, W., Lv, J.: Location-aware targeted influence blocking maximization in social networks. In: 2019 28th International Conference on Computer Communication and Networks (ICCCN), pp. 1–9. IEEE (2019)

Deep Learning-Based Task Offloading for Vehicular Edge Computing

Feng Zeng[1(✉)], Chengsheng Liu[1], Junzhe Tangjiang[1], and Wenjia Li[2]

[1] School of Computer Science and Technology, Central South University,
Changsha 410083, Hunan, China
`fengzeng@csu.edu.cn`
[2] Department of Computer Science, New York Institute of Technology, New York,
NY 10023, USA

Abstract. With widely used of computation intensive vehicular applications, Vehicular Edge Computing (VEC) plays an increasing important role in providing computation service for vehicles, and task scheduling has direct impact on task offloading performance. In this paper, we analyze the scheduling of tasks in VEC, propose a deep learning-based task scheduling mechanism, and design a model suitable for the prediction of task scheduling success probability and offloading delay. The performance of the model is evaluated with a large amount of data compared to the SVM-based task scheduling algorithm, the proposed mechanism has the offloading failure rate decreased by 40% .

Keywords: Internet of vehicles · Vehicular Edge Computing · Task offloading · Deep learning

1 Introduction

With the rapid development of information technology, the vehicles have gradually evolved to the intelligent devices, equipped with many sensors and on-board computing units to achieve autonomous driving, intelligent navigation and other functions [1, 2]. A large number of sensors (e.g. cameras, GPS, radar, etc.) generate huge amounts of data, which often cannot be fully processed in the local on-board computing unit due to the limited resource [3]. Although the cloud can provide computation services for vehicles, the service latency is difficult to meet the requirements of Quality of Service (QoS) for the emerging intelligent applications, since the cloud servers are far away from the vehicles [4]. For low latency of computing services, the servers can be placed on the locations near to vehicles, and the edge network is formed to provide low-latency computing services for vehicles, which is recently emerged Vehicular Edge Computing (VEC) [5].

In a VEC system, a vehicle can offload all or part of its computation tasks to an edge server for execution, and subsequently obtain the results, thus breaking the limits of the vehicle's own computing power [6]. A typical VEC system usually consists of three parts [7], and the first part is the vehicles in which the vehicular devices generate a large

© Springer Nature Switzerland AG 2021
Z. Liu et al. (Eds.): WASA 2021, LNCS 12939, pp. 291–298, 2021.
https://doi.org/10.1007/978-3-030-86137-7_32

amount of data in real time, and the data is processed locally or offloaded to the VEC servers for processing. The second part includes Road Side Units (RSUs), edge servers, communication base stations, etc. It is the edge of the Internet, closest to that where the data is generated, and can provide limited, fast and low-cost computing services for vehicle users. The third part is the cloud, which usually refers to the computing services provided by cloud computing vendors, and the cloud can be considered to have unlimited computing resources.

Due to a large number of vehicles requesting VEC service, the traffic and computing resources in a VEC network usually change in real time. With the rising of the demand for VEC, the competition for computing resources becomes more and more intense. Therefore, how to schedule computing resources to meet the vehicular computation demand becomes the key problem to overcome. In this paper, we focuses on the intelligent scheduling of tasks, and the deep learning-based methods are proposed to predict the success probability of task offloading and its service delay. With the efficient prediction, the best policy is selected for task offloading.

2 Related Work

In the VEC, vehicles can offload all or part of their computing tasks to edge or cloud servers via wireless communication. The techniques related to task offloading have been extensively researched, which involve issues such as when to offload tasks, how to offload tasks, and where to offload tasks, and so on. In this paper, we focus on the task scheduling problem of VEC, and investigate and evaluate the policy of task offloading for the best QoS.

To address the task scheduling problem in VEC, Sun et al. [8] proposed an adaptive learning task scheduling algorithm (ALTO) based on a multi-armed gambling machine (MAB) to minimize the offloading delay for the dynamic network environment in VEC. The ALTO algorithm works in a distributed manner where the offloading vehicle and the offloaded vehicle do not need to exchange accurate state information (e.g., channel state, computational workload, etc.).

Wang et al. [9] proposed a multi-user and non-cooperative task offloading game as a way to adjust the task offloading probability of each vehicle in VEC, and considered factors such as the distance from the vehicle to the access point (RSU) and the communication method between the vehicles. Based on this computation offloading game model, the authors construct a distributed response algorithm to maximize the utility of each vehicle and show that the strategy can converge to a unique Nash equilibrium.

Liu et al. [10] proposed a matching algorithm-based task scheduling method to minimize network latency. The matching algorithm can provide an effective solution for complex and dynamic network environments. Vehicles obtain decisions by sending matching requests to the RSU, but these requests add additional overhead to the system, slowing down offloading decisions, and the model assumes a fixed value of network latency, which does not adapt to the real-world environment of dynamically changing networks.

Feng et al. [11] proposed a federated vehicle and cloud (HVC) architecture in which vehicles can offload tasks to neighboring vehicles, RSUs and cloud servers to extend their own computing power. Based on the proposed architecture, the authors propose a real-time algorithm for task scheduling which aims to reduce the failure rate of task offloading and reduce the use of the cellular network.

Sonmez et al. [12] proposed a machine learning-based task scheduling mechanism with a two-stage scheduling process. In the first stage, a classification model based on a multi-layer perceptron (MLP) predicts the success of task offloading. In the second stage, a Support Vector Machine (SVM)-based regression model predicts the service delay of task offloading based on the success of the prediction result in the first stage. With the two stages, the task is offloaded to the node with the shortest service delay.

In contrast to existing research works, in this paper, we adopt deep learning methods for the performance prediction of task scheduling. With the powerful representation capability of neural networks, the underlying association of task information can be mined without designing complex features, and the performance of the model can be improved, thus improving the efficiency of task scheduling.

3 Deep Learning Based Task Offloading

In this paper, we propose a deep learning-based task scheduling mechanism, as shown in Fig. 1. When a vehicle user requests for task offloading, three trained deep learning models are used to make the optimal decision according to the task's features, the surrounding environment, etc. Each model has two outputs, one is the success/failure probability of task offloading, and the other is the estimated service delay of task offloading.

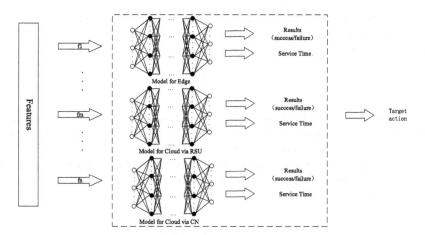

Fig. 1. Deep learning based task scheduling

The deep learning model proposed in this paper is shown in Fig. 2, which consists of two main parts including Feature Generation and Wide & Deep model.

Feature Generation Model: The feature generation DNN model is a non-linear model. With the deepening of the model layers, the model learns a cross-section of high-dimensional features, which makes the model have a relatively good generalization ability. In contrast, the linear model which has a relatively strong memory ability and learns shallow features. Usually, some artificial features are designed to strengthen the model's expressive ability, and crossing the features is used to generate artificial features, as shown in (1):

$$\phi_k(X) = \prod_{i=1}^{d} x_i^{c_{ki}} c_{ki} \in \{0, 1\}, \tag{1}$$

Where x_i represents a feature, and c_{ki} is a binary variable. The above method limits the number of features which can cross at most two, thus generating features with low order crossings.

In this paper, the EdgeCloudsim [15] platform is used to conduct simulation experiments to obtain raw data for task scheduling to train the models. Deep learning, compared to traditional machine learning, does not usually require feature engineering. With the powerful expressive power of neural networks, neural networks are usually able to automatically extract features from raw data.

WIDE and DEEP Model: The WIDE & DEEP model is used to predict whether a task will be successfully offloaded to the cloud or edge by adopting a specific offloading strategy and the processing time required to offloading. The model is divided into two main parts, the WIDE and DEEP. The WIDE part uses a linear model shown in (2).

$$y = w^T[x, \phi(x)] + b \tag{2}$$

The accepted input is the fused features generated after feature crossover, where x denotes the original features, $\phi(x)$ denotes the crossover features, and the DEEP model partly uses a non-linear model, i.e. the traditional DNN model, shown in (3).

$$a^{l+1} = f\left(W^l a^l + b^l\right) \tag{3}$$

In (3), W^l, a^l and b^l denote respectively the l layer's weight, activation output and bias, and f is the activation function. The input features accepted by the DEEP model are fused features from the original features and some of the crossover features.

The outputs of the WIDE and DEEP models are combined and fed into a state classifier, and a time regressor, where the classifier uses cross-entropy as the loss function, and the outputs are:

$$p = \sigma\left(w_{wide}^T[x, \phi(x)] + w_{deep}^T a^{lf} + b\right), \tag{4}$$

Where σ is the sigmoid activation function, and $\phi(x)$ is the crossover feature, and a^{lf} is the activation value of the last layer of the DNN network. The regressor uses the mean square error as the loss function and the output is:

$$t = w_{wide}^T[x, \phi(x)] + w_{deep}^T a^{lf} + b. \tag{5}$$

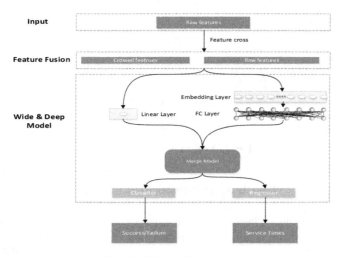

Fig. 2. Wide & Deep model

4 Simulation

4.1 Parameters Setting

The system simulation is based on the EdgeCloudSim platform (hereinafter referred to as the platform), which can realize the simulation of vehicle movement, and the simulation of vehicle movement model is set up as shown in Fig. 3. The whole road is designed as a 16 km oval section, and the RSU is deployed to achieve full coverage of the whole section, with each RSU designed to cover a 400 m section, and 40 RSUs can be deployed to meet the system requirements. In order to better simulate the real movement of vehicles, the 16 km elliptical road section is divided into 40 segments according to 400 m, and the 40 segments are evenly assigned three different speeds, namely 20 km/h, 40 km/h and 60 km/h. During the initialization stage of the system, the vehicles are evenly initialized on the 16 km circular road, and it is ensured that during the operation of the system, the total number of vehicles in the whole will not change. As the road sections have been given different speeds, the vehicle density in the low speed area will be greater than in the high speed area, which is more in line with the real life situation, indicating that the area is a hot spot and traffic congestion has occurred.

The platform allows for the simulation of vehicle movements in addition to other system variables such as network parameters. In order to better simulate the real environment, the task parameters generated by the vehicle are shown in Table 1 and Table 2 below. The simulation divides the tasks into three categories: navigation tasks, assisted driving tasks and entertainment tasks, and they account for 35%, 35% and 30% of the overall tasks respectively. The generation intervals of the three types of tasks are set to 3 s, 5 s and 40 s respectively, with navigation tasks being the most intensive, assisted driving tasks the second most intensive, and infotainment tasks the most sparse; the task lengths of the three types of tasks are set to 3 GI, 10 GI and 5 GI respectively, with GI representing the number of instructions to be executed by the task and the number of computing resources required by the task.

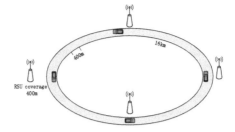

Fig. 3. Vehicle movement model

Table 1. System simulation task parameters

	Specific gravity (%)	Interval(s)	Upload/download volume (KB)	Maximum time delay (s)	Length of assignment (GI)
Navigation tasks	35	3	20/20	0.5	3
Assisted driving tasks	35	4	40/20	1	10
Infotainment tasks	30	40	20/80	2	5

Table 2. Other parameters of the system simulation

Parameters	Value
WAN Network Bandwidth	1000 Mbs
WLAN network bandwidth	100 Mbs
CN Network Bandwidth	10 Mbs
RSU coverage radius	200 m
VEC execution speed	800 GIPS
Cloud execution speed	3000 GIPS
Number of vehicles	100–2200 (vehicles)
Number of simulation rounds	100

4.2 Simulation Results and Analysis

In the simulation, the impact of each algorithm on the offload success rate was tested, as shown in Fig. 4. The offload success rate is one of the most important performance metrics in VEC. If the edge server is full and cannot accept new tasks, or the edge network is congested, it may lead to task execution failure. We use the random scheduling algorithm (Random) as the benchmark algorithm, which represents the worst-case task offloading. From Fig. 4, it can be observed that the average task offload failure rate gradually increases as the number of vehicles increases. This is because as the number of vehicles increases, the network becomes more congested and the load on the edge servers and cloud centre servers becomes higher.

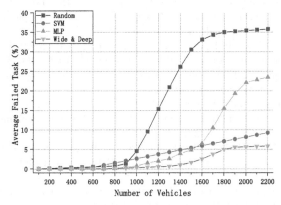

Fig. 4. Impact of different algorithms on task scheduling

From Fig. 4, it can also be observed that the SVM, MLP, and Wide & Deep based task scheduling algorithms, all outperform the benchmark algorithm, while the Wide & Deep model proposed in this paper has the best performance. The Wide & Deep model is able to make more accurate predictions about the outcome of task scheduling by leveraging the powerful generalization ability of deep neural networks and the memory capability of linear units, thus greatly improving the success rate of task offloading. The above simulation results show that in the worst case, the proposed Wide & Deep-based task scheduling algorithm reduces the average task offload failure rate by nearly 88% compared to the benchmark algorithm, nearly 40% compared to the SVM-based task scheduling algorithm, and nearly 75% compared to the MLP-based task scheduling algorithm.

5 Summary

In this paper, we analyze the scheduling of tasks in VEC, propose a deep learning-based task scheduling mechanism, and design a model suitable for task scheduling result prediction. The performance of the model is evaluated with a large amount of data. Scheduling of tasks in in-vehicle edge computing is a challenging problem because task scheduling is an online problem where tasks are generated in real time and the scheduling mechanism must ensure that tasks are scheduled to the appropriate nodes to improve VEC performance. The deep learning-based algorithm proposed in this paper can significantly reduce the average task offloading failure rate.

References

1. Olariu, S.: A survey of vehicular cloud research: trends, applications and challenges. IEEE Trans. Intell. Transp. Syst. **21**(6), 2648–2663 (2019)
2. Foh, C.H., Kantarci, B., Chatzimisios, P., Wu, J., Gao, D.: IEEE access special section editorial: advances in vehicular clouds. IEEE Access **4**, 10315–10317 (2016)
3. Liu, L., Chen, C., Pei, Q., Maharjan, S., Zhang, Y.: Vehicular edge computing and networking: a survey. Mob. Networks Appl. **26**, 1145–1168 (2020)
4. Feng, J., Liu, Z., Wu, C., Ji, Y.: AVE: autonomous vehicular edge computing framework with ACO-based scheduling. IEEE Trans. Veh. Technol. **66**(12), 10660–10675 (2017)
5. Abbas, N., Zhang, Y., Taherkordi, A., Skeie, T.: Mobile edge computing: a survey. IEEE Internet Things J. **5**(1), 450–465 (2017)
6. Raza, S., Wang, S., Ahmed, M., Anwar, M.R.: A survey on vehicular edge computing: architecture, applications, technical issues, and future directions. Wireless Commun. Mob. Comput. **2019**, 3159762-1-3159762–19 (2019)
7. Rasheed, A., Chong, P.H.J., Ho, I.W.H., Li, X.J., Liu, W.: An overview of mobile edge computing: architecture, technology and direction. KSII Trans. Internet Inf. Syst. (TIIS) **13**(10), 4849–4864 (2019)
8. Sun, Y., et al.: Adaptive learning-based task offloading for vehicular edge computing systems. IEEE Trans. Veh. Technol. **68**(4), 3061–3074 (2019)
9. Wang, Y., et al.: A game-based computation offloading method in vehicular multiaccess edge computing networks. IEEE Internet Things J. **7**(6), 4987–4996 (2020)
10. Liu, P., Li, J., Sun, Z.: Matching-based task offloading for vehicular edge computing. IEEE Access **7**, 27628–27640 (2019)
11. Feng, J., Liu, Z., Wu, C., Ji, Y.: Mobile edge computing for the internet of vehicles: offloading framework and job scheduling. IEEE Veh. Technol. Mag. **14**(1), 28–36 (2018)
12. Sonmez, C., Tunca, C., Ozgovde, A., et al.: Machine learning-based workload orchestrator for vehicular edge computing. IEEE Trans. Intell. Transp. Syst. **22**(4), 2239–2251 (2020)
13. Zeng, F., Chen, Q., Meng, L., Wu, J.: Volunteer assisted collaborative offloading and resource allocation in vehicular edge computing. IEEE Trans. Intell. Transp. Syst. **22**(6), 3247–3257 (2020)
14. Zeng, F., Chen, Y., Yao, L., Wu, J.: A novel reputation incentive mechanism and game theory analysis for service caching in software-defined vehicle edge computing. Peer-to-Peer Netw. Appl. **14**, 467–481 (2021)
15. Sonmez, C., Ozgovde, A., Ersoy, C.: Edgecloudsim: an environment for performance evaluation of edge computing systems. Trans. Emerg. Telecommun. Technol. **29**(11), e3493 (2018)

Hacks Hit the Phish: Phish Attack Detection Based on Hacks Search

Yunyi Zhang[1,2] and Shuyuan Jin[1,2(✉)]

[1] School of Computer Science and Engineering, Sun Yat-sen University, Guangzhou, China
zhangyy333@mail2.sysu.edu.cn, jinshuyuan@mail.sysu.edu.cn
[2] Cyberspace Security Research Center, Peng Cheng Laboratory, Shenzhen, China

Abstract. Phishing is a simple but fatal cyber-attack that deceives users to visit a fake website to steal sensitive information such as username, password, and other credentials. The search engine-based phishing detection approaches provide interpretability and credibility well. While, the limitation of these approaches is that it is difficult to choose an accurate search string to collect valid information. The uncertain search results caused by search strings will influence the detection accuracy. This paper proposes a Hacks search based phishing detection approach—Hacks Hit the Phishing (HHP), in which the Hacks search is an advanced search syntax provided by search engines. The approach not only collects valid information accurately by Hacks search syntax, but also can detect phishing sites hosted on compromised servers by the resource decision strategy. From the experimental results, it is observed that HHP achieved an accuracy of 98.3% in Alexa, and 95.59% in openphish.

Keywords: Phishing attack · Search engine · Anti-phishing

1 Introduction

Phishing is a deception attack that attackers deceive users to visit a fake website that mimics a legitimate site, which is identified cyber-threat in 1996. Phishing can be achieved in many ways such as email, website, malware, voice, etc. According the 2020 Q1 report [1] published by Anti-Phishing Working Group (APWG), the trend of phishing attacks highlights three features: 1) popularization of phishing topic, where attackers set the hot issue as the topic of phishing to improve the success of attacks, like COVID-19 topics; 2) consistent goals, where the mail and software as a service are still the most popular target; 3) specialization of attack techniques, where 75% phishing sites apply HTTPS. As shown in Fig. 1, the proportion has exceeded 70%.

Researches are in progress for different stages of phishing, 1) phishing prevention, which improves user ability to recognize phishing by training; 2) phishing detection, which detects the phishing actions by different detection techniques to prevent attacks; 3) phishing handing, which ranks the threat level by analyzing phishing and prioritize high-risk attacks [2].

© Springer Nature Switzerland AG 2021
Z. Liu et al. (Eds.): WASA 2021, LNCS 12939, pp. 299–309, 2021.
https://doi.org/10.1007/978-3-030-86137-7_33

There are many detection approaches that rely on URLs, page source codes, and third-party data. The third-party based features provide interpretability and credibility well, which play an important role in phishing detection. The third-party data comes from search engines, WHOIS, or passive DNS, etc. Nevertheless, there exist two main challenges in the search engine-based approach: 1) for different search strings, there is a huge difference in search results, which will affect the judgment of phishing; 2) many implementations fail to detect phishing sites hosted on compromised servers. The compromised server refers to the server was attacked and controlled by attackers. To resolve these problems, this paper presents HHP, in which the Hacks search is an advanced search syntax provided by search engines. And the approach leverages index decision and resource decision to mitigate the problem of URL redirection and to counter the phishing sites hosted on compromised servers.

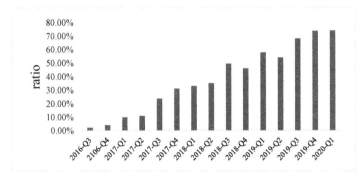

Fig. 1. The ratios of HTTPS in phishing sites

The contributions of this paper are as follows:

- The HHP was proposed to detect phishing attacks, which applies advanced search syntax that search engines provided to get the right search results.
- Index decision and resource decision strategies were proposed to mitigate the problems of third-party domain name reputations stole caused by URL redirection and detect the phishing sites hosted on compromised servers.

The rest of this paper is organized as follows: Sect. 2 shows the background for phishing. Section 3 explains the detail of the proposed work. Section 4 presents the analysis of experiments for the approach. Section 5 concludes this paper.

2   Background

2.1   Anti-phishing Techniques

One area of work in the literature used white/black list to detect phishing sites. These techniques are simple and straightforward with high accuracy and low system cost. But there exist some obvious disadvantages, for instance, the list needs to be updated continuously and they cannot prevent zero-day attacks. To mitigate the problems, LungHao et al. [3] proposed a updating blacklist framework—PhishTrack, which updates blacklist by collecting multiple sources of blacklist. To improve the accuracy of blacklist, Bell et al. [4] measured three famous phishing datasets, Google Safe Browsing (GSB), PhishTank (PT), and OpenPhish (OP) from different aspects, such as numbers, re-add, overlap etc.

Another area explores the URL features to detect phishing sites. Gu et al. [5] extracted the URL features and applied Bayesian network and support vector machine to achieve phishing detection. Based on CANTINA, Xiang et al. [6] proposed CANTINA+, which designs eight features involving search engine, HTML etc.

Visual and page content features can also be used for phishing detection. Liu et al. [7] put forward a visual feature based phishing detection method, which compares the DOM and style of webpage with legitimate sites. For the page content, Zhang et al. [8] extracted the page keywords by TFIDF algorithm and then check whether the target is absent in the search results of keywords.

2.2 Hacks Search

Google Hacks, is an information gathering technique using the advanced search syntax of the google search engine. Through Google Hacks, we can accurately collect information for a specified site. We use google advanced operator to control the search results. The operation syntax as follow:

operator: search string

The common advanced operators are shown in Table 1.

Table 1. The common advanced operator

Advanced operator	Description	Sample
site:	Limit the search results to specified domain names or sites	site:example.com
intile:	Limit the search results that page title contains specified search string	intile:login
inurl:	Limit the search results that URL contains specified search string	inurl:login.php

3   HHP: Design and Implementation

This section describes the detailed design and implementation of the proposed HHP.

3.1   Motivation

The phishing detection approaches based on search engine inherit the reputation of search engines, where search engines prefer to index pages that are of high value to users. The point here is, an accurate search string is necessary. Many search string generation methods have been developed. Common ones of search string include the domain name, page titles, and the "keywords" attribute. However, the effect of these search strings is uncertain, which may acquire irrelevant data. Figure 2 shows the search results of applying "the domain name + keywords" as a search string (as shown in Fig. 2(1)) and "the domain names" (as shown in Fig. 2(2)). Search engines will match the search string as much as possible, while the "keywords" attribute contains so redundant information that misleads search engines, thereby, we cannot find the target site in search results in Fig. 2(1), and there is just one result in Fig. 2(2) that can match the target site. Moreover, it is difficult to get search strings related to page contents. To obtain the search string, it is necessary to obtain all the content of the page.

The simple comparison strategy that checks whether the target site is absent in search results is no longer working. The number of phishing sites hosted on compromised serves is on the rise. Hosting a phishing site on compromised servers not only can extend the survival life of phishing pages, but also carries the reputation of original sites, which may bypass protective measures that rely on the reputation of third-party.

To resolve the issues, this paper proposes a Hacks search based phishing detection approach, which applies advanced search syntax to obtain accurate data of target sites. And the approach leverages index decision and resource decision strategies to mitigate the problem of third-party domain name reputations stole caused by URL redirection and detect the phishing sites hosted on compromised servers.

(1)   (2)

Fig. 2. The search results of different search strings

3.2 Design

Hacks Search Pattern Generation. The standard format of URL is as follow:

$$\text{protocol:}//\text{hostname}[:\text{port}]/\text{path}/[;\text{parameters}][?\text{query}]\#\text{fragment}$$

The hostname refers to domain names, which indicates the location of hosts. Domain names in modern Internet have become an important digital asset of the company. The path is the specific location where the target resource is stored. Through the Hacks search syntax, we can obtain accurate information of target sites by limiting the domain name and paths. Here, we generate two search patterns:

For the situation that the URL contains paths, we have

site: domain inurl : startpath

For the path is absent in URLs, we have

site: domain

For example, for "http://example.com/img/hello.jpg", we have

site: example.com inurl : img

For "http://example.com", we have

site: domain

Detection. For each unlabelled URL, the first step is to determine whether the URL is redirected, which will lead to a different judge process. Then, the search results enter the two core decision-making modules, namely index decision and resource decision, to obtain detection results. Figure 4 depicts the detection processes.

Index Decision. There exist different decision conditions for redirected URLs and non-redirected URLs. For redirected URLs, we first record the original unlabelled URL and the redirected URL, and make a Hacks search separately. Then, we compare whether the index counts of two search results are in an order of magnitude, which can mitigate the problem that attackers steal the domain reputations by URL redirection. If the index counts are not in an order of magnitude, we label the site phishing. Alternatively, we check whether the index counts are zero and if so, we label the site phishing, else we need to make resource decision. For non-redirected URLs, we check whether the index counts are zero directly.

Resource Decision. The index decision may fail to detect phishing sites hosted on compromised servers. So, the paper proposes the decision indicators aimed at resource features, including types and paths. The development of a legitimate site will follow the development specifications, and there will be a fixed storage location for each resource. However, attackers may locate the phishing page in a casual path. Figure 3 shows a simple example of calculation process of resource type consistency (RTC) and resource path similarity (RPS). When there exist multiple URLs, we will obtain a list for RTC and RPS respectively. For the list of RPS $PS = \{p_1, p_2, \ldots, p_n\}$, where n takes ten or twenty generally, there is RPSV

$$\text{RPSV} = \begin{Bmatrix} 1, & 1 \in PS \\ 0, & 1 \notin PS \end{Bmatrix}$$

When the RPSV $= 1$, the site be labelled legitimate, else phishing.

For the list of RTC TC $= \{t_1, t_2, \ldots t_n\}$, where n takes ten or twenty generally, we calculate the RTCV

$$RTCV = \frac{|\{t_i | t_i > 0.5, \quad \forall t_i \in TC\}|}{|TC|}$$

And, we set the resource path similarity threshold R, when the RTCV is greater than R, the site be labelled legitimate, else phishing.

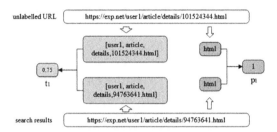

Fig. 3. The calculation process of RTC and RPS

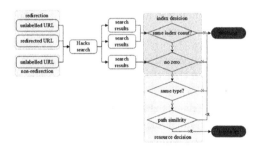

Fig. 4. The detection processes

3.3 Implementation

Figure 5 depicts the overview of HHP, which consists of search pattern generation, Hacks search, and detection. The implementation of HHP is given in Table 2.

Search pattern generation parses the unlabelled URL to generate specified search strings, and then combines the Hacks search syntax to obtain search patterns.

Hacks search makes restricted search by the advanced search function search engines provided. Most of search engines support the advanced search function, like Google, Baidu, Bing, etc. Based on the prior study [9], we choose the Google search engine in our experiments.

Detection uses the search results to make judgments, based on index decision and resource decision strategies. The index decision compares the index counts of search results, which can find phishing sites that steal the reputation of original sites by redirection or that hosted on attackers' servers. The resource decision takes advantage of the resource features to detect the phishing sites hosted on compromised servers. For resource path similarity, we choose 0.2 to the threshold, if the RTCV is less than 0.2, the site will be labelled phishing. When the threshold is 0.2, the best effect can be obtained in our experiments, as Sect. 4.2 shown.

Fig. 5. The overview of HHP

Table 2. Algorithm of HHP

The algorithm of HHP
Input: target URL
Output: status of the URL
Domain_Status ← NULL
Is_Redirection ← redirectionDecision (URL)
Old_URL ← URL, Result_N_Re ← 0
If Is_Redirection then
Old_URL, Re_URL ← getUrl(URL)
Result_N_Re, Result_URL_Re ← search(Re_URL)
End if
Result_N_Old, Result_URL_Old ← search(Old_URL)
If Result_N_Re ⊕ Result_N_Old==0 ‖ (Result_N_Old==0 && Result_N_Re==0) then
Domain_Status ← Phishing
Return Domain_Status
else
Ftscore ← filetypeScore(Old_URL,Result_URL_Old)
If Ftscore==0 then
Domain_Status ← Phishing
Return Domain_Status
End if
Psimilarity ← pathSimilarity(Old_URL,Result_URL_Old)
If Psimilarity < threshold then
Domain_Status ← Phishing
Return Domain_Status
End if
Domain_Status ← Legitimate
End if
Return Domain_Status

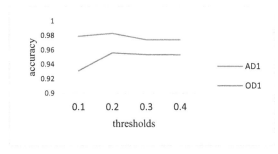

Fig. 6. The accuracy of different thresholds

4 Experiments

4.1 Datasets

To evaluate the performance of HHP, the experimental datasets come from two aspects. The legitimate dataset is the Alexa and the phishing dataset is collected from openphish. The datasets are divided into 4 sets:

- AD1: list of legitimate sites with Alexa Rank ranking from 1 to 1000.
- AD2: list of legitimate sites with Alexa Rank ranking from 1000 to 5000.
- AD3: list of legitimate sites with Alexa Rank ranking from 500000 to 505000.
- OD1: list of phishing sites in openphish collected from 13 Jan, 2021.

4.2 Threshold Setting

In this section, we will identify the threshold of resource path similarity. The goal of resource path similarity is to detect the phishing sites hosted on compromised servers, where the basic idea is the normativeness of project development. Figure 6 demonstrates the trend of accuracy under different thresholds on AD1 and OD1. As we can see, the trends are consistent, where the best effect can be obtained when threshold is 0.2. So, we choose the 0.2 as our threshold in experiments.

4.3 Comparison of Experimental Results

In this section, we evaluate the effect of HHP on different datasets and compare HHP with existing approaches, LDP and Jail-phish. LDP is a search engine based lightweight phishing detection system, which extracts the top-level domain and page titles as its search string and checks whether the target site is absent in search results to identify phishing sites. And, Jail-phish, a search engine-based phishing detection technique, advances the generation of the search string and the analysis of search results, which can detect the phishing site hosted on compromised servers.

The experiment results are shown in Table 3. Pages titles are a necessary element in LDP and Jail-phish. However, we discover that the difficulty of extracting page titles rises with lower ranking in Alexa in experiments, even more than 60% pages are failed to obtain their titles in AD3. This situation influences the accuracy of LDP and Jail-phish. On the other hand, to detect the phishing sites hosted on compromised servers, Jail-phish needs page data to calculate the similarity. However, there exist a lot of pages that are failed to request. Figure 7 shows the accuracy of different approaches in different datasets. The effect of LDP and Jail-phish fluctuates greatly, which verify that they were influenced by the rank of sites. While, due to the accurate search results provided by the Hacks search technique, the change of site ranking has a little effect on HHP.

Table 3. The experiment results of different approaches

Method	Dataset	Legitimate	Phishing	No title	Accuracy
LDP	AD1	882	118	391	0.882
	AD2	3403	595	1489	0.8512
	AD3	3406	1594	2313	0.6812
	OD1	95	1219	901	0.9277
Jail	AD1	891	77	389	0.8919
	AD2	3345	386	1659	0.8365
	AD3	3954	801	2454	0.791
	OD1	17	1245	883	0.9475
HHP	AD1	981	17	–	0.983
	AD2	3910	71	–	0.9822
	AD3	4618	383	–	0.9234
	OD1	54	1256	–	0.9559

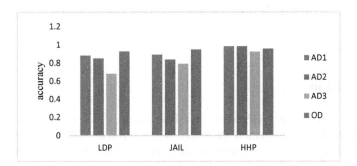

Fig. 7. The accuracy in different datasets

4.4 Discussion

Time Cost. Phishing detection is cost-sensitive, and we need to reduce the browsing delay as much as possible. The time cost box chart is shown in Fig. 8. The time cost of HHP is lower in AD1, where most of results are concentrated in 20 s. But, the time cost of HHP becomes bigger than LDP and Jail-phish in OD1, which is caused by the extra verification to promote the accuracy. Overall, compared with legitimate sites, the proportion of phishing sites is small, so the HHP still has the advantage over LDP and Jail-phish in the real situation.

URL Redirection. The URL redirection is a website development technique, which can redirect the target URL to another address to advance the availability of websites. In our experiments, we discover that attackers apply the redirection to steal the reputation of third-party domain name for bypassing the phishing detection. There exist several methods to archive redirection, including 1) short-link service, which provides the service that shortens a long links to improve the friendliness of URL; 2) status code, which is the traditional way, like 301, 302, etc.; 3) JavaScript script, which is concealed way and needs to load the pages to execute it to find the land pages. And, we discover some phishing sites are redirected Google or other popular sites. We guess that the phishing sites are taken over to stop attacks.

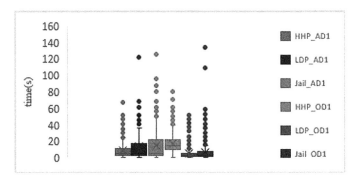

Fig. 8. The cost time box chart of different approaches

5   Conclusion

In this paper, we proposed HHP to detect phishing attacks, which applied advanced search syntax to collect site information accurately. We analyzed the URL redirection problem that steals third-party domain reputation and proposed an index decision strategy to mitigate it. To acquire the ability to detect the phishing site hosted on compromised servers, we designed and implemented a resource decision strategy. Our experimental results reveal that HHP achieved an accuracy of 98.3% in Alexa, and 95.59% in openphish.

Acknowledgement. This work was supported by the National key research and development program of China (Grant No. 2018YFB1800705), the National Natural Science Foundation of China (Grant No. 61672494).

References

1. APWG: Phishing Activity Trends Report. APWG (2020)
2. Heijden, A., van der, A.L.: Cognitive triaging of phishing attacks. In: Heninger, N., Traynor, P. (eds.) 28th USENIX Security Symposium, USENIX Security 2019, Santa Clara, CA, USA, 14–16 August 2019, pp. 1309–1326. USENIX Association (2019)
3. Lee, L.-H., Lee, K.-C., Chen, H.-H., Tseng, Y.-H.: POSTER: proactive blacklist update for anti-phishing. In: Proceedings of the 2014 ACM SIGSAC Conference on Computer and Communications Security, pp. 1448–1450. Association for Computing Machinery, New York (2014). https://doi.org/10.1145/2660267.2662362
4. Bell, S., Komisarczuk, P.: An analysis of phishing blacklists: Google safe browsing, OpenPhish, and PhishTank. In: Proceedings of the Australasian Computer Science Week Multiconference. Association for Computing Machinery, New York (2020). https://doi.org/10.1145/3373017.3373020
5. Nguyen, L.A.T., To, B.L., Nguyen, H.K., Nguyen, M.H.: An efficient approach for phishing detection using single-layer neural network. In: 2014 International Conference on Advanced Technologies for Communications (ATC 2014), pp. 435–440 (2014). https://doi.org/10.1109/ATC.2014.7043427
6. Xiang, G., Hong, J., Rose, C.P., Cranor, L.: CANTINA+: a feature-rich machine learning framework for detecting phishing web sites. ACM Trans. Inf. Syst. Secur. 14(2), 1–28 (2011)
7. Wenyin, L., Xiaotie, D., Guanglin, H., Fu, A.Y.: An antiphishing strategy based on visual similarity assessment. IEEE Internet Comp. 10, 58–65 (2006)
8. Zhang, Y., Hong, J.I., Cranor, L.F.: Cantina: a content-based approach to detecting phishing web sites. In: Proceedings of the 16th International Conference on World Wide Web, pp. 639–648. Association for Computing Machinery, New York (2007). https://doi.org/10.1145/1242572.1242659
9. Jain, A.K., Gupta, B.B.: Two-level authentication approach to protect from phishing attacks in real time. J. Ambient Intell. Humanized Comput. 9(6), 1783–1796 (2018)

The Sensor-Cloud System and Node Reliability Analysis

Lingbo Jin, Xian Lu, and Fangming Shao[(✉)]

Department of Mathematics, East China University of Science and Technology,
Shanghai 200237, China
fmshao@ecust.edu.cn

Abstract. The sensor-cloud system (SCS) integrates sensors, sensor networks and cloud systems to manage sensors, collect and process data, and make decisions based on the processed data. And SCS reliability pertains to systems that can be modeled as graphs whose nodes and/or edges have associated probabilities of being operational. In particular, we analyze the reliability of nodes or a group of nodes in the SCS network. It refers to the probability that all the target nodes can be connected. In this paper, we give the network model of k-target nodes, and its reliability based on the structure of the SCS network and the node unreliability theory. For the computational complexity of the k-target reliability calculation, we use the Monte Carlo method to estimate network reliability based on the representation of the path between two nodes in a graph by the adjacency matrix. The simulation results show that we can effectively analyze the large-scale SCS network, and the proposed algorithm has reached the ideal accuracy.

Keywords: Sensor-cloud system · k-target reliability · Node reliability · Reliability estimation · Monte Carlo algorithm

1 Introduction

In the field of network reliability, research on node reliability is very common. Generally speaking, the node reliability of a graph refers to the probability that the induced subgraphs of all operating nodes are connected when each node fails independently with exactly the same probability and the edge is completely reliable [1]. Node reliability problems are very common in ac-networks, wireless sensor networks, sensor cloud systems (SCS) and other special networks.

The network reliability model has been widely used in many SCS systems. Due to the high tolerance of the SCS network to failures and abnormalities, the reliability analysis of the SCS network is a difficult task.

Another problem in traditional network reliability theory is to assume that all nodes will not fail, and the edges will fail independently. Some types of reliability have also been studied including all-terminal reliability, two-terminal reliability, and k-terminal reliability. The k-terminal reliability is concerned about the successful communication between all pairs of network nodes belonging to a pre-specified subset K. As its name

© Springer Nature Switzerland AG 2021
Z. Liu et al. (Eds.): WASA 2021, LNCS 12939, pp. 310–317, 2021.
https://doi.org/10.1007/978-3-030-86137-7_34

implies, the all-terminal reliability of a graph G is the special case of k-terminal reliability where the set of specified nodes is the entire operational nodes. The two-terminal reliability polynomial is defined as the probability that the two specific nodes are in the same connected component when each edge or each node fails independently with the same probability. Recently, some new reliability model and algorithm are proposed. Such as, Zhang [2] presented the model of k-reliability, define cascading failures based on k-reliability, and proposed an algorithm to calculate k-reliability for estimation of potential cascading failures. The problem of precise calculation of both these characteristics is known to be NP-hard. For solving network probabilistic connectivity and its average pairwise connectivity, Kuo [3] proposed an efficient method for evaluating the terminal-pair reliability based on an edge expansion tree and using an OBDD (ordered binary decision diagram). Migov [4] propose the parallel methods, which are based on the well-known factoring method. The effectiveness of the algorithm is proved in some related works.

On the basis of the theory analysis about common searching node method, Li [5] gave us a further research on new improved searching node method which can resolve the problem of network system reliability calculation in the certain rang. A traditional accurate evaluation method of k-terminal reliability is to find all the minimum paths or minimum cut sets [6]. The limitation of this method is that it cannot display excessive minimum paths or minimum cuts when the number of network edges increases. For the failure probability of a single computer system and communication facility, an approximate calculation of network reliability is given [7]. The Monte Carlo simulation method has been widely used in large-scale networks other than high-probability networks [8, 9]. And there are effective MCS algorithms for highly reliable networks such as conditional MCS methods, approximate zero variance importance sampling [10] and combinations of these methods [11].

Recently, Mo [12] focused on the problem of k-terminal network reliability evaluation and proposed a network simplification method to simplify the large-scale network structure, so as to reduce the difficulty of reliability calculation and facilitate the reliability analysis of network structure. In this article, we use the method of network simplification to calculate and analyze the reliability of the SCS network based on the reliability of node. Then we propose a Monte Carlo simulation algorithm to estimate the reliability and get the ideal result.

The rest of this article is organized as follows: Sect. 2 introduces definitions and concepts. Section 3 gives the algorithm steps. Section 4 we calculate two SCS network examples to verify the accuracy of the calculation and use this method to estimate the reliability of a uniformly optimal graph. Finally, Sect. 5 gives conclusions.

2 Problem Formulation and System Model

Due to the high fault tolerance of SCS network, the reliability analysis of SCS network is very important for SCS system. Different models are built into application-level indicators or network-level indicators, where application-level metrics usually involve successful communication between a set of specified vertices through at least one failure-free path or tree [13]. For example, in universal healthcare applications, the medical sensor cloud infrastructure uses various medical toolkits to monitor the patient's physiological information in real time, and sequentially upload the sensed data to the cloud server for specific processing and storage, so patients can get basic diagnosis and treatment methods without going to the hospital [14]. In this network, there is always a set of important target nodes, such as a group of sensor nodes distributed in each patient's heart, they have common attributes, but they are not related to each other. We focus on these important target nodes and analyze its reliability, and describe this problem with the following mathematical model.

Generally, a sensor-cloud system can be regarded as a graph G (V, E, K), where V is the node set, E is the edge set of this network and $K \subseteq V$ is the target node set which is the set consised of the important nodes and as a node subset and $|K| = k$. We assume that all target nodes and all edges are perfect and each non-target node of $V - K$ fails independently with the same failure probability $q = 1 - p$, where p is the operating probability of a node. The problem can convert to analyze the k-target reliability problem of networks. Thus, we have the following definition:

Definition 1. Suppose the k-target nodes and all edges of a graph G never fail, and all non-target nodes have the same failure probability $1 - p$, the reliability of sensor-cloud system is.

$$Rel(G) = \sum_{r=1}^{n-k} S_r p^r (1 - p)^{n-k-r} \tag{1}$$

where S_r is the number of connected subgraphs composed of r non-target nodes and k target nodes and their related edges.

Compared with the traditional definition of reliability, its precise algorithm is still very complicated, we give the following example. Let G be a network in Fig. 1, $V = \{1, 2, 3, 4, 5, 6, 7\}$, $E = \{(1, 4), (1, 5), (2, 4), (2, 5), (2, 6), (2, 7), (3, 4), (3, 6)\}$, and $K = \{1, 2, 3\}$.

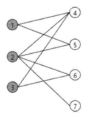

Fig. 1. An example network (The target node is filled with gray).

From the Definition 1, we have the following nine cases of connected subgraphs, so we can get $S_1 = 1$ corresponded to (1) in Fig. 2, $S_2 = 4$ corresponded to (2) (3) (4) (5) in Fig. 2, $S_3 = 4$ corresponded to (6) (7) (8) (9) in Fig. 2, $S_4 = 1$ corresponded to (10) in Fig. 2. Its reliability is $Rel(G) = 1 - (1 - p)^4 - 3p(1 - p)^3$.

Computational complexity of the k-target reliability calculation is still NP-hard. It is essential for designing fast approximation algorithm to compute reliability of large-scale network.

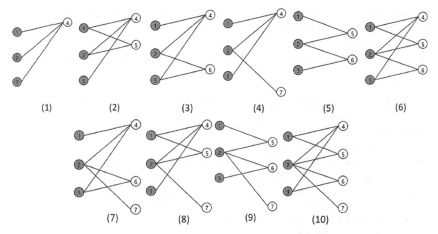

Fig. 2. The connected subgraphs of the network in Fig. 1.

3   MC Algorithm Design

The Monte Carlo algorithm is used to evaluate the system reliability of SCS benchmark networks. Based on the path correspondence between the adjacency matrix and the graph, the adjacency matrix is changed according to the structure adjustment after the network simplified, and the connectivity of the network is judged by the power operation of the matrix. The detailed process of the Monte Carlo algorithm is as follows:

First step is to set three variables, the number of successful experiments SE (the initial value is 0), the number of experiments that have been carried out CE (the initial value is 0) and the total number of experiments T (a constant which is large enough). We assume that there are n nodes in graph G, and we use v_1, v_2, v_3, ..., v_n to represent each node in graph G, then the node set V becomes $V = \{ v_1, v_2, v_3, ..., v_n \}$. We can get its adjacency matrix Z the elements in which are only represented by 0 and 1 (for example, if there is an edge between v_1 and v_2, then $z_{12} = 1$, otherwise $z_{12} = 0$).

The second step is to deal with the non-target nodes in the graph. For each non-target node v_i of G, we randomly generate a number a_i from the uniformly distributed interval $(0, 1)$ and if $a_i > p$, we get Z' in which we make them as 0 to the values of the row and column associated with the corresponding node in the adjacency Z.

In the third step, we first analyze the adjacency matrix Z', if one of the target elements in Z' is 0, it indicates that there is a pair of target nodes cannot be connected with each other, so we need continue to power Z' to get Z'^2, and repeat the previous judgment process until we find that none of the target elements are zero in a power matrix of $Z'^{\,l}$ where l refers to the limited path length or the power of a matrix ($1 \leq l \leq |V' - K|$).

The fourth step is to say if we can find the adjacency matrix satisfying the condition within the range of l, it means that we have carried out a successful experiment; if we can't find the adjacency matrix satisfying the condition, the number of successful experiments remained unchanged.

Finally, we repeat steps 2, 3 and 4 until reaching the predetermined number of experiments. We will get the reliability of the network is equal to $Rel(G) = SE/T$ (T is the simulation number).

These are the calculation steps of Monte Carlo algorithm. Let's use a table to describe it.

Algorithm : Monte Carlo algorithm evaluate the $Rel(G)$—the reliability of SCS network
Input: $G, p, SE = 0, CE = 0, T$.
Output: $Rel(G)$—the reliability of SCS network
Step 1: Number each node in the graph with $v_1, v_2, v_3, ..., v_n$, then the corresponding adjacency matrix Z is generated.
Step 2: Generating the number a_i is randomly generated in the uniform interval $[0, 1]$ for each non-target node and getting the new adjacency matrix Z'.
Step 3: Judge the target element in $Z'^l (1 \leqslant l \leqslant |V - K|)$. (1) If yes, $SE = SE + 1$, $CE = CE + 1$; (2) If no, $SE = SE$, $CE = CE + 1$.
Step 4: Repeat steps 2 and 3 until $CE == T$. The $Rel(G) = SE/T$.

This algorithm can limit the error rate to less than 1% in the following analysis.

4   Examples and Results Analysis

The reliability estimation of k-target networks is an NP-hard problem, and we use the SCS networks to verify the relationship between Monte Carlo algorithm and accurate algorithm. What is the accurate algorithm? According to the definition of reliability in Sect. 2, we can directly count the number of S_r and substitute it into the formula (1).

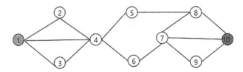

Fig. 3. This is a kind of network structure obtained by selecting two nodes as target in the original SCS benchmark network.

There is an effective subgraph (denoted by W) of the SCS network when two target nodes selected in Fig. 3. We use two algorithms to calculate its reliability, the results are as follows (suppose $p = 0.9$, $T = 10000$):

The target node of this example is $\{1, 10\}$. According to the definition, we can accurately calculate its reliability Rel_1 as 0.8756. The table gives the estimated value Rel_2 and the corresponding error rate ($|(Rel_1 - Rel_2)/Rel_1|$). According to the table, the average error rate between the estimated value and the accurate value is not more than 1%. If we switch to a network with more target nodes, what will the performance of the algorithm be like? We use another three target network to verify it (Table 1).

Table 1. The estimated and compared results of SCS network with two target nodes.

Estimated	0.8640	0.8758	0.8654	0.8625	0.8710
Error rate (%)	1.16	0.61	0.03	0.81	1.16
Estimated	0.8703	0.8685	0.8722	0.8687	0.8603
Error rate (%)	0.39	1.50	0.79	0.53	1.75
Estimated average		0.8679	Error rate average (%)		0.88

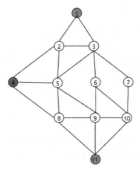

Fig. 4. This is a kind of network structure obtained by selecting three nodes as target in the original SCS benchmark network.

There is an effective subgraph (denoted by H) of the SCS network with three target nodes shown in Fig. 4. We use two algorithms to calculate its reliability, the results are as follows (suppose $p = 0.9$, $T = 10000$):

Table 2. The two algorithm results of SCS network with three target nodes.

Target node	Exact value	Estimated value	Error rate (%)
{1, 4, 11}	0.9825	0.9861	0.411

The first column in Table 2 indicates the target node, the second column represents the accurate value of the network reliability, the third column gives the estimate which is the average of ten repeated estimates, and the fourth column gives the average error rate of the two values. The results show that the average error rate of Monte Carlo algorithm for reliability estimation is no more than 1%.

In these two examples, Monte Carlo algorithm has a low error in the estimation of network reliability. Then, when the network structure becomes larger, will the algorithm still be accurate? Let's test it with a larger segment of SCS networks.

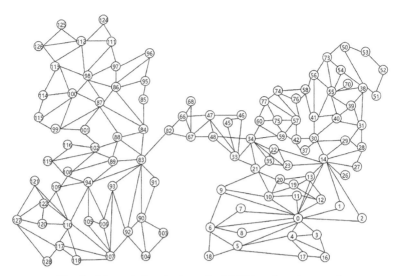

Fig. 5. A large induced subgraph of SCS benchmark network

We use Monte Carlo method to estimate a large induced subgraph of the SCS network, as shown in Fig. 5, and the results are as follows (It is assumed that $p = 0.9$):

Table 3. The results of Monte Carlo algorithm for the large induced subgraph.

Target node	Rel_1	Rel_2	Error rate (%)
{50, 128}	0.999999	0.999879	0.0124
{74, 88}	0.998899	0.994649	0.4254
{5, 30, 114}	0.989998	0.987958	0.2060
{2, 52, 100}	0.989888	0.993006	0.3151
{70, 128}	0.890998	0.889171	0.1827

The first column of Table 3 shows the location of the target node, the second column 'Rel_1' is the known reliability results, the third column 'Rel_2' is the reliability calculated by our method, and the fourth column is the error rate of the two results.

According to the data in Table 3, the Monte Carlo calculation results are very close to the known reliability in high probability networks. This shows that Monte Carlo algorithm is still applicable in large SCS networks.

5   Conclusion

Reliability theory is concerned mainly with computing the probability that a complex system is functional given the failure probabilities of its elements. We focus on the

k-target reliability of networks based on the reliability of nodes, which involves the successful communication between all pairs of network nodes belonging to a pre-specified subset K. Since the k-target network reliability evaluation is known to be an NP-hard problem, Monte Carlo algorithm is proposed to estimate the reliability of large-scale sensor-cloud network and achieve the ideal accuracy. In the future, we can further use this algorithm to analyze and optimize the SCS network.

References

1. Goldschmidt, O., Jaillet, P., LaSota, R.: On reliability of graphs with node failures. Networks **24**, 251–259 (1994)
2. Zhang, Z., An, W., Shao, F.: Cascading failures on reliability in cyber-physical system. IEEE Trans. Reliab. **65**, 1745–1754 (2016)
3. Yeh, F.M., Kuo, S.Y.: OBDD-based network reliability calculation. Electron. Lett. **33**(9), 759–760 (1997)
4. Migov, D.A., Rodionov, A.S.: Parallel implementation of the factoring method for network reliability calculation. In: International Conference on Computational Science and Its Applications. Springer, Cham (2014). https://doi.org/10.1007/978-3-319-09153-2_49
5. Li, Y.: Study of Reliability for Network System Based on Intelligent Calculation. Computer Technology and Development (2006)
6. Yeh, W.C.: An improved sum-of-disjoint-products technique for the symbolic network reliability analysis with known minimal paths. Rel. Eng. Syst. Saf. **2**(92), 260–268 (2007)
7. Nsler, H.E., Mcauliffe, G.K., Wilkov, R.S.: Exact calculation of computer network reliability. Networks **4**(2), 95–112 (2010)
8. Yan, K., Zhong, C., Ji, Z., Huang, J.: Semi-supervised learning for early detection and diagnosis of various air handling unit faults. Energy Build. **181**, 75–83 (2018)
9. Yan, K., Ma, L., Dai, Y., Shen, W., Ji, Z., Xie, D.: Cost-sensitive and sequential feature selection for chiller fault detection and diagnosis. Int. J. Refrig. **86**, 401–409 (2018)
10. L'Ecuyer, P., Rubino, G., Saggadi, S., Tuffin, B.: Approximate zerovariance importance sampling for static network reliability estimation. IEEE Trans. Reliab. **60**(3), 590–604 (2011)
11. Cancela, H., L'Ecuyer, P., Rubino, G., Tuffin, B.: Combination of conditional Monte Carlo and approximate zero-variance importance sampling for network reliability estimation. In: Simulation Conference (2010)
12. Mo, Y., et al.: Network simplification and K-target reliability evaluation of sensor-cloud systems. IEEE Access. **8**, 177206–177218 (2020)
13. Mo, Y., Xing, L., Guo, W., Cai, S., Zhang, Z., Jiang, J.: Reliability analysis of IoT networks with community structures. IEEE Trans. **1**(7), 304–315 (2020)
14. Wang, T., Li, Y., Fang, W.: A comprehensive trustworthy data collection approach in sensor-cloud system. IEEE Trans. (2018)

Reinforcement Learning Based Seamless Handover Algorithm in SDN-Enabled WLAN

Jianjun Lei[1]([envelope]) [iD], Xin Liu[1] [iD], Ying Wang[1] [iD], Xunwei Zhao[2] [iD], and Ping Gai[2] [iD]

[1] School of Computer Science and Technology, Chongqing University of Posts and Telecommunications, Chongqing 400065, China
leijj@cqupt.edu.cn
[2] State Grid Information and Telecommunication Group CO., LTD., Beijing 102211, China
{zhaoxunwei,gaiping}@sgitg.sgcc.com.cn

Abstract. In Wireless Local Area Network (WLAN), Station (STA) performs handover according to received signal strength indication (RSSI), which results in long handover delay and inability during selecting the best Access Point (AP). This paper proposes T-DQN (enhanced Throughput based on Deep Q-Network), a novel intelligent handover algorithm based on deep reinforcement learning (DRL), which is modeled as a Markov decision process (MDP) and enables network to dynamically handover according to current network states. Meanwhile, the T-DQN not only considers the STA throughput, but also takes into account system throughput and fairness of Basic Service Set (BSS) during the handover process. Moreover, we employ the software defined network (SDN) to perform a centralized control and seamless handover of network. Simulation results demonstrate that the T-DQN can effectively improve STA throughput and system throughput, and also achieve the lower packet loss rate, which outperforms some traditional handover schemes.

Keywords: WLAN · SDN · Reinforcement learning · Handover

1 Introduction

WLAN has been widely used because of its high data-rate and convenience [1]. In traditional handover scheme, When RSSI between STA and AP is lower than threshold, handover is triggered [2]. And it takes a lot of time for STA to complete the process of associating with target AP. In recent years, the emergence of software-defined networking (SDN) technology is promoting network architecture. SDN decouples control and data layers of network, and controller provides programmable interfaces that administrators can control and manage network through it [3, 4].

In this paper, we propose an intelligent seamless handover algorithm based on DRL. Firstly, we design a network architecture based on software defined wireless network (SDWN). Wherein, the STA is associated with a unique logic AP (LAP), and therefore the soft handover of STA is operated only by removing and adding LAP on AP. Secondly, we propose T-DQN handover algorithm, which can choose the trigger time of handover

© Springer Nature Switzerland AG 2021
Z. Liu et al. (Eds.): WASA 2021, LNCS 12939, pp. 318–326, 2021.
https://doi.org/10.1007/978-3-030-86137-7_35

and the better target AP according to current network condition. Finally, we design a sophisticated reward mechanism for our proposed T-DQN algorithm that considers not only the throughput of STA itself, but also the system throughput and the fairness of BSS that the STA is associating. The simulation results verify that our proposed algorithm improves greatly the network performance in terms of throughput and packet loss rate.

2 Related Work

In traditional WLAN handover process, the communication between STA and AP will be interrupted for a few seconds [5]. In [6], the authors show that communication interruption is between 13 ms and 30 ms during handover process. In IEEE 802.11 protocol, a complete handover process is divided into three parts: scanning, authentication, and reassociation. Some documents suggest enhancing scanning phase to reduce the total handover delay. In [7], APs are equipped with dual interfaces, one of interfaces broadcasts beacon frames to scan channels through channel used by AP. Although this method can reduce scanning delay, AP's two interfaces will cause additional expenses. In [8], the authors use the neighbor graph model, which is used to store working channels of neighbor APs and construct neighbor graph of APs, but when neighbor APs are distributed in all channels, this method does not decrease scanning delay. In [9], the algorithm equips a redundant AP for each AP, and the redundant AP collects channel states for whole system, Although the mechanism reduces the number of STA scanning channels, however, redundant APs cause waste of resources. In [10], the authors propose a scheme that uses multiple physical APs to provide multiple transmission paths for a STA. Although it improves network performance, also faces very complex flow scheduling problem. In [11], the authors propose an architecture that combines SDN, deep neural network, recurrent neural network, and convolutional neural network, and present a handover algorithm based on Q-learning, although this algorithm improves throughput of mobile STA, it does not consider system throughput.

3 Proposed Algorithm

3.1 System Model

This section mainly introduces network scenarios. We consider an environment, which contains N STAs and M APs. All STAs continuously send data to APs. Since we focus on handover problem under the same frequency deployment scenario, all APs are located on same channel. In addition, our algorithm is based on the SDWN architecture, so the controller controls and monitors all STAs and APs, as shown in Fig. 1. The controller obtains the RSSI of all BSSs through OpenFlow protocol. If the RSSI of some BSSs is too low to be measured, we will set their value as a lower value than the minimum measured value.

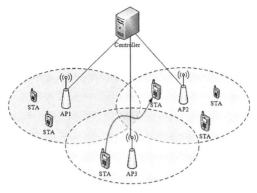

Fig. 1. Network scenario

3.2 System Architecture and Modules

In order to overcome limitations and challenges of handover algorithms in WLAN, we propose a SDWN-based network architecture, as shown in Fig. 2. This architecture separates control layer from data layer, allowing the controller to logically concentrate the control network to achieve network programmability. The DQN architecture includes three layers: physical layer, control layer and application layer.

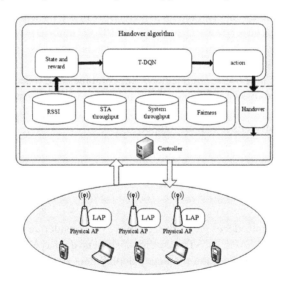

Fig. 2. DQN architecture

Data layer is mainly responsible for following functions: 1) Using LAP technology to achieve seamless handover; 2) forming network topology and data transmission between nodes; 3) transmitting real-time network information to control layer through southbound interface. Controller layer is mainly responsible for following functions: 1) Obtaining underlying network states information through OpenFlow protocol; 2) assigning LAP to STA; 3) Controlling handover of STA. When the STA accesses the network, the controller will detect whether the STA connects a LAP, and will assign a unique LAP for the STA if it still does not. In addition, the controller controls handover of STA by removing or adding LAP on AP, so the entire handover process is transparent to STA. Application layer is mainly responsible for following functions: 1) Obtaining information through northbound interface as the input to algorithm; 2) passing the input of algorithm through a fully connected neural network to estimate the next action; 3) outputting the command to control handover of the entire network.

3.3 Handover Algorithm

MDP Model. The construction of MDP is based on agent and environment, and its elements include state, action and reward. Wherein, the current network system is used as environment and controller is used as agent, so controller is the decision maker and the learner in reinforcement learning system.

The state space contains all network states and is defined as:

$$S = \{s_1, s_2, s_3, \ldots, s_n, \ldots\} \tag{1}$$

The state of the STA collected by the controller from the network at time t is defined as:

$$s_t = \{RSSI_1, RSSI_2, \ldots, RSSI_{M-1}, RSSI_M\} \tag{2}$$

Where M is the number of APs. $RSSI_1$ represents RSSI between STA and AP_1.

In addition, the agent obtains different rewards by taking actions, and we set action space as A:

$$A = \{a_1, a_2, \ldots, a_{M-1}, a_M\} \tag{3}$$

The action space has M dimensions, so M is the number of APs, a_i means that STA handover to AP_i. If the algorithm selects AP that STA is associated with, the STA does not handover; if unavailable AP is selected, the environment will give a negative feedback to the controller.

The reward at time t is defined as:

$$r_t = w_1 \left(\sum_{j=1}^{M} T_j^t - \sum_{j=1}^{M} T_j^{t-1} \right) + w_2 T_{k,j}^t (1 - \sigma) \tag{4}$$

w_1 and w_2 are weights, and $w_1 + w_2 = 1$. T_j^t represents the throughput of AP_j at time t, and $\sum_{j=1}^{M} T_j^t$ is the system throughput, T_j^t is defined as:

$$T_j^t = \sum_{i=1}^{N} T_{i,j}^t \tag{5}$$

N is the number of STAs associated with AP_j, $T_{i,j}^t$ is the throughput from STA_i to AP_j. $\sum_{i=1}^{N} T_{i,j}^t$ represents the sum of the throughput of all STAs associated with AP_j, which is also the throughput of BSS_j. STA_k is observation STA. σ is the throughput fairness of BSS_j:

$$\sigma = \sqrt{\frac{\sum_{i=1}^{N}\left(T_{i,j}^t - \overline{T}_j^t\right)^2}{N}} \tag{6}$$

At time t, STA_i is sending data to AP_j, $T_{i,j}^t$ represents the throughput of STA_i. $\overline{T}_j^t$ is the average throughput of AP_j, $\overline{T}_j^t$ be calculated as:

$$\overline{T}_j^t = \frac{1}{N}\sum_{i=1}^{N} T_{i,j}^t \tag{7}$$

T-DQN. In T-DQN, the input of algorithm is RSSI between STA and AP, and the output is association between STA and target AP. The algorithm initializes experience pool D, its maximum capacity is B, and then preprocesses environment, and inputs state to the evaluation network and the evaluation network returns all Q values in state. In this algorithm, the action is selected according to greedy strategy, that is, a random action with probability ε is selected, and vice versa, action with the highest Q value is selected. After selecting an action, the controller executes action, and updates states and receives rewards. Next, the algorithm stores experience in experience pool, then randomly extracts experience from experience pool, calculates loss function, and then performs gradient descent to minimize loss. Finally, for every step, the evaluation network passes the parameters to the target network until the entire training finishes.

Algorithm 1: T-DQN algorithm

Inputs: State information, s_t
Output: Association with target AP, a_t
1: Initialize experience pool D to capacity B
2: Initialize the scenario parameters M, A
3: Initialize the statistic parameters Z, ε_0, γ, α, β, few_steps
4: Initialize evaluation network Q with random parameters θ
5: Initialize the target network $\hat{Q}$ with $\hat{\theta} = \theta$
6: Read state s_t
7: $\varepsilon = \varepsilon_0$
8: **for** $t = 1$ **to** Z **do**
9:　Input s_t to evaluation network and output the Q-values of actions
10:　Randomly select actions a_t from A with ε-greedy strategy
11:　$\varepsilon = \varepsilon * \beta$
12:　Execute action a_t, handover to target AP
13:　Obtain rewards r_t by calculating real-time throughput of STAs
14:　Next state s_{t+1}
15:　Store transition (s_t, a_t, r_t, s_{t+1}) in D
16:　Sample minibatch of transition (s_j, a_j, r_j, s_{j+1}) from D
17:　Perform gradient descent s on $(r_j + \gamma \max \hat{Q}\left(s_{j+1}, a_{j+1}; \theta\right) - Q(s_j, a_j; \theta))^2, a_{j+1} \in A$
18:　$s_t = s_{t+1}$
19:　Every few_steps step, update target network with $\hat{\theta} = \theta$
20: **end for**

---

4 Performance Evaluation

4.1 Simulation Settings

In this section, we use Mininet-WiFi to evaluate the performance of T-DQN and compare with a traditional handover algorithm based on RSSI and DCRQN [11] algorithm based on DQN. WLAN is deployed in a space with an area of 200 m * 200 m. All STAs are connected to network during simulation and continuously send data of different priorities to AP. At first, one of STAs is in moving state as observation station, and the other STAs and APs are in static state. Observation station is advancing at a constant speed from a fixed starting point at a speed of 0.5 m/s. The parameters used in the simulation are shown in Table 1.

Table 1. Simulation parameters

Parameters	Value	Parameters	Value
STA Number	13	Frequency band	2.4 GHz
AP Number	9	Protocol	IEEE 802.11g
CCA Threshold	−62 dBm	Channel	1
Propagation Loss Model	Log distance	Receiving gain	5 dBm
Transmitting power	21 dBm	Transmitting gain	5 dBm

4.2 Simulation Results

STA Throughput. In order to verify the throughput performance of T-DQN algorithm, we let the STA governed by UDP and TCP protocols to transmit data respectively. Figure 3(a) and Fig. 3(b) show throughput changes of mobile STA using TCP and UDP streams to send data.

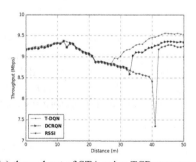
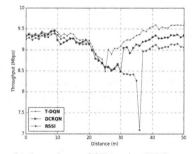

(a) throughput of STA using TCP streams   (b) throughput of STA using UDP streams

Fig. 3. STA throughput performance of the three algorithms under different streams

When mobile STA uses TCP to send data, T-DQN, DCRQN and RSSI handover at 27 m, 33 m, and 41 m. When mobile STA uses UDP to send data, algorithms T-DQN, DCRQN, and RSSI handover at 25 m, 30 m, and 36 m. Because UDP is unreliable transmission, when UDP transmission is used, throughput of STA fluctuates greatly per second. Because RSSI is traditional handover scheme, change scheme needs that STA disconnect previous connection before handover to new AP, so handover delay is longer. It can be observed that no matter whether UDP or TCP stream is used to transmit data, T-DQN handover earlier than DCRQN and RSSI. After handover, the AP can provide higher bandwidth.

System Throughput. The Fig. 4(a) and Fig. 4(b) show changes in the system throughput of TCP and UDP streams. At the beginning of simulation, there was no handover, the system throughput of the three algorithms changes similarly, but as observation STA moved, the link between STA and current connection gradually slackened, resulting in a slight decrease in system throughput. T-DQN, DCRQN and RSSI algorithms handover in sequence because T-DQN selects APs with the better performance for associating and triggers handover in time, which makes reasonable use of network resources and improves the system throughput.

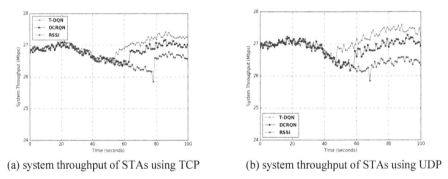

(a) system throughput of STAs using TCP   (b) system throughput of STAs using UDP

Fig. 4. System throughput of the three algorithms under different streams

Packet Loss Rate. Figure 5 shows change in packet loss rate of mobile STA. In RSSI algorithm, STA will disconnect from current AP during handover, and then associates with the other target AP. The entire process is controlled by STA, so handover delay is very long and results in a packet loss rate as high as 83%. DCRQN and T-DQN adopt SDWN-based network architecture, and controller is responsible for performing STA handover, and can perform seamless handover.

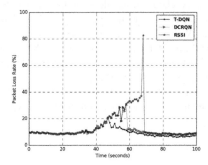

Fig. 5. Packet loss rate of mobile STA

5 Conclusion

In this paper, we propose a seamless handover algorithm for WLAN based on SDN and DQL. We present a network architecture that can utilize the controller as the agent and considers the system throughput, STA throughput and fairness of BSS as the reward of DQL. Meanwhile, the agent can interact dynamically with the environment when the STA's handover occurs, and thus an optimal policy capable of maximizing the long-term returns is eventually obtained. Finally, the simulation results by Mininet-WiFi platform demonstrate that our proposed algorithm can significantly improve the performance of handover in terms of the throughput and the packet loss rate.

References

1. Coronado, E., Gomez, B., Riggio, R.: A network slicing solution for flexible resource allocation in SDN-BASED WLANs. In: 2020 IEEE Wireless Communications and Networking Conference Workshops, WCNCW, pp. 1–2. IEEE, Seoul (2020)
2. Lei, J., Tao, J., Yang, S.: Joint AP association and bandwidth allocation optimization algorithm in high-dense WLANs. Future Internet 10(8), 73–87 (2018)
3. Ahmad, S., Mir, A.H.: Scalability, consistency, reliability and security in SDN controllers: a survey of diverse SDN controllers. J. Netw. Syst. Manage. 29(1), 1–59 (2020). https://doi.org/10.1007/s10922-020-09575-4
4. Lembke, J., Ravi, S., Eugster, P., et al.: RoSCo: robust updates for software-defined networks. IEEE J. Sel. Areas Commun. 38(7), 1352–1365 (2020)
5. Feirer, S., Sauter, T.: Seamless Handover in Industrial WLAN Using IEEE 802.11k. In: 2017 IEEE 26th International Symposium on Industrial Electronics, ISIE, pp. 1234–1239. IEEE, Edinburgh (2017)
6. Fernández, Z., Seijo, Ó., Mendicute, M., et al.: Analysis and evaluation of a wired/wireless hybrid architecture for distributed control systems with mobility requirements. IEEE Access 7, 95915–95931 (2019)
7. Jeong, J.P., Park, Y.D., Suh, Y.J.: An efficient channel scanning scheme with dual-interfaces for seamless handoff in IEEE 802.11 WLANs. IEEE Commun. Lett. 22(1), 169–172 (2018)
8. Ma, H., Zhou, Z., Chen, X.: Leveraging the power of prediction: predictive service placement for latency-sensitive mobile edge computing. IEEE Trans. Wireless Commun. 19(10), 6454–6468 (2020)

9. Sun, Y., Liu, Y., Jiang, L.: A scheme of seamless handover in wireless communications based on sentinel mechanism. In: 2019 15th International Wireless Communications and Mobile Computing Conference, IWCMC, pp. 1725–1730. IEEE, Tangier (2019)
10. Guimaraes, R.S., García, V.M., Mello, R.C., et al.: An SDN-NFV orchestration for reliable and low-latency mobility in off-the-shelf WiFi. In: ICC 2020–2020 IEEE International Conference on Communications, ICC, pp. 1–6. IEEE, Dublin (2020)
11. Han, Z., Lei, T., Lu, Z., et al.: Artificial intelligence based handoff management for dense WLANs: a deep reinforcement learning approach. IEEE Access 7, 31688–31701 (2019)

Attack Traffic Detection Based on LetNet-5 and GRU Hierarchical Deep Neural Network

Zitian Wang[1] , ZeSong Wang[1] , FangZhou Yi[1] , and Cheng Zeng[1,2,3(✉)]

[1] School of Computer Science and Information Engineering, Hubei University,
Wuhan 430062, China
`zc@hubu.edu.cn`
[2] Hubei Province Engineering Technology Research Center for Software Engineering,
Wuhan 430062, China
[3] Hubei Engineering Research Center for Smart Government and Artificial
Intelligence Application, Wuhan 430062, China

Abstract. The paper converts the network traffic information about a single-channel grayscale image as input data. In addition, a deep hierarchical network model is designed, which combines LetNet-5 and GRU neural networks to analyze traffic data from both time and space dimensions. At the same time, two networks can be trained simultaneously to achieve better classification results because of the reasonable network association method. This paper uses the CICID2017 dataset, which contains multiple types of attacks and is time-sensitive. The experimental results show that, through the combination of deep neural networks, the model can classify attack traffic with extremely high accuracy.

Keywords: Attack traffic detection · Multi-dimensional layered network · CNN network · GRU network

1 Introduction

In this age, deep learning network has been widely used, including network intrusion detection[1]. Few researchers consider the influence of time on network intrusion detection. The detection process is improved compared with the detection without considering the time characteristics, but the improvement in accuracy is limited [2]. Based on the above research results, this paper makes further optimization and attempts, and achieves better results in the time dimension, while ensuring high accuracy.

Supported by National Natural Science Foundation of China 61977021.
Supported by National Natural Science Foundation of China 61902114.
Supported by Hubei Province Technological Innovation Foundation 2019ACA144.

© Springer Nature Switzerland AG 2021
Z. Liu et al. (Eds.): WASA 2021, LNCS 12939, pp. 327–334, 2021.
https://doi.org/10.1007/978-3-030-86137-7_36

2   Related Works

In the previous research, the network traffic information is processed as one-dimensional data, and some scholars creatively splice the network traffic information as two-dimensional data [3]. The experimental results show that the classification method can achieve a good classification effect when the training set is large enough. Based on the time characteristics of network traffic information, some scholars have proposed a recursive neural network model for deep learning [4]. By studying the temporal characteristics of network traffic information, the error rate can be reduced by 5% based on the traditional machine learning model. Because of the obvious advantages of the LSTM network in processing time-series data compared with the traditional RNN network, some scholars try to classify network traffic data based on LSTM network [5]. It is proved that the LSTM network has the potential to analyze network traffic information.

3   Methodology

In this section, we establish a layered deep network model to detect attract network traffic. The model consists of two different neural network algorithm models. The first layer is letnet-5 convolutional neural network to extract the spatial characteristics of the stream, and the second layer is the GRU network to extract the temporal characteristics of the stream. By adjusting the output of the first layer network, the two networks can be trained at the same time. Before elaborating the model in detail, we first declare how to preprocess the network traffic data.

3.1   Data Preprocessing

Compared with traditional feature engineering, we only need to keep all the information in the network traffic packet and map it to the corresponding format to meet the classification requirements. The data package comes from the capture software and is displayed in hexadecimal.

1. data: Through the early research [6], it show that the fields of Ethernet layer, MAC source address, MAC destination address and protocol version do not need to be the characteristics of network traffic data. These data need to be removed which has an impact on our detection.
2. split: All data are divided according to address, port and time information. Because of a large number of data packets, split cap software [7] can be used to achieve packet splitting.
3. convert: Statistics show that more than 90% of the data streams contain less than 10 packets, and the rest of the data streams contain more than 10 packets. If the length of the network traffic packet is less than 160 bytes, select to add 0 to 160 bytes at the end. At the same time, to make the features more universal, we select the top 10 packets in each data stream. If the number of data packets is insufficient, we will supplement the data packets with all 160 bytes of data as 0. After this conversion, we get 1600 bytes of raw data.

3.2   CNN Model

CNN convolution neural network has good spatial awareness and has achieved excellent results in image processing [8]. The preprocessed data is equivalent to a single-channel 40×40 grayscale image. More complex convolution network models such as ResNet [9]and VGGNet [10] need to add a lot of data to the analysis of this image. Given that the proportion of abnormal traffic in network traffic analysis is too low, if you choose to use an overly complex identification network, it will easily lead to over-fitting of the identification network and reduce the accuracy of model prediction. So we chose an improved LetNet-5 network for handwritten number recognition, which uses a model similar to our scenario, with single-channel low-pixel images.

In the hidden layer of the CNN network, we use two convolution layers and two maximum pooling layers to extract the spatial characteristics of the original network traffic data. After processing, the original single-channel 40×40 pictures are converted to 8×8 pictures with 64 channels. After fully expanding them, we get the 4096-dimensional vector and transfer it to the output layer of the CNN network. The output layer uses the full junction layer, and the full junction layer uses 1600 neurons. This transformation preserves the same dimensionality of the original data after it is extracted. Considering the occurrence of over-fitting, deletion after the fully connected layer inactivates some neurons, a process that is completely random to ensure the reliability of the experimental results.

3.3   GRU Model

In the scenario of attack traffic detection, packets are forwarded in a time sequence, and due to the delay in transmission, there is a sequence of packets at the receiving end. In addition, the number of packets sent within a timestamp also varies dynamically. The above characteristics indicate that network traffic data has time characteristics and are suitable for research using recursive neural networks. Due to design flaws in general RNN networks, all incoming information from the previous layer is recorded as valid information by default. This paper uses the GRU network structure. As an improvement of the RNN network, the same gate control is used to forget and select the information from the previous moment. It is better than the RNN network in dealing with long-time series problems [11]. In this paper, the GRU network is used to extract the time feature of the original stream data automatically, and the GRU network uses two-layer unit to extract the time feature. Each cell of GRU includes 256 hidden layer units, and the activation function of each layer uses S-type function for nonlinear operation. The last layer of GRU network uses the fully connected layer, and the number of neurons in the fully connected layer is equal to the number of flow categories.

3.4   Deep Hierarchical Network

The research shows that network traffic data contains a large number of features [12]. In the past operation, researchers are used to defining part of the characteristics to study. In the first mock exam, however, the selection is just passable and the information is not well utilized. Using the combination of CNN and GRU network, this paper analyzes all the information from the time and space of network traffic and realizes the comprehensive mining of the characteristics in the flow. In order to train the two networks at the same time, the output format of CNN is set to meet the input format of the GRU network. According to the design of this paper, each stream extracts the first 10 packets and each packet extracts the first 160 bytes, which are mapped to the GRU network, corresponding to the time step and input size respectively. Finally, we use a softmax classifier, which can output the classification probability of each stream, and map the experimental results to the corresponding categories according to the highest probability. The loss function used in the model is the mean square loss function, and the trained optimizer [13] uses an adaptive matrix for gradient descent. The model structure is shown in Fig. 1.

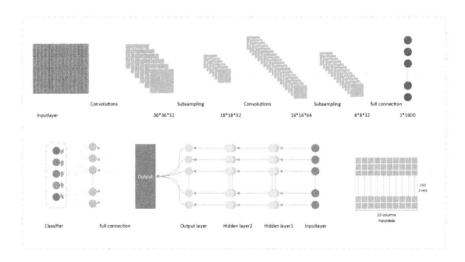

Fig. 1. Deep hierarchical network model.

4   Experiments

4.1   Data

The CICID2017 data set is open source provided by the Canadian Institute of Cyber Security. Considering the reliability of the training results, we selected the top ten attack traffic and normal traffic as our training set and test set, ensuring that each type contains at least two thousand traffic data.

4.2   Calculation Process

The two deep networks in this article are connected to perform operations. First, starting from the CNN network, after data preprocessing, we have obtained a 40×40 single-channel grayscale image. The kernel size used in the first layer convolution operation is 32 5×5; the kernel size used in the second layer convolution operation is 64 3×3, a total of 64. After transformation, the original data is downsampled to $8 \times 8 \times 64$, and finally, 1600-dimensional features can be output through the fully connected layer. Combining 10 continuous data packets is the requirement of our selection of features and the input requirement of the GRU network. This article artificially sets the time step of each training of the GRU network to 10, so that a 10×160 matrix is obtained as the GRU network Enter the content. The GRU network structure has two layers and each layer contains 256 neurons. Since the data first passes through the CNN network and then the GRU network, the CNN network will be trained first in the forward training process. The loss calculated in the reverse process of training the GRU network will be calculated first and then the CNN network will be calculated. The reason for this design is to link the temporal and spatial characteristics of the data so that the performance of the classifier can be higher.

4.3   Experimental Results

In order to comprehensively consider the performance of the model and compare it with other models, this paper tests the two-class and multi-class performance of the model. The content of the two-classification experiment is to classify normal traffic and attack traffic, and does not require the specific types of attack traffic to be classified, while the multi-class experiment requires the specific types of attack traffic to be classified. Table 1 records the average results after multiple binary classification experiments, and Table 2 records the average results after multiple classification experiments. This article focuses on comparing the possible effects of different time series networks on the experimental results, and chooses three types of neural networks: RNN, LSTM, and GRU for comparison.

Table 1. Multiple binary classification

Metrics	Accuracy	Precision	Recall	F1-measure	Time
RNN	0.9976	0.9978	0.9963	0.9971	149.45
LSTM	0.9980	0.9987	0.9958	0.9972	244.20
GRU	0.9966	0.9988	0.9917	0.9952	240.40
CNN	0.9986	0.9975	0.9991	0.9983	234.66
CNN+RNN	0.9977	0.9947	0.9990	0.9968	338.27
CNN+LSTM	0.9981	0.9958	0.9994	0.9976	449.31
CNN+GRU	**0.9992**	**0.9993**	**0.9995**	**0.9991**	439.85

Table 2. Multiple classification

Metrics	Accuracy	Precision	Recall	F1-measure	Time
RNN	0.9953	0.9973	0.9993	0.9983	156.98
LSTM	0.9965	0.9974	0.9997	0.9986	245.16
GRU	0.9976	0.9979	0.9997	0.9989	246.41
CNN	0.9975	0.9986	0.9994	0.9990	236.19
CNN+RNN	0.9957	0.9986	0.9983	0.9984	352.70
CNN+LSTM	0.9963	0.9979	0.9997	0.9988	453.07
CNN+GRU	**0.9977**	**0.9991**	**0.9998**	**0.9992**	442.20

Tables 1 and 2 records the results of 20,000 iterations of the model. As shown in the table, the improved depth hierarchical network model proposed in this paper has advantages in each index and has obvious advantages inaccuracy. Compared with the model of combining CNN network and LSTM network proposed by previous scholars [14], our model not only has advantages of inaccuracy but also reduces the convergence rate. According to the data in Table 1 and Table 2, we can see that the accuracy has been improved by 0.1%, and the training time has been shortened by about 10 s. Compared with training the deep neural network separately, the hierarchical structure reduces the convergence speed of the whole model by nearly 10%, and improves the efficiency significantly when training the large data model. At the same time, we find that our model does not have obvious advantages in multi-classification problems, and many indicators of GRU and CNN models are very close to our model. However, in the two-class problem, our model can get considerable advantages on each index. We think that the reason for this is probably that the amount of data in the multi-classification problem is not enough to make the model fully understand the characteristics of each kind of attack traffic, and the index of the multi-classification experiment is lower than that of the two-classification model as a whole. This also shows that the model proposed in this paper is suitable for the treatment of large data problems. When the amount of data is sufficient, the advantages of the model proposed in this paper in accuracy and convergence speed will be obvious. The extremely high accuracy rate of the artificial model in this article is due to the following reasons:

1. In each data packet, after transforming the original one-dimensional network traffic information into a two-dimensional single-channel grayscale image, combining the originally distant features is beneficial to algorithm analysis to obtain new features. Generally, algorithms for one-dimensional data mainly study the relationship between the front and back of the data. If the two parts of the data are too far apart, it is difficult for existing algorithms to combine the two parts as a combination of features for classification. When the data is processed as a graph, through the convolution operation of the

convolution kernel, this paper realizes the combined analysis of a variety of distant features.

2. Since this article takes the first ten data packets for each data stream for analysis, it is obvious that for each data stream, there are certain timing characteristics before these ten data packets. For this reason, this article adds a GRU neural network based on the improvement of the recurrent neural network to analyze the temporal correlation between the input data.

3. It is necessary to combine the two neural networks for training. If it is a horizontal splicing method, each network is trained separately, and the classification results of the two networks are combined into the final classification result according to certain weight distribution. To further supplement the experimental results, this article supplements other indicators in the horizontal splicing mode. The number of iterations of the horizontal stitching experiment is the same as that of the layered model, and the weights predicted by the two models are 50% each. According to supplementary experiments as Table 3 shows, it can be found that the horizontal stitching method has no obvious effect on the detection results, and some indicators are even inferior to the results of the model training separately.

Table 3. Horizontal splicing model

Metrics	Accuracy	Precision	Recall	F1-measure
CNN+RNN_binary	0.9959	0.9966	0.9973	0.9970
CNN+LSTM_binary	0.9963	0.9979	0.9977	0.9988
CNN+GRU_binary	0.9979	0.9988	0.9987	0.9988
CNN+RNN_multiple	0.9947	0.9976	0.9973	0.9974
CNN+LSTM_multiple	0.9954	0.9979	0.9987	0.9976
CNN+GRU_multiple	0.9967	0.9981	0.9988	0.9981

5 Conclusion

This paper proposes a hierarchical network model based on LetNet-5 and GRU to detect attack traffic. According to the characteristics of network traffic data, this paper selects some continuous data packets in each network flow and converts certain data in each data packet into a single-channel grayscale image as input data for network attack traffic detection. The data selected in this way not only retains the timing relationship between the same stream data packet but also fully combines the characteristics of the data in each data packet. Tested by CICIDS2017, the model proposed in this paper can reach a very high level in terms of accuracy, precision, recall rate, and F1-measurement. Compared with the combined deep neural network model with close performance indicators, the model proposed in this paper has an advantage in convergence speed. Based on the above characteristics of the model, this article believes that the model is suitable for network attack traffic detection in the case of big data, such as in a data center.

Besides, the model also has room for further improvement. Considering that the data of the attack traffic in the real situation is less, the model can be further optimized to use fewer data to train the model while ensuring the detection effect of the model.

References

1. Zeng, Y., Gu, H., Wei, W., Guo, Y.: $Deep-full-range$: a deep learning based network encrypted traffic classification and intrusion detection framework. IEEE Access **7**, 45182–45190 (2019)
2. Yeo, M., et al.: Flow-based malware detection using convolutional neural network. In: 2018 International Conference on Information Networking (ICOIN), pp. 910–913. IEEE (2018)
3. Zhou, H., Wang, Y., Lei, X., Liu, Y.: A method of improved CNN traffic classification. In: 2017 13th International Conference on Computational Intelligence and Security (CIS), pp. 177–181. IEEE (2017)
4. Yuan, X., Li, C., Li, X.: Deepdefense: identifying DDoS attack via deep learning. In: 2017 IEEE International Conference on Smart Computing (SMARTCOMP), pp. 1–8. IEEE (2017)
5. Kim, J., Kim, J., Thu, H.L.T., Kim, H.: Long short term memory recurrent neural network classifier for intrusion detection. In: 2016 International Conference on Platform Technology and Service (PlatCon), pp. 1–5. IEEE (2016)
6. Denning, D.E.: An intrusion-detection model. IEEE Trans. Softw. Eng. **2**, 222–232 (1987)
7. Taylor, V.F., Spolaor, R., Conti, M., Martinovic, I.: Robust smartphone app identification via encrypted network traffic analysis. IEEE Trans. Inf. Forensics Secur. **13**(1), 63–78 (2017)
8. Girshick, R., Donahue, J., Darrell, T., Malik, J.: Rich feature hierarchies for accurate object detection and semantic segmentation. In: Proceedings of the IEEE Conference on Computer Vision and Pattern Recognition, pp. 580–587 (2014)
9. He, K., Zhang, X., Ren, S., Sun, J.: Deep residual learning for image recognition. In: Proceedings of the IEEE Conference on Computer Vision and Pattern Recognition, pp. 770–778 (2016)
10. Liu, Z., Li, J., Shen, Z., Huang, G., Yan, S., Zhang, C.: Learning efficient convolutional networks through network slimming. In: Proceedings of the IEEE International Conference on Computer Vision, pp. 2736–2744 (2017)
11. Fu, R., Zhang, Z., Li, L.: Using LSTM and GRU neural network methods for traffic flow prediction. In: 2016 31st Youth Academic Annual Conference of Chinese Association of Automation (YAC), pp. 324–328. IEEE (2016)
12. Ahuja, R.K., Magnanti, T.L., Orlin, J.B.: Network flows: Theory. Algorithms, and Applications, 526 (1993)
13. Kingma, D.P., Ba, J.: Adam: a method for stochastic optimization. arXiv preprint arXiv:1412.6980 (2014)
14. Zhang, Y., Chen, X., Jin, L., Wang, X., Guo, D.: Network intrusion detection: based on deep hierarchical network and original flow data. IEEE Access **7**, 37004–37016 (2019)

Real-Time and Consistent Route Update Based on Segment Routing for NFV-enabled Networks

Wanchen Wang, Hongli Xu, Gongming Zhao$^{(\boxtimes)}$, and Liusheng Huang

School of Computer Science and Technology, University of Science and Technology
of China, Hefei 230027, Anhui, China
{wwc0316,zgm1993}@mail.ustc.edu.cn,
{xuhongli,lshuang}@ustc.edu.cn

Abstract. In NFV-enabled networks, it is necessary to frequently update the flow's route to ensure that the network continues performing well due to flow dynamics. In previous SFC route update schemes, the optimization goal mainly focused on the load balance of the network (e.g., VNF and link) and seldom paid attention to the update delay. Therefore, these schemes either take a too long time or have very high rule-space costs; they can't be used in a large or frequently changed network. When we update the SFC route, we face two challenges: real-time update and path consistency guarantee. Specifically, most flows have a short duration, so route updates that take a too long time will make the new route unsuitable for the current network's workload. Path consistency requires that only one route configuration is used for packets in the update process. Otherwise, in-flight packets might meet with forwarding errors (e.g., loops). In this paper, we propose to use segment routing technology to deal with the problem of path inconsistent. We formalize the real-time SFC route update problem (RSRU) by jointly optimizing the update delay and the load of VNF. Then we design an algorithm called RBRU based on randomized rounding to solve it with a bounded approximate ratio. The simulation results show that RBRU can reduce the update delay by 41.3%–57.9% compared with the comparison algorithms when achieving a similar VNF load balancing effect.

Keywords: Network function virtualization · Service function chain · Route update · Segment routing

1 Introduction

The emerging technology of network function virtualization (NFV) has recently shifted how network functions (NFs) are implemented by moving NFs from dedicated hardware to commercial general-purpose servers, which overcome the high cost and inflexibility of hardware NFs devices [5]. Today's networks are widely distributed with specialized NFs (e.g., firewalls and load-balancers). These NFs

© Springer Nature Switzerland AG 2021
Z. Liu et al. (Eds.): WASA 2021, LNCS 12939, pp. 335–344, 2021.
https://doi.org/10.1007/978-3-030-86137-7_37

provide users with various services rather than just forward users' packets and network traffic usually needs to pass through multiple NFs in a particular order called service function chain (SFC) [10]. Due to the dynamic change of the network flow, we need to update the flows' routes frequently to make better use of the network resources. There are two main challenges: real-time update and path consistency guarantee. 1) Real-time updates. According to [7], we know that the duration of most flows in the network is very short. For example, more than 80% of the flow last less than 10s. Therefore, if route updates take a long time (e.g., the 30s), the new route selection may not be applicable to the current network's workload. 2) Path consistency guarantee. We need to ensure that the packet uses the original route configuration before route update and the updated route configuration after route update [15].

Different from traditional networks, SFC routing may have routing loops and other problems [12]. Thus, the solution of route update in traditional networks can't be directly applied to NFV-enabled networks. In the SFC route update research, the schemes are mainly divided into ordered scheduling and two-phase-commit. Ordered scheduling [8,14] generally divides the update sequence of flows by calculating the dependency relationship between flows and ensures that each round of update meets the consistency of the path. However, this scheme can't guarantee that such an update sequence exist, so its applicability is limited. Moreover, it doesn't consider the update delay, so it is not suitable for scenes sensitive to update delay. Two-phase-commit [6,13] generally refers to that update the internal switch's rules in the first phase, and the ingress switch's rules are updated in the second phase. It requires all switches to keep both old and new path rules and tags in-flight packets to determine whether to use the new path rules or the old. This scheme can achieve a very low update delay, but each switch has to keep double the flow table entries, which is not applicable for large networks and switch with limited rule-space.

To satisfy these two requirements for SFC route update, we propose using segment routing technology to ensure path consistency firstly. Segment routing (SR) is a source routing technique [1]. In a nutshell, the complete information of the flow's path will be inserted into the package header through a table entry on the flow's source node. Other nodes read the path information in the header to determine the forwarding action. When we update the flow's path information, we just need to update the table entry on the source node, which naturally avoids the in-flight packet using the mixed rule and causing path inconsistency. As for the demand of real-time update, we formalize the SFC route update problem as an integer programming, which takes the update delay as the constraint, and pursues a better path redistribute for the flow within the limited update delay. We use the load balancing effect of VNFs as a criterion to measure the performance of the new path allocation.

In summary, we propose to use SR technology to solve the real-time SFC route update problem in the NFV-enabled network. The main contributions of this paper are summarized as follows:

- We propose to use SR technology to solve the problem of path inconsistency and give a formal definition of the real-time SFC route update problem.
- We design an algorithm based on randomized rounding to solve the real-time and consistent SFC route update problem.
- We evaluate the proposed algorithm through simulation tests and the results show that our algorithm performs better than the comparison algorithms.

2   Preliminaries and Problem Formulation

2.1   Network and Flow Models

An NFV-enabled network consists of a set of switches, $V = \{v_1, ..., v_n\}$, with $n = |V|$, a collection of server hosts, $H = \{h_1, ..., h_p\}$, with $p = |H|$, and a cluster of controllers. Therefore, the network topology is modeled as $G = \{H \cup V, E\}$, where E is the set of links which connects these devices.

A set of VNF instances is denoted as $F = \{f_1, ..., f_q\}$, with $q = |F|$. We define $c(f)$ as the capacity of VNF instance f. We denote the flows based on originator-destination pairs as $\gamma \in \Gamma$, with $m = |\Gamma|$. The intensity of the flow γ represented by $c(\gamma)$. We define the set of different source nodes of all flows as S and $S \subseteq V$. Further, we define Γ_s as the set of flows with s as their source node. The path set is defined as P, where each path is a sequence of switches and server hosts. Each flow γ will be assigned a set of feasible paths P_γ, each path of which satisfies the flow's SFC requirement.

2.2   Segment Routing Framework for SFC Route Update

SR uses segment ID (SID) to tag VNF services in NFV-enabled networks, which allows us to pay less attention to the routing between each VNF and focus on selecting VNF service segments. This greatly simplifies the SFC route decision. For example, a simple NFV-enabled network is shown in Fig. 1, where different segments are used to tag switches and VNF services. The solid red line represents the path assigned to a flow with SFC requirements of {FW, IDS}. We can use a segment list (SL) {6002, 2001, 6003, 2003, 6004} to completely express the path information of this flow. Then, this flow's source node 6001 will install the corresponding table entry, which will insert SL into this flow's packet header.

However, inserting SL into the packet's header will introduce the consumption of header space. We must consider the challenge of header space occupation for real-time route updates based on the following two observations: 1) the length of SL is related to the length of SFC requirements. SR defines service segments to tag VNF services, and the service segment has a local meaning for each device. Therefore, a service segment is typically combined with a node segment to ensure delivery to the server node [4]. Assuming that the SFC requirement's length is k, at least $2 \cdot k + 1$ segments are required to fully express the SFC path. 2) Some switches may not support a large label stack (less than 5) [9], and in a medium NFV-enabled network, the average length of SFC is about 5 [16].   We

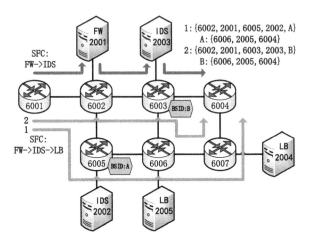

Fig. 1. A simple NFV-enabled network. There are two flow's SFC paths: the solid red line and the solid blue line (the blue line ignores the path through VNF). Each flow's SFC requirements are shown in the figure. Switch 6005 and switch 6003 are installed with SR policy entries (BSID: A and BSID: B). Path and entry details are listed on the upper right of the figure.

propose useing stitch node and binding-SID (BSID) to solve this problem [2]. For example, the solid blue line 1 in Fig. 1 represents the path of a flow with SFC requirement {FW, IDS, LB} (ignore the path to VNF for simplicity). The original SL is {6002, 2001, 6005, 2002, 6006, 2005, 6004}, the length of which is more than 5. With the help of stitch node 6005 and BSID: A, source node 6001 only insert SL {6002, 2001, 6005, 2002, A} into the package header. Then stitch node 6005 installs a table entry (this entry represented by BSID: A), which will insert the remaining SL {6006, 2005, 6004} into the package header.

According to the above description, we extended the definition of set S to merge the source node set of all flows denoted as $SourceN$ and all Stitch Node set defined as $StitchN$ into a new set S, that is $S = \{SourceN \cup StitchN\}$.

2.3 Problem Formulation

In this section, we define the real-time SFC route update (RSRU) problem. We use $x_\gamma^p \in \{0, 1\}$ to denote whether flow γ choose path $p \in P_\gamma$. When updating route, the controller updates the table entries of corresponding switches, which introduces the update delay. Because of SR's source routing nature, we only need to update the table entries on the node $s \in S$. Thus, we define $UpdateDelay_s$ to represent the update delay introduced on the node s. Accordingly, we formulate the RSRU problem as follows:

$$\min \quad \lambda$$

$$\text{S.t.} \begin{cases} \sum_{p \in \mathcal{P}_\gamma} x_\gamma^p = 1, & \forall \gamma \in \Gamma \\ \sum_{\gamma \in \Gamma} \sum_{f \in p: p \in \mathcal{P}_\gamma} x_\gamma^p \cdot s(\gamma) \leq \lambda \cdot c(f), & \forall f \in F \\ UpdateDelay_s = \sum_{\gamma \in \Gamma_s} \sum_{p \in \mathcal{P}_\gamma} x_\gamma^p \cdot d_{\gamma,s}^p, & \forall s \in S \\ UpdateDelay_s \leq DelayLimited, & \forall s \in S \\ x_\gamma^p \in \{0, 1\}, & \forall p, \gamma \end{cases} \qquad (1)$$

The first set of inequalities denotes that a flow must be assigned on one path from the set of feasible paths. The second set of inequalities states that the sum of flows' intensity processed by each VNF instance can't be larger than $\lambda \cdot c(f)$, where λ is the maximum load rate for all VNFs. The goal of the problem is to minimize λ. The third set of equalities and the fourth set of inequalities represent constraints on the update delay, where $DelayLimited$ is a preset update delay threshold value for all source nodes and stitch nodes. $d_{\gamma,s}^p$ represents the delay of updating the table entry on node s when the path of flow γ is updated from the original path to path p. $d(s, \gamma, p)$ is defined as follows:

$$d_{\gamma,s}^p = \begin{cases} d_m & N(p) = N(p_\gamma^o) \ and \ p \neq p_\gamma^o \ , \ s \in S \\ d_i & N(p) \neq N(p_\gamma^o) \ , \ s \in StitchN \\ 0 & otherwise \end{cases} \qquad (2)$$

where p_γ^o represents the original route configuration of flow γ. $N(p_\gamma^o)$ and $N(p)$ represent the source node or stitch node in the path. For node $s \in S$, if $p \neq p_\gamma^o$, we need to modify the table entry on node s, so the update delay $d_{\gamma,s}^p$ is d_m. For stitch node $s \in StitchN$, if the stitch nodes of the original and new paths are different, we need insert a new table entry on the new stitch node, so the update delay $d_{\gamma,s}^p$ is d_i. For example, in Fig. 1, when the blue path is updated from 1 to 2, we need to insert a new table entry represented by BSID: B in the new stitch node 6006. So the update delay introduced for 6006 is d_i. In other cases, $d_{\gamma,s}^p$ is 0. For current commodity switches [6], the delay for flow table insert and modify operations are typically 5ms and 10ms, respectively.

Theorem 1. *The RSRU problem is NP-hard.*

Proof. The proof of Theorem 1 is omitted because of space limitation.

3 Algorithm Design

3.1 A Rounding-Based Algorithm for RSRU

To solve the RSRU problem, we design an algorithm called RBRU based on randomized rounding. We first consider a relaxed version of the RSRU problem, where each flow is splittable. Specifically, the binary variable x_γ^p is relaxed to a decimal variable so that the problem becomes a linear program. The relaxed version linear program is formulated as follows:

$$\min \quad \lambda$$

$$S.t. \begin{cases} \sum_{p\in\mathcal{P}_\gamma} x^p_\gamma = 1, & \forall\gamma\in\Gamma \\ \sum_{\gamma\in\Gamma}\sum_{f\in p:p\in\mathcal{P}_\gamma} x^p_\gamma \cdot s(\gamma) \leq \lambda \cdot c(f), & \forall f\in F \\ UpdateDelay_s = \sum_{\gamma\in\Gamma_s}\sum_{p\in\mathcal{P}_\gamma} x^p_\gamma \cdot d^p_{\gamma,s}, & \forall s\in S \\ UpdateDelay_s \leq DelayLimited, & \forall s\in S \\ x^p_\gamma \in [0,1], & \forall p,\gamma \end{cases} \tag{3}$$

Algorithm 1. RBRU: Rounding-based Algorithm for RSRU problem

1: **Step 1: Sloving the Relaxed RSRU Problem**
2: Construct a linear program in Eq. (1) as relaxed RSRU
3: Obtain the optimal solution $\widetilde{x}^p_\gamma$
4: **Step 2: Determing the Flow's Route Selection**
5: Derive an integer solution $\widehat{x}^p_\gamma$ by randomized rounding
6: **for** each flow $\gamma\in\Gamma$ **do**
7:     set a random number $ran\_num \in [0,1]$
8:     **for** each feasible path $p\in\mathcal{P}_\gamma$ **do**
9:         subtract the value of ran_num from the value of $\widetilde{x}^p_\gamma$
10:        **if** $ran\_num \leq 0$ **then**
11:            set $\widehat{x}^p_\gamma = 1$
12:        **else**
13:            set $\widehat{x}^p_\gamma = 0$
14:        **end if**
15:    **end for**
16: **end for**
17: appoint the path p for flow $\gamma\in\Gamma$ if $\widehat{x}^p_\gamma = 1$

The RBRU algorithm is divided into two main steps. The first step is to solve the linear programming described above. We can get the optimal solution in polynomial time, denoted as $\widetilde{x}^p_\gamma$. At the same time, the optimal result is denoted by $\widetilde{\lambda}$. In the second step, by using the randomized rounding method, we can get the integer solution, defined as $\widehat{x}^p_\gamma$. For each flow, the algorithm sets $\widehat{x}^p_\gamma$ to 1 with the probability of $\widetilde{x}^p_\gamma$ and guarantee that only one path from the set of feasible paths will be selected as the target route for each flow. The RBRU algorithm is formally described in Alg. 1.

3.2 Performance Analysis of RBRU Algorithm

Theorem 2. *The proposed RBRU algorithm achieves the approximation factor of $\frac{3\ln n}{\alpha} + 3$ for VNF capacity constraints.*

Theorem 3. *The proposed RBRU algorithm achieves the approximation factor of $\frac{3\ln n}{\alpha} + 3$ for route update delay constraints*

Proof. Since the space is limited, the proof of Theorem 2 and is Theorem 3 omitted here.

4   Performance Evaluation

4.1   Simulation Setting

In the simulation, we choose the Monash campus network topology as running examples, which contains 100 switches and 200 hosts. We randomly generate flows' (or requests) source address, destination address, and SFC requirements. For the flow size, 20% of the top-ranked flows may be responsible for more than 80% of the total traffic [3]. The simulation includes four different VNF instances, then randomly combined these into four SFC policies with different lengths, from which the flow randomly selects the SFC requirements. The capacity of each VNF instance is 1 Gbps. Since the theoretical number of feasible paths for each SFC policy is exponential, we prune the set of feasible paths with the help of the idea in [12] to speed up the running time of the algorithm.

4.2   Performance Metrics and Benchmarks

In the simulation, we mainly choose two performance metrics to evaluate performance: The Maximum VNF Load Ratio and Update Delay, respectively. Then we select two benchmarks to compare our algorithm. For the first benchmark, we choose SR plus greed strategy, called SRG. Specifically, the algorithm greedily selects the path with the lowest VNF load to minimize the maximum VNF load ratio when selecting a new path for each flow. The second benchmark, called FLUS [11], is a routing update algorithm based on SR technology for SDN. When updating a new path for a flow, the algorithm will reuse the old path segment to pursue a shorter update delay. We add constraints that meet the requirements of SFC on this basis.

4.3   Simulation Results

We mainly run three groups of simulation experiments on Monash campus network topology to verify the performance of our algorithm RBRU to deal with the RSRU problem. In the first group of simulation experiments, the number of network flow is set to 6k, and the maximum VNF load ratio is about 0.99 before route update. Figure 2 shows the experimental result, where the abscissa value is the update delay constraint, and the ordinate value is the maximum VNF load ratio. We can see that with the increase of update delay, the value of the maximum VNF load ratio is gradually decreasing and approaching the optimal solution of 0.5. Finally, the minimum update delay of RBRU, FLUS, and SRG algorithm to reach the optimal solution is 0.8s, 1.8s, and 1.6s, respectively. Then, when the update delay is limited to 0.8s, we calculate the cumulative distribution diagram of all NFV loads and compare RBRU and FLUS algorithm. The results are shown in Fig. 4. It can be seen that the NFV load balancing effect obtained by the RBRU algorithm is better than that of the FLUS algorithm. Then, when the maximum VNF load ratio reaches the optimal solution of 0.5, we calculate the cumulative distribution diagram of the required update delay of

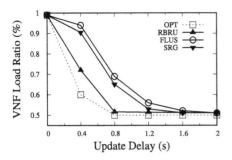

Fig. 2. VNF Load Ratio vs. Update Delay with 6k flows

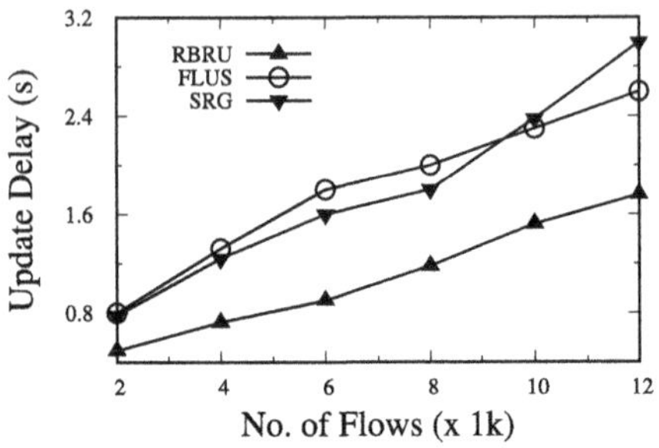

Fig. 3. Update Delay vs. No. of flows

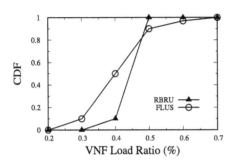

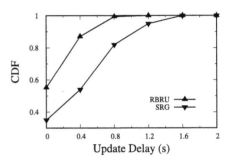

Fig. 4. CDF vs. VNF Load Ratio

Fig. 5. CDF vs. Update Delay

all node $s \in S$ and compare RBRU and SRG algorithm. The results are shown in Fig. 5. Compared with SRG, the update delay distribution introduced by the RBRU algorithm is more concentrated. Because we consider both the VNF load and update delay constraints, our algorithm can achieve better results.

In the second group of simulation experiments, we take the number of flows as the dependent variable and then record the minimum update delay required when routing updates to the optimal solution. The results are shown in Fig. 3. It can be seen that RBRU has the smallest curve slope, followed by FLUS (the more flows, the more available old path segments), and SRG has the largest.

Through the above simulation results, we can draw the following conclusions. Compared with FLUS, RBRU can achieve a better NFV load balancing effect under the same update delay. Specifically, for example, in Fig. 1, compared with the comparison algorithm, our algorithm can reduce the NFV load ratio by 26.2%–30.1%. Compared with SRG, RBRU can obtain the optimal NFV load balancing effect under a smaller update delay. Specifically, for example, in Fig. 1, compared with the comparison algorithm, our algorithm can reduce the update delay by 41.3%–57.9%.

5 Conclusion

In this paper, we propose a real-time and consistent SFC route update scheme based on SR technology in the NFV-enabled network and use stitch node to solve the problem of packet header space occupied in SR. We formalized the RSRU problem and propose an algorithm called RBRU based on randomized rounding to solve it. Through simulation results, the performance of the RBRU algorithm is better than the comparison algorithms.

References

1. Abdullah, Z.N., Ahmad, I., Hussain, I.: Segment routing in software defined networks: a survey. IEEE Commun. Surv. Tutorials **21**(1), 464–486 (2018)
2. Clarence, F., Kris, M., Ketan, T.: Segmentation Routing Part I. Posts & Telecom Press, Beijing (2017)
3. Curtis, A.R., Mogul, J.C., Tourrilhes, J., Yalagandula, P., Sharma, P., Banerjee, S.: Devoflow: scaling flow management for high-performance networks. In: Proceedings of the ACM SIGCOMM 2011 Conference, pp. 254–265 (2011)
4. Filsfils, C., Nainar, N.K., Pignataro, C., Cardona, J.C., Francois, P.: The segment routing architecture. In: 2015 IEEE Global Communications Conference (GLOBECOM), pp. 1–6. IEEE (2015)
5. Han, B., Gopalakrishnan, V., Ji, L., Lee, S.: Network function virtualization: challenges and opportunities for innovations. IEEE Commun. Mag. **53**(2), 90–97 (2015)
6. Jin, X., et al.: Dynamic scheduling of network updates. ACM SIGCOMM Comput. Commun. Rev. **44**(4), 539–550 (2014)
7. Kandula, S., Sengupta, S., Greenberg, A., Patel, P., Chaiken, R.: The nature of data center traffic: measurements & analysis. In: Proceedings of the 9th ACM SIGCOMM conference on Internet measurement, pp. 202–208 (2009)
8. Katta, N.P., Rexford, J., Walker, D.: Incremental consistent updates. In: Proceedings of the Second ACM SIGCOMM Workshop on Hot Topics in Software Defined Networking, pp. 49–54 (2013)
9. Kitsuwan, N., Oki, E., Kurimoto, T., Urushidani, S.: Single tag scheme for segment routing in software-defined network. Telecommun. Syst. **74**(2), 173–184 (2020). https://doi.org/10.1007/s11235-019-00645-w
10. Kuo, T.W., Liou, B.H., Lin, K.C.J., Tsai, M.J.: Deploying chains of virtual network functions: on the relation between link and server usage. IEEE/ACM Trans. Networking **26**(4), 1562–1576 (2018)
11. Luo, L., Yu, H., Luo, S., Zhang, M., Yu, S.: Achieving fast and lightweight SDN updates with segment routing. In: 2016 IEEE Global Communications Conference (GLOBECOM), pp. 1–6. IEEE (2016)
12. Qazi, Z.A., Tu, C.C., Chiang, L., Miao, R., Sekar, V., Yu, M.: Simple-fying middlebox policy enforcement using SDN. In: Proceedings of the ACM SIGCOMM 2013 Conference on SIGCOMM, pp. 27–38 (2013)
13. Reitblatt, M., Foster, N., Rexford, J., Schlesinger, C., Walker, D.: Abstractions for network update. ACM SIGCOMM Comput. Commun. Rev. **42**(4), 323–334 (2012)
14. Vissicchio, S., Cittadini, L.: Flip the (flow) table: Fast lightweight policy-preserving SDN updates. In: IEEE INFOCOM 2016-The 35th Annual IEEE International Conference on Computer Communications, pp. 1–9. IEEE (2016)

15. Wang, S., Li, D., Xia, S.: The problems and solutions of network update in SDN: a survey. In: 2015 IEEE Conference on Computer Communications Workshops (INFOCOM WKSHPS), pp. 474–479. IEEE (2015)
16. Zhao, G., Xu, H., Liu, J., Qian, C., Ge, J., Huang, L.: Safe-me: Scalable and flexible middlebox policy enforcement with software defined networking. In: 2019 IEEE 27th International Conference on Network Protocols (ICNP), pp. 1–11. IEEE (2019)

Privacy-Preserving Auction for Heterogeneous Task Assignment in Mobile Device Clouds

Xufeng Jiang[1,2], Xuhao Pei[1,2], Dawei Tian[1,2], and Lu Li[2,3(✉)]

[1] Nanjing Tech University, Nanjing, China
[2] School of Information Engineering, Yancheng Teachers University, Yancheng, China
lil@yctu.edu.cn
[3] Suzhou Research Institute, University of Science and Technology of China, Suzhou, China

Abstract. In the past several decades, despite the continuous improvement of mobile devices, mobile applications requiring resources are still beyond its capacity to be completed on a single device. Due to high fairness and distribution efficiency, cloud auctions of mobile device allocation has recently attracted a lot of attention. However, most of them focus on efficiency but ignore the privacy-preserving issues in cloud auction process, which will have a significant impact on the authenticity of auctions. In this paper, we propose PAHTA, a privacy-preserving auction for heterogeneous task assignment in mobile device clouds by using Yao's garbled circuits and homomorphic encryption. Meanwhile, we design a set of sub-protocols to support secure arithmetic operations, including secure division protocol and secure selection protocol. We further analyze the security and effectiveness of the system theoretically and prove that it can ensure sufficient and strong privacy protection under the semi-honest adversary model. Based on a large number of experiments, these results are consistent with the theoretical analysis.

Keywords: Cloud auction · Heterogeneous task assignment · Yao's garbled circuits · Privacy-preserving

1 Introduction

Despite the increased capabilities of mobile devices, mobile applications that require resources exceeds the number of tasks that can be accomplished by a single device. As such, mobile device cloud (MDC), an environment that enables computation-intensive tasks to be performed among a set of nearby mobile devices, provides a promising architecture to support real-time mobile applications. The resource shortage ofzhe mobile devices can be alleviated by offloading resource-intensive applications from mobile devices to remote cloud servers, where long-distance communication can lead to communication delays and highly power consumption. Generally, utilizing the unused resources of

© Springer Nature Switzerland AG 2021
Z. Liu et al. (Eds.): WASA 2021, LNCS 12939, pp. 345–358, 2021.
https://doi.org/10.1007/978-3-030-86137-7_38

the nearby mobile devices in MDCs can achieve better system performance, e.g., reducing the latency and network congestion with short-range communications [2]. To solve the task assignment problem as well as social welfare, task allocation auction mechanism in MDCs aims that are designed to stimulate bidders to bid their true valuations of the resource requirements of the tasks, and the resource availabilities at mobile devices. Unfortunately, from a security perspective, the cloud auction mechanism for task assignment is weak in terms of privacy. Third-party auctioneers are not always trustworthy as well as bidders are commercial competitors. They may abuse sensitive information exposed in the auction for their own benefit. In a real auction, a bidder's bid reflects his or her true valuation of the task, which may be a trade secret closely related to winning auction profits, so bidders are reluctant to disclose this information to the auctioneer and competing bidders. By using historical bidding prices, auctioneers may manipulate the auction, and bidders may lie about their bids to get higher profits, which violates the authenticity of the original auction mechanism.

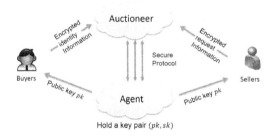

Fig. 1. Framework of our protocol.

Motivated by the above observations, in this paper, we propose a privacy-preserving and truthful heterogeneous auction in Mobile Device Clouds. We focus on a truthful auction mechanism proposed recently [1], where the tasks (or saying the owners of the tasks) act as the buyers of mobile resources, and the mobile devices owning the resources act as the sellers or bidders. In the rest of the paper, we use the terminology of buyers and tasks, sellers, bidders and mobile devices, interchangeably. Our privacy-preserving cloud auction framework is depicted in Fig. 1. Sellers wish to keep its private auction during the bidding period. They send encrypted information to the cloud auctioneer, and the cloud agent which helps the auctioneer with the auction provides encrypted services. We assume that both the auctioneer and the agent are semi-honest entities, meaning that they will run the protocol exactly as they are specified without any deviation, but will try to learn additional information from their protocol. In addition, we also assume the auctioneer and the agent may not collude with each other, that is, they are independently established organizations. In this work, the ultimate goal is that the auctioneer and the agent do not know the identity of the seller, the bid price, the number of resources and other information except the final auction result, while the results are the same as that of the original auction mechanism.

The above studies inspire us to design a Privacy-preserving Auction for Heterogeneous Task Assignment (PAHTA) in mobile device clouds for encrypted data. In heterogeneous task model, each task is assumed to require different amounts of resources for execution. We have solved the following challenges when designing this system. In order to solve the problem of full privacy protection in the semi-honest model, we use Yao's protocol [14], which has the fast running speed and high security, to turn the auction process into the garbled circuits. Additionally, to be able to effectively compute encrypted data form of nonlinear polynomials, we combine Yao's protocol with homomorphic encryption to design a secure division protocol and a secure selection protocol. Our contributions are articulated as follows.

- We are the first to propose privacy-preserving auction for heterogeneous task assignment in mobile device clouds. Compared with the state-of-the-art mechanisms, PAHTA can preserve both sellers' bid privacy and number of resources privacy by using both homomorphic encryption and Yao's garbled circuits [14].
- By taking advantages of Yao's protocol, we design a set of sub-protocols to support secure ciphertext arithmetic operations: secure division protocol and secure selection protocol. These protocols can also be served as key building blocks for the problem of secure spectrum auction.
- We theoretically prove that our protocol is secure under the semi-honest adversary model. To further demonstrate its practicality, we implement the prototype of PAHTA and conduct extensive experiments to evaluate its performance. The experimental result is consistent with the theoretical analysis.

The rest of the paper is organized as follows. Section 2 presents the problem statement and Sect. 3 introduces background knowledge. Section 4 presents the protocols for PAHTA. We analyze the security and complexity of the proposed protocols in Sect. 5, and report the experimental results in Sect. 6. Finally, Sect. 7 discusses some related works and Sect. 8 concludes the paper.

2   Problem Statement

We review a truthful auction mechanism for task assignment in mobile device clouds [1]. In this auction model, the tasks requiring the resources for executions act as the buyers, while the mobile devices owning the resources act as the sellers. To assist the matching between the buyers and sellers, a trusted third party auctioneer is necessary to administrate the trading. The detail of the auction process is described as follow.

Step1: Cost per Unit Resource. Each seller/device d_i submit a truthful bid $b_{i,j}$ for each task/buyer t_j to the auctioneer. We define a parameter $\beta_{i,j}$, named cost per unit resource, as follows:

$$\beta_{i,j} = \frac{b_{i,j}}{r_j} \tag{1}$$

In general, the bid with smaller cost per unit resource should have higher chance to win the bid. Let $\widetilde{T}$ as the set of the tasks that have been assigned with mobile devices so far, and $\overline{B}$ as the set of the bids that can still be chosen as the winning bids so far.

Step2: Winning Bids Determination. The Auctioneer select the least cost per unit resource among the bids in $\overline{B}$. That is $\beta_{i_1,j_1} = min\{\beta_{i,j}|b_{i,j} \in \overline{B}\}$. This bid b_{i_1,j_1} is one of the winning bids, i.e., $x_{i_1,j_1} = 1$, and allocate the task t_{j_1} to mobile device d_{i_1}, i.e., $\widetilde{T} = \widetilde{T} \cup \{t_{j_1}\}$. Correspondingly, the auctioneer remove this bid β_{i_1,j_1} from $\overline{B}$ and then remove bids that may violate the resource constraint of the device, or the bids that are useless for future task allocations. That is, remove the bid $b_{i,j}$ from $\overline{B}$, if $b_{i,j}$, satisfies any of the following two conditions: (1) Task t_j has already been allocated with mobile device in the previous step. As such, the bids to task t_j become useless, and should be removed. (2) The resource left at device d_i is not enough to support the other task in $T - \widetilde{T}$. That is,

$$R_i - \sum_{j=1}^{m} x_{i,j} r_j < \{r_{j'}|t_{j'} \in T - \widetilde{T}\} \tag{2}$$

Continue the above process, until all the tasks are allocated with mobile device, i.e., $\widetilde{T} = T$.

Step3: The Payment for Winning Bids. The winning bids selected in the above process can be store in $B_W = \{b_{i,j}|b_{i,j} = 1\}$. The payment of winning bid $b_{i,j} \in B_W$ is then decided as follows: (1) Remove bid $b_{i,j}$ from the consideration bids in $\overline{B}$. That is, $\overline{B} = \cup_{i=1}^{n} B_i - \{b_{i,j}\}$. (2) Re-select the winning bids from set $\overline{B}$ as in Step2, until the task t_j is allocated with a mobile device, e.g., $d_{i'}$. That is, the bid $b_{i',j}$ wins its bid for task t_j without the presence of bid $b_{i,j}$. (3) Set the payment for device $d_i's$ winning bid $b_{i,j}$ determined in Step2 as $b_{i',j}$. Continue the above process, until considering all the winning bids in B_W.

3 Primitives

For privacy-preserving the above auction process, we use the following primitives: Paillier homomorphic cryptosystem [15], oblivious transfer and Yao's garbled circuits.

3.1   Paillier Cryptosystem

The encryption function is defined as $E_{pk}(m,r) = (1+N)^m \times r^N \bmod N^2$, Where $m \in Z_n$ is a message for encryption, N is a product of two large prime numbers p and q, g generates a subgroup of order N, and r is a random number in Z_N^*. The public key for encryption is (N,g) and the private key for decryption is (p,q). The detail of decryption function D with private key sk can be found in [15]. The properties of the Paillier cryptosystem include homomorphic addition, which means it satisfying: $D_{sk}(E_{pk}(m_1) * E_{pk}(m_2)) = m_1 + m_2 \bmod N$.

3.2   Oblivious Transfer

Oblivious transfer (OT) [17] protocol facilitates the secret exchange between two parties. To be specific, in a parallel 1-out-of-2 OT protocol of κ β-bit strings, denoted as OT_β^κ, for $i = 1, ..., \kappa$, the sender inputs a pair of β-bit strings $m_i^0, m_i^1 \in \{0,1\}^\beta$ and the receiver inputs κ choice bits $\zeta_i \in \{0,1\}$. By following the protocol, the receiver learns the chosen strings $m_i^{\zeta_i}$ without any knowledge of the unchosen strings $m_i^{1-\zeta_i}$, and the sender knows nothing about which encrypted string is accessed.

3.3   Garbled Circuits

With a clever use of garbled circuits and oblivious transfer protocol, we develop the secure comparison protocol to compare two encrypted numbers securely. Yao's garbled circuits [14] were proposed for secure two-party computation, and have been proved to be practical and secure. Two parties with inputs a and b respectively, can jointly compute an arbitrary function $\psi(a,b)$ without leaking any private information beyond the outcome itself. In the garbled circuits protocol, one party (the circuit *generator*) first converts a circuit computing ψ into an encrypted version, then sends the generated circuits and the input to the other party. The other party (the circuit *evaluator*) obliviously computes the output of the circuit without learning any intermediate values. During the protocol execution, the oblivious transfer protocol will be invoked to transmit the input from one party to the other.

Now we itemize the functionalities of some important basic circuits [16,18]:

- **EQ:** The equal circuit takes as input two l-bit values x and y, and output a bit σ, such as if $x == y$, $\sigma = 1$; otherwise, $\sigma = 0$.
- **MIN:** The minimum circuit takes as input n l-bit values $x_1, x_2, ..., x_n$, and output a l-bit z, such as $z = min\{x_1, x_2, ..., x_n\}$.
- **SUB:** The subtraction circuit takes as input two l-bit values x and y, and outputs a l-bit values z, such as $z = x - y$.
- **MUX:** The multiplexer circuit takes as input two l-bit values x and y, and an extra bit σ, and outputs a l-bit values z, such that: if $\sigma = 0$, $z = x$; otherwise, $z = y$. Specially, we will invoke the MUX circuit using input x, 1^l and σ, which is often used to remove invalid bids and assigned tasks and devices.

– **XOR:** The xor circuit takes as input n a bit values $x_1, x_2, \ldots, x_n$, and output a bit z, such as $z = x_1 \oplus x_2 \oplus \ldots \oplus x_n$.

Table 1. Summary of notations

T	The set of tasks to be considered (i.e., buyers);
D	The set of mobile devices (i.e., sellers);
m	The total number of tasks in T (i.e., buyers);
n	The total number of mobile devices in D (i.e., sellers);
t_j	The j-th task in T (i.e., buyer);
d_i	The i-th mobile device in D (i.e., seller);
R_i	The maximum amount of resources that can be provided by d_i;
r_j	The number of resources required for task t_j;
$b_{i,j}$	The cost claimed by d_i for executing task t_j
B_i	The set of the seller d_i submits its bids for all tasks;
$\mathbb{B}$	The set of all the bids submitted by the sellers in D;
β	The set of costs per unit resource;
W	The set of winning matching pair (device d_i, task t_j);
P	The set of the payment for all winning pairs W;

4   PAHTA

In this section, we propose a privacy-preserving auction for heterogeneous task assignment in MDCs. As mentioned above, our design rationale is based on the original scheme [1]. However, the technical difficulty is to execute the auction on the secret-shared data in a data oblivious manner. To achieve this, we improve the original auction mechanism to make it data-oblivious by using secure division protocol ($SecureDIV$) and secure Selection protocol ($SELEC$), which are be described in the last two subsections (Subsects. 4.4 and 4.5). We assume that bids of sellers and the amount of resource are l-bits binaries. The main auction scheme consists of the following phases.

The agent initializes the key pair (pk, sk) of Paillier cryptosystem, and then publishes the public key pk and holds the private key sk himself. With using the public key pk, each seller d_i encrypts his bids B_i and the amount of resources R_i. After encrypting, all ciphertexts are sent to the auctioneer, who carries out the following privacy-preserving scheme, with the help of the agent. The final auction results will be revealed by the auctioneer and the agent cooperatively. After that, we elaborate a data-oblivious task assignment, and present a privacy-preserving auction for heterogeneous task assignment (PAHTA) protocol as shown in Alogrithm 1 and Alogrithm 2. Table 1 shows some notations and symbols that are used extensively in this paper.

4.1 Cost per Unit Resource

After receiving sets $\mathbb{B}$, $\mathbb{R}$, $\mathbb{r}$ from buyers and sellers, the auctioneer runs secure division protocol with the agent to obtain cost per unit resource $\beta_{i,j} = b_{i,j}/r_j$. To secret-shared data in the auctioneer and agent, they execute the oblivious transfer protocol to obtain the garbled values corresponding to input $\mathbb{B}, \mathbb{R}, \mathbb{r}, \beta$. All subsequent operations are completed by them in the garbled circuit.

Algorithm 1. PAHTA(1)

Input:

    Auctioneer: Encrypted bids $\mathbb{B}$, encrypted sellers' resources $\mathbb{R}$,

             tasks' resources required $\mathbb{r}$.

    Agent: $\mathbb{r}$ and key pair (pk, sk);

Output:

    Auctioneer: The location of the winning bids X_w and the task T_w .

    Agent: $\perp$

Step1: Cost Per Unit Resource:

1: $\beta = SecureDIV(\mathbb{B}, \mathbb{r})$

2: The auctioneer runs oblivious transfer protocol with the agent to obliviously obtain the garbled values corresponding to input $\mathbb{B}, \mathbb{R}, \mathbb{r}, \beta$.

Step2: Winning bids determination:

3: $R \leftarrow \mathbb{R}; r \leftarrow \mathbb{r}; X_w \leftarrow \varnothing; T_w \leftarrow \varnothing; \mathscr{B} \leftarrow \beta; w \leftarrow 0$

4: **For** $k = 1$ **to** m $(\forall i \in [1,n], j \in [1,m])$

5:     $\beta_{min} = MIN\{\beta_{i,j}\}$,

6:     $x_{i,j} = EQ\{\beta_{min}, \beta_{i,j}\}, X = \{x_{i,j}\}$;

7:     $\sigma_j = nXOR(x_{1,j}, x_{2,j}, ..., x_{n,j}), \boldsymbol{\sigma} = \{\sigma_{i,j}\}$;

8:     $r_j = MUX(r_j, 1^l, \sigma_j), \boldsymbol{r} = \{r_{i,j}\}$;

9:     $Sum = SELECT(r, \sigma)$;

10:     $\delta_i = nXOR(x_{1,j}, x_{2,j}, ..., x_{n,j})$;

11:     $R'_i = MUX(0, Sum, \delta_i)$;

12:     $R_i = SUB(R_i, R'_i)$;

13:     $\tau_{i,j} = CMP(R_i, r_j)$;

14:     $\beta_{i,j} = MUX(\beta_{i,j}, 1^l, \tau_{i,j})$;

15:     $\beta_{i,j} = MUX(\beta_{i,j}, 1^l, \sigma_j)$;

16:     $X_w = X_w \cup X; T_w = T_w \cup \boldsymbol{\sigma}$;

17: **End For**;

18: Repeat the above Step2 until all tasks are allocated or all sellers do not have sufficient resources.

4.2 Winning Bids Determination

This step is mainly to determine the winning bids. Firstly, the auctioneer and agent initialize the data R, r and backup from β to $\mathscr{B}$. Then, they use MIN circuit to obliviously find the least cost per unit resource β_{min} in β, which is one of the winning bids. To secretly know the loaction of this winning bid. They use

EQ circuit to find the location of β_{min}. Next, they delete the currently assigned task by setting its resources to the maximum number 1^l (line 7, 8) and update winning seller' the remaining of resources (line 9–12). The details are as follows:

- They select the number of resources res currently assigned to the task by the $SELECT$ circuit.
- To find the winning seller, they xor for each column of the location set X.
- Calculating the vendor's resource allocation vector R'_i, the resource left at the winning seller is $R_i - R'_i$.

Note that we need to remove the bid $\beta_{i,j}$ from β, which satisfies any of the following two conditions: (1) Task t_j has already been allocated with the seller in the previous steps (line 14). (2) The resource left at device d_j is not enough to support any other task (line 15). Finally, let X_w and T_w denote the collections of the location of the winning bids and the winning tasks correspondingly.

The above process is repeated until all tasks are allocated or all sellers do not have sufficient resources. To help calculate, we leverage three arrays of binary flags, $\sigma_j, \delta_i, \tau_{i,j}$, with $i \in [1, n], j \in [1, m]$ as follows (We assume a task t_q is assigned to a device d_p, i.e., $x_{p,q} = 1$):

σ_q : indicates whether the task t_q is assigned currently ($\sigma_q = 1$) or not ($\sigma_q = 0$) (line 7).

δ_p : indicates whether the seller d_p successfully assigned a task currently ($\delta_p = 1$) or not ($\delta_p = 0$) (line 10).

$\tau_{p,q}$: indicates whether the number of resources required r_q a task t_q is less than or equal to the resources R_p of a seller d_p, i.e., $r_q \leq R_p(\tau_{p,q} = 1)$ or not ($\tau_{p,q} = 0$) (line 13).

4.3   The Payment for Winning Bid

In this step, we mainly introduce how to obliviously decide the payment of each device/seller for its winning bids. The main idea is to record all the results of the second run and then find another winning bid, which have the same task.

We restore the original data (line 3) and then remove the current winning bid $b_{d,t}$ (line 4). Repeat Step2 with using R, r, β as input and output another winning set $(X'_{w'}, T'_{w'})$ (line 5). Then obliviously find winning seller allocating the same task t_k in the turn (line 6–9). The details are as follows:

- Based on the results of the previous step, we use $SELECT$ circuit to select all the winning original bids $S = \{S_{k'}\}_{k'=1}^{w'}$ in original bid set B.
- To find the same task location σ_k from $T'_{w'}$, i.e., if $\sigma_k = \sigma'_{k'}, \theta_{k'} = 1$; otherwise, $\theta_{k'} = 0$.
- With the sets S and θ, we can compute the payment amount p_k of currently winning bid's $b_{d,t}$.

The auctioneer and agent reveal X_k cooperatively to get the winning pair (device d_{x_k}, task t_{y_k}). However, if p_k is 0, they need to set the payment amount is $b_{d,t}$. It is noted that the payment bid that loses in the above subsection is paid by 0, i.e., if $x_{i,j} = 0$, $p_k = 0$.

Algorithm 2. PAHTA(2)

Input:
  Auctioneer: The location of the winning bids X_w and the task T_w.
  Agent: r and key pair (pk, sk);
Output:
  Auctioneer: The payment P and winning pairs $W = \{(d_{x_k}, t_{y_k})\}_{k=1}^{w}$
  Agent: $\perp$
Step3: The payment for winning bid:
1: $P \leftarrow \varnothing; W \leftarrow \varnothing$;
2: **For** $k = 1$ **to** w
3:     $B \leftarrow \mathbb{B}; R \leftarrow \mathbb{R}; r \leftarrow \mathrm{r}; \beta \leftarrow \mathscr{B}$;
4:     $\beta = MUX(\beta, 1^l, X_k)$;
5:     Execute Step2$(R, r, \beta) \rightarrow (X'_{w'}, T'_{w'})$;
6:     **For** $k' = 1$ **to** w'
7:         $S_{k'} = SELECT(X'_{k'}, B)$;
8:         $\theta_{k'} = EQ(\sigma_k, \sigma'_{k'})$;
9:     **End For**;
10:    $p_k = SELECT(S, \theta)$;
11:    Reveals X_k cooperatively to get winning pairs (d_{x_k}, t_{y_k});
12:    $W = W \cup (d_{x_k}, t_{y_k})$;
13:    Reveals p_k cooperatively;
14:    **If**$(p_k == 0)$
15:        Decrypt the payment bid $b_{d,t}$ of (d_{x_k}, t_{y_k});
16:        $p_k = b_{d,t}; P = P \cup p_k$;
17:    **else** $P = P \cup p_k$;
18:    **End If**;
19: **End For**;
20: Return P, W;

4.4   Secure Division Protocol

One party Alice holds a l-bit binary encrypted data $[\![a]\!]$ and a plaintext b, and need to achieve $[\![a/b]\!]$. Meanwhile, another party Bod holds the Paillier key pk and sk. Instead of sending $[\![a]\!]$ directly to Bob, Alice first masks them with a k-bit random number r^1 via the additively homomorphic property (i.e., $[\![a + r^1 * b]\!] = [\![a]\!] * [\![r^1]\!]^b$). After receiving $[\![a + r^1 * b]\!]$ from Alice, Bob uses the private key pk for decryption and then calculates $(a + r^1 * b)/b$. Finally, Bob re-encrypts and returns the result to Alice, who conducts the following computation: $[\![a/b]\!] = [\![a/b + r^1]\!] \cdot [\![r^1]\!]^{-1}$.

4.5   Secure Selection Protocol

To support secure selection in garbled circuits, we leverage Yao's garbled circuits (GC). Based on MUX and XOR circuits, we construct a secure selection circuit ($SELECT$) (Fig. 2) for securely computing the result of selection. Specially, this circuit takes as input two arrays $X = x_1, x_2, \ldots, x_n$ which each is l-bis binary and $\sigma = \sigma_1, \sigma_2, \ldots, \sigma_n$ which each is l-bits binary and output a l-bits values z, such that: if $\sigma_i = 1$ and other $\sigma_j = 0$ $(j \neq i), z = x_j$.

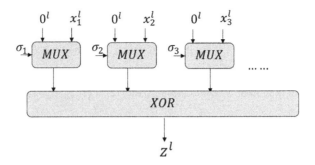

Fig. 2. The structure of $SELECT$ circuit

5   Analysis

5.1   Complexity Analysis

The main cost in the protocol is to execute Yao's garbled circuits. Because the XOR gate is nearly free [19], the computation cost of Yao's protocol is typically determined by the number of non-XOR gates. Note that the bit length of garbled input is l.

- Step1: The main cost of this step is the secure division protocol, Auctioneer need to do nm encryptions and multiplications for the ciphertext, and Agent need to do nm decryptions.
- Step2: The MIN circuits (line 5) need to at most nml non-free gate. The EQ circuit (line 9) needs to at most nml non-free gate. The MUX circuits (line 11 & 14 & 17) need to at most $(mn + m + n)l$ non-free gate. Line 12 use the secure selection protocol in Alg. 1, which leads to at most $2ml$ non-free gate. The SUB circuit (line 15) needs to at most nl non-free gate and the CMP circuits (line 16) needs to at most nml non-free gate. Besides, this step requires to execute at most m times to find all the winning bids, which leads to the total cost of this step $(6nm^2 + 3m^2 + 2nm)l$ non-free gate operations.
- Step3: For each winning bid, this step requires to repeat step2, which leads to at most $(6nm^2 + 3m^2 + 2nm)l$ non-free gate. The MUX circuit (line 24) needs to at most mnl non-free gate. The secure selection protocol (line 27 & 30) needs to execute at most m times, which leads to at most $2nm^2l + 2ml$ non-free gate, The EQ circuit (line 28) needs to require at most m^2l non-free gate. Besides, this step requires to execute at most m times for each winning bid, which leads to the total cost of this step $(8nm^3 + 4m^3 + 3nm^2 + 2m^2)l$ non-free gate operations.

5.2   Security Analysis

As all the messages transmited during our protocol are either ciphertexts which are encrypted by using the public key which is belonged to other party under the paillier encrypted system, or circuit labels during the execution of Yao's protocol, according to the proof of [20], our protocol is secure in the semi-honest adversary model.

6   Experiments

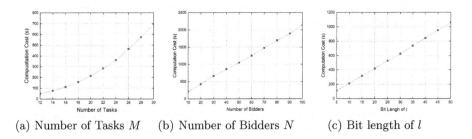

(a) Number of Tasks M (b) Number of Bidders N (c) Bit length of l

Fig. 3. Computation cost induced by PAHTA

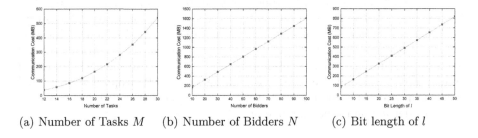

(a) Number of Tasks M (b) Number of Bidders N (c) Bit length of l

Fig. 4. Communication cost induced by PAHTA

We implement our protocol (PAHTA) on top of FastGC [16], a Java-based framework for garbled circuit computation. In our experiments, we simulate the auctioneer and the agent with two processes on a computer with an Intel Core CPU of 6-core operating at 2.20 GHz processor and 16 GB RAM, and Windows 10 operating system with Java Runtime Engine (JRE) 1.7. We use Paillier encryption with 1024-bit modulus, and 80-bit wire labels for garbled circuit, which provides an 80-bit security level.

The number of buyers varies from 10 to 100, and the number of sellers varies from 2 to 20. The number of the resources of a task and a mobile device are generated randomly in the intervals $[0,10)$ and $[0,100)$. We set the default value of seller/bidder number N, task number M and bit length of l as 10, 20 and 10, respectively. In our simulation, we focus on the following performance metrics:

(1) Computation overhead: Total CPU time spent by the servers of Auctioneer and Agent. (2) Communication overhead: Total message volume (data size of all messages sent between the two parties).

Figure 3 and Fig. 4 illustrates the computation and communication overhead of PAHTA. In each set of evaluation, we vary the number of tasks, bidders or change the bit length while fixing other factors. As shown in Fig. 3(a) and Fig. 4(a), when the number of bidders N is 10, the computation and communication costs of tasks M range from 49 to 693 s and from 37MB to 540MB. These curves of M grow super-linearly, while grow quasi-linearly in the number of bidders N and the bit length l. These results are consistent with our theoretical analysis that the complexity of PAHTA is $O(NM^3l)$.

7 Related Work

There exist a number of privacy-preserving designs for conventional auctions, such as [10–13]. However, most of these studies [11–13] did not preserve privacy in the sense of cryptography, i.e., they leaked some information about bids beyond auction results (not necessary the exact bid values). The study [10] did preserve privacy in the sense of cryptography as our work, but it provided a secure auction framework without any concrete secure auction design.

Furthermore, secure spectrum auctions have been extensively studied in recent years. Wang et al. [6,7] propose a series of auction schemes by building secure mixed protocols based on multiple cryptographic primitives. The works in [3,4] focus on how to protect bid values with no regard for bidders' location privacy. Besides, the work [5] provide a privacy-preserving solution for cloud auction, but it relies on great-depth garbled circuits, causing an impractical computation and communication cost. Cheng et al. [8,9] propose a secure and lightweight spectrum auction framework by secret sharing, which involves a lot of secret sharing multiplication operations.

8 Conclusion

In this paper, we propose a privacy-preserving framework for heterogeneous task assignment auction in an oblivious way. Technically, We design a set of sub-protocols to support secure arithmetic operations (i.e., secure division protocol and secure selection protocol). We theoretically prove that these protocols are secure in the semi-honest model. Through analysis and extensive experiments, we plan to extend our framework to support a variety of secure auction schemes in the future.

Acknowledgment. This work was partially supported by Natural Science Foundation of China (Grant No. 61602400) and Jiangsu Provincial Department of Education (Grant NO. 16KJB520043).

References

1. Wang, X., Chen, X., Wu, W.: Towards truthful auction mechanisms for task assignment in mobile device clouds. In: INFOCOM 2017, pp. 1–9. IEEE, Atlanta (2017)
2. Kao, Y., Krishnamachari, B., Ra, M., Bai, F.: Hermes: latency optimal task assignment for resource-constrained mobile computing. In: INFOCOM 2015, pp. 1894–1902. IEEE, Hong Kong (2015)
3. Chen, Z., Huang, L., Li, L., Yang, W., Miao, H., Tian, M., Wang, F.: Ps-trust: provably secure solution for truthful double spectrum auctions. In: INFOCOM 2014, pp. 1249–1257. IEEE, Toronto (2014)
4. Chen, Z., Wei, X., Zhong, H., Cui, J., Xu, Y., Zhang, S.: Secure, efficient and practical double spectrum auction. In: IWQoS 2017, pp. 1–6. IEEE/ACM, Vilanova i la Geltru (2017)
5. Chen, Z., Chen, L., Huang, L., Zhong, H.: On privacy-preserving cloud auction. In: SRDS 2016, pp. 279–288. IEEE, Budapest (2016)
6. Wang, Q., Huang, J., Chen, Y., Tian, X., Zhang, Q.: Privacy-preserving and truthful double auction for heterogeneous spectrum. Trans. Networking (TON) **27**(2), 848–861 (2019)
7. Wang, Q., Huang, J., Chen, Y., Wang, C., Xiao, F., Luo, X.: Prost: privacy-preserving and truthful online double auction for spectrum allocation. TIFS **14**(2), 374–386 (2018)
8. Cheng, K., Wang, L., Shen, Y., Liu, Y., Wang, Y., Zheng, L.: A lightweight auction framework for spectrum allocation with strong security guarantees. In: INFOCOM 2020, pp. 1708–1717. IEEE, Toronto (2020)
9. Cheng, K., Shen, Y., Zhang, Y., Zhu, X., Wang, L., Zhong, H.: Towards efficient privacy-preserving auction mechanism for two-sided cloud markets. In: ICC, 2019, pp. 1–6. IEEE, Shanghai (2019)
10. Naor, M., Pinkas, B., Sumner, R.: Privacy preserving auctions and mechanism design. In: EC 1999, pp. 129–130. ACM, Denver Colorado (1999)
11. Peng, K., Boyd, C., Dawson, E., Viswanathan, K.: Robust, Privacy protecting and publicly verifiable sealed-bid auction. In: ICICS 2002, pp. 147–159. Springer (2002)
12. Suzuki, K., Yokoo, M.: Secure generalized vickrey auction using homomorphic encryption. In: Wright, R.N. (ed.) FC 2003. LNCS, vol. 2742, pp. 239–249. Springer, Heidelberg (2003). https://doi.org/10.1007/978-3-540-45126-6_17
13. Yokoo, M., Suzuki, K.: Secure generalized vickrey auction without third-party servers. In: Juels, A. (ed.) FC 2004. LNCS, vol. 3110, pp. 132–146. Springer, Heidelberg (2004). https://doi.org/10.1007/978-3-540-27809-2_17
14. Yao, C.-C.: How to generate and exchange secrets. In: SFCS 1986, pp. 162–167. IEEE, Toronto (1986)
15. Paillier, P.: Public-key cryptosystems based on composite degree residuosity classes. In: EUROCRYPT 1999, pp. 223–238. Springer (1999)
16. Huang, Y., Evans, D., Katz, J., Malka, L.: Faster secure two-party computation using garbled circuits. In: USENIX Security 2011
17. Even, S., Goldreich, O., Lempel, A.: A randomized protocol for signing contracts. Commun. ACM **28**(6), 637–647 (1985)
18. Kolesnikov, V., Sadeghi, A.-R., Schneider, T.: Improved garbled circuit building blocks and applications to auctions and computing minima. In: Garay, J.A., Miyaji, A., Otsuka, A. (eds.) CANS 2009. LNCS, vol. 5888, pp. 1–20. Springer, Heidelberg (2009). https://doi.org/10.1007/978-3-642-10433-6_1

19. Kolesnikov, V., Schneider, T.: Improved garbled circuit: free XOR gates and applications. In: Aceto, L., Damgård, I., Goldberg, L.A., Halldórsson, M.M., Ingólfsdóttir, A., Walukiewicz, I. (eds.) ICALP 2008. LNCS, vol. 5126, pp. 486–498. Springer, Heidelberg (2008). https://doi.org/10.1007/978-3-540-70583-3_40
20. Lindell, Y., Pinkas, B.: A proof of security of Yao's protocol for two-party computation. J. Cryptol. **22**(2), 161–188 (2009)

Deep Reinforcement Learning for DAG-based Concurrent Requests Scheduling in Edge Networks

Yaqiang Zhang$^{1,2(\boxtimes)}$, Ruyang Li^{1,2}, Zhangbing Zhou^4, Yaqian Zhao^{1,3}, and Rengang Li^{1,3}

^{1} State Key Laboratory of High-End Server and Storage Technology, Jinan 250101, China
^{2} Inspur (Beijing) Electronic Information Industry Co., Ltd, Beijing 100085, China
{zhangyaqiang,liruyang}@inspur.com
^{3} Inspur Electronic Information Industry Co., Ltd, Jinan 250101, China
^{4} China University of Geosciences (Beijing), Beijing 100083, China

Abstract. The explosive growth of mobile edge users causes potential pressure for achieving their delay-sensitive requests in edge networks. Moreover, the incoming requests with task-dependency, which can be represented as Directed Acyclic Graphs (DAG), are hard to deal with effectively. In this paper, we intend to mitigate the DAG-based concurrent requests scheduling problem in an online manner. An Markov Decision Process (MDP) model is constructed for the proposed problem, where requests are split into a set of tasks and are assigned to different edge servers in terms of their status. To optimize the scheduling policy in each time slot while minimizing the long term system delay, we propose a Deep Reinforcement Learning (DRL)-based mechanism to promote the scheduling policy and make decision in each step. Extensive experiments are conducted, and evaluation results demonstrate that our proposed DRL technique can effectively improve the long-term performance of scheduling system, compared with other mechanisms.

Keywords: DAG-based user request · Edge network · Deep Reinforcement Learning · Delay sensitive

1 Introduction

As a new paradigm towards 5G time, the edge computing technique has developed rapidly in recent years. A large amount of end users have been connected to the edge networks, and have access to the services provided by the edge servers. The advantages of edge computing are apparent as it shortens the delay that occurs when users require to access computing resources from remote cloud [1–3]. Meanwhile, the high bandwidth provided by edge networks allows users to offload their computing tasks to the nearby edge servers, where data transmission

© Springer Nature Switzerland AG 2021
Z. Liu et al. (Eds.): WASA 2021, LNCS 12939, pp. 359–366, 2021.
https://doi.org/10.1007/978-3-030-86137-7_39

does not need to go through the backbone network. The cooperation and collaboration between edge servers drive the achievement of task-dependency request which is composed of a variety of different services and functions and can be represented as Directed Acyclic Graphs (DAG). The user side sends the data and requests, while network edge processes data and provides required services.

Aiming to improve the Quality of Experience (QoE) in user side or the efficiency in edge network, advanced techniques have been widely developed when a user's computation task is transferred to the edge network. When scheduling user requests with complex structure, it is critical to consider the logical sequence and the time constraints among tasks of a request [4,5]. In some studies considering the static environment, the execution location and resource allocation of all tasks are configured before the request is scheduled, and never changed once decided. While for the researches in dynamic environments, requests are structured as multiple phase, and at each phase, the appropriate tasks are scheduled according to the current environment. There are few studies focusing on concurrent multi-user requests in a dynamic manner, where scheduling multiple tasks at a same phase is quite complex, and the status of each sub-task in different requests may affect the scheduling of other tasks [6–8].

To address the existing challenges mentioned above, we propose to schedule the concurrent requests in an online manner. The purpose is to optimize the long-term average system delay while improving the task completion that meet their time constraints. Main contributions of this paper are summarized as follows:

- We formulate the concurrent requests scheduling problem as an MDP model, where tasks from different user requests could be marked at the same stage if they are ready to execute. System states include the status of edge networks and tasks information, and actions are scheduling decisions for a set of tasks. The system states are updated constantly along with the chosen actions.
- A DDQN-based tasks scheduling mechanism is proposed, in which two Q-value networks are maintained. Tricks of action selection and Q-value calculation are applied, where the optimal action in the current network is adopted to calculate the Q-value of the target network. The mentioned techniques could improve the convergence efficiency of the Q-value networks.

This paper is organized as follows. Section 2 describes the system model. Section 3 constructs an MDP model for the online DAG-based requests scheduling problem. The proposed DDQN-based concurrent requests optimization mechanism is discussed in Section 4. Section 5 presents the experiments we conducted to evaluate the proposed mechanism and Section 6 concludes this work.

2   System Model

2.1   User Request Model

A user request REQ discussed in this paper has a structure like a DAG and it consists of two parts: a set of sub-tasks and a set of time constraints between them. It can be expressed as $REQ = \{\{SubTask_k\}_{k \in \mathbb{K}}, \{t_w\}_{w \in \mathbb{W}}\}$ where $\mathbb{K}$ is the set of sub-tasks $SubTask$ in this REQ and $\mathbb{W}$ is the set of edges with time constraint t_w between sub-tasks. For convenience, we use task to represent sub-task later in this paper. A $SubTask$, which is represented as a node in a DAG, contains three parts: a set of required data $\{Dt_n\}$ from different edge servers $n \in \mathbb{N}$, a set of input links $\mathbb{W}_i$ with time constraint t_w and the computation resource $Proc$ required by the task: $SubTask_k = \{\{Dt_n\}_{n \in \mathbb{N}}, \{t_w\}_{w \in \mathbb{W}_i}, Proc\}$.

Figure 1 shows an example of a DAG-based request structure. For any task in a request, there must be some kinds of data that are obtained from other resources. $t_1, t_2...$ mentioned in Fig. 1 are time constraints between tasks. Two $SubTasks$ connected by an edge mean that the subsequent task need to be executed at time period t_w after the pre-ordered task finished.

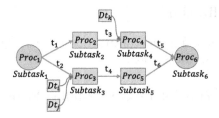

Fig. 1. DAG-based user request structure.

2.2 Tasks Scheduling Model

As a DAG-based user request is composed of a set of tasks, scheduling the whole execution process for one time may cause more delay. Therefore, the request needs to be split and each task should be dynamically scheduled.

Tasks Queue. A discrete timeline is introduced with the equal length time slots. In the beginning of each time slot, there is a certain probability that one or no request will arrive in the system. A user request is firstly divided into separate tasks according to the structure, and each task can be executed independently by an ES. The sign that a task can be executed is that all its previous tasks have been fully completed. A queue of tasks is built to sort the priority of tasks to be scheduled and the execution order of task queues is subject to the First-In First-Out (FIFO) rule. There exist two situations for a task being queued: 1) The task has no antecedent task in its request structure, i.e., it is the starting node; 2) All the antecedent tasks of the task have been completed.

Delay Calculation. ESs connect each other by adopting the Orthogonal Frequency Division Multiple Access (OFDMA) technique and the network communication mode between servers is two-way propagation mode. B_{ij} denotes the bandwidth between two edge servers ES_i and ES_j, and there is a system delay d_{ij} that is influenced by the network condition. Assuming that a package with size of S will be transmitted between edge servers, we can simplify the calculation of transmission time as $TD_{ij}(S) = \frac{S}{B_{ij}} + d_{ij}$. The processor of each edge server can process a task at one time. Delay of task processing is proportional to the amount of required data received by the server. F denotes CPU frequency of an edge server, and Z denotes the number of CPU cycles required to process a unit of data. If a task with data of size S has been processed, the processing time TP is shown as $TP(S) = \frac{Z*S}{F}$. The total time consumption D_n^t of a ready task at time slot t can be determined by the wait time, transfer time and execution time occurred in an ES_n: $T_{waiting} + TD + TP$, where $T_{waiting}$ needs to be considered when the channel or processor is occupied by other tasks.

3   Problem Definition

The objective function and model construction for the scheduling optimization problem are proposed in this section.

3.1   Objective Function of Tasks Scheduling Edge System

The purpose is to minimize the long term average delay in edge networks, while improving the rate of tasks completely executed within their temporal constraints. The objective function can be formulated as follows:

$$\min_{a_t, T \to \infty} \frac{1}{T} \sum_{t=0}^{T} \frac{1}{|\mathbb{N}_t|} \sum_{n \in \mathbb{N}_t} D_n^t \ s.t. \ \mathbb{N}_t \in \mathbb{N} \tag{1}$$

where $\mathbb{N}_t$ denotes the sub-collation of ESs that are assigned with tasks following the scheduling action a_t in time slot t and $|\mathbb{N}_t|$ denotes the number of edge servers in this set. The term $\frac{1}{|\mathbb{N}_t|} \sum_{n \in \mathbb{N}_t} D_n^t$ in formula (1) represents the average delay of all the edge servers participating in task scheduling at a certain time slot, which reflects the average latency level of the edge system at that stage.

3.2   MDP Model

An MDP is firstly applied to describe the sequential decision making problem mathematically in a dynamic environment. The key elements of the MDP are shown as follows:

System State. State information of the edge networks can be given as: $s_t = \{(C_i^t, L_{i,j}^t)_{i,j \in \mathbb{N}}, Qu_t\}$, where C_i^t denotes the computation resources occupation of ES_i at time t and $L_{i,j}^t$ indicates the network condition from edge server i to j. Besides, the queue Qu_t saves the tasks information that are ready for execution and will be updated in the beginning of each time slot. State changes when an action is taken or just over time.

Actions. Actions in this paper are defined as simultaneous decisions made for the execution of multiple tasks and it is defined as: $a_t = \{Qu_t\}_{|\mathbb{N}_t|} \rightarrow \{A_{\mathbb{N}}^{\mathbb{N}_t}\}$, where $\{A_{\mathbb{N}}^{\mathbb{N}_t}\}$ is an arrangement of the set $\mathbb{N}_t$ which is no larger than $|\mathbb{N}|$. If there are more than $|\mathbb{N}|$ tasks in Qu_t, only the first $|\mathbb{N}|$ tasks are taken into consideration, and the rest will be deferred to the next time slot.

Reward. Based on the ultimate goal of minimizing the long term average delay in edge network and improve the QoE of users, we give the reward R in this paper as: $R = \frac{1}{|\mathbb{N}_t|} \sum_{n \in \mathbb{N}_t} D_n^t$ which is part of the objective function. R represents the average delay caused by ESs in a decision phase, leading to a better performance with smaller reward.

4   Algorithm Design

When the scale of actions and states in the problem is very small, the tabular method can be used to find the actions corresponding to the optimal value function. In this paper, both the environment state and the action set have a large scale, especially the environment state, which is a high-dimensional continuous variable and cannot be enumerated. Therefore, an approximate method like DQN can be applied. In a DQN pipeline, Q-value function can be approximated by a parameter network: $\hat{Q}(s, a, \omega) \approx Q(s, a)$, where $\hat{Q}$ can be expressed by a deep neural network. ω is the parameter of the neural network, whose input is the feature of state and the output is Q-value corresponding to actions. DQN makes the parameter ω converge by training the network. Therefore, the corresponding loss function needs to be established. A replay buffer $\mathbb{D}$ is used to store system historical data in the form of tuples consisting of states, actions and rewards. We randomly sample no more than M tuples like $[s_m, a_m, R_m, s_m']$ from $\mathbb{D}$ to form a subset and each tuple m in the subset can be used to calculate the target Q-value, while the mean square error loss function $L(\omega)$ is set as:

$$\frac{1}{M} \sum_{m=1}^{M} [R_m + \gamma \hat{Q}'(s_m', \arg\min_{a'} \hat{Q}(s_m', a', \omega), \omega') - \hat{Q}(s_m, a_m, \omega)]^2 \qquad (2)$$

In order to improve the performance of the original DQN method, an improved version based on double Q network called Double DQN (DDQN) is considered. Two neural networks with the same structure are established, where the so-called current network $\hat{Q}$ is responsible for selecting the actions and updating the parameters ω of the network. Another one is the target network $\hat{Q}'$, which is responsible for calculating the target Q-value. Since the two networks have the same structure, in every certain stage, complete values of parameters ω in the current network are assigned to the parameters ω' in target network. In the loss function (2), the optimal Q-value is not directly selected in the calculation of the target Q-value. It selects the actions $\arg\min_{a'} \hat{Q}(s_m', a', \omega)$ that can obtain the optimal Q-value of the current network and calculated of the target network with a' as input.

Algorithm 1. DDQN-based Multi-Tasks Scheduling Algorithm

1: Randomly initialize the parameter ω of current Q-value function network $\hat{Q}(s, a, \omega)$

2: Initialize the parameter $\omega' = \omega$ of target Q-value function network $\hat{Q}'(s, a, \omega')$
3: Initialize the experience replay buffer $\mathbb{D}$ and the batch size M
4: Initialize the parameter ϵ, γ, and frequency C
5: Initialize the state s
6: **while** *looptime* $T < MAX$ **do**
7:     Take s as the input of $\hat{Q}(s, a, \omega)$
8:     Choose the action a according to ϵ-greedy based on $\hat{Q}(s, a, \omega)$
9:     Take action a in state s, get the reward R and transmit to a new state s'
10:    $\mathbb{D} \leftarrow [s,a,R,s']$
11:    **if** $|\mathbb{D}| \geq M$ **then**
12:       Randomly sample M records from $\mathbb{D}$
13:       Update ω using mini-batch SGD according to (2)
14:       **if** $T\%C == 0$ **then**
15:          $\omega' = \omega$
16:       **end if**
17:    **end if**
18:    $s = s'$
19: **end while**

The algorithm flow is shown in Algorithm 1. The parameter ω of current Q-value network is randomly set during initialization and ω' of target network is the same as ω. A suitable batch size M, a frequency of parameter copy C and the initialized ϵ and γ are given before training (lines 1–5). At the iteration phase, the observed system state s is put into $\hat{Q}(s, a, \omega)$ and the output are Q-value of all the available actions. An action with the minimal Q-value is chosen according to ϵ-greedy strategy. Then it takes the selected action a, and the system transfers to a new state s' while a immediately reward is calculated (lines 7–9). A tuple of $[s, a, R, s']$ is stored in experience replay buffer $\mathbb{D}$ (line 10). While the number of elements in $\mathbb{D}$ is larger than batch size M, randomly sample M records from $\mathbb{D}$ and update ω according to (2), in which a mini-batch SGD is applied (lines 11–13). Every C times the parameter ω is copied to ω' (lines 14–16). At the end of each loop-time, transfer s to s' (line 18).

5   Implementation and Evaluation

5.1   Experiment Settings

The number of edge servers N is set from 2 to 6 in the proposed evaluation settings. F representing the frequency of server processor is set to 1GHz-3GHz, correspondingly. It is assumed that 40 CPU cycle is needed for dealing with a byte of data. The channel data transmission capacity among servers is set to 1MBytes per time unit. We also set the length of time slot is a time unit and the system delay is set from 0.01 to 0.1 time unit. In order to verify the performance of the proposed mechanism in different scenarios, we apply different user request arrival probability in each time slot from 20% to 100%. We explore the performance of the proposed DDQN-based mechanism, original DQN and a random strategy under different scenarios.

5.2   Experimental Evaluation

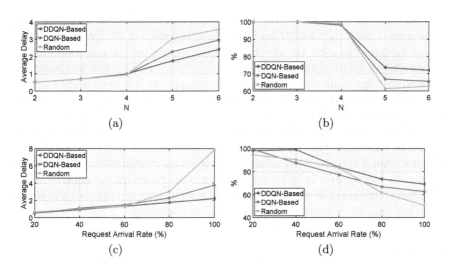

Fig. 2. Performance on average delay and tasks completion rate.

Figure 2(a), 2(b) compare the performance of different scheduling mechanisms with the change of number of edge servers, respectively. With the increase in the number of edge servers, average system delay shows an upward trend in Fig. 2(a), while task completion rate in Fig. 2(b) experiences a downward trend. Obviously, the proposed DDQN-based mechanism can provide a better scheduling decision when there are more edge servers in system, leading to a slow increases in delay and decreases in task completion rate, while the DQN and random mechanism have significant changes when the number of edge servers is greater than 4. This indicates that the system state will become much more complex with more edge servers joined, and more alternative decisions will be made, resulting in a certain decline in the performance of mentioned scheduling mechanisms.

Figure 2(c), 2(d) show the variation trend of mechanism performances under different arrival rates of user requests, respectively. In Fig. 2(c), when the probability of user requests generation increases, average system delay in DDQN is lower than DQN based scheduling mechanism, while the delay generated by random mechanism is significantly higher than that of the other mechanisms. The random is close to other mechanisms only when the task arrival rate is small. The proposed mechanism can still choose the better decision when the task intensity increases, so as to ensure the delay of user request and ensure a certain stability of the system. In Fig. 2(d), task completion rate shows a downward trend in curves. The DDQN and DQN can maintain a relative high task completion rate as much as possible, while the decline of the random strategy is obvious.

6   Conclusion

In order to reduce the long-term average delay of tasks while satisfying internal temporal constraints of DAG-based user requests, a DDQN-based mechanism is proposed to solve the concurrent task scheduling optimization problem. Specifically, an MDP model is constructed, and the strategy of task scheduling is obtained through reinforcement learning technique. As it is hard to deal with the scenarios with high-dimension environment description and large-scale actions, the combination of reinforcement learning and deep learning successfully solve the real-time online scheduling problem of user requests based on DAG in multi-edge servers network. Extensive experiments have been conducted, and the comparisons among the proposed mechanism, baseline mechanism and DQN-based mechanism are figured in the present work. Our technique is superior to the DQN-based and random strategy in terms of delay, user request completion rate and other indicators for the task scheduling performance.

References

1. Shi, W., Cao, J., Zhang, Q., Li, Y., Xu, L.: Edge computing: vision and challenges. IEEE Internet Things J. **3**(5), 637–646 (2016)
2. Jiang, W., Li, M., Zhou, X., Qu, W., Qiu, T.: Multi-user cooperative computation offloading in mobile edge computing. In: Wireless Algorithms, Systems, and Applications, 15th International Conference (WASA), pp. 182–193 (2020)
3. Pawani, P., Jude, O., Madhusanka, L., Mika, Y., Tarik, T.: Survey on multi-access edge computing for internet of things realization. IEEE Commun. Surv. Tutorials **20**(4), 2961–2991 (2018)
4. Zhang, Y., Meng, L., Xue, X., Zhou, Z., Tomiyama, H.: Qoe-constrained concurrent request optimization through collaboration of edge servers. IEEE Internet Things J. **6**(6), 9951–9962 (2019)
5. Liu, Y., et al.: Dependency-aware task scheduling in vehicular edge computing. IEEE Internet Things J. **7**(6), 4961–4971 (2020)
6. Topcuoglu, H., Hariri, S., Wu, M.Y.: Performance-effective and low-complexity task scheduling for heterogeneous computing. IEEE Trans. Parallel Distrib. Syst. **13**(3), 260–274 (2002)
7. Wu, F., Wu, Q., Tan, Y.: Workflow scheduling in cloud: a survey. J. Supercomputing **71**(2015), 3373–3418 (2015)
8. Jia, M., Cao, J., Yang, L.: Heuristic offloading of concurrent tasks for computation-intensive applications in mobile cloud computing. In. IEEE Conference on Computer Communications Workshops (INFOCOM WKSHPS), vol. 2014, pp. 352–357 (2014)

Generative Adversarial Scheme Based GNSS Spoofing Detection for Digital Twin Vehicular Networks

Hong Liu[1]([✉]), Jun Tu[1] , Jiawen Liu[1], Zhenxue Zhao[2], and Ruikang Zhou[3]

[1] School of Software Engineering, East China Normal University, Shanghai, China
hliu@sei.ecnu.edu.cn
[2] School of Economics and Management, Wuhan University, Wuhan, China
zhaozx-xs@petrochina.com.cn
[3] China Electronics Standization Institute, Beijing, China

Abstract. Digital twin vehicular network is an emerging architecture to realize vehicle communications. Anti-GNSS-spoofing becomes a challenging issue due to the growing automotive intelligence. However, the anti-spoofing methods are faced with several challenges: the additional cost of anti-spoofing devices, the limited computation resource within the vehicles, the lack of abnormal data, and model bias. To solve these problems, a generative adversarial scheme based anti-spoofing method is proposed for digital twin vehicular networks. The scheme consists of two deep-learning models of the generator and the detector, which generates pseudo normal data and detects spoofing. The LSTM model is introduced as the generator model, which fabricate the abnormal data with the GNSS/CAN/IMU data from Comma2k19. The DenseNet is introduced as the detector model, which make prediction on the basis of latitude, longitude, speed, steering angle and acceleration forward. The generative adversarial scheme is implemented for performance analysis, which indicates that the proposed scheme is suitable for digital twin vehicular applications.

Keywords: GNSS spoofing · Digital twin · Automotive security

1 Introduction

Vehicles are becoming more and more connected and intelligent with the advances in 5G and big data technologies. However, due to the vehicles' large attack surface, cybersecurity attacks can cause life-threatening situations, which highlights the need for efficient security monitoring and intrusion detection systems [1–4]. Among the cybersecurity attacks, the GNSS (Global Navigation Satellite System) spoofing has a great influence towards vehicle security. The misleading location and speed would lead the vehicles to wrong place, which causes accidents. The anti-spoofing methods needs the computing power, which vehicles are not deployed with. In order to address this issue, the digital twin

© Springer Nature Switzerland AG 2021
Z. Liu et al. (Eds.): WASA 2021, LNCS 12939, pp. 367–374, 2021.
https://doi.org/10.1007/978-3-030-86137-7_40

vehicular network becomes an emerging issue for future vehicular applications. Maintaining twins of vehicle components enables edge computing units to continuously monitor the vehicle-related sensor data, detect the spoofing message and send feedback to the vehicles in turn [5,6].

As to the challenges, we proposed the generative adversarial scheme based anti-spoofing method. The main contributions are as follows.

- The digital twin is introduced as the reflection of real driving vehicles. The edge computing unit utilizes the sensor data contained with digital twins to complete the anti-spoofing task, which is difficult to the computing unit within vehicles. It is not necessary to add the computing hardware to the vehicles, which means a great cost.
- The proposed method is based on the machine learning and sensor data within vehicles without additional hardware facilities, which is low-budget and transplantable. The factory do not need to add cost to deploy the additional anti-spoofing hardware towards vehicles. The method is also not constrained to the vehicles with particular hardware, which could be utilized by most vehicles.
- The proposed method includes generator and detector. The generator could generate the pseudo data to solve the problem of abnormal data source. The detector is not only trained with training dataset, but also with pseudo data. So the detector would not be biased to the training dataset, and could detect the unknown attacks with the help of pseudo data generated by the generator.

The remainder of this paper is organized as follows. Section 2 outlines the related work. Section 3 presents the system model including various components used in the solution. Section 4 describes the proposed solution. The implementation and performance analysis are discussed in Sect. 5. Finally, Sect. 6 summarizes the conclusion.

2   Related Work

Ling Xiao *et al.* [7] proposed an anti-spoofing method to detect spoofing interference, using the pseudo-range double-differences (PRDD) measurements of two receivers; the method recognizes spoofing signal by analysing the differences between PRDD measurements and expected PRDD estimations. Based on the differences, a spoofing decision variable is deduced. And the statistical characterization of the variable is analysed. The methods mentioned above rely on just one parameter which is not enough to detect spoofing. It is necessary to introduce multiple parameters to detect the spoofing comprehensively.

The anti-spoofing methods using additional hardware facilities are subdivided into Antenna array-based, angle of arrival-based, Subspace projection-based, Signal arrival direction-based and Signal quality monitoring-based. The samples are given as follows. Zhang *et al.* [8] proposed a spoofing TDOA estimation method based on differential code phase (DCP), and established a DCP-based TDOA model and its estimation error model. Ali *et al.* [9] proposed a spoofing detection algorithm that uses joint signal quality monitoring techniques and residual signal monitoring. The methods above utilize the additional hardware facilities, which is an additiional cost to the vehicle. As to vehicles, it is better to use the devices deployed on vehicles to detect the GNSS spoofing, without additional hardware.

In our work, at first we anaylze the multiple parameters from GNSS, CAN, and IMU to detect the GNSS spoofing, without additional hardware devices. In addition, we introduce the generative adversarial scheme which generate the pseudo data and detect GNSS spoofing. The detection model would not be biased to the training dataset, because the pseudo data is introduced to train the detection model.

3   System Model

3.1   Digital Twin Based Vehicular Network Architecture

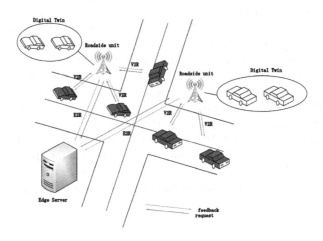

Fig. 1. Digital twin based vehicular network architecture

Figure 1 presents the digital twin based vehicular network architecture.

The network architecture would be described as two layers: physical layer and digital layer.

– *Physical Layer:* The driving vehicles are made up of cellular hotpot, GNSS(Global Navigation Satellite System), pilot device and human driver. The commands within the pilot device is from the feedback from roadside unit, so it does not demand high level hardware within vehicles. The cellular hotpot provide the pilot device with the transmission towards roadside units. The transmission might be implemented with 5G LTE sim card. The vehicle could communicate with digital twins in this way. GNSS provides pilot device with the latitude, longitude and speed through inner cables. The pilot

Table 1. Notations

Notation	Description
v_*	The driving vehicle
rsu_*	The roadside unit
$req_*(t)$,	The request from v_* at time t
lat_*,	The latitude
lon_*,	The longitude
t_*,	The target next state of the given sequence
N	The number of states
$prop$	The output logits of the dense layer
θ	Softmax activation generating vector

device receives feedback from roadside units and provides the human drivers with advice about driving. The human driver control the speed and location according to the pilot device. The human could not perfectly behave as the advice from pilot device, so there is driver model within the edge server, and the pilot device make compensatement towards vehicles.

– *Digital Layer:* In the digital layer, the digital twins are generated with massive data transmitted from vehicles. The following are the function modules with the digital layer. The map module contains the maps which consists of road type, road length, road direction, and the speed limitation. The module would receive location from the GNSS on vehicles and locate the vehicle within the map. The driving model predict the vehicle path with the speed and location from vehicles. The human behaviour module compare the vehicle condition with the driving plan and make compensatement towards vehicle. The power module anaylze the driving condition and send the report to the pilot device (Table 1).

4   Generative Adversarial Scheme

The proposed anti-GNSS-spoofing method consists of two neural network models called pseudo normal data generator and spoofing detector. At first, the pseudo normal data generator is trained in advance using normal data to produce outputs that mimic real data called pseudo normal data. Then, the generator generates pseudo normal data that will be used as abnormal data for training the detection model. After that, the detection model is trained to determine whether a given sample is from the real dataset or the generated pseudo normal dataset.

Architecture of the Generator Model. The generator model is based on LSTM(Long-Short Term Memory), which is a representative kind of recurrent neural networks (RNNs). Long Short-term Memory (LSTM) is an RNN architecture designed to be better at storing and accessing information than standard RNNs. LSTM has recently given state-of-the-art results in a variety of sequence processing tasks, including stock price and channel state information [10,11].

The input to the generator model is a sequence of states $[s_{t_0}, s_{t_1}, \ldots]$. The LSTM-based model is trained to guess which $s_{t_{i+1}}$ is the most probable as the following state at each time step based on the given sequence of states. Since RNNs have an internal state that contains the context of the previously seen elements, predicting the next state is available on basis of the given sequence of states.

In detail, the vehicle state vector is fed to the LSTM layer with 256 units. The LSTM layer extracts the context of a given sequence. Then, the dense layer outputs logits predicting the log-likelihood of the next state. Therefore, the output size of the dense layer is the same as the length of the state vector. The prediction of the next state is derived by sampling from this probability distribution.

Training the Generator Model. The generator model predict the class of the next state based on the given previous state of the LSTM layer and the input state of time steps. The categorical cross-entropy loss function is used as the dense layer outputs a probability over the states.

$$Cross\ Entropy = -\sum_{i}^{N} t_i \log(\theta_i) \tag{1}$$

The N refers to the number of states. The t_i represents the target next state of the given sequence. The θ is computed as:

$$\theta_i = \exp^{prop_i} \bigg/ \sum_{i=1}^{N} \exp^{prop_i} \ (i = 0, \ldots, N). \tag{2}$$

The softmax activation above normalizes a N-dimensional vector *prop* to a N-dimensional vector θ in the range (0, 1) of which the sum is 1. The vector *prop* represents the output logits of the last dense layer.

Generating State Sequence. Once the generator model is trained, it is able to generate state sequences that mimic the real state sequence. We can generate state sequence by feeding states of time steps to the generator model. The generator model predicts the distribution of the next state based on the given state sequence. Then, the index of the next state is obtained by sampling from the predicted probability distribution.

Abnormal Data Detection. We used the Dense Convolutional Network (DenseNet) by Gao Huang et al. as our detection model [12], which contains shorter connections between layers close to the input and those close to the output. DenseNet alleviate the vanishing-gradient problem, strengthen feature propagation, encourage feature reuse, and substantially reduce the number of parameters.

The detection model is trained through supervised learning using pseudo normal data, generated by the generator model, and normal data from dataset. Accordingly, training the detection model is considered as a binary classification problem. Samples of normal data and pseudo normal data are labeled as 0 and 1 respectively.

Similar to training the generator model with categorical cross entropy, we used the binary cross-entropy loss to train the detection model, because the detection model classifies the input samples into two classes, normal and abnormal. The binary cross-entropy loss is calculated by Eq. 1, where N is set to 2 because of the number of output classes.

5   Implementation and Performance Analysis

5.1   Dataset

We take comma2k19 as our dataset, which is proposed by Harald Schafer et al. [13].

In our study, we take the dataset from GNSS, CAN, and IMU. The GNSS dataset includes satellite system data from u-box and Qcom, which consists of latitude, longitude, speed, timestamp, height and angle. The CAN dataset consists of CAN timestamp, speed and steering angle. The IMU dataset consists of the accelerometer from three directions.

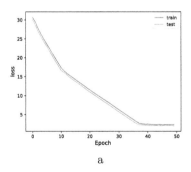
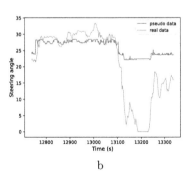

a   b

Fig. 2. The training process of generator model (a) and The difference between pseudo and real steering angle (b)

5.2   Experiment

The samples are described as time, latitude, longitude, speed, steering angle, acceleration forward, wihch is fed into the LSTM based generator model. The LSTM layer outputs 256 units. The LSTM model is trained to predict the next state, given sequence of state. Figure 2(a) show the training process of generator model.

The trained generator model is utilized to fabricate the state sequence. For example, Fig. 2(b) shows the difference between pseudo and real steering angle sequence.

The pseudo data generated by generator and normal data from dataset are fixed to train the DenseNet based detection model. Table 2 represents the training results.

Table 2. Model summary

Parameter	Value
Total params	133,663
Trainable params	126,217
Class accuracy (training dataset)	0.98
Class accuracy (test dataset)	0.97

6   Conclusions

This work proposed a generative adversarial scheme based anti-spoofing method for digital twin vehicular networks. The edge computing unit monitor the digital twins to detect the spoofing. The LSTM based generator model generates pseudo data from Comma2k19, while the DenseNet based detector model classifies the pseudo normal data with normal data. The additional hardware facilities are not necessary, which make the method low-budget and transplantable. The generator model generates abnormal data, which is appropriate to a limited data environment, common in real-world problems. The detector model is trained with pseudo normal data and data from training dataset, which solves the problem of model bias. The experimental result demonstrates that the generative adversarial scheme based model trained by the proposed method has great ability to detect spoofing and is suitable for the digital twin vehicular network. Although the result of this study still needs further performance improvements to be deployed in real-world applications for now, this study presents the possibility of a comprehensive model based on generative adversarial scheme that can detect the spoofing without being biased to the training data.

Acknowledgment. This work is funded by the National Key R&D Program of China (2020AAA0107800), National Natural Science Foundation of China (62072184). This work is partially supported by the Project of Science and Technology Commitment of Shanghai (19511103602, 20511106002).

References

1. Javed, A.R., Usman, M., Rehman, S.U., Khan, M.U., Haghighi, M.S.: Anomaly detection in automated vehicles using multistage attention-based convolutional neural network. IEEE Trans. Intell. Transp. Syst. **22**(7), 1–10 (2020)
2. Dennis, K.N., Larson, U.E.: Conducting forensic investigations of cyber attacks on automobile in-vehicle networks. Int. J. Digital Crime Forensics **1**(2), 28–41 (2009)
3. Chowdhury, A., Karmakar, G., Kamruzzaman, J.: Trusted autonomous vehicle: measuring trust using on-board unit data. In: 2019 18th IEEE International Conference On Trust, Security And Privacy. In Computing And Communications/13th IEEE International Conference on Big Data Science and Engineering (Trust-Com/BigDataSE), pp. 787–792 (2019)
4. Sergio, M., Giuli, T.J., Lai, K., Baker, M.: Mitigating routing misbehavior in mobile ad hoc networks. In: Proceedings of the 6th Annual International Conference on Mobile Computing and Networking, pp. 255–265 (2000)
5. Rassõlkin, A., Vaimann, T., Kallaste, A., Kuts, V.: Digital twin for propulsion drive of autonomous electric vehicle. In: 2019 IEEE 60th International Scientific Conference on Power and Electrical Engineering of Riga Technical University (RTUCON), pp. 1–4 (2019)
6. Ríos, J., Morate, F.M., Oliva, M., Hernandez-Matias, J.: Framework to support the aircraft digital counterpart concept with an industrial design view. Int. J. Agile Syst. Manage. **9**, 212–231 (2016)
7. Xiao, L., Li, X., Wang, G.: GNSS spoofing detection using pseudo-range double differences between two receivers. In: 2019 IEEE 7th International Conference on Computer Science and Network Technology (ICCSNT), pp. 498–502 (2019)
8. Zhang, Z., Zhan, X., Zhang, Y.: GNSS spoofing localization based on differential code phase. In: 2017 Forum on Cooperative Positioning and Service (CPGPS), pp. 338–344 (2017)
9. Ali, K., Manfredini, E.G., Dovis, F.: Vestigial signal defense through signal quality monitoring techniques based on joint use of two metrics. In: 2014 IEEE/ION Position, Location and Navigation Symposium - PLANS 2014, pp. 1240–1247 (2014)
10. Istiake Sunny, M.A., Maswood, M.M.S., Alharbi, A.G.: Deep learning-based stock price prediction using LSTM and bi-directional LSTM model. In: 2020 2nd Novel Intelligent and Leading Emerging Sciences Conference (NILES), pp. 87–92 (2020)
11. Li, S., Wang, Q., Liu, X., Chen, J.: Low cost LSTM implementation based on stochastic computing for channel state information prediction. In: 2018 IEEE Asia Pacific Conference on Circuits and Systems (APCCAS), pp. 231–234 (2018)
12. Huang, G., Liu, Z., van der Maaten, L., Weinberger, K.Q.: Densely connected convolutional networks (2018)
13. Schafer, H., Santana, E., Haden, A., Biasini, R.: A commute in data: the comma2k19 dataset (2018)

Spatial Sketch Configuration for Traffic Measurement in Software Defined Networks

Da Yao[1], Hongli Xu[1(✉)], Haibo Wang[2], Liusheng Huang[1], and Huaqing Tu[1]

[1] School of Computer Science and Technology,
University of Science and Technology of China, Hefei, Anhui, China
{yddzf,fx364117,thq527}@mail.ustc.edu.cn, {xuhongli,lshuang}@ustc.edu.cn
[2] Department of Computer and Information Science and Technology,
University of Florida, Gainesville, FL, USA
wanghaibo@ufl.edu
http://staff.ustc.edu.cn/~xuhongli/int/

Abstract. Flow-level traffic statistics information plays a vital role for many applications, such as network management, attack detection and packet engineering. Compared with TCAM-based counting and packet sampling, sketches can provide flow-level traffic estimation with bounded error using compact data structures, thus have been widely used for traffic measurement. Under many practical applications, several different sketches should be deployed on each switch to support various requirements of traffic measurement. If each arrival packet is measured by all sketches on a switch (*i.e.*, without sketch configuration), it may lead to redundant measurement, and cost massive CPU resource, especially with increasing traffic amount. Due to limited computing capacity on most commodity switches, heavy traffic measurement overhead will seriously interfere with the basic rule operations, especially when some switches need to deal with many new-arrival flows or update routes of existing flows. To address this challenge, we propose a spatial sketch configuration problem for the general case. As a case study, we present optimal sketch configuration for proportional fairness with per-switch computing capacity constraint (SCP), so that each sketch can measure enough flows without unduly restricting the number of flows measured by other sketches in the network. Due to the NP-hardness of this problem, a greedy-based algorithm with approximation ratio 1/3 is presented, and its time complexity is analyzed. We implement the proposed sketch configuration solution on the platform. The extensive simulation results and the experimental results show that the proposed algorithm can measure traffic of 44%–91% more flows compared with the existing solutions with CPU resource constraint.

Keywords: Software defined networks · Traffic measurement · Sketch configuration · Flow-level statistics · Approximation

ⓒ Springer Nature Switzerland AG 2021
Z. Liu et al. (Eds.): WASA 2021, LNCS 12939, pp. 375–389, 2021.
https://doi.org/10.1007/978-3-030-86137-7_41

1 Introduction

A lot of applications benefit from an accurate view of flow-level traffic statistics in a software defined network (SDN). For example, many data centers implement dynamic scheduling of flow routing based on traffic statistics [1]. An accurate global view of individual flows' traffic also helps to achieve better QoS [2], such as higher throughput, and lower latency. Moreover, traffic statistics information is important for network management, such as accounting management, and performance management [3–5].

There are three different ways for traffic measurement, TCAM-based counting [6,7], packet sampling [8,9], and sketches [10,11]. However, due to limited size of TCAM and SRAM on a commodity SDN switch [12], both TCAM-based counting and packet sampling can only achieve coarse-grained traffic measurement [13]. Though measurement accuracy can be improved by increasing the TCAM size or sampling rate, the memory/computing resource usage will dramatically increase and pose scalability issues, especially in high-speed networks [14]. On the contrary, sketches can provide fine-grained traffic measurement for individual flows. Unlike the other two measurement solutions, sketches can summarize traffic statistics of all packets using compact data structures with fixed-size memory, while incurring only bounded estimation errors [14]. Many sketch-based solutions have been proposed in the literature to address different measurement requirements [10,11].

Unfortunately, it is challenging to deploy sketches in practice for two reasons. 1) Sketches (e.g., Count-Min [15]) are only primitives and usually can not provide the flow ID, which restricts its usage for network management. Instead, they should be supplemented with additional operations to fully support a measurement task. 2) Sketches are often task specific, and a sketch only measures one simple object, such as heavy hitters and traffic changes detection. To implement various measurement requirements, the SDN controller usually requires different types of statistics knowledge from switches. For example, OpenSketch [13] deploys Count-Min, k-ray, and Bloom filter sketches on each switch to implement various applications, e.g., heavy hitters, traffic changes detection, and traffic counting.

Besides, if a packet is measured/processed by all the sketches at a switch upon its arrival, the total measurement overhead per packet may be massive, not to mention that today's networks require very high throughput (e.g., beyond 10 Gbps). Moreover, OpenFlow capable switches usually have only limited processing power [16], which needs to be shared by different operations, e.g., rule insertion/deletion/modification, statistics collection, and traffic measurement. The testing results in [12] have shown that the switch can complete only 275 flow setups per second even without any traffic load. If traffic measurement on sketches costs 50% CPU utilization, the switch can only complete 137 flow setups per second, let alone forward packets.

Therefore, *it is important to perform efficient traffic measurement with limited per-switch computing overhead*, so that basic rule operations on each switch will not be interfered, especially for high-speed networks. Though some works, *e.g.*, [17], use the hash value of a packet's 5-tuple to distribute traffic measurements among switches, it requires all packets to carry their ingress-egress pairs, which are not available in practical networks [18], and also requires massive memory cost for auxiliary information.

Inspired by the fact that a flow will pass through several switches from its source to destination, we propose to solve the problem by determining which sketches (not all sketches) will be turned on (or be enabled) at each switch such that a flow can be measured by all required sketches in a distributed manner without violating per-switch computing capacity constraint. Our objective is to derive the statistics information of more flows processed by each kind of sketch so as to draw a more accurate view of traffic statistics. Specifically, we consider the optimization of proportional fairness, so that each kind of sketch can measure many flows without unduly restricting the number of flows measured by other sketches. This optimization metric has been widely adopted in different applications, such as association control [19], rate control [20,21], and resource allocation [22]. *We should note that this paper does not design a new sketch for traffic measurement, but focuses on efficient sketch configuration among all switches.* The main contributions of this paper are:

1. We formulate a spatial sketch configuration with per-switch computing capacity constraint and present a case study of an optimal sketch configuration with per-switch computing capacity constraint for proportional fairness (SCP) problem. The complexity of this problem is analyzed.
2. We then present an efficient algorithm with approximation ratio 1/3 based on the greedy 0–1 knapsack method, and analyze the time complexity of the proposed algorithm.
3. The extensive simulation results show that our proposed algorithm can measure traffic of 44%–91% more flows compared with the existing solution. Besides, our proposed algorithm can make a good tradeoff between the CPU resource and the number of flows.

The rest of this paper is organized as follows. Section 2 introduces the network/sketch models and formulates the SCP problem. We propose an efficient algorithm for SCP and give the detailed performance analysis in Sect. 3. The simulation results are reported in Sect. 4. We conclude the paper in Sect. 5.

2   Preliminaries

In this section, we first introduce some typical sketches and motivate the problem by presenting microbenchmark on software implementations of these sketches. Then we show our solution with an intuitive example. Last, we formally formulate the spatial sketch configuration problem and present a case study of an optimal sketch configuration for proportional fairness problem.

2.1   Testing Results for Sketches' Overhead

This section will test the sketch's computing overhead per packet on the open virtual switch (OVS) [23], and the average number of CPU cycles (or CPU cycles for abbreviation) is adopted as the metric. In our experiment, our OVS runs on a VMware with 1 GB of RAM and 3.7 GHz of CPU frequency, and the sketches are integrated with the OVS. Since packet forwarding costs CPU resource through the OVS, we should avoid this impact on the sketch measurement overhead. To this end, packet forwarding is disabled during the testing. We mainly test the measurement overhead per packet for six sketches, Bloom Filter, Count-Min, k-ary, Cold Filter, CountSketch, and MRAC, respectively. Each of these sketches has 5 rows and 2000 columns, except of Bloom Filter with 1 row and 2000 columns. For each sketch, we take a test during a minute, and count the number, denoted as g, of measured packets on this sketch. Let G be the CPU frequency. Then, we obtain its average CPU cycles for sketch measurement is $\frac{60 \cdot G}{g}$. The number of CPU cycles for six kinds of sketches is listed in Table 1. Obviously, the measurement overhead of CountSketch (350) is much more than that of Count-Min (78), for CountSketch needs additional heap operations besides updating.

Table 1. Number of CPU cycles for per packet's measurement

Bloom filter	Count-min	K-ary	Cold filter	CountSketch	MRAC
77	78	81	150	350	404

2.2   A Motivation Example for Sketch Configuration

In this section, we give an example to motivate our solution. As shown in Fig. 1, there are three flows $\{\gamma_1, \gamma_2, \gamma_3\}$ in the network. We assume that the arrival rate of each flow is 10 packets per second. The controller requires to deploy two sketches $\{s_1, s_2\}$ for all three flows. For simplicity, the measurement overhead of each sketch per packet is denoted as 1 unit. In the left plot of Fig. 1, two sketches are enabled on each switch. As a result, the measurement overhead on switches v_1, v_3, v_4, and v_5 is 40 packets per second. Through proper sketch configuration, each switch just enables one sketch at most, as illustrated in the right plot of Fig. 1. Therefore, there only need 4 sketches for measurement of flows γ_1, γ_2, and γ_3, and the maximum measurement overhead among all switches is reduced. Specifically, the measurement overhead on switches v_1, v_3, v_4, and v_5 is reduced to 20 packets per second, as described in Table 2.

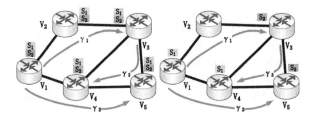

Fig. 1. An example of sketch configuration. *Left plot*: without sketch configuration; *right plot*: with proper sketch configuration.

Motivated by this example, we should enable a subset of sketches on each switch for efficient traffic measurement. To this end, there are two different ways. One is called *sketch placement* [24]. That is, the controller only places those proper (or enabled) sketches on switches. The other is sketch configuration. That is, all sketches are pre-deployed on a switch, and the state of each sketch can be dynamically configured (on or off) by the controller. The first way is memory efficient, for each switch only keeps a subset of all sketches. However, network traffic is dynamic and ever-changing [18], and the sketch placement needs to be adjusted based on the observed traffic statistics with an online manner to meet the capacity constraints. The former, unfortunately, hinders such processes as the sketch software needs to be compiled to work again.

Table 2. Illustration of measurement overhead on switches

	v_1	v_2	v_3	v_4	v_5
Without configuration	40	20	40	40	40
With configuration	20	0	20	20	20

2.3 General Optimization of Sketch Configuration

An SDN typically consists of a logically-centralized controller and a set of switches, $V = \{v_1, ..., v_n\}$, with $n = |V|$. These switches comprise the data plane of an SDN. Thus, the network topology of the data plane can be modeled by G. Note that the logical controller may be a cluster of distributed controllers [25], which help to balance the control overhead among these controllers. Since we focus on the per-switch measurement overhead, the number of controllers will not significantly impact this metric. For simplicity, we assume that there is only one controller.

We define the spatial sketch configuration problem. Under the general SDN framework, we denote the flow based on originator-destination (OD) pairs as $\Gamma = \{\gamma_1, ..., \gamma_m\}$, with $m = |\Gamma|$. For simplicity, we assume that each flow will be forwarded through only one path. With the advantage of centralized control in an SDN, the controller knows all the installed rules on switches, thus mastering the route path of each OD-pair/flow. Let P_{γ_k} denote the path of flow γ_k. The set of flows (or pairs) passing through switch v_i is denoted as Γ_i. In an SDN network, each switch can count the number of forwarded packets through port statistics, and we can derive the total number of forwarded packets on a switch by adding them together. We denote the set of packets passing through switch v_i as $\mathcal{P}_i$.

To fulfill different application requirements, we assume that each switch has deployed a set of q sketches, denoted as $\mathcal{S} = \{s_1, ..., s_q\}$. These sketches are able to measure traffic for different objects. For sketch s_j, its measurement/computing overhead per packet is denoted as $c(s_j)$, which can be measured by the number of CPU cycles. We will configure the status (on or off) of each sketch on a switch. If the status of a sketch is on, we call this sketch "enable". To avoid the additional control on switches, we assume that each arrival packet will be measured by all enabled sketches on this switch. As a result, the total measurement overhead on each switch v_i is denoted as $c(v_i)$. Due to limited computing power on each switch, we expect a given fraction (*e.g.*, 30%) of computing capacity for traffic measurement. Thus, the computing overhead for traffic measurement on switch v_i should not exceed the threshold C_i.

In many applications, such as flow spread and traffic change detection, it is expected that more flows can be measured. In the following, if all packets of a flow are measured by sketch s_j, we call that this flow is *covered* by sketch s_j. $f(\gamma_k)$ denotes the value of attributes (*e.g.* traffic size) of flow γ_k and H_j denotes the lower bound of the attributes of measured flows. In Sect. 2.4, we study a special case of optimal sketch configuration for proportional fairness for better network performance.

Accordingly we formalize the spatial sketch configuration problem as follows:

$$\max\ G(H_1, ..., H_q)$$

$$S.t. \begin{cases} \sum_{v_i \in P_{\gamma_k}} x_i^j \geq z_k^j, & \forall \gamma_k, s_j \\ \sum_{\gamma_k \in \Gamma} z_k^j \cdot f(\gamma_k) \geq H_j, & \forall s_j \\ c(v_i) = \sum_{s_j \in \mathcal{S}} x_i^j \cdot c(s_j) \cdot |\mathcal{P}_i| \leq C_i, & \forall v_i \\ x_i^j, z_k^j \in \{0, 1\}, & \forall s_j, v_i, \gamma_k \end{cases} \tag{1}$$

where x_i^j denotes the result of sketch configuration by the controller. That is, if $x_i^j = 1$, the sketch s_j is enabled on switch v_i. Otherwise, its status is off. The first set of inequalities denotes whether flow γ_k is covered ($z_k^j = 1$) by sketch s_j or not. The second set of inequalities ensures that the attribute of measured flows (*e.g.*, the number of measured flows or the traffic amount of measured flows) by sketch s_j is not less than H_j, where $f(\gamma_k)$ represents the attributes of measured flows, *e.g.*, traffic information. For example, if we let $f(\gamma_k)$ be 1, this set of inequalities means that sketch s_j can measure at least H_j flows. The third set of inequalities means the cost on each switch v_i should not exceed its computation threshold C_i. The objective is to maximize the function $G(H_1, ..., H_q)$, which refers to the attributes of measured flows.

2.4 A Case Study of Optimal Sketch Configuration for Proportional Fairness

In this section, we consider a special case (aiming to make an optimal sketch configuration for proportional fairness) of the general sketch configuration.

Based on the basic description in Sect. 2.3, after sketch configuration, the total number of covered flows by sketch s_j is denoted as β_j. We set $f(\gamma_k)$ as 1 and H_j as β_j. Due to CPU resource constraint on commodity SDN switches, we may not cover all flows. One natural objective is to maximize the minimum number of covered flows among all sketches, *i.e.*, max-min fairness. This fairness manner is simple, but may reduce the total number of covered flows measured by all these sketches. Thus, our goal is to propose an optimal sketch configuration in a proportional fairness manner [19,26]; the configuration allows each sketch measuring enough flows without unduly restricting the number of flows measured by other sketches, *i.e.*, $\max \sum_{j=1}^{q} \log \beta_j$.

According to Eq. (1), we formalize the problem of sketch configuration problem with the limited CPU capacity (SCP). The objective function of proportional fairness can be referred to the definition in [26].

$$\max \quad \sum_{j=1}^{q} \log \beta_j$$

$$S.t. \begin{cases} \sum_{v_i \in P_{\gamma_k}} x_i^j \geq z_k^j, & \forall \gamma_k, s_j \\ \sum_{\gamma_k \in \Gamma} z_k^j \geq \beta_j, & \forall s_j \\ c(v_i) = \sum_{s_j \in S} x_i^j \cdot c(s_j) \cdot |\mathcal{P}_i| \leq C_i, & \forall v_i \\ x_i^j, z_k^j \in \{0,1\}, & \forall s_j, v_i, \gamma_k, \end{cases} \quad (2)$$

The definition of x_i^j is same as that in Eq. (1). The first set of inequalities denotes whether flow γ_k is covered ($z_k^j = 1$) by sketch s_j or not. The second set of inequalities ensures that at least β_j flows will be covered by sketch s_j. The third set of inequalities means the cost on each switch v_i should not exceed C_i, in which C_i is the reserved computing capacity for traffic measurement on switch v_i. The objective is to optimize the proportional fairness among all sketches.

Theorem 1. *The SCP problem defined in Eq. (2) is NP-hard.*

Proof. Assuming that there is only one switch in a network, only some specified sketches can be selected to cover flows passing through the switch with the CPU constraint. That is, this becomes a 0–1 knapsack problem [27], which is NP-Hard. Since the case that there is only one switch in a network is a special case of our problem, the SCK problem is NP-Hard too.

3 Algorithm Design of Proportional Fairness

Due to the NP-hardness, the SCP problem cannot be solved in polynomial time. In this section, we propose an efficient algorithm, and analyze its approximation factor.

Algorithm 1. SCK: Sketch Configuration using 0-1 Knapsack
_____
1: $V =$ a set of all switches.
2: **for** each switch $v_i \in V$ **do**
3:     **for** each sketch $s_j \in \mathcal{S}$ **do**
4:         $p(s_j^i) = \log |\Gamma_i|$
5:         $c(s_j^i) = c(s_j) \cdot |\mathcal{P}_i|$
6:     **end for**
7: **end for**
8: **while** $|V| > 0$ **do**
9:     **Step 1: Choosing a switch with maximum profit**
10:     Regard every switch v_i as a package and compute the profit $p(v_i)$ using greedy 0-1 knapsack [27]
11:     Select switch v_i with the maximum profit
12:     The enabled sketch set on switch v_i is denoted as $\mathcal{S}'$
13:     Set the status of each sketch in $\mathcal{S}'$ on, and others off
14:     The flow set covered by $s_j \in \mathcal{S}'$ is denoted as $\overline{\Pi}_j$
15:     $V = V - \{v_i\}$
16:     **Step 2: Updating the profit of each sketch**
17:     **for** each switch $v_i \in V$ **do**
18:         **for** each sketch $s_j \in \mathcal{S}$ **do**
19:             $p(s_j^i) = \log |\Gamma_i \cup \overline{\Pi}_j| - \log |\overline{\Pi}_j|$
20:         **end for**
21:     **end for**
22: **end while**
_____

3.1   Algorithm Design

In this section, we present a sketch configuration (SCK) algorithm based on 0–1 knapsack [27] for proportional fairness. The detailed description of the SCK algorithm is given in Algorithm 1. Initially, the profit of each sketch on switch v_i is $\log |\Gamma_i|$ (Line 4), where Γ_i denotes the set of flows passing through switch v_i. The cost of each sketch s_j on switch v_i is denoted as $c(s_j^i) = c(s_j) \cdot |\mathcal{P}_i|$, where $c(s_j)$ is the computing overhead per packet and $\mathcal{P}_i$ denotes the set of packets through switch v_i. The algorithm mainly consists of iterations, each of which is divided into two steps. In the first step, for each switch, we compute the maximum profit using the greedy 0–1 knapsack method [27] under a computing cost constraint (Line 10). Then, we choose a switch, denoted as v_i, with the maximum profit, determine the set of enable sketches on switch v_i, and update the set of covered flows by these sketches. In the second step, we update the profit for each sketch s_j on switch v_i as $p(s_j^i) = \log |\Gamma_i \cup \overline{\Pi}_j| - \log |\overline{\Pi}_j|$ (Line 19), where $\overline{\Pi}_j$ denotes the current set of flows covered by sketch s_j.

3.2   Greedy Method for the 0–1 Knapsack Problem [28]

As described above, the 0–1 knapsack algorithm is a core module for the SCK algorithm. For each switch v_i, we regard each sketch s_j as an item, whose profit and cost are denoted as $p(s_j^i)$ and $c(s_j^i)$, respectively. Our objective is to maximize the total profit of the selected items with a total cost constraint C_i. The knapsack algorithm first computes the profit-cost ratio for each sketch s_j as: $\delta(s_j^i) = \frac{p(s_j^i)}{c(s_j^i)}$. Then, we sort all the sketches by the decreasing order of their profit-cost ratios. Finally, we check each sketch to determine whether this sketch will be selected or not with cost constraint. The formal algorithm is described in Algorithm 2.

Algorithm 2. Greedy Method for 0-1 knapsack on switch v_i

1: **for** each sketch $s_j \in \mathcal{S}$ **do**

2:     Compute the profit-cost ratio as $\delta(s_j^i) = \frac{p(s_j^i)}{c(s_j^i)}$

3: **end for**

4: Sort the sketches by the decreasing order of their profit-cost ratios

5: **for** each sketch $s_j \in \mathcal{S}$ **do**

6:     **if** $c(s_j^i) \leq C_i$ **then**

7:         $p(v_i) = p(v_i) + p(s_j^i)$

8:         $C_i = C_i - c(s_j^i)$

9:     **end if**

10: **end for**

3.3   Performance Analysis

We first prove a simple conclusion, which will serve performance analysis of the SCK algorithm. Assume that Y and Z are arbitrary non-empty sets.

Lemma 1. $\log |Y_1 \cup Z| + \log |Y_2 \cup Z| \geq \log |Y \cup Z| + \log |Z|$, where $Y_1 \cup Y_2 = Y$, and $Y_1 \cap Y_2 = \phi$.

Proof. Assume that $|Y| = y$ and $|Z| = z$. Moreover, $|Y_1 \cup Z| = z + y_1$, and $|Y_2 \cup Z| = z + y_2$. Then, we have $|Y \cup Z| = z + y_1 + y_2$. Obviously, $(z + y_1) \cdot (z + y_2) \geq z \cdot (z + y_1 + y_2)$. As a result, $\log |Y_1 \cup Z| + \log |Y_2 \cup Z| \geq \log |Y \cup Z| + \log |Z|$.

Now, we give the following lemma. Given a set Y, we consider a division $\{Y_1, ..., Y_n\}$ of set Y. That is, $Y_1 \cup ... \cup Y_n = Y$, and $Y_i \cap Y_j = \phi$, $\forall i, j$.

Lemma 2. $\sum_i (\log |Y_i \cup Z| - \log |Z|) \geq \log |Y \cup Z| - \log |Z|$.

Proof. We prove this lemma by induction on variable n. When $n = 1$ or 2, the lemma is proved. We assume that the lemma is proved for any $n \leq k$. Now, we consider the case $n = k + 1$.

$$\sum_{i=1}^{k+1}(\log|Y_i \cup Z| - \log|Z|) = \sum_{i=1}^{k-1}(\log|Y_i \cup Z| - \log|Z|) + (\log|Y_k \cup Z| - \log|Z|)$$
$$+ (\log|Y_{k+1} \cup Z| - \log|Z|) \geq \sum_{i=1}^{k-1}(\log|Y_i \cup Z| - \log|Z|) + (\log|(Y_k \cup Y_{k+1}) \cup Z| - \log|Z|)$$
$$\geq \log|(Y_1 \cup ... \cup Y_{k+1}) \cup Z| - \log|Z| \qquad (3)$$
$$= \log|Y \cup Z| - \log|Z|$$

Note that the third and fourth inequalities follow by the induction as $n = 2$ and $n = k$, respectively.

Let Q_i and Q_i' be two vectors of flow sets passing through switch v_i as follows: $Q_i = [Q_{i,1}, ..., Q_{i,q}]$ and $Q_i' = [Q_{i,1}', ..., Q_{i,q}']$, where $Q_{i,j}$ and $Q_{i,j}'$ are both sets of flows covered by sketch s_j on switch v_i. We define the profit of Q_i as $\omega(Q_i) = \sum_{j=1}^{q} \log|Q_{i,j}|$. For simplicity, we also define a vector operation as follows:

$$\omega(Q_i \uplus Q_i') = \sum_{j=1}^{q} \log|Q_{i,j} \cup Q_{i,j}'| \qquad (4)$$

The incremental profit from vectors Q_i' to Q_i is:

$$\omega(Q_i \backslash Q_i') = \omega(Q_i \uplus Q_i') - \omega(Q_i') = \sum_{j=1}^{q} (\log|Q_{i,j} \cup Q_{i,j}'| - \log|Q_{i,j}'|) \qquad (5)$$

In the following, Q_G denotes a vector of flow sets covered by all sketches after the SCK algorithm. In the lth iteration of SCK, G_l' denotes the vector of flow sets covered by all sketches, and the incremental profit is denoted as X_l'. Obviously $X_l' = \omega(G_l' \backslash \uplus_{i=1}^{l-1} G_i')$. For simplicity, the optimal solution for SCP is denoted as OPT.

Lemma 3. *The SCK algorithm can achieve the approximation ratio $1/3$ for the SCP problem.*

Proof. Let α be the approximation ratio of the greedy algorithm for 0–1 knapsack. Consider an instant that the SCK algorithm has executed l-1 iterations. In the lth iteration, the algorithm chooses the switch $v_{l'}$. Assume that the optimal solution will select a vector of covered flow sets, denoted as O_l, from switch $v_{l'}$. If we choose O_l instead of G_l' in this iteration, the incremental profit becomes $\omega(O_l \backslash \uplus_{i=1}^{l-1} G_i')$, denoted as X''_l. Obviously, we have $X_l' \geq \alpha \cdot X_l'' = \alpha \cdot \omega(O_l \backslash \uplus_{i=1}^{l-1} G_i') \geq \alpha \cdot \omega(O_l \backslash Q_G)$. It follows

$$\omega(Q_G) = \sum_{l=1}^{n} X_l' \geq \sum_{l=1}^{n} \alpha \cdot \omega(O_l \backslash Q_G) = \alpha \cdot \sum_{l=1}^{n} \omega(O_l \backslash Q_G) \geq \alpha \cdot \omega(\uplus_{l=1}^{m} O_l \backslash Q_G)$$
$$= \alpha \cdot \sum_{l=1}^{n} [\omega(O_l \uplus Q_G) - \omega(Q_G)] \geq \alpha \cdot [\omega(\uplus_{l=1}^{n} O_l \uplus Q_G) - \omega(Q_G)]$$
$$= \alpha \cdot [\omega(OPT \uplus Q_G) - \omega(Q_G)] \geq \alpha \cdot [\omega(OPT) - \omega(Q_G)]$$

Thus, we have

$$\omega(Q_G) \geq \frac{\alpha}{1+\alpha} \cdot \omega(OPT) \tag{6}$$

Since the greedy method achieves the approximation ratio $1/2$ for 0–1 knapsack [27], by Eq. (6), the SCK algorithm can achieve the approximation ratio $1/3$ for SCP.

4 Performance Evaluation

In this section, we first introduce the metrics and benchmarks for performance comparison (Sect. 4.1). We then evaluate our proposed algorithm by comparing with the random method through simulations (Sect. 4.2).

4.1 Performance Metrics and Benchmarks

In this paper, we expect to measure more flows with proportional fairness, which benefits different applications, *e.g.*, traffic engineering, with the constraint of CPU processing capacity through efficient sketch configuration. Thus, we adopt the following metric in our numerical evaluations.

1. *Flow cover ratio (FCR)*. The controller computes the number of covered flows by each sketch. The flow cover ratio is defined as the number of covered flows dividing the number of all flows in the network. We denote the flow cover ratio of each sketch as $\theta_j = \beta_j/m$, where β_j is the number of flows covered by sketch s_j and m is the number of flows in the network. In this paper, we measure three metrics of FCR, the average, the maximum and the minimum, respectively. For example, the average flow cover ratio is $\overline{\theta} = \sum_{j=1}^{q} \theta_j/q$.

According to [29], it considers the memory allocation of multiple sketches for accurate traffic measurement. We consider the CPU resource allocation of multiple sketches instead of memory allocation in the paper. Specifically, the controller will choose sketches in order to cover as many as flows configured on each switch with the CPU processing capacity constraint. The detailed algorithm called *SCREAM* is referred to [29,30]. Besides, we compare the proposed SCK algorithm with the random solution, denoted as *RND*, through both simulations and prototype experiments. Specifically, the controller will randomly choose sketches configured on each switch with the CPU processing capacity constraint.

4.2 Simulation Evaluation

Simulation Setting. In the simulations, as running examples, we select two practical and typical topologies: one for campus networks and the other for data center networks. The first topology, denoted as (a), contains 100 switches, 200 servers and 397 links from [31]. The second one is the fat-tree topology [32], denoted as (b), which has been widely used in many data center networks.

The fat-tree topology has in total 80 switches (including 16 core switches, 32 aggregation switches, and 32 edge switches) and 192 servers. To observe the impact of different traffic traces on the measurement performance, we adopt two types of traffic traces. One is the 2–8 distribution. Specifically, the authors of [12] have shown that less than 20% of the top-ranked flows may be responsible for more than 80% of the total traffic. The other is that the traffic size of each flow follows the Gaussian distribution. We adopt six kinds of sketches, Count-Min, CountSketch, Bloom Filter, Cold Filter, MRAC and k-ary, respectively, in our simulation. The sketch computing overhead per packet is listed in Table 1. By observing the configuration of some commodity SDN switches, $e.g.$, H3C and Pica8, the switch's CPU capacity is set as 3 GHz, and we assume that at most 50% CPU capacity will be allocated for traffic measurement. We execute each simulation 100 times, and take the average of the numerical results.

Simulation Results. We run two groups of simulations to check the effectiveness of the SCK algorithm. The first group of four simulations observes the FCR by changing the CPU capacity constraints from 0.5 GHz to 1.5 GHz. We generate 30K flows by default in the network. Figures 2 and 3 show that the average flow cover ratio is increasing with enhanced CPU capacity constraints for all algorithms. Our SCK algorithm can significantly improve the flow cover ratio compared with SCREAM and RND. Specifically, given the CPU capacity constraint of 1 GHz, the average FCR by our SCK algorithm is 0.89, while SCREAM and RND achieve the average FCRs only about 0.67 and 0.48, respectively, by the Fig. 2. That is, our proposed algorithm can improve the average flow cover ratio by 33% and 85% compared with SCREAM and RND. Moreover, the average FCR of SCK is always near to the optimal result with the CPU capacity increasing. For example, the average FCR of SCK is about 96% of that of the optimal result under the CPU capacity constraint of 1 GHz in Fig. 2.

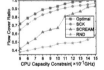 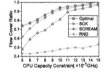 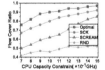 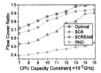

Fig. 2. Flow cover ratio vs. CPU capacity constraint under 2–8 distribution with topology (a)

Fig. 3. Flow cover ratio vs. CPU capacity constraint under 2–8 distribution with topology (b)

Fig. 4. Flow cover ratio vs. CPU capacity constraint under Gaussian distribution with topology (a)

Fig. 5. Flow cover ratio vs. CPU capacity constraint under Gaussian distribution with topology (b)

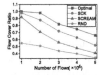 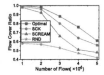 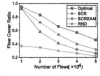 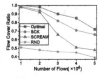

Fig. 6. Flow cover ratio vs. number of flows under 2–8 distribution with topology (a)

Fig. 7. Flow cover ratio vs. number of flows under 2–8 distribution with topology (b)

Fig. 8. Flow cover ratio vs. number of flows under Gaussian distribution with topology (a)

Fig. 9. Flow cover ratio vs. number of flows under Gaussian distribution with topology (b).

Figures 4 and 5 plot the FCR under the Gaussian traffic distribution. The trend of these curves is similar as that of curves in Figs. 2 and 3. We find that our SCK algorithm can improve the average FCR by 30% compared with SCREAM under the CPU capacity constraint of 1 GHz by Figs. 4 and 5. When the CPU capacity constraint is 1 GHz, we observe that SCK can improve the average FCR by 51%–89% compared with the RND algorithm by Figs. 4 and 5. Moreover, the average FCR of SCK is always near to the optimal result with the CPU capacity increasing. For example, the average FCR of SCK is about 90% of that of the optimal result under the CPU capacity constraint of 1 GHz.

In the second simulation set, we observe the FCR by changing the number of flows from 10K to 50K. By default, we set the CPU capacity constraint as 0.8 GHz. Figures 6, 7, 8 and 9 show that the average flow cover ratio is decreasing with more flows in the network. Specifically, when there are 30K flows in the network, the average FCR of SCK is 0.72 by the left plot and 0.85 by the right plot in Fig. 7. Moreover, SCK can improve the average FCR 30%–78% compared with SCREAM and RND by Fig. 6 and 7. Besides, the average FCR of SCK is at least 79% of that of the optimal result with the number of flows increasing in Figs. 6 and 7. That is, SCK can achieve the similar performance with the optimal result.

From these simulation results in Figs. 2, 3, 4, 5, 6, 7, 8 and 9, we can make the following conclusions. First, our algorithm achieves the similar measurement performance compared with the optimal result. For example, the average FCR of SCK is about 96% of that of the optimal result under the CPU capacity constraint of 1 GHz in Figs. 2 and 3. Second, our SCK algorithm can achieve better flow cover ratio than SCREAM and RND. For example, our SCK algorithm can improve the average flow cover ratio by 30%–91% compared with SCREAM and RND by Fig. 2. According to SCREAM [29,30], the flows covered by the applied sketchs hould meet the requirements of a certain kind of sketch in a certain order before choosing the next one, which makes a large gap in the number of flows covered by all types of sketch. Thus, our SCK algorithm performs better than SCREAM and RND on proportional fairness.

5   Conclusion

In this paper, we studied how to perform optimal sketch configuration on switches for proportional fairness. We proposed the SCP problem, and designed an efficient algorithm with approximation ratio 1/3 for this problem. We implemented the proposed algorithm on our SDN platform, and the simulation results showed high efficiency of our proposed algorithm. In the future, we will study the trade-off between sketch's memory cost, measurement accuracy and computing cost for more practical designs.

References

1. Hong, C.-Y., et al.: Achieving high utilization with software-driven wan. In: ACM SIGCOMM, pp. 15–26 (2013)
2. Li, D., Shang, Y., Chen, C.: Software defined green data center network with exclusive routing. In: IEEE INFOCOM, pp. 1743–1751 (2014)
3. Wang, B., Zheng, Y., Lou, W., Hou, Y.T.: DDoS attack protection in the era of cloud computing and software-defined networking. Comput. Netw. **81**, 308–319 (2015)
4. Yan, Q., Yu, F.R., Gong, Q., Li, J.: Software-defined networking (SDN) and distributed denial of service (DDoS) attacks in cloud computing environments: A survey, some research issues, and challenges. IEEE Commun. Surv. Tutorials **18**(1), 602–622 (2016)
5. Agarwal, S., Kodialam, M., Lakshman, T.: Traffic engineering in software defined networks. In: IEEE INFOCOM, pp. 2211–2219 (2013)
6. Su, Z., Wang, T., Xia, Y., Hamdi, M.: Flowcover: Low-cost flow monitoring scheme in software defined networks. In: Global Communications Conference (GLOBE-COM), pp. 1956–1961. IEEE (2014)
7. Xu, H., Yu, Z., Qian, C., Li, X.-Y., Liu, Z.: Minimizing flow statistics collection cost of sdn using wildcard requests. In: INFOCOM 2017-IEEE Conference on Computer Communications, IEEE. pp. 1–9. IEEE (2017)
8. Estan, C., Keys, K., Moore, D., Varghese, G.: Building a better netflow. ACM SIGCOMM Comput. Commun. Rev. **34**(4), 245–256 (2004)
9. Phaal, P., Lavine, M.: sflow version 5. http://www.sflow.org/sflow_version_5.txt. Accessed July 2004
10. Kumar, A., Xu, J., Wang, J.: Space-code bloom filter for efficient per-flow traffic measurement. IEEE J. Sel. Areas Commun. **24**(12), 2327–2339 (2006)
11. Li, T., Chen, S., Ling, Y.: Per-flow traffic measurement through randomized counter sharing. Netw. IEEE/ACM Trans. **20**(5), 1622–1634 (2012)
12. Curtis, A.R., Mogul, J.C., Tourrilhes, J., Yalagandula, P., Sharma, P., Banerjee, S.: DevoFlow: scaling flow management for high-performance networks. ACM SIGCOMM Comput. Commun. Rev. **41**(4), 254–265 (2011)
13. Yu, M., Jose, L., Miao, R.: Software defined traffic measurement with opensketch. In: the 10th USENIX Symposium on Networked Systems Design and Implementation, pp. 29–42 (2013)
14. Huang, Q., et al.: Sketchvisor: robust network measurement for software packet processing. In: Proceedings of the Conference of the ACM Special Interest Group on Data Communication, pp. 113–126. ACM (2017)

15. Cormode, G., Muthukrishnan, S.: An improved data stream summary: the count-min sketch and its applications. J. Algorithms **55**(1), 58–75 (2005)
16. Wang, A., Guo, Y., Hao, F., Lakshman, T., Chen, S.: Scotch: elastically scaling up SDN control-plane using vswitch based overlay. In: Proceedings of the 10th ACM International on Conference on emerging Networking Experiments and Technologies, pp. 403–414. ACM (2014)
17. Sekar, V., Reiter, M.K., Willinger, W., Zhang, H., Kompella, R.R., Andersen, D.G.: csamp: a system for network-wide flow monitoring. In: NSDI, vol. 8, pp. 233–246 (2008)
18. Yu, Y., Qian, C., Li, X.: Distributed and collaborative traffic monitoring in software defined networks. In: Proceedings of the third workshop on HotSDN, pp. 85–90. ACM (2014)
19. Li, W., et al.: AP association for proportional fairness in multirate WLANs. IEEE/ACM Trans. Netw. (TON) **22**(1), 191–202 (2014)
20. Wang, X., Kar, K.: Cross-layer rate control for end-to-end proportional fairness in wireless networks with random access. In: Proceedings of the 6th ACM International Symposium on Mobile ad hoc Networking and Computing, pp. 157–168. ACM (2005)
21. Alizadeh, M., et al.: Data center tcp (dctcp). ACM SIGCOMM Comput. Commun. Rev. **41**(4), 63–74 (2011)
22. Wang, S., Huang, F., Wang, C.: Adaptive proportional fairness resource allocation for of dm-based cognitive radio networks. Wirel. Netw. **19**(3), 273–284 (2013)
23. Open vswitch http://openvswitch.org/
24. Liu, Z., Manousis, A., Vorsanger, G., Sekar, V., Braverman, V.: One sketch to rule them all: Rethinking network flow monitoring with univmon. In: Proceedings of the 2016 conference on ACM SIGCOMM 2016 Conference, pp. 101–114. ACM (2016)
25. Wang, T., Liu, F., Guo, J., Xu, H.: Dynamic SDN controller assignment in data center networks: stable matching with transfers. In: Proceedings of INFOCOM (2016)
26. Li, L., Pal, M., Yang, Y. R.: Proportional fairness in multi-rate wireless lans. In: INFOCOM 2008. The 27th Conference on Computer Communications. IEEE, pp. 1004–1012. IEEE (2008)
27. Gupta, A.: Approximations algorithms (2005)
28. Deng, C.S., Liang, C.Y.: Mixed coding greedy differential evolution algorithm for 0–1 knapsack problem. Comput. Eng. **35**(23), 24–26 (2009)
29. Moshref, M., Yu, M., Govindan, R., Vahdat, A.: Scream: sketch resource allocation for software-defined measurement. In: CoNEXT, Heidelberg, Germany (2015)
30. Kwak, J., Kim, Y., Lee, J., Chong, S.: Dream: dynamic resource and task allocation for energy minimization in mobile cloud systems. IEEE J. Sel. Areas Commun. **33**(12), 2510–2523 (2015)
31. The network topology from the monash university. http://www.ecse.monash.edu.au/twiki/bin/view/InFocus/LargePacket-switchingNetworkTopologies
32. Al-Fares, M., Loukissas, A., Vahdat, A.: A scalable, commodity data center network architecture. In: ACM SIGCOMM Computer Communication Review, vol. 38, no. 4, pp. 63–74. ACM (2008)

Estimating Clustering Coefficient of Multiplex Graphs with Local Differential Privacy

Zichun Liu[✉], Hongli Xu[✉], Liusheng Huang[✉], and Wei Yang

School of Computer Science and Technology, University of Science and Technology of China, Hefei 230026, Anhui, China
lzc223@mail.ustc.edu.cn, {xuhongli,lshuang,qubit}@ustc.edu.cn

Abstract. Multiplex graph analysis occupies a prominent position in many real-world applications, such as commodity recommendation, marketing and pandemic tracking. Due to the existence of untrusted data curators, it is in urgent need to design decentralized privacy mechanisms for analyzing multiplex graphs. Local differential privacy(LDP) is an emerging technique for preserving decentralized private data, which has drawn a great deal of attention from academic and industrial fields. The potential of LDP has been proved in various graph analysis tasks in recent researches. However, existing LDP studies may result in insufficient privacy preservation and heavy computation burden for multiplex graphs. In this paper, we introduce an eclectic privacy definition for multiplex graphs. Under this definition, we propose a randomized mechanism, called $RALL$, to estimate clustering coefficient of multiplex graphs with lower computation cost and higher protection strength. Furthermore, we present a post-processing method to improve the estimation accuracy. The effectiveness and efficiency of $RALL$ mechanism are validated through extensive experiments.

Keywords: Local differential privacy · Multiplex graphs · Clustering coefficient

1 Introduction

Graph analysis occupies a prominent position in socializing, trading and biology. Through mining multidimensional data contained in these graphs, data curators can make profits in many applications, such as commodity recommendation [11], marketing [3] and pandemic tracking [1]. However, along with the rapid expansion of machine learning and big data, centralized databases are becoming increasingly unreliable for storing sensitive graph data. Therefore, it is in urgent need to design alternative decentralized privacy mechanism.

Since its inception, the emerging technique *Local differential Privacy* [5] has drawn a great deal of attention from academic and industrial fields. Without

© Springer Nature Switzerland AG 2021
Z. Liu et al. (Eds.): WASA 2021, LNCS 12939, pp. 390–398, 2021.
https://doi.org/10.1007/978-3-030-86137-7_42

requiring trusted data curators, LDP provides strong and rigorous preservation for decentralized private data. Furthermore, after LDPGen [9] brings LDP to graph data, the potential of LDP has been proved in various graph analysis tasks [10,13,15], which makes graph LDP a research hotspot. Graph LDP researches are mainly based on two solutions, Laplace mechanism [6] and Randomized Response [12], respectively. Laplace based methods are applicable to general problems, but perform poor in certain analysis tasks requiring neighboring information [14]; RR based methods protect structural information in graphs, but cause a denser graph problem [9], which could be more severe in multiplex graphs. A recent research [15] manages to combine the advantages of these two solutions. However, directly applying these mechanisms from monolayer graphs to multiplex graphs may suffer from heavy computation cost. Furthermore, most graph LDP researches focus on edge LDP, but practical scenarios of multiplex graphs raise the demand for new privacy definition. For example, in a social network, individuals are linked with different kinds of relations: friendship, partnership, membership, coworker-ship, vicinity, kinship or sexual relations, and some of these relation labels are also sensitive, so they may require both their links and labels to be protected.

To overcome these obstacles, we review the conventional node-based [8] and edge-based [2] privacy definition in graphs, and propose an eclectic granularity definition for multiplex graphs, which strikes balance between utility and privacy. Under this definition, we present *RALL* mechanism to deal with the high computation cost and excessive noise introduced by the characteristic of multiplex graphs. As a byproduct of aggregating perturbed statistics, we also design a post-processing method to further improve estimation accuracy. Our contributions can be summarized as follows:

- We propose layer local differential privacy definition for multiplex graphs.
- We formulate the problem of estimating clustering coefficient of multiplex graphs under local differential privacy.
- We utilize the relations between adjacency matrix and degree sequence to improve estimation accuracy.
- We present the RALL mechanism, and validate its effectiveness and efficiency based on extensive experiments with two comparative methods.

The rest of this paper is organized as follows. Section 2 introduces preliminaries. Section 3 describes the details of *RALL* mechanism. Section 4 illustrates the experimental results. Section 5 concludes the paper.

2   Preliminaries

2.1   Multiplex Graphs

A multiplex graph, $\mathcal{G} = \{G_\alpha | \alpha \in \{1, ..., m\}\}$ is defined as m layers of graphs, where each layer is an undirected graphs $G_\alpha = (V_\alpha, E_\alpha)$, with V_α representing the nodes in layer α and E_α representing edges in layer α. Clustering coefficient quantifies the tendency of nodes to form triangles, and such an important measure can be extended to multiplex graphs. The general clustering coefficient definition of a given node i is the ratio of *existing* links and the *largest possible* links between neighbors of i. For node $i \in V$, let $\mathcal{N}_\alpha(i)$ be the set containing neighbors of i in layer α, and $\mathcal{L}_\alpha(i) = \{(j, k) \in E_\alpha$ and $k, j \in \mathcal{N}_\alpha(i)\}$ is the set of existing links between neighbors. Then the formal definition of *clustering coefficient* is given below:

$$C_{\mathcal{M}}(i) = \frac{2\sum_{\alpha=1}^m |\mathcal{L}_\alpha(i)|}{\sum_{\alpha=1}^m |\mathcal{N}_\alpha(i)|(|\mathcal{N}_\alpha(i)| - 1)} \tag{1}$$

2.2 Local Differential Privacy on Graphs

Local Differential Privacy. (LDP) has been the standard local privacy preservation method since its inception [5]. Without relying on the assumption of a trusted data curator, each user perturbs private data with LDP mechanism in his/her own devices, and then sends the perturbed results to the server, thus preserving privacy locally. To protect private graph data, LDP on graph leads to two variant definitions: *node LDP* [8] and *edge LDP* [2]. Node LDP provides stronger privacy preservation than edge LDP, but the resulting estimation utility is poor. Edge LDP reaches better utility, yet providing insufficient privacy protection in some practical scenarios. However, in Multiplex graph, the granularity of privacy can be divided more finely, thus we propose *layer LDP* to protect both edges and layers for multiplex graphs.

Definition 1 *(Layer Local Differential Privacy): A randomized mechanism $\mathcal{A}$ satisfies ϵ-layer local differential privacy, if and only if for any two neighboring lists $\mathcal{N}, \mathcal{N}'$ differing in one layer, and any $\ell \in Range(\mathcal{A})$,*

$$Pr[\mathcal{A}(\mathcal{N}) = \ell] \le exp(\epsilon) \cdot Pr[\mathcal{A}(\mathcal{N}') = \ell]$$

3 The RALL Mechanism

3.1 Overview

In this section, we present our *RALL* mechanism as in Fig. 1. For each individual, *RALL* is locally executed to randomize two statistics. After the two randomization processes, the perturbed adjacency lists and degree sequences are sent to server. As in server side, the correlated neighboring lists and degree sequences are utilized to enhance the understanding of local graph structures. We denote the edge with two nodes reporting (1,1), (1,0)(or (0,1)), (0,0) in adjacency matrix as full edge, half edge and empty edge respectively, and the perturbed edges are considered to be accepted/rejected under the constraints of related degree sequences. With the post-processing method in estimation component, denser graph problem in *RNL* [9] is mitigated, thus better estimation of clustering coefficients is obtained.

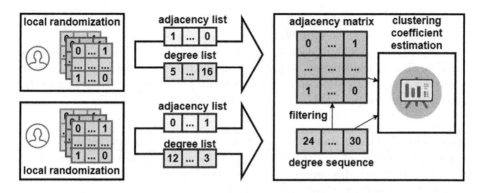

Fig. 1. Model of estimating clustering coefficient of multiplex graph with RALL.

3.2   Projection and Randomization

Data Pre-processing. Two statistics are essential in clustering coefficient estimation [4]: adjacency matrix of projection graph and degree sequences. Given a multiplex graph $\mathcal{G}$, an edge in projection graph $\mathcal{A}_{proj(\mathcal{G})}$, only when the nodes of this edge are linked in some layer, the formal definition is given bellow:

$$
a_{ij} = \begin{cases} 1, if\ a_{ij}^{\alpha} = 1\ for\ some\ 1 \le \alpha \le m \\ 0, otherwise \end{cases}
$$

Adjacency List Randomization. Instead of flipping m vectors in RR [12], we manage to flip one vector with GRR [7]. The core idea is treating the layer information α as label of edges from $[0, 1, 2, ..., m]$, where $[1, 2, ..., m]$ represent m layers respectively and an extra value 0 represents a disconnected edge. Therefore the multiplex graph $\mathcal{G}(i)$ can be encoded as an n-dimensional adjacency vector $\bar{A}(i)$, where each bit $\bar{a}_i$ is a label from $[0, 1, 2, ..., m]$. So one edge exists in projection graph($a_{ij} = 1$) when the label of this edge lies in $[1, 2, ..., m]$, otherwise $a_{ij} = 0$. When changing one existing edge label $\bar{a}_i$ of original graph, the probabilities of the label being reserved, flipped in $[1, 2, ..., m]$ and flipped as 0 are $\frac{e^{\epsilon}}{e^{\epsilon}+m}$, $\frac{1}{e^{\epsilon}+m}$, and $\frac{1}{e^{\epsilon}+m}$ respectively. Therefore the probability of one edge being reserved in projection graph is $p = \frac{e^{\epsilon}+m-1}{e^{\epsilon}+m}$. Similarly, the probability of non-edge node pair being flipped as an edge in projection graph is given as $q = \frac{m}{e^{\epsilon}+m}$. By relating projection adjacency bit with edge values in adjacency list $\bar{A}(i)$, we propose the *randomized aggregated labels*(RAL) method as follows:

$$
Pr[\tilde{a}_{ij} = 1] = \begin{cases} \dfrac{e^{\epsilon} + m - 1}{e^{\epsilon} + m} & ,if\ a_{ij} = 1 \\ \dfrac{m}{e^{\epsilon} + m} & ,if\ a_{ij} = 0 \end{cases} \tag{2}
$$

Degree Sequence Randomization. Degree perturbation adopts Laplace mechanism, with bounded maximum degree θ in truncated graph, the sensitive of degree aggregation is 2θ. Through adding noises drawn from $Lap(\frac{2\theta}{\epsilon})$ to the aggregated degree from different layers, the perturbed degree sequence is given by $\tilde{d}_\alpha(i) = d_\alpha(i) + Lap(2\theta/\epsilon)$.

The detailed randomization component of $RALL$ mechanism is presented in Algorithm 1, the privacy budget ϵ is divided into two parts ϵ_1 and ϵ_2 for adjacency list perturbation and degree sequence perturbation. According to the sequential composition, $RALL$ mechanism satisfies $(\epsilon_1 + \epsilon_2)$-LDP.

Algorithm 1. Graph Randomization Component of RALL mechanism

Input: Multiplex graph $\mathcal{G}(i)$, Privacy budget ϵ, Layer size m, Maximum degree θ
Output: Perturbed adjacency list $\tilde{\mathcal{N}}_{proj(\mathcal{G})}(i)$ and Degree list $\tilde{d}(i)$
1: project and truncate origin multiplex graph
2: **for** each bit in adjacency list $\bar{a}_i \in \bar{A}(i)$ **do**
3:    flip bit in $\mathcal{A}_{proj(\mathcal{G})}(i)$ with probability

$$Pr[\tilde{a}_{ij} = 1] = \begin{cases} \dfrac{e^{\epsilon_1} + m - 1}{e^{\epsilon_1} + m} & , if\ a_{ij} = 1 \\ \dfrac{m}{e^{\epsilon_1} + m} & , if\ a_{ij} = 0 \end{cases}$$

4: **end for**
5: perturb degree sequence as $\tilde{d}_\alpha(i) = d_\alpha(i) + Lap(2\theta/\epsilon_2)$
6: **return** $\tilde{\mathcal{N}}_{proj(\mathcal{G})}(i)$ and $\tilde{d}(i)$

3.3 Clustering Coefficient Estimation

After collecting the randomized data from all users, the general working process of edge filtering is as follows: full edges, denoting as $\tilde{a}_{ij} = \tilde{a}_{ji} = 1$, are accepted with the probability $p_f = min(\frac{\tilde{d}(i)}{|\mathcal{N}_\alpha(i)|}, 1)$, and those full edges that exceed the corresponding degree are randomly truncated. And half edges, where $\tilde{a}_{ij}\ xor\ \tilde{a}_{ji} = 1$, are accepted with the Chung-Lu edge probability $p_h = \frac{\tilde{d}(i)\tilde{d}(j)}{\sum_k \tilde{d}(k)}$, which is also used in LDPGen [9]. Based on the filtering procedure, the probability of one edge being reserved can be calculated as $p_e = p^2 p_f + 2pq p_h$, and the probability of one non-edge being flipped can be calculated as $q_e = q^2 p_f + 2pq p_h$, where $p = \frac{e^\epsilon + m - 1}{e^\epsilon + m}$ and $q = \frac{m}{e^\epsilon + m}$.

During the estimation procedure, the denominator of Eq. 1, which is $\sum_{\alpha=1}^m |\mathcal{N}_\alpha(i)|(|\mathcal{N}_\alpha(i)| - 1)$, can be easily derived from perturbed degree $\tilde{d}_\alpha(i)$, and the numerator $\sum_{\alpha=1}^m |\mathcal{L}_\alpha(i)|$ can be calculated as follows. Note that the nodes in local graph $G(i)$ can be classified in 3 sets, $\mathcal{L}_\alpha(i)$, $\mathcal{N}_\alpha(i) - \mathcal{L}_\alpha(i)$ and others, where $\mathcal{L}_\alpha(i)$ represents the set of two neighbors j, k have edge e_{jk}, and $\mathcal{N}_\alpha(i) - \mathcal{L}_\alpha(i)$ represents neighbors without an direct edge, and others are disconnected nodes. So the expected value of $|\tilde{\mathcal{L}}_\alpha(i)|$ can be calculated by the following parts:

1. Two neighbors of i are originally in $\mathcal{L}_\alpha(i)$, so three edges are reserved with p_e^3;

Algorithm 2. Clustering Coefficient Estimation Component of RALL mehanism

---

Input: Privacy budget ϵ, Perturbed Adjacency list $\tilde{\mathcal{N}}_{proj(\mathcal{G})}$ and Degree list $\tilde{d}$
Output: Estimated clustering coefficient $\tilde{C}_{proj(\mathcal{G})}$ of multiplex graph under ϵ-LDP
1: **for** each node $i \in [1, 2, ..., n]$ **do**
2:      **for** each node $j \in [1, 2, ..., n]$ **do**
3:          filtering adjacency matrix
4:          **if** $\tilde{a}_{ij} = \tilde{a}_{ji} = 1$ **then**
5:              randomly accept the full edges with $p_f = min(\frac{\tilde{d}(i)}{|\mathcal{N}_\alpha(i)|}, 1)$
6:          **end if**
7:          **if** $\tilde{a}_{ij}$ *xor* $\tilde{a}_{ji} = 1$ **then**
8:              randomly accept the half edges with $p_h = \frac{\tilde{d}(i)\tilde{d}(j)}{\sum_k \tilde{d}(k)}$
9:          **end if**
10:     **end for**
11: **end for**
12: **for** each node $i \in [1, 2, ..., n]$ **do**
13:     calculate the existing links set edges $\sum_{\alpha=1}^{m} |\tilde{\mathcal{L}}_\alpha(i)|$
14:     estimate $\mathcal{L}_\alpha^*(i)$ based on equation 3
15:     get an unbiased estimation of clustering coefficient $C_{proj(\mathcal{G})}^*(i) = \frac{2|\mathcal{L}_\alpha^*(i)|}{\tilde{d}(i)(\tilde{d}(i)-1)}$
16: **end for**
17: **return** estimated $C_{proj(\mathcal{G})}^*$

---

2. Two neighbors of i are originally in $\mathcal{N}_\alpha(i) - \mathcal{L}_\alpha(i)$, so two edges are reserved and one edge is flipped with $p_e^2 q_e$;
3. One neighbor is originally in $\mathcal{N}_\alpha(i) - \mathcal{L}_\alpha(i)$ and the other is disconnected node, so one edge is reserved and two edges are flipped with $p_e q_e^2$;
4. Two nodes are disconnected nodes, so three edges are flipped with q_e^3.

Hence, the number of existing links between neighbors $|\mathcal{L}_\alpha^*(i)|$ is estimated as:

$$|\mathcal{L}_\alpha^*(i)| = \frac{1}{p_e^2(p_e - q_e)}(|\tilde{\mathcal{L}}_\alpha(i)| - \binom{d}{2}p_e^2 q_e - \binom{d}{1}\binom{n-d-1}{1}p_e q_e^2 \\ - \binom{n-d-1}{2}q_e^3) \tag{3}$$

4   Experimental Evaluation

To evaluate the performance of *RALL*, we implement two alternative methods: *DCC* and *RNLL*. *DCC* exploits noisy degree as in [9]; while *RNLL* integrates RNL mechanism and Laplace mechanism as in [15].

4.1   Experiment Setting

General Setting. The three methods are simulated on multiple synthetic Watts Strogatz random graphs, which captures the structure of many real world networks. To generally cover practical scenarios, the layer of multiplex graphs m

ranges from 2 to 8, the maximum degree θ of each layer ranges from 5 to 25, the rewiring probability of W-S random graphs ranges from 0.1 to 0.7, the number of nodes is 1000 and the privacy budget ranges from 0.1 to 5.0, with $\epsilon_1 = \epsilon_2 = \epsilon/2$.

Each setting is simulated 100 times, and the results are average value of these simulations. In each simulation, m single W-S random graphs are generated and merged into a multiplex graph.

Performance Metric. *Root Mean Square Error* (RMSE) is adopted to evaluate the accuracy of clustering coefficient estimation on multiplex graph:

$$\sqrt{\frac{1}{n}\sum_{i=1}^{n}(C_{\mathcal{G}}(i) - \tilde{C}_{proj(\mathcal{G})}(i))^2}$$

4.2   Results

We illustrate the results by separately varying Layer size m, Maximum degree θ and rewiring probability p.

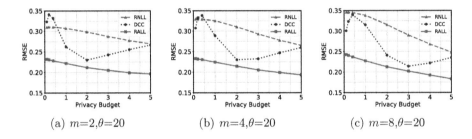

(a) $m=2,\theta=20$ (b) $m=4,\theta=20$ (c) $m=8,\theta=20$

Fig. 2. Estimation errors of clustering coefficient with different m

Layer Size m. With maximum degree bound $\theta = 20$, and layer size m ranges from 2 to 8, Fig. 2 presents the results with different privacy budget ϵ. As m increases, the error of three methods also increased, in which $RALL$ is rarely affected by m and $RNLL$ suffers from changing m. In general, $RALL$ outperforms the other two methods when changing layer size m.

Maximum Degree θ. With layer size $m = 6$, maximum degree θ ranges from 10 to 20, Fig. 3 presents the results with different privacy budget ϵ. As θ increases, the estimation error of three methods are decreasing slower, which indicates the effect of noises introduced by θ, and DCC suffers from changing θ. In general, $RALL$ outperforms the other two methods when changing Maximum degree θ.

Graph Models. With layer size $m = 4$, maximum degree $\theta = 20$, we change the rewiring probability in W-S graph model, to cover more practical scenarios. When setting rewiring probability as $p = 0.1$, 0.3 and 0.7, the related clustering coefficient is around 0.59, 0.42 and 0.26 respectively. Figure 4 presents the

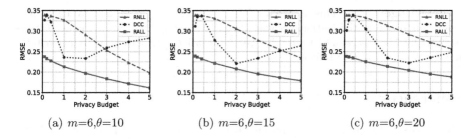

(a) $m=6,\theta=10$ (b) $m=6,\theta=15$ (c) $m=6,\theta=20$

Fig. 3. Estimation errors of clustering coefficient with different θ

results. When the clustering coefficient decreases, the error of three methods also decreases, in which DCC is unstable in different settings. In general, $RALL$ outperforms the other two methods when changing Graph models.

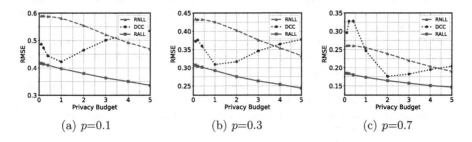

(a) $p=0.1$ (b) $p=0.3$ (c) $p=0.7$

Fig. 4. Estimation errors of clustering coefficient with different graph

In summary, it is feasible to estimate clustering coefficients of multiplex graphs under layer LDP, and the estimation of our $RALL$ is more accurate and more stable than DCC and $RNLL$. The error of DCC method is fluctuated in most simulations, and a possible reason may be: when privacy budget is limited, the main error comes from introduced noise, so the overall error is decreasing; as privacy budget increases, the error of missing neighboring information is taking up more percentage, thus the overall error starts to increase instead.

5   Conclusion

In this paper, we propose layer local differential privacy for multiplex graphs, which strikes a balance between utility and privacy. Furthermore, we present $RALL$ mechanism to estimate clustering coefficient with reduced computation cost and improved protection strength, and we evaluate the effectiveness and efficiency of $RALL$ mechanism through extensive experiments.

Acknowledgements. This research of Liu, Huang, Xu, Yang and Wang is partially supported by the National Science Foundation of China (NSFC) under Grants 61822210, U1709217, and 61936015; by Anhui Initiative in Quantum Information Technologies under No. AHY150300.

References

1. Al-garadi, M., Khan, M., Varathan, K.D., Mujtaba, G., Al-Kabsi, A.M.: Using online social networks to track a pandemic: a systematic review. J. Biomed. Inf. **62**, 1–11 (2016)
2. Blocki, J., Blum, A., Datta, A., Sheffet, O.: The johnson-lindenstrauss transform itself preserves differential privacy. In: 2012 IEEE 53rd Annual Symposium on Foundations of Computer Science, pp. 410–419 (2012)
3. Chen, W., Wang, C., Wang, Y.: Scalable influence maximization for prevalent viral marketing in large-scale social networks. In: Proceedings of the 16th ACM SIGKDD International Conference on Knowledge Discovery and Data Mining (2010)
4. Criado, R., Flores, J., Amo, A.G.D., Gómez-Gardeñes, J., Romance, M.: A mathematical model for networks with structures in the mesoscale. Int. J. Comput. Math. **89**, 291–309 (2012)
5. Duchi, J.C., Jordan, M.I., Wainwright, M.J.: Local privacy and statistical minimax rates. 2013 51st Annual Allerton Conference on Communication, Control, and Computing (Allerton), p. 1592 (2013)
6. Dwork, C., McSherry, F., Nissim, K., Smith, A.D.: Calibrating noise to sensitivity in private data analysis. In: TCC (2006)
7. Kairouz, P., et al.: Extremal mechanisms for local differential privacy. Adv. Neural Inf. Process. Syst. **27**, 2879–2887 (2014)
8. Kasiviswanathan, S., Nissim, K., Raskhodnikova, S., Smith, A.D.: Analyzing graphs with node differential privacy. In: TCC (2013)
9. Qin, Z., Yu, T., Yang, Y., Khalil, I.M., Xiao, X., Ren, K.: Generating synthetic decentralized social graphs with local differential privacy. In: ACM Conference on Computer and Communications Security (2017)
10. Sun, H., et al.: Analyzing subgraph statistics from extended local views with decentralized differential privacy. In: Proceedings of the 2019 ACM SIGSAC Conference on Computer and Communications Security, pp. 703–717 (2019)
11. Wang, Z., Liao, J., Cao, Q., Qi, H., Wang, Z.: Friendbook: a semantic-based friend recommendation system for social networks. IEEE Trans. Mob. Comput. **14**, 538–551 (2015)
12. Warner, S.: Randomized response: a survey technique for eliminating evasive answer bias. J. Am. Stat. Assoc. **60**(309), 63–6 (1965)
13. Wei, C., Ji, S., Liu, C., Chen, W., Wang, T.: Asgldp: Collecting and generating decentralized attributed graphs with local differential privacy. IEEE Trans. Inf. Forensics Secur. **15**, 3239–3254 (2020)
14. Ye, Q., Hu, H., Au, M.H., Meng, X., Xiao, X.: Lf-gdpr: a framework for estimating graph metrics with local differential privacy. IEEE Trans. Knowl. Data Eng. p. 1 (2020). https://doi.org/10.1109/TKDE.2020.3047124
15. Ye, Q., Hu, H., Au, M., Meng, X., Xiao, X.: Towards locally differentially private generic graph metric estimation. In: 2020 IEEE 36th International Conference on Data Engineering (ICDE), pp. 1922–1925 (2020)

New Rectangle Attack Against SKINNY Block Cipher

Jiyan Zhang$^{(\boxtimes)}$, Ting Cui, and Chenhui Jin

PLA SSF Information Engineering University, Zhengzhou, China

Abstract. The issue of security and privacy plays an important role in the wireless networks and directly affects the wide application of wireless network systems. In order to protect the confidentiality of data for wireless networks, especially for the wireless sensor networks, a series of lightweight ciphers have been proposed in recent years. SKINNY, a family of lightweight block cipher, is designed in such scenario with competitive performance and security guarantees. SKINNY-128-256 is a widely used version as underlying primitive in NIST's Lightweight Cryptography (LWC) project. In this paper, we consider the security of SKINNY-128-256 under related-tweakey rectangle attack. Based on an 18-round related-tweakey boomerang distinguisher composed of two 9-round differential characteristics, a 23-round related-tweakey rectangle attack is proposed by expanding forward for 3-round and extending backwards for 2-round. Our attack utilize the incompleted diffusion property of MixColumns operation of SKINNY to reduce the times of exhaustive key search. To the best of our knowledge, this attack efficiently reduces the costs compared to the currently known attacks on 23-round SKINNY-128-256, especially the data complexity is considerably less than the existing results.

Keywords: Wireless sensor networks · Lightweight cryptography · SKINNY · Cryptanalysis · Rectangle attack

1 Introduction

Wireless networks have received much attention over the last ten years. With the rapid development of wireless networks, many fields employ wireless network devices including smart homes, intelligent transportation, etc. However, most of these devices work in resource constrained and untrustable environments, e.g. the wireless sensor networks (WSN). In such scenario, how to protect the data security and privacy is an indispensable issue. In order to fulfill the security requirements, lightweight cryptography emerges as a safety-protection strategy. Lightweight cryptography is a subfield of cryptography that aims to provide solutions tailored for resource-constrained devices. Therefore, lightweight ciphers are suitable for using in wireless sensor network devices where many traditional ciphers designed for desktop/server environments are not fit. Under this motivation, many lightweight primitives have been proposed, such as PRESENT [1],

© Springer Nature Switzerland AG 2021
Z. Liu et al. (Eds.): WASA 2021, LNCS 12939, pp. 399–409, 2021.
https://doi.org/10.1007/978-3-030-86137-7_43

SIMON [2], GIFT [3] and SKINNY [4], to meet the requirements in the resource-constrained environment.

SKINNY is a family of lightweight tweakable block cipher proposed at Crypto 2016. Its design intention is not only to provide the implemented performance no lower than SIMON, but also to ensure stronger security margin against the well known classical attacks, e.g. differential attacks [5], linear attacks [6] and integral attacks [7]. There are 6 variants in the SKINNY family supporting two block lengths $n = 64$-bit and 128-bit and the tweakey lengths of each can be either n, $2n$ and $3n$, namely SKINNY-64-64, SKINNY-64-128, SKINNY-64-192, SKINNY-128-128, SKINNY-128-256 and SKINNY-128-384. Since it was proposed, each variant of SKINNY has been analyzed by various cryptanalysis techniques including impossible differential attacks [8–10] and rectangle attacks [9,11,12].

SKINNY-128-256 is a widely used version in the SKINNY family. In the LWC standardization project held by NIST, SKINNY-128-256 is an appealing choice as the underlying primitive in the design of lightweight authenticated encryption with associated data (AEAD). ForkAE [13] is a second round candidate, which employs SKINNY-128-256 to design PAEF-ForkSkinny-128-256 and SAEF-ForkSkinny-128-256. SKINNY-AEAD [14] provides an alternative scheme for processing short inputs based on SKINNY-128-256. Beierle et al. also utilized SKINNY-128-256 combined with the sponge construction to design a hashing scheme called SKINNY-HASH. In addition, Romulus [15], one of the finalist candidates announced by NIST on March 2021, employs SKINNY-128-256 as the underlying tweakable block cipher of the two versions Romulus-N3 and Romulus-M3 to achieve the goal of lightweight, efficient and highly secure.

In this paper, we present a related-tweakey rectangle attack against the 23-round SKINNY-128-256. We choose an 18-round practical boomerang distinguisher from a set of boomerang distinguisher of SKINNY-128-256 proposed by Hadipour et al. [12], whose probability is $2^{-40.77}$. The reason we choose this 18-round boomerang distinguisher is that it can not only extend a better attack but also require less data complexity than others. In order to conduct the 23-round attack, we extend three rounds at the beginning and extend two rounds at the end of the distinguisher. Since the key schedule of SKINNY is linear, the tweakey difference of extend rounds can be computed from the distinguisher. In the attack, the incompleted diffusion property of MixColumns operation of SKINNY is utilized to reduce the costs of exhaustive key search. Taken together, we can achieve the attack with a time complexity of $2^{213.26}$ 23-round SKINNY-128-256 encryptions, a data complexity of $2^{84.39}$ chosen plaintexts and 2^{96} memory complexity. This is the best cryptanalytic result against the 23-round SKINNY-128-256 and the comparison with previous attacks is listed in Table 1. Note that Hadipour et al. propose a 24-round attack in [12], which employs a 21-round boomerang distinguisher with the probability of $2^{-116.43}$. But even if it can degenerate into a 23-round attack, the data complexity seems more expensive than the attack we presented. In other words, our attack is competitive with the existing results.

Table 1. Summary of the attacks against SKINNY-128-256

Rounds	Technique	Data	Time	Memory	References
22	Rectangle	2^{127}	$2^{235.6}$	2^{127}	[9]
23	Impossible differential	$2^{124.47}$	$2^{251.47}$	2^{248}	[9]
23	Impossible differential	$2^{124.41}$	$2^{243.41}$	$2^{155.41}$	[10]
23	Rectangle	$2^{84.39}$	$2^{213.26}$	2^{96}	This paper
24	Rectangle	$2^{125.21}$	$2^{209.85}$	$2^{125.54}$	[12]

The rest of the paper is organized as follows. Section 2 gives a brief description of SKINNY-128-256 and the rectangle attack. Section 3 presents the 23-round related-tweakey rectangle attack against SKINNY-128-256. Section 4 concludes this paper.

2 Preliminaries

2.1 Brief Description of the SKINNY-128-256 Block Cipher

SKINNY-128-256 is a well-known variant in the SKINNY family, which takes a 128-bit block size and a 256-bit tweakey size. Its internal state can be seen as a 4×4 byte-matrix indexed by

$$\begin{bmatrix} 0 & 1 & 2 & 3 \\ 4 & 5 & 6 & 7 \\ 8 & 9 & 10 & 11 \\ 12 & 13 & 14 & 15 \end{bmatrix}$$

Each round of SKINNY-128-256 operates the 128-bit state matrix with the following five transformations: SubCells (SC), AddConstants (AC), AddRoundT-weakey (ART), ShiftRows (SR) and MixColumns (MC). Since the AddConstants operation has no effect in our attack, we omit it here and the details of other operations are described as follows.

- SubCells (SC): Each cell applies a nonlinear substitution (an 8-bit S-box S) to update the state. For more details of the 8-bit S-box, please refer to [4].
- AddRoundTweakey (ART): For the first two rows of the state matrix, each cell applies the xor operation with the round tweakey. The round tweakey TK_i in the i-th round is computed by $tk_i^1 \oplus tk_i^2$. Concretely, the update of tk_i^1 is applying a permutation $P_T = [9, 15, 8, 13, 10, 14, 12, 11, 0, 1, 2, 3, 4, 5, 6, 7]$ on the cell positions of the tweakey arrays. Similarly, tk_i^2 applies the P_T first and each cell of the first two rows is updated with an LFSR: $(x_0||x_1||x_2||x_3||x_4||x_5||x_6||x_7) \rightarrow (x_1||x_2||x_3||x_4||x_5||x_6||x_7||x_0 \oplus x_2)$.
- ShiftRows (SR): For the i-th row ($i = 0, 1, 2, 3$) of the state, rotate i positions to the right to update the state.

- MixColumns (MC): For each column, premultiply a binary matrix $\mathbb{M}$ to update the state, where $\mathbb{M}$ and the inverse $\mathbb{M}^{-1}$ are listed below.

$$\mathbb{M} = \begin{bmatrix} 1 & 0 & 1 & 1 \\ 1 & 0 & 0 & 0 \\ 0 & 1 & 1 & 0 \\ 1 & 0 & 1 & 1 \end{bmatrix}, \mathbb{M}^{-1} = \begin{bmatrix} 0 & 1 & 0 & 0 \\ 0 & 1 & 1 & 1 \\ 0 & 1 & 0 & 1 \\ 1 & 0 & 0 & 1 \end{bmatrix}$$

We define the following notations used in our attack. X_i represents the state before SC, Y_i represents the state after SC and AC, Z_i represents the state after ART and W_i represents the state after MC in the i-th round. Denote TK_i as the round tweakey used in the i-th round. The diagram of one round SKINNY-128-256 encryption with the tweakey schedule is shown in Fig. 1.

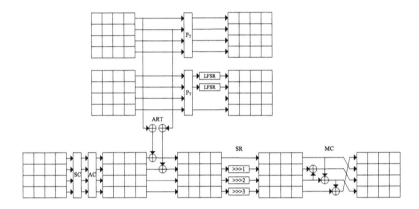

Fig. 1. One round SKINNY-128-256 encryption with the tweakey schedule

2.2 Rectangle Attack

The rectangle attack [16] is evolved from the boomerang attack [17], which handles in a chosen-plaintext scenario. In this attack, attackers attempt to concatenate two short differential trails to find a high-probability differential distinguisher. The target cipher E is usually divided into two parts E_0 and E_1, i.e. $E = E_1 \circ E_0$. In the related-key setting, assume that the difference α propagates to the difference β under the key difference $\triangle K$ on E_0 with probability p, while the difference γ propagates to the difference δ under the key difference ∇K on E_1 with probability q. Let $K_1 \oplus K_2 = \triangle K$, $K_3 \oplus K_4 = \triangle K$ and $K_1 \oplus K_3 = \nabla K$, then giving a pair of plaintexts with the difference α and the key difference $\triangle K$, the probability satisfying the following differentials is $Pr[E_{K_3}^{-1}(E_{K_1}(x) \oplus \delta) \oplus E_{K_4}^{-1}(E_{K_2}(x \oplus \alpha) \oplus \delta) = \alpha] = p^2 q^2$.

A series of works are devoted to improving the probability of the boomerang distinguisher in previous literature [18–21]. A recent work was presented by Cid et al. at Eurocrypt 2018 [22], which proposed a new cryptanalysis tool called boomerang connectivity table (BCT) to evaluate the probability of the boomerang distinguisher. Soon after, Wang et al. presented a boomerang difference table (BDT) to improve this work further [23]. Independently, Song et al. proposed a general framework to search high-probability boomerang distinguishers [12, 24].

3   Related-Tweakey Rectangle Attack on 23-Round SKINNY-128-256

In this section, we present a related-tweakey rectangle attack on 23-round SKINNY-128-256. In this attack, we follow the attack framework in [11]. We first select an 18-round boomerang distinguisher from a set of boomerang distinguishers of SKINNY-128-256 proposed by Hadipour et al. [12]. We have two considerations in choosing the boomerang distinguisher. On the one hand, the 18-round boomerang distinguisher is practical with a probability of $Pr = 2^{-40.77}$, which a right quartet satisfying it can be verified. On the other hand, the probability of boomerang distinguisher is the main factor that affects the data complexity in the rectangle attack, i.e. a high-probability distinguisher will lead an attack with lower data complexity. The selected 18-round boomerang distinguisher is listed in the following (Table 2).

Table 2. Specification of the 18-round boomerang distinguisher

$\triangle X$	0x00000000000000000000000000200000
$\triangle tk^1$	0x00000000000000000002000000000000
$\triangle tk^2$	0x00000000000000000080000000000000
$\triangle TK$	0x00000000000000000082000000000000
∇X	0x40400040004000000000184000400040
∇tk^1	0x0000000000000000000000000000f800
∇tk^2	0x0000000000000000000000000000cf00
∇TK	0x00000000000000000000000000003700

We extend three rounds at the beginning of the 18-round distinguisher and add two rounds at the end to obtain the 23-round attack, which is shown in Fig. 2. Note that in the last round of this attack, the SR and MC operations can be omitted. Before describing the attack procedure, we recall the lemma below.

Lemma 1. [9] The 8-bit S-box S of SKINNY-128-256 satisfies the following property: for each non-zero input difference $\triangle_{in}$ and out difference $\triangle_{out}$, there exists one solution on average such that $S(x) \oplus S(x \oplus \triangle_{in}) = \triangle_{out}$.

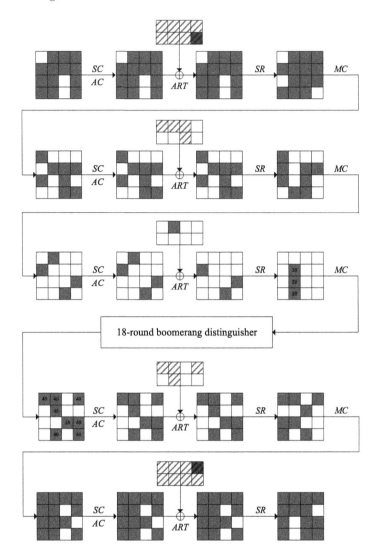

Fig. 2. A 23-round related-tweakey rectangle attack against SKINNY-128-256

Since the tweakey schedule is linear, we can deduce the corresponding tweakey difference of the extended round. Specifically, the tewakey differences in the extended rounds are $\triangle TK_1 = 0x0000000000000042$, $\triangle TK_2 = 0x0000000000000000$, $\triangle TK_3 = 0x0082000000000000$, $\nabla TK_{22} = 0x0000000000000000$ and $\nabla TK_{23} = 0x0000003800000000$, respectively.

Generally, the rectangle attack can be parted into two phases. The first phase is to collect data to construct required quartet for the attack and the second phase is the key recovery phase which is to recover the involved key in the attack. Suppose E_b represent the three extended rounds at the beginning and

E_f represent the two extend rounds at the end. Denote r_b as the number of unknown bits in the plaintexts difference of E_b and m_b as the number of involved sub-tweakey bits needed to guess in E_b. Similarly, we denote r_f as the number of unknown bits in the ciphertexts difference of E_f and denote m_f as the number of involved sub-tweakey bits needed to guess in E_f. Thus, according to Fig. 2, we have $r_b = 13 \times 8 = 104$ bits, $m_b = 12 \times 8 = 96$ bits, $r_f = 13 \times 8 = 104$ bits and $m_f = 12 \times 8 = 96$ bits. Note that we omit the MC operation in the last round. In order to obtain s right quartets satisfying the 18-round distinguisher, we construct $y = \sqrt{s} \cdot 2^{128/2-r_b}/\sqrt{Pr} = \sqrt{s} \cdot 2^{-19.62}$ plaintexts structure, where each structure contains $2^{r_b} = 2^{104}$ chosen plaintexts. Then, encrypt the plaintexts in each structure under the related tweakey $TK1$, $TK2$, $TK3$ and $TK4$ with the relationship $TK2 = TK1 \oplus \triangle TK_1$, $TK3 = TK1 \oplus \triangledown TK_1$, and $TK4 = TK3 \oplus \triangle TK_1$, and obtain the four corresponding plaintext-ciphertext sets $(P_1, C_1) \in L_1$, $(P_2, C_2) \in L_2$, $(P_3, C_3) \in L_3$ and $(P_4, C_4) \in L_4$. Further, insert L_2 and L_4 into the hash tables H_1 and H_2 indexed by the r_b bits of plaintexts.

In our attack, let the expected number of right quartets s equal 1. Guess the $m_b = 96$ bits of sub-tweakeys involved in E_b, then partially encrypt plaintext $P_1 \in L_1$ under E_b, and partially decrypt it under the sub-tweakeys with difference $\triangle TK_1$ after xoring the difference $\triangle X$ to get P_2. Next, search H_1 to find the collision $P_2 \in L_2$ and record the pair (P_1, C_1) and (P_2, C_2) in the set S_1, i.e. $S_1 = \{(P_1, C_1, P_2, C_2) : (P_1, C_1) \in L_1, (P_2, C_2) \in L_2, E_b(P_1, TK1) \oplus E_b(P_2, TK2) = \triangle X\}$. In the same way, the set S_2 can be constructed, i.e. $S_2 = \{(P_3, C_3, P_4, C_4) : (P_3, C_3) \in L_3, (P_4, C_4) \in L_4, E_b(P_3, TK3) \oplus E_b(P_4, TK4) = \triangle X\}$. Under each guessed key, the size of S_1 and S_2 are both $M = y \cdot 2^{r_b} = 2^{84.39}$. Here we can do a preliminary filtration to reduce the size of possible quartets. Concretely, let the 24 (128-r_f) zero difference bits be the index of C_1 and C_2 and insert S_1 into the hash table H_3, then for each element of S_2, search H_3 to find the collision that $C_1 \oplus C_3 = 0$ and $C_2 \oplus C_4 = 0$ in the corresponding 48 bits respectively. After this filter, the number of remaining quartets is about $M^2 \times 2^{-2 \times (128-r_f)} = 2^{120.78}$.

Next, initialize a list of $2^{m_f} = 2^{96}$ counters, each of which corresponds to a guess of the 96 bits sub-tweakeys involved in the last two rounds. Then, the key recovery procedure is described as follows by using the remaining quartets.

Step 1. We first deal with the ciphertexts pair (C_1, C_3). From the incompleted diffusion property of MixColumns, we can establish the eight equations.

$$\triangle W_{22}[2] = 0 = \triangle X_{23}[2] \tag{1}$$

$$\triangle W_{22}[4] = 0 = \triangle X_{23}[4] \oplus \triangle X_{23}[8] \oplus \triangle X_{23}[12] \tag{2}$$

$$\triangle W_{22}[5] = 0 = \triangle X_{23}[5] \oplus \triangle X_{23}[9] \oplus \triangle X_{23}[13] \tag{3}$$

$$\triangle W_{22}[7] = 0 = \triangle X_{23}[7] \oplus \triangle X_{23}[11] \oplus \triangle X_{23}[15] \tag{4}$$

$$\triangle W_{22}[10] = 0 = \triangle X_{23}[6] \oplus \triangle X_{23}[14] \tag{5}$$

$$\triangle W_{22}[11] = 0 = \triangle X_{23}[7] \oplus \triangle X_{23}[15] \tag{6}$$

$$\triangle W_{22}[13] = 0 = \triangle X_{23}[1] \oplus \triangle X_{23}[13] \tag{7}$$

$$\triangle W_{22}[15] = 0 = \triangle X_{23}[3] \oplus \triangle X_{23}[15] \tag{8}$$

Since $X_{23}[8, 9, 10, 11, 12, 13, 14, 15]$ is not involved with the sub-tweakeys, it can be computed by the ciphertexts directly. Moreover, we have already known the value of $\triangle X_{23}[6, 11, 14] = 0$, which means the above Eqs. (1) and (5) can not provide additional information and the Eqs. (4) and (6) are equivalent. Thus, the value of $\triangle X_{23}[1, 3, 4, 5, 7]$ can be determined by $X_{23}[8, 9, 10, 11, 12, 13, 14, 15]$, i.e. $\triangle X_{23}[1] = \triangle X_{23}[13]$, $\triangle X_{23}[3] = \triangle X_{23}[15]$, $\triangle X_{23}[4] = \triangle X_{23}[8] \oplus \triangle X_{23}[12]$, $\triangle X_{23}[5] = \triangle X_{23}[9] \oplus \triangle X_{23}[13]$ and $\triangle X_{23}[7] = \triangle X_{23}[11] \oplus \triangle X_{23}[15]$. And because the difference at the position of Y_{23} can be computed by the ciphertexts, we can know the difference before and after the operation SC. According to Lemma 1, we can obtain a solution for $TK_{23}[1, 3, 4, 5, 7]$ on average, respectively.

Step 2. Since the value of $TK_{23}[1, 5]$ have known, we can partially decrypt to obtain the information of the second column of X_{23}, and then after the inverse of MC, the values and corresponding differences can be computed at the position of $W_{22}[1, 9]$. Since the value of $\triangle Y_{22}[1]$ can be deduced by $\triangle W_{22}[1]$ and the value of $\triangle X_{22}[1]$ can be obtained from the 18-round boomerang distinguisher, we can get one solution of $TK_{22}[1]$ on average. The difference $\triangle Y_{22}[9]$ can be deduced by $\triangle W_{22}[9]$ and it can be mapped to the difference $\triangle X_{22}[11]$ with the probability of 2^{-8}, which can filter the quartets and about $2^{120.78} \times 2^{-8} = 2^{112.78}$ quartets remaining. At the same time, we check the corresponding ciphertext pair (C_2, C_4) to make a further filter under the conditiona $\triangle W_{22}[1] \xrightarrow{2^{-8}} \triangle X_{22}[1] = 0x40$, $\triangle W_{22}[9] \xrightarrow{2^{-8}} \triangle X_{11}[1] = 0x40$ and $\triangle W_{22}[5, 13] = 0$. For the random case, the probability that satisfying both of above conditions is 2^{-32}. Therefore, about $2^{112.78} \times 2^{-32} = 2^{80.78}$ are remaining.

Step 3. The knowledge of $TK_{23}[3, 7]$ support us to compute the fourth column of X_{23} and we can get the value and its difference at the position of $W_{22}[3]$. The difference $\triangle W_{22}[3]$ maps to the difference $\triangle X_{22}[3]$ after the inverse transformations with the probability of 2^{-8}. In addition, since the value of $W_{22}[3]$ has computed by decryption, we can obtain one solution of $TK_{22}[3]$ on average. Then, similar to the Step 2, we also check the ciphertext pair (C_2, C_4) to filter the remaining quartets. Different from Step 2, since $\triangle W_{22}[7] = \triangle X_{23}[7] \oplus \triangle X_{23}[11] \oplus \triangle X_{23}[15]$, $\triangle W_{22}[11] = 0 = \triangle X_{23}[7] \oplus \triangle X_{23}[15]$ and $\triangle X_{23}[11] = 0$, we have $\triangle W_{22}[7] = \triangle W_{22}[11]$, i.e. $\triangle W_{22}[7]$ and $\triangle W_{22}[11]$ is related. Thus, the probability satisfying the conditions $\triangle W_{22}[7] = 0$ and $\triangle W_{22}[11] = 0$ for the random case is 2^{-8}, instead of 2^{-16}. Besides, the probability that both $\triangle W_{22}[3] \xrightarrow{2^{-8}} \triangle X_{22}[3] = 0x40$ and $\triangle W_{22}[15] = 0$ hold is 2^{-16}. Hence, there are $2^{80.75} \times 2^{-24} = 2^{56.78}$ quartets remain after this step.

Step 4. Deal with the first column of X_{23}. Since $\triangle W_{22}[8]$ maps to $\triangle X_{22}[10]$ with a probability of 2^{-8}, there are about $2^{56.78} \times 2^{-8} = 2^{48.78}$ quartets remain. Further, guess the 8 bits unknown sub-tewakey of $TK_{23}[0]$. For each possible guess, we can determine the value and its difference at the position $W_{22}[0]$. With the knowledge of $\triangle X_{22}[0] = 0x40$, we can get one solution of $TK_{22}[0]$ on average according to Lemma 1. Moreover, $\triangle W_{22}[12]$ can be computed by partially decrypted with $TK_{23}[0]$ and the probability is 2^{-8} from $\triangle W_{22}[12]$

mapping to $\triangle X_{22}[13] = 0x40$. Therefore, about $2^{48.78} \times 2^8 \times 2^{-8} = 2^{48.78}$ quartets remain. Utilizing the known value of $TK_{23}[0, 4]$ and $TK_{22}[0]$, we partially decrypt the ciphertexts pair (C_2, C_4) and check whether the conditions $\triangle X_{22}[0] = 0x40$, $\triangle W_{22}[4] = 0$, $\triangle X_{22}[10] = 0x18$ and $\triangle X_{22}[13] = 0x40$ hold or not. After the filter, there are about $2^{48.78} \times 2^{-32} = 2^{16.78}$ quartets remain.

Step 5. Guess the 16 bits unknown sub-tweakey of $TK_{23}[2, 6]$ and partially decrypt the third column of X_{23}, we can get the value and difference at the position of $W_{22}[6, 14]$. Combined with $\triangle X_{22}[5] = 0x40$, on average one solution of $TK_{22}[5]$ will be obtained. The probability that $\triangle W_{22}[14]$ maps to $\triangle X_{22}[15]$ after the inverse transformations is 2^{-8}. Decrypt the ciphertexts pair (C_2, C_4) partially with $TK_{22}[5]$ and $TK_{23}[2, 6]$ and check whether the condition $\triangle X_{22}[5, 15] = 0x40$ holds. Therefore, about $2^{16.78} \times 2^{16} \times 2^{-8} \times 2^{-16} = 2^{8.78}$ quartets are remaining.

Step 6. Using the remaining quartets to count for the 96 bits sub-tweakeys involved in E_f. Here, the right quartet will be remained under the right sub-tweakey and the other cases are considered as random behavior. Select the top 2^6 counters to be the candidates, which indicates a 90-bit advantage delivered. Then, exhaustively search the remaining $256 - m_b - m_f = 64$ unknown key bits of the master key.

Complexity Analysis. The data complexity is $4 \times y \times 2^{r_b} = 2^{84.39}$ chosen plaintexts. In order to construct the quartets, we need $3 \times 2^{m_b} \times M = 2^{181.97}$ looking-up-table operations. In the process of key recovery, the main time complexity is dominated by Step 1 and Step 2, which is equals to $2^{96} \times 2^{120.78} \times 2 = 2^{217.78}$ one-round decryption of SKINNY-128-256. In comparison, the time complexity generated in Step 3 to 5 is negligible. In Step 6, the needed complexity is $2^{96} \times 2^6 \times 2^{64} = 2^{166}$ encryptions. Thus, the total time complexity is $2^{213.26}$ 23-round SKINNY-128-256 encryptions. The memory complexity is bounded by the size of H_1, H_2, H_3, S_1, S_2 and the 96 bits counter, which is $5M + 2^{m_f} \approx 2^{96}$.

4 Conclusion

In this paper, we discuss the security of 23-round SKINNY-128-256 against the related-tweakey rectangle attack. Our attack is based on the boomerang distinguishers proposed in [12], but the choice of boomerang distinguisher in the attack is careful, which makes the attack has an advantage in the costs, especially in the data complexity. In the attack process, we utilize the incompleted diffusion property of MixColumns operation to reduce the guess of unknown key. Finally, we receive an attack with a data complexity of $2^{84.39}$ chosen plaintexts and a time complexity of $2^{213.26}$ encryptions, which improves the results against 23-round SKINNY-128-256. We believe that the presented analysis provides a better understanding of SKINNY-128-256.

Acknowledgement. This work is supported by the National Natural Science Foundation of China (No. 61772547, 61802438, 61902428, 61602514) and the National Cryptography Development Fund (No. MMJJ20170125).

References

1. Bogdanov, A., et al.: PRESENT: an ultra-lightweight block cipher. In: Paillier, P., Verbauwhede, I. (eds.) CHES 2007. LNCS, vol. 4727, pp. 450–466. Springer, Heidelberg (2007). https://doi.org/10.1007/978-3-540-74735-2_31
2. Beaulieu, R., Shors, D., Smith, J., Treatman-Clark, S., Weeks, B., Wingers, L.: The SIMON and SPECK lightweight block ciphers. In: Proceedings of the 52nd Annual Design Automation Conference, San Francisco, CA, USA, 7–11 June 2015, pp. 175:1–175:6 (2015)
3. Banik, S., Pandey, S.K., Peyrin, T., Sasaki, Yu., Sim, S.M., Todo, Y.: GIFT: a small present. In: Fischer, W., Homma, N. (eds.) CHES 2017. LNCS, vol. 10529, pp. 321–345. Springer, Cham (2017). https://doi.org/10.1007/978-3-319-66787-4_16
4. Beierle, C., et al.: The SKINNY family of block ciphers and its low-latency variant MANTIS. In: Robshaw, M., Katz, J. (eds.) CRYPTO 2016. LNCS, vol. 9815, pp. 123–153. Springer, Heidelberg (2016). https://doi.org/10.1007/978-3-662-53008-5_5
5. Biham, E., Shamir, A.: Differential cryptanalysis of DES-like cryptosystems. J. Cryptol. **4**(1), 3–72 (1991). https://doi.org/10.1007/BF00630563
6. Nyberg, K.: Linear approximation of block ciphers. In: De Santis, A. (ed.) EUROCRYPT 1994. LNCS, vol. 950, pp. 439–444. Springer, Heidelberg (1995). https://doi.org/10.1007/BFb0053460
7. Knudsen, L., Wagner, D.: Integral cryptanalysis. In: Daemen, J., Rijmen, V. (eds.) FSE 2002. LNCS, vol. 2365, pp. 112–127. Springer, Heidelberg (2002). https://doi.org/10.1007/3-540-45661-9_9
8. Tolba, M., Abdelkhalek, A., Youssef, A.M.: Impossible differential cryptanalysis of reduced-round SKINNY. In: Joye, M., Nitaj, A. (eds.) AFRICACRYPT 2017. LNCS, vol. 10239, pp. 117–134. Springer, Cham (2017). https://doi.org/10.1007/978-3-319-57339-7_7
9. Liu, G., Ghosh, M., Song, L.: Security analysis of SKINNY under related-tweakey settings (long paper). IACR Trans. Symmetric Cryptol. **2017**(3), 37–72 (2017)
10. Sadeghi, S., Mohammadi, T., Bagheri, N.: Cryptanalysis of reduced round SKINNY block cipher. IACR Trans. Symmetric Cryptol. **2018**(3), 124–162 (2018)
11. Zhao, B., Dong, X., Meier, W., Jia, K., Wang, G.: Generalized related-key rectangle attacks on block ciphers with linear key schedule: applications to SKINNY and GIFT. Des. Codes Crypt. **88**(6), 1103–1126 (2020). https://doi.org/10.1007/s10623-020-00730-1
12. Hadipour, H., Bagheri, N., Song, L.: Improved rectangle attacks on SKINNY and CRAFT. IACR Cryptology ePrint Archive Report 2020/1317 (2020)
13. Andreeva, E., Lallemand, V., Purnal, A., Reyhanitabar, R., Roy, A., Vizár, D.: Forkcipher: a new primitive for authenticated encryption of very short messages. In: Galbraith, S.D., Moriai, S. (eds.) ASIACRYPT 2019. LNCS, vol. 11922, pp. 153–182. Springer, Cham (2019). https://doi.org/10.1007/978-3-030-34621-8_6
14. Beierle, C., et al.: SKINNY-AEAD and skinny-hash. IACR Trans. Symmetric Cryptol. **2020**(S1), 88–131 (2020)
15. Iwata, T., Khairallah, M., Minematsu, K., Peyrin, T.: Duel of the titans: the Romulus and Remus families of lightweight AEAD algorithms. IACR Trans. Symmetric Cryptol. **2020**(1), 43–120 (2020)
16. Biham, E., Dunkelman, O., Keller, N.: The rectangle attack — rectangling the serpent. In: Pfitzmann, B. (ed.) EUROCRYPT 2001. LNCS, vol. 2045, pp. 340–357. Springer, Heidelberg (2001). https://doi.org/10.1007/3-540-44987-6_21

17. Wagner, D.: The boomerang attack. In: Knudsen, L. (ed.) FSE 1999. LNCS, vol. 1636, pp. 156–170. Springer, Heidelberg (1999). https://doi.org/10.1007/3-540-48519-8_12

18. Biham, E., Dunkelman, O., Keller, N.: New results on boomerang and rectangle attacks. In: Daemen, J., Rijmen, V. (eds.) FSE 2002. LNCS, vol. 2365, pp. 1–16. Springer, Heidelberg (2002). https://doi.org/10.1007/3-540-45661-9_1

19. Biryukov, A., De Cannière, C., Dellkrantz, G.: Cryptanalysis of SAFER++. In: Boneh, D. (ed.) CRYPTO 2003. LNCS, vol. 2729, pp. 195–211. Springer, Heidelberg (2003). https://doi.org/10.1007/978-3-540-45146-4_12

20. Biryukov, A., Khovratovich, D.: Related-key cryptanalysis of the full AES-192 and AES-256. In: Matsui, M. (ed.) ASIACRYPT 2009. LNCS, vol. 5912, pp. 1–18. Springer, Heidelberg (2009). https://doi.org/10.1007/978-3-642-10366-7_1

21. Dunkelman, O., Keller, N., Shamir, A.: A practical-time related-key attack on the KASUMI cryptosystem used in GSM and 3G telephony. In: Rabin, T. (ed.) CRYPTO 2010. LNCS, vol. 6223, pp. 393–410. Springer, Heidelberg (2010). https://doi.org/10.1007/978-3-642-14623-7_21

22. Cid, C., Huang, T., Peyrin, T., Sasaki, Yu., Song, L.: Boomerang connectivity table: a new cryptanalysis tool. In: Nielsen, J.B., Rijmen, V. (eds.) EUROCRYPT 2018. LNCS, vol. 10821, pp. 683–714. Springer, Cham (2018). https://doi.org/10.1007/978-3-319-78375-8_22

23. Wang, H., Peyrin, T.: Boomerang switch in multiple rounds. Application to AES variants and deoxys. IACR Trans. Symmetric Cryptol. 2019(1), 142–169 (2019)

24. Song, L., Qin, X., Hu, L.: Boomerang connectivity table revisited. Application to SKINNY and AES. IACR Trans. Symmetric Cryptol. 2019(1), 118–141 (2019)

Optimal Convergence Nodes Deployment in Hierarchical Wireless Sensor Networks: An SMA-Based Approach

Jiahuan Yi, Kezhong Jin, Yu Xu, and Zhenzhou Tang$^{(\boxtimes)}$

College of Computer Science and Artificial Intelligence, Wenzhou University,
Wenzhou 325035, Zhejiang, China

Abstract. This paper investigates the optimal deployment of the convergence nodes in hierarchical wireless sensor networks (WSNs) since it plays an essential role in the performance of hierarchical WSNs, especially for those where the locations of sensing nodes are determined. By optimizing the locations of the convergence layer nodes, two optimization objectives are considered under the premise of ensuring that all sensing nodes are effectively connected: one is to minimize the total transmission power of sensing nodes, and the other is to make the energy consumption of the sensing nodes as balanced as possible to prolong the life of WSNs. These optimization problems are non-convex and NP-hard. To solve them, this paper proposes an optimization scheme based on the state-of-the-art swarm intelligence algorithm, namely the slime mould algorithm (SMA). The simulation results show that the SMA-based deployment scheme can dramatically reduce the total power of the sensing nodes and balance the energy consumption among sensing nodes.

Keywords: Wireless sensor networks · Optimal deployment · SMA

1 Introduction

For large scale wireless sensor networks (WSNs), hierarchical structures are typically preferred due to the strong scalability and stability [1,2]. A hierarchical WSN generally includes convergence nodes (CNs) and sensing nodes (SNs). An SN is mainly responsible for collecting information, and then forwarding it to the associated convergence node. And a CN collects data from the associated SNs and delivers them to servers. Typically, SNs are powered by batteries and it is not practical to replace or recharge them. While CNs are much less in number compared to SNs and typically have stable power supplies.

The deployment of CNs plays an important role in the performance of hierarchical WSNs and has aroused great interests. Reference [3] studied the deployment of heterogeneous wireless directional sensor networks in a three-dimensional intelligent city. A new distributed parallel multi-objective evolutionary algorithm

© Springer Nature Switzerland AG 2021
Z. Liu et al. (Eds.): WASA 2021, LNCS 12939, pp. 410–417, 2021.
https://doi.org/10.1007/978-3-030-86137-7_44

was proposed to optimize the coverage, connectivity quality, lifetime, connectivity and reliability. In [4], the deployment of sensor nodes and relay nodes in industrial environments is studied with the objectives of optimizing the security, lifetime and coverage. In [5], a WSN is applied to air pollution mapping, which solves the optimization problem of sensor deployment. On the premise of ensuring network connectivity and considering node perception error, two kinds of air pollution map layout models are derived by using the integer linear programming method. Reference [6] proposed a distributed parallel coevolutionary multi-objective large-scale evolutionary algorithm to optimize the WSN deployment in the three-dimensional (3D) cabin space of a super large crude oil carrier to improve the coverage, network lifetime and reliability. In [7], a real coverage model of 3D environment based on Bresenham line of sight is proposed, and multi-objective genetic algorithm is used to solve the problem with the number and location of sensors as the target.

In this paper, we aim to optimize the deployment of CNs for the hierarchical WSN where the locations of SNs are determined due to the explicit requirements of the monitoring area. The goal is to make the total Tx power of the sensing layer node as low as possible, or make the Tx power of the sensing layer node as balanced as possible. Studies in [8] and [9] also investigated the optimal deployment of CNs in hierarchical clustering WSNs, however, the objective was to achieve the full coverage of SNs with the lowest total power of CNs, but not SNs. It makes more sense to lower the power consumption of SNs rather than CNs since it is the SNs rather than CNs that are power constrained.

The above optimization problems are both non-convex and NP-hard, so it is difficult to obtain analytical solutions by using classical optimization theory. Therefore, this paper introduces a state-of-the-art swarm intelligence optimization algorithm (SIOA): slime mould algorithm (SMA) [10] to search for the approximate optimal solutions of the optimization problems. SIOAs have been proved to be highly effective in solving complicated optimization problems [11–13]. Moreover, this paper fully considers the non-uniformity of the actual deployment environment, that is, there are various obstacles within the deployment environment, which cause different degrees of attenuation to the wireless signals. It should be noted that although we only concern two-dimensional deployment scenarios in this work, it is straightforward to extend the proposed scheme to 3D scenarios by adding the value of z-axis as an additional decision variable.

The performance of the SMA-based optimized deployment mechanism are verified by sufficient simulations. The simulation results show that, compared with the traditional uniform distribution wireless sensor model, the SMA-based optimal convergence layer deployment scheme can significantly reduce the total transmission power of the sensing layer nodes and balance the energy consumption among sensing layer nodes on the premise that all sensing layer nodes are covered by the signal.

The rest of this paper is organized as follows: Sect. 1 introduces the system model of wireless sensor network and the mathematical model of the optimization problem. Section 2 describes the detailed process of SMA based hierarchical wireless sensor network aggregation layer topology optimization mechanism. Section 3 describes the simulation experiment and gives the optimized results. Finally, Sect. 4 summarizes the paper.

2   System Model

Consider a hierarchical WSN deployed in the two-dimensional area M which is divided into two layers, namely the sensing layer and the convergence layer. We assume that there are N_s sensing nodes (SNs) in the sensing layer, denoted as $\mathbb{S} = \{\mathrm{SN}_1, \mathrm{SN}_2, \ldots, \mathrm{SN}_{N_s}\}$ and $N_c \{N_c \ll N_s\}$ convergence nodes (CNs) in the convergence layer, denoted as $\mathbb{C} = \{\mathrm{CN}_1, \mathrm{CN}_2, \ldots, \mathrm{CN}_{N_c}\}$. Each CN associates with at least one SN while each SN can be associated to only one CN.

We divide the two-dimensional area M into m×m grids. Each grid is covered by one SN, that is, $N_s = m^2$. It is assumed that each SN is located in the center of the small square. The position of SN_i $(i = 1, 2, \cdots, N_s)$ is denoted as $L_{\mathrm{SN}_i} = (x_{\mathrm{SN}_i}, y_{\mathrm{SN}_i})$, and its Tx power is denoted as p_i $(p_{\min} \leq p_i \leq p_{\max})$. The position of CN_j $(j = 1, 2, \ldots, N_c)$ is $L_{\mathrm{CN}_j} = (x_{\mathrm{CN}_j}, y_{\mathrm{CN}_j})$. The receiving sensitivity of a CN is p_0. Meanwhile, we assume that each wireless link between a SN and a CN is bidirectional under the same transmission power, that is, as long as the signal of SN_i can effectively cover CN_j , the signal of CN_j can also effectively cover SN_i.

In this paper, the propagation attenuation of wireless signal from SN_i to CN_j is modeled as $\alpha = \beta_0 + 10\gamma \lg \frac{d_{i,j}}{d_0} + \beta_1$, where γ represents the attenuation factor, which depends on the surrounding environment; β_0 represents the attenuation of its signal caused by obstacles; d_0 is the reference distance; β_1 is the received power of d_0 at the reference distance; $d_{i,j} = \sqrt{\left(x_{\mathrm{SN}_i} - x_{\mathrm{CN}_j}\right)^2 + \left(y_{\mathrm{SN}_i} - y_{\mathrm{CN}_j}\right)^2}$ is the distance from SN_i to CN_j.

In order to better simulate the real environment, the target area M is set as a non-uniform environment, that is, there are various obstacles within M. These obstacles cause addition attenuation. If the line from SN_i to CN_j, denoted as $L_{i,j}$ passes through an obstacle, the attenuation caused by this obstacle is then taken into account.

The Boolean expression to judge whether SN_i is effectively covered by CN_j is as follows:

$$C\left(\mathrm{SN}_i, \mathrm{CN}_j\right) = \begin{cases} 1, & \text{if } p_i - \alpha \geq p_0 \\ 0, & \text{otherwise} \end{cases} \tag{1}$$

Consequently, the indicator that whether SN_i is covered by at least one CN can be defined as $C\left(\mathrm{SN}_i\right) = 1 - \prod_{\mathrm{CN}_j \in G} \left[1 - C\left(\mathrm{SN}_i, \mathrm{CN}_j\right)\right]$, and the coverage rate of the sensing nodes can be expressed as $E(S, G) = \frac{1}{N_s} \sum_{\mathrm{SN}_i \in S} C\left(\mathrm{SN}_i\right)$.

We use the variance to evaluate the energy consumption balance among sensing nodes, which is calculated as $\sigma = \frac{1}{N_s} \sum_{\mathrm{SN}_i \in S} (p_i - \bar{p})^2$, where $\bar{p} = \frac{1}{N_s} \sum_{\mathrm{SN}_i \in S} p_i$ represents the average power of the sensing nodes.

The optimization problem in this paper is to optimize the locations of the convergence nodes on the premise of ensuring the full coverage of the sensing nodes, so that 1) the total transmission power of the sensing nodes can be minimized, and 2) the transmission power can be balanced as far as possible. Therefore, the mathematical model of the optimization problem is defined as follows:

$$OP1 : \min_{\mathbf{L}_{CN}} \left(\sum_{SN_i \in S} p_i \right)$$

$$OP2 : \min_{\mathbf{L}_{CN}} \sigma \qquad (2)$$

$$\text{s.t. } E\left(S, G\right) = 1$$

where $\mathbf{L}_{\mathrm{CN}} = \left\{ (x_{\mathrm{CN}_1}, y_{\mathrm{CN}_1}), (x_{\mathrm{CN}_2}, y_{\mathrm{CN}_2}), \cdots, (x_{\mathrm{CN}_{N_c}}, y_{\mathrm{CN}_{N_c}}) \right\}$ is the location vector for convergence nodes, the constraint is the full coverage requirement.

3   SMA Based Optimal Deployment Scheme

The location vector of CNs ($\mathbf{L}_{\mathrm{CN}}$) is mapped to the position of a slime mould in the super dimensional space. That is, each individual in the swarm represents a candidate solution of (2). Slime moulds approach food according to the smell in the air which is interpreted as the fitness in the optimization algorithm. In this paper, the fitness is defined as follows:

$$\mathcal{F}(\mathbf{L}_{\mathrm{CN}}) = \begin{cases} OP1 : & \sum_{SN_i \in S} p_i, \\ OP2 : & \sigma. \end{cases} \qquad (3)$$

The approach behavior and contraction mode of the ith slime mould in the swarm in the tth iteration can be modeled as

$$\mathbf{L}_{\mathrm{CN}}(t+1, i) = \begin{cases} r_0 \left(\mathbf{B}_u - \mathbf{B}_l \right) + \mathbf{B}_l, r_1 < z \\ \mathbf{L}_{\mathrm{CN}}^{\mathrm{best}}(t) + \mathbf{v}_b \cdot \left(w \cdot \mathbf{L}_{\mathrm{CN}}^A(t) - \mathbf{L}_{\mathrm{CN}}^B(t) \right), r_1 \geq z, r_2 < p \\ \mathbf{v}_c \cdot \mathbf{L}_{\mathrm{CN}}(t, i), r_1 \geq z, r_2 \geq p \end{cases} \qquad (4)$$

The variables and vectors involved in (4) are explained as follows. $\mathbf{B}_u$ and $\mathbf{B}_l$ are upper and lower bound of location coordinates. r_0, r_1 and r_2 are random values within the range of $[0, 1]$. z is a predefined threshold. $\mathbf{L}_{\mathrm{CN}}(t, i)|_{N_p \times 2N_c}$ is the ith individual in the tth iteration and N_p is the population size. $\mathbf{L}_{\mathrm{CN}}^{\mathrm{best}}(t)$ is the best individual, that is, the individual achieves the best fitness by the tth iteration. $\mathbf{V}_b$ and $\mathbf{V}_c$ are two random factors where $|\mathbf{v}_b| \leq \operatorname{arctanh} \left(-\frac{t}{\max_t t} + 1 \right)$ and $|\mathbf{v}_c| \leq \frac{t}{\max_t t}$, respectively. $t = 1, 2, \ldots, \mathrm{iter}_{\max}$ is the current iteration and $\mathbf{L}_{\mathrm{CN}}^A(t)$ and $\mathbf{L}_{\mathrm{CN}}^B(t)$ represent two individuals randomly selected from the swarm. p can be calculated as:

$$p = \tanh |\mathcal{F}(t, i) - \mathcal{F}_{\mathrm{best}}(t)|, i = 1, 2, \ldots, N_p \qquad (5)$$

where $\mathcal{F}(t, i)$ returns the fitness of the ih individual in $\mathbf{L}_{\mathrm{CN}}(t)$, $\mathcal{F}_{\mathrm{best}}(t) = \mathcal{F}\left(\mathbf{L}_{\mathrm{CN}}^{\mathrm{best}}(t) \right)$. w is the fitness weight vector which can be calculated as:

$$\overline{w\left(\mathbf{I}_{\mathcal{F}}(i)\right)} = \begin{cases} 1 + r \cdot \log \left(\frac{\mathcal{F}_{\mathrm{best}}(t) - \mathcal{F}(t, i)}{\mathcal{F}_{\mathrm{best}}(t) - \mathcal{F}_{\mathrm{worst}}(t)} + 1 \right), & \text{condition} \\ 1 - r \cdot \log \left(\frac{\mathcal{F}_{\mathrm{best}}(t) - \mathcal{F}(t, i)}{\mathcal{F}_{\mathrm{best}}(t) - \mathcal{F}_{\mathrm{worst}}(t)} + 1 \right), & \text{others} \end{cases} \qquad (6)$$

where $r \in [0,1]$ is a random value, the condition indicates that $\mathcal{F}\left(\mathbf{L}_{\mathrm{CN}}^{i}(t)\right)$ ranks first half of the population, $\mathcal{F}_{\mathrm{worst}}(t)$ is the worst fitness value obtained in the iterative process currently, $\mathbf{I}_{\mathcal{F}}$ denotes the sequence of fitness values sorted in ascending order.

The pseudo code of the SMA-based optimal CN deployment scheme is summarized in Algorithm 1.

Algorithm 1. SMA-based optimal CN deployment scheme.

Initialize N_p, iter$_{\max}$, $t \leftarrow 0$ and the CN positions $\mathbf{L}_{\mathrm{CN}}(t,i), \forall i \in [1, N_p]$;
while $(t \leq$ iter$_{\max})$ **do**
    for each individual i in the population **do**
        Calculate $\mathcal{F}(t,i)$ by (3);
    end for
    $\mathbf{L}_{\mathrm{CN}}^{\mathrm{best}}(t) \leftarrow \arg\min_{\mathbf{L}_{\mathrm{CN}}} \mathcal{F}(t)$;
    $\mathcal{F}_{\mathrm{best}}(t) \leftarrow \mathcal{F}(\mathbf{L}_{\mathrm{CN}}^{\mathrm{best}}(t))$;
    Calculate $\mathbf{w}$ by (6);
    $t \leftarrow t+1$;
    for each individual i in the population **do**
        Update p by (5);
        Randomly update $\mathbf{v}_b$ and$\mathbf{v}_c$;
        Update $\mathbf{L}_{\mathrm{CN}}(t,i)$ by (4);
    end for
end while
return $\mathcal{F}_{\mathrm{best}}(t)$, $\mathbf{L}_{\mathrm{CN}}^{\mathrm{best}}(t)$;

4　Simulation Experiment

In this study, a two-dimensional space M of $100\,\mathrm{m} \times 100\,\mathrm{m}$ is simulated and divided into 20×20 grids, as shown in Fig. 1(a). One sensing node is placed in the center of each grid. Initially, 36 convergence nodes are evenly placed in the target area (green triangles in Fig. 1(a)). In order to better simulate the heterogeneous environment in real life, we also add some common obstacles in the simulation space. The attenuation introduced by load bearing walls, rick walls and wooden walls is 30 dB, 15 dB and 10 dB respectively. The maximum and minimum powers of sensing layer node are 23.5 dBm and 1 dBm, respectively. The attenuation factor (γ) is 3, the reference distance (d_0) is 1 m.

We assume that each SN knows the location of the associated CN and always adjusts its Tx power to the lowest value which ensures a reliable connection. In the initial layout, the minimum total Tx power of the sensing nodes is 10680.39 mW. The association between the convergence nodes and the sensing nodes is shown in Fig. 1(a). The Tx power of each sensing node is shown in Fig. 1(b). It can be observed that the TX powers of sensing nodes are distributed over a considerable large range. The Tx power variance is 1127.76.

4.1   Optimization on Total Tx Power

Firstly, the deployment of convergence nodes is optimized with the objective of minimizing the total Tx power of sensing nodes by the proposed SMA-based scheme. The population size is 500 and the maximum number of iteration is 2000. The optimization process is shown in Fig. 1(c). It can be seen from the figure that in the first 500 iterations, slime moulds are looking for a higher quality food source, and the total Tx power remains unchanged. With the continuous iteration of the algorithm, it can be seen that the total Tx power of the sensing nodes is significantly reduced. The total Tx power remains stable after about 1800 iterations, with the value of 6032.16 mW. Compared with the total Tx power of 10680.39 mW before optimization, a 43.52% reduction is achieved. The optimized locations of the convergence nodes and the association between the sensing nodes and convergence nodes are shown in Fig. 1(d).

4.2   Optimization on Energy Consumption Balance

Then, we optimize the deployment of the convergence nodes to minimize the variance of the TX powers of the sensing nodes, so that the energy consumption of the sensing nodes can be balanced. The optimization process is shown in Fig. 1(e). Similarly, it can be observed that the variance of the Tx power starts to drop after 500 iterations and remains stable at the value of 166.72 after about 1500 iterations, which is only 14.78% of the original. Figure 1(f) depicts the distribution of the TX powers of the sensing nodes after optimization. Compared with Fig. 1(b), the TX powers is much more balanced at this time. The optimized locations of the convergence nodes and the association between the sensing nodes and convergence nodes are shown in Fig. 1(d).

We further evaluated the survival rate of sensing nodes and the survival time of the WSN. It is assumed that each sensing node has the same total energy $(1 \times 10^4 \text{ J})$ and that each sensing node transmits and receives data for a period of 10 ms per second. A sensing node is considered dead if its energy decreases to 0. In addition, the whole WSN is considered dead if 30% of the sensing nodes die.

Figure 1(h) compares the survival rate and the network survival time between the traditional uniform deployment and the optimized one. It can be found that the death rates drop significantly in the optimized deployed WSNs compared with the uniformly deployed WSN. The uniformly deployed WSN stops working (30% of SNs run out of energy) after 307056 s, while as a contrast, only 4% and 1.75% of SNs die in the OP1-optimized scenario (OP1) and the OP2-optimized scenario (OP2) by then, respectively. The OP1-optimized WSN can survive for 892536 s. And the OP2-optimized WSN lives much longer than the other two. It continues working for up to 1020668 s.

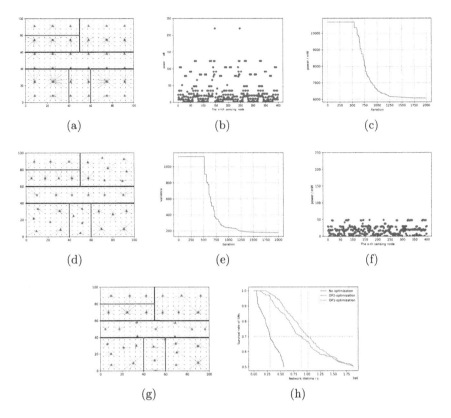

Fig. 1. (a) Initial deployment and associations between SNs and CNs, (b) Tx powers of SNs in initial deployment, (c) OP1: Converge curve of the total Tx power of SNs, (d) OP1: Associations between SNs and CNs, (e) OP2: Converge curve of the total Tx power of SNs, (f) OP2: Tx powers of SNs, (g) OP2: Associations between SNs and CNs, (f). Survival rate of SNs.

5 Conclusion

In this paper, we propose an optimized convergence node deployment scheme for hierarchical WSNs based on SMA. The objectives are to minimize the total Tx power or balance the power consumption among sensing nodes on the premise of full coverage of the sensing nodes.

Moreover, this paper fully considers various obstacles which introduce additional signal attenuation within the target area. Experimental results show that the optimal deployment scheme can greatly reduce the total energy consumption of the sensing nodes, promote the energy consumption balance among sensing nodes, and prolong the network lifetime.

Acknowledgement. This work was supported in part by the Zhejiang Provincial Natural Science Foundation of China under Grants No. LZ20F010008 and No. LY19F010010, in part by Fundamental Scientific Research Project of Wenzhou City under Grants No. G20180008.

References

1. Baronti, P., Pillai, P., Chook, V.W., Chessa, S., Gotta, A., Hu, Y.F.: Wireless sensor networks: a survey on the state of the art and the 802.15.4 and ZigBee standards. Comput. Commun **80**(7), 1655–1695 (2007)
2. Rawat, P., Singh, K.D., Chaouchi, H., Bonnin, J.M.: Wireless sensor networks: a survey on recent developments and potential synergies. J. Supercomput. **68**(1), 1–48 (2013). https://doi.org/10.1007/s11227-013-1021-9
3. Cao, B., Zhao, J., Yang, P., Yang, P., Liu, X., Zhang, Y.: 3-D deployment optimization for heterogeneous wireless directional sensor networks on smart city. IEEE Trans. Industr. Inf. **15**(3), 1798–1808 (2019)
4. Cao, B., Zhao, J., Gu, Y., Fan, S., Yang, P.: Security-aware industrial wireless sensor network deployment optimization. IEEE Trans. Industr. Inf. **16**(8), 5309–5316 (2020)
5. Boubrima, A., Bechkit, W., Rivano, H.: On the deployment of wireless sensor networks for air quality mapping: optimization models and algorithms. IEEE/ACM Trans. Netw. **27**, 1629–1642 (2019)
6. Cao, B., Zhao, J., Yang, P., Lv, Z., Liu, X., Min, G.: 3-D multiobjective deployment of an industrial wireless sensor network for maritime applications utilizing a distributed parallel algorithm. IEEE Trans. Industr. Inf. **14**(12), 5487–5495 (2018)
7. Saad, A., Senouci, M.R., Benyattou, O.: Toward a realistic approach for the deployment of 3D wireless sensor networks. IEEE Trans. Mobile Comput. (2020)
8. Zhi, Z., Chen, X., Li, C., Tang, Z.: Multi-objective optimization on deployment of convergence layer in hierarchical clustering wireless sensor networks. Chin. J. Sens. Actuators **33**(4), 571–578 (2020)
9. Liu, P., Meng, X., Tang, S., Tang, Z.: Optimization on 3D deployment of hierarchical heterogeneous wireless sensor networks: an adaptive FOA approach. Chin. J. Sens. Actuators **33**(7), 1033–1040 (2020)
10. Li, S., Chen, H., Wang, M., Heidari, A.A., Mirjalili, S.: Slime mould algorithm: a new method for stochastic optimization. Future Gener. Comput. Syst. **111**, 300–323 (2020)
11. Liu, P., Hu, Q., Jin, K., Yu, G., Tang, Z.: Toward the energy-saving optimization of WLAN deployment in real 3-D environment: a hybrid swarm intelligent method. IEEE Syst. J. 1–12 (2021)
12. Fan, J., Tang, Z., Hu, Q.: Predicting vacant parking space availability: an SVR method with fruit fly optimisation. IET Intell. Transp. Syst. **12**(10), 1414–1420 (2018)
13. Zhou, M., Lin, F., Hu, Q., Tang, Z., Jin, C.: AI-enabled diagnosis of spontaneous rupture of ovarian endometriomas: a PSO enhanced random forest approach. IEEE Access **8**, 132253–132264 (2020)

A Virtual-Potential-Field-Based Cooperative Opportunistic Routing Protocol for UAV Swarms

Mengfan Yan, Lei Lei$^{(\boxtimes)}$, Shengsuo Cai, and Jie Wang

College of Electronic and Information Engineering, Nanjing University of Aeronautics and Astronautics, Nanjing 211106, China
{mengfan.yan,leilei,caishengsuo,wangjie199696}@nuaa.edu.cn

Abstract. Due to highly dynamic links and unstable wireless channels, designing reliable and efficient routing protocols for UAV swarm networks is challenging. In this paper, a modified virtual potential field method is developed to coordinate the UAV swarm and provide local topology information. Both coordination and mutual influence between UAVs are taken into consideration for virtual force calculation. Next, a new Virtual-Potential-Field-based Cooperative Opportunistic Routing (VPFCOR) protocol is proposed. VPFCOR comprehensively combines three main metrics for candidate ordering, i.e., forwarding distance, virtual force and remaining energy. With these metrics, VPFCOR can effectively adapt to different tasks, take smaller routing overhead and meet the real-time requirement. Simulation results are presented to obtain the optimal parameter settings and validate the effectiveness of our proposed protocol.

Keywords: Virtual potential field · Opportunistic routing · UAV swarms

1 Introduction

Unmanned Aerial Vehicle (UAV) is an emerging technology that can be harnessed for military, public and civil applications, e.g., military confrontation, fire rescue, agricultural monitoring, and logistics transportation. UAV swarm networks have the characteristics of high node mobility and fast topology changes, resulting in highly dynamic links and unstable wireless channels. In order to achieve effective cooperation and information exchange between multiple UAVs, it is essential to design an effective routing protocol for message transmission in multi-hop UAV swarm networks [1]. Traditional routing protocols include two main processes, i.e., route discovery and routing table maintenance. However, due to highly dynamic links and unstable wireless channels, the

This work was supported in part by the National Natural Science Foundation of China (No. 61902182), the Natural Science Foundation of Jiangsu Province of China (No. BK20190409), the Aeronautical Science Foundation of China (No. 2016ZC52029), Qing Lan Project of Jiangsu Province of China, China Postdoctoral Science Foundation (No. 2019TQ0153), and the Foundation of CETC Key Laboratory of Aerospace Information Applications of China (No.SXX18629T022).

© Springer Nature Switzerland AG 2021
Z. Liu et al. (Eds.): WASA 2021, LNCS 12939, pp. 418–428, 2021.
https://doi.org/10.1007/978-3-030-86137-7_45

use of traditional routing protocol in UAV swarm networks will generate a huge routing overhead and lead to a decline in the overall performance of the network. In addition, since the energy of a UAV is usually limited, the signal strength decays exponentially with the increase of distance. Thus, we also need to consider the impact of the remaining energy of UAVs.

Opportunistic Routing (OR) [2] provides a method to solve such issues. By dynamically selecting the forwarder from a set of multiple receivers, opportunistic routing can significantly reduce the number of packet retransmissions caused by link failures. It also eliminates the need to maintain expensive topology information. However, which node should be chosen from the candidate relay set in each forwarding process is very challenging. A good choice can make routing more efficient. In the literature, the most widely used method is candidate ordering [3] based on one of the following metrics: hop count, geographic distance, Expected Transmission Times (ETX), Expected Transmission Time (ETT), and coding gain. However, considering of a single metric will cause drastic depletion of UAVs' onboard energy which reduces the overall network performance. Zhao et al. considers multiple metrics and proposes a Topology and Link Quality-aware Geographical Opportunistic Routing (TLG-OR) protocol [4]. However, it needs to collect and maintain a lot of topology information. Many other techniques are adopted to improve the performance of OR including mobility modeling, topology awareness, and link quality characterization [5, 6]. However, the effectiveness of these methods depends heavily on the quality and quantity of topology related information collection. Besides, Sang et al. predicted the position of a UAV to facilitate opportunistic communication. However, it only considers the movement of the UAV independently without consider the influence of surrounding nodes.

In this work, we propose a new virtual-potential-field-based cooperative opportunistic routing (VPFCOR) protocol for multi-hop UAV swarm networks. The main contributions are in two folds. Firstly, a modified virtual potential field method is developed to coordinate the UAV swarm and provide local topology information. Different from traditional methods that only consider the impact of the environment on individual UAV, we consider both coordination and mutual influence between UAVs. Secondly, considering both swarm cooperation and opportunistic communication, VPFCOR comprehensively combines three main metrics for candidate ordering, i.e., forwarding distance, virtual force and remaining energy. Specially, with the help of virtual force, nodes' movement information is effectively predicted to form a more accurate candidate relay set without missing some nodes. In general, VPFCOR has the following advantages: (1) VPFCOR can adapt to different tasks with flexible weights of different metrics and provide good performance of UAV swarm network; (2) The routing overhead is small because only local topology information is required; (3) The real-time requirement is guaranteed with the help of highly efficient virtual potential field technique.

2   Virtual Potential Field for UAV Swarm

In this section, we introduce a modified virtual potential field method by taking account of the coordination and mutual influence between UAVs. Virtual potential field has the advantage of simple, efficient and smooth trajectory planning [7]. The algorithm does not need to search the global trajectory, thus the planning time is short. The efficiency is high, and the real-time requirements is guaranteed.

The basic virtual potential field method is to abstract the environment of the intelligent individual into a virtual potential field, and the individual is moved by the force in the virtual potential field. In general, there are two basic forces, i.e., attraction and repulsion. The superposition of attraction and repulsion vectors form a resultant force, and the individual moves towards the target point under the effect of the resultant force. However, in UAV swarm, due to fast-moving speed and large number of UAVs, swarm topology changes rapidly, resulting in complex and dynamic network. Simple attraction and repulsion cannot satisfy the accurate description of the force situation of a UAV in the swarm. In this work, three main forces are considered for UAV swarm network, i.e., guidance force (generated by the destination), topology force (generated by neighboring UAVs) and obstacle avoidance force (generated by obstacles).They are shown in Fig. 1. The combination of three forces is the resultant force of the UAV.

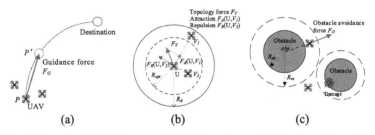

Fig. 1. Virtual force in the UAV swarm: (a) Guidance force; (b) Topology force; (c) Obstacle avoidance force.

2.1 Guidance Force

When the UAV is moving, the goal can be a temporary point in the path planning process or the destination of the entire swarm movement. The guidance force is the force that navigate UAV to reach the designated point. The UAV in Fig. 1(a) has planned a motion path in advance. The UAV is currently at point P and its coordinate is $P\,(x_p, y_p, z_p)$. The UAV knows that it should be in $P'\,(x_{p'}, y_{p'}, z_{p'})$ at the next moment with path plan. At the moment, the value of guidance force $\overrightarrow{F_G}$ can be calculated by:

$$F_G = k_G \sqrt{\left(x_p - x_{p'}\right)^2 + \left(y_p - y_{p'}\right)^2 + \left(z_p - z_{p'}\right)^2} \tag{1}$$

where k_G is the guidance force gain. The direction is the vector direction from P to P'. The guidance force in Fig. 1(a) is the largest at the beginning of the movement, and gradually decreases when it approaches the intermediate temporary point P', so as to form a good and stable network topology before the next move. If a UAV does not plan the path in advance, it will be affected by the guidance force from the destination and move directly to it.

2.2 Topology Force

UAV swarm is composed of a large number of UAV nodes, and two UAVs within a certain range will generate interaction forces. The interaction force between UAVs is defined as topology force. The topology force not only plays a key role in maintaining the topology of the swarm, but also effectively prevent the UAVs from being too close to cause collisions.

Figure 1(b) illustrates the attraction and repulsion of the topology force within neighboring nodes, i.e., nodes U and V (V_1, V_2, ..., V_n). Note that R_d is the detection range of a UAV, and R_{opt} is the optimal distance of two neighboring UAVs. If the distance between UAVs U and V is less than R_d, they will move close by attraction. However, if the distance is less than R_{opt}, they will be away from each other by repulsion. When the distance between UAVs is R_{opt}, two forces between them cancel out each other. At a certain moment, UAV V will have at most one force acting on UAV U.

The values of attraction $\overrightarrow{F_A(U,V_1)}$ and repulsion $\overrightarrow{F_R(U, V_2)}$ between UAVs U and V can be expressed by:

$$F_A(U, V_1) = k_A\big[D(U, V_1) - R_{opt}\big] \quad R_{opt} \leq D(U, V_1) \leq R_d \qquad (2)$$

$$F_R(U, V_2) = k_R \cdot \left[\frac{1}{D(U, V_2)^2} - \frac{1}{R_{opt}^2}\right] \quad 0 < D(U, V_2) < R_{opt} \qquad (3)$$

where k_A and k_R are the attractive and repulsive gain coefficient, respectively. D (U, V) is the Euclidean distance between UAVs U and V. The direction of $\overrightarrow{F_A(U, V_1)}$ is the vector direction from U to V_1 and the direction of $\overrightarrow{F_R(U, V_2)}$ is the vector direction from V_2 to U.

We define UAVs with distance less than R_d from UAV U as $N(U)$. The topology force on UAV U is calculated by:

$$\overrightarrow{F_T} = \alpha_A \sum_{V \in N(U)} \overrightarrow{F_A(U, V)} + \alpha_R \sum_{V \in N(U)} \overrightarrow{F_R(U, V)} \quad 0 \leq \alpha_A, \alpha_R \leq 1 \qquad (4)$$

where α_A and α_R are attraction and repulsion weight, respectively. By adjusting the relationship between α_A and α_R, the best effect of topology force can be obtained in different swarm environments.

2.3 Obstacle Avoidance Force

In many scenarios, UAV swarm often encounters obstacles such as mountains and buildings while moving. In the virtual potential field, the area that threatens UAVs is abstracted into a geometric obstacle. The force that hinders the movement is defined as obstacle avoidance force. The obstacle avoidance force acts on UAVs in the form of repulsion. In this paper, we assume that a UAV detects obstacles based on its own sensors and shares the information with other UAVs. We define the set of obstacles around UAV U as O(U).

In Fig. 1(c), we abstract irregular obstacles into circles. The dangerous distance of the obstacle is defined as R_{ds}. Distance between the UAV and the center of obstacle needs to be kept greater than R_{ds} or the UAV is damaged. The required distance of obstacle avoidance reactions from the center of obstacle is defined as R_{re}. When distance from the obstacle to the UAV is less than R_{re}, the UAV will be subject to repulsion from the obstacle. For a UAV U, the value of obstacle avoidance force $\overrightarrow{F_O}$ it receives from the obstacle *obs* can be expressed by:

$$F_O(\text{U}, obs) = k_O \cdot [R_{re} - D(\text{U}, obs)] \, R_{ds} \leq D(\text{U}, obs) \leq R_{re} \tag{5}$$

where k_O is the obstacle avoidance gain coefficient, and D (U, *obs*) is the distance between the current UAV and the center of the obstacle. The direction of $\overrightarrow{F_O}$ is the vector direction from *obs* to U. Then the sum of all obstacle avoidance forces on U is:

$$\overrightarrow{F_O} = \sum_{obs \in O(\text{U})} \overrightarrow{F_O(\text{U}, obs)} \tag{6}$$

We add up the three forces in (1), (4), and (6) to achieve the resultant force $\overrightarrow{F_{RS}}$:

$$\overrightarrow{F_{RS}} = \beta_G \overrightarrow{F_G} + \beta_T \overrightarrow{F_T} + \beta_O \overrightarrow{F_O} \quad 0 \leq \beta_G, \beta_T, \beta_O \leq 1 \tag{7}$$

where β_G, β_T and β_O are the weight coefficient of guidance force, topology force and obstacle avoidance force, respectively. The UAV is moved by the force in the virtual potential field. In different scenarios, the optimal resultant force can be achieved by changing the ratio between β_G, β_T and β_O.

3   The Virtual-Potential-Field-Based Cooperative Opportunistic Routing Protocol

This section introduces the VPFCOR protocol. VPFCOR takes into account forwarding distance, virtual force and remaining energy to make a joint consideration. In order to minimize overhead and duplicate transmissions, VPFCOR optimizes the candidate relay set according to these metrics.

3.1   Candidate Ordering

Assume that the one-hop transmission distance at source node i is R_{tx}. Within R_{tx}, the relay node set of source node i is defined as N_i (j), where j represents nodes in this set $(j = 1, 2, 3, ..., n)$.

Forwarding Distance
The purpose of opportunistic routing is to forward data packets to the destination node faster and better. The best relay selection should consider the relative position of candidate relay node and destination node, so that each transmission can advance towards the destination node as much as possible. Then it can reduce the number of network transmission hops and improve the overall network performance.

We define D (i, d) as the Euclidean distance from the source node i to the destination node d. For N_i (j), the distance to the source node i is D $(i, N_i$ $(j))$ and the distance to the destination node d is $D(N_i(j), d)$. The forwarding distance of candidate relay nodes $March(N_i(j))$ is the projection of $D(N_i(j), d)$ on $D(i, d)$. It is expressed by:

$$March(N_i(j)) = \frac{D^2(i, N_i(j)) + D^2(i, d) - D^2(N_i(j), d)}{2 \times D(i, d)} \tag{8}$$

To facilitate subsequent calculations, the normalized distance $Mar(N_i(j))$ of the candidate relay nodes $N_i(j)$ is:

$$Mar(N_i(j)) = \frac{March(N_i(j))}{R_{tx}} \tag{9}$$

Virtual Force

In the virtual potential field, the UAV node is affected by three forces: the guidance force from destination, the topology force from other UAV nodes and the obstacle avoidance force from obstacles. When selecting the best candidate relay for a node, not only the current position but also the motion of the candidate relay nodes must be considered.

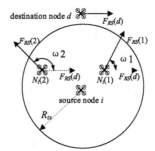

Fig. 2. Angle of virtual force between nodes.

As shown in Fig. 2, there are source node i, relay nodes $N_i(1)$, $N_i(2)$, and destination node d. For the source node i, the forwarding distances of nodes $N_i(1)$ and $N_i(2)$ are similar. It is not appropriate to select the best relay node only from the perspective of forwarding distance. For a dynamic topology, if the node carrying data can move toward the destination node, it can reduce the number of network hops to a certain extent and effectively improve the performance of the network. Figure 2 shows virtual forces of the candidate relay nodes $N_i(1)$, $N_i(2)$ and the destination node d in the UAV swarm. The expression of angle ω_j between them is:

$$\omega_j = \cos^{-1}\left(\frac{\overrightarrow{F_{RS}(j)} \cdot \overrightarrow{F_{RS}(d)}}{\left|\overrightarrow{F_{RS}(j)}\right| \times \left|\overrightarrow{F_{RS}(d)}\right|}\right) \tag{10}$$

According to (10), the value range of ω_j of the candidate relay nodes is $[0, \pi]$. Smaller ω_j indicates that the virtual force directions of the candidate relay node and the destination node are more consistent. When ω_j is closer to π, it indicates that the movement direction of the candidate relay node and the destination node is approximately opposite. To facilitate calculation, the virtual force angle between them is normalized by:

$$Vir(N_i(j)) = \frac{\pi - w_j}{\pi} \tag{11}$$

Remaining Energy

UAVs are usually powered by batteries and the energy a UAV possessed is limited. Therefore, when prioritizing candidate relay nodes, the remaining energy of the UAV needs to be included in the evaluation criteria. Distributing the forwarding task to the UAV nodes with more remaining energy can effectively extend the swarm networks duration and improve overall network performance.

The remaining energy of a UAV is E_0. If it is selected as a relay node, the remaining energy will be E_0' after time t. In order to ensure that the UAV node retains enough energy to work, the minimum threshold of energy is E_{min}. For convenience of calculation, the remaining energy of the UAV node is normalized. The normalized remaining energy of node j is represented by $Ene\ (N_i\ (j))$ and its expression is:

$$Ene(N_i(j)) = \begin{cases} 0 & E_0 \leq E_{min} \\ \frac{E_0' - E_{min}}{E_0 - E_{min}} & E_0 > E_{min} \end{cases} \tag{12}$$

The priority equation of $N_i\ (j)$ is:

$$\begin{cases} Val(N_i(j)) = \gamma_M Mar(N_i(j)) + \gamma_V Vir(N_i(j)) + \gamma_E Ene(N_i(j)) \\ \gamma_M + \gamma_V + \gamma_E = 1 \end{cases} \tag{13}$$

where γ_M, γ_V, and γ_E are the weight coefficient of forwarding distance, virtual force and remaining energy. The node with greater $Val(N_i(j))$ has higher priority. We use the timer-based coordination method. The response of the candidate relay node with the highest priority can prevent the response of others with lower priority. If a candidate relay node hears the response before the timer expires, it will give up forwarding, otherwise it will reply after the timer expires. In different tasks, the weighting coefficients should be adjusted for the specific environment. In different network environments, it is necessary to find the best coefficient allocation scheme, which can effectively improve the overall performance of the network.

3.2 Candidate Filtering

Due to the high-speed mobility of UAVs and the rapid change of topology, data packets will be repeatedly transmitted between several nodes, resulting in a waste of network resources. Although including more candidates in the candidate relays set provides higher resiliency, it is often better to limit the number of candidate relays in order to minimize overhead and duplicate transmissions [8]. Therefore we optimize the candidate relay set according to (9), (11) and (13). When the forwarding distance $Mar\ (N_i\ (j))$ is a negative number, it indicates that the candidate relay node is in the opposite direction to the destination node. In order to avoid data transmission in the opposite direction, this node will not reply or forward packets. Similarly, when the remaining energy of a candidate relay node is lower than the preset threshold E_{min}, the node will also give up forwarding. During the movement of the UAV swarm, obstacles will cause UAVs to split briefly. There may be no candidate relay nodes in the filtered candidate relays set. When the node carrying data has no candidate relays set, the node will enter the "store-carry-forward" mode and continue to move, waiting for the next motion to try routing discovery again.

4 Performance Evaluation

Table 1. Parameter settings.

Parameter	Value
Simulation area	6000 m × 6000 m
Target coordinate	(5000, 5000)
Maximum speed of UAV V_{max}	20 m/s
Obstacle coordinates	(2500, 2500), (3500, 2500)
Number of UAVs	30
Initial energy of UAV E_0	10000
Minimum energy threshold E_{min}	1000

In the simulation, we design a UAV swarm motion scenario with obstacle avoidance. The parameter settings are shown in Table 1. UAVs are randomly distributed in the range of 2000 m × 2000 m, moving towards the target under the action of virtual force. The final trajectory is shown in Fig. 3. When the UAV swarm passes through obstacles, avoidance force plays a major role. It is divided into two subgroups. After bypassing obstacles, they recombine a whole under the action of topology force.

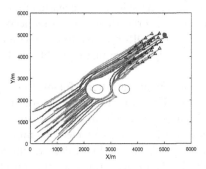

Fig. 3. Moving path of the UAV swarm.

The source node and destination node are randomly generated. The data packet will be forwarded by other nodes in the UAV swarm and finally received by the destination node. The simulation time is 200 s. When selecting the forwarding node, the node carrying the data packet will use the VPFCOR opportunistic routing strategy to select the best relay node. It can be seen from Sect. 3 that the performance of the VPFCOR routing protocol is affected by the distribution relationship of γ_M, γ_V and γ_E. Figure 4(a) gives average forwarding times of different coefficient combinations. We can find that combinations giving all weights to forwarding distance or virtual force lead to more forwarding times. In this scenario, combination VPFCOR-1 ($\gamma_M = 0.6$, $\gamma_V = 0.3$, $\gamma_E = 0.1$) has the least forwarding times. To further analyze the performance of VPFCOR in different moments of the simulation, we choose another combination VPFCOR-2 ($\gamma_M = 0.6$, $\gamma_V = 0.3$, $\gamma_E = 0.1$) as comparison. Meanwhile, we compare our VPFCOR with the classic Extremely Opportunistic Routing (ExOR) and TLG-OR in terms of times of entering "store-carry-forward" mode, average forwarding times and average end-to-end delay.

Figure 4(b) shows times of nodes entering the "store-carry-forward" mode. In the simulation process, this mode is mainly triggered when the UAV swarm encounters obstacles. Message transmission utilizing movement of UAV will consume a lot of time and we should reduce times of nodes entering the mode. The traditional opportunistic routing strategies TLG-OR and ExOR have 9 and 11 times respectively. Compared with traditional routing protocols, VPFCOR-1and VPFCOR-2 takes into account the virtual force and reduce times, reducing the delay caused by interrupt. When the UAV swarm networks topology changes frequently and the swarm motion path is relatively random, appropriately increasing the weight of virtual force can obtain better network performance.

Figure 4(c) shows the average forwarding times at different moments. Traditional opportunistic routing ExOR is a classic routing protocol considering hops. In the initial stage, UAVs move in a relatively fixed topology under the action of virtual forces. ExOR can complete data transmission with less forwarding times. However, when encountering obstacles, the movement of UAV adversely affects its performance. The current relay node selection is often not optimal at the next moment. TLG-OR considers too many factors and they change quickly, the forwarding times is greater than that of other routing protocols. When the UAV swarm encounters obstacles and divides, there is a certain improvement of performance. VPFCOR considers the virtual force of UAV nodes on the basis of the forwarding distance. In the network scenario of nodes moving and topology changing, the average number of forwarding times is reduced and the overall network performance is improved. In VPFCOR-2, virtual force plays a major role. Although the forwarding times is generally higher than that of VPFCOR-1, it is hardly affected by obstacles.

Time delay is one of the important criteria for measuring network performance. Figure 4(d) shows the average delay of a packet of the four protocols. ExOR does not consider the influence of distance and movement factors on relay selection. As can be seen from the figure, because VPFCOR-1 considers the impact of UAV movement on topology changes, the network delay of it is lower than traditional opportunistic routing. In the initial stage of this simulation scenario, since the trajectory of the UAV swarm

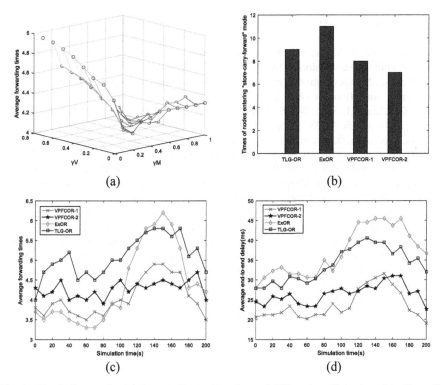

Fig. 4. Simulation results: (a) Average forwarding times of different coefficient combinations; (b) Times of nodes entering "store-carry-forward" mode; (c) Average forwarding times; (d) Average end-to-end delay.

is relatively fixed and the randomness is small, an appropriate increase in the weight coefficient of the forwarding distance can effectively improve the network performance. The VPFCOR-2 takes too much virtual force into consideration and sacrifices the benefits of distance. In the initial stage of the swarm movement, the topology basically does not change, resulting in a higher delay in the UAV swarm networks when using this strategy.

5 Conclusion

The design of routing schemes is essential and mandatory to better assist packet transmission of UAV swarm networks. In this paper, we first modified the virtual potential field method to calculate the virtual forces of a UAV in the swarm. The influence of obstacles, targets and surrounding UAVs are considered to calculate the guidance force, topology force and obstacle avoidance force. Next, a new virtual-potential-field-based cooperative opportunistic routing protocol is proposed by taking into account the influence of forwarding distance, virtual force and remaining energy comprehensively. Simulation results are presented to validate the effectiveness of our proposed protocol. In our future work, we will combine virtual force and forwarding distance with other QoS metrics, e.g., delay and link quality. It is also an interesting attempt.

References

1. Gupta, L., Jain, R., Vaszkun, G.: Survey of important issues in UAV communication networks. IEEE Commun. Surv. Tutorials **18**(2), 1123–1152 (2016)
2. Chakchouk, N.: Survey on opportunistic routing in wireless communication networks. IEEE Commun. Surv. Tutorials **17**(4), 2214–2241 (2015)
3. Hsu, C.J., Liu, H.I., Seah, W.K.G.: Opportunistic routing - a review and the challenges ahead. Comput. Netw. **55**(15), 3592–3603 (2011)
4. Zhao, Z., Rosario, D., Braun, T.: Topology and Link quality-aware Geographical opportunistic routing in wireless ad-hoc networks. In: 2013 9th International Wireless Communications and Mobile Computing Conference (IWCMC), pp. 1522–1527. IEEE, Sardinia, Italy (2013)
5. Hong, L., Guo, H., Liu, J., Zhang, Y.: Toward swarm coordination: topology-aware inter-UAV routing optimization. IEEE Trans. Veh. Technol. **69**(9), 10177–10187 (2020)
6. Sang, Q., Wu, H., Xing, L., Ma, H., Xie, P.: An energy-efficient opportunistic routing protocol based on trajectory prediction for FANETs. IEEE Access **8**, 192009–192020 (2020)
7. Liu, Y., Zhao, Y.: A virtual-waypoint based artificial potential field method for UAV path planning. In: 2016 IEEE Chinese Guidance, Navigation and Control Conference (CGNCC), pp. 949–953. IEEE, Nanjing, China (2016)
8. Zeng, K., Yang, Z., Lou, W.: Opportunistic routing in multiradio multi-channel multi-hop wireless networks. IEEE Trans. Wirel. Commun. **9**(11), 512–3521 (2010)

Social-Interaction GAN: Pedestrian Trajectory Prediction

Shiwen Zhang[1,2] , Jiagao Wu[1,2(✉)], Jinbao Dong[1,2] , and Linfeng Liu[1,2]

[1] School of Computer Science, Nanjing University of Posts and Telecommunications,
Nanjing 210023, China
{jgwu,liulf}@njupt.edu.cn
[2] Jiangsu Key Laboratory of Big Data Security and Intelligent Processing,
Nanjing 210023, China

Abstract. With the increasing number of intelligent autonomous systems in human society, the ability of such systems to perceive, understand and anticipate human behaviors becomes increasingly important. However, the pedestrian trajectory prediction is challenging due to the variability of pedestrian movement. In this paper, we tackle the problem with a deep learning framework by applying a generative adversarial network (GAN) and introduce a model called Social-Interaction GAN (SIGAN). Specially, we propose a novel Social Interaction Module (SIM) to dispose the human-human interactions, which combines the location and velocity features of the pedestrians in a local area. Extensive experiments show that our proposed model can obtain state-of-the-art accuracy.

Keywords: Pedestrian trajectory prediction · Generative adversarial network · Social interaction

1 Introduction

The problem of pedestrian trajectory prediction based on the deep learning method has renewed interest in recent years. The prediction of pedestrians' trajectories in crowded scenes [1,2] is highly valuable for social robot navigation [3], self-driving [4] and intelligent tracking [5,6]. Its goal is to generate the future locations of each pedestrian based on the previously trajectory. However, the pedestrian trajectory prediction is difficult to be realized because of the complex movement behaviors of pedestrians especially in crowded scenes [17].

Existing pedestrian trajectory prediction algorithms can be grouped into two categories: hand-crafted features based methods [11–15] and deep learning based methods. Hand-crafted features based methods mainly depend on the manually designed behavioral model functions [14,15] and hand-crafted settings of pedestrian properties. These methods cannot reliably predict the future trajectories in

Supported by National Natural Science Foundation of China (NSFC) Nos. 61872191 and 41571389.

more complicated scenes because it is difficult to combine all movement patterns into one model and is invalid for the prediction of long trajectories. Therefore, deep learning based methods are introduced to overcome the above issues.

The RNNs-based methods [9,10,22] and GANs-based methods [8,16] are the most commonly used in the trajectory prediction. With regard to the RNN-based methods, Xu et al. [9] predict the future trajectories by exerting LSTMs and introducing the "spatial affinity" to measure the importance of different pedestrians for the target pedestrian. However, the forecast of human behaviors remains a multimodel problem because there may not be one single correct future prediction for the pedestrian trajectory prediction given a partial history. In RNNs-based methods, they usually tend to minimize the L2 distance from the ground truth future trajectory to predict the only one future trajectory. However, in GAN-based methods, we can predict multiple acceptable trajectories. Among these trajectories, we choose the "best" one as the prediction result. Besides, the adversarial loss enables the prediction model to overcome the limitation of L2 loss and potentially learns the distribution of acceptable trajectories that can fool the discriminator.

Gupta et al. [8] propose Social GAN that consists of an LSTM-based Encoder-Decoder Generator with a pooling module and an LSTM-based Discriminator. However, both CIDNN and Social GAN have some shortcomings in modelling the human-human interactions due to the following reasons: (i) It is not enough to consider only the location to measure the social interactions, while the motion information (such as velocity) is also neglected. (ii) It is not appropriate to use all pedestrians' information in the same scene for the pooling process. The global information of all pedestrians contains too much useless information (such as the historical trajectories of a faraway pedestrian) which probably worsens the prediction results.

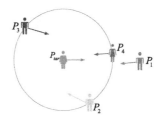

Fig. 1. The motivation illustration that pedestrians are influenced by other pedestrians with the different locations and different velocities.

As is shown in Fig. 1, note that although two pedestrians P_3 and P_4 have the equal distance to the target pedestrian P_{tar}, their influence on the trajectory prediction of the target pedestrian may be different. There are several reasons: (i) In Fig. 1, although the Euclidean distance from P_4 to P_{tar} is the same to that from P_3 to P_2, P_4 has a greater influence on the prediction result due to their velocity relation : pedestrians walking fast and moving towards the target may greatly affect the target pedestrian. (ii) Besides, if the distance between the pedestrians is very long, then there is little influence on the target pedestrian.

In this paper, we consider both the spatial information and the motion information as the spatial-temporal affinity of pedestrians for the trajectory prediction of the target pedestrian. Besides, we deal with the global interaction problem by proposing a new local pooling mechanism. The contributions of this paper are concluded as follows:

(1) We propose a deep learning framework called Social-Interaction GAN (SIGAN) for pedestrian trajectory prediction, and SIGAN uses a novel Social Interaction Module (SIM), which considers the information of locations, motions and interactions of neighboring pedestrians.
(2) We define a new spatial-temporal affinity, which combines the locations and velocity features of all pedestrians, as a measurement of human-human interaction influence. In addition, we propose a local pooling mechanism that can constrain the human-human interaction influence in a suitable scope.
(3) Extensive experiments on several real-world crowd datasets show that our model can obtain state-of-the-art accuracy in pedestrian trajectory prediction.

2   Related Work

We introduce deep learning based methods for trajectory prediction in this part.

2.1   RNNs Based Trajectory Prediction

Alahi *et al.* [10] propose the Social-LSTM (S-LSTM) model mainly considering human-human interactions. This model combines the behavior of neighboring pedestrians within a large neighborhood by a social pooling way. Su *et al.* [19] propose to deploy LSTM networks with social-aware recurrent Gaussian processes to model the complex uncertainties of the crowd and achieve good performance. But both of them do not treat the pedestrians differently. In *CIDNN* [9], Xu *et al.* disposes the global interactions by introducing spatial affinity that takes the spatial relationship as the interactions information. But this information lack of current velocity is not enough to model the interaction with other pedestrians. Furthermore, we should notice that human-human interactions only happen if the distance is not far. The global interaction may not be suitable.

2.2   GANs-Based Trajectory Prediction

The Generative Adversarial Network [20] (GAN) is composed of a generator and discriminator. However, the original GAN belongs to unsupervised learning and it would generate samples randomly due to the weak controllability. Therefore, Conditional GAN [7] (CGAN) is proposed to overcome this limitation by adding the extra information to guide the generation process. As for trajectory prediction, the extra information is the pedestrians' observed location coordinates.

Based on CGAN, Gupta *et al.* propose Social GAN and apply variety loss to encourage the network to produce multiple diverse future trajectories by considering all the pedestrians involved in a scene. However, the method disposing human-human interactions is too simple that they may not capture the human-human interactions. And in *Sophie* [16], the author applies the social-attention to dispose the social-interactions with GAN model. However, both of two take all pedestrians into consideration and this may worsen the predicted results. Therefore, this motivates us a new way to consider merging the possible factors.

3   Prediction Model

3.1   Problem Definition

In this paper, the pedestrian is taken as the agent. The goal of pedestrian trajectory prediction is to predict the future trajectories of all the agents involved in a scene by observing the agents' past trajectories. Assume that there are n agents $\{P_1, P_2, ..., P_n\}$ in a scene, the observed past trajectories for all the agents are denoted by $\{X_1, X_2, ..., X_n\}$ and the predicted trajectories are denoted by $\{\hat{Y}_1, \hat{Y}_2, ..., \hat{Y}_n\}$. Among them, the observed trajectory of P_i for several time steps $t \in [1, t_{obs}]$ is defined as $X_i = \{X_i^1, X_i^2, ..., X_i^t\}$ where $X_i^t = (x_i^t, y_i^t)$ is the location coordinate of agent P_i at the t-th time step. Similarly, the predicted location coordinate of agent P_i at the time step $t \in [t_{obs} + 1, t_{obs} + t_{pred}]$ is expressed as $\hat{Y}_i^t = (\hat{x_i^t}, \hat{y_i^t})$, and the predicted trajectory of agent P_i is defined as $\hat{Y}_i = < \hat{Y}_i^{t_{obs}+1}, \hat{Y}_i^{t_{obs}+2}, ..., \hat{Y}_i^{t_{obs}+t_{pred}} >$. The ground truth of the predicted location coordinate of agent P_i at the time step $t \in [t_{obs} + 1, t_{obs} + t_{pred}]$ is defined as $Y_i^t = X_i^t$. The coordinates of a trajectory are obtained in the same time interval, therefore, the velocity of agent P_i at the t-th time step can be defined as $V_i^t = (x_i^t - x_i^{t-1}, y_i^t - y_i^{t-1})$.

3.2   Social-Interaction GAN

The structure of Social-Interaction GAN is shown in Fig. 2. The model consists of a Generator (G) and a Discriminator (D). The G network inputs the multiple agents' past trajectories and outputs the predicted future trajectories of all agents. G network has three components: an Encoder, a Decoder and a Social Interaction Module (SIM). The Encoder is comprised of two sub-encoders: Location Encoder and Motion Encoder. Besides, SIM is a module to dispose human-human interactions, and the Decoder is taken as the output part of G.

Generator: Generator observes past trajectories $X_1, X_2, ..., X_n$ of all the agents and predicts the future trajectory.

Encoder: The Encoder includes Location Encoder and Motion Encoder. In Location Encoder, a fully connected layer is provided to embed the observed coordinate of each agent at time step t (*e.g.*, X_i^t) into a higher dimension vector $O_i^t \in R^{32}$, and then these high-dimension vectors are taken as the input of the LSTM according to the following recurrence:

$$O_i^t = fc_1 \left(X_i^t; W_O \right)$$
$$G_i^t = LSTM_1 \left(G_i^{t-1}, O_i^t; W_{encoder} \right) \tag{1}$$

where $fc_1(\cdot; \cdot)$ is used as embedding function and W_O represents the embedding weight. The LSTM is shared between the agents. $G_i^t \in R^{32}$ is the encoded location vector, and is typically initialized as 0.

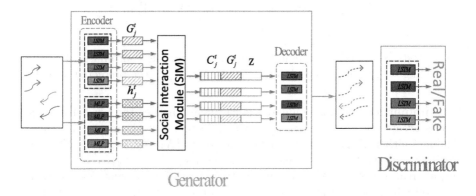

Fig. 2. The overview of our proposed Social-Interaction GAN model where the Generator network exhibits an Encoder-Decoder architecture with n agents.

In Motion Encoder, a 3-layer MLP with Relu activation is used to encode the observed coordinate and velocity of each agent at time step t (*e.g.*, X_i^t) and (*e.g.*,V_i^t) to get a motion vector $h_i^t \in R^{64}$ with the following formula:

$$h_i^t = MLP \left(X_i^t, V_i^t; W_1, W_2, W_3 \right) \tag{2}$$

where W_1, W_2, W_3 represent the weights of the 3-layer MLP, respectively. For each agent, we sequentially feed its past trajectory into the Location Encoder and the Motion Encoder to obtain the high-dimension location and motion vectors.

SIM: A module called Social Interaction Module (SIM) is designed by considering different social interactions, and a new measurement spatial-temporal affinity is introduced to consider the influence of location and velocity on the target agent. We also propose a new local pooling mechanism that takes into account the influence from a certain boundary on the target agent and obtain an influence vector denoted by C_i^t. The details of SIM will be described in Sect. 3.4.

Decoder: The Decoder is taken as the trajectory generation. Similar to Location Encoder, the Decoder of the G network also uses LSTM. However, we need to combine information from the encoder to effectively propose human-human interactions. As aforementioned above, we deal with these interactions via an SIM. The traditional GAN takes the noise as input and then it generates the output. However, in our method, we take the output of the Encoder as a condition by initializing the hidden states of the LSTM-Decoder:

$$S_i^t = \left[fc_2 \left(G_i^t, C_i^t; W_c \right), z \right] \tag{3}$$

where $fc_2(\cdot; \cdot)$ denotes a fully connected layer, W_c denotes the corresponding weight, and z denotes the Gauss noise. After initializing the decoder states by Eq. (4), we can obtain the predicted trajectory as follows:

$$\begin{aligned} S_i^t &= LSTM_2 \left(S_i^{t-1}, fc_3 \left(X_i^{t-1}; W_{co} \right); W_{dec} \right) \\ \hat{Y}_i^t &= fc_4 \left(S_i^t; W_p \right) \end{aligned} \tag{4}$$

where $fc_3(\cdot; \cdot)$ is used as an embedding function for the coordinates, W_{co} is an embedding weight, W_{dec} is a decoder weight and W_p is the predicted weight.

Discriminator: The discriminator is to judge whether the predicted trajectory is acceptable. D observes the past trajectories of all agents and then it combines either all generated future trajectories $\{X_1, X_2, ..., X_n, \hat{Y}_1, \hat{Y}_2, ..., \hat{Y}_n\}$ or all ground truth of the future trajectories $\{X_1, X_2, ..., X_n, Y_1, Y_2, ..., Y_n\}$. It outputs real or fake labels for the future trajectory of each agent. We use LSTM to encode the input of the Discriminator and use a full connected layer to judge the predicted trajectory.

Loss Function: The loss function includes adversarial loss and $L2$ loss:

$$L = \max_D L_{CGAN} \left(G, D \right) + \lambda L_{L2} \left(G \right) \tag{5}$$

where λ is the balance factor for balancing the adversarial loss and the $L2$ loss and L_{CGAN} is the adversarial loss. The adversarial loss is written as follows:

$$L_{CGAN} = \sum_{i \in scene} \left[log(D \left(Y_i, X_i \right)) + log(1 - D \left(G \left(z, X_i \right), X_i \right)) \right] \tag{6}$$

$D(Y_i, X_i)$ and $D(G(z, X_i))$ represent the probabiltiy that the ground truth and the predicted future trajectories are real, respectively. The $L2$ loss is expressed as:

$$L_{L2} \left(G \right) = \min_m ||Y_i - \hat{Y}_i||_2 \tag{7}$$

The $L2$ loss is set to ensure the diversity of the trajectories generated by the generator. When calculating the position offset loss, we will sample m times that we generate m samples for each observed agent, and select the data with the smallest loss to optimize the back propagation of network.

3.3   Details of Social Interaction Module

SIM is to capture the human-human interaction, which consists of 2 parts: Spatial-temporal Affinity part and Local Pooling part. SIM takes the encoded location and motion vectors as input to calculate the influence of each agent to a target agent. Without loss of generality, we mark the target agent as P_i.

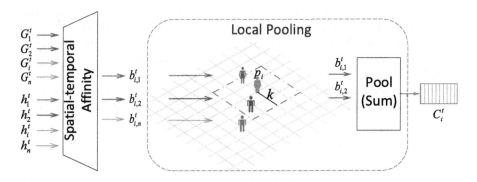

Fig. 3. The architecture of the Social Interaction Module with $2k \times 2k$ grid size.

For the Spatial-temporal Affinity part, as aforementioned, the movement of a target agent from the current frame to next frame is related to all agents' motion, including the location and velocity influences from each agent. Thus, a straightforward way is to linearly combine the location and motion features of all agents for displacement prediction. Therefore, in Spatial-temporal Affinity part, we propose the spatial-temporal affinity as the weight to measure the influence of each agent to the target agent. According to the output of the Motion Encoder, for any agent P_j, we define its spatial-temporal affinity to the target agent P_i at the time step t as $a_{i,j}^t$, i.e.,

$$a_{i,j}^t = \frac{\exp\left(\langle h_i^t, h_j^t \rangle\right)}{\sum_j \exp\left(\langle h_i^t, h_j^t \rangle\right)} \tag{8}$$

where $\langle h_i^t, h_j^t \rangle$ is an inner production operation between h_i^t and h_j^t. We take a softmax way to normalize $a_{i,j}^t$ falling into the interval $[0,1]$ and use it as the spatial-temporal affinity measurement. This formula takes both spatial factors and velocity factors into consideration. When the spatial-temporal affinity becomes larger, the target could be influenced more greatly. Besides, it is obvious to find that $a_{i,j}^t$ and $a_{j,i}^t$ are different, and this is because the movement of each agent is based on itself as well as *velocity and location of its neighbors. Hence, by combining spatial-temporal affinity and encoded location vector, interaction influence information to the target agent P_i cause by P_j is denoted by $b_{i,j}^t$:

$$b_{i,j}^t = a_{i,j}^t \cdot G_j^t \tag{9}$$

For the Local Pooling part, we need a compact representation that combines the information from all neighboring interaction influence. As we know, the movement of the target agent will only be affected by the neighboring agents. For example, as shown in Fig. 3, there exist 3 agents adjacent to the target agent P_i. Usually, only the nearer 2 neighbor agents (inside the green box) can influence the target agent P_i, which the farther neighbor agent (outside the green box) cannot. Different agents have different influence level on the target agents future trajectories. This phenomenon indicates that the agents walking from different directions or with different velocity in different locations have different influence to the target agent. To this end, we propose the local pooling scheme to combine these factors into our consideration for trajectory prediction.

To implement the local pooling, we set a grid-based neighborhood that is centered at each target agent's position for each target agent. Then, we can get the interaction influence from other agents to the target agent P_i as follows:

$$C_i^t = \sum_{j \in N_i(k)} b_{i,j}^t \tag{10}$$

where $C_i^t \in R^{32}$ and $N_i(k)$ is the neighbor set of the target agent P_i within $2k \times 2k$ grid size. It can be seen that the size k is an important parameter in the local pooling, which represents the influence scope of all agents. In this paper, we set the $k = 1, 2, ..., 20$, and train our model for different values of k. Finally, we choose the optimal value of k which yields the best prediction results.

4   Experiments

We evaluate SIGAN on two public pedestrian-trajectory datasets: ETH and UCY. We follow the same data preprocessing strategy as S-LSTM and SGAN. All data is converted into a world coordinate system and then interpolated to obtain values every 0.4 s. Here, we observe the trajectories in 8 time steps ($t_{obs} = 8$) to predict the trajectories in the following 8 time steps ($t_{pred} = 8$). In addition, we also implement a leave-one-out splitting strategy on the datasets. During the experiments, we train our network using 4 subsets and test it on the remaining 1 subset.

4.1   Experimental Setup

All the models are trained over 300 epochs with Adam optimizer and learning rate is 0.001. Our model is built using Python 3.6 on Pytorch 0.4 and trained with an NVIDIA RTX-2080 GPU. Like SGAN, we also set $m = 20$ in $L2$ loss.

4.2   Evaluation Metrics

We use Average Displacement Error (ADE) and Final Displacement Error (FDE) as the metrics to measure the performance of different methodS. ADE is defined as the average distance between the positions in the predicted and ground truth trajectories of all agents. FDE is the distance between the predicted destination and the actual destination of a agent.

4.3 Baselines and Evaluation Metrics

To assess the performance of SIGAN, besides S-LSTM, SGAN and CIDNN, we also compare SIGAN against two basic motion prediction approaches like:

- Linear: A baseline method based on linear regression. This method assumes that each pedestrian walks in a straight path.
- LSTM: The basic LSTM-based trajectory prediction method does not consider any social interactions.

4.4 Quantitative Results

In this section, we discuss the results obtained by SIGAN.

As we have mentioned above, SIGAN has considered the two factors including the velocity and location of pedestrians that would influence their movement. Then, we demonstrate the validity of SIGAN. To demonstrate the validity of SIGAN, we first give the prediction results in Table 1 and Table 2. Except Linear prediction on HOTEL dataset, SIGAN outperforms ADE and FDE especially on ETH dataset.

Table 1. Prediction results of all methods. The results are ADE/FDE in meters (a smaller result is better) when $t_{obs} = 8$ and $t_{pred} = 8$.

Dataset	Linear	LSTM	S-LSTM	SGAN	**SIGAN**
ETH	0.84/1.60	0.70/1.45	0.73/1.48	0.61/1.22	**0.52/1.09**
HOTEL	**0.35/0.60**	0.55/1.17	0.49/1.01	0.48/0.95	0.43/0.93
UNIV	0.56/1.01	0.36/0.77	0.41/0.84	0.36/0.75	**0.30/0.70**
ZARA1	0.41/0.74	0.25/0.53	0.27/0.56	0.21/0.42	**0.17/0.39**
ZARA2	0.53/0.95	0.31/0.65	0.33/0.70	0.27/0.54	**0.21/0.51**
Average	0.54/0.98	0.43/0.914	0.45/0.918	0.386/0.776	**0.326/0.724**

Table 2. Prediction results of CIDNN and SIGAN when $t_{obs} = 5$ and $t_{pred} = 5$.

Method	ETH	HOTEL	UNIV	ZARA1	ZARA2	AVERAGE
CIDNN	**0.09**	0.12	0.12	0.15	0.10	0.116
SIGAN	0.10	**0.10**	**0.11**	**0.12**	0.09	**0.104**

4.5   Evaluation of Different Part of the SIM Module

Spatial Affinity vs. Spatial-Temporal Affinity. In Fig. 3, the Spatial-temporal Affinity part of SIM takes both location and velocity of agents into consideration as the spatial-temporal affinity. In CIDDN, only spatial affinity is considered. We compare the two strategies on human-human interactions in Table 3:

Table 3. Comparison on different definitions of affinity when $t_{obs} = 8$ and $t_{pred} = 8$. We denote Spatial Affinity as SA and Spatial-temporal Affinity as STA.

Affinity	ETH	HOTEL	UNIV	ZARA1	ZARA2	AVERAGE
SA	0.59/1.17	0.48/0.99	0.33/0.75	0.19/0.43	0.24/0.55	0.366/0.778
STA	**0.52/1.09**	**0.43/0.93**	**0.30/0.70**	**0.17/0.39**	**0.21/0.51**	**0.326/0.724**

Every pedestrian's movement will be influenced by the neighboring pedestrians. Pedestrians walk from different directions with different velocity and whether they are far or nearby, and these issues have been taken into consideration. From Table 3, we can see that the affinity with both spatial and velocity information will better capture the current relative states of each pedestrian.

Local Pooling vs. Global Pooling. Pedestrians are influenced by those around them in a local area to avoid collisions. Here, we set a $2k \times 2k$ grid neighborhood for each target agent, and $k = 1, 2, ..., 20$. A different value of k gives rise to a different prediction result. We set the best prediction result as the final result and record the corresponding k.

We can see in Fig. 4 and Fig. 5, in the process of enlarging the k value, ADE and FDE first decrease and then increase, and finally they almost remain despite of the value of k since all agents have already been taken into consideration.

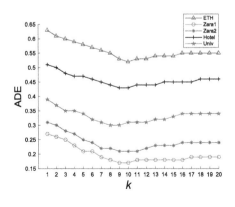   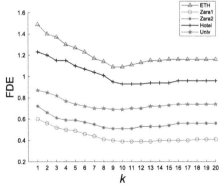

Fig. 4. The ADE values with k.   **Fig. 5.** The FDE values with k.

SIGAN always achieves the best prediction results when the k is set to 9 or 10. This is because when k is small (e.g., $k < 9$), few social interactions would occur. However, if the value of k is large (e.g., $k > 10$), too many useless interactions will worsen the prediction results. SGAN is a method that considers the global interactions. However, in our proposed SIGAN, even though we consider the global interactions (e.g., $k = 20$), we can still get better prediction results than SGAN, which indicates that the combination of location and velocity has an extremely important influence on the pedestrian trajectory prediction.

5 Conclusion

In this work, we propose a GAN-based model with a novel SIM module to deal with the pedestrian trajectory prediction, along with a new spatial-temporal affinity which combines every agent's location and velocity. Besides, we propose a pooling mechanism with a suitable scope. Experimental results for the ADE, FDE demonstrate that our model outperforms other methods in terms of accuracy and collision avoidance.

References

1. Grant, J., Flynn, P.: Crowd scene understanding from video. ACM Trans. Multimedia Comput. Commun. Appl. **13**(2), 1–23 (2017)
2. Alahi, A., Ramanathan, V., Li, F.F.: Socially-aware large-scale crowd forecasting. In: Proceedings of the IEEE Conference on Computer Vision and Pattern Recognition, pp. 2203–2210. IEEE (2014)
3. Liu, J., Wang, G., Hu, P., Duan, L.-Y., Kot, A. C.: Global context-aware attention LSTM networks for 3D action recognition. In: Proceedings of the IEEE Conference on Computer Vision and Pattern Recognition, pp 1647–1656 (2017)
4. Deo, N., Rangesh, A.: How would surround vehicles move? A unified framework for maneuver classification and motion prediction. arXiv:1801.06523 (2018)
5. Bagautdinov, T., Alahi, A., Fleuret, F., Fua, P., Savarese, S.: Social scene understanding: end-to-end multi-person action localization and collective activity recognition. In: Proceedings of the International Conference on Computer Vision and Pattern Recognition, pp. 3425–3434. IEEE (2016)
6. Ballan, L., Castaldo, F., Alahi, A., Palmieri, F., Savarese, S.: Knowledge transfer for scene-specific motion prediction. In: Leibe, B., Matas, J., Sebe, N., Welling, M. (eds.) ECCV 2016. LNCS, vol. 9905, pp. 697–713. Springer, Cham (2016). https://doi.org/10.1007/978-3-319-46448-0_42
7. Mirza, M., Osindero, S.: Conditional generative adversarial nets. arXiv preprint arXiv:1411.1784 (2014)
8. Gupta, A., Johnson, J., Fei-Fei, L., Savarese, S., Alahi, A.: Social GAN: Socially acceptable trajectories with generative adversarial networks. In: Proceedings of the IEEE International Conference on Computer Vision and Pattern Recognition, pp. 2255–2264. IEEE (2018)
9. Xu, Y., Piao, Z., Gao, S.: Encoding crowd interaction with deep neural network for pedestrian trajectory prediction. In: Proceedings of the IEEE Conference on Computer Vision and Pattern Recognition, pp. 5275–5284. IEEE (2018)

10. Alahi, A., Goel, K., Ramanathan, V., Robicquet, A., Fei-Fei, L.: Social LSTM: human trajectory prediction in crowded spaces. In: Proceedings of the IEEE Conference on Computer Vision and Pattern Recognition, pp. 5275–5284. IEEE (2016)
11. Helbing, D., Molnar, P.: Social force model for pedestrian dynamics. Phys. Rev. E **51**(5), 4282 (1995)
12. Mehran, R., Oyama, A., Shah, M.: Abnormal crowd behavior detection using social force model. In: Proceedings of the IEEE Conference on Computer Vision and Pattern Recognition, pp. 935–942. IEEE (2009)
13. Yamaguchi, K., Berg, A., Ortiz, L., Berg, T.: Who are you with and where are you going? In: Proceedings of the IEEE Conference on Computer Vision and Pattern Recognition, pp. 1345–1352. IEEE (2011)
14. Yi, S., Li, H., Wang, X.: Understanding pedestrian behaviors from stationary crowd groups. In: Proceedings of the IEEE Conference on Computer Vision and Pattern Recognition, pp. 3488–3496. IEEE (2015)
15. Antonini, G., Bierlaire, M., Weber, M.: Discrete choice models of pedestrian walking behavior. Transportation Research Part B: Methodological, pp. 667–687(2006)
16. Sadeghian, A., Kosaraju, V., Sadeghian, A., Hirose, N., Savarese, S.: Sophie: An attentive GAN for predicting paths compliant to social and physical constraints. arXiv preprint arXiv:1806.01482 (2018)
17. Vemula, A., Muelling, K., Oh, J.: Modeling cooperative navigation in dense human crowds. In: IEEE International Conference on Robotics and Automation, pp. 1685–1692. IEEE (2017)
18. Ballan, L., Castaldo, F., Alahi, A., Palmieri, F., Savarese, S.: Knowledge transfer for scene-specific motion prediction. In: Leibe, B., Matas, J., Sebe, N., Welling, M. (eds.) ECCV 2016. LNCS, vol. 9905, pp. 697–713. Springer, Cham (2016). https://doi.org/10.1007/978-3-319-46448-0_42
19. Su, H., Zhu, J., Dong, Y., Zhang, B.: Forecast the plausible paths in crowd scenes. In: Proceedings of the Twenty-Sixth International Joint Conference on Artificial Intelligence, IJCAI-17, pp. 2772–2778. (2017)
20. Goodfellow, I., et al.: Generative adversarial nets. In: Advances in Neural Information Processing Systems, pp. 2672–2680 (2014)
21. Du, Y., Wang, W., Wang, L.: Hierarchical recurrent neural network for skeleton based action recognition. In: Proceedings of the IEEE Conference on Computer Vision and Pattern Recognition, pp. 1110–1118. IEEE (2015)
22. Liu, J., Shahroudy, A., Xu, D., Wang, G.: Spatio-temporal LSTM with trust gates for 3D human action recognition. In: Leibe, B., Matas, J., Sebe, N., Welling, M. (eds.) ECCV 2016. LNCS, vol. 9907, pp. 816–833. Springer, Cham (2016). https://doi.org/10.1007/978-3-319-46487-9_50

An Intelligent Wallpaper Based on Ambient Light for Human Activity Sensing

Chenqi Shi[1(✉)], Tao Li[1], and Qiang Niu[1,2(✉)]

[1] School of Computer Science and Technology, China University of Mining and Technology, Xuzhou 221116, China
{shichenqi,li_t,niuq}@cumt.edu.cn
[2] China Mine Digitization Engineering Research Center, Ministry of Education, Xuzhou 221116, China

Abstract. Using visible light for indoor human sensing has received a great deal of attention. Existing researches on visible light sensing have two limitations: (a) relying on a specific light (b) small sensing range. In this paper, using the light reflection model, we propose a human activity sensing system based on ambient light named Sensing-Wallpaper (SenWp). It could realize whole room human sensing using Photo-Diode (PD) hidden in the wallpaper without offline training or specific light. In the SenWp system, human activity sensing model is proposed to capture human activity semantic information and enhance signal characteristics. We have conducted a large number of experiments in three typical indoor environments. The accuracy of human activity sensing reaches 96%. Moreover, in the absence of artificial light, just using natural light, the activity sensing range can reach 6m. We also have conducted long-term research in real life to prove the potential of the system in practice.

Keywords: Ambient light · Training-free · Visible light sensing (VLS)

1 Introduction

At present, a growing number of surveillance cameras have been installed in houses, nursing homes, and hospitals to monitor the activity status and living habits of indoor human [1,2]. However, the privacy violation caused by cameras has attracted lots of attention. To avoid privacy issues, existing research works mainly use radio signals, such as Wi-Fi [6], ultrasonic wave [7] and visible light [5] to sense indoor human activities.

Traditional visible light sensing work mostly requires a specific light source [5]. Majeed *et al.* using LED luminaires locate indoor human [4]. Sensing with fixed light source is limited in practical application. For visible light positioning

This work was supported by the National Natural Science Foundation of China (No. 51674255).

Z. Liu et al. (Eds.): WASA 2021, LNCS 12939, pp. 441–449, 2021.
https://doi.org/10.1007/978-3-030-86137-7_47

work using ambient light, its sensing distance is still very limited. For example, Faulkner *etal*. localizes a target based on received signal strength of the ambient light [3]. In [2] can only achieve the human positioning with a distance of 1–2 m. The main reason is that the multi-path effect of ambient light affected by human activities can be easily buried in noise, and it is challenging to extract activities semantic information from ambient light. This paper firstly presents a novel sensing model using ambient light to push the human activity sensing range from the current 1–2 m to house level (5–6 m), bridging the gap between lab prototype and actual deployment.

This paper designs a human activity sensing system based on ambient light named Sensing-Wallpaper(SenWp), which obtains the ambient light intensity through the Photo-Diode (PD) hidden in the wallpaper to recognition human activity. The main contributions of the paper can be summarized as follows.

(1) To the best of our knowledge, this is the first system that uses ambient light reflection model to detect human activity in all over the room without wearable devices or offline training.
(2) To realize room-wide human activity sensing, we proposed human activity sensing model to accurately capture human activity semantic information and enhance signal characteristic.
(3) We have conducted extensive experiments in three typical indoor environments. The accuracy of SenWp in recognition human activities reached 96%, which proves the effectiveness and robustness of the system.

The rest of this paper is organized as follows. Section 2 gives an overview of our system design. Section 3 introduces the human activity sensing model of our system. Section 4 presents the implementation and experimental results and future directions followed by a conclusion in Sect. 5.

2   System Overview

SenWp is a low-cost and non-intrusive human activity sensing system. The system uses the PD hidden in the wallpaper to sense the location and activity status of the human. The key steps for SenWp are as follows:

(1) Detect whether there is human activity in the room. If human activity is detected, record the current period as the "active period" and mark the PD that perceives the activity.
(2) According to PD changes, determine whether the behavior that occurs during the "activity period" is "walking", "falling", or "light source switching". Otherwise, it is recorded as an "in-situ activity" behavior.
(3) Record the duration of the "activity period" and infer information such as the human walking speed. Make judgments on the living habit of the human according to the rule of human activities.

3   Human Activity Sensing Model

This section will describe how SenWp recognizes the type and duration of human actions without offline training in detail.

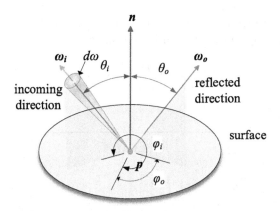

Fig. 1. The incoming light reaches the surface of the object.

3.1 Multi-path Effect Caused by Human Activity

In radiology, the function that describes how surfaces reflect light is called the "Bidirectional Reflectance Distribution Function" (BRDF). We use $f(p, \omega_i, \omega_0)$ to represent the BRDF of the surface of the object.

$$f(p, \omega_i, \omega_0) = \frac{dL_o(p, \omega_o)}{dE_i(p, \omega_i)} \tag{1}$$

Where, $dE_i(p, \omega_i)$ represents the differential value of the irradiance of the incident ray reaching point p in the direction of ω_i, and $dL_o(p, \omega_o)$ represents the differential value of the irradiance of the reflected ray leaving point p in the direction of ω_o, as shown in Fig. 1. According to the definition of radiance L and irradiance E:

$$L = \frac{d^2\phi}{dA_\perp d\omega} = \frac{d^2\phi}{dA\cos\theta_i d\omega}, E = \frac{d\phi}{dA} \tag{2}$$

Substitute Eq. (2) into Eq. (1) to get:

$$f(p, \omega_i, \omega_0) = \frac{dL_o(p, \omega_o)}{L_i(p, \omega_i)\cos\theta_i d\omega_i} \tag{3}$$

According to Eq. (3), integral within a solid angle Ω_i of the incident ray can be obtained as follows. Where Ω_i is equal to $2\pi^+$.

$$L_o(p, \omega_o) = \int_{\Omega_i} f(p, \omega_i, \omega_o) L_i(p, \omega_i)\cos\theta_i d\omega_i \tag{4}$$

The reflectivity of the luminous flux is equal to the ratio of the luminous flux of the reflected ray to that of the incident ray. Denoted by the symbol ρ, defined as:

$$\rho(p, \Omega_i, \Omega_0) = \frac{d\phi_0}{d\phi_i} \tag{5}$$

Then, according to the definition of irradiance E, i.e. Eq. (2), the differential of luminous flux (incoming ray) can be obtained:

$$d\phi_i = dA \int_{\Omega_i} L_i \cos \theta_i d\omega_i \qquad (6)$$

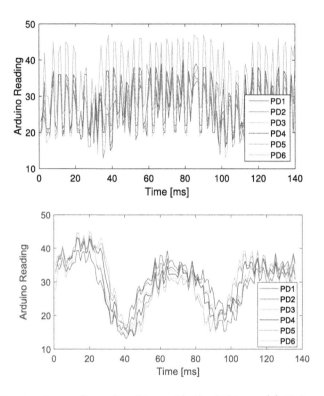

Fig. 2. Light intensity reading of walking with the light on. (a) Before denoise. (b) After denoise.

3.2   Time-Segment Algorithm Based on Light Intensity

There is a significant difference in noise signals when using daylight and lighting source. First, we filter the light intensity signal. The daylight source will slowly change with the time of the day. The illumination light source has periodic high-frequency light signal oscillations due to a high-frequency flicker that cannot be distinguished by the human eye. Fig. 2(a) shows the light intensity of walking in a ceiling-lit room before noise reduction. Figure 2(b) shows the light intensity waveform after noise reduction.

Next, we extract the characteristics of the "activity period" to determine the type of activity. We mainly carry out two aspects of work: extracting temporal features and enhancing amplitude features. First, analyze the time domain

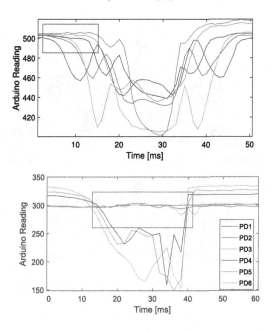

Fig. 3. (a) Light intensity when a person is walking. (b) Light intensity changes as a human fall.

characteristics of each PD channel. Record whether the light intensity of each PD channel changes when the current "active period" appears and if there are changes, record the sequence of PD changes. Then, the inner product operation is performed on the denoised light intensity signal, enhancing its expression without losing signal characteristics.

3.3   Amplitude Coupling Time-Domain Recognition algorithm

SenWp system can recognize "Walk", "Fall" activities through the activity recognition model based on amplitude and time domain coupling. We first study the state where there is only one target activity in the room. We did a slight swinging arm movement at different positions from the PD. Experiments show that the light intensity reading of the PD is reduced by at least 5%. Therefore, we regard the light intensity change of more than 5% as the activity recognition threshold.

The light intensity changes caused by each action are different. Therefore, the SenWp system first learns the characteristic light intensity of each action. The light intensity change of "Walk" is shown in Fig. 3(a). It can be observed that each light intensity channel changes in the sequence of position, and the change curve of each channel is same roughly. The light intensity of the "Fall" is shown in Fig. 3(b).

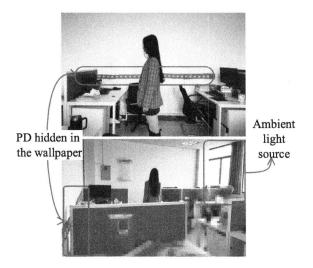

Fig. 4. Example environment of SenWp system.

4   Experiment

4.1   Experiment Setting

The SenWp system uses cheap ELECFANS 5 mm photo-diodes connect to the ready-made Arduino Uno as the receiving device. The interval between PDs is 10 cm, and they are installed on a wall with a height of one meter from the ground. The sampling frequency of PD can be adjusted through Arduino. The sampling frequency of PD on the SenWp system is 10 Hz. To evaluate the performance of SenWp, we conducted experiments in an office with window, as shown in Fig. 4.

There are more furniture, tables, chairs, and electronic equipment in the room, so the source of ambient light is more complicated due to the influence of multi-path effects. The SenWp system is equipped with light-weight experimental equipment on a wall to monitor human activities in the room, the activity status of human, and whether there is a dangerous situation. We invited six volunteers from the team as experimenters to verify the robustness of the SenWp system.

4.2   Distinguishing Activities

Walk Sensing. Table 1 shows the sensing results of the SenWp system when people are walking. The accuracy of walking sensing is about 95%, and the FNR is about 5%. In reality, some large-scale in-situ activities will be recognized as walking. For example, when a person walks perpendicularly to the wallpaper, the distance between the person and the wallpaper gradually becomes longer during the walking process. Resulting in no change in light intensity of the PD near the edge, and walking will be recognized as a fall. We further evaluated the walk sensing performance of the SenWp system for different participants. As shown in Table 1, the accuracy of different participants is similar.

Table 1. Impact of different participants of walking.

Participant	1	2	3	4	5	6
Accuracy [%]	95.1	95.5	94.4	95.6	96.1	94.9
FNR [%]	5.31	5.70	5.28	6.18	4.74	5.91

Fall Sensing. Table 2 shows the overall performance of human fall sensing. The accuracy of fall sensing is about 97%, and the FNR is about 4%. Some large-scale in-situ activities will be recognized as falls. For example, in the sitting state, the light intensity changes caused by rapid arm raising and lowering actions are very similar to falling, and both cause a significant change in a particular PD in a short time. Besides, missed cases are primarily because the participant is far away from the wallpaper in the case of using a top-lamp as the light source.

Table 2. Impact of different participants of fall.

Participant	1	2	3	4	5	6
Accuracy [%]	95.1	95.5	94.4	95.6	96.1	94.9
FNR [%]	5.31	5.70	5.28	6.18	4.74	5.91

Impact of Different Heights. In this experiment, to verify the impact of the height of the PD installation on the recognition results, we fixed the wallpaper PD in three cases of 0.5 m, 1 m, and 1.5 m used two indicators of accuracy FNR to evaluate the SenWp performance. Fig. 5(a) shows the precision of human action recognition at these three heights, and (b) is the FNR of human activity recognition. It can be seen that the recognition precision is the highest in 1 meter, and the FNR is the lowest at this time. We think that this is due to the arm and spine that are the most active joints during human activities. This position is generally 1 m above and below the ground. Therefore, the best location for PDs in wallpaper is 1 m.

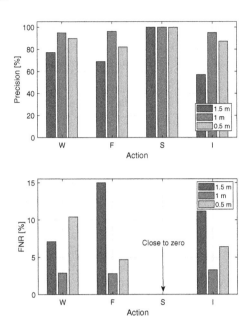

Fig. 5. Impact of PDs height on SenWp performance. (a) Precision. (b) FNR.

5 Conclusion

This paper proposes a training-free human activity sensing system based on ambient light intensity. We proceed from coarse activity determination by judging the "rest period" and "active period". Next, we identify activities based on the amplitude coupling time-domain recognition algorithm. Then, we conducted a large number of experiments in three typical indoor environments to demonstrate the potential of the system in practice. For walk sensing, the accuracy is 95%, and the FNR is 5%. The accuracy of fall recognition is 97%, and the FNR is 4%. We believe that the SenWp system can provide valuable data sets for analyzing and inferring people's living habits, physical conditions, emergencies, and even emotions.

References

1. Chen, W., et al.: Robust dynamic hand gesture interaction using LTE terminals. In: 2020 19th ACM/IEEE International Conference on Information Processing in Sensor Networks (IPSN), pp. 109–120. IEEE (2020)
2. Faulkner, N., Alam, F., Legg, M., Demidenko, S.: Smart wall: passive visible light positioning with ambient light only. In: 2019 IEEE International Instrumentation and Measurement Technology Conference (I2MTC), pp. 1–6. IEEE (2019)
3. Faulkner, N., Alam, F., Legg, M., Demidenko, S.: Watchers on the wall: passive visible light-based positioning and tracking with embedded light-sensors on the wall. IEEE Trans. Instrum. Meas. **69**(5), 2522–2532 (2019)

4. Majeed, K., Hranilovic, S.: Performance bounds on passive indoor positioning using visible light. J. Lightwave Technol. **38**(8), 2190–2200 (2020)
5. Nguyen, V., Ibrahim, M., Rupavatharam, S., Jawahar, M., Gruteser, M., Howard, R.: Eyelight: light-and-shadow-based occupancy estimation and room activity recognition. In: IEEE INFOCOM 2018-IEEE Conference on Computer Communications, pp. 351–359. IEEE (2018)
6. Niu, K., Zhang, F., Chang, Z., Zhang, D.: A fresnel diffraction model based human respiration detection system using COTS Wi-Fi devices. In: Proceedings of the 2018 ACM International Joint Conference and 2018 International Symposium on Pervasive and Ubiquitous Computing and Wearable Computers, pp. 416–419 (2018)
7. Sun, K., Zhao, T., Wang, W., Xie, L.: Vskin: sensing touch gestures on surfaces of mobile devices using acoustic signals. In: Proceedings of the 24th Annual International Conference on Mobile Computing and Networking, pp. 591–605 (2018)

Adaptive Data Transmission and Task Scheduling for High-Definition Map Update

Jiaxi Liu[1](✉), Zhen Wang[1], Chi Zhang[1](✉), Chengjie Gu[1], Miao Pan[2],
and Xia Zhang[3]

[1] School of Information Science and Technology, University of Science
and Technology of China, Hefei 230027, China
{jxliu01,wang1992}@mail.ustc.edu.cn, {chizhang,gcj}@ustc.edu.cn
[2] Department of Electrical and Computer Engineering, University of Houston,
Houston, TX 77204, USA
mpan2@uh.edu
[3] School of Computer Science and Technology, Wuhan University of Technology,
Wuhan 430070, China
zhang_xia@whut.edu.cn

Abstract. In recent years, high-definition (HD) maps are considered to be significant complements to the on-board sensors of autonomous vehicles. Due to the highly dynamic characteristic of HD map, how to update HD maps fast and efficiently has become the pivotal issue which attracts great attentions. Currently, most of the research on this issue focuses on the crowdsourcing protocol design or specific updating method meanwhile disregarding the need of communication and computing resource in HD map update. Therefore, in this paper, we propose an integrated update framework including both an adaptive data transmission scheme and an adaptive task scheduling scheme to realize fast data collection and fast data processing for HD map update. To the best of our knowledge, this is the first work that addresses the problem of HD map update which takes the need of communication and computing resource into consideration. In this paper, we firstly illustrate the system architecture of our HD map update framework. Based on that, to realize fast data collection, we propose an adaptive data transmission scheme, which optimizes the transmission rate on different links of each vehicle considering the wireless channel capacity and fronthaul link capacity of the access points. Besides, to realize fast data processing, we propose an adaptive task scheduling scheme, which enables cooperative computing between the edge nodes and cloud computing server, considering the constraints of computing capacity and backhaul link capacity. To the end, we carry out simulations to verify the effectiveness of our proposed policies.

This work was supported by the Natural Science Foundation of China (NSFC) under Grants 61871362 and U19B2023, and by the Strategic Priority Research Program of Chinese Academy of Sciences under Grant XDA17040517.

Z. Liu et al. (Eds.): WASA 2021, LNCS 12939, pp. 450–462, 2021.
https://doi.org/10.1007/978-3-030-86137-7_48

Keywords: High-definition map update · Adaptive data transmission · Cooperative computing

1 Introduction

Recently, autonomous driving, which is expected to liberate drivers physically and improve traffic safety and efficiency, has attracted great interest from both the academia and industry [5]. However, the intrinsic hardware constraints of the on-board sensors of autonomous vehicles bring great risks on driving safety under extreme conditions [1]. Therefore, high-definition (HD) maps, which is composed of comprehensive, detailed, and real-time environment information, come to be the key complements to the sensor-based autonomous driving system [12]. Compared with the digital navigation map used by humans, the HD map, which is originally designed for machines, is endowed with a larger data volume and higher update frequency. For instance, the update frequency of HD map data used by HERE reaches a level of hours [3]. In the era of digital navigation maps, map providers update maps using dedicated mapping vehicles equipped with a suite of high-accuracy sensors. Due to the high cost and the limited number of such vehicles, the digital navigation map can only be updated in several years, indicating that this approach cannot be applied to HD maps. To conquer these shortcomings, crowdsourcing, which aims to leverage the millions of vehicles already on the road to detect the changes, is deemed as the most promising substitute paradigm to keep the HD map up-to-date.

Currently, many efforts have been devoted to updating HD maps by crowdsourcing. In [9], Pannen et al. proposed a method to predict the probability of change and update HD map with crowdsourced data and training datasets. In [7], Liebner et al. proposed a method to create crowdsourced HD map patches through graph-based simultaneous localization and mapping (SLAM). In [6], in order to improve the reliability of map updating, Kim et al. designed an observation learner algorithm to cope with the uncertainty of the crowdsourced data. It is worth noting that the crowdsourcing update process of HD map can be generally divided into two phases, a data collection phase and a data processing phase, namely. However, most of the work mentioned above only focuses on the data processing method of HD map update without caring about the specific computing resources needed by their methods. Meanwhile, how to collect data fast and efficiently to support their methods is also neglected. In fact, for the data collection phase, the latency occurred during which has a great impact on the update performance. However, how to conquer the data collection latency in HD map update is still an open issue. Besides, for the data processing phase, there are two typical computing frameworks proposed, a cloud-based pattern and an edge-based pattern, namely. The cloud-based pattern refers that vehicles upload their sensing data to the remote cloud map server continuously via their Over-The-Air (OTA) interfaces. The cloud map server calculates updates using such collected sensing data and then dispatches update packets on demand. Currently, the cloud-based pattern is the mainstream way and adopted by many commercial map providers [2,3]. However, with the increase on complexity and latency requirements of HD map, the cloud-based pattern will be restricted by extra transmission latency resulting from the uncertainty of the backhaul links. Hence, the edge-based pattern is proposed to tackle this dilemma, in which local updates can be conducted locally without transferring. However, edge-based pattern also risks meeting the latency requirements when burst update tasks occur. Thus, an adaptive cooperation framework that combines the advantages of both cloud and edge is expected by the data processing phase of HD map update.

Based on above analysis, we hence propose an integrated update framework including both an adaptive data transmission scheme and an adaptive task scheduling scheme to realize fast data collection and fast data processing for HD map update. The main contributions of our work can be listed as follows.

- To our best of knowledge, this is the first work that addresses the HD map update problem which takes the need of communication and computing resource into consideration.
- We illustrate the system architecture of our update framework. Based on that, we propose an adaptive transmission scheme and an adaptive task scheduling scheme to minimize the data collection latency and data processing latency in HD map update, respectively.
- Specifically, in data collection phase, we optimize the transmission rate on different links of each vehicle. In data processing phase, we enable an efficient cooperation between the cloud and the edge.
- Extensive simulations have been conducted to verify the effectiveness of our proposed framework.

2   System Architecture

As Fig. 1 shows, the system architecture of our proposed update framework mainly includes three layers, the vehicle layer, the edge layer, and the cloud layer, namely. The vehicle layer accounts for data collection for map updates and the edge layer and cloud layer account for data processing for map updates in a cooperative way.

- **Vehicle Layer:** The vehicle layer comprises ordinary crowdsourcing automobiles. Since the update process of different edge nodes is independent, we consider the vehicles within the coverage of one edge node. Let $\mathcal{V}_j = \{v_{j1}, v_{j2}, \ldots v_{jV_j}\}$ denote the set of crowdsourcing vehicles of edge node j, where V_j represents the number of crowdsourcing vehicles at edge node j. For simplicity, we assume that the update tasks have already been generated and perception tasks have already been allocated to vehicles. Then, we assume that the vehicles always upload all their sensing data to the edge node in a stream way. The generation rate of sensing data at vehicle v_{jn} is denoted as G_{jn}. In order to improve transmission efficiency and avoid frequent handovers caused by the mobility of vehicles, we allow a vehicle to upload sensing data to multiple access points of edge node j simultaneously for the sake of coordinated multipoint reception (CoMP) technique [11].

- **Edge Layer:** We envision J independent edge nodes in the system, denoted as $\mathcal{J} = \{1, 2, \ldots, J\}$. Each edge node is equipped with an edge server and K access points, which can be denoted as S_j and $\mathcal{B}_j = \{b_{j1}, b_{j2}, \ldots, b_{jK}\}$, respectively. The edge server connects with the access points with wired fronthaul links. The fronthaul link capacity of access point b_{jk} is denoted as W_{jk}^{front}. Besides, the computing capacity of edge node j can be denoted as F_j. To realize low-latency updates, we assume each edge node can split and offload part of the update tasks according to the instructions given by the cloud computing server, which means such tasks can be partially computed at the edge node and partially computed at the cloud computing server in a parallel way. We denote the generated update task set at edge node j as $\mathcal{N}_j = \{n_{j1}, n_{j2}, \ldots, n_{jN_j}\}$, where N_j indicates that there are N_j update tasks at edge node j. Each task can be described by a tuple $n_{jp} = \{L_{jp}, C_{jp}\}$, where L_{jp} represents the input sensing data size and C_{jp} indicates the number of CPU cycles which are required to process one-bit sensing data of this task. We define the computing resource allocated to task n_{jp} by edge node j as f_{jp}^e (in CPU Cycle/s).
- **Cloud Layer:** The cloud layer consists of a cloud map server and a cloud computing server. The cloud map server can send update requests to edge nodes and receive updates from edge nodes. The cloud computing server can supervise the running status of all edge nodes and make decisions on the task splitting strategy of each task from each edge node and the computing resource allocation strategy of itself and the edge nodes. We denote the cloud computing server as S_0, which connects with all the edge nodes individually via backhaul links. The backhaul link capacity from the cloud computing server to the edge node j is denoted as W_j^{back}. The computing capacity of the cloud computing server can be represented as F_c and the computing resource allocated to offloaded task n_{jp} can be denoted as f_{jp}^c (in CPU Cycle/s). Since the cloud map server only triggers updates at edge nodes or receives updates from edge nodes, we neglect its effects in the process of update computing.

3 Adaptive Data Transmission

The latency of an edge node computing an update task includes two parts. The first part refers to the latency incurred when the edge server obtains the sensing data via the access points from the vehicles, which is defined as data collection latency. The second part refers to the latency incurred when the edge server processes the sensing data and fulfills an update, which is defined as data processing latency. In this section, we focus on minimizing the data collection latency through an adaptive data transmission scheme.

3.1 Latency Analysis

Since the vehicles can communicate with multiple access points using the CoMP technique and the sensing data collected by each vehicle are firstly streamed

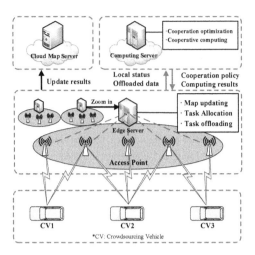

Fig. 1. System architecture.

to the access points and then aggregated at the edge server, we use an under-saturated service-demand traffic model [4] to express the data collection latency of the system. A basic formulation of the under-saturated service-demand model follows:

$$D \propto \frac{L}{R_{ij} - r_{ij}}, \tag{1}$$

where D refers to the latency, L denotes the packet size, R_{ij} denotes the path capacity, and r_{ij} represents the allocated rate, based on which the latency can be represented as the inverse of the residual capacity at each link. In this work, for simplicity, we firstly assume the vehicles have already been associated with proper access points through a feasible mobility management policy. Then we denote the uploading rate and available capacity of the link from vehicle v_{jn} to access point b_{jk} as r_{nk}^j and R_{nk}^j, respectively. Based on above, the uploading rate at the fronthaul link of access point b_{jk} can be denoted as $r_k^j = \sum_{n \in \mathcal{V}_j(k)} r_{nk}^j$, in which $\mathcal{V}_j(k)$ represents the set of vehicles connected with access point b_{jk}. In sum, the data collection latency generated from vehicles to access points at edge node j can be defined as

$$d_{jk} = \frac{1}{G_j} \sum_{k \in \mathcal{B}_j} \sum_{n \in \mathcal{V}_j(k)} \frac{r_{nk}^j}{R_{nk}^j - r_{nk}^j}, \tag{2}$$

where $G_j = \sum_{n \in \mathcal{V}_j} G_{jn}$ is the sum of the sensing data generation rate of all vehicles at edge node j. The data collection latency generated from access points to the edge server S_j can be defined as

$$d_{kS_j} = \frac{1}{G_j} \frac{r_k^j}{W_{jk}^{front} - r_k^j}. \tag{3}$$

Therefore, we formulate the total data collection latency as follows,

$$d_j^{coll} = \sum_{k \in \mathcal{B}_j} (d_{jk} + d_{kS_j}). \tag{4}$$

3.2 Problem Formulation

To fulfill the adaptive data transmission at different links, we now formulate a problem to minimize the data collection latency at edge node j. Since the data collection phase at different edge nodes is independent, the optimization of data transmission can also be implemented at each edge server independently. Thus, we illustrate the adaptive data transmission problem over one edge node for example as follows.

$$\min_{r_{nk}^j} d_j^{coll}, \tag{5a}$$

$$\text{s.t.} \sum_{b_k \in B_j(n)} r_{nk}^j = G_{jn}, \forall n \in \mathcal{V}_j, j \in J \tag{5b}$$

$$0 \le \sum_{n \in \mathcal{V}_j} r_{nk}^j \le W_{jk}^{front}, \forall k \in \mathcal{B}_j, j \in J \tag{5c}$$

$$0 \le r_{nk}^j \le R_{nk}^j, \forall k \in \mathcal{B}_j, n \in \mathcal{V}_j, j \in J. \tag{5d}$$

In problem (5), constraint (5b) implies that the sum of the allocated rate at different links of a vehicle should be equal to the sensing data generation rate of itself, in which $\mathcal{B}_j(n)$ indicates the set of access points connected with vehicle v_{jn}. Constraints (5c) and (5d) ensure that the allocated rate at each link should be non-negative but not exceed the link capacity.

3.3 Proposed Solution

Given the definition of MCF problem in [4], problem (5) can be kept as a special case of MCF problem, in which a common destination and multiple sources are considered. Due to its prohibitive complexity, we develop a modified flow derivation method to obtain the optimal rate allocation scheme through iterative convergence. The key idea of the proposed algorithm is to transfer part of the rate allocated on the congestive link to the "shortest link" among the remains. Without loss of generality, in our method, we use the first-order derivative of the latency to describe the path cost [4]. Let $cost_{nk}^j$ denote the cost of path

(v_{jn}, b_{jk}, S_j), which can be expressed as

$$
\begin{aligned}
cost_{nk}^j &= \frac{\partial d_j^{\text{coll}}}{\partial r_{nk}^j} + \frac{\partial d_j^{\text{coll}}}{\partial r_k^j} \\
&= \frac{1}{G_j} \left(\frac{R_{nk}^j}{\left(R_{nk}^j - r_{nk}^j \right)^2} + \frac{W_{jk}^{front}}{\left(W_{jk}^{front} - \sum_{v_{jn} \in \mathcal{V}_j(k)} r_{nk}^j \right)^2} \right).
\end{aligned}
\tag{6}
$$

The proposed algorithm mainly includes two steps, which can be described as follows.

1. **Find a Feasible Solution:** For each vehicle at edge node j, find the "shortest" path $\pi(v_{jn}, b_{jk}, S_j)$ using the metric defined in (6) and let $r_{nk}^j = G_{jn}$. If the allocated rate exceeds the path capacity, transfer λr_{nk}^j to the "shortest" path in the remaining links until the path capacity constraint is met, where $0 < \lambda < 1$. The path cost should be updated after each allocation and transfer.
2. **Find the Optimal Solution:** Begin with an iteration. For each vehicle at edge node j, transfer part of its allocated rate on each path to the current "shortest" path meanwhile updating the path cost. The iteration will not end until the data collection latency converged.

4   Adaptive Task Scheduling

After obtaining the sensing data collected by vehicles, the sensing data will be preprocessed by the edge server and formed into a series of individual packets, each of which is kept as input data of a specific update task. In this section, we neglect the impact of preprocessing on latency and mainly focus on minimizing the data processing latency through an adaptive task scheduling scheme between the edge and the cloud.

4.1   Latency Analysis

In this paper, for a specific update task, our adaptive scheduling scheme mainly includes three aspects: how to split the task, how to allocate computing resources at the edge node to the remaining part, and how to allocate computing resources at the cloud computing server to the offloaded part. Denote $\alpha_{jp} \in [0,1]$ as the splitting ratio of update task n_{jp}, which indicates the data proportion that is offloaded to the cloud computing server. Then the number of CPU cycles needed for processing the remaining part can be represented as $(1-\alpha_{jp})L_{jp}C_{jp}$. Therefore, the computing latency for processing the remaining part of data at the edge server can be expressed as

$$
d_{jp}^e = \frac{(1-\alpha_{jp})L_{jp}C_{jp}}{f_{jp}^e}.
\tag{7}
$$

Furthermore, we assume that the backhaul link capacity W_j^{back} of each edge node is sufficient enough to scale with the number of tasks. Thus, we denote W_{jp} as the allocated backhaul capacity for task n_{jp}. Therefore, the transmission latency for the offloaded part can be expressed as

$$d_{jp}^t = \frac{\alpha_{jp} L_{jp} C_{jp}}{W_{jp}}. \tag{8}$$

When receiving the offloaded data from an edge node, the cloud computing server will begin to compute the offloaded task in a parallel way. Therefore, the computing latency for processing the offloaded part of data at cloud computing server is given by

$$d_{jp}^c = \frac{\alpha_{jp} L_{jp} C_{jp}}{f_{jp}^c}. \tag{9}$$

Without loss of generality, we assume the computing of remaining data can be performed in parallel with the transmission of the offloaded data. However, the cloud computing server usually cannot begin to compute until the transmission ends [13]. Besides, given the data size of the computing result is small [8], we neglect the latency incurred during feedback of cloud computing server. In sum, the overall data processing latency of task n_{jp} can be given by

$$d_{jp}^{comp} = \max\{d_{jp}^e, d_{jp}^t + d_{jp}^c\} \tag{10}$$

4.2 Problem Formulation

To fulfill the optimal task splitting strategy and computing resource allocation strategy at both edge nodes and cloud computing server, we now formulate the following problem to minimize the data processing latency of all edge nodes.

$$\min_{\alpha_{jp}, f_{jp}^e, f_{jp}^c} \sum_{j \in J} \sum_{p \in N_j} d_{jp}^{comp}, \tag{11a}$$

$$\text{s.t.} \quad 0 \leq \alpha_{jp} \leq 1, \forall p \in \mathcal{N}_j, j \in \mathcal{J}, \tag{11b}$$

$$\sum_{p \in \mathcal{N}_j} f_{jp}^e = F_j, \forall j \in \mathcal{J}, \tag{11c}$$

$$\sum_{j \in J} \sum_{p \in \mathcal{N}_j} f_{jp}^c \leq F_c. \tag{11d}$$

The optimization variables in problem (11) include the task splitting ratio $\{\alpha_{jp}\}$ and the computing resource allocation $\{f_{jp}^e, f_{jp}^c\}$. Constraint (5c) and (11d) imply the allocated computing resources at edge node and cloud computing server should not exceed its total available computing capacity, respectively.

4.3 Proposed Solution

Note that the objective function in problem (11) is so complicated that we cannot solve it directly. Inspired by work [10], we find that given a computing resource allocation strategy f_{jp}^e and f_{jp}^c, the optimal task splitting ratio α_{jp}^* can be expressed with f_{jp}^e and f_{jp}^c. Thus, we firstly derive the expression of α_{jp}^* using f_{jp}^e and f_{jp}^c. Then, we reformulate the problem and obtain the closed-form optimal computing resource allocation strategy f_{jp}^{e*} and f_{jp}^{c*} through Lagrange multiplier method.

Considering the definition of d_{jp}^e, d_{jp}^t, d_{jp}^c and d_{jp}^{comp}, we can find that $d_{jp}^e = \frac{(1-\alpha_{jp})L_{jp}C_{jp}}{f_{jp}^e}$ decreases with α_{jp} and $d_{jp}^t + d_{jp}^c = \alpha_{jp}L_{jp}(\frac{1}{W_{jp}} + \frac{C_{jp}}{f_{jp}^c})$ increases with α_{jp}. Recall that $d_{jp}^{comp} = \max\{d_{jp}^e, d_{jp}^t + d_{jp}^c\}$, we find that d_{jp}^{comp} first decreases and then increases with α_{jp}. Thus, the minimum value of d_{jp}^{comp} can be achieved when $d_{jp}^e = d_{jp}^t + d_{jp}^c$. Then, the optimal task splitting ratio α_{jp} can be derived as

$$\alpha_{jp}^* = \frac{f_{jp}^e C_{jp} W_{jp}}{f_{jp}^e(f_{jp}^c + C_{jp}W_{jp}) + f_{jp}^c C_{jp}W_{jp}}. \tag{12}$$

By applying (12) to (10), the data processing latency of task n_{jp} can be rewritten as

$$d_{jp}^{comp*} = \frac{L_{jp}(C_{jp}f_{jp}^c + C_{jp}^2 W_{jp})}{f_{jp}^e f_{jp}^c + C_{jp}W_{jp}\left(f_{jp}^e + f_{jp}^c\right)}. \tag{13}$$

Then, the problem (11) can be reformulated as

$$\min_{f_{jp}^e, f_{jp}^c} \sum_{j \in J} \sum_{p \in N_j} d_{jp}^{comp*},$$

$$\text{s.t.} \quad (11b), (11c). \tag{14}$$

Now we apply the Lagrange multiplier method to solve the problem (14). Firstly, we introduce Lagrange multipliers $\gamma_j \geq 0$ and $\phi \geq 0$. Then, the partial Lagrange function for the problem (14) can be formulated as

$$La = \sum_{j \in \mathcal{J}} \sum_{p \in \mathcal{N}_j} d_{jp}^{comp*} + \sum_{j \in \mathcal{J}} \gamma_j \left(\sum_{p \in \mathcal{N}_j} f_{jp}^e - F_j \right)$$

$$+ \phi \left(\sum_{j \in \mathcal{J}} \sum_{p \in \mathcal{N}_j} f_{jp}^c - F_c \right). \tag{15}$$

Let $\{f_{jp}^{e*}, f_{jp}^{c*}\}$ be the optimal computing resource allocation strategy.the respective Karush−Kuhn−Tucker (KKT) conditions can be derived as follows.

$$\frac{\partial La}{\partial f_{jp}^{e*}} = L_{jp}C_{jp} \left(\frac{f_{jp}^{c*} + C_{jp}W_{jp}}{f_{jp}^{e}fjp^{c*} + C_{jp}W_{jp}\left(f_{jp}^{e*} + f_{jp}^{c*}\right)} \right)^2$$
$$+\gamma_j^* \begin{cases} \geq 0, f_{jp}^{e*} = 0, \\ = 0, f_{jp}^{e*} > 0 \end{cases} \tag{16}$$

$$\frac{\partial La}{\partial f_{jp}^{c*}} = -\frac{L_{jp}C_{jp}^3 W_{jp}^2}{\left(f_{jp}^{e*}f_{jp}^{c*} + C_{jp}W_{jp}\left(f_{jp}^{e*} + f_{jp}^{c*}\right)\right)^2}.$$
$$+\phi^* \begin{cases} \geq 0, f_{jp}^{c*} = 0, \\ = 0, f_{jp}^{c*} > 0 \end{cases} \tag{17}$$

$$\gamma_j^* \left(\sum_{p \in \mathcal{N}_j} f_{jp}^{e*} - F_j \right) = 0, \sum_{p \in \mathcal{N}_j} f_{jp}^{e*} \leq F_j, \gamma_j^* \geq 0, \forall j \in \mathcal{J}. \tag{18}$$

$$\phi^* \left(\sum_{j \in \mathcal{J}} \sum_{p \in \mathcal{N}_j} f_{jp}^{c*} - F^c \right) = 0, \sum_{j=1}^{J} \sum_{i=1}^{I_j} f_{jp}^{c*} \leq F_c, \phi^* \geq 0. \tag{19}$$

Based on the aforementioned conditions, the optimal computing resource allocation strategy can be derived as

$$\begin{cases} f_{jp}^{e*} = \max(0, \sqrt{\frac{L_{jp}C_{jp}}{\gamma_j^*}} - \left(1 - \sqrt{\frac{\phi^*}{\gamma_j^*}}\right)C_{jp}W_{jp}), \\ f_{jp}^{c*} = \max(0, \sqrt{\frac{\gamma_j^*}{\phi^*}} - 1)C_{jp}W_{jp}. \end{cases} \tag{20}$$

5   Simulations

5.1   Settings

We assume there are 1 cloud computing server and 3 edge nodes in the system. Each edge node, accounting for map update in its own service area independently, includes one edge server and 5 access points. The instantaneous computing capacity of the cloud computing server and edge node follows the uniform distribution in the range $[150, 600]$ GHz and $[0.5, 5]$ GHz, respectively. The backhaul link capacity allocated for each offloaded task, W_{jp}, follows the uniform distribution in the range $[5, 50]$ Mbps. The fronthaul link capacity W_{jk}^{front} follows the uniform distribution in the range $[10, 50]$ Mbps. For the data collection phase, we assume that there are 15 vehicles recruited for crowdsourcing at each edge node. Each vehicle can connect with 3 access points simultaneously at most.

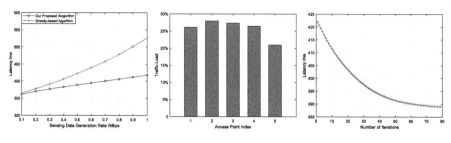

Fig. 2. Data generation rate versus latency

Fig. 3. Traffic load ratio of one edge node

Fig. 4. Iteration versus optimized latency

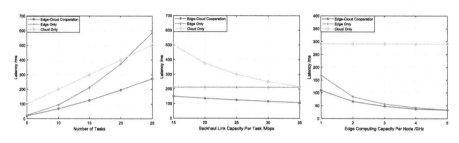

Fig. 5. Number of tasks versus latency

Fig. 6. Backhaul capacity versus latency

Fig. 7. Edge computing capacity versus latency

The link capacity from a vehicle to an access point follows the uniform distribution in the range $[1, 5]$ Mbps. The sensing data generation rate of each vehicle is assumed to be 0.5 Mbps. For the data processing phase, we assume that there are 15 update tasks having been triggered at each edge node, each of which has a 0.5 Mb sensing data packet as input. And the computing workload for one-bit sensing data, C_{jp}, follows the uniform distribution in the range $[500, 1500]$ CPU cycles per bit.

5.2 Evaluation and Analysis

In our simulations, we perform sufficient experiments to verify the effectiveness of our proposed algorithms for fast data allocation and fast data processing, respectively. Specifically, for the data collection phase, we compare the proposed modified flow deviation method with a distributed greedy-based data transmission method and further show the relationship between the data collection latency and the number of vehicles. For the data processing phase, we compare the proposed task scheduling scheme with an edge-only scheme and a cloud-only scheme, based on which we further investigate the impact of the number of tasks, the edge computing capacity, and the backhaul link capacity on the data processing latency. Figure 2 illustrates the data collection latency of one edge node and Fig. 3 demonstrates the load balancing effects achieved by our proposed algorithm. It can be seen that our proposed data transmission scheme outperforms the greedy-based counterpart with the increase of the sensing data generation rate of each vehicle. Figure 4 shows the convergence of our proposed algorithm. Besides, for the data processing phase, Fig. 5, Fig. 6, and Fig. 7 illustrate the superiorities of our proposed edge-cloud cooperation scheme in terms of the average data processing latency of the edge nodes. Additionally, Fig. 5 shows that the edge-only scheme can barely meet the latency requirement when handling burst update tasks, which proves the necessity of our proposed adaptive task scheduling scheme between the edge and the cloud. Furthermore, Fig. 6 indicates that the performance gap between edge computing and cloud computing is mainly determined by backhaul link capacity while keeping the computing resource fixed. Finally, Fig. 7 implies that the performance gap between our proposed cooperation scheme and edge only scheme decreases with the increase of edge computing capacity, due to the fact that most of the tasks will be processed locally if the edge computing capacity reaches a certain level.

6   Conclusion

In this paper, we propose an integrated update framework including both an adaptive data transmission scheme and an adaptive task scheduling scheme to realize fast data collection and fast data processing for HD map update. Specifically, based on our proposed system architecture, we firstly optimize the transmission rate on different links of each vehicle to realize fast data collection. Then, we determine the task splitting strategy at each edge node and the computing resource allocation strategy at both the edge nodes and the cloud computing server to realize fast data processing. To the end, we carry out simulations to verify the effectiveness of our proposed policies.

References

1. Automated vehicles require intelligent HD maps for reliable and safe driving. https://nds-association.org/hd-maps/. Accessed 12 Aug 2020
2. Extending the vision of automated vehicles with HD Maps and ADASIS. https://download.tomtom.com/open/banners. Accessed 30 Mar 2020
3. The future of maps: technologies, processes, and ecosystem. https://www.here.com/sites/g/files/odxslz166/files/2019-01/. Accessed 30 Mar 2020
4. Fratta, L., Gerla, M., Kleinrock, L.: The flow deviation method: An approach to store-and-forward communication network design. Networks 3(2), 97–133 (1973)
5. Hussain, R., Zeadally, S.: Autonomous cars: research results, issues, and future challenges. IEEE Commun. Surv. Tutorials 21(2), 1275–1313 (2018)
6. Kim, K., Cho, S., Chung, W.: HD map update for autonomous driving with crowd-sourced data. IEEE Robot. Autom. Lett. 6(2), 1895–1901 (2021). https://doi.org/10.1109/LRA.2021.3060406

7. Liebner, M., Jain, D., Schauseil, J., Pannen, D., Hackelöer, A.: Crowdsourced HD map patches based on road model inference and graph-based slam. In: 2019 IEEE Intelligent Vehicles Symposium (IV), pp. 1211–1218 (2019). https://doi.org/10.1109/IVS.2019.8813860

8. Luo, S., Chen, X., Wu, Q., Zhou, Z., Yu, S.: HFEL: joint edge association and resource allocation for cost-efficient hierarchical federated edge learning. IEEE Trans. Wirel. Commun. **19**(10), 6535–6548 (2020)

9. Pannen, D., Liebner, M., Hempel, W., Burgard, W.: How to keep HD maps for automated driving up to date. In: 2020 IEEE International Conference on Robotics and Automation (ICRA), pp. 2288–2294 (2020). https://doi.org/10.1109/ICRA40945.2020.9197419

10. Ren, J., Yu, G., He, Y., Li, G.Y.: Collaborative cloud and edge computing for latency minimization. IEEE Trans. Veh. Technol. **68**(5), 5031–5044 (2019)

11. Sawahashi, M., Kishiyama, Y., Morimoto, A., Nishikawa, D., Tanno, M.: Coordinated multipoint transmission/reception techniques for LTE-advanced [coordinated and distributed MIMO]. IEEE Wirel. Commun. **17**(3), 26–34 (2010). https://doi.org/10.1109/MWC.2010.5490976

12. Seif, H.G., Hu, X.: Autonomous driving in the icity—HD maps as a key challenge of the automotive industry. Engineering **2**(2), 159–162 (2016)

13. Wang, Y., Sheng, M., Wang, X., Wang, L., Li, J.: Mobile-edge computing: partial computation offloading using dynamic voltage scaling. IEEE Trans. Commun. **64**(10), 4268–4282 (2016)

Research on Path Planning for Relay Drones with Multiple Constraints

Di Xu[1(✉)] and Hongyan Qian[1,2]

[1] College of Computer Sciences and Technology, Nanjing University of Aeronautics and Astronautics, Nanjing, China
xuyouye@nuaa.edu.cn
[2] Collaborative Innovation Center of Novel Software Technology and Industrialization, Nanjing, China

Abstract. There are many applications of UAV relay networks in large-scale and long-distance scenarios. In such applications, reasonable path planning is conducive to reducing the travel distance and improving the adaptability of UAV networks. We propose a path planning algorithm for UAVs based on the formulation of an optimization problem, with the objectives of maintaining connectivity, minimizing the required movements and avoiding the deployment of more relay UAVs than necessary. The heuristic algorithm is compared to other methods in terms of the quality of solution.

Keywords: UAV relay networks · Path planning · Mobility control

1 Introduction

Early uses of Unmanned Aerial Vehicles (UAVs) were characterized by the use of a single large UAV for a task [1]. Different from the single UAV system, the multi-UAV system has the advantages of lower acquisition and maintenance cost, stronger scalability and higher speedup. In order to deal with coverage expansion and the system capacity increase in wireless communication networks, multi-UAV systems are often used as relays. Compared with traditional relay networks, UAV relay networks can overcome terrain obstacles for relay location deployment [2] and establish communication links with the shorter time.

In [3], satisfied with collision avoidance, limited communication and UAV kinematic constraints, the optimal UAV motion plan is obtained by decentralized receding horizon control, which is solved by particle swarm optimization with elite mechanism. However, this paper does not take into account that the mission UAV travels a long distance with the limited number.

UAV path planning plays an important role in flight missions. There are many research publications on UAV path planning. The main focus of this research in [4] is to determine the optimal trajectories of the UAVs to maintain communication at all times under the constraint that the total distance travelled by all

© Springer Nature Switzerland AG 2021
Z. Liu et al. (Eds.): WASA 2021, LNCS 12939, pp. 463–470, 2021.
https://doi.org/10.1007/978-3-030-86137-7_49

UAVs is minimum. However, the approach does not pay attention to the motion performance of the UAV, such as speed, acceleration, etc.

Tropistic RRT*, which is a sampling based path planning method is proposed in [5]. It improves the efficiency of the path planning by restricting the sampling space to approach the goal position just like the phototropism of plants. Although Tropistic RRT* performs much better than other RRT* variants in terms of the cost of path, the convergence speed and the memory usage, it does not discuss that many agents move under the constraint of maintaining communication links.

As we know so far, many papers [6–8] only concern about the single UAV's path planning and do not deal with the path planning of multiple relay UAVs. Our work discusses a path planning algorithm based on movement prediction and simple geometric principles, with the objectives of maintaining connectivity, the number of drones and moving distance. The distributed approaches control the movement of multiple relay drones, so that all relay drones can obtain the desired path.

The main work of this paper are as follows: first, we tackle a simple yet sound technical problem with an analytical approach; second, we propose a combination of UAV movement control algorithms, the CMPPG algorithm can obtain the minimum movement distance under the premise of maintaining connectivity. To ensure there is no excess number of drones in the air, we optimize the position of the relay UAVs by PPPR algorithm.

2   Problem Description

It is assumed that relay drones are deployed in a chain, so as to obtain a connected path between MU and GCS. GCS, MU and RUs are respectively denoted by u_G, u_0, $\{u_r\}_{r=1}^n$. And $p_i = (x_i, y_i)$, $p_i = (x_{i'}, y_{i'})$, for $i \in u_0 \cup \{u_r\}_{r=1}^n$ respectively represent the initial position and the final position of the mobile node. The coordinates of the fixed node is $p_G = (x_G, y_G)$.

In order to simplify the description, some new definitions are introduced: first, the node on the side of the GCS is defined as the upstream node (UN), and the node on the other side is the downstream node (DN); second, for any pair of neighbor nodes, the upstream node is called the passive node (PN), and the other is the active node (AN). The mobility of AN affects the movement of PN. All drones are assumed to fly at a fixed altitude H and have a maximum speed v_{max}. In this wireless network, the communication range of all nodes is R.

RUs adopt the method of incremental deployment. There is a special circumstance that an unnecessary additional RU is increased to maintain connectivity. Supposed that the number of RUs deployed at time t is $Num(t)$, the network is connected. Thus the number of RUs at time $t + 1$ is divided into the following two cases:

$$Num(t + 1) = \begin{cases} Num(t), & connected \\ Num(t) + 1, & otherwise \end{cases} \quad (1)$$

If $\|p_i(t + 1) - p_0(t + 1)\|_2 < [Num(t) + 1] \cdot R$, the condition *connected* is established. $\|\cdot\|_2$ is the function to calculate the distance between two nodes.

The optimization problem is described by the following equations:

$$min \left\{ \sum_{t=0}^{T} \sum_{i=1}^{N_{max}} \|p_i(t+1) - p_i(t)\|_2 \right\} \qquad (2a)$$

s.t.

$$\|p_i(t+1) - p_{i+1}(t+1)\|_2 \leq R \qquad (2b)$$

$$\|p_i(t+1) - p_0(t+1)\|_2 < (Num(t)+1) \cdot R \qquad (2c)$$

$$v_i(t) \leq v_{max} \qquad (2d)$$

During the flight time, (2a) is an objective function, it represents the minimum moving distance of all RUs. (2b) forces the link between PN and AN at the next time to remain connected. (2c) ensures that the number of RUs in the air is minimal. (2d) specifies the maximum speed cannot exceed v_{max}.

3   Algorithm Scheme

In order to maintain connectivity between the pair, the movement prediction algorithm is used which is based on simple kinematic rules. The algorithm uses the AN position updates, thus the time must be discretized into time steps. Supposed that Δt equals 1 and the position of AN at time t is $p_i(t) = [x_i(t), y_i(t)]$, so its next position coordinate is:

$$\begin{cases} x_i(t+1) = x_i(t) + [v_{x_i}(t) + \frac{1}{2}a_{x_i}(t) \cdot \Delta t] \cdot \Delta t \\ y_i(t+1) = y_i(t) + [v_{y_i}(t) + \frac{1}{2}a_{y_i}(t) \cdot \Delta t] \cdot \Delta t \end{cases} \qquad (3)$$

where $v_{x_i}(t)$ means the speed of node i at time t, and $a_{x_i}(t)$ is the acceleration.

Furthermore, we set up two states of the UAV: *hover* and *move*. After PN predicts the future position of AN at the next time, PN needs to determine whether it will change the motion state. The judgment is relatively simple: First, calculating the distance d_{ij} in accordance with the following equation:

$$d_{ij} = \sqrt{([x_j(t) - x_i(t+1)]^2 + [y_j(t) - y_i(t+1)]^2)} \qquad (4)$$

Second, the distance is judged to be less than the maximum communication distance d_{max}/R. PN keeps hovering if it is less than d_{max}/R. Otherwise, it is necessary to calculate the next position:

$$\begin{cases} cos\theta = \frac{|x_i(t+1) - x_j(t)|}{d_{ij}} \\ sin\theta = \frac{|y_i(t+1) - y_j(t)|}{d_{ij}} \\ \Delta d = d_{ij} - d_{max} \\ x_j(t+1) = x_j(t) - \Delta d \cdot cos\theta \\ y_j(t+1) = y_j(t) - \Delta d \cdot sin\theta \end{cases} \qquad (5)$$

Each PN moves at their speeds within the same update time:

$$v_j = min \left\{ \frac{\|p_j(t+1) - p_j(t)\|_2}{\Delta t}, v_{max} \right\} \tag{6}$$

As $host_{N_{max}}$ detects that it disconnected with $host_G$ at time $t+1$, the situation of *connected* in Eq. (1) will be judged, if connected, all relay drones need to set their states to *hover* and start the PPPR algorithm in the control module, so as to optimize the position of relay nodes in the same time step; otherwise, an additional UAV needs to be arranged and set its ID to N+1, N_{max} should update to N+1 as well. The core pseudo code is shown in Algorithm 1.

Algorithm 1. Connectivity Maintenance Path Points Generation (CMPPG) Algorithm

---

Input:
    The target location of MU
Output:
    Path points of each RU at each time step
1: **Initialization:**
        Number 0,1,2... N for each UAV;
        Position coordinates of each UAV at time t;
        Step length of update time;
2: **for** n **do** $= 0, 1, 2, ... N_{max}$
3:     **if** $n = 0$ **then**
4:         Send message containing its current position to its upstream node;
5:     **end if**
6:     **else if** $n = N_{max}$ **and** $\|P_{N_{max}} - P_G\| > R$ **then**
7:         **case:** *connected* set all RUs to *hover* and start the PPPR.
8:         **case:** *otherwise* add a new RU and set $N_{max} = N + 1$
9:     **end if**
10:    **else**
11:        Receive message from $j = i - 1$;
12:        Calculate the next position of j with (3);
13:        Calculate d_{ij} between node j at $t+1$ and node i at t with (4);
14:        **if** $d_{ij} > d_{max}$ **then**
15:            Set i's state to *move*;
16:            Calculate i's next position and its velocity with (5)(6);
17:        **else**
18:            Set i's state to *hover*;
19:        **end if**
20: **end for**
21: **return** The path of each RU that is formed by path points.

When the link between the GCS and its downstream neighbor node is disconnected, we can add a UAV to expand the communication range or adjust the position of relay nodes. Although the CMPPG algorithm guarantees the minimum travel distance with the constraint of connectivity, its deficiency causes an unlimited increase in the number of UAVs. To ensure the minimization of UAV increments, we propose the PPPR algorithm running in each RU shown in Fig. 1.

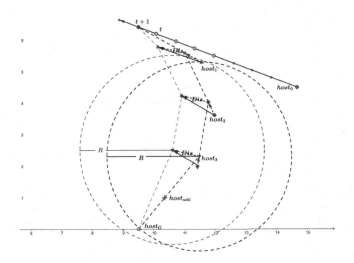

Fig. 1. Moving method based on the characteristics of parallelogram

The message includes the distance Dis that the UAV should move and the relevant trigonometric functions of the heading angle α. Both of them can be calculated by (5). As long as each relay node receives these information and combines with the predicted position at time $t + 1$, the actual target position optimized at time $t + 1$ can be obtained. The relevant pseudo code is shown in Algorithm 2.

4   Simulation Experiment and Result

We use Matlab software to verify the performance of our algorithm scheme. Given the initial position of each UAV in advance (See Fig. 2). The position of the ground node is (300,0). The coordinates of MU is (540,380). Relay nodes are distributed in the right half of the line $X = 300$. First, MU is notified by GCS to the target location (200,300) near the fixed ground node. Final positions of all nodes are shown in Fig. 2(a). Next, we give a further target position (60,400). In this case, GCS needs to make the decision of adding a UAV or adjusting the position. The UAV movement trajectory without PPPR algorithm is shown in Fig. 2(b).

Algorithm 2. Path Points Parallel Relocation (PPPR) Algorithm

---

Input:
    Position coordinates of each UAV at time t
Output:
    Optimized path points at time $t + 1$
1: **for** n **do** $= 0, 1, 2, ...N_{max}$
2:     **if** $n \,! = 0$ **then**
3:         **if** TimeOut (T_{adjust}) **then**
4:             Convert hover-state into move-state;
5:         **end if**
6:         **else**
7:             Receive message Dis from its UN;
8:             Use (5) to calculate $cos\alpha, sin\alpha$;
9:             Calculate the adjusted next position with the predicted position.
10:     **end if**
11: **end for**
12: **return**

In order to observe the optimized discrete path points more clearly, the second experiment resets the update time twice as long as the previous ones. The results without PPPR algorithm is shown in Fig. 3(a), and the path optimized by the PPPR algorithm is shown in Fig. 3(b).

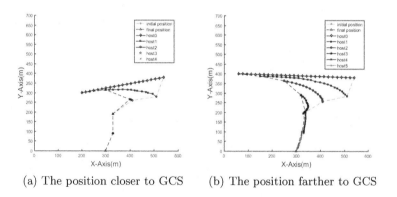

(a) The position closer to GCS   (b) The position farther to GCS

Fig. 2. MU moves to different positions

According to the experiments, the movement trajectories of the relay nodes are affected by the initial topology configuration and the target position of MU. In the coordinate axis, when the slope of the trajectory of MU is negative, all relay nodes move away from the GCS. At this situation, a new UAV is added to keep the entire network connected. Moreover, if the distance between the final position and the initial position is long enough, the trajectories will be infinitely close to the ones of their downstream neighbor.

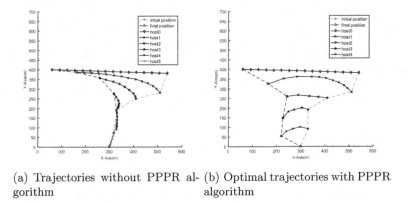

(a) Trajectories without PPPR algorithm

(b) Optimal trajectories with PPPR algorithm

Fig. 3. Comparision between with PPPR and without PPPR

Furthermore, we observe that the closer the nodes to the MU, the greater the distance they move on the X-axis, and the smaller the distance on the Y-axis. When using the PPPR algorithm, the relay nodes can be adjusted. Under the strong constraint of maintaining connectivity, the scheme increases the moving speed so that RUs can move away from their upstream neighbor quickly in the X-axis direction, and move close to GCS at a slower speed in the Y-axis direction.

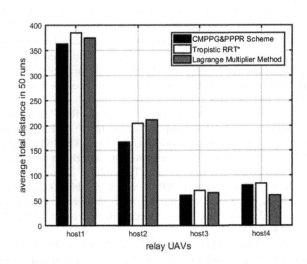

Fig. 4. Comparision among three schemes for the minimum distance

In order to further verify the effectiveness of the combination of CMPPG and PPPR algorithm. We introduce Tropistic RRT* and Lagrangian function method for the minimum value. The results are reported in Fig. 4. It shows that our algorithm scheme ensures $host1 - host3$ have the shortest moving distance at each time step and obtains satisfactory results in the shorter total moving distance. $host4$ used Lagrangian function method have a better result than our approaches, but the total income can make the final result ignore the loss of $host4$. It can be inferred that with the increase of the number of UAVs, the income in the total distance will be more obvious.

5   Conclusion

Deploying UAV networks in long-distance scenarios is obviously beneficial. This paper studies the minimum travel distance of all relay UAVs under the constraints of connectivity and the minimum number. Therefore, we have developed an effective combination of UAV movement control algorithms, the CMPPG algorithm based on prediction can obtain the minimum movement distance with the constraint of maintaining connectivity. The PPPR algorithm optimize the position of the relay UAVs without an excess number. Multiple sets of simulation data show the effectivity of our algorithm.

References

1. Gupta, L., Jain, R., Vaszkun, G.: Survey of important issues in UAV communication networks. IEEE Commun. Surv. Tutorials **18**(2), 1123–1152 (2015)
2. Bekmezci, I., Sahingoz, O.K., Temel, Ş: Flying ad-hoc networks (FANETs): a survey. Ad Hoc Netw. **11**(3), 1254–1270 (2013)
3. Zhu, Q., Zhou, R., Zhang, J.: Connectivity maintenance based on multiple relay UAVs selection scheme in cooperative surveillance. Appl. Sci. **7**(1), 8 (2017)
4. de Silva, R., Rajasinghege, S.: Optimal desired trajectories of UAVs in private UAV networks. In: 2018 International Conference on Advanced Technologies for Communications (ATC), pp. 310–314 (2018)
5. Wang, J., Li, C.X., Chi, W., Meng, M.Q.: Tropistic RRT*: an efficient planning algorithm via adaptive restricted sampling space. In: 2018 IEEE International Conference on Information and Automation (ICIA), pp. 1639–1646 (2018)
6. Chen, J., Li, M., Yuan, Z., Gu, Q.: An improved A* algorithm for UAV path planning problems. In: 2020 IEEE 4th Information Technology, Networking, Electronic and Automation Control Conference (ITNEC), vol. 1, pp. 958–962 (2020)
7. Zhou, Z., Zhang, C., Xu, C., Xiong, F., Zhang, Y., Umer, T.: Energy-efficient industrial Internet of UAVs for power line inspection in smart grid. IEEE Trans. Ind. Inf. **14**(6), 2705–2714 (2018)
8. Sánchez-García, J., Reina, D.G., Toral, S.L.: A distributed PSO-based exploration algorithm for a UAV network assisting a disaster scenario. Fut. Gener. Comput. Syst. **90**, 129–148 (2019)

A Reinforcement Model Based Prioritized Replay to Solve the Offloading Problem in Edge Computing

Wenrui Liu, Cong Wang[(✉)], Jiazhi Mi, He Luan, and Yixin Luo

Northeastern University at Qinhuangdao, Qinhuangdao, China
congw@neuq.edu.cn

Abstract. Mobile edge computing is widely applied to help mobile devices to improve its data processing speed. However, one of its main challenges is how to generate computation offloading decision effectively and quickly in the complex wireless scenario. In this paper, we aim to build up a multiple user devices application scenario, where each device performs binary computation offloading policy which is executed in the local device or offloaded to a cloud server via the wireless network. A model based on deep reinforcement learning is proposed to optimize computation offloading decisions. First, the weighted rate of offloading computation is introduced to be a reward in the Q function. Second, offloading decisions are generated from a deep Q-network (DQN) with batch normalization layers. At last, the deep Q-network is trained with a designed prioritized replay policy. Experimental results indicate the proposed model generates the optimal offloading decisions in a short time and gets faster convergence speed on the weighted rate.

Keywords: Mobile edge computing · Binary computation offloading · Deep reinforcement learning · Prioritized replay

1 Introduction

MEC is a new technology that provides cloud services and IT services to mobile device users in a short distance [1]. Traditional network operators are only responsible for controlling transmission flow, like forwarding and packet filtering. However, the MEC server is deployed at every base station in mobile edge computing. Therefore, network operators also play an important role in providing services for mobile device users. MEC platform decreases the network latency through providing storage service and computation capabilities for mobile edge networks, of which key point is the computation offloading and computational resource allocation.

We assume that the mobile edge computing network only performs the binary computation offloading strategy, which means every computing assignment from the mobile device is either performed in the local device or offloaded to the cloud server entirely. In order to optimally adapt to the computation offloading decision and wireless and computing resource allocation, the complex scenario where wireless channel varies from

© Springer Nature Switzerland AG 2021
Z. Liu et al. (Eds.): WASA 2021, LNCS 12939, pp. 471–478, 2021.
https://doi.org/10.1007/978-3-030-86137-7_50

time to time is considered. This requires the rapid solution of complex combinatorial optimization problems in channel coherence time, which is difficult to be achieved by traditional numerical optimization methods. While reinforcement learning relies on deep neural network to learn from training samples, an optimal mapping from state space to action space is finally produced. A distributed DRL based offloading model for mobile edge networks, called DDLO, is proposed [2]. However, due to the exhaustive searching nature of DQN when selecting actions in each iteration, it is not suitable to deal with the problem of high-dimensional action space [3].

DROO, an online offloaded model based on DRL, is proposed to make the weighted calculation rate of wireless power maximum that supplies Multi-Access edge computing networks with binary computing offload [4]. The model learns from the past offloading experience and improves the offloading actions generated by DNN through reinforcement learning. A method of quantified order preserved and self-adapting parameter setting are designed to achieve fast convergence of the model. Compared with the traditional optimal computing approaches, the DROO model completely eliminates the demand to solve complex mixed integer programming problems. However, the main problem is that the mobile devices will make it harder for DROO to converge and leads to large fluctuations in the final weighted calculation rate.

In this paper, we aim to estimate a DRL based model for a large number of mobile devices in MEC computation offloading and resource allocation system. A Deep Q Network (DQN) is embedded in the model to set up the value function of Q-learning, which evaluates the current channel gains and computation offloading decision totally. Batch normalization (BN) is used to avoid internal covariate shift, which helps DQN learns faster with a greater learning rate [5]. Prioritized replay takes the place of random sample while sampling transitions from memory, which leads to a higher possibility of acceptance of qualified experience [6]. At last, this DRL based model shows better convergence and shorter learning time to generate the optimal binary computation offloading decision.

2 Modeling on Binary Computation Offloading Policy

Consider that a wireless powered mobile edge computing network consists of an eNB (eNodeB) and N user equipment (UE). The MEC server is deployed on the eNB, and each UE undertakes a computing intensive task. It is up to the UE to decide whether to execute the task in the local device or offload it to the MEC server. Since UE is a wireless Internet of things device with low battery capacity, it is necessary to receive radio energy before performing computing tasks.

The system time is divided into several equal length continuous time frames. In each time frame T, the time division multiplexing (TDD) is used by eNB to transmit radio energy or data in the same band. h_i is used to represent the wireless channel gain between eNB and UE. At the beginning of each frame time, it takes each UE the same time aT to receive the power transmitted wirelessly, where $a \in [0, 1]$. After receiving the power, UE performs its computation task and completes the task before the end of the current time frame. Each UE will get a different computing weight w_i. The higher the w_i, the faster the computation rate allocated by UE. When executing computation tasks, UE has two kinds of computing decisions: it is completely executed in the local device, or it is completely offloaded to MEC and executed by MEC. $x_i \in \{0, 1\}$ is used to represent the behavior of UE_i, where $x_i = 0$ represents the local computation, and $x_i = 1$ represents the offloading computation, and τ_i is the time proportion of the computation offloading of UE_i.

It is assumed that h_i only changes with time, and other parameters such as w_i remain unchanged. $r_{L,i}^*(a)$ is the local computation rate, and $r_{O,i}^*(a, \tau_i)$ is the offloading computation rate, which is considered to equal the data offloading rate. Therefore, the weighted computation rate of each time frame is equal to

$$Q(h, x, \tau, a) = \sum_{i=1}^{N} w_i \big((1 - x_i) r_{L,i}^*(a) + x_i r_{O,i}^*(a, \tau_i) \big) \tag{1}$$

This non-convex problem can be optimized into a convex problem [4]:

$$Q^*(h, x) = \max_{\tau, a} Q(h, x, \tau, a) \tag{2}$$

where $\sum_{i=1}^{N} \tau_i + a \leq 1, a \geq 0, \tau_i \geq 0, \forall i \in N$.

In this way, the convex problem can be solved in two steps. First step is to determine an offloading computation policy, and the second step is to allocate resource, which generates the optimal solution (h, x, τ, a) at last.

2.1 System Model

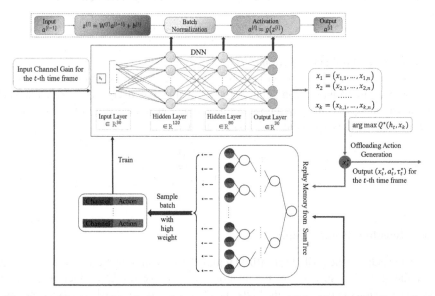

Fig. 1. Architecture of the designed deep reinforcement model for binary offloading policy

As shown in Fig. 1, we propose a model that is able to generate the optimal binary computation offloading policy quickly. The model consists of two parts. One is offloading action generation, and the other is offloading policy update. In the offloading action generation stage, the channel gain h_t of the current time frame t is input into the DNN to explore K group candidate computation offloading actions, and then the optimal solution x_t^* is chosen from the state space. Next comes the offloading policy update stage. (h_t, x_t^*) is sent as a new sample to the memory, after which each sample is assigned a priority. At the end, a batch of samples is selected with Prioritized Replay and sent to DNN for training.

2.2 Offloading Action Generation

Initially, the number of UE is N, and the number of quantized actions is set to $K = N$. In the t-th time frame, after K is updated, the channel gain h_t is input to DNN, and then K group relaxed variables $\widehat{x_t}$ based on the current computation offloading policy π_{θ_t} can be obtained.

Next, via the quantized function

$$g_k : \widehat{x_t} \rightarrow \{x_k | x_k \in \{0, 1\}^N, k = 1, 2, \ldots, K\} \tag{3}$$

The K group relaxed variables $\widehat{x_t}$ produces K group candidate offloading policy $\{x_k\}$. The Q value of each candidate action is

$$Q^*(h, x) = \max_{\tau, a} Q(h, x, \tau, a) \tag{4}$$

The offloading action corresponding to the maximum Q value defined as:

$$x_t^* = \arg \max_{x_i \in \{x_k\}} Q^*(h_t, x_i) \tag{5}$$

which is the final offloading action.

Since the internal covariate shift phenomenon occurs when the depth of NN deepens, which makes the weighted computation rate Q unable to converge as expected, a batch normalization layer is inserted between linear function and activation function of each layer of DNN, that is, each dimension is changed as

$$\hat{x}^{(k)} = \frac{x^{(k)} - E\left[x^{(k)}\right]}{\sqrt{Var\left[x^{(k)}\right]}} \tag{6}$$

2.3 Offloading Policy Update

In order to achieve the goal of prioritized replay during sampling, SumTree is introduced to be the basic data structure of the memory. The sample (h_t, x_t^*), which is generated from the previous step, is given the highest priority $p = (e + \varepsilon)^\alpha$, where ε is a very small number to ensure that $p \neq 0$. p and (h_t, x_t^*) are stored in the leaf nodes of SumTree.

When training DNN, a batch of samples are selected from SumTree according to their priorities, and the sampling probability is defined as

$$p(i) = \frac{p_i^\alpha}{\sum_k p_k^\alpha} \tag{7}$$

where p_i is proportional to $|\delta_i|$, and defined as the different value of the label and the prediction of DNN. The larger $|\delta_i|$ is, the larger the gap between the label and the prediction is, the more valuable it is for DNN to learn, and the higher the probability of the sample being extracted. This sampling mechanism is called prioritized replay. In this paper, we define the parameters of prioritized replay as $\varepsilon = 0.01$ and $\alpha = 0.6$. The weight of importance sampling is

$$w_j = \left(\frac{P_j}{min_i P_i}\right)^{-\beta} \tag{8}$$

After the weight $\{w\}$ of this batch of samples are calculated, the weighted cross entropy loss function

$$L(\theta_t) = -\frac{1}{|T_t|} \sum_{t \in T_t} w_t \left((x_T^*)^T \log f_{\theta_t}(h_T) + (1 - x_T^*)^T \log(1 - f_{\theta_t}(h_T)) \right) \tag{9}$$

is used in DNN for backpropagation, where $|T_t|$ represents the dimension of T_t. Every δ time frame, SumTree can collect abundant samples. With prioritized replay, samples with high priorities are selected and input into DNN. After DNN training, θ_t and π_{θ_t} are updated to θ_{t+1} and $\pi_{\theta_{t+1}}$ respectively, which can be used to generate offloading action x_{t+1} in the next time frame.

Algorithm 1: An prioritized replay based algorithm to solve binary offloading policy

---

Input: Wireless channel gain h_t at each time frame t, the number of
quantized actions K;

Output: Offloading action x_t^*, and the corresponding optimal resource
allocation a_t, τ_t for each time frame t;

1   Initialize the NN with batch normalization;
2   Set iteration number M and the training interval δ;
3   **for** $t = 1$ to M **do**
4   Generate a relaxed offloading action $\hat{x}_t = f_{\theta_t}(h_t)$;
5   Quantize $\hat{x}_t$ into K binary actions $\{x_k\} = g_K(\hat{x}_t)$;
6   Compute $Q^*(h_t, x_k)$ for each of $\{x_k\}$;
7   Select the best action $x_t^* = \arg\max_{\{x_k\}} Q^*(h_t, x_k)$;
8   Add (h_t, x_t^*) with highest priority to SumTree;
9   **if** $t \bmod \delta = 0$ **then**
10   Sample data set $\{(h_\tau, x_\tau^*) | \tau \in T_t\}$ from the SumTree ac-
            cording to normalized priorities $\{P_j\}$;
11   Compute w_j for every sample from the batch;
12   Train the NN with weighted Cross Entropy Loss;
13   Update samples' priorities $\{p_j\}$ in SumTree;
14   **end if**
15 **end for**
16 **return** x_t^*, a_t, τ_t

The proposed algorithm is able to generate the optimal computation offloading
action according to h_t of current time frame, and select high qualified experience from
$\{(h_t, x_t^*) | t \in T\}$ to learn, so as to update the computation offloading policy of the proposed model. With prioritized replay instead of random replay, DNN can learn multiple
groups of with large gaps between predicted value and practical value more efficiently,
which ensures that the computation offloading policy can converge quickly and the
fluctuation after convergence is in a very small range.

3   Performance Evaluation

In this section, a scenario of multiple user devices and an eNB where MEC server is
located is assumed to estimate the performance of our model. The energy receiver at

each user device is set as P2110 Powerharvester, and the energy transmitter at the eNB is considered to work as Powercast TX91501-3W with $P = 3$ W. For each time frame t with N user devices, the wireless channel gain $h_t = \left[h_1^t, \cdots, h_N^t \right]$ is harvested from a Rayleigh fading channel model as $h_i^t = \overline{h_i}\alpha_i^t$, where $\overline{h_i}$ follows the free space path loss algorithm, and α_i^t follows an exponential distribution.

In the simulation, we consider two conditions respectively to compare our proposed model with other DRL based models. One of the two conditions is with medium quantities of user devices, and the other is with large quantities of user devices.

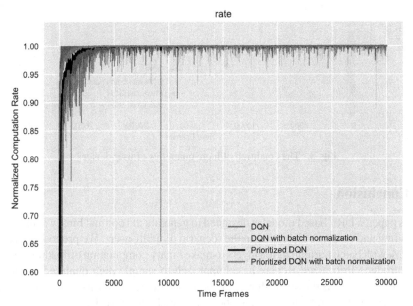

Fig. 2. The condition of medium quantities of user devices

As shown in Fig. 2, the normalized computation rate of the four DRL based models is performing similarly when user devices are not too much. As shown in Fig. 3, when amount of user devices becomes larger, the proposed model is slower than other DQN based model at the start of the experiment. Because Prioritized Replay the proposed model uses is applied with ε-greedy policy that samples from $\left\{ \left(h_t, x_t^* \right) \middle| t \in T \right\}$ only according to its $|\delta_i|$, which leads to samples with greater $|\delta_i|$ but lower learning quality. However, the proposed model shows a faster convergence speed than the DQN based model in the middle and late stage of the experiment, which reflects that samples with lower learning quality has been removed from the memory and the deep Q-network is growing more stable to generate better computation offloading decisions.

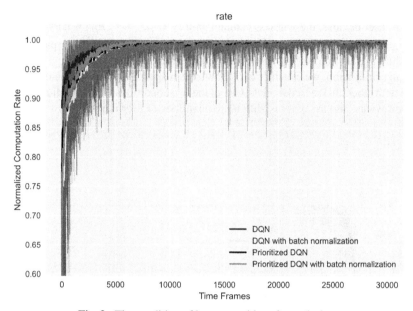

Fig. 3. The condition of large quantities of user devices

4   Conclusion

In this paper, a DRL based model is designed to generate the optimal binary computation offloading and resource allocation in the scenario of multi-users. We propose a Deep Q-network with batch normalization layers to make binary computation offloading decision and introduce Prioritized Replay based approach to sample high qualified experience from the memory. As the result shows, the proposed model performs better convergence and shorter learning time to access the best-weighted rate of MEC.

References

1. Yuyi, M., Jun, Z., Khaled, L.: Dynamic computation offloading for mobile-edge computing with energy harvesting devices. IEEE J. Sel. Areas Commun. **34**(12), 3590–3605 (2016)
2. Huang L., Feng X., Feng A., Huang Y., Qian P.: Distributed deep learning-based offloading for mobile edge computing networks. Mobile Netw. Appl. (2018). https://doi.org/10.1007/s11036-018-1177-x
3. Lillicrap, T., Hunt, J., Pritzel, A., et al.: Continuous control with deep reinforcement learning. In: ICLR (2016)
4. Liang, H., Suzhi, B., Yingjun, Z.: Deep reinforcement learning for online computation offloading in wireless powered mobile-edge computing networks. IEEE Trans. Mob. Comput. **19**(11), 2581–2593 (2020)
5. Ioffe, S., Szegedy, C.: Batch normalization: accelerating deep network training by reducing internal covariate shift. In: Proceedings of the 32nd International Conference on Machine Learning, pp.448–456. JMLR.org, Lille (2015)
6. Schaul, T., Quan, J., Antonoglou, I., et al.: Prioritized experience replay. Computer Science (2015)

Authentication System Based on Fuzzy Extractors

Mingming Jiang[1,2], Shengli Liu[1,2,4(✉)], Shuai Han[2,3], and Dawu Gu[1]

[1] Department of Computer Science and Engineering, Shanghai Jiao Tong University, Shanghai 200240, China
{jiangmingming,slliu,dalen17,dwgu}@sjtu.edu.cn
[2] State Key Laboratory of Cryptology, P.O. Box 5159, Beijing 100878, China
[3] School of Cyber Science and Engineering, Shanghai Jiao Tong University, Shanghai 200240, China
[4] Westone Cryptologic Research Center, Beijing 100070, China

Abstract. In this paper, we research on client-server authentication system without local key storage. We take advantage of the available fuzzy extractor technology to design a client-server authentication system. Our authentication system is built from a fuzzy extractor and a digital signature scheme. Fuzzy extractor is in charge of key generation/reproduction during the client enrollment and client-server authentication stages. The client only stores some public information generated during enrollment procedure. When doing authentication, the extracted key can be reproduced with this public information. Then we use the challenge-response to implement the authentication, which is supported by the digital signature. Overall, our client-server authentication system relaxes the requirement of random sources, and gets rid of the risk of key leakage and key abuse since key storage is not needed.

Keywords: Authentication system · Fuzzy extractor · Digital signature

1 Introduction

Advances in computer technology and wireless network technology have paved the way for online services. Via mobile phone, electronic pad, or computer, people can surge on Internet to access these services – glancing news on Web, shopping at Amazon, watching online movies, playing games with unknown people in the cyberspace, etc. As for the service providers, they control resources to open only to subscribed users. As a result, it is necessary for the remote servers to identify subscribed clients before granting them access to the services.

In general, authentication systems are mainly based on cryptographic algorithms. They are classified into two types: those from symmetric-key cryptographic algorithms and those from asymmetric-key cryptographic algorithms. With symmetric-key cryptography, the implementation of authentication requires

© Springer Nature Switzerland AG 2021
Z. Liu et al. (Eds.): WASA 2021, LNCS 12939, pp. 479–490, 2021.
https://doi.org/10.1007/978-3-030-86137-7_51

the communication parties (i.e. server and client) to share a secret key through an enrollment procedure. In this case, both the client and server need to store the secret key locally and privately. While with asymmetric-key algorithms, authentication requires that clients generate their own public key and secret key pairs, so only the client needs to store the secret key locally for the later authentication. In both authentication systems, complicated key management is involved in the client-server system, including key generation, key transportation, key storage, etc.

In Fig. 1, we formalize a general authentication system based on asymmetric-key algorithms, which includes three procedures: Setup, Enrollment and Authentication. The Setup phase determines some public parameters of the system. The Enrollment allows the client to register in the system and generate its own public information and secret key. After key generation, the secret key needs to be stored by the client, since it will be used in the later authentication of the client.

To ensure the security of the authentication system, the secret key is always assumed to be uniformly distributed. However, in reality, it is hard to find a truly random uniform source, which makes the key generation an uneasy task. Moreover, after key generation, the secret key needs to be stored locally and privately for authentication use, which brings the risk of key leakage. Two natural questions arise:

Q1. *Can we make use of the fuzzy sources that are inherent in nature to implement authentication?*

Q2. *Can we design an authentication system such that the client does not store the secret key after enrollment?*

Our Contribution. We answer these questions in the affirmative. As we mention, perfect sources rarely exist. But if we relax the requirement of sources from being perfect to possessing high entropy, we are able to find many choices, such as bio-metric information (fingerprint, iris, face) [12,13], physical unclonable functions [14], quantum bits [5], etc.

In this paper, we resort to fuzzy extractors to solve the problem. The notion of fuzzy extractor was proposed in [7] by Dodis et al. A fuzzy extractor allows one to extract a nearly uniform key from a fuzzy source along with some public helper strings, and reproduce the key with the public helper strings. In this paper, we propose a fuzzy-extractor-based authentication system, which makes use of fuzzy sources, thus the key involved in the authentication is not necessarily stored by the clients. The framework of our proposed fuzzy-extractor-based authentication system (FEA system for short) is illustrated in Fig. 2.

We present a generic construction of our novel authentication system from two building blocks, a fuzzy extractor and a digital signature scheme. Taking the abundant choices of efficient fuzzy extractors and digital signatures in the literature [1–4,6,8,9,16], our construction admits numerous concrete instantiations.

The remaining parts of this paper are organized as follows. Section 2 will introduce some preliminaries used in our construction. In Sect. 3, our fuzzy-extractor-based authentication system is proposed and an in-depth security proof will be given in Sect. 4. In Sect. 5, we conclude the paper.

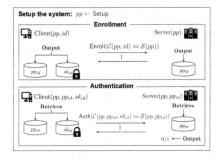

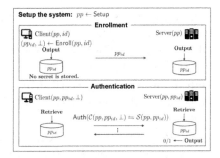

Fig. 1. The interaction of authentication systems.

Fig. 2. The interaction of our proposed FEA authentication system.

2 Preliminaries

Let n denote the security parameter throughout the paper. Let $\mathsf{negl}(n)$ denote a negligible function of n. "PPT" abbreviates probabilistic polynomial time. Denote by $x \leftarrow_\$ \mathcal{X}$ the procedure of sampling x from set $\mathcal{X}$ uniformly at random. If $\mathcal{D}$ is distribution, $x \leftarrow \mathcal{D}$ means that x is sampled according to $\mathcal{D}$. Let $y \leftarrow \mathcal{A}(x)$ denote the execution of algorithm $\mathcal{A}$ on input x. Let $\mathsf{dis}(w, w')$ denote the distance of w and w' in a metric space $\mathcal{M}$. By $\mathsf{Adv}_{\mathsf{X},\mathcal{A}}^{\mathsf{Y}}(\cdot)$ we denote the advantage function of algorithm $\mathcal{A}$ in Y-security experiment for scheme X. Define $\mathsf{Adv}_{\mathsf{X}}^{\mathsf{Y}}(n) := \max_{\mathsf{PPT}\mathcal{A}} \mathsf{Adv}_{\mathsf{X},\mathcal{A}}^{\mathsf{Y}}(n)$. By $(a \mid b) \leftarrow \mathsf{Protocol}(\mathcal{A} \leftrightharpoons \mathcal{B})$, we denote the protocol is executed between $\mathcal{A}$ and $\mathcal{B}$, and $\mathcal{A}$ outputs a and $\mathcal{B}$ outputs b.

2.1 Fuzzy Extractor

We recall the concept of fuzzy extractor proposed by Dodis et al. [7] as well as some related definitions.

Definition 1 (Metric Space [7]). *A metric space is a set $\mathcal{M}$ along with a distance function $\mathsf{dis}: \mathcal{M} \times \mathcal{M} \rightarrow [0, \infty)$, such that for all $x, y, z \in \mathcal{M}$, the following properties hold: (1) $\mathsf{dis}(x, y) \geq 0$ and $\mathsf{dis}(x, y) = 0$ if and only if $x = y$; (2) $\mathsf{dis}(x, y) = \mathsf{dis}(y, x)$; (3) $\mathsf{dis}(x, z) \leq \mathsf{dis}(x, y) + \mathsf{dis}(y, z)$.*

In this paper, we will focus on a specific Hamming metric, where $\mathcal{M} = \{0, 1\}^n$ and dis is the Hamming distance between two binary strings, i.e., the number of positions at which the corresponding bits are different.

Definition 2 (Min-entropy). *For a random variable X over set $\mathcal{X}$, the min-entropy of X is defined as $\mathsf{H}_\infty(X) = -\log_2(\max_{x \in \mathcal{X}} \Pr[X = x])$.*

Fuzzy extractor consists of two algorithms, namely, a generation algorithm FE.Gen and a reproduction algorithm FE.Rep. It allows one to extract a pseudorandom string R from a sample w of source W, then successfully reproduce

R from another sample w' which is close to w. In the following, we recall the formal definition from [7], but we relax the security requirement of FE from information theoretical security to computational security, which admits more practical instantiations of FE.

Definition 3 (Fuzzy Extractor [7]). *Let $\mathcal{M}$ be a metric space with a distance function* dis. *An $(\mathcal{M}, m, l, t, \epsilon)$-fuzzy extractor* FE = (FE.Gen,FE.Rep) *consists of a pair of PPT algorithms.*

- *$(R, P) \leftarrow$ FE.Gen(w): FE.Gen takes a string $w \in \mathcal{M}$ as the input and outputs an extracted string $R \in \{0,1\}^l$ together with a public helper string P.*
- *$R' \leftarrow$ FE.Rep(w', P): FE.Rep takes a string $w' \in \mathcal{M}$ and a public string P as inputs, then outputs a reproduced string $R' \in \{0,1\}^l$.*

Correctness. *For all $w, w' \in \mathcal{M}$ with $\mathsf{dis}(w, w') \leq t$, all $(R, P) \leftarrow$ FE.Gen(w), it holds that FE.Rep$(w', P) = R$.*

ϵ-Security. *For any distribution W over $\mathcal{M}$, if $H_\infty(W) \geq m$, then for any PPT adversary $\mathcal{A}$, its advantage defined below satisfies*

$$\mathsf{Adv}_{\mathsf{FE},\mathcal{A}}(n) := |\Pr[\mathcal{A}(P, R_0) \Rightarrow 1] - \Pr[\mathcal{A}(P, R_1) \Rightarrow 1]| \leq \epsilon,$$

where $(R_0, P) \leftarrow$ FE.Gen(w) for $w \leftarrow W$, and $R_1 \leftarrow_\$ \{0,1\}^l$.

Fuzzy extractor can be generically constructed from secure sketch and strong extractor [7], and has many efficient instantiations (e.g., based on DDH assumptions [17] or LPN assumptions [11]).

2.2 Digital Signature

We recall the syntax of digital signature and its existential unforgeability under chosen-message attack (EUF-CMA security for short).

Definition 4 (Digital Signature [10]). *A digital signature scheme* SIG = (SIG.Setup, SIG.Gen, SIG.Sign, SIG.Vrfy) *consists of a tuple of PPT algorithms.*

- *$pp \leftarrow$ SIG.Setup(1^n): SIG.Setup takes as input the security parameter 1^n and outputs a public parameter pp.*
- *$(vk, sk) \leftarrow$ SIG.Gen(pp): SIG.Gen takes as input a public parameter pp, and outputs a pair of verification key and signing key (vk, sk). We will sometimes make the randomness r consumed by the probabilistic algorithm SIG.Gen(pp) explicitly, and write $(vk, sk) \leftarrow$ SIG.Gen$(pp; r)$.*
- *$\sigma \leftarrow$ SIG.Sign(sk, m): SIG.Sign takes as input a signing key sk and a message $m \in \{0,1\}^*$, and outputs a signature σ.*
- *$b \leftarrow$ SIG.Vrfy(vk, m, σ): SIG.Vrfy takes as input a verification key vk, a message m and a signature σ. It outputs a bit b, with $b = 1$ indicating acceptance and $b = 0$ indicating rejection.*

Correctness. *For all $pp \leftarrow$ SIG.Setup(1^n), all $(vk, sk) \leftarrow$ SIG.Gen(pp), all $m \in \{0,1\}^*$, and all $\sigma \leftarrow$ SIG.Sign(sk, m), it holds that SIG.Vrfy$(vk, m, \sigma) = 1$.*

EUF-CMA Security. *For any PPT adversary $\mathcal{A}$, its advantage $\mathsf{Adv}_{\mathsf{SIG},\mathcal{A}}^{\mathsf{euf\text{-}cma}}(n) := \Pr[\mathbf{Exp}_{\mathsf{SIG},\mathcal{A}}^{\mathsf{euf\text{-}cma}}(1^n) \Rightarrow 1]$ is negligible in the security parameter n, where $\mathbf{Exp}_{\mathsf{SIG},\mathcal{A}}^{\mathsf{euf\text{-}cma}}(1^n)$ is the security experiment as shown in Fig. 3.*

$\mathbf{Exp}_{\mathsf{SIG},\mathcal{A}}^{\mathsf{euf\text{-}cma}}(1^n)$	$\mathcal{O}_{\mathrm{SIGN}}(m)$:
$pp \leftarrow \mathsf{SIG.Setup}(1^n)$. $(vk, sk) \leftarrow \mathsf{SIG.Gen}(pp)$.	$\sigma \leftarrow \mathsf{SIG.Sign}(sk, m)$.
MList := ∅. //Record messages from signing queries.	MList := MList ∪ $\{m\}$.
$(m^*, \sigma^*) \leftarrow \mathcal{A}^{\mathcal{O}_{\mathrm{SIGN}}(\cdot)}(pp, vk)$.	Return σ.
If $(m^* \notin \mathsf{MList}) \wedge (\mathsf{SIG.Vrfy}(vk, m^*, \sigma^*) = 1)$: Return 1;	
Else: Return 0.	

Fig. 3. The EUF-CMA security experiment $\mathbf{Exp}_{\mathsf{SIG},\mathcal{A}}^{\mathsf{euf\text{-}cma}}(1^n)$ for SIG.

2.3 Authentication System

We present the formal definition for a Client-Server asymmetric authentication system.

Definition 5. *A Client-Server authentication system* CSAuth = (Setup, Enroll, Auth) *consists of a setup algorithm* Setup, *an enrollment protocol* Enroll *and an interactive authentication protocol* Auth.

- $pp \leftarrow$ Setup(1^n): *The* Setup *algorithm takes as input the security parameter* 1^n *and outputs a public parameter pp for the scheme.*
- $((pp_{id}, sk_{id}) \mid pp_{id}) \leftarrow$ Enroll$(\mathcal{C}(pp, id) \rightleftharpoons \mathcal{S}(pp))$: *The* Enroll *protocol is executed between a client $\mathcal{C}$ who has (pp, id) and the server $\mathcal{S}$ who has pp. After the execution of* Enroll, *the client will output an identity-related public string pp_{id} and a secret key sk_{id}, and the server will output pp_{id}.*
- $b \leftarrow$ Auth$(\mathcal{C}(pp, pp_{id}, sk_{id}) \rightleftharpoons \mathcal{S}(pp, pp_{id}))$: *The* Auth *protocol is executed between a client $\mathcal{C}$ who has (pp, pp_{id}, sk_{id}) and the server $\mathcal{S}$ who has (pp, pp_{id}). At the end of the execution, $\mathcal{S}$ will output a bit b, with $b = 1$ indicating that the client $\mathcal{C}$ passes the authentication and $b = 0$ a failure.*

Correctness. For all $pp \leftarrow$ Setup(1^n), all client identities id, and all $((pp_{id}, sk_{id}) \mid pp_{id}) \leftarrow$ Enroll$(\mathcal{C}(pp, id) \rightleftharpoons \mathcal{S}(pp))$, it holds that Auth$(\mathcal{C}(pp, pp_{id}, sk_{id}) \rightleftharpoons \mathcal{S}(pp, pp_{id})) = 1$.

Security. For any PPT stateful adversary $\mathcal{A}$ who has access to an oracle $\mathcal{O}_{\mathcal{C} \rightleftharpoons \mathcal{S}}(\cdot)$, its advantage $\mathsf{Adv}_{\mathsf{CSAuth},\mathcal{A}}(n) := \Pr[\mathbf{Exp}_{\mathsf{CSAuth},\mathcal{A}}(1^n) \Rightarrow 1]$ is negligible in the security parameter n, where the oracle $\mathcal{O}_{\mathcal{C} \rightleftharpoons \mathcal{S}}(\cdot)$ and the security experiment $\mathbf{Exp}_{\mathsf{CSAuth},\mathcal{A}}(1^n)$ are shown in Fig. 4.

$\mathbf{Exp}_{\mathsf{CSAuth},\mathcal{A}}(1^n)$:
  $pp \leftarrow \mathsf{Setup}(1^n)$. $\mathsf{List} := \emptyset$.
  $id^* \leftarrow \mathcal{A}^{\mathcal{O}_{\mathcal{C} \leftrightharpoons \mathcal{S}}(\cdot)}(pp)$.
  If $\nexists(id^*, \cdot, \cdot) \in \mathsf{List}$:
    $((pp_{id^*}, sk_{id^*}) \mid pp_{id^*}) \leftarrow \mathsf{Enroll}(\mathcal{C}(pp, id^*) \leftrightharpoons \mathcal{S}(pp))$;
    $\mathsf{trans}_{id^*}^{\mathsf{Enroll}} := \mathsf{transcript}(\mathsf{Enroll}(\mathcal{C}(pp, id^*) \leftrightharpoons \mathcal{S}(pp)))$;
    $\mathsf{List} := \mathsf{List} \cup \{(id^*, \mathsf{trans}_{id^*}^{\mathsf{Enroll}}, sk_{id^*})\}$.
  If $\mathsf{Auth}(\mathcal{A}^{\mathcal{O}_{\mathcal{C} \leftrightharpoons \mathcal{S}}(\cdot)}(pp, \mathsf{trans}_{id^*}^{\mathsf{Enroll}}) \leftrightharpoons \mathcal{S}(pp, pp_{id^*})) = 1$:
    Return 1;
  Else: Return 0.

$\mathcal{O}_{\mathcal{C} \leftrightharpoons \mathcal{S}}(id)$
  If $\exists(id, \mathsf{trans}_{id}^{\mathsf{Enroll}}, sk_{id}) \in \mathsf{List}$ for some id:
    Retrieve $(id, \mathsf{trans}_{id}^{\mathsf{Enroll}}, sk_{id})$ from List.
  If $\nexists(id, \cdot, \cdot) \in \mathsf{List}$:
    $((pp_{id}, sk_{id}) \mid pp_{id}) \leftarrow \mathsf{Enroll}(\mathcal{C}(pp, id) \leftrightharpoons \mathcal{S}(pp))$;
    $\mathsf{trans}_{id}^{\mathsf{Enroll}} := \mathsf{transcript}(\mathsf{Enroll}(\mathcal{C}(pp, id) \leftrightharpoons \mathcal{S}(pp)))$;
    $\mathsf{List} := \mathsf{List} \cup \{(id, \mathsf{trans}_{id}^{\mathsf{Enroll}}, sk_{id})\}$.
  $\mathsf{trans}_{id}^{\mathsf{Auth}} := \mathsf{transcript}(\mathsf{Auth}(\mathcal{C}(pp, pp_{id}, sk_{id}) \leftrightharpoons \mathcal{S}(pp, pp_{id})))$.
  Return $(\mathsf{trans}_{id}^{\mathsf{Enroll}}, \mathsf{trans}_{id}^{\mathsf{Auth}})$.

Fig. 4. The security experiment $\mathbf{Exp}_{\mathsf{CSAuth},\mathcal{A}}(1^n)$. Here $\mathsf{transcript}(\mathsf{Enroll}(\mathcal{C}(pp, id) \leftrightharpoons \mathcal{S}(pp)))$ and $\mathsf{transcript}(\mathsf{Auth}(\mathcal{C}(pp, pp_{id}, sk_{id}) \leftrightharpoons \mathcal{S}(pp, pp_{id})))$ denote the transcripts of the enrollment and authentication protocols executions between client $\mathcal{C}$ and server $\mathcal{S}$ respectively.

3   Our Proposed Authentication System

We are now ready to construct our fuzzy-extractor-based authentication system (FEA system for short), which is built from a fuzzy extractor and a digital signature scheme.

More precisely, the building blocks underlying our construction are as follows.

- Let $\mathsf{FE} = (\mathsf{FE.Gen}, \mathsf{FE.Rep})$ be a $(\mathcal{W}, m, l, t, \epsilon)$ fuzzy extractor, where $\mathcal{W}$ is a metric space with a distance function dis.
- Let $\mathsf{SIG} = (\mathsf{SIG.Setup}, \mathsf{SIG.Gen}, \mathsf{SIG.Sign}, \mathsf{SIG.Vrfy})$ be an EUF-CMA secure signature scheme, with $\{0,1\}^l$ the randomness space for $\mathsf{SIG.Gen}$.

Our fuzzy-extractor-based authentication system $\mathsf{FEA} = (\mathsf{FEA.Setup}, \mathsf{FEA.Enroll}, \mathsf{FEA.Auth} = (\mathsf{FEA.Challenge}, \mathsf{FEA.Response}, \mathsf{FEA.Vrfy}))$ is defined in Fig. 5. See also Fig. 6 for a framework view of our proposed FEA system played between a client $\mathcal{C}$ and a server $\mathcal{S}$.

Our FEA system works in a Client-Server system as follows. Let W be a distribution over metric space $\mathcal{W}$, representing a fuzzy source. The source W can be bio-metric like people's fingerprints, iris, face, etc. We assume that each client id has its own efficient sampling algorithm, which samples elements from the source W, i.e., $w \leftarrow \mathsf{Sample}_{id}(W)$. Here Sample_{id} is just the reading of the fingerprint, iris scan, or face scan for client id. We note that only the client id can invoke its own Sample_{id} algorithm. It is reasonable to assume that the distance between different samples from a same person is bounded by some threshold t. Hence, for each client id, we assume that two samples $w, w' \leftarrow \mathsf{Sample}_{id}(W)$ have distance no more than t with overwhelming probability, i.e., $\mathsf{dis}(w, w') \leq t$.

- **System Setup.** The system is setup by $pp \leftarrow \mathsf{FEA.Setup}(1^n)$, and the public parameter pp is published to all clients and servers.
- **Client Enrollment.** When a client id enrolls in the system, it invokes $(pp_{id}, \bot) \leftarrow \mathsf{FEA.Enroll}(pp, id)$. More precisely, the client id samples $w \leftarrow \mathsf{Sample}_{id}(W)$ with its own sampling algorithm Sample_{id}, then uses the generation algorithm of fuzzy extractor to distill a secret string R_{id} and a public

$pp \leftarrow$ FEA.Setup(1^n):	$(pp_{id}, \perp) \leftarrow$ FEA.Enroll(pp, id):	$b \leftarrow$ FEA.Auth($\mathcal{C}(pp, pp_{id}, \perp) \leftrightarrows \mathcal{S}(pp, pp_{id})$)
$pp \leftarrow$ SIG.Setup(1^n).	$w \leftarrow$ Sample$_{id}(W)$.	$ch \leftarrow$ FEA.Challenge(pp_{id}).
Return pp.	$(R_{id}, P_{id}) \leftarrow$ FE.Gen(w).	$\sigma \leftarrow$ FEA.Response(pp, pp_{id}, ch).
	$(vk_{id}, sk_{id}) \leftarrow$ SIG.Gen($pp; R_{id}$).	$b \leftarrow$ FEA.Vrfy(pp, pp_{id}, ch, σ).
	$pp_{id} = (id, P_{id}, vk_{id})$.	Return b.
	Return ($pp_{id}, sk_{id} := \perp$).	
$ch \leftarrow$ FEA.Challenge(pp_{id}):	$\sigma \leftarrow$ FEA.Response(pp, pp_{id}, ch):	$b \leftarrow$ FEA.Vrfy(pp, pp_{id}, ch, σ):
Parse $pp_{id} = (id, P_{id}, vk_{id})$.	$w' \leftarrow$ Sample$_{id}(W)$.	Parse $pp_{id} = (id, P_{id}, vk_{id})$.
$r \leftarrow_\$ \{0,1\}^n$.	Parse $ch = (P_{id}, r)$.	If SIG.Vrfy(vk_{id}, ch, σ) = 1:
Return $ch := (P_{id}, r)$.	$R'_{id} \leftarrow$ FE.Rep(w', P_{id}).	Return 1;
	$(vk'_{id}, sk'_{id}) \leftarrow$ SIG.Gen($pp; R'_{id}$).	Else: Return 0.
	$\sigma \leftarrow$ SIG.Sign(sk'_{id}, ch).	
	Return σ.	

Fig. 5. The algorithms (FEA.Setup, FEA.Enroll, FEA.Auth) involved in our FEA authentication system with FEA.Auth = (FEA.Challenge, FEA.Response, FEA.Vrfy), built from fuzzy extractor FE and digital signature SIG. Here W is a distribution over metric space $\mathcal{W}$ (representing a fuzzy source such as peoples's fingerprint, iris, face), and Sample$_{id}$ is an efficient sampling algorithm owned by the client id (representing a reading of the fingerprint, iris scan, or face scan for client id).

helper string P_{id}, i.e., $(R_{id}, P_{id}) \leftarrow$ FE.Gen(w). The secret string R_{id}, as randomness, is in turn used in the key generation algorithm of the signature scheme to get a pair of verification key and signing key (vk_{id}, sk_{id}), i.e., $(vk_{id}, sk_{id}) \leftarrow$ SIG.Gen($pp; R_{id}$). The client sends the id-related public information $pp_{id} = (id, P_{id}, vk_{id})$ to the server. We stress that the client only stores pp_{id} locally and publicly, and never stores the secret signing key sk_{id}. This frees the clients from secret key storage and management, and addresses the issues of secret key leakage and abuse.

- **Authentication between client and server.** The authentication protocol works in four stages.
  - **Service Request from Client.** When the client asks services from the server, it will send its identity id to the server.
  - **Challenge from Server.** The server retrieves $pp_{id} = (id, P_{id}, vk_{id})$ from its database. To identify the legacy of the client, the server generates a challenge for the client via $ch \leftarrow$ FEA.Challenge(pp_{id}). More precisely, it will choose an element $r \leftarrow_\$ \{0,1\}^n$ randomly and send $ch := (P_{id}, r)$ to the client as a challenge.
  - **Response from Client.** After obtaining the challenge $ch = (P_{id}, r)$, the client will prepare a response σ to the server via FEA.Response(pp, pp_{id}, ch). More precisely, the client re-samples w' from the source via $w' \leftarrow$ Sample$_{id}(W)$. Then it invokes the reproduce algorithm of fuzzy extractor with w' and the public helper string P_{id}, i.e., $R'_{id} \leftarrow$ FE.Rep(w', P_{id}). Then, the client uses R'_{id} as the randomness to obtain (vk'_{id}, sk'_{id}) again via SIG.Gen($pp; R'_{id}$). The client will use sk'_{id} to sign the challenge and reply the signature $\sigma \leftarrow$ SIG.Sig(sk'_{id}, ch) as the response to the server.

- **Services from Server.** After obtaining the response σ from the client, the server will invoke the verification algorithm FEA.Vrfy, which is exactly SIG.Vrfy (vk_{id}, ch, σ). If the verification succeeds, the server provides services to the client; otherwise, the server aborts and the client fails to get the services.

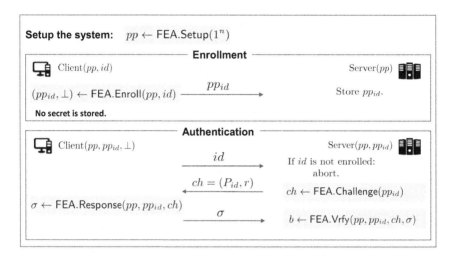

Fig. 6. The framework of our proposed FEA authentication system.

Recall that as long as $\mathsf{dis}(w, w') \leq t$, the correctness of FE makes sure that $R'_{id} = R_{id}$, hence $(vk'_{id}, sk'_{id}) = (vk_{id}, sk_{id})$. Consequently, σ will be a signature signed with sk_{id}, which is coupled with vk_{id} held by the server. By the correctness of SIG, the server always outputs 1. This shows the correctness of our FEA.

In the next section, we will prove the security of our FEA authentication system.

4   Security Proof of Our FEA Authentication System

Theorem 1. *Suppose that the fuzzy source $\mathcal{W}$ has distribution W with at least m-bit min-entropy, i.e., $\mathsf{H}_\infty(W) \geq m$. Let $\mathsf{FE} = (\mathsf{FE.Gen}, \mathsf{FE.Rep})$ be a $(\mathcal{W}, m, l, t, \epsilon)$-fuzzy extractor. Let $\mathsf{SIG} = (\mathsf{SIG.Setup}, \mathsf{SIG.Gen}, \mathsf{SIG.Sign}, \mathsf{SIG.Vrfy})$ be a digital signature with EUF-CMA security, where the random space for $\mathsf{SIG.Gen}$ is $\{0, 1\}^l$. For our authentication system FEA defined in Fig. 4, the advantage of any PPT adversary $\mathcal{A}$ satisfies*

$$\mathsf{Adv}_{\mathsf{FEA}, \mathcal{A}}(n) = \Pr[\mathbf{Exp}_{\mathsf{FEA}, \mathcal{A}}(1^n) \Rightarrow 1] \leq (Q + 1)\epsilon + Q \cdot 2^{-n} + Q \cdot \mathsf{Adv}_{\mathsf{SIG}}^{\mathsf{euf\text{-}cma}}(n),$$

where Q is number of oracle queries made by $\mathcal{A}$.

Proof. The proof goes with three games Game_0, Game_1 and Game_2. The security experiment $\mathbf{Exp}_{\mathsf{FEA},\mathcal{A}}(1^n)$ and Game_i, $i \in \{0,1,2\}$, are defined in Fig. 7. We will show that these games are computationally indistinguishable by the following three lemmas.

$\underline{\mathbf{Exp}_{\mathsf{FEA},\mathcal{A}}(1^n)}$ // $\boxed{\mathsf{Game}_0,}$ $\boxed{\mathsf{Game}_1,}$ $\boxed{\mathsf{Game}_2}$

// $pp \leftarrow$ FEA.Setup(1^n)
$\quad pp \leftarrow$ SIG.Setup(1^n).
$\quad$ List $:= \emptyset$, $\boxed{\text{rList} := \emptyset}$.
$\quad id^* \leftarrow \mathcal{A}^{\mathcal{O}_{c\rightleftharpoons s}(\cdot)}(pp)$.
$\quad$ If $\exists (id, pp_{id^*}, R_{id^*}, w^*) \in$ List:
$\quad\quad$ Retrieve $(id, pp_{id^*}, R_{id^*}, w^*)$ from List;
$\quad$ If $\nexists (id^*, pp_{id^*}, R_{id^*}, w^*) \in$ List:
// $(pp_{id^*}, \perp) \leftarrow$ FEA.Enroll(pp, id^*)
$\quad\quad w^* \leftarrow$ Sample$_{id^*}(W)$.
$\quad\quad (R_{id^*}, P_{id^*}) \leftarrow$ FE.Gen(w^*).
$\quad\quad \boxed{R_{id^*} \leftarrow_\$ \{0,1\}^l.}$
$\quad\quad (vk_{id^*}, sk_{id^*}) \leftarrow$ SIG.Gen$(pp; R_{id^*})$.
$\quad\quad pp_{id^*} = (id^*, P_{id^*}, vk_{id^*})$.
$\quad\quad$ List $=$ List $\cup\, (id^*, pp_{id^*}, R_{id^*}, w^*)$.
$\quad r^* \leftarrow_\$ \{0,1\}^n$.
$\quad$ If $r^* \in$ rList:
$\quad\quad$ Abort.
$\quad \sigma^* \leftarrow \mathcal{A}^{\mathcal{O}_{c\rightleftharpoons s}(\cdot)}(id^*, ch^* = (P_{id^*}, r^*))$.
$\quad$ If FEA.Vrfy$(pp, pp_{id^*}, vk_{id^*}, ch^*, \sigma^*) = 1$:
$\quad\quad$ Return 1;
$\quad$ Else: Return 0.

$\mathcal{O}_{c\rightleftharpoons s}(id)$:
$\quad$ If $\exists (id, pp_{id}, R_{id}, w) \in$ List:
$\quad\quad$ Retrieve (id, pp_{id}, R_{id}, w) from List;
$\quad\quad$ Parse $pp_{id} = (id, P_{id}, vk_{id})$.
$\quad$ If $\nexists (id, pp_{id}, R_{id}, w) \in$ List:
$\quad\quad$ // $(pp_{id}, \perp) \leftarrow$ FEA.Enroll(pp, id)
$\quad\quad w \leftarrow$ Sample$_{id}(W)$;
$\quad\quad (R_{id}, P_{id}) \leftarrow$ FE.Gen(w).
$\quad\quad \boxed{R_{id} \leftarrow_\$ \{0,1\}^l.}$
$\quad\quad (vk_{id}, sk_{id}) \leftarrow$ SIG.Gen$(pp; R_{id})$.
$\quad\quad pp_{id} := (id, P_{id}, vk_{id})$.
$\quad\quad$ Return pp_{id}.
$\quad\quad$ List $:=$ List $\cup \{(id, pp_{id}, R_{id}, w)\}$.
$\quad$ // $ch \leftarrow$ FEA.Challenge(pp_{id})
$\quad\quad r \leftarrow_\$ \{0,1\}^n$.
$\quad\quad \boxed{\text{rList} := \text{rList} \cup \{r\}.}$
$\quad\quad ch := (P_{id}, r)$.
$\quad$ // $\sigma \leftarrow$ FEA.Response(pp, pp_{id}, ch)
$\quad\quad w' \leftarrow$ Sample$_{id}(W)$.
$\quad\quad$ Parse $ch = (P_{id}, r)$.
$\quad\quad R'_{id} \leftarrow$ FE.Rep(w', P_{id}).
$\quad\quad \left(\begin{array}{l} \text{If dis}(w, w') \leq t: \\ \quad R'_{id} = R_{id}. \end{array}\right)$
$\quad\quad (vk'_{id}, sk'_{id}) \leftarrow$ SIG.Gen$(pp; R'_{id})$.
$\quad\quad \sigma \leftarrow$ SIG.Sign(sk'_{id}, ch).
$\quad$ // $b \leftarrow$ FEA.Vrfy$(pp, pp_{id}, ch, \sigma)$
$\quad\quad$ If SIG.Vrfy$(vk_{id}, ch, \sigma) = 1$: $b := 1$;
$\quad\quad$ Else: $b := 0$.
$\quad\quad$ Return $(pp_{id}, (ch, \sigma, b))$.

Fig. 7. Game sequences $\mathsf{Game}_0, \mathsf{Game}_1, \mathsf{Game}_2$ for the security proof of Theorem 1. Here Game_0 contains the $\boxed{\text{text}}$ part, Game_1 contains both $\boxed{\text{text}}$ and $\boxed{\text{text}}$ parts, and Game_2 contains all of the $\boxed{\text{text}}$, $\boxed{\text{text}}$ and $\boxed{\text{text}}$ parts.

First, we claim that Game_0 behaves identically as $\mathbf{Exp}_{\mathsf{FEA},\mathcal{A}}(1^n)$. The difference between $\mathbf{Exp}_{\mathsf{FEA},\mathcal{A}}(1^n)$ and Game_0 lies in the generation of R_{id} when the oracle invokes algorithm FEA.Response. In $\mathbf{Exp}_{\mathsf{FEA},\mathcal{A}}(1^n)$, the oracle invokes

$R'_{id} \leftarrow$ FE.Rep(w', P_{id}). In Game$_0$, the oracle will first retrieve the value of stored R_{id} which is recorded when Enroll algorithm invokes $(R_{id}, P_{id}) \leftarrow$ FE.Gen(w). Then the oracle checks whether the distance between the stored w and the input w' is no more than the threshold t. If dis$(w, w') \leq t$, the oracle will make use of the stored value R_{id} in the execution of FEA.Response. According to the correctness of FE, upon any oracle query id, the oracle has the same reply to $\mathcal{A}$ no matter in $\mathbf{Exp}_{\mathsf{FEA},\mathcal{A}}(1^n)$ or in Game$_0$. Therefore, Game$_0$ has the same functionality as $\mathbf{Exp}_{\mathsf{FEA},\mathcal{A}}(1^n)$, and we have

$$\Pr[\mathbf{Exp}_{\mathsf{FEA},\mathcal{A}}(1^n) \Rightarrow 1] = \Pr[\mathsf{Game}_0 \Rightarrow 1]. \tag{1}$$

Lemma 1. $|\Pr[\mathsf{Game}_0 \Rightarrow 1] - \Pr[\mathsf{Game}_1 \Rightarrow 1]| \leq (Q+1)\epsilon.$

Proof. The only difference between Game$_0$ and Game$_1$ lies in the generation of R_{id}. In Game$_0$, R_{id} is generated by FE.Gen. In Game$_1$, R_{id} is chosen from $\{0,1\}^l$ uniformly at random (once for each id, then record $(id, P_{id}, vk_{id}, R_{id}, w)$). In both games, there are Q queries to the oracle $\mathcal{O}_{\mathcal{C}=\mathcal{S}}(id)$. For each query id, the challenger will generate a value of R_{id}. Moreover, the challenger also generates R_{id^*} for the target id^* chosen by $\mathcal{A}$. Therefore, there are at most $Q+1$ generations of R_{id}. Define Game$_{0.j}$, $j \in \{0, 1, \dots, Q\}$, which is identical to Game$_0$ except that in the first j oracle queries, the oracle will choose random R_{id} if id has never been queried. Game$_{0.Q+1}$ is defined similarly, all R_{id} including R_{id^*} generated by oracle are randomly chosen. Obviously,

$$\mathsf{Game}_{0.0} = \mathsf{Game}_0, \quad \mathsf{Game}_{0.Q+1} = \mathsf{Game}_1. \tag{2}$$

Next, we show that for $j \in \{0, 1, \dots, Q\}$

$$|\Pr[\mathsf{Game}_{0.j} \Rightarrow 1] - \Pr[\mathsf{Game}_{0.j+1} \Rightarrow 1]| \leq \epsilon, \tag{3}$$

according to the ϵ-security of fuzzy extractor.

Given any PPT $\mathcal{A}$ such that $\mathsf{Adv}_{(j,j+1),\mathcal{A}} = |\Pr[\mathsf{Game}_{0.j} \Rightarrow 1] - \Pr[\mathsf{Game}_{0.j+1} \Rightarrow 1]|$, we construct another PPT algorithm $\mathcal{B}$ who has the same advantage for the security of FE. Let the challenge of $\mathcal{B}$ be $(\hat{P}, \hat{R})$, which is either generated by $(\hat{P}, \hat{R}) \leftarrow$ FE.Gen(w) or $\hat{P}$ is generated by FE.Gen(w) but $\hat{R}$ is randomly chosen from $\{0,1\}^l$. Then $\mathcal{B}$ invokes $pp \leftarrow$ FEA.Setup(1^n) and sends pp to $\mathcal{A}$. When $\mathcal{A}$ queries oracle $\mathcal{O}_{\mathcal{C}=\mathcal{S}}(\cdot)$ with id, $\mathcal{B}$ will behave just exactly the original oracle except that for the first $j-1$ different id's, $\mathcal{B}$ chooses random elements from $\{0,1\}^l$ as the values of R_{id}'s. For the j-th id (which is different from the first $j-1$ id's), $\mathcal{B}$ sets $R_{id} := \hat{R}$. Finally, $\mathcal{B}$ returns 1 to its own challenger if $\mathcal{A}$ wins (i.e., the game outputs 1).

If $\mathcal{B}$'s challenge $(\hat{P}, \hat{R})$ is generated by FE.Gen(w), $\mathcal{B}$ simulates Game$_{0.j-1}$ perfectly for $\mathcal{A}$; otherwise, $\mathcal{B}$ simulates Game$_{0.j}$. Therefore,

$$|\Pr[\mathsf{Game}_{0.j} \Rightarrow 1] - \Pr[\mathsf{Game}_{0.j+1} \Rightarrow 1]| = |\Pr[(\hat{P}, \hat{R}) \leftarrow \mathsf{FE.Gen}(w) : \mathcal{B}(\hat{P}, \hat{R}) \Rightarrow 1]$$
$$- \Pr[(\hat{P}, \hat{R}) \leftarrow \mathsf{FE.Gen}(w); \hat{R} \leftarrow_\$ \{0,1\}^l : \mathcal{B}(\hat{P}, \hat{R}) \Rightarrow 1]| \leq \epsilon,$$

due to the ϵ-security of FE. This proves (3).

Finally, Lemma 1 follows from (2) and (3).   □

Lemma 2. $|\Pr[\mathsf{Game}_1 \Rightarrow 1] - \Pr[\mathsf{Game}_2 \Rightarrow 1]| \leq Q \cdot 2^{-n} = \mathsf{negl}(n).$

Proof. The only difference between Game_1 and Game_2 is the occurrence of "Abort". Recall that Game_2 will abort if $r^* \in \mathsf{rList}$. If "Abort" does not happen, Game_1 and Game_2 are identical. According to the difference lemma [15],

$$|\Pr[\mathsf{Game}_1 \Rightarrow 1] - \Pr[\mathsf{Game}_2 \Rightarrow 1]| \leq \Pr[\mathsf{Abort}]. \qquad (4)$$

Note that r^* is uniformly chosen from $\{0,1\}^n$ and there are at most Q values in rList since adversary $\mathcal{A}$ queries the $\mathcal{O}_{\mathcal{C}\rightleftharpoons\mathcal{S}}(id)$ at most Q times. Therefore, $\Pr[\mathsf{Abort}] = \Pr[r^* \in \mathsf{rList}] \leq Q \cdot 2^{-n}$. Together with (4), Lemma 2 follows.   □

Lemma 3. $\Pr[\mathsf{Game}_2 \Rightarrow 1] = Q \cdot \mathsf{Adv}_{\mathsf{SIG}}^{\mathsf{euf\text{-}cma}}(n).$

Due to the space limitation, we omit the proof of Lemma 3, which can be found in the full version.

Combining the three lemmas above and (1), we finish the proof of Theorem 1 which shows the security of our FEA authentication system proposed in Sect. 3.   ■

5   Conclusion

In this paper, we propose a generic black-box construction of client-server authentication system from fuzzy extractors and digital signatures. The security of the authentication system relies on the security of fuzzy extractor and unforgeability of the signature scheme. It allows the client to authenticate itself to the server with help of its fuzzy source like bio-metric information (fingerprint, face, iris, etc.) or PUF (physical uncloneable function). Meanwhile, such construction allows the clients to store only public information instead of secret keys. Fuzzy extractors provide us a new idea on extracting nearly random and reproducible secret keys from these fuzzy sources. Then we design a challenge-response protocol from digital signature, whose secret signing key can be generated or reproduced by the fuzzy extractor.

Our novel fuzzy-extractor-based authentication system addresses the issues of secret key leakage and abuse, and makes the key storage and key management easy for the clients, thus increases the practicability and security of authentication systems. Due to the abundant choices of efficient fuzzy extractors and digital signatures in the literature, our construction admits a variety of specific client-server authentication systems.

Acknowledgement. Shengli Liu and Mingming Jiang were partially supported by Guangdong Major Project of Basic and Applied Basic Research (2019B030302008) and National Natural Science Foundation of China (NSFC No. 61925207). Shuai Han was partially supported by National Natural Science Foundation of China (Grant No. 62002223), Shanghai Sailing Program (20YF1421100), and Young Elite Scientists Sponsorship Program by China Association for Science and Technology. Dawu Gu was partially supported by National Key Research and Development Project 2020YFA0712300.

References

1. Bai, S., et al.: MPSign: a signature from small-secret middle-product learning with errors. In: Kiayias, A., Kohlweiss, M., Wallden, P., Zikas, V. (eds.) PKC 2020. LNCS, vol. 12111, pp. 66–93. Springer (2020). https://doi.org/10.1007/978-3-030-45374-9

2. Barbareschi, M., Barone, S., Mazzeo, A., Mazzocca, N.: Efficient reed-muller implementation for fuzzy extractor schemes. In: DTIS 2019, pp. 1–2. IEEE (2019)

3. Bellare, M., Miner, S.K.: A forward-secure digital signature scheme. In: Wiener, M. (ed.) CRYPTO 1999. LNCS, vol. 1666, pp. 431–448. Springer, Heidelberg (1999). https://doi.org/10.1007/3-540-48405-1_28

4. Bellare, M., Rogaway, P.: The exact security of digital signatures-how to sign with RSA and Rabin. In: Maurer, U. (ed.) EUROCRYPT 1996. LNCS, vol. 1070, pp. 399–416. Springer, Heidelberg (1996). https://doi.org/10.1007/3-540-68339-9_34

5. Bennett, C.H., Shor, P.W.: Quantum information theory. IEEE Trans. Inf. Theory **44**(6), 2724–2742 (1998)

6. Chang, D., Garg, S., Hasan, M., Mishra, S.: Cancelable multi-biometric approach using fuzzy extractor and novel bit-wise encryption. IEEE Trans. Inf. Forensics Secur. **15**, 3152–3167 (2020)

7. Dodis, Y., Reyzin, L., Smith, A.: Fuzzy extractors: how to generate strong keys from biometrics and other noisy data. In: Cachin, C., Camenisch, J.L. (eds.) EUROCRYPT 2004. LNCS, vol. 3027, pp. 523–540. Springer, Heidelberg (2004). https://doi.org/10.1007/978-3-540-24676-3_31

8. Gao, Y., Su, Y., Xu, L., Ranasinghe, D.C.: Lightweight (reverse) fuzzy extractor with multiple reference PUF responses. IEEE Trans. Inf. Forensics Secur. **14**(7), 1887–1901 (2019)

9. Karati, S., Das, A., Roychowdhury, D., Bellur, B., Bhattacharya, D., Iyer, A.: Batch verification of ECDSA signatures. In: Mitrokotsa, A., Vaudenay, S. (eds.) AFRICACRYPT 2012. LNCS, vol. 7374, pp. 1–18. Springer, Heidelberg (2012). https://doi.org/10.1007/978-3-642-31410-0_1

10. Katz, J., Lindell, Y.: Introduction to Modern Cryptography, Second Edition. CRC Press, Boca Raton (2014)

11. Li, Y., Liu, S., Gu, D., Chen, K.: Reusable fuzzy extractor based on the LPN assumption. Comput. J. **63**(12), 1826–1834 (2020)

12. Mai, G., Cao, K., Lan, X., Yuen, P.C.: Secureface: face template protection. IEEE Trans. Inf. Forensics Secur. **16**, 262–277 (2021)

13. Nandakumar, K., Jain, A.K., Pankanti, S.: Fingerprint-based fuzzy vault: implementation and performance. IEEE Trans. Inf. Forensics Secur. **2**(4), 744–757 (2007)

14. Satamraju, K.P., Malarkodi, B.: A PUF-based mutual authentication protocol for internet of things. In: ICCCS 2020, pp. 1–6. IEEE (2020)

15. Shoup, V.: A Computational Introduction to Number Theory and Algebra. Cambridge University Press, Cambridge (2006)

16. Ueno, R., Suzuki, M., Homma, N.: Tackling biased PUFs through biased masking: a debiasing method for efficient fuzzy extractor. IEEE Trans. Comput. **68**(7), 1091–1104 (2019)

17. Wen, Y., Liu, S., Han, S.: Reusable fuzzy extractor from the decisional Diffie-Hellman assumption. Des. Codes Cryptogr. **86**(11), 2495–2512 (2018)

Performance Analysis of V2V-Based Vehicular Platoon with Modified CACC Scheme

Siyuan Zhou[1,2], Liangliang Xiang[1(✉)], and Guoping Tan[1,2]

[1] School of Computer and Information, Hohai University, Nanjing, China
{siyuan.zhou,ll.xiang,gptan}@hhu.edu.cn
[2] Jiangsu Intelligent Transportation and Intelligent Driving Research Institute, Nanjing, China

Abstract. By exploiting vehicle-to-vehicle (V2V) communication in vehicular platoon system, the platoon members could receive the real-time vehicle dynamics information of the leader vehicle and the preceding vehicle, which can be utilized to control the vehicles' acceleration. However, the interference and the channel uncertainty of V2V communication can impair the communication delay, which deteriorate the vehicle's ability to maintain the desired velocity and the inter-vehicle distance. This paper performs a joint communication and control analysis of a platoon with the modified cooperative adaptive cruise control (mCACC) scheme. Specifically, the delay requirement to ensure the stability of the platoon control system is derived in the mCACC scheme. Then, the communication delay of the V2V communication links is analytically investigated by combining stochastic geometry and queuing theory. Subsequently, a reliability of the platoon communication system is obtained, which reveals the probability that the V2V communication delay can satisfy the delay requirement of the control system for maintaining the platoon stability. Simulation results validate the theoretical results and present the impact of the critical parameters on the platoon performance.

Keywords: Autonomous vehicular platoon · Cooperative adaptive cruise control · String stability · Communication delay

1 Introduction

As one of the vehicle-to-vehicle (V2V)-enabled applications, the autonomous vehicular platoon (hereafter referred to as platoon) can effectively decrease the safe following distance while maintaining the high vehicle speed. Besides, platoon also depends on the advanced management scheme in the control domain, which is known as cooperative adaptive cruise control (CACC). In V2V enabled CACC

This work was supported in part by the National Natural Science Foundation of China (No. 61701168, 61832005, 61571303), the China Postdoctoral Science Funded Project (No. 2019M651672).

The original version of this chapter was revised: The Figure 3 has been corrected by adding a blue dotted line to the graph. The correction to this chapter is available at https://doi.org/10.1007/978-3-030-86137-7_63

scheme, vehicles can simultaneously sense the speed, acceleration, steering information of other vehicles. With such information, the vehicles determine their behavior in order to maintain the platoon formation. If the V2V communication is considered ideal in platoon, a leader-predecessor-follower platooning system is proposed in [1]. A modified CACC (mCACC) scheme, introduced in [2], largely mitigates the impact of actuation lag on platoon performance which is a big limiting factor for achieving short vehicle spacing. In the practical system, the V2V communication suffers from the co-channel interference and the wireless channel uncertainty. [3] develops a modeling framework for carrier sense multiple access coordinated inter-vehicle communication. [4] introduces a communication model for multi-platooning scenarios and presents a probabilistic performance analysis of the inter-platoon communications. However, these work fails to consider the impairment of the platoon control performance due to the V2V communication uncertainty.

Specifically, on the one hand, the accurate platoon control depends upon the high performance of the V2V communication. On the other hand, the performance of the V2V communication in platoon is determined by the specific platoon control scheme. Thus, the control scheme and the V2V communication are complementary and inseparable, which needs to be jointly analyzed. Recently, [5] proposes a framework for optimizing a platoon's operation by jointly considering the delay and the vehicle's control system. Nevertheless, the dynamic information from the leader vehicle of the platoon is not taken into account in [5]. The constant spacing-based platooning systems, such as mCACC platoon, cannot guarantee the string stability if platoon members only use the preceding vehicle's information [1, 2]. Moreover, the control scheme in [5] only considers the effect of the speed difference with the preceding vehicle. However, in the mCACC scheme, the information of the acceleration, speed, as well as the location of the preceding and leader vehicles should be jointly considered in order to improve the platoon stability [2].

In this paper, a joint communication and control analysis framework is introduced to perform a systematic analysis for the platoon equipped with the mCACC control scheme. Assuming the platoon members can receive information from both the leader vehicle and the preceding vehicle, we investigate the relationship between the platoon stability and the V2V communication delay. To the best of authors' knowledge, this is the first study that focuses on the joint communication and control of the mCACC scheme.

2   System Model

In the V2V-based platoon system, each vehicle could receive the dynamic information from the leader and the preceding vehicles. The leader vehicle broadcasts its position, speed, and acceleration information to the whole platoon, and the broadcasting is interfered by the leader vehicles in other platoons. The preceding car transmits its acceleration information via unicast to the following car, and the unicasting is interfered by the non-platoon cars. In addition, the position

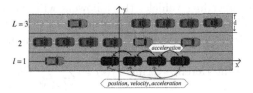

Fig. 1. A traffic scenario: red vehicles-the desired platoon, yellow vehicles-other platoons, blue vehicles-non-platoon vehicles in the proximity of the desired platoon. (Color figure online)

and speed information of the preceding vehicle is obtained via on-board sensors of the following car. Based on the received and the observed information, the vehicle controls its acceleration rate in order to keep the platoon stability.

As shown in Fig. 1, we consider the desired platoon is composed of $N+1$ vehicles and a traffic scenario consisting of L lanes. The desired platoon is on the l-th lane. In order to characterize the stochastic pattern of the vehicle distribution, we use 1D Poisson Point Processes (PPP) to model the distribution of vehicles on each lane. The individual vehicles at the front of the platoon are defined as the set Φ_0 with density λ_0, and the individual vehicles at the rear of the platoon are defined as the set Φ_1 with density λ_1. On other lanes, the individual vehicles are defined as the set Ψ_h with density $\lambda_h, h \in \{1, 2, \ldots, l-1, l+1, \ldots, L\}$. Similarly, we define the leader cars of other platoons at the front of the desired platoon as the set Φ_0^* with density λ_0^*, and the corresponding vehicles set at the rear of the platoon is defined as Φ_1^*, with density λ_1^*. On other lanes, we define the leader cars of other platoons as the set Ψ_h^* with density λ_h^*. A coordinate system is centered on the front bumper of the desired vehicle in the platoon. For the vehicles on the l-th lane, the coordinates can be expressed as $(x, 0)$, where x is the distance between the vehicle and the origin. For vehicles on the other lanes, the coordinates can be expressed as $(x, (h-l)d)$, where d is the lane width and h is the lane index.

2.1 Communication Model

For the V2V link between the preceding vehicle and the desired vehicle, an orthogonal frequency-division multiple access (OFDMA) scheme is considered. Specifically, the base station assigns N orthogonal subcarriers to the vehicles in the platoon, and the interference only comes from the vehicles outside the platoon. In the platoon, we model the V2V channel from the preceding car as independent Nakagami fading channel to characterize a wide range of fading environments for V2V links. We assume that each vehicle has the same transmit power P. The received power at follower $i \in N$ from the preceding car is $P_{i-1,i}(t) = Pg_{i-1,i}(t)(d_{i-1,i}(t))^{-\alpha}$, where $g_{i-1,i}(t)$ follows a Gamma distribution with shape parameter m, $d_{i-1,i}(t)$ is the distance between the preceding vehicle and the desired vehicle, and α is the path loss exponent. For the

V2V link from the preceding vehicle, the followers will encounter interference from the V2V links from other individual autonomous vehicles. We model these interference channels as independent Rayleigh fading channels. Consequently, for V2V links from the preceding vehicle, the interference at vehicle i is the sum of two following interference terms: $I_1(t) = \sum_{i \in h} \sum_{c = \Psi_i} P h_{c,i}(t)(d_{c,i}(t))^{-\alpha}$ and $I_2(t) = \sum_{i=1}^{2} \sum_{c = \Phi_i} P h_{c,i}(t)(d_{c,i}(t))^{-\alpha}$, where $I_1(t)$ denotes interference from non-platoon vehicles on lane h, while $I_2(t)$ denotes interference from non-platoon vehicles on lane l. $h_{c,i}(t)$ refers to the channel gain from vehicle c to i at time t, which follows an exponential distribution. The SINR of the V2V link from the preceding vehicle to vehicle i will be:

$$\gamma_{i-1,i}(t) = \frac{P_{i-1,i}(t)}{I_1(t) + I_2(t) + \sigma^2} \tag{1}$$

where σ^2 is the variance of Gaussian noise.

Similarly, we model the broadcast channel from the leader vehicle as Rayleigh fading channel. The received power at follower $i \in N$ from the leader car is $P_{0,i}(t) = P h_{0,i}(t)(d_{0,i}(t))^{-\alpha}$, where $h_{0,i}(t)$ refers to the channel gain from the leader vehicle to vehicle i at time t and $d_{0,i}(t)$ is the distance between the leader vehicle and the desired vehicle. For braodcast link from the leader car, the interference comes from broadcasts from other platoon leaders. We also model these channels as Rayleigh fading channels so that the interference at vehicle i is the sum of $I_3(t)$ and $I_4(t)$. $I_3(t) = \sum_{i \in h} \sum_{c = \Psi_i^*} P h_{c,i}(t)(d_{c,i}(t))^{-\alpha}$ and $I_4(t) = \sum_{i=1}^{2} \sum_{c = \Phi_i^*} P h_{c,i}(t)(d_{c,i}(t))^{-\alpha}$, where $I_3(t)$ indicates interference from other platoon leader cars on lane h, and $I_4(t)$ indicates interference from other platoon leaders on lane l. Consequently, the SINR of the broadcast link from the leader vehicle to vehicle i will be:

$$\gamma_{0,i}(t) = \frac{P_{0,i}(t)}{I_3(t) + I_4(t) + \sigma^2} \tag{2}$$

2.2   mCACC Scheme

In practical terms, the acceleration computed as the output of the CACC controller is not applied immediately due to the actuation lag. Compared to conventional CACC control algorithms that transmit instantaneous acceleration values, mCACC scheme that transmits desired acceleration values can significantly reduce the negative impact of actuation lag on platoon performance. The instantaneous acceleration is obtained via sensors on the vehicle tyres, while the desired acceleration is the output of the mCACC controller.

For the i-th vehicle in the platoon, the desired vehicle spacing including the length of the vehicle from the preceding car is defined as L. The spacing error of the i-th vehicle, which indicates the difference between the instantaneous vehicle spacing and the desired vehicle spacing, is $\varepsilon_i(t) = x_i(t) - x_{i-1}(t) + L$, where $x_{i-1}(t)$ and $x_i(t)$ are the position of the $i-1$-th and the i-th vehicle at time t in the platoon.

Since the communication delay deteriorates the vehicle's ability to maintain the desired vehicle spacing, we introduce the time delay $\tau_{i,0}(t)$ and $\tau_{i,i-1}(t)$ that indicate the communication delays in the mCACC scheme. Assuming the desired acceleration of the i-th platoon car is $\ddot{x}_{i,des}(t)$, which denotes the second order derivative of the desired position of the i-th platoons vehicles. The desired acceleration of the i-th car is mainly determined by the desired acceleration of the leader and preceding cars, the speed difference with the leader car, the speed difference and the spacing error with the preceding car, is:

$$\ddot{x}_{i,des}(t) = (1 - C_1)\ddot{x}_{i-1,des}\left(t - \tau_{i,i-1}(t)\right) + C_1\ddot{x}_{0,des}\left(t - \tau_{i,0}(t)\right)$$
$$- \left(2\xi - C_1\left(\xi + \sqrt{\xi^2 - 1}\right)\right)\omega_n\dot{\varepsilon}_i(t) \tag{3}$$
$$- \left(\xi + \sqrt{\xi^2 - 1}\right)\omega_n C_1\left(v_i(t) - v_0(t - \tau_{i,0}(t))\right) - \omega_n^2\varepsilon_i(t)$$

where $\dot{\varepsilon}_i(t) = \dot{x}_i(t) - \dot{x}_{i-1}(t)$, $\dot{\varepsilon}_i(t)$ denotes the first order derivative of the i-th vehicle spacing error. In the above equation, the desired acceleration of the i-th vehicle in the mCACC platoon is determined by five terms: The first and second terms indicate the desired acceleration of the preceding and the leader cars, the third and fourth terms indicate the speed difference with the preceding and the leader cars, and the fifth term reflects the impact of spacing error with the preceding vehicle. C_1, ξ and ω_n are three separate control parameters. The parameter C_1 is responsible to weigh the contribution of the leader's speed and acceleration which has a value between 0 and 1. Gain ξ is the damping ratio and can be set to one for critical damping. Gain ω_n is the bandwidth of the controller. For the sake of analytical simplicity, we define that $\tau(t)=\max\left(\tau_{i,0}(t), \tau_{i,i-1}(t)\right)$ and replace both $\tau_{i,0}(t)$ and $\tau_{i,i-1}(t)$ with $\tau(t)$.

3   Performance Analysis of the V2V-Based Platoon

3.1   Delay Requirements Based on String Stability Analysis

String stability is one of important evaluation criteria for the mCACC system of a platoon. String stability is a group property that describes the interaction between vehicles in a platoon, which constrains the spacing errors from diverging as the errors propagate towards the tail of the platoon. A large body of literature has analyzed string stability in different platoon scenarios and with different CACC spacing control strategies [6,7]. In this paper, we perform a string stability analysis of the mCACC scheme with the aim of deriving the delay requirements for a wireless communication system that guarantees the string stability of the platoon control system. For a platoon, the string stability of interconnected vehicles requires: $\|\varepsilon_1\|_\infty \geq \|\varepsilon_2\|_\infty \geq \ldots \geq \|\varepsilon_N\|_\infty$. Let $E_i(s)$, $E_{i-1}(s)$ denote the

Laplace transform of $\varepsilon_i(t)$, $\varepsilon_{i-1}(t)$, the spacing error transfer function between adjacent vehicles is defined as follows: $G_i(s) = \frac{E_i(s)}{E_{i-1}(s)} = \frac{\mathcal{L}(\varepsilon_i(t))}{\mathcal{L}(\varepsilon_{i-1}(t))}, i = 2, \ldots, N$.

The mathematical expression for the string stability can be equated to $|G_i(j\omega)| \leq 1$. To derive this expression in mCACC scheme, let us recall (3) and formulate a similar equation for the $i-1$-th vehicle, too. Then we can get the formula for the desired acceleration difference between the i-th and $i-1$-th vehicles

$$
\begin{aligned}
\ddot{\varepsilon}_{i,des}(t) = \ddot{x}_{i,des}(t) - \ddot{x}_{i-1,des}(t) = & (1 - C_1)\ddot{\varepsilon}_{i-1,des}(t - \tau(t)) \\
& - \left(2\xi - C_1\left(\xi + \sqrt{\xi^2 - 1}\right)\right) \omega_n\left(\dot{\varepsilon}_i(t) - \dot{\varepsilon}_{i-1}(t)\right) \\
& - \left(\xi + \sqrt{\xi^2 - 1}\right)\omega_n C_1\dot{\varepsilon}_i(t) - \omega_n^2\left(\varepsilon_i(t) - \varepsilon_{i-1}(t)\right)
\end{aligned}
\tag{4}
$$

Assuming that the engine reacts to the desired acceleration signal as a first order inertial system, we can express the desired acceleration difference as the sum of the instantaneous acceleration difference and a first order increment. Thus, we can write the following equation:

$$
\begin{aligned}
\ddot{\varepsilon}_i(t) + \varsigma\dddot{\varepsilon}_i(t) = & (1 - C_1)\left(\ddot{\varepsilon}_{i-1}(t - \tau(t)) + \varsigma\dddot{\varepsilon}_{i-1}(t - \tau(t))\right) \\
& - \left(2\xi - C_1\left(\xi + \sqrt{\xi^2 - 1}\right)\right)\omega_n\left(\dot{\varepsilon}_i(t) - \dot{\varepsilon}_{i-1}(t)\right) \\
& - \left(\xi + \sqrt{\xi^2 - 1}\right)\omega_n C_1\dot{\varepsilon}_i(t) - \omega_n^2\left(\varepsilon_i(t) - \varepsilon_{i-1}(t)\right)
\end{aligned}
\tag{5}
$$

where $\ddot{\varepsilon}_i(t)$ represents the second order derivative of the spacing error of the i-th car. With the help of the Laplace transform and its time domain differential theorem, we can derive the spacing error transfer function of the proposed mCACC control system:

$$
\begin{aligned}
G_i(s) = \frac{E_i(s)}{E_{i-1}(s)} = & \frac{(1 - C_1)\left(s^2 + \varsigma s^3\right)e^{-s\tau(t)}}{\left(s^2 + \varsigma s^3\right) + 2\xi\omega_n s + \omega_n^2} \\
& - \frac{\left(2\xi - C_1\left(\xi + \sqrt{\xi^2 - 1}\right)\right)\omega_n s - \omega_n^2}{\left(s^2 + \varsigma s^3\right) + 2\xi\omega_n s + \omega_n^2}
\end{aligned}
\tag{6}
$$

The vehicle platoon is string stable if $|G_i(j\omega)| \leq 1$. Thus, we can conclude that when C_1, ξ, ω_n and ς are satisfied within a certain range, in order to ensure that the platoon control system satisfies string stability, the delay time $\tau(t)$ must satisfy the following condition: $\tau(t) \leq \kappa(C_1, \xi, \omega_n, \varsigma)$, where $\kappa(C_1, \xi, \omega_n, \varsigma)$ (hereafter referred to as κ) is a function of C_1, ξ, ω_n and ς. As shown in the above inequality, as long as the delay time is less than the threshold κ, then the string stability of the mCACC platoon control system can be guaranteed. Due the numerator and denominator in equation (6) are cubic polynomials with respect to s, it is difficult to derive κ directly. Therefore, in the subsequent work, we perform the derivation while fixing some of the control parameters.

3.2 End-to-end Latency Analysis of the Wireless Network

From the analysis in the previous subsection, we have obtained the maximum delay threshold for the platoon control system to remain stable. To jointly analyze the communication and control performance of the platoon, it is necessary to quantify the end-to-end delay of the vehicle. In mCACC scheme, the vehicle i in the platoon needs to receive dynamic information from both the leader vehicle and the preceding vehicle. For the broadcast link between the leader vehicle and the desired vehicle in the platoon, it is interfered with by the broadcast links of the leader vehicles in other platoons. For the unicast link between the preceding vehicle and the desired vehicle, it receives interference from other non-platoon vehicles. We derive the CCDF for SINR introduced by (1):

$$F_1(\theta) = P(\gamma_{i-1,i} > \theta) = P\left(g_{i-1,i} > \frac{\theta\left(\sigma^2 + I_1(t) + I_2(t)\right)d_{i-1,i}^{-\alpha}}{P}\right)$$

$$\overset{(a)}{\approx} \sum_{k=1}^{\beta}(-1)^{k+1}\binom{\beta}{k}\exp\left(\frac{-k\eta\theta d_{i-1,i}^{\alpha}}{P}\sigma^2\right)\mathcal{L}_1\left(\frac{k\eta\theta d_{i-1,i}^{\alpha}}{P}\right)\mathcal{L}_2\left(\frac{k\eta\theta d_{i-1,i}^{\alpha}}{P}\right)$$

(7)

where $\eta=\beta(\beta!)^{-\frac{1}{\beta}}$, the change in (a) is based on the approximation of tail probability of a Gamma function, Binomial theorem and follows the definition of Laplace transform. $\mathcal{L}_1(s)$ and $\mathcal{L}_2(s)$ denote the Laplace transforms of $I_1(t)$ and $I_2(t)$, respectively, as follows:

$$L_1(s) = E_\psi\left[\exp\left(-s\sum_{i\in h}\sum_{c\in\psi_i}Ph_{c,i}(t)(d_{c,i}(t))^{-\alpha}\right)\right]\overset{(a)}{=}\prod_{i\in h}E_{\psi_i}\left[\prod_{c\in\psi_i}\frac{1}{1+sPd_{c,i}^{-\alpha}}\right]$$

(8)

$$\overset{(b)}{=}\prod_{i\in h}\exp\left[-\lambda_i\int_{|l-i|d}^{\infty}\left(1-\frac{1}{1+sPr^{-\alpha}}\right)\frac{2x}{\sqrt{x^2-(l-i)^2l^2}}dx\right]$$

where step (a) follows from the assumption of Rayleigh channel where the channel gain follows the exponential distribution. $d_{c,i}$ is replaced with x in step (b). Similarly,

$$\mathcal{L}_2(s) = \exp\left[-\lambda_0\int_{x_0-x_i}^{\infty}\left(1-\frac{1}{1+sPx^{-\alpha}}\right)dx\right]$$

$$\times \exp\left[-\lambda_1\int_{x_i-x_N}^{\infty}\left(1-\frac{1}{1+sPx^{-\alpha}}\right)dx\right]$$

(9)

We can use a similar analysis to derive the CCDF for SINR for the broadcast link from the leader vehicle:

$$F_2(\theta) = P(\gamma_{0,i} > \theta) \approx \exp\left(\frac{-\theta d_{0,i}^{\alpha}}{P}\sigma^2\right)\mathcal{L}_3\left(\frac{\theta d_{0,i}^{\alpha}}{P}\right)\mathcal{L}_4\left(\frac{\theta d_{0,i}^{\alpha}}{P}\right)$$

(10)

where $\mathcal{L}_3(s)$, $\mathcal{L}_4(s)$ denote the Laplace transforms of $I_3(t)$ and $I_4(t)$. Similarly, they can be obtained by replacing λ_0, λ_1 and λ_j in Eq. (8) and (9) with λ_0^*, λ_1^* and λ_j^*.

In our scenario, we only consider the transmission delay at the transceiver. The total time delay from the preceding vehicle to the desired vehicle of a V2V link in the platoon is modeled as the time spent in the queue Q_1 and the delay from the leader vehicle is modeled as the time spent in the queue Q_2 according to queuing theory. The queue Q_1 and Q_2 include the queuing delay and the transmission delay at the transceiver. Queue Q_1 and Q_2 can be modelled as an similar M/G/1 queue, assuming that arriving packets follow a Poisson process with rate λ_a and the queue has a infinite capacity buffer and a first-come, first-served policy. We use D_1 and D_2 to denote the service time of a single packet in queue Q_1 and queue Q_2 respectively. The mean and variance of D_1 can be expressed as

$$E\left(D_1\right) = \int_0^\infty \frac{SN}{\omega \log_2(1+\theta)} f_1(\theta) d\theta \tag{11}$$

$$Var\left(D_1\right) = \int_0^\infty \frac{S^2 N^2}{\omega^2 \left(\log_2\left(1+\theta\right)\right)^2} f_1(\theta) d\theta - \left(\int_0^\infty \frac{SN}{\omega \log_2\left(1+\theta\right)} f_1(\theta) d\theta\right)^2 \tag{12}$$

where S is the packet size in bits, and $f_1(\theta) = -\frac{dF_1(\theta)}{d\theta}$.

Therefore, according to the well-known Pollaczek-Khinchine formula, we can derive the average of the delay value T_1 in queue Q_1, including transmission delay and waiting time, as.

$$\bar{T}_1 = \frac{\rho_1 + \lambda_a \mu_1 Var(D_1)}{2(\mu_1 - \lambda_a)} + \frac{1}{\mu_1} \tag{13}$$

where $\mu_1 = 1/E\left(D_1\right)$, $\rho_1 = \lambda_a E(D_1)$. In a similar way, we can derive the average of the delay value T_2 in queue Q_2.

3.3   Analysis of Wireless Network Reliability

Wireless network reliability to measure the performance of a wireless network that can guarantee the stability of a platoon control system is proposed, so that the performance of a platoon's control and communication systems can be jointly assessed. The reliability of a wireless network is defined as the probability that the instantaneous delay in the wireless network meets the control system delay requirements.

When the rate of incoming packets in the queue is small, the queuing delay is negligible compared to the transmission delay, and the delay of the wireless system is mainly determined by the transmission delay. With the help of Eq. (7) and Shannon's Theorem, an approximate formula for the reliability of the wireless system is derived as shown below:

$$P = P(T_1 < \kappa) \cdot P(T_2 < \kappa) \tag{14}$$

$$
P(T_1 < \kappa) = \sum_{k=1}^{\beta} (-1)^{k+1} \binom{\beta}{k} \exp \left(\frac{-k\eta \left(2^{\frac{SN}{\omega\kappa}} - 1 \right) d_{i-1,i}^{\alpha}}{P} \sigma^2 \right)
$$

$$
\mathcal{L}_1 \left(\frac{k\eta \left(2^{\frac{SN}{\omega\kappa}} - 1 \right) d_{i-1,i}^{\alpha}}{P} \right) \mathcal{L}_2 \left(\frac{k\eta \left(2^{\frac{SN}{\omega\kappa}} - 1 \right) d_{i-1,i}^{\alpha}}{P} \right) \tag{15}
$$

$$
P(T_2 < \kappa) = \exp \left(\frac{-\left(2^{\frac{SN}{\omega\kappa}} - 1 \right) d_{0,i}^{\alpha}}{P} \sigma^2 \right) \mathcal{L}_3 \left(\frac{\left(2^{\frac{SN}{\omega\kappa}} - 1 \right) d_{0,i}^{\alpha}}{P} \right) \mathcal{L}_4 \left(\frac{\left(2^{\frac{SN}{\omega\kappa}} - 1 \right) d_{0,i}^{\alpha}}{P} \right) \tag{16}
$$

4   Simulation Results and Analysis

In order to verify the validity of the theoretical analysis, this section presents a simulation of the entire system with the aid of the Matlab/Simulink tool. In the simulation scenario, we consider a 4-lane, 10-km long highway, with the mCACC platoon of 9 vehicles travelling on one of the lanes. There are other platoons and individual cars in our scenario. The remaining relevant simulation parameters are listed in Table 1.

Table 1. Parameter values used for simulation

Parameters	Values	Parameters	Values
Number of lanes: L	4	Label of platoon lane: l	1
Width of lanes: d	3.7 m	Number of followers in the platoon: N	8
Length of the vehicles	5 m	Weight of the controller: C_1	$3 - \sqrt{5}$
Damping ratio: ξ	1	Bandwidth of the controller: ω_n	0.5
Transmission power: P	27 dBm	Nakagami parameter: β	3
Path loss exponent: α	3	Noise variance: σ^2	−174 dBm/Hz
λ_a (packets/s)	10	μ_1 (packets/s)	10,000

Under the parameter assumptions in Table 1, we can conclude the following: The string stability of the system can be guaranteed if the maximum delay of the V2V link in the platoon satisfies: $\tau(t) \leq \kappa = \frac{(18-6\sqrt{5})\varsigma+16-8\sqrt{5}}{(\sqrt{5}-2)\varsigma+13-6\sqrt{5}}$ $(0 \leq \varsigma \leq 0.412)$. This equation shows that as the actuation lag value increases, smaller delay value can be tolerated while guaranteeing the string stability of the system. In particular, when $\varsigma = 0.4$ s, the value of κ is 171.1 ms. We model the uncertainty of wireless system delay in the V2V links as a time-varying delay in the range $(0,171.1)$ ms. At the initial moment of the simulation, all vehicles in the platoon have the same initial speed, 130 km/h. The interval between two adjacent vehicles is 7 m. The desired vehicle spacing is $L = 7$ m. To verify the string stability, we let the leader car do a uniform deceleration with a deceleration of 2 m/s^2 at t=0−9.5 s and a uniform acceleration of 1.5 m/s^2 at t = 9.5−28s. From Fig. 2 we can observe that the spacing error becomes smaller as the errors propagate towards the tail of the platoon and converges to zero, thus indicating that the delay threshold ensures the string stability of the platoon.

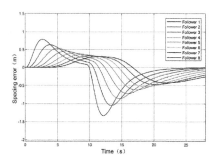

Fig. 2. Simulation result of spacing errors.eps

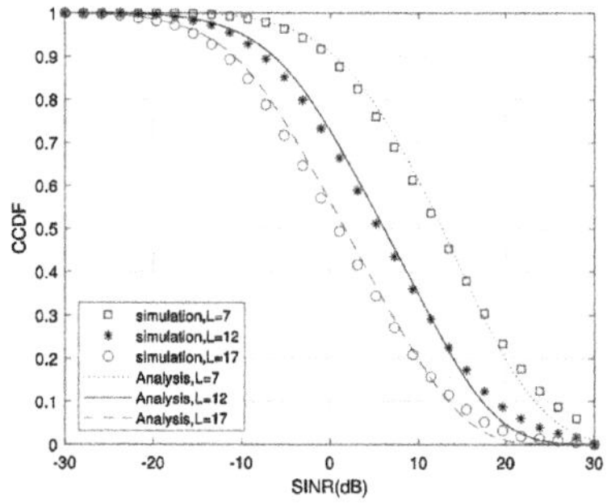

Fig. 3. The CCDF with the SINR derived in (7)

We set the desired spacing between two adjacent vehicles as 7 m, 12 m, and 17 m to obtain the CCDF with the corresponding SINR derived in (7). From Fig. 3 we can observe that the simulation results match the analytical results, thus ensuring the validity of the quantitative time delay in the V2V link derived based on Eq. (14). In addition, Fig. 3 shows that the probability of the SINR exceeding 10 dB is approximately 0.62 at $L = 7$ m, while this probability drops to 0.36 and 0.19 at $L = 12$ and $L = 17$ m, thus illustrating that the greater the spacing between the vehicles in the platoon, the weaker the signal strength received by the vehicle from the preceding vehicle, resulting in a reduced probability of the SINR being at a higher value.

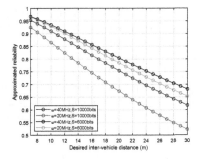

Fig. 4. Approximated reliability for platoon with different disired inter-vehicle distance.

Figure 4 shows the approximate reliability introduced by Eq. (14) for several different packet sizes and total transmission bandwidth scenarios. We can observe the general trend that the approximate reliability of the communication between vehicles gradually decreases as the desired inter-vehicle distance in the platoon increases. In addition, we can draw the following two conclusions: the larger the transmitted packets, the smaller the approximate reliability for the same inter-vehicle spacing and total transmission bandwidth, and similarly, the larger the total bandwidth, the larger the approximate reliability can be. In addition, we can obtain the values of the relevant parameters in order to achieve a specific reliability index. Due to space limitations, we do not explain them all.

5 Conclusion

In this paper, the communication and control performance of a modified CACC platoon is jointly analyzed. We perform a string stability analysis of the platoon to derive the maximum delay requirement to ensure platoon stability, after which the end-to-end delay of the V2V link using stochastic geometry and queuing theory is determined. In addition, we derive the approximate reliability of the communication system that is to guarantee the stability of the control system. Based on this reliability, the effect of the relevant control parameters, inter-vehicle distance, packet size, and total transmission bandwidth on the platoon is analyzed. This work has provided valuable guidance on the design of control and communication system for the mCACC platoon.

References

1. Zhang, Y., Wang, M., Hu, J., Bekiaris-Liberis, N.: Semi-constant spacing policy for leader-predecessor-follower platoon control via delayed measurements synchronization. In: Proceedings of the 21st IFAC World Congress (2020)
2. Sybis, M., et al.: Communication aspects of a modified cooperative adaptive cruise control algorithm. IEEE Trans. Intell. Transp. Syst. **20**(12), 4513–4523 (2019)

3. Farooq, M.J., ElSawy, H., Alouini, M.S.: Modeling inter-vehicle communication in multi-lane highways: a stochastic geometry approach. In: 2015 IEEE 82nd Vehicular Technology Conference (VTC2015-Fall), pp. 1–5. Boston, MA, USA (2015). https://doi.org/10.1109/VTCFall.2015.7391025
4. Peng, H., Li, D., Abboud, K., Zhou, H., Zhao, H., Zhuang, W., Shen, X.: Performance analysis of IEEE 802.11 p DCF for multiplatooning communications with autonomous vehicles. IEEE Trans. Veh. Technol. **66**(3), 2485–2498 (2016)
5. Zeng, T., Semiari, O., Saad, W., Bennis, M.: Joint communication and control for wireless autonomous vehicular platoon systems. IEEE Trans. Commun. **67**(11), 7907–7922 (2019)
6. Lazar, C., Tiganasu, A.: String stable vehicle platooning using adaptive cruise controlled vehicles. IFAC-PapersOnLine **52**(5), 1–6 (2019)
7. Feng, S., Zhang, Y., Li, S.E., Cao, Z., Liu, H.X., Li, L.: String stability for vehicular platoon control: definitions and analysis methods. Annu. Rev. Control. **47**, 81–97 (2019)

Leveraging Fine-Grained Self-correlation in Detecting Collided LoRa Transmissions

Wenwei Li[1], Bin Hu[1], Xiaolei Zhou[1,2(✉)], and Shuai Wang[1]

[1] School of Computer and Science Technology, Southest University, Nanjing, China
{213170186,binhu,shuaiwang}@seu.edu.cn
[2] The Sixty-Third Research Institute, National University of Defense Technology,
Changsha, China
zhouxiaolei@nudt.edu.cn

Abstract. Recently LoRa has become one of the most attractive Low Power Wide Area Network (LPWAN) technologies and is widely applied in many distinct scenarios, such as health monitoring and smart factories. However, affected by the signal collision of uplink transmissions, a base station fails to decode concurrent transmissions. To solve this challenge and improve the performance of the base station, it is necessary to detect the collided transmission accurately. Existing researches focus on extracting the corresponding payload from collided signals based on the information of detected preamble. In this paper, we present FSD, a novel approach that achieves an effective preamble detection from collided LoRa packets, which exploits the inherent fine-grained similarity of LoRa. We implement and evaluate the design on commodity LoRa devices and USRP B210 base stations. The experiment results show that the accuracy and precision are improved by up to 20% than the continue peaks detection method and time-domain cross-correlation method.

Keywords: Internet of things · LoRa · Collided transmissions

1 Introduction

LoRa, as one of the representatives of Low Power Wide Area Network (LPWAN) technologies, has become a widely-used communication platform in IoT and is applied in many successful LoRa based applications in various scenarios [7]. Due to the characteristic of long-distance, a large number of LoRa devices are deployed in the same area, which leads to severe signal collisions. Since the transmission of the end device fails to be correctly detected, it is challenging to demodulate collisions. It is a critical factor that causes the degradation of network performance.

To resolve this issue, it is necessary to detect collided packets and locate the boundary of signals correctly, i.e. preamble detection. Existing approaches of detecting LoRa preamble are summarized into the following two categories:

© Springer Nature Switzerland AG 2021
Z. Liu et al. (Eds.): WASA 2021, LNCS 12939, pp. 503–511, 2021.
https://doi.org/10.1007/978-3-030-86137-7_53

time-domain approaches and frequency-domain approaches. The time-domain
approaches exploit cross-correlation with standard upchirp in time domain [9].
The frequency-domain approaches address this problem through multiple similar
continue peaks detection [2,4,5]. These techniques have the capability to detect
preamble of collided transmissions, but they are limited in burst traffic scenarios.
In addition, the time-domain cross-correlation approach is severely affected by
carrier frequency offset (CFO), intensive isomorphic and heterogeneous interference.

In this paper, we present FSD, which utilizes the fine-grained self-correlation
in the frequency domain to detect preamble in concurrent LoRa transmissions.
To extract the preamble effectively, the core idea of this work is to leverage fine-
grained self-correlation in the frequency domain. There are several challenges in
practice including (i) the fragmentation of correlation in the case of high concur-
rency, and (ii) the high computational overhead caused by a mass of correlation
calculations. In FSD, the dichotomy method is used to gradually reduce the window and the storage of intermediate computation results is utilized to simplify
time complexity. The contributions of FSD are summarized as follows

- To the best of our knowledge, the proposed design called FSD is the first to
  consider the fine-grained self-correlation from the preamble part in frequency
  domain of dechirped LoRa signal. It requires no hardware changes and takes
  advantage of preamble's own correlation as well as LoRa's modulation characteristics.
- We design the dichotomy algorithm dividing the window and simplify the
  correlation calculation to address the fragmentation of correlation and energy
  consumption limits.
- We evaluate FSD with commodity nodes (i.e., SX1280) and USRP B210. The
  experiment results show that the performance of FSD is improved by up to
  20% than the continue peaks detection and the time domain cross correlation
  method.

2   Background and Motivation

In this section, we briefly introduce the basic knowledge of LoRa and then elaborate on where the idea comes from.

2.1   Primer of LoRa

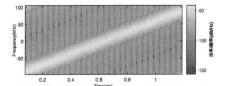

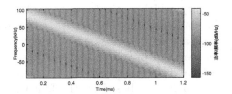

Fig. 1. Spectrogram of an upchirp.   **Fig. 2.** Spectrogram of a downchirp.

LoRa adopts Chirp Spread Spectrum (CSS) modulation scheme to modulate the signal. As shown in Fig. 1, the frequency of a standard upchirp signal increases linearly from -BW/2 to BW/2, where BW is bandwidth. The conjugate of this signal is a standard downchirp as shown in Fig. 2. The value of a LoRa symbol is determined by its initial frequency. The modulated signal of a symbol S is represented as [1]

$$X_S(t) = \begin{cases} e^{j2\pi(\frac{B}{2T_s}t^2 + B(\frac{S}{2^{SF}} - \frac{1}{2})t)} & 0 \le t < t_{turn} \\ e^{j2\pi(\frac{B}{2T_s}t^2 + B(\frac{S}{2^{SF}} - \frac{3}{2})t)} & t_{turn} \le t < T_s \end{cases} \quad (1)$$

where T_s is the duration of a chirp and B is the bandwidth. SF denotes spreading factor which indicates the number of binary bits a chirp can represent. And t_{turn} is the time when the frequency peaks.

The dechirp process in LoRa demodulation is represented as follows

$$Y_S(t) = X_S(t) \cdot X_0^*(t) = \begin{cases} e^{j2\pi(\frac{BS}{2^{SF}})t} & 0 \le t < t_{turn} \\ e^{j2\pi(\frac{BS}{2^{SF}} - B)t} & t_{turn} \le t < T_s \end{cases} \quad (2)$$

Ideally, we see exactly one frequency component after performing the Fast Fourier Transform (FFT). The bin index of the frequency is S. However, we generally see the index is desultorily shifted.

2.2   Preamble in Collided Transmissions

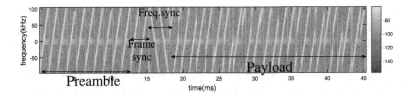

Fig. 3. Spectrogram of a LoRa package.

As shown in Fig. 3, the LoRa physical frame structure mainly consists of preamble, frame sync (i.e., sync word), freq. sync (i.e., SFD), optional header, and payload [10]. Among them, the preamble is composed of consecutive identical upchirp, which motivates us to exploit it, and the length is variable depending on the configuration. The accuracy of preamble detection is greatly affected when there are signal collisions. In terms of conflict structure, it may be a collision between the preamble and the preamble, the preamble and the payload, the SFD, and the preamble, or an arbitrary superposition of the previous cases [11].

Our idea is based on the following observations. Ideally (i.e., no frequency offset), the symbol from the preamble shows a peak close to bin0 in the frequency domain after performing dechirp and FFT. Time offset causes the same chirp is divided into two windows, but the bin of the same chirp in these two windows is close, and the peak value is divided into one high and one low [8]. Meanwhile the preamble as a whole shows a high degree of similarity due to the same interference and having the same structure. Considering this phenomenon. In this work, the correlation is calculated separately for consecutive windows considering splitting odd and even windows.

3   Main Design

We turn this idea into concrete things in this section. The design overview is shown in Fig. 4.

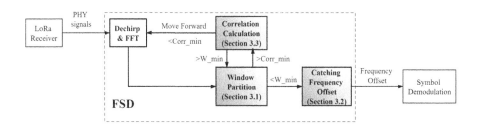

Fig. 4. The overview of the FSD architecture.

3.1   Partition Window

In Sect. 2.2, when there are signal collisions, we know that a minimum window exists for the preamble after the dechirp and FFT, and one or more similar peaks exist in each of the minimum windows of several consecutive reception windows. In general, the size of this window does not exceed 3 and in most cases they exist at the same bin, i.e., the window size is reduced to 1. This is the reason for the high performance of the continuous peak detection method. The present work here generally considers the case where the window size is larger than 1. In order to simplify the complexity of the algorithm and extract the window accurately, this work mainly adopts the classical divide-and-conquer idea to divide the window. We denote N_p as the number of chirps in a preamble, and the specific steps are as follows. First, we divide the received signal into N_p windows for dechirp and FFT. We denote the result as $w_i, i = 1, 2, \cdots, N_p$. Then we split the window evenly into two parts, i.e., w_i^l, w_i^r. Since the minimum window may be exactly at the junction of our two windows, it is necessary for the two windows to cover a length of each other, and the size of that length is the size of the minimum window. We assume N_p is even for convenient explanation. Similar results are obtained in the odd case. Then we calculate normalized correlation for $[w_1^l, w_3^l, \cdots, w_{N_p-1}^l], [w_1^r, w_3^r, \cdots, w_{N_p-1}^r], [w_2^l, w_4^l, \cdots, w_{N_p}^l], [w_2^r, w_4^r, \cdots, w_{N_p}^r]$. The result is represented as $corr_o^l$, $corr_o^r$, $corr_e^l$, $corr_e^r$, respectively.

$$w_i = \begin{cases} w_i^l & max(min(corr_o^l), min(corr_e^l)) >= corr_{min} \\ w_i^r & max(min(corr_o^r), min(corr_e^r)) >= corr_{min} \end{cases} \tag{3}$$

Here, we calculate the correlation coefficient matrix separately, and take the minimum value of the odd and even window sequence respectively, and then obtain the maximum correlation degree for comparison. The reason we take the minimum value is that if there's a preamble, we have to get a certain correlation across all of these windows. After taking the minimum value, it can be decided that there is no preamble in that window group. The maximum correlation is taken for comparison because the correlations obtained from odd and even windows tend to be inconsistent, as we introduced in Sect. 2.2, and the smaller correlations may be caused by window misalignment, i.e., time offset or superposition of multiple collided chirp signals, so this work chooses to take the larger correlations as the basis for judgment.

We repeat this process until the window size is smaller than w_{min}. w_{min} depends on the spreading factor, which is generally larger than 2. If this value is equal to 1, our method will be essentially equivalent to the continuous peak detection method. The reason for using this partitioning algorithm is that we cannot determine where this window is located. Simply traversing it once, similar to the continuous peak detection method, can not give us this window, and to fully exploit the information contained in the signal. We need to gradually reduce the window from the largest to the smallest. If this minimum window exists, the correlation in the whole reception window is lower than the correlation corresponding to the minimum window but exceed normal. So if we calculate a quite low correlation in the first step, we do not need to approach further down. If there is a high correlation, we can gradually approximate the left and right boundaries of the minimum window by dichotomizing.

It is noted that this partitioning algorithm used in this work is not the only method. For example, we can also calculate the correlation by taking a window of the minimum window size in the receiving window and sliding it continuously afterwards. Or we can also combine the two and perform a dichotomy first, followed by a continuous sliding, which is also a direction we can optimize.

3.2   Catching Frequency Offset

We now have a minimum correlation window that contains multiple possible frequencies that we need. Due to the limit of frequency resolution and uncertain frequency offset, we observe that a peak that should be at one bin might split into 2–3 bin, which often happens in practical scenarios. At this point, we have trouble distinguishing it from multiple preambles coexisting, and we choose to combine several bins into the same bin by taking the median.

3.3   Correlation Calculation

In fact, there are many methods to calculate correlation in different fields and scenarios. Among them, the Schmidl-Cox algorithm and its variations are most classical and widely used. We try some common methods such as distance-based correlation, linear correlation, and cosine correlation, but the experimental results are not satisfactory. In this paper, we define our correlation coefficient as follows

$$Corr(i,j) = \begin{cases} 1 & i == j \\ \max_{0 \le k < L} \left(\dfrac{\sum_{n=1}^{L-k} w_i(k+n) \cdot w_j^*(n)}{\sqrt{\sum_{n=1}^{L} w_i(n) \cdot w_i^*(n) \cdot \sum_{n=1}^{L} w_j(n) \cdot w_j^*(n)}} \right) & i < j \\ Corr(j,i) & i > j \end{cases} \quad (4)$$

where L denotes the size of w_i. This calculation method is also derived from the Schmidl-Cox algorithm. The first reason for normalization is that we need to remove the influence of the difference in spectral coefficients on the correlation calculation, and the second reason is that we have the process of taking the maximum and minimum values for comparison afterwards, and we need a uniform range to make a reasonable comparison.

When calculating the correlation of any two different windows, we translate the two windows relative to each other and find the maximum of the product sum of the overlapping intervals as the correlation measure, and normalize the value by dividing it with the product sum of the window and itself. Note that the product sum of the sliding sequences of different windows is used again in the subsequent subwindow correlation calculations. Hence we store them to reduce the overall computational overhead. And since we take the minimum value of the values in the matrix when we compare the correlation later, we can end the computation of all elements of the matrix as soon as the result is 0, and determine directly that there is no preamble. In addition, we do not need to store the matrix, because in the end all we need is the minimum value of the matrix, so we only need to store a minimum value and iterate over it.

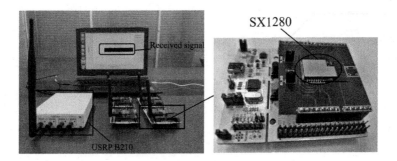

Fig. 5. Our experiment devices

4   Performance Evaluation

We implement and evaluate our method with cross-correlation in time domain approach and continue peaks detection method on USRP B210 and LoRa commodity nodes(i.e., SX1280) as shown in Fig. 5. We use GNU Radio to control USRP B210 to collect and process signals and use MATLAB to analyze them offline. In the following experiments, the frequency band we use is all 2.4 GHz, the SF is 8, the bandwidth is 203.125 KHz, and the preamble length is 6 chirp. The LoRa node transmitted the signal at random intervals of one to two seconds. We compare offset accuracy rate (OAR) and packet detection ratio (PDR) under different conditions to examine the performance of these methods.

4.1   Main Performance

To compare the main performance of our method with other methods, as shown in Fig. 6 and Fig. 7, we increase the number of nodes from 1 to 5. As we see, cross-correlation in the time domain approach detects almost all when the number of nodes is less than 4. However, as there are collisions, the signals in the time domain is severely damaged, the performance of detecting preamble drops rapidly. For the continue peaks detection method, the detection packet and the offset accuracy decline rapidly but then stabilize. Our FSD always maintains over 90% PDR and over 80% OAR, which has stable performance in the changing context of collision.

4.2   Impact of SNR

In order to study the influence of noise on these methods, we use five nodes with different signal-to-noise ratios (SNR) to do a comparative experiment. We reach a similar conclusion in the SNR experiment with five-node collisions as shown in Fig. 9. The low SNR is less than 0 dB, the medium SNR is between 0 and 10 dB, and the high SNR is greater than 10 dB. The average packet detection ratio of the continue peaks detection method is 70% at different SNR. It is seen that the influence of noise on this method is very limited, the changing SNR

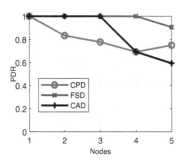

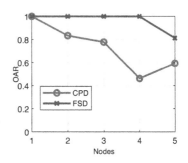

Fig. 6. PDR with different number of nodes.

Fig. 7. OAR with different number of nodes.

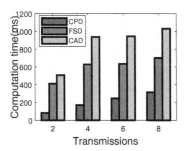

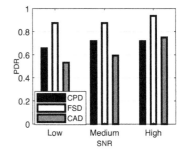

Fig. 8. Computation overhead with different transmissions.

Fig. 9. PDR with different SNR in five-node collisions.

does not cause much fluctuation in the PDR. And cross-correlation in the time domain approach, to the contrary, under the influence of low SNR, decreases significantly.

4.3 Computation Overhead

The other thing that we are very concerned about is whether the complexity of our algorithm is acceptable. We do experiments which add up the number of transmission by calculating their computation time as shown in Fig. 8. Our FSD method also brings high complexity with higher accuracy than the continue peaks detection method, but it is still within the acceptable range from the results.

5 Conclusion

In this paper we present a novel approach called FSD, which exploit the fine-grained self-correlation in preamble based on LoRa modulate scheme. FSD greatly improves the accuracy and precision of detection by up to 20% at the expense of certain computation cost as experiments show.

Acknowledgment. This work was supported in part by National Natural Science Foundation of China under Grant No. 61902066, Natural Science Foundation of Jiangsu Province under Grant No. BK20190336, China National Key R&D Program 2018YFB2100302 and Fundamental Research Funds for the Central Universities under Grant No. 2242021R41068.

References

1. Ghanaatian, R., Afisiadis, O., Cotting, M., Burg, A.: Lora digital receiver analysis and implementation. In: IEEE International Conference on Acoustics, Speech and Signal Processing, pp. 1498–1502. IEEE (2019)
2. Hu, B., Yin, Z., Wang, S., Xu, Z., He, T.: SCLoRa: leveraging multi-dimensionality in decoding collided LoRa transmissions. In: IEEE 28th International Conference on Network Protocols, pp. 1–11. IEEE (2020)
3. Eletreby, R., Zhang, D., Kumar, S., Yagan, O.: Empowering low power wide area networks in urban settings. In: Proceedings of the Conference of the ACM Special Interest Group on Data Communication, pp. 309–321. ACM (2017)
4. Xia, X., Zheng, Y., Gu, T.: FTrack: parallel decoding for LoRa transmissions. In: Proceedings of the 17th Conference on Embedded Networked Sensor Systems, pp. 192–204. ACM (2019)
5. Wang, X., Kong, L., He, L., Chen, G.: mLoRa: a multi-packet reception protocol in LoRa networks. In: IEEE 27th International Conference on Network Protocols, pp. 1–11. IEEE (2019)
6. Xu, Z., Luo, J., Yin, Z., He, T., Dong, F.: S-MAC: achieving high scalability via adaptive scheduling in LPWAN. In: IEEE INFOCOM 2020-IEEE Conference on Computer Communications, pp. 506–515. IEEE (2020)
7. Augustin, A., Yi, J., Clausen, T., Townsley, W.M. : A study of LoRa: long range and low power networks for the internet of things. Sensors **16**(9), 1466 (2016)
8. Tong, S., Xu, Z., Wang, J.: CoLoRa: enabling multi-packet reception in LoRa. In: IEEE INFOCOM 2020 - IEEE Conference on Computer Communications, pp. 2303–2311. IEEE (2020)
9. Gamage, A., Liando, J.C., Gu, C., Tan, R., Li, M.: LMAC: efficient carrier-sense multiple access for LoRa. In: Proceedings of the 26th Annual International Conference on Mobile Computing and Networking, pp. 1–13. IEEE (2020)
10. Robyns, P., Quax, P., Lamotte, W., Thenaers, W.: A multi-channel software decoder for the LoRa modulation scheme. In: IoTBDS, pp. 41–51. IEEE (2018)
11. Rahmadhani, A., Kuipers, F.: When LoRaWAN frames collide. In: Proceedings of the 12th International Workshop on Wireless Network Testbeds, Experimental Evaluation and Characterization, pp. 89–97. ACM(2018)

Blockchain Oracle-Based Privacy Preservation and Reliable Identification for Vehicles

Pin Lv[1,2,3], Xuetao Zhang[1], Jing Liu[1], Tingting Wei[1], and Jia Xu[1,2,3(✉)]

[1] School of Computer, Electronics and Information, Guangxi University,
Nanning 530004, China
{lvpin,xujia}@gxu.edu.cn

[2] Guangxi Key Laboratory of Multimedia Communications and Network Technology,
Nanning 530004, China

[3] Guangxi Colleges and University Key Laboratory of Parallel and Distributed
Computing, Nanning 530004, China

Abstract. Vehicle identity authentication is an important research topic in the field of intelligent transportation. Existing vehicle identity authentication schemes solve the privacy and authentication problem using encryption, but they cannot detect whether a vehicle has malicious behavior while identifying the vehicle. To solve the above problems, a novel vehicle reliable identification scheme based on blockchain oracle is proposed in this paper. The scheme includes a trusted vehicle registration model, a data source reliability model, and an off-blockchain data aggregation model. Specifically, the trusted vehicle registration model divides the registered vehicles into ordinary vehicles and new vehicles. Ordinary vehicles use decentralized oracle technology to combine the on-blockchain smart contract with the off-blockchain real world, while new vehicles are constrained by an additional punishment mechanism. The data source reliability model uses an indicator voting and a resource quantification protocol to ensure the reliability of third-party data sources, and uses (t,n) threshold signature and elliptic curve cryptography (ECC) to guarantee privacy when accessing the information of vehicles and drivers from third-party data sources. The off-blockchain data aggregation model uses multi-attribute analytic hierarchy process to aggregate the third-party data of vehicles and drivers. We implement the scheme in the Solidity Remix integrated development environment and Python environment. The results show that the scheme can effectively guarantee the privacy of vehicles and drivers, and also can achieve credibility, reliability, and fairness.

Keywords: Blockchain · Oralce · Reliable identification ·
Off-blockchain data aggregation · Intelligent transportation

This research is funded by Special funds for Guangxi BaGui Scholars, National Natural Science Foundation of China under Grant Nos. 62062008 and 62062006, Guangxi Natural Science Foundation under Grant Nos. 2019JJA170045, 2018JJA170194, 2018JJA170028.

Z. Liu et al. (Eds.): WASA 2021, LNCS 12939, pp. 512–520, 2021.
https://doi.org/10.1007/978-3-030-86137-7_54

1   Introduction

According to statistics, most of the traffic accidents are caused by bad behavior of drivers or poor vehicle conditions. Traffic restrictions on such drivers or vehicles can effectively improve road safety. The road traffic management systems can employ the vehicle's own various sensors, on-board unit (OBU) and nearby roadside unit (RSU) to perceive the vehicle, condition and the driver, thereby it can restrict the travel of unscrupulous drivers and vehicles. Most of these road traffic management systems use centralized servers to store data, which are vulnerable to data modification, privacy leakage, or single point of failure. Hence, the availability of the systems is not high.

The applications of decentralized blockchain technology in the field of the Internet of vehicles (IoV) gradually attract great attention from academics and industries in the transportation field. The essence of blockchain is to solve the problem of trust and reduce the cost of trust. Several papers [1–3] explore the applications of blockchain on the Internet of vehicles and verify the feasibility of blockchain in IoV. A few schemes [4–6] solve the security problem of user data, but do not solve the privacy protection of user data in IoV. User data requests in the blockchain are all in the form of transactions, and all of the transaction information are publicly recorded in the blocks of the blockchain. Therefore, many researchers begin to focus on data privacy protection in the blockchain. Some research works [7–9] propose privacy protection schemes for the privacy protection problem of blockchain in IoV.

However, the existing privacy protection schemes mainly focus on the verification of identity information, and do not consider the driving habits of drivers and vehicle conditions of local or cross-domain vehicles. Therefore, in consideration of these shortcomings of the existing schemes, a vehicle reliable identify scheme based on blockchain oracle is proposed in this paper. The scheme uses smart contracts and external data sources to identify of vehicles or drivers when they join the system. However, the blockchain cannot initiate network calls to access external data sources when executing smart contracts. The blockchain oracle is used as a two-way bridge connecting the real-world and smart contracts. The data source reliability model ensures the credibility of the oracle data source. Moreover, information of the vehicles and drivers and data sources of our scheme are encrypted, and are verified to protect their privacy while performing credible identification. This scheme not only protects the privacy of participants and data sources, but also ensures the reliability of data source, and realizes multi-data source credibility identification.

In summary, our contributions of this paper are as follows:

- We propose a vehicle reliable identify scheme based on blockchain oracle, which can reduce the bad driving behavior of malicious vehicles or drivers.
- We use indicator voting and resource quantification protocol to design a data source reliability model. The model adds elliptic curve cryptography (ECC) and (t,n) threshold signature to protect user privacy while verifying whether the data source is legal, and solve the problem of unreliability of the oracle data source.

– We use the multiple attribute analytic hierarchy process (AHP) to design a data aggregation model to calculate a weight and a comprehensively score of the acquired data. It can improve the verification efficiency of the blockchain and the communication efficiency.

The rest of this paper is arranged as follows. The related theoretical knowledge is described in Sect. 2. The system architecture is introduced in Sect. 3. The scheme of the vehicle reliability identification is given in Sect. 4. The performance of the scheme is analyzed in Sect. 5, and this paper is concluded in Sect. 6.

2   Related Concepts

With in-depth study, the blockchain and oracle technology derived many of the concepts. In order to better distinguish these concepts, the related key concepts are explained.

2.1   Blockchain

Blockchain is the core supporting technology of the digital cryptocurrency systems such as Bitcoin [10]. In the blockchain, there is no central control of the entire network-entities or nodes. Once the data is stored online, it can not be deleted or modified. The blockchain consists of four important parts:

(1) **Hash Function:** With help of hash functions, the original data or transaction record is encoded as a string composed of numbers and letters of a specific length, and it recorded in the blockchain.
(2) **Block:** As a part of the blockchain, a block generally includes two parts: block header and block body. The block header contains basic information of the block connection such as the current version number, the address of the previous block, and the target hash value of the current block. The block body uses a tree structure to encapsulate transactions over a period of time [11].
(3) **Time Stamp:** It is an important proof that blockchain cannot modify and forge data blocks, the block header contains the time to write data.
(4) **Chain Structure:** Blocks are stored as a unit. According to the time sequence of blocks, blocks are connected into a chain.

2.2   Smart Contract

The concept of smart contract is proposed by Szabo in 1994 [12]. The smart contract is coded, stored in the contract address and called by the transaction command. The execution of the smart contract is opened to the whole network.

2.3   Blockchain Oracle

The oracle can be used as a middleware to connect the smart contract on-blockchain to the off-blockchain real world. Blockchain is a certain and closed system environment. Blockchain can only obtain data within the chain but cannot get data from real world outside the chain. The execution of a smart contract needs a trigger condition, such as external events or states in the real world. Hence, oracle is designed to achieve this goal.

2.4   Encryption Algorithm

(1) **Elliptic Curve Cryptography (ECC):** ECC is proposed by Koblitz and Miller in 1985. Based on the mathematical elliptic curve, an asymmetric encryption algorithm for public secret key encryption is proposed.

(2) **(t, n) Threshold Signature:** According to the definition of the (t, n) threshold signature scheme $(1 \leq t \leq n)$, if any t signers in the group agree jointly to sign a message, a valid group signature for the message can be generated, on behalf of the entire group, equal to the size of a single signature.

3   System Architecture

The system architecture can be described in six parts. As is shown in Fig. 1.

- **User:** The users are vehicles or drivers who want to join the system and members of the verification committee. Vehicles and drivers registration based on user roles into two categories: new vehicles or drivers and ordinary vehicles or drivers.
- **Road-Side Unit (RSU):** The RSU is located on the roadside, deployed by the vehicular services providers, RSU verifies the encrypted and obfuscated messages sent by the users and performs a pre-aggregate operation.
- **Trustworthy Data (TD):** The TD is a third-party data source. After the blockchain consensus, we trust to get third-party data sources.
- **Trusted Vehicle Registration Model:** The trusted vehicle registration model is to ensure the identity of the joined vehicle or driver.
- **Data Source Reliability Model:** The data source reliability model is to ensure the reliability and privacy of third-party data sources.
- **Off-blockchain Data Aggregation Model:** The off-blockchain aggregation model is to aggregate third-party information about vehicles or drivers.

4   Vehicle Reliability Identification Scheme

Blockchain oracle-based reliable identification scheme for vehicles is described in this section, including trusted vehicle registration model, data source reliability model and off-blockchain data aggregation model. Data security and privacy protection are also introduced.

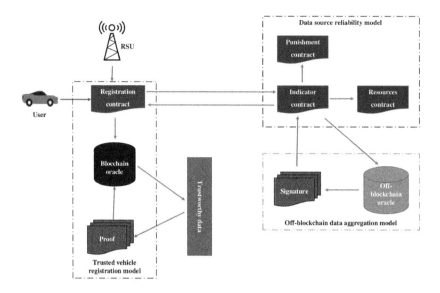

Fig. 1. System architecture

4.1   Trusted Vehicle Registration Model

In the trusted registration model, the vehicle must be registered with a hash value uniquely identified by the base station and an electronic signature attached to the RSU. The identity of the vehicle is confirmed by the roadside node, and the identity of the driver is used the in-vehicle camera to recognize the driver and communicate with the roadside node for confirmation.

The traffic blockchain system obtained the data from the data source and perform (t,n) threshold signature, then, send it to the traffic blockchain system for validation and data aggregation. Vehicles in bad condition or drivers with bad driving records cannot be verified by the traffic blockchain system. They must pay a certain amount of deposit in advance to join the system, and as a key monitoring object when driving, in order to reduce traffic accidents.

4.2   Data Source Reliability Model

In this paper, the consensus of blockchain is used to determine the trust of multiple data sources. The model uses indicator voting smart contracts to determine the indicators of vehicles and drivers. Resource quantification smart contracts are used to filter reliable data sources for selected indicators. The most reliable data source as is selected the third-party data source.

Indicator Voting Smart Contract. Users in the system can log in to the voting system to vote. For different users, the voting indicators are also different. In the voting system, voting indicators are also called candidate indicators, which represent the identity verification information of the vehicle and the driver. Candidate indicators for vehicles include vehicle condition, accident rate,etc. Candidate indicators for drivers include credit, reputation,etc. These identity authentication information also need to be decided by the voting system through member consensus voting.

Resources Quantitative Smart Contract. An indicator may correspond multiple third-party data sources. All third-party data sources are referred to as resources. Resource quantification matrix is expressed as $C_M = \{M_1, M_2, \cdots, M_n\}$, where M means the resource and n is the index of each resource. The resource quantitative rating standard is the rule for voters to vote on resources C_M. Resource quantification is the use of resource quantification rating standard to digitize resources. Resource rating standard and resource quantization matrix are shown in Table 1 and Table 2.

Table 1. Resource rating standard

Evaluation value	Comment	Grade
$C_i > 3.5$	Excellent	A1
$2.5 < C_i \leq 3.5$	Good	A2
$1.5 \leq C_i \leq 3.5$	Average	A3
$C_i \leq 1.5$	Poor	A4

Table 2. Resource quantization matrix

C_M	M_1	M_2	$\cdots$	M_n
M_1	r_{11}	$\cdots$	$\cdots$	r_{1n}
M_2	$\cdots$	$\cdots$	$\cdots$	$\cdots$
$\cdots$	$\cdots$	$\cdots$	$\cdots$	$\cdots$
M_n	r_{n1}	$\cdots$	$\cdots$	r_{nn}

Blockchain oracle transfers the resource quantization matrix to off-blockchain, thus authentication calculation and data aggregation are conducted off-blockchain.

4.3   Off-Blockchain Data Aggregation Model

The resource quantization matrix, normalized, to determine the weights M_i, where $\sum_{i=1}^{n} M_i = 1$, $M_i \geq 0$, $i = 1, 2, \cdots, n$. Verification calculations on the determined weights are also performed. The purpose of verification calculations is to test the rationality of the weight division.

The obtained indicator voting matrix and the resource quantization matrix are aggregated into a value, which is also called a threshold. The principle is to multiply the weight matrix and the resource matrix respectively, and add them together. Comparing the obtained threshold value with Table 1, a scoring grade, is explored to judge whether the vehicle or driver has behaviors that harms traffic safety.

5 Experiments and Security Analysis

Smart Contract Function. Indicator voting smart contract and resource quantification smart contract are implemented using the Solidity language. The smart contract is tested in the Solidity Remix integrated development environment. Indicator voting smart contract and resource quantification smart contract are deployed, compiled and tested in the JavaScript VM framework. The oracle of the vehicle reliability identification smart contract uses the chainlink platform to connect the smart contract and the external data source API, and the Link token is used to access the external data sources. The off-blockchain data aggregation uses the oracle adapter and the Python language.

Message Integrity and Authentication. The blockchain oracle uses the (t, n) threshold signature algorithm when accessing external data sources. When the data source D_i signs the message m, it chooses a random number k_i, and calculates $r_i = g_i^k \ mod \ p$. Hence, $s_i = x_i m' - k_i r_i \ mod \ (p-1)$. Each data source member calculates $R = \prod_{i=1}^{n} r_i \ mod \ p$. Denote y_i as the public key of D_i, $M = \prod_{D_i \in s_i} y_i \ mod \ p$, $r \neq M$.

If (m, M, s, r, R) is the legal signature of the message m by t members in the signature group member set S, the blockchain oracle verifies whether it satisfies the formula (1).

$$g^s r^r = (y \times R^{-1})^{h(m,r)} \bullet M^r \ mod \ p \quad (r \neq M) \tag{1}$$

Security. The aggregated value of the off-blockchain data is sent to registered users while using elliptic curve encryption to sign the information data m as (r,s). Research work [13] shows that the security of a 160-bit elliptic key is equivalent to a 1024-bit RSA key, and its cracking difficulty is exponential, thus, the security is very high.

Anonymity. Only the blockchain oracle knows the identity of the t data source members participating in the signature. The system as a verifier can only verify whether the signature is correct, and does not know who participates in the signature.

6   Conclusion

In this paper, a novel vehicle reliable identification scheme based on blockchain oracle and smart contract was proposed, for the local and cross-domain vehicles to achieve trusted registration. Also, privacy protection of vehicle identity information and third-party data sources was realized through the (n, t) threshold signature algorithm and the elliptic curve encryption (ECC) algorithm. The oracle mechanism solved the problem that the smart contract cannot sense third-party data sources, which led to the inability to assess the user behavior and predict their future behaviors. This solution improved road safety. Through experimental analysis and evaluation, the scheme was proven to have feasibility.

References

1. Hernández-Ramos, J., et al.: Toward a lightweight authentication and authorization framework for smart objects. IEEE J. Sel. Areas Commun. **33**(4), 690–702 (2015). https://doi.org/10.1109/JSAC.2015.2393436
2. Hussein, D., Bertin, E., Frey, V.: A community-driven access control approach in distributed IoT environments. IEEE Commun. Mag. **55**(3), 146–153 (2017). https://doi.org/10.1109/MCOM.2017.1600611CM
3. Shen, W., Lu, L., Cao, X., et al.: Cooperative message authentication in vehicular cyber-physical systems. IEEE Trans. Emerg. Top. Comput. **1**(1), 84–97 (2013). https://doi.org/10.1109/TETC.2013.2273221
4. Sultan, A., Mushtaq, M.A., Abubakar, M.: IOT security issues via blockchain: a review paper. In: Proceedings of the 2019 International Conference on Blockchain Technology, ICBCT 2019, pp. 60–65. Association for Computing Machinery, New York, NY, USA (2019)
5. Alphand, O., Amoretti, M., Claeys, T., et al.: IoTChain: a blockchain security architecture for the Internet of Things. In: 2018 IEEE Wireless Communications and Networking Conference (WCNC). IEEE (2018)
6. Dorri, A., Kanhere, S.S., Jurdak, R., Gauravaram, P.: LSB: a lightweight scalable blockchain for IoT security and anonymity. J. Parallel Distrib. Comput. **134**, 180–197 (2019). https://doi.org/10.1016/j.jpdc.2019.08.005
7. Ding, S., Cao, J., Li, C., et al.: A novel attribute-based access control scheme using blockchain for IoT. IEEE Access **7**, 38431–38441 (2019). https://doi.org/10.1109/ACCESS.2019.2905846
8. Ouaddah, A., Elkalam, A.A., Ouahman, A.A.: Towards a novel privacy-preserving access control model based on blockchain technology in IoT. In: Rocha, A, Serrhini, M., Felgueiras, C. (eds.) Europe and MENA Cooperation Advances in Information and Communication Technologies. Advances in Intelligent Systems and Computing, vol 520. Springer, Cham (2017). https://doi.org/10.1007/978-3-319-46568-5_53
9. Nandan Mohanty, S., et al.: An efficient lightweight integrated blockchain (ELIB) model for iot security and privacy. Fut. Gener. Comput. Syst. **102**, 1027–1037 (2020). https://doi.org/10.1016/j.future.2019.09.050
10. Yuan, Y., Wang, F.Y.: Current status and prospects of blockchain technology development. Zidonghua Xuebao/Acta Automatica Sinica **42**(4), 481–494 (2016). (in Chinese). https://doi.org/10.16383/j.aas.2016.c160158

11. Makhdoom, I., Abolhasan, M., Abbas, H., et al.: Blockchain's adoption in IoT: the challenges, and a way forward. J. Netw. Comput. Appl. **125**, 251–279 (2019). https://doi.org/10.1016/j.jnca.2018.10.019
12. Haiwu, H., An, Y., Zehua, C.: Survey of smart contract technology and application based on blockchain. J. Comput. Res. Develop. **55**(11), 2452–2466 (2018). (in Chinese)
13. Kumar, A., Aggarwal, A., Charu: performance analysis of manet using elliptic curve cryptosystem. In: International Conference on Advanced Communication Technology (ICACT) (2012)

Objects Perceptibility Prediction Model Based on Machine Learning for V2I Communication Load Reduction

Pin Lv[1,2,3], Yuebin He[1], Jinlei Han[1], and Jia Xu[1,2,3]✉

[1] School of Computer, Electronics and Information, Guangxi University,
Nanning 530004, China
xujia@gxu.edu.cn
[2] Guangxi Key Laboratory of Multimedia Communications and Network Technology,
Nanning 530004, China
[3] Guangxi Colleges and University Key Laboratory of Parallel and Distributed Computing,
Nanning 530004, China

Abstract. Autonomous driving is becoming prevalent and important for enhancing road safety. Sensor-based perception on vehicles is the main technology in autonomous driving systems. The environmental perception by individual vehicle has the limitations on coverage and detection accuracy. This issue can be solved by sending environmental information from the roadside infrastructure to autonomous vehicles. However, it results in a heavy communication load. In this paper, we present a machine learning based model to predict whether an autonomous vehicle can perceive an object. The prediction result can help roadside infrastructures to send the cooperative information selectively, and finally reduces the network load. The experiments prove that the accuracy of the model reaches 93%, and the V2I communication load reduction is up to 55%.

Keywords: Vehicle-to-infrastructure · Autonomous driving · Cooperative perception · Machine learning · Object detection

1 Introduction

Recently, autonomous driving and CAVs (connected and autonomous vehicles) attract much attention due to its safety and efficiency [1, 2], and is expected to reduce traffic congestion and fatal accidents. Generally, the main component of CAVs include environment perception, route scheduling, decision-making and communication (with other CAVs or surrounding infrastructure). As the source of information that other modules require, environment perception is usually considered as the critical and fundamental task.

This research is funded by Special funds for Guangxi BaGui Scholars, National Natural Science Foundation of China under Grant Nos. 62062008 and 62062006, Guangxi Natural Science Foundation under Grant Nos. 2019JJA170045, 2018JJA170194, 2018JJA170028

Z. Liu et al. (Eds.): WASA 2021, LNCS 12939, pp. 521–528, 2021.
https://doi.org/10.1007/978-3-030-86137-7_55

However, sensing precision is prone to be influenced by occlusion and distance, CAVs can hardly obtain complete environmental information by themselves. To solve such problem, cooperative perception with V2I (vehicles to infrastructure) communication is proposed. The accuracy of perception can be improved significantly by exchange messages with roadside nodes [3], but such method is also constrained by the capacity of transmission at the same time. In order to reduce the load of V2I communication and avoid the redundancy of perception information, it is a practical solution for the roadside infrastructure to transmit object information selectively. Specifically, the infrastructure can only broadcast the messages which the autonomous vehicles cannot perceive by themselves. In this case, it is necessary for roadside infrastructure to predict whether the objects are perceptible for the CAVs.

In this paper, we propose a neural network model to predict the perceptibility of objects. Base on the model, roadside infrastructure can broadcast the unperceived information to autonomous vehicles selectively. We train the model and verify the accuracy on real dataset, and evaluate the model by IOU (intersection-over-union) as an indicator. Finally, we verify the reduction of communication load by SUMO (Simulation of Urban Mobility) traffic simulator.

V2I-based cooperative sensing has been studied in recent years. B. Rebsamen et al. [4] set up a roadside infrastructure to send messages to self-driving cars to let them slow down when pedestrians appear at the intersection, W. Liu et al. [5] evaluate the risk level through special roadside infrastructure, there by autonomous vehicles can effectively avoid danger by combining their own perception information and risk level from the roadside infrastructure. In [4, 5], the roadside infrastructure sends message to each self-driving car rather than sending selectively. Reference [6], the V2I communication load is reduced by a trajectory prediction approach. T. Noguchi et al. [7] use V2I communication for target tracking tasks, and the tracker broadcasts the handover request message to the surrounding vehicles and infrastructure before the object is lost. However, the perceptibility of objects is not considered in above works.

The contributions of this paper are as follows:

1) We propose a neural network model to predict the perceptibility of objects for autonomous vehicles.
2) We train the model and verify the accuracy on real dataset, and verify the effectiveness of the model by SUMO simulator.

The rest of the paper is organized as follows. The system model of this paper is introduced in Sect. 2, the training process of the model is described in Sect. 3. In Sect. 4, we verify the accuracy of the model, and the model is evaluated by IOU and V2I communication load reduction. Finally, we make a conclusion in Sect. 5.

2   System Model

As shown in Fig. 1, a neural network consists of four layers is used as the predicted model. The first layer is input layer which contains external factors such as the distance between vehicles and objects. There are two hidden layers after the input layer, and each of them contains 64 and 32 neurons respectively. The output of each hidden layer is the input of the next layer through the Relu activation function. The third output layer maps the output to 0 or 1 through the Sigmoid function to get the final result.

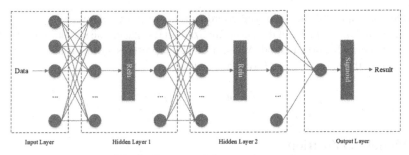

Fig. 1. Structure of the neural network

3 Model Training

The model training of this paper is based on the KITTI dataset [8], which provides a large number of real scenes data. KITTI dataset is currently one of the most important public datasets in the field of autonomous driving. In this section, we reconstruct an object-detection algorithm PointRCNN [9], which is based on the KITTI dataset, to obtain the positions of predicted objects, self-rotation angles of objects and other information. In order to match each object in the KITTI dataset with the detection result, the deviation of the object center position δ on 2D plane is considered as a control condition. Firstly, the label of each object from the KITTI dataset is traversed to record the Velodyne coordinate x_a and z_a of them. The object is considered to be detected when the predicted coordination (x_p, z_p) satisfies formula (1).

$$|x_a - x_p| < \delta, |z_a - z_p| < \delta \tag{1}$$

In the next step, the factors that may affect object perception in Table. 1 are selected as input parameters.

Table 1. The detail of input parameters

Parameter	Physical meaning	Range
x, y, z	The coordinates of the object	[0, 100]
w, h, l	The width, height and length of object	[0, 20]
o	The degree of occlusion	{0, 1, 2,3}
θ	Self-rotation angle of object	$[-\pi, \pi]$
t	The degree of truncation	{0, 1}

Because values of the Velodyne coordinate (x, y, z) are relatively larger than the vehicle size (w, h, l), the input data is normalized. In this paper, the standard deviation is used as the normalization method. Assuming that μ represents the mean and σ represents the variance, the normalization formula is as follow.

$$x_{normal} = (x - \mu)/\sigma \qquad (2)$$

4   Model Verification

4.1   Accuracy of the Model

In this section, experiments are conducted to verify the influence of external factors on whether the object can be detected. The neural network described in Sect. 2 is used for training, and 20% of the KITTI dataset is divided as the testing set. The model is trained 120 epochs with the learning rate of 0.005, and verified on the testing set every 5 epochs. The accuracy and the loss recorded during the training process are depicted in Fig. 2(a) and Fig. 2(b) respectively.

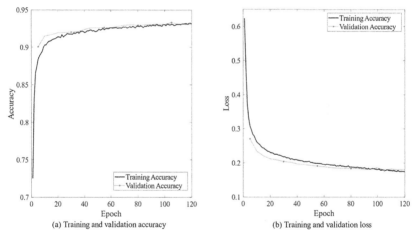

(a) Training and validation accuracy   (b) Training and validation loss

Fig. 2. The accuracy and loss of neural network

The results reveal that the external factors have a great influence on the perceptibility of the objects. After the training, the prediction accuracy on the testing set and training set reaches 93%. It is possible to accurately predict whether the target can be detected in the perception task according to these factors.

4.2   Comparative Test

In this section, we respectively remove the parameter in each row of Table 1 and set of (o, θ, t) to set up six control groups.

The training is conducted under the same neural network, and the accuracy of prediction on the training set and the testing set during the training process is recorded, as shown in Fig. 3(a) and Fig. 3(b). The proportion of positive samples is used as the control condition baseline which is 0.678.

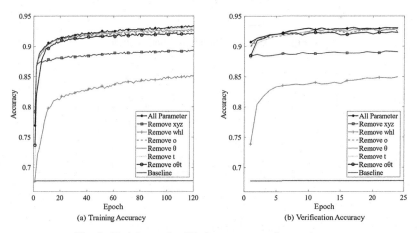

(a) Training Accuracy   (b) Verification Accuracy

Fig. 3. Training and validation accuracy of control group

According to the testing results, the following conclusions can be drawn. Firstly, the size information of the object has the greatest impact on the prediction result. After removing the object size information (w, h, l), the prediction accuracy is reduced to 0.85. Secondly, the position of the object will also affect the prediction result obviously. After removing the position information (x, y, z), the prediction accuracy is reduced to less than 0.9. The occlusion degree, the object's self-rotation angle, and the truncation degree are removed respectively, and each factor has little effect on the prediction accuracy, but when remove these three factors at the same time, it results in a slight decrease in the prediction accuracy.

4.3 Evaluation of the Model

In this section, IOU (Intersection-over-Union) [10] is used as a metric to evaluate the effectiveness of the neural network model. 2D-IOU is usually used as a precision indicator in object perception tasks.

The Area definition in IOU calculation is show in Fig. 4, and the IOU calculation formula is as follows.

$$IOU = \frac{InterArea}{DetectionResult + GroundTruth - InterArea} \tag{3}$$

We use all the existing data (including the training set and testing set) as input of the neural network in Sect. 2, and obtain the prediction result of whether each object can be detected, then compare it with the actual label and get two sets of Ture Positive (TP)

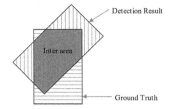

Fig. 4. Area definition in IOU calculation

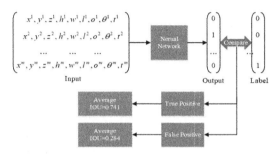

Fig. 5. The process of evaluation

and False Positive (FP). Finally, we calculate the average IOU of the object detection in the two sets respectively. The process of evaluation is sketched in Fig. 5.

TP sets include detected objects which are predicted as positive samples by the neural network. On the contrary, FP sets include undetected objects which are predicted as positive samples by the neural network. According to the calculation result, the average IOU value of the FP set is 0.284 while the average IOU value of the TP set is 0.741.

Two conclusions can be drawn according to the result above:

1) The model has a high accuracy in prediction, so that communication load of roadside infrastructure can be reduced by sending messages selectively.
2) Though roadside infrastructure sends messages to some vehicles which can perceive objects by themselves, the messages is also helpful for them because they have a low IOU value in perception.

4.4 Simulation Results

In this section, the number of CPM (cooperative-perception-message) is used to evaluate the reduction of V2I communication load. The simulation is based on SUMO [11] traffic simulator. As shown in Fig. 6, four lanes are set up and vehicles appeared randomly at the starting point of the lane at each moment. The neural network is used to predict the perceptibility of each vehicle, and the roadside infrastructure broadcast information of imperceptible vehicles in each epoch.

The number of arriving vehicles within the range of the roadside infrastructure gradually increases over the epochs. Suppose that one specified unit of CPM contains the

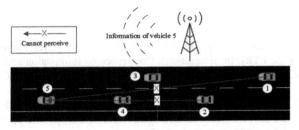

Fig. 6. The simulation scenario

information of one object, the numbers of broadcast CPMs under two comparative methods are recorded. One method is broadcasting all the information of vehicles in the coverage area of infrastructure, and the other one is broadcasting the information of imperceptible vehicles selectively. The result of the simulation is shown in Fig. 7.

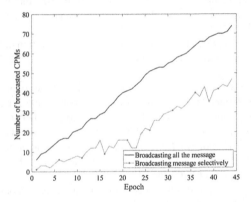

Fig. 7. Effectiveness of V2I communication load reduction

The simulation experiment proves that the number of CPMs can be significantly reduced according to the neural network model. The average reduction of CPMs reaches 55%.

5 Conclusion

In this paper we proposed a model to predict whether object can be detected by an autonomous vehicle. It was proved through experiments that the model had a high accuracy. When the roadside infrastructure predicted that the autonomous vehicle cannot perceive an object according to the model, it sent the object information to the vehicles, which improved the perception range of the autonomous vehicle and reduced the communication load of roadside infrastructure. The effectiveness of the model was proved by simulation experiment.

References

1. Min, K., Han, S., Lee, D., Choi, D., Sung, K., Choi, J.: SAE level 3 autonomous driving technology of the ETRI. In: International Conference on Information and Communication Technology Convergence, pp. 464–466 (2019). https://doi.org/10.1109/ICTC46691.2019.893 9765

2. Okuyama, T., Gonsalves T., Upadhay, J.: Autonomous driving system based on deep Q learning. In: International Conference on Intelligent Autonomous Systems, pp. 201–205 (2018). https://doi.org/10.1109/ICoIAS.2018.8494053

3. Aoki, S., Higuchi, T., Altintas, O.: Cooperative perception with deep reinforcement learning for connected vehicles. In: IEEE Intelligent Vehicles Symposium (IV), pp. 328–334 (2020). https://doi.org/10.1109/IV47402.2020.9304570

4. Rebsamen, B., et al.: Utilizing the infrastructure to assist autonomous vehicles in a mobility on demand context. In: TENCON 2012 IEEE Region 10 Conference, pp. 1–5 (2012). https://doi.org/10.1109/TENCON.2012.6412285.

5. Liu, W., Muramatsu, S., Okubo, Y.: Cooperation of V2I/P2I communication and roadside radar perception for the safety of vulnerable road users. In: 16th International Conference on Intelligent Transportation Systems Telecommunications, pp. 1–7, (2012). https://doi.org/10.1109/ITST.2018.8566704

6. Boquet, G., et al.: Trajectory prediction to avoid channel congestion in V2I communications. In: 28th Annual International Symposium on Personal, pp. 1–6 (2017). https://doi.org/10.1109/PIMRC.2017.8292325

7. Noguchi, T., Ting, Y.C., Yoshida, M., Ramonet, A.G.: Real-time cooperative vehicle tracking in VANETs. In: 29th International Conference on Computer Communications and Networks, pp. 1–6 (2020). https://doi.org/10.1109/ICCCN49398.2020.9209650

8. KITTI dataset Homepage. http://www.cvlibs.net/datasets/kitti/raw_data.php

9. Shi, S., Wang, X., Li, H.: PointRCNN: 3D object proposal generation and detection from point cloud. In: IEEE/CVF Conference on Computer Vision and Pattern Recognition, pp. 770–779 (2019). https://doi.org/10.1109/CVPR.2019.0008

10. Zhou, et al.: IoU loss for 2D/3D object detection. In: International Conference on 3D Vision, pp. 85–94 (2019). https://doi.org/10.1109/3DV.2019.00019

11. Krajzewicz, D., Erdmann, J., Behrisch, M., Bieker, L.: Recent development and applications of SUMO - simulation of urban mobility. Int. J. Adv. Syst. Measur. 5, 128–138 (2012)

KESAR: A High-Accuracy Prediction Algorithm and Solar-Aware Routing Strategy for Outdoor WSN

Dongchao Ma[✉], Xiaofu Huang, Xinlu Du, and Li Ma

School of Information, North China University of Technology, Beijing, China
madongchao1980@wo.cn

Abstract. The high energy density of sunlight makes solar wireless sensor networks (WSN) have advantages in outdoor monitoring applications. Two key technologies are applied: 1) Solar energy prediction and 2) Energy-aware routing strategy. Affected by frequently changing weather, shadows of buildings, trees, and other factors, the accuracy of existing prediction algorithms is relatively low, and the lifetime is not very satisfactory when the existing predictions are used as a support basis for routing. Thus, this paper proposes a prediction algorithm based on revised machine learning, and propose an adjustable routing strategy to achieve long-term stable monitoring. Experimental results show that the accuracy of prediction can be increased by up to 72.7%, and the network lifetime can be extended by at least 9.8%.

Keywords: Solar WSN · Internet of Things · Long-term stable monitoring · Extend outdoor WSN lifetime

1 Introduction

The motivation of this paper comes from the actual deployment of outdoor solar WSN. When our group deploys a monitoring system in the old Shougang Industrial Park (Project of Beijing Education Grid Phase II), it is found that the system is difficult to work stably. After analyzing the logs, some problems are discovered: 1) The accuracy of existing energy prediction algorithms decreases when used in outdoors. 2) The routing strategy is not reasonable enough. Following is a brief analysis.

Firstly, during periods when the weather is relatively stable (e.g., several consecutive sunny days), the predicted energy of some sensors is close to the actual values (prediction accuracy up to 80%), but some others differed greatly. During periods when the weather is relatively frequently changing (e.g., rain and sunshine alternate in a short time), the accuracy generally decreased to less than 67.1%. According to this phenomenon, we find sensors that can be predicted accurately are in open locations (e.g., no shaded, or shaded for a short time) or under stable weather, and sensors that can not be predicted

This work was supported by the National Key Research and Development Program of China under Grant 2018YFB1800302 and Beijing Natural Science Foundation (4212018, KZ201810009011).

Z. Liu et al. (Eds.): WASA 2021, LNCS 12939, pp. 529–536, 2021.
https://doi.org/10.1007/978-3-030-86137-7_56

accurately are in shaded locations (e.g., shaded by buildings and trees for a long time) or under frequently changing weather. We have tried to collect training data at deployment locations of each node, but the work overhead is too high.

Secondly, another important reason for the high node mortality comes from the routing strategy. Initially, we try to use the existing energy-aware routing strategies [1, 2], and the network traffic does tend to the nodes with more remaining and predicted energy. This is consistent with the goal of balancing network energy consumption. However, the topology is frequently adjusted with the energy consumption of nodes, increasing the overhead. At the same time, the routing computation burden of the controller is increased. Moreover, some energy-aware routing algorithms focus on uniform energy consumption and prolonging the lifetime of the first dead node (LTS 1: Lifetime Standard 1 [3]), even increasing the number of hops to transmit data around the distance. However, the application scenarios of solar WSN are quite different. Even if a small number of nodes die, they will be revived after a short period of sunlight. The WSN lifetime standard of "a certain percentage of nodes die (LTS 2: Lifetime Standard 2 [4])" is more applicable to solar WSN.

In summary, the following issues need to be resolved: 1) How to improve the accuracy of prediction for outdoor sensors. 2) How to design a suitable routing strategy for solar WSN. The main contributions of this paper are as follows.

1. We propose an energy prediction algorithm. Considering the environment of small sensors deployed outdoors, it can improve the prediction accuracy.
2. We propose an solar-aware routing strategy(SAR). It can adjust the routing goals under different sunlight conditions, calculate the topological connection matrix, effectively reduce node mortality, and achieve long-term stable working.
3. We introduce weighted parameters, transform the routing model into a convex model, and give a lightweight solution.

The rest of this paper is organized as follows. Section 2 provides the related works and the motivation. Section 3 describes the proposed algorithms. Section 4 analyzes the effects of the proposed algorithms. Section 5 presents the conclusions.

2   Related Work and Motivation

2.1   Energy Prediction Algorithm

Existing prediction algorithms can be divided into two categories: probability statistics and machine learning based algorithms. The algorithms based on probability statistics predict the energy based on historical data of various statistical transformations [2, 5, 6]. The algorithms based on machine learning use the neural network, reinforcement learning, and other methods [7, 8]. Muhammad et al. [5] propose IPro to predict the average solar radiation in the future. A model named ANN-Linear that combines neural network and a linear model is proposed [7]. ANN predicts the energy within 12 h, and the linear model predicts the energy after 12 h.

Machine learning based models are more capable of adapting to weather changes than those based on probability statistics. However, most of them are trained based on uniform environmental characteristics (e.g., wind speed, sunlight conditions in open locations, cloud coverage, etc.). It ignores the multi-scale characteristics of solar radiation (e.g., the change rate of different weather), as well as the differences of each small sensor individual deployment environment (e.g., shades of buildings and trees). The overhead of collecting training sets node by node is too high. Therefore, there is still room to improve the accuracy of existing predictions in outdoor practical applications.

2.2 Energy-Aware Routing Strategy

Most energy-aware routing strategies are based on the topology deployment and traffic distribution of the network layer [1, 2, 9–11]. Lu T. *et al.* [1] propose EEDSRS, with the goal of maximizing network energy efficiency. R. Zhang *et al.* [2] propose maxUtility to adjust the collection frequency and routing by observing the strength of correlation between collected data.

We have tried to apply the above strategies, but find the following problems: 1) The goal of maximizing network energy efficiency will increase node death rate. 2) Frequent topology oscillations increase the overhead (e.g., the routing announcement, recalls, etc.). 3) When the sunlight conditions are poor, the small sensors have limited energy storage and harvest little energy, the routing goal of balancing network energy consumption increases the overhead of data forwarding (e.g., the number of routing hops increases). Although the first dead node appears late, a large number of nodes die in a short time. Therefore, when existing energy-aware routing strategies are applied outdoors, there is room to improve environmental adaptability.

3   System Model

3.1   High-Accuracy Energy Prediction

When we apply the existing predictions to outdoor WSN, we find that the predictions would be inaccurate when 1) the weather changes frequently and 2) nodes are shaded. It is found that the harvested energy is approximately equal to a constant P_{in_shade} (about 1.14 W/m^2) when nodes are shaded. It has little relationship with sunlight and weather conditions. Therefore, a prediction algorithm is introduced as follows.

Prediction Without the Shades: K-Means + Elman (KE). Because of the complexity and diversity of weather data, before prediction, the data need to be analyzed for cross-correlation and selected that are closely associated with harvested energy. We use K-means to classify the characteristics into K clusters. To determine the optimal number of clusters K, we compare the accuracy through RMSE based on the validation set comparison. when $K = 3$, RMSE $= 30.6692$ is the minimum. It means the dataset characteristic has 3 trends with strong correlations. We use Elman to train the 3 clusters with strong correlations, respectively. We determine the number of training round *epoch* and hidden layer neurons based on validation set comparison.

KE can improve the weather adaptation capability and achieve high accuracy without considering the shades. However, only using KE cannot avoid the impact of environmental factors such as shades on the energy harvest. Next, the following will analyze environmental factors to solve the inaccurate prediction when nodes are shaded.

Prediction with the Shades: KE-Revise. We propose a shadow judgment algorithm (SJM) in previous work [16]. This paper intends to introduce a prediction solution. Firstly, without considering the shades, we analyze the short-term and long-term characteristics based on fluctuation and the multi-scale effect of solar irradiance, and perform cross-correlation analyze of historical solar irradiance. Then we combine the recurrent neural network to train data with a strong correlation. Finally, we incorporate the impact of individual deployment environment to revise the predicted results that haven't considered the shades. This is expected to improve accuracy effectively. The flow chart of the KE-revise proposed in this paper is shown in Fig. 1.

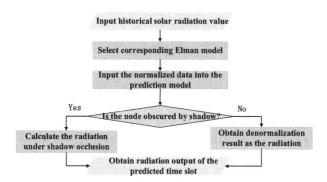

Fig. 1. High-accuracy energy prediction algorithm flow chart.

3.2 Solar-Aware Routing Strategy

We abstract the outdoor WSN into a directed graph $G = (V \cup \{S\}, E)$, where V is the set of n sensors, and S is the sink node. E is an edge between two nodes. Each sensor is powered by solar and consumes its energy on data sending and receiving. Sensors transmit data to the sink through the logical links in a multi-hop manner. Let $\Phi(i)$ denote the set of son nodes, $\Theta(i)$ denote the set of parent nodes. $\sum_{j \in \Phi(i)} f_{ji,t}$ is the amount of data send by son nodes at time t to sensor i (in byte). $\sum_{j \in \Theta(i)} f_{ij,t}$ is the amount of data send by sensor i to parent nodes at time t (in byte). e_{re} and e_{tr} are the energy consumption of each sensor receiving and sending data (in J/time). m is the amount of data collected by the sensor (in byte/time). $E_{i,t}$, $U_{i,t}$ and $C_{i,t}$ are the remaining energy, harvested energy and consumed energy of sensor i at time t (in J). In this paper, we introduce the energy consumption ratio (*ECR*). By calculating the ratio of $C_{i,t}$ to $(E_{i,t} + U_{i,t})$, find the node with max *ECR* in the network. $C_{i,t}$ and $ECR_{i,t}$ are calculated as follows.

$$C_{i,t} = \left\lceil \frac{\sum_{j \in \Phi(i)} f_{ji,t}}{m} \right\rceil e_{re} + \left\lceil \frac{\sum_{j \in \Theta(i)} f_{ij,t}}{m} \right\rceil e_{tr} \tag{1}$$

$$ECR_{i,t} = \frac{C_{i,t}}{E_{i,t} + U_{i,t}} \tag{2}$$

The solar-aware routing strategy proposed in this paper is as follows: when the sunlight conditions are good, the routing adjusts the goal to minimize node energy consumption with max *ECR*. When the sunlight conditions are poor, the routing adjusts the goal to save energy. Doing so can not only prolong the lifetime, but also reduce the number of topology oscillations and enhance the stability of the topology. The SAR proposed in this paper is as follows.

$$minimize(a \cdot maxECR) + b \cdot \left\| \sum_{j \in \Phi(i)} sgn(f_{ji,t}) \right\|_0) \tag{3}$$

$$subject\ to : \sum_{j \in \Phi(i)} f_{ji,t} \le c_i \tag{4}$$

$$\sum_{j \in \Phi(i)} f_{ji,t} > 0 \tag{5}$$

$$\sum_{j \in \Theta(i)} f_{ij,t} > 0 \tag{6}$$

$$\sum_{j \in \Theta(i)} f_{ij,t} - \sum_{j \in \Phi(i)} f_{ji,t} = m, m \ge 0 \tag{7}$$

$$\sum_{j \in \Phi(i)} sgn(f_{ji,t}) \le z, sgn(w) = \begin{cases} 1, w > 0 \\ 0, w = 0 \end{cases}, \tag{8}$$

The $sgn(f_{ji,t})$ is means whether there is data transmit between the node j and i. When there is no data transmission, $sgn(f_{ji,t}) = 0$, otherwise, $sgn(f_{ji,t}) = 1$. $\sum_{j \in \Phi(i)} sgn(f_{ji,t})$ represents the number of son nodes that transmit data to the parent node i. $\|\sum_{j \in \Phi(i)} sgn(f_{ji,t})\|_0$ means the number of parent nodes in network. Constraint (4) indicates the amount of data received by sensor i does not exceed c_i. Constraint (5) indicates there is data received by sensor i. Constraint (6) indicates there is data sent by sensor i. Constraint (7) is the traffic balance equation. Constraint (8) indicates sensor i can have at most z son nodes at time t. The model uses a, b to adjust the network goals.

$sgn(f_{ji,t})$ and l_0-norm in SAR make the model non-convex. Therefore, some transformations are needed to transform it into a convex model approximately. Obviously, On the right side of Formula (3), $\|\sum_{j \in \Phi(i)} sgn(f_{ji,t})\|_0$ equals to $\|\sum_{j \in \Phi(i)} f_{ji,t}\|_0$. But the l_0-norm $\|\sum_{j \in \Phi(i)} f_{ji,t}\|_0$ is still difficult to solve. Stephen P. Boyd, a well-known expert in convex optimization theory, proposes a breakthrough in 2008 to solve this kind of l_0-norm problem [14]. The problem $\|\sum_{j \in \Phi(i)} f_{ji,t}\|_0$ is translated into another problem as $\sum_{i \in \Phi(j)} \sum_{j \in \Theta(i)} \omega_{ji} f_{ji,t}$ and then uses the iterative algorithm in Sect. 2.2 of [14] to solve it. Thus, we can get the convex model as follows.

$$minimize(a \cdot max\ ECR + b \cdot \sum_{i \in \Phi(j)} \sum_{j \in \Theta(i)} \omega_{ji} f_{ji,t}) \tag{9}$$

subject to: (4)–(8).

The above problem is a convex optimization problem, which can be solved by cvx tool in Matlab, and the computational complexity is relatively low.

4   Performance Evaluation

In this section, KE and KE-Revise are compared with IPro [3] and ANN [5]. SAR is compared with EEDSRS [1] and maxUtility [2]. The solar radiation is obtained from the data of Denver published by the national renewable energy laboratory (NREL) [15].

4.1 Simulations

Figure 2 shows the experimental results of three prediction algorithms predict the solar radiation of Denver for 31 days in January 2019. The line graph shows the prediction data for consecutive 4 days in January, and the bar graph shows the error MAE for 31 days in January. Figure 2(a) verifies the accuracy of KE (without revise) when the weather changes frequently, and nodes are not shaded. Figure 2(b) verifies the accuracy of KE-Revise when the weather changes frequently and the node shaded by buildings.

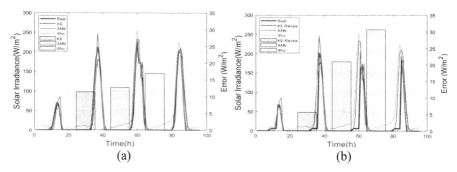

Fig. 2. Comparison of errors when the weather changes frequently and nodes are not shaded (a), when the weather changes frequently and nodes are shaded during a period of time (b).

LTS 2 is more suitable for solar WSN. Figure 3(a) is to verify the effect under LTS 2 (30% of nodes die, network dies). In Fig. 3(a), when the routing is EEDSRS or maxUtility, only introducing KE-Revise can extend the network lifetime by nearly double. If SAR is adopted, KESAR (KE-Revise + SAR) extends the network lifetime by 15.4%–20.6% compared to only introduce KE-Revise.

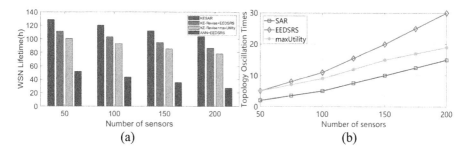

Fig. 3. Network lifetime under LTS 2 (a) and the number of oscillations (b).

The number of topological oscillations is compared under LTS 2. The experimental result is shown in Fig. 3(b). The number of topological oscillations of SAR is reduced by 33.3%–60%.

4.2 Real Node Experiments

In Fig. 4(a), the MAE of KE-Revise, ANN, and IPro are 2.0, 9.9, and 10.4. The results show that KE-Revise indeed has higher accuracy when applied outdoors.

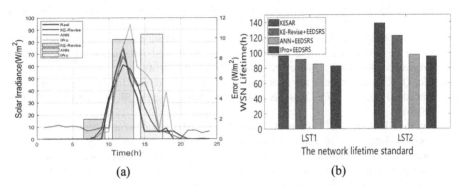

Fig. 4. Comparison of prediction errors in outdoor (a), and Network lifetime in outdoor (b).

To verify the effect of KESAR in outdoor, we deploy these sensors in a partially shaded environment. Figure 4(b) shows the network lifetime under both LTS 1 and LTS 2. KE-Revise + EEDSRS has a 7%–10% increase in lifetime. Due to the high accuracy of KE-Revise, which drives topology to adjust in time, and the lifetime is increased by 25.6%–28.9% under LTS 2.

5 Conclusions

This paper proposes a machine learning based prediction algorithm (KE-Revise) and an energy-aware routing strategy (SAR). Experimental results show that the lifetime of WSN can be extended by 9.8%–42.5%.

References

1. Lu, T., Liu, G., Chang, S.: Energy-efficient data sensing and routing in unreliable energy-harvesting wireless sensor network. In: 2018 Wireless Networks, vol. 2018, no. 24, pp. 611–625 (2018)
2. Zhang, R., Peng, J., Xu, W., Liang, W., Li, Z., Wang, T.: Utility maximization of temporally correlated sensing data in energy harvesting sensor networks. IEEE Internet Things J. 6(3), 5411–5422 (2019)
3. Dietrich, I., Dressler, F.: On the lifetime of wireless sensor networks. ACM Trans. Sensor Netw. 5(1), 1–39 (2009)
4. Madan, R., Cui, S., Lall, S., Goldsmith, A.: Cross-layer design for lifetime maximization in interference-limited wireless sensor networks. IEEE Trans. Wireless Commun. 5(11), 3142–3152 (2006)

5. Muhammad, Khaliq, Q.H., Umber, S., Muhammad, S., Andreas, P., Marios, L.: Harvested energy prediction schemes for wireless sensor networks: performance evaluation and enhancements. In: 2017 Wireless Communications and Mobile Computing, vol. 2017, no. 10, pp. 1–14 (2017)

6. Cammarano, A., Petrioli, C., Spenza, D.: Online energy harvesting prediction in environmentally powered wireless sensor networks. in IEEE Sens. J. **16**(17), 6793–6804 (2016)

7. Bao, Y., Wang, X., Liu, X., Zhou, S., Niu, Z.: Solar radiation prediction and energy allocation for energy harvesting base stations. In: 2014 IEEE International Conference on Communications (ICC), Sydney, NSW, pp. 3487–3492 (2014)

8. Liu, Q., Zhang, Q.: Accuracy improvement of energy prediction for solar-energy-powered embedded systems. IEEE Trans. Very Large Scale Integration (VLSI) Syst. **24**(6), 2062–2074 (2016)

9. Du, R., Gkatzikis, L., Fischione, C., Xiao, M.: On Maximizing sensor network lifetime by energy balancing. IEEE Trans. Control Network Syst. **5**(3), 1206–1218 (2018)

10. Dehwah, A.H., Shamma, J.S., Claudel, C.G.: A distributed routing scheme for energy management in solar powered sensor networks. Ad Hoc Networks **67**, 11–2 (2017)

11. Yang, G., Liang, T., He, X., Xiong, N.: Global and local reliability-based routing protocol for wireless sensor networks. IEEE Internet Things J. **6**(2), 3620–3632 (2019)

12. Zhang, Y., Wang, X., Tang, H.: An improved elman neural network with piecewise weighted gradient for time series prediction. Neurocomputing **359**(9), 199–208 (2019)

13. Ma, D., Zhang, C., Sun, X., Ma, L.: An adjustable model in data collection scenario for WSN. In: 2017 IEEE International Symposium on Parallel and Distributed Processing with Applications and 2017 IEEE International Conference on Ubiquitous Computing and Communications (ISPA/IUCC), Guangzhou, pp. 282–289 (2017)

14. Boyd, S.P., et al.: Enhancing sparsity by reweighted l1 minimization. J. Fourier Anal. Appl. **2008**(12), 877–905 (2008)

15. "Measurements and Instrumentation Data Center (midc), National Renewable Energy Laboratory (NREL). http://www.nrel.gov/midc/Author, F.: Article title. Journal 2(5), 99–110 (2016)

16. Hu, Y., Ma, D., Huang, X., Du, X., Xiao, A.: SWAF: a distributed solar wsn adaptive framework. In: Qiu, M. (ed.) ICA3PP 2020. LNCS, vol. 12452, pp. 465–479. Springer, Cham (2020). https://doi.org/10.1007/978-3-030-60245-1_32

Blockchain Empowered Federated Learning for Medical Data Sharing Model

Zexin Wang[1], Biwei Yan[2], and Yan Yao[1(✉)]

[1] School of Computer Science and Technology, Qilu University of Technology
(Shandong Academy of Sciences), Jinan 250351, China
`yaoyan@qlu.edu.cn`
[2] School of Mathematical Science, Qufu Normal University, Qufu 273165, China

Abstract. In medical fields, data sharing for patients can improve the collaborative diagnosis and the complexity of traditional medical treatment process. Under the condition of data supervision, federated learning breaks the restrictions between medical institutions and realizes the sharing of medical data. However, there are still some issues. For example, lack of trust among medical institutions leads to the inability to establish safe and reliable cooperation mechanisms. For another example, malicious medical institutions destroy model aggregation by sharing false parameters. In this paper, we propose a new federated learning scheme based on blockchain architecture for medical data sharing. Moreover, we propose an intelligent contract to verify the identity of participants and detect malicious participants in federated learning. The experimental results show that the proposed data sharing scheme provides a credible participation mechanism for medical data sharing based on federal learning, and provides both higher efficiency and lower energy consumption as well.

Keywords: Blockchain · Federated learning · Medical data sharing · Smart contract

1 Introduction

Artificial intelligence is now capable of processing huge amounts of data, which has already achieved great success in various fields such as speech recognition, face recognition, and image recognition [1–3]. With the help of artificial intelligence, cancer can be diagnosed earlier, which is also beneficial to patients. In the past few years, we have witnessed the rapid development of artificial intelligence in the field of medicine. The success of these artificial intelligence technologies is based on a great deal of data. However, the training of these systems requires a lot of data to obtain a satisfactory performance [4]. Hospital data usually exists in the form of data island. The non-circulation of medical data makes it difficult to collect massive medical data, which affects the effectiveness of machine learning training model and the development and application of Wise medical.

© Springer Nature Switzerland AG 2021
Z. Liu et al. (Eds.): WASA 2021, LNCS 12939, pp. 537–544, 2021.
https://doi.org/10.1007/978-3-030-86137-7_57

Federated learning can protect patients' privacy and break data islands. However, it has several imitations as follows:

- Since the participants in the federal study come from different medical organizations, there is a lack of trust between each other. How to establish a safe and reliable cooperation mechanism in the absence of mutual trust is a problem that needs to be solved urgently in practical applications.
- A single central server is prone to a single point of failure, resulting in irreparable losses.
- The data shared by participants lacks a corresponding quality verification mechanism, and malicious participants may provide wrong model parameters, thus disrupting the learning process.

Blockchain can provide a reliable mechanism. Through the authorization mechanism and identity management of the alliance chain, mutually untrustworthy medical institutions are integrated as participants to establish a safe and credible cooperation mechanism. For malicious participants who provide false data destruction models, they can be prohibited from participating in data sharing through the management node in the alliance chain. In addition, the blockchain can avoid the single point of failure of traditional federated learning.

The fusion and complementarity of the two technologies can effectively solve the demand for data sharing under the protection of privacy in the field of medical data, and fully tap the added value of medical data. The main contributions of this paper is as follows:

- We propose a safe and reliable cooperation mechanism for participants who lack trust in sharing medical data based on federated learning with the blockchain network.
- A medical data sharing model based on blockchain and federated learning is proposed.
- A smart contract is designed to detect false model parameters, and penalize malicious participants to avoid false parameters from destroying the entire model.

The rest of the paper is organized as follows: Sect. 2 depicts the related work. Section 3 presents our proposed models. Section 4 discusses intelligent contract design and experimental data analysis. Finally, the conclusion is depicted in Sect. 5.

2   Related Work

Federated learning can solve the "data island" problem through privacy protection and efficient processing, while the blockchain provides an incentive mechanism, a completely decentralized approach, and powerful anti-poisoning capabilities.

In [5], Kim proposed a blockchain joint learning architecture, in which local learning model updates can be exchanged and verified. Qu et al. [6] used federated learning and blockchain to develop a decentralized paradigm for big data-driven cognitive computing.

To solve the security and privacy issues, Lu et al. designed a secure data sharing architecture that supports blockchain in [7]. By merging the privacy-preserving joint learning, the data sharing problem is expressed as a machine learning problem. Martinez et al. [8] used blockchain to record and reward joint learning contributions and reward participants based on the cost of training data.

3 Data Sharing Model

In this section, we propose a reliable data sharing model for the collaboration between various participants in medical data sharing, based on blockchain.

3.1 Overall Scheme

The whole scheme is divided into two parts: local and aggregation, as shown in Fig. 1.

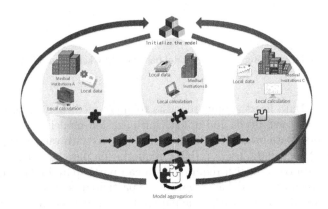

Fig. 1. Overall scheme

Local Part: Two or more medical institutions install the initialized models on their respective terminals. The model of individual medical institution is the same. Afterwards, participants can use the local medical data to train the model. Because of the different medical data of each medical institution, the final model trained by the terminal also has different model parameters.

Aggregation Part: Different model parameters will be uploaded to the blockchain at the same time. The blockchain will summarize and update the model parameters, and upload the updated parameters to the blockchain again. Each medical institution updates the local model and starts the next iteration. The above process will be repeated until the convergence of the entire training process.

3.2   Medical Data Sharing Model

Figure 2 presents a medical data sharing model based on blockchain and federated learning. The model includes data users, data providers, model aggregator, smart contracts, and blockchain networks. The blockchain network provides a reliable platform for all participants, to share medical data, and different medical institutions train the final model through federal learning cooperation.

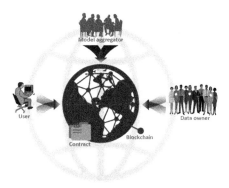

Fig. 2. Medical data sharing business model based on blockchain and federated learning

1) Data users: Data users submit requests to share medical data in blockchains based on their own needs and upload initialization models
2) Data owners: Data owners are medical institutions with various types of medical data. When data users publish requests for data or images of certain diseases, data owners with required data can participate in sharing data.
3) Model aggregators: Model aggregators are participants in the model. They do not share medical data, but participate in the aggregation model stage in the sharing process. The data provider trains the model locally and uploads it, the model aggregator aggregates uploaded multiple models, and then provides the data provider with a local model update service until the model gradient reaches the threshold.
4) Blockchain: Blockchain establishes a safe and reliable cooperation mechanism for participants lacking mutual trust. The request and initialization model for shared data is broadcast to all other nodes through the blockchain network. Then, the data provider that satisfies the request stores the locally trained model in the block, so that all model aggregators can retrieve the stored model. The model is constantly updated until it meets the needs of data users.

5) Smart contract: In the process of medical data sharing, participants need to be authenticated first, and then join the blockchain to participate in the sharing activities. Through the identity authentication intelligent contract, a trusted sharing environment for federal learning is established. By recording the parameters of the local training model shared by the data provider through the block chain, the intelligent contract can detect the data provider whose model quality is not up to standard.

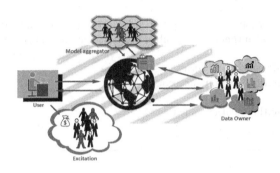

Fig. 3. Data sharing process

In general, a single sharing process as follows (Fig. 3):

Step 1: The data user makes a request to share medical data and update the initialization model. The data request and initialization model will generate a transaction in the blockchain, and all participants can see the data use request made by the data user.

Step 2: Data owners download the initialization model,and train the model locally with their own medical data.

Step 3: Data providers upload the trained model to blockchain. Smart contract detect the quality of the model automatically, so as to ensure that no malicious participants share false parameters to destroy the training of the overall model, and record the required model in the block chain.

Step 4: The aggregated model is uploaded to the blockchain again by the model aggregator. Each data owner updates to the local and continues to train the model locally, which is an iterative process.

Step 5: After the aggregation model parameters meet the preset requirements, a medical data sharing process ends. Data users can provide corresponding rewards for data providers and model aggregators.

3.3   Identity Verification Smart Contract

Participants first enter the blockchain network and register. Each participant has a unique and non-copyable id. After the registration is completed, the participant will have its own id and identity certification private key, and the identity certification public key will not be issued. It is stored in the authentication smart contract. When a participant initiates a transaction, the authentication smart contract is called first, and the corresponding public key is found according to the id. Only the registered participants in the blockchain network can participate in sharing legally.

Algorithm 1. Identity Verification

Input: participant id, authentication private key
Output: result
  1: Identity information = authentication private key (participant id)
  2: Verify message = authentication public key (authentication private key (participant id))
  3: **if** Identity information = Verify message **then**
  4:    result = authentication succeeded
  5: **else**
  6:    result = authentication failed
  7: **end if**
  8: **return** *result*

3.4 Malicious Participants Detected Smart Contracts

Assume that local data has been processed locally, and the parameters to be uploaded have been generated. Smart contracts make different judgments based on different types of medical models. If it is a classification model, F-score is used as the evaluation criterion for the model's quality. F-score can give consideration to the accuracy rate and recall rate of the model at the same time. The weight of accuracy rate and recall rate can be adjusted by adjusting the value of β (≤ 1). If it is an image segmentation model, the Dice coefficient is used as the evaluation standard of whether the model reaches the standard, and the Dice coefficient is used to measure the performance of the segmentation model. This indicator is also widely used in the medical field.

For models shared by different participants, different evaluation values will be generated, considering the difference of data set sizes or hardware. These evaluation values will be compared with predefined thresholds of the evaluation values in the smart contract. Malicious participant detection consists of two smart contracts, one is used for the detection of the primary contract, and the other for the evaluation of the parameter generated sub-contract. Both the primary contract and the sub-contract are written and deployed separately in the blockchain and invoked through their addresses.

The detection of model parameters through smart contract can avoid the destroy of false model parameters to the overall model aggregation effect. Smart contract provides a quality detection mechanism for medical data sharing based on federated learning, and automatic detection without the participation of a third party has higher security and faster efficiency. The detection of model parameters by smart contract can avoid the damage of model aggregation effect by false model parameters. Smart contracts provide a quality detection mechanism for federated learning-based sharing of medical data, which is an automatic detection without the participation of the third party, with higher security and efficiency.

4 Experiment Analysis

We conduct simulation experiments on the proposed scheme. Considering the timeliness of medical data sharing and the limitation of local equipment performance, we conduct efficiency and energy consumption tests to prove that our scheme is feasible. We tested it on the Linux operating system using Hyperledger Fabric. We carried out simulation experiments on the proposed plan. Taking into account the timeliness of medical data sharing and local equipment performance limitations, we conducted efficiency and energy consumption tests to prove that our scheme is feasible. We used Hyperledger Fabric as the environment to test in the Linux operating system.

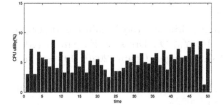

Fig. 4. CPU occupancy rate

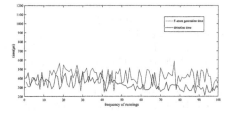

Fig. 5. Malicious participant detection efficiency

We conducted 100 tests and the experimental results are shown in Fig. 4. As can be seen from Fig. 4, CPU utilization is around 6%, resulting in fluctuations of about 2%, within an acceptable range. The results show that the resource consumption of our proposed scheme is low.

We deployed the malicious participants to smart contract in blockchain, and the experimental results are shown in Fig. 5. Generally speaking, the consumption of the sub-contract and the main contract is close. In general, the main contract takes less time than the sub-contract. The time fluctuation range is within 200 ms, and within a controllable range.

5 Conclusion

A novel medical data sharing model is proposed in this paper which combines federated learning and blockchain technology. The main purpose of the combining the federated learning and blockchain technology is to provide a trusted participation environment as well as high-quality data. Considering the timeliness of medical data sharing and the performance limitations of participants' local equipment, this model has high efficiency and low energy consumption. It can be better applied to the sharing of medical data and give full play to the value of medical data.

Acknowledgments. This work is partially supported by National Key R&D Program of China (Grant No. 2019YFB2102600), NSFC (Grants No. 61832012, 61771289), the Key Research and Development Program of Shandong Province (Grant No. 2019JZZY020124), the Pilot Project for Integrated Innovation of Science, Education and Industry of Qilu University of Technology (Shandong Academy of Sciences) (Grant No. 2020KJC-ZD02), and the Key Program of Science and Technology of Shandong (Grant No. 2020CXGC010901).

References

1. Pouyanfar, S., et al.: A survey on deep learning: algorithms, techniques, and applications. ACM Comput. Surv. **51**(5), 92:1–92:36 (2019)
2. Hatcher, W.G., Yu, W.: A survey of deep learning: platforms, applications and emerging research trends. IEEE Access **6**, 24411–24432 (2018)
3. Trask, A.W.: Grokking Deep Learning (2019)
4. Yan, B., Yu, J., Wang, Y., Guo, Q., Chai, B., Liu, S.: Blockchain-based service recommendation supporting data sharing. In: Yu, D., Dressler, F., Yu, J. (eds.) WASA 2020. LNCS, vol. 12384, pp. 580–589. Springer, Cham (2020). https://doi.org/10.1007/978-3-030-59016-1_48
5. Kim, H., Park, J., Bennis, M., Kim, S.-L.: Blockchained on-device federated learning. IEEE Commun. Lett. **24**(6), 1279–1283 (2020)
6. Qu, Y., Pokhrel, S.R., Garg, S., Gao, L., Xiang, Y.: A blockchained federated learning framework for cognitive computing in industry 4.0 networks. IEEE Trans. Industr. Inf. **17**(4), 2964–2973 (2020)
7. Yunlong, L., Huang, X., Dai, Y., Maharjan, S., Zhang, Y.: Blockchain and federated learning for privacy-preserved data sharing in industrial IoT. IEEE Trans. Ind. Inf. **16**(6), 4177–4186 (2020)
8. Martinez, I., Francis, S., Hafid, A.S.: Record and reward federated learning contributions with blockchain. In: 2019 International Conference on Cyber-enabled Distributed Computing and Knowledge Discovery (CyberC), pp. 50–57. IEEE (2019)
9. Qu, Y., et al.: Decentralized privacy using blockchain-enabled federated learning in fog computing. IEEE Internet Things J. **7**(6), 5171–5183 (2020)
10. Wang, Y., Yu, J., Yan, B., Wang, G., Shan, Z.: BSV-PAGS: blockchain-based special vehicles priority access guarantee scheme. Comput. Commun. **161**, 28–40 (2020)
11. Yunlong, L., Huang, X., Zhang, K., Maharjan, S., Zhang, Y.: Blockchain empowered asynchronous federated learning for secure data sharing in internet of vehicles. IEEE Trans. Veh. Technol. **69**(4), 4298–4311 (2020)

A Deep Learning Based Intelligent Transceiver Structure for Multiuser MIMO

Anming Dong[1]($\boxtimes$), Wenqi Cui[1], Jiguo Yu[1], Sufang Li[1], Yao Huang[1], Tong Zhang[2], and You Zhou[3]

[1] School of Computer Science and Technology, Qilu University of Technology (Shandong Academy of Sciences), Jinan 250353, China
anmingdong@qlu.edu.cn, jiguoyu@sina.com
[2] School of Computer Science, Qufu Normal University, Rizhao 276826, China
[3] Shandong HiCon New Media Institute Co., Ltd., Jinan 25000, Shandong, China

Abstract. Precoding and post-processing are necessary technical steps for information recovery of multiple-input multiple-output (MIMO) systems, which can effectively suppress interference between data streams and improve system capacity and resource utilization. However, it is not trivial to design the precoders for multiuser MIMO system and the complexity of the traditional precoding algorithms is usually very high. Deep learning sheds new light to overcome this challenge via data-driven solutions. In this paper, we study the intelligent information transmission technique for a multiuser MIMO broadcast channel network based on deep learning (DL). We propose a DL-based intelligent transceiver structure in this work. The proposed structure is composed of a DL network at the transmitter that played the role of precoder and a post-decoding DL network with a radio transformer network (RTN) at the receiver. Given the channel state information at the transmitter, the proposed intelligent transceiver is trained through the symbols drawn from a discrete constellation by decreasing the mean-squared error (MSE) loss. Simulation results show the proposed intelligent structure is capable of suppressing the inter-stream and inter-user interference adaptively through the training.

Keywords: Transceiver design · Deep learning · Multiuser MIMO · Broadcast channel · Beamforming · Radio transformer network

This work was supported in part by the National Key R&D Program of China under grant 2019YFB2102600, the National Natural Science Foundation of China (NSFC) under Grants 61701269, 61832012, 61771289 and 61672321, the Shandong Provincial Natural Science Foundation under Grant ZR2017BF012, the Key Research and Development Program of Shandong Province under Grants 2019JZZY010313 and 2019JZZY020124, the program for Youth Innovative Research Team in University of Shandong Province under grant 2019KJN010, the Pilot Project for Integrated Innovation of Science, Education and Industry of Qilu University of Technology (Shandong Academy of Sciences) under Grant 2020KJC-ZD02.

© Springer Nature Switzerland AG 2021
Z. Liu et al. (Eds.): WASA 2021, LNCS 12939, pp. 545–552, 2021.
https://doi.org/10.1007/978-3-030-86137-7_58

1   Introduction

With the rapid development of wireless communication, the demand for data transmission is also increasing [1–4]. In modern wireless communication systems, multiple input multiple output (MIMO) technology is widely used due to its potential in spectral efficiency and reliability brought by the space dimensions of multiple antennas [5–7]. In a MIMO system, multiple data streams are transmitted in parallel through spatial duplexing. Since multiple data streams are simultaneously transmit over the air at the same time, there will exist inter-stream and inter-user interference. It is well known that the interference is a bottleneck factor that limits the efficiency and reliability of the MIMO systems. It is thus important to deal with the effect of interference when designing a MIMO communication system [8–10].

In recent years, deep learning (DL) techniques have been intensively studied in many areas, such as image processing, machine vision, natural language processing and speech recognition, etc. [11–13]. It has also gained considerable attention in the area of wireless communication, since it is able to represent complex communication systems that are indescribable with explicit mathematical models [14]. A lot pioneering work has been carried out in such area, including MIMO channel estimation [15–17], MIMO detection [18], channel coding, resource allocation [19], etc. These DL algorithms achieve lower complexity or better performance than traditional algorithms, which shows the huge potential of deep learning in the field of wireless communication.

In the research work of [20], the MIMO communication system was first regarded as an end-to-end deep learning model. The DL-based communication system is interpreted as an autoencoder that performs end-to-end refactoring tasks while optimizing transmitters and receivers and learning signal coding. In DL theory, an autoencoder describes a deep neural network to find a low-dimensional representation of its input in a specific intermediate layer, thereby allowing reconstruction at the output with minimal error. The DL-based communication system can be represented and implemented by using an autoencoder and training it from a data set in an offline style. The trained autoencoder can be directly applied online in an actual system. The DL-based communication systems can optimize end-to-end performance through deep network neural networks, which is fundamentally different from the block structure of traditional communication systems.

DL-based MIMO system can be regarded as a black box for optimization. As without considering expert knowledge such as channel state information (CSI) [21], DL-based MIMO system still have room for improvement in performance. In the research of [22], by adding full CSI to the transmitter input and local CSI to the receiver input, better performance than traditional baseline algorithms can be achieved. In order to effectively improve the performance of DL-based MIMO systems, Radio Transformer Network (RTN) was proposed and applied to DL-based receiver design, which combined expert knowledge and obtained better performance results [14,23]. The RTN can significantly enhance the signal processing capability of DL-based MIMO systems and accelerate the convergence speed of the loss function. The experimental results in [20] and [21] prove that the MIMO system has better performance than the traditional baseline algorithm in terms of bit error rate.

In this paper, we propose a DL-based intelligent transceiver structure for a MIMO Broadcast Channel (BC) network. In the proposed transmission structure, the transmitter is composed of an encoder network and a precoding network. The former performs a transforming for the input symbols, and the latter performs further coding for the output of the encoder network by combining the CSI. This structure is inspired by the traditional precoding module, and its purpose is to effectively suppress inter-stream interference. This is different from the classical end-to-end DL MIMO structure proposed in [20], where the output of the encoder at the transmitter side is sent to the antennas directly. At the receiver side, we adopt the RTN structure for decoding enhancement. The simulation results show that the proposed DL-based MIMO transmission structure outperforms the classical schemes.

2 System Model

Since multiple terminals at the receiver cannot share information, the terminals cannot coordinate signal detection. In order to realize multi-user communication, signal pre-processing must be performed at the base station transmitting end through precoding to suppress spatial multi-user interference, so that each user can distinguish its own signal and realize multi-user communication.

In this paper, we consider a MU-MIMO BC system shown by Fig. 1, which consists of a transmitter with N_t antennas and K receivers, each of which is equipped with N_r antennas. We assume the k-th receiver desires d_k data streams, such that the transmitter sends $D = \sum_{k=1}^{K} d_k$ symbols at one transmission. We arrange the symbols as one vector $\mathbf{s} = [\mathbf{s}_1^T, \mathbf{s}_2^T, \dots, \mathbf{s}_K^T]^T \in \mathcal{C}^{D \times 1}$, where $\mathbf{s}_k = [s_{k,1}, s_{k,1}, \dots, s_{k,d_k}]^T$ is the symbol vector for the k-th user. Without getting confused, we denote the symbol vector $\mathbf{s} = [s_1, s_2, \dots, s_D]$. In this work, we assume the symbols are draw from a discrete constellation set $\mathcal{M}$ with the cardinality of $|\mathcal{M}| = M$. At the transmitter, the symbol vector is precoded by a matrix $\mathbf{V} = [\mathbf{V}_1, \mathbf{V}_2, \dots, \mathbf{V}_K] \in \mathcal{C}^{N_t \times D}$, where $\mathbf{V}_k \in \mathcal{C}^{N_t \times d_k}$ is the precoding matrix for the k-th user. After the channel prorogation, the received signal at the each receiver side is denoted as

$$\mathbf{y}_k = \mathbf{H}_k \mathbf{V} \mathbf{s} + \mathbf{n}_k = \mathbf{H}_k \sum_{j=1}^{K} \mathbf{V}_j \mathbf{s}_j + \mathbf{n}_k = \mathbf{H}_k \mathbf{V}_k \mathbf{s}_k + \mathbf{H}_k \sum_{j=1, j \neq k}^{K} \mathbf{V}_j \mathbf{s}_j + \mathbf{n}_k \quad (1)$$

where $\mathbf{H}_k$ is the $N_r \times N_t$ matrix of complex channel gains, and $\mathbf{n}_k \in \mathcal{C}^{N_r \times 1}$ is the zero-mean complex additive white Gaussian noise (AWGN) vector. The received signal $\mathbf{y}_k$ is then sent to the decode module to recover the corresponding symbols at the k-th receiver.

By observing the received signal (1), we know there are inter-user interference denoted by the middle term of the right hand side of the equation. Traditionally,

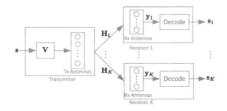

Fig. 1. MU-MIMO BC system

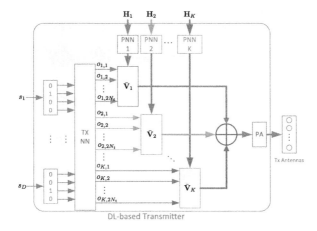

Fig. 2. DL-based transmitter structure for the MU-MIMO BC system

the precoding matrix **V** and decoding filters should be carefully designed to suppress the inter-user interference, such as the work in [8,9,24]. Different from the traditional precoding and decoding methods that derive the transmit matrix and receive filters using the convex optimization theory in a manual way, we attempt to develop an adaptive transceiver optimization method through the deep learning mechanism.

3   Structure of DL-Based MU-MIMO

In this section, we propose the DL-based transceiver structure fo the MU-MIMO BC system. For the considered MU-MIMO BC system, we assume the full CSI is available to the transmitter.

As is shown in Fig. 2, the transmitter maps the symbol vector of each user into a one-hot vector, i.e., s_k is mapped to a corresponding one-hot vector. We concatenate the one-hot vectors of all users as an input vector to a neural network, such as $[0\ 1\ 0\ 0 \cdots 0\ 1\ 0\ 0]^T$ shown in Fig. 2. The concatenated one-hot vector is then fed into a neural network labeled as *TX NN*. The output signals of the TX NN, i.e., $o_{k,i}, \forall k = 1, \ldots, K, i = 1, \ldots, 2N_t$, are divided into K groups, each of which consists of N_t signals. The grouped signal vectors are

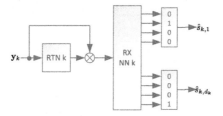

Fig. 3. DL based MU-MIMO BC receiver

then multiplied by the matrices $\bar{\mathbf{V}}_k \in \mathcal{C}^{2N_t \times 2N_t}, \forall k$, which are the outputs of K precoding neural networks (PNNs). For the k-th PNN, the input is the channel matrix $\mathbf{H}_k$ and the output is reshaped as a matrix with size of $2N_t \times 2N_t$. It is noted that the PNNs is used to mimic the interference suppressing procoding. All the signals are then merged to form a superimposed signal vector, which is normalized and powered by the power amplifier (PA) module. The powered signal is finally emitted through the TX antennas.

At the receiver side, the received signal at the k-th user is first fed to a RTN network, and then sent into the RX NN, as shown by Fig. 3. The output of the RX NN is then used to recover the one-hot vectors. This process is similar to our previous work in [25].

We adopt the supervised learning scheme to train the neural networks, by the randomly generated training symbols. The mean-square error (MSE) loss function is used as the optimization criterion, which is written as

$$Loss_{MSE} = \frac{1}{N} \sum_{k=1}^{K} \sum_{i=1}^{d_k} \sum_{n=1}^{N} ||s_{k,i}(n) - \hat{s}_{k,i}(n)||^2 , \qquad (2)$$

where N is the number of samples.

4 Simulation

In this section, we evaluate the proposed DL-based transceiver through simulations. The NNs presented in the structure are implemented using the Keras framework in Python 3.6 [26]. Without loss of generality, the Rayleigh fading channel is adopted in this work, the constellation set $\mathcal{M}$ is the QPSK set and we assume $d_k = d, \forall k$.

In Fig. 4, we show the BER performance of the proposed structure. The classical precoding schemes, including the Singular Value Decomposition (SVD) and Minimum Mean Square Error (MMSE), are adopted as the performance benchmarks. The parameters are set as $N_t = 4$, $N_r = 2$, $K = 2$, $d = 2$. It is shown that the proposed scheme (precoding+RTN) outperforms the traditional SVD precoding and MMSE precoding schemes.

In Fig. 5 and Fig. 6, we show the constellation points at the TX and RX antennas after $epoch = 100$ iterations under $SNR = 20\,\mathrm{dB}$, respectively. It can

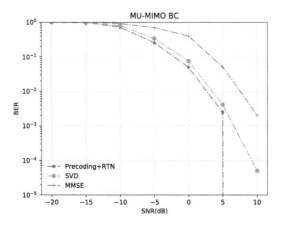

Fig. 4. BER of the MU-MIMO BC system consisting of QPSK modulation with $N_t = 4, N_r = 2, K = 2, d = 2$.

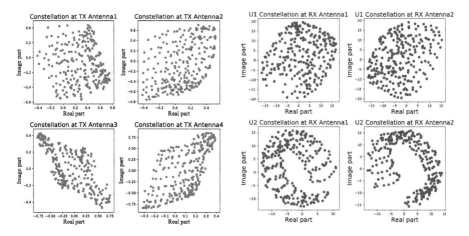

Fig. 5. Learned transmit constellations in MU-MIMO BC system at each antenna with QPSK modulation and $N_t = 4, N_r = 2, K = 2, d = 2, SNR = 20$ db, *epoch* = 100.

Fig. 6. Learned received constellations in MU-MIMO BC system at each user with QPSK modulation and $N_t = 4, N_r = 2, K = 2, d = 2, SNR = 20$ db, *epoch* = 100.

be observed that the transmitted signals and the received signal at the antennas are scattered after being trained. This implies that the interference among the data symbols are suppressed by the training.

5   Conclusion

In this paper, we proposed a DL-based transceiver structure for MIMO broadcasting systems. The DL-based transmitter was consists of multiple neural networks that plays the role of interference suppressing precoding process. At the receive side, the received signals are sent to a RTN network to further eliminate the interference. Experimental results show that the proposed DL-based structure outperforms the traditional precoding algorithms with respect to the BER performance.

References

1. Chen, Q., Cai, Z., Cheng, L., Gao, H.: Low-latency data aggregation scheduling for cognitive radio networks with non-predetermined structure. IEEE Trans. Mob. Comput. **20**, 2412–2426 (2020)
2. Cai, Z., Ji, S., He, J., Wei, L., Bourgeois, A.G.: Distributed and asynchronous data collection in cognitive radio networks with fairness consideration. IEEE Trans. Parallel Distrib. Syst. **25**(8), 2020–2029 (2013)
3. Cai, Z., Ji, S., He, J., Bourgeois, A.G.: Optimal distributed data collection for asynchronous cognitive radio networks. In: 2012 IEEE 32nd International Conference on Distributed Computing Systems, pp. 245–254. IEEE (2012)
4. Lu, J., Cai, Z., Wang, X., Zhang, L., Li, P., He, Z.: User social activity-based routing for cognitive radio networks. Pers. Ubiquit. Comput. **22**(3), 471–487 (2018)
5. Andrews, J.G., et al.: What will 5G be? IEEE J. Sel. Areas Commun. **32**(6), 1065–1082 (2014)
6. Larsson, E.G., Edfors, O., Tufvesson, F., Marzetta, T.L.: Massive MIMO for next generation wireless systems. IEEE Commun. Mag. **52**(2), 186–195 (2014)
7. Chen, S., Sun, S., Xu, G., Su, X., Cai, Y.: Beam-space multiplexing: practice, theory, and trends, from 4G TD-LTE, 5G, to 6G and beyond. IEEE Wirel. Commun. **27**(2), 162–172 (2020)
8. Dong, A., Zhang, H., Yuan, D., Zhou, X.: Interference alignment transceiver design by minimizing the maximum mean square error for MIMO interfering broadcast channel. IEEE Trans. Veh. Technol. **65**(8), 6024–6037 (2015)
9. Dong, A., Zhang, H., Wu, D., Yuan, D.: QoS-constrained transceiver design and power splitting for downlink multiuser MIMO SWIPT systems. In: 2016 IEEE International Conference on Communications (ICC), pp. 1–6. IEEE (2016)
10. Zhao, N., et al.: Secure transmission via joint precoding optimization for downlink MISO NOMA. IEEE Trans. Veh. Technol. **68**(8), 7603–7615 (2019)
11. LeCun, Y., Bengio, Y., Hinton, G.: Deep learning. Nature **521**(7553), 436–444 (2015)
12. Goodfellow, I., Bengio, Y., Courville, A.: Deep Learning. MIT Press (2016)
13. Liang, Y., Cai, Z., Yu, J., Han, Q., Li, Y.: Deep learning based inference of private information using embedded sensors in smart devices. IEEE Netw. **32**(4), 8–14 (2018)
14. O'Shea, T., Hoydis, J.: An introduction to deep learning for the physical layer. IEEE Trans. Cogn. Commun. Netw. **3**(4), 563–575 (2017)
15. Liu, Z., Zhang, L., Ding, Z.: An efficient deep learning framework for low rate massive MIMO CSI reporting. IEEE Trans. Commun. **68**, 4761–4772 (2020)
16. Ma, X., Gao, Z.: Data-driven deep learning to design pilot and channel estimator for massive MIMO. IEEE Trans. Veh. Technol. **69**(5), 5677–5682 (2020)
17. Kim, H., Kim, S., Lee, H., Jang, C., Choi, Y., Choi, J.: Massive MIMO channel prediction: Kalman filtering vs. machine learning. IEEE Trans. Commun. **69**, 518–528 (2020)

18. Shao, M., Ma, W.-K.: Binary MIMO detection via homotopy optimization and its deep adaptation. arXiv preprint arXiv:2004.12587 (2020)
19. Zhang, J., Dong, A., Yu, J.: Intelligent dynamic spectrum access for uplink underlay cognitive radio networks based on q-learning. In: Yu, D., Dressler, F., Yu, J. (eds.) WASA 2020. LNCS, vol. 12384, pp. 691–703. Springer, Cham (2020). https://doi.org/10.1007/978-3-030-59016-1_57
20. O'Shea, T.J., Erpek, T., Clancy, T.C.: Deep learning based MIMO communications. arXiv preprint arXiv:1707.07980 (2017)
21. He, H., Jin, S., Wen, C.-K., Gao, F., Li, G.Y., Xu, Z.: Model-driven deep learning for physical layer communications. IEEE Wirel. Commun. **26**(5), 77–83 (2019)
22. Song, J., Häger, C., Schröder, J., O'Shea, T., Wymeersch, H.: Benchmarking end-to-end learning of MIMO physical-layer communication. arXiv preprint arXiv:2005.09718 (2020)
23. O'Shea, T.J., Pemula, L., Batra, D., Clancy, T.C.: Radio transformer networks: Attention models for learning to synchronize in wireless systems. In: 2016 50th Asilomar Conference on Signals, Systems and Computers, pp. 662–666. IEEE (2016)
24. Zhang, H., Dong, A., Jin, S., Yuan, D.: Joint transceiver and power splitting optimization for multiuser MIMO SWIPT under MSE QoS constraints. IEEE Trans. Veh. Technol. **66**(8), 7123–7135 (2017)
25. Cui, W., Dong, A., Cao, Y., Zhang, C., Yu, J., Li, S.: Deep learning based MIMO transmission with precoding and radio transformer networks. Procedia Comput. Sci. **187**, 396–401 (2021)
26. Gulli, A., Pal, S.: Deep Learning with Keras. Packt Publishing Ltd. (2017)

GreenAP: An Energy-Saving Protocol for Mobile Access Points

Zouyu Liu, Xiaowei Qin$^{(\boxtimes)}$ 🆔, and Guo Wei

CAS Key Laboratory of Wireless-Optical Communications,
University of Science and Technology of China, Hefei, China
liuzouyu@mail.ustc.edu.cn, qinxw@ustc.edu.cn

Abstract. With the rapid advancement of the information age, an increasing number of people have started using Wi-Fi tethering, which can turn their mobile phones into mobile access points (APs) to meet their networking needs anywhere. However, the existing energy-saving mechanisms in IEEE 802.11 mainly aim at stations (STAs) and rarely consider APs. To solve the problem of mobile APs' high energy consumption, we propose an energy-saving protocol for mobile APs, called GreenAP. On the one hand, the protocol is compatible with the original IEEE 802.11 standard. On the other hand, the adaptive strategy in the protocol ensures that the energy consumption of the AP is reduced without affecting the user experience. The energy-saving AP protocol is implemented in NS-2. The experimental results show that GreenAP-3 can enable APs' sleep duration up to 74.7% when the traffic intensity is low, and the energy consumption can be reduced by 64.6% with small packet delay. In the case of high traffic intensity, the protocol can ensure less packet delay by adaptively adjusting APs' sleep time, which guarantees that the user experience is not affected under any circumstances.

Keywords: IEEE 802.11 · Energy-saving protocol · Mobile access points · Wi-Fi Tethering · NS-2

1 Introduction

With the development of chip manufacturing processes and software systems, more and more portable wireless devices, such as smart watches and tablets, have become popular in recent years. Because the power consumption of accessing the Internet through a cellular interface is often several times that of a Wi-Fi interface, most smart devices only have the ability to access the Internet via Wi-Fi. Currently, mobile phones can use the Wi-Fi interface as mobile access points (APs) of nearby smart devices [1,2], which is also known as Wi-Fi tethering by the public. The mobile APs have gradually become an important bridge between

This work was supported by the National Key Research and Development Program of China, 2018YFA0701603.

© Springer Nature Switzerland AG 2021
Z. Liu et al. (Eds.): WASA 2021, LNCS 12939, pp. 553–565, 2021.
https://doi.org/10.1007/978-3-030-86137-7_59

other smart devices and the Internet, which solves the needs of these intelligent devices for networking anywhere.

Reducing the energy consumption of Wi-Fi is a hot topic all the time, because improving the endurance of mobile phones is a very important aspect of improving user experience. However, in general scenarios, APs are assumed to be supported by AC power. Therefore, lots of research related to energy-efficient mechanisms only aims at wireless devices as stations (STAs) and rarely considers them as APs, such as [15–17]. According to power save mode (PSM) implemented in the IEEE 802.11 standard [3], an STA can negotiate with an AP to wake up after a certain period of sleep, and then it enters the sleep state again after completing data reception. However, when the mobile phone is used as an AP, the Wi-Fi transceiver module is always in receiving idle state, even when there is no traffic. As a result, a large amount of power is wasted and the battery life of the mobile phone is shortened, which makes the user experience extremely unfriendly.

At present, the research on energy-saving mechanisms for APs can be divided into two types. One is adjusting transmission power of APs, such as [13,14]. However, it is hard to change mobile devices' transmission power in reality. The other is designing a sleep scheduling mechanism of APs, which is more likely to deploy in our mobile phones. DozyAP [4] is the first to study the energy consumption of smart terminals as Wi-Fi hotspots. The paper proposes a sleep request mechanism. However, this mechanism is difficult to operate in practice because it requires complicated changes at both the AP and STAs, and it causes a large packet delay. POEM [5] and SleepAP [6] also propose some different sleep polling mechanisms, but the actual deployment of them also has the aforementioned implementation problems. A different solution is proposed in [7]. It allows STA to automatically update the network allocation vector (NAV) through designing a special sleep frame, thus ensuring that no uplink data occurs during the AP sleeps. However, it only uses fixed sleep parameters and cannot adaptively adjust the sleep time according to the traffic conditions of the STA. Therefore, the user experience will be affected in the case of heavy traffic.

This paper proposes an energy-saving protocol for mobile APs with two important considerations. First, the AP sleep timer's backoff strategy and adaptive sleep time selection strategy are designed in the energy-saving AP protocol. The backoff strategy will delay the transmission of APs' sleep indication frames to reduce data delay when STAs send uplink traffic. The selection strategy enables the AP to adaptively select the appropriate sleep time according to the average traffic statistics, which can reduce packet delay. The design of two strategies ensures that, no matter which traffic mode the STA is in, it will not affect the user experience. Second, by designing the AP sleep indication frame on the original MAC frame, it does not change the basic structure of the original MAC frame, so it is compatible with the IEEE 802.11 standard.

There are four main contributions in this paper. First, we propose an energy-saving AP protocol based on existing IEEE 802.11 framework to reduce energy consumption of mobile APs. Second, optimized sleep strategies are designed in the protocol framework. The results show that the adaptive method can ensure that, APs can obtain higher energy-saving benefits while not having a huge impact on packet delay. Third, because the current chips do not support the AP to enter sleep mode, we designed and verified the protocol in NS-2, which is the mainstream network simulation tool. Fourth, through adjusting the parameter values, we simulated several scenarios, including single station and multiple stations. Under various traffic patterns, experimental results show that the designed energy-saving protocol reduces energy consumption of the APs by up to 64.60% with little packet delay.

The rest of this paper is organized as follows. Section 2 describes the energy-saving AP protocol and introduces the optimized sleep strategies. Section 3 shows how to implement the simulation in NS-2 and the experimental results under various test scenarios. Finally, we conclude this paper in Sect. 4.

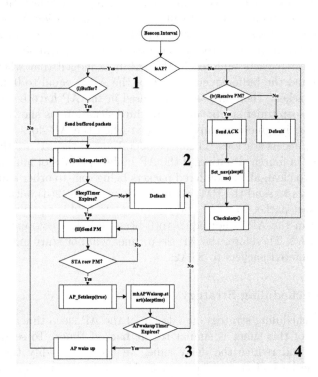

Fig. 1. Program diagram of energy-saving AP protocol. The design is divided into four parts.

2 Energy-Saving Protocol for Mobile APs

The design of the overall energy-saving AP protocol can be described in conjunction with the program diagram in Fig. 1, which is divided into four parts:

(i) the judgment of whether there is a buffered packet in the AP, (ii) the sleep scheduling strategy, (iii) the design of the sleep indication frame called PM sent by the AP, and (iv) the process after the STA receives the PM frame. These parts are described as follows.

2.1   Buffer Judgment

There are four different situations: one is single station connecting to an AP without buffered packets; two is single station connecting to an AP with buffered packets; three is multiple stations connecting to an AP without buffered packets; four is multiple stations connecting to an AP with buffered packets.

In first situation, as shown in Fig. 2(a), when there is no packet in the buffer, the AP's buffer queue length is equal to 0 and then the AP sleep timer starts to work. If the timer expires, the AP will send a sleep indication frame called PM (to be described in Sect. 2.3), which means the AP can start to sleep. In second situation, as shown in Fig. 2(b), the energy-saving STA will send a PS-POLL frame to request packets buffered in the AP. It is judged that when moredata is equal to 0 and the buffer queue length of the AP is equal to 0 after sending the buffered packets, then all packets buffered in the AP have been sent. After that, the AP sleep timer starts timing. In third situation, as shown in Fig. 2(c), the nonbuffered judgment is only performed when the AP does not buffer the packets of any access stations. Then, the operations of the AP are the same as a single station. In fourth situation, if the AP buffers packets of multiple stations, then it needs to clean all the buffered packets being sent to other stations before the AP prepares to send the PM frame. As shown in Fig. 2(d), although the AP has sent the last packet to STA1 and the moredata field is equal to 0, the buffer queue length in the AP is not equal to 0 because it has not sent the buffered packets to STA2. Therefore, the AP sleep timer will not start until the AP has sent all the buffered packets to STA2.

2.2   Sleep Scheduling Strategy

In the sleep scheduling strategy, the design of the AP sleep timer is a key part. The function of this timer is similar to the backoff timer. To send the packet preferentially and reduce the delay time, we need to modify the calculation method of the backoff time. The backoff timer selects a random value in the contention window as the backoff count value, and the AP sleep timer directly selects the contention window as the backoff count value. The specific design is as follows, where the initial waiting interval T, the increased contention window N and the maximum sleep time S are the adjustable parameters.

To avoid conflicts caused by multiple stations accessing the network at the same time, the core mechanism adopted in IEEE 802.11 is carrier sense multiple access with collision avoidance (CSMA/CA) [3]. The specific way to achieve conflict avoidance is to set a contention window and then roll back randomly [12]. When the sleep timer encounters uplink data from the STA, the channel is busy and then the sleep timer suspends timing. The next contention window is

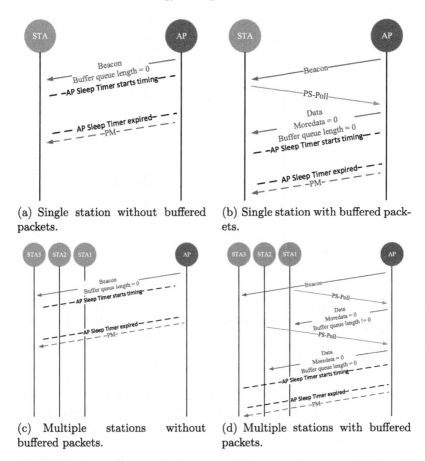

(a) Single station without buffered packets.

(b) Single station with buffered packets.

(c) Multiple stations without buffered packets.

(d) Multiple stations with buffered packets.

Fig. 2. Judgment flags that AP has no buffered packets, and then the AP sleep timer starts timing in two scenarios. One scenario is the AP connected to a single station. The other scenario is the AP connected to multiple stations. (PM: Sleep indication frame of AP that we designed. ACK and other frames are not drawn in the figure.)

increased by N time slots. Therefore, when encountering high traffic intensity, the contention window of the PM frame continues to increase in order to reduce the transmission of the PM frame. The design allows the AP to sleep less and reduce packet delay. Figure 3 specifically demonstrates that, after the AP receives multiple uplink data sent by the STA, the AP sleep timer increases its contention window each time and delays the transmission of the PM frame. The AP does not enter the sleep state until no uplink data is sent for a period of time.

After the AP sleeps for S ms for the first time and then wakes up, the initial duration of the AP sleep timer is set to T ms. When the STA transmits a packet, the contention window of the PM frame will increase and then the timing duration will increase. When there is no packet to transmit, the timer expires and then the AP sends a PM frame to sleep. When T is very small,

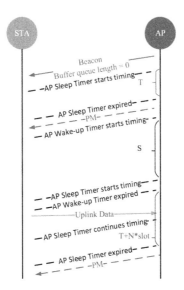

Fig. 3. Backoff mechanism of the AP sleep timer in NS-2. When the STA sends uplink data, the AP needs to backoff N slots and then send the PM. (PM: Sleep indication frame of the AP that we designed, T: Initial waiting interval, N: Increased competition window, S: Maximum sleep time.)

this design scheme ensures that the AP has more sleep time in a low traffic pattern, improving the AP's energy-saving effect. When T is large, the packet delay of the STA can be reduced, but the energy-saving benefit will also be reduced. Therefore, the adjustment of three parameters can change the energy-saving benefits and average packet delay. To obtain the best compromise in performance, we design three parameter selection schemes to schedule the PM frame as follows.

Traverse and Selection of Parameter Values. To determine a set of more suitable values, the first method traverses parameter values. The steps are as follows:

– Select different traffic patterns to test the percentage of sleep duration and packet delay.
– Manually adjust the parameters for multiple tests and compare the performance. As a result, S = 30, N = 100, T = 0.002 are the best values under different traffic conditions. They meet the requirements of higher energy-saving benefits while not having too much impact on data delay.

Dynamic Change. The second method dynamically changes the waiting contention window and automatically adjusts N. The steps are as follows:

Table 1. Sleep parameters corresponding to traffic statistics.

Pareto	Average number of packets	Range	Parameter value
0/100	1.02	<10	10
10/90	9.98	<10	10
20/80	23.94	10–80	20
30/70	30.75	10–80	20
40/60	39.66	10–80	20
50/50	47.40	10–80	20
60/40	64.77	10–80	20
70/30	69.55	10–80	30
80/20	82.35	>80	30
90/10	90.23	>80	30
100/0	99.40	>80	30

- Monitor the channel every 20 ms while the AP sleep frame is waiting to be sent.
- When the AP finds uplink data, the waiting contention window size is increased by 10. If there is no uplink data, the waiting contention window size is reduced by 10.

Adaptive Adjustment. The third method adjusts the parameter S adaptively according to the previous traffic statistics. The steps are as follows:

- As shown in Table 1, the average number of packets sent by low, medium, and high traffic patterns determines the threshold and the corresponding parameters.
- Count the number of packets reaching each beacon and store them in an array A. The average number of packets of the Nth beacon is calculated based on the average number of packets of the previous N-1 beacon interval of the array A.
- Then, select the parameter value of the Nth time according to the flow interval of the average grouping number, and then take out the corresponding parameter.
- Repeat the previous two steps for each beacon interval.

2.3 Sleep Indication Frame

Figure 4 shows the MAC frame format of the existing IEEE 802.11 protocol. The AP's sleep indication frame PM added in the protocol is a multicast frame. When the PM frame is sent, it will be sent to all STAs connected to the AP. In the PM frame, the key point that we design is setting the original field Duration/ID

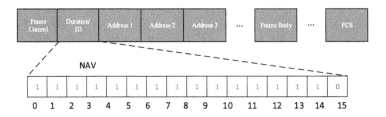

Fig. 4. MAC frame format in IEEE 802.11.

of the MAC frame header, which occupies 2 bytes. As shown in Fig. 4, when the 15th bit of this field is set to 0, the field represents the Network Allocation Vector (NAV). Therefore, the maximum value of the NAV is 32768 microseconds. When we calculate the sleep time of the AP, since the maximum NAV is approximately 32 ms, the AP sleep time should be taken as the lower of the remaining time and the maximum NAV. After the AP sends the PM frame and then receives the ACK frame from the STA, it starts to sleep.

2.4 STA Process After Receiving the PM

After the STA successfully receives the PM frame, it will perform the following steps:

- First, the STA obtains the Duration/ID field in the PM frame and then makes the NAV of the STA equal to the sleep time according to its value. When the STA receives the PM frame and sends the ACK frame, the NAV timer starts to work. During this time, the STA monitors whether the channel is busy, thus it does not try to send the uplink traffic before the NAV timer expires. The AP sleep duration does not exceed the maximum value of the NAV, which ensures that there is no uplink traffic while the AP is asleep, so the AP can sleep safely without packet loss [8].
- If the AP enters sleep mode, then the STA also enters sleep mode after receiving the PM frame, and it automatically wakes up after the sleep duration expires to monitor the arrival of the next PM frame.

3 Performance Evaluation

3.1 Implementation

We implement the energy-saving AP protocol in NS-2. The energy model of NS-2 records the remaining energy of each wireless node, and the energy parameter settings of each wireless node are shown in Table 2. For the energy parameters, this paper refers to energy consumption under 3.3V power supply in [9] and sets the initial battery energy of each node to 1000J. The literature [10], [11] found that the "ON/OFF" model based on the Pareto distribution can simulate actual web traffic. Therefore, the traffic generator based on the Pareto "ON/OFF" model is selected to simulate real network applications in NS-2. In this model, the "ON" and "OFF" intervals conform to the Pareto distribution, and the traffic is only generated in the "ON" state. The following two scenarios (to be described in Sects. 3.2 and 3.3) are verified by five different traffic patterns, as shown in Table 3. After completing each simulation, we used Gawk to extract useful information from the data generated in the wireless tracking file. Finally, three performance indicators are obtained: the sleep duration, energy consumption and average packet delay.

Table 2. Energy parameters in NS-2 for calculating energy consumption

Parameter	Value
Initial energy	1000 J
Tx power	0.990 W
Rx power	0.825 W
Idle power	0.825 W
Sleep power	0.0297 W

Table 3. Five different traffic intensity parameters in NS-2 (L: Low traffic intensity, M: Medium traffic intensity, MH: Between medium and high traffic intensity, H: High traffic intensity, F: Full load traffic intensity).

	L	M	MH	H	F
Burst_time_(ms)	0	20	50	80	100
Idle_time_(ms)	100	80	50	20	0
PacketSize_(byte)	512	512	512	512	512
Rate(Kb/s)	4096	4096	4096	4096	4096

For comparison, we tested three sleep scheduling strategies proposed in Sect. 2.2 and recorded their performance indicators. The first sleep strategy, GreenAP-1, selected a fixed set of good values by simply traversing all parameter values. The second sleep strategy, GreenAP-2, dynamically changed the waiting competition window and automatically adjusted the parameter N. The third sleep strategy, GreenAP-3, adjusted the parameter S adaptively according to the previous traffic statistics. As a result, the best sleep scheduling strategy is GreenAP-3, based on the performance comparison in Sects. 3.2 and 3.3. GreenAP-1 has the highest energy-saving benefit under MH traffic, and GreenAP-2 has the highest energy-saving benefit under L and M traffic, but they both cause more packet delay. However, GreenAP-3 sacrifices only a small energy-saving benefit to keep the packet delay at a low value, achieving the best compromise between energy-saving effects and user experiences.

3.2   Single Station

The topology structure built in this scenario is an AP and an STA. The STA establishes an association with the AP through passive scanning.

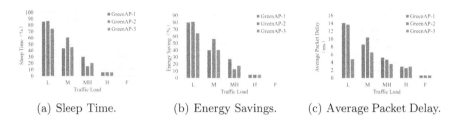

(a) Sleep Time.   (b) Energy Savings.   (c) Average Packet Delay.

Fig. 5. Energy and delay performance under five traffic intensities when an STA is connected with an AP. The figures compare the performance indicators of three sleep scheduling strategies obtained in NS-2 (GreenAP-1, GreenAP-2 and GreenAP-3).

As shown in Fig. 5, when the STA sends packets to the AP at L and M traffic intensity, GreenAP-2 has the highest percentage of sleep duration, reaching 86.7%, which corresponds to an 80.9% reduction in energy consumption. When the STA sends packets to the AP with ML traffic, the sleep duration of GreenAP-1 accounts for the highest percentage, reaching 29.9%, which saves 27.2% energy. Because GreenAP-3 sleeps for a shorter time under these traffic patterns, the sleep duration and energy consumption are up to 16.3% lower than those of GreenAP-1 and GreenAP-2. On the contrary, the average delay of GreenAP-3 is only 4.8 ms at low traffic, which is 68.5% lower than GreenAP-1 and GreenAP-2, with 14.1 ms and 13.7 ms, respectively. GreenAP-3 also maintains the lowest packet delay under the other two conditions.

When the STA sends packets to the AP with H traffic or F traffic, the sleep duration of the AP under the three sleep strategies is essentially the same, less than 10%, and the energy savings is less than 5%. Additionally, the packet delay is reduced to less than 3 ms, which indicates that the AP rarely enters the sleep state ensuring the quality of service for users. When traffic becomes highest, the backoff mechanism of the designed AP sleep timer ensures that

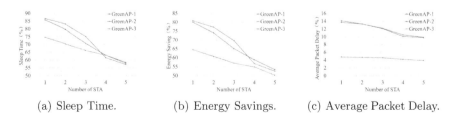

(a) Sleep Time.   (b) Energy Savings.   (c) Average Packet Delay.

Fig. 6. Energy and delay performance with multiple stations (1 5). L traffic intensity is selected in this scenario.

the energy-saving AP protocol does not have much impact on the packet delay through sending fewer PM frames. The above results show that, in the state of data transmission, packet delay of hotspots can be controlled according to the number of packets, and the energy-saving benefits can be guaranteed as users are unaware of transmission delay.

3.3 Multiple Stations

In this scenario, two, three, four, and five STAs are constructed to connect to the AP for testing, and each station establishes an association with the AP through passive scanning. The test results are shown in Fig. 6.

When the number of STAs connecting to the AP changes from two to five, the sleep duration of GreenAP-1 decreases from 79.8% to 57.9%, and the energy consumption changes accordingly by 20.7%. The percentage of GreenAP-2 sleep duration decreases from 83.2% to 57.0%, and the energy consumption changes by 24.7% accordingly. The percentage of GreenAP-3 sleep duration decreases from 70.4% to 58.5%, and the energy consumption changes by 10.5% accordingly. These results show that, as the accessing number of STAs increases, the APs go to sleep less frequently, and the energy savings also decrease. This is due to the increase in network activity after more stations are connected, thus the number of uplink packets received by the AP is more than in the case of a single station. At the same time, GreenAP-3 has a smaller change in energy consumption as the number of connected STAs increases, compared to GreenAP-1 and GreenAP-2, because it adaptively changes parameters in the sleep scheduling strategy according to the previous traffic conditions. Therefore, GreenAP-3 exhibits superior performance.

Moreover, as the number of STAs increases, the packet delay of GreenAP-1 and GreenAP-2 is reduced from 14.1 ms to 9.9 ms and 13.7 ms to 9.8 ms, respectively, while the packet delay of GreenAP-3 remains at 4 ms. This shows that the strategy in GreenAP-3 greatly decreases the impact of the APs' sleeping on packet delay, allowing the APs to save energy without influencing user experience.

Based on the above results, in the case of multiple stations access, GreenAP-3, the third solution for adaptively adjusting sleep parameters, still performs better when considering energy consumption and average packet delay. Especially in the case of low data traffic, when the AP energy consumption is reduced by only approximately 16.5% compared with the first and second schemes, the average packet delay decreases by approximately 66.0%. Therefore, GreenAP-3 is not only suitable for ordinary low-traffic scenarios but also low-traffic but delay-sensitive applications such as games.

4   Conclusion

With the popularization of Wi-Fi tethering, mobile APs are widely used. We design an energy-saving AP protocol and verify the protocol in NS-2. Based on compatibility with the original IEEE 802.11 protocol, we design three different sleep scheduling strategies in the energy-saving AP protocol. The protocols are tested in two scenarios with five different traffic types. Through comparison of the simulation results, the optimal sleep scheduling strategy GreenAP-3 is selected, which can adaptively adjust the sleep parameters according to the previous received traffic and achieve the best compromise between APs' energy-saving benefits and the packet delay.

References

1. Sharma, A., et al.: Cool-Tether: energy efficient on-the-fly wifi hot-spots using mobile phones. In: Conference on Emerging Network Experiment and Technology. ACM, pp. 109–120 (2009)
2. Keshav, K., Indukuri, V.R., Venkataram, P.: Energy efficient scheduling in 4G smart phones for Mobile Hotspot application. In: 2012 National Conference on Communications (NCC), Kharagpur, pp. 1–5 (2012)
3. Wireless LAN Medium Access Control (MAC) and Physical Layer (PHY) specifications. IEEE Std 802.11, 2007
4. Han, H., Liu, Y., Shen, G., Zhang, Y., Li, Q., Tan, C.C.: Design, realization, and evaluation of DozyAP for power-efficient wi-fi tethering. IEEE/ACM Trans. Networking **22**(5), 1672–1685 (2014)
5. Lim, W., Shin, K.G.: POEM: minimizing energy consumption for WiFi tethering service. IEEE/ACM Trans. Networking **24**(6), 3785–3797 (2016)
6. Jung, K.-H., Jeong, J.-P., Suh, Y.-J.: Sleeping mobile AP: a novel energy efficient Wifi tethering scheme. Wireless Netw. **21**(3), 963–980 (2014). https://doi.org/10.1007/s11276-014-0798-7
7. Jung, K., Qi, Y., Yu, C., Suh, Y.: Energy efficient Wifi tethering on a smartphone. In: IEEE INFOCOM 2014 - IEEE Conference on Computer Communications, Toronto, ON, pp. 1357–1365 (2014)
8. Politis, A.C., Hilas, C.S.: CTS-to-self as a protection mechanism for the no acknowledgment protocol in VoIP WLANs. Contemporary Eng. Sci. **11**(29), 1421–1435 (2018)
9. Kamerman, A., Monteban, L.: WaveLAN®-II: a high-performance wireless LAN for the unlicensed band. Bell Labs Techn. J. **2**(3) (1997)
10. Adas, A.: Traffic models in broadband networks. IEEE Commun. Mag. **35**(7), 82–89 (1997)
11. Crovella, M.E., Bestavros, A.: Self-similarity in World Wide Web traffic: evidence and possible causes. IEEE/ACM Trans. Networking **5**(6), 835–846 (1997)
12. Goodman, J., Greenberg, A.G., Madras, N., March, P.: Stability of binary exponential backoff. In: Proceedings of the 17-th Annual ACM Symposium on Theory of Computing, May 1985
13. Thangadorai, K.K., et al.: Intelligent and adaptive machine learning-based algorithm for power saving in mobile hotspot. In: 2020 IEEE 17th Annual Consumer Communications & Networking Conference (CCNC), Las Vegas, NV, USA, pp. 1–6 (2020)
14. Saranappa, R.K., Joseph, V.B.E., Das, D.: Dynamic power saving techniques for mobile hotspot. In: 2018 15th IEEE Annual Consumer Communications & Networking Conference (CCNC), Las Vegas, NV, pp. 1–2 (2018)

15. Manweiler, J., Roy Choudhury, R.: Avoiding the rush hours: WiFi energy management via traffic isolation. IEEE Trans. Mob. Comput. **11**(5), 739–752 (2012)
16. Rozner, E., Navda, V., Ramjee, R., Rayanchu, S.: NAPman: network-assisted power management for Wifi devices. In: Proceedings of the 8th International Conference on Mobile Systems, Applications, and Services 2010
17. Qiao, D., Shin, K.G.: Smart power-saving mode for IEEE 802.11 wireless LANs. In: Proceedings IEEE 24th Annual Joint Conference of the IEEE Computer and Communications Societies, vol. 3, pp. 1573–1583 (2005)

A Robust Algorithm for Multi-tenant Server Consolidation

Boyu Li[1], Xueyan Tang[2], and Bin Wu[1(✉)]

[1] College of Intelligence and Computing, Tianjin University, Tianjin, China
{boyulee,binw}@tju.edu.cn
[2] School of Computer Science and Engineering, Nanyang Technological University,
Singapore, Singapore
asxytang@ntu.edu.sg

Abstract. We study server consolidation problems in the cloud under conditions of simultaneous failure of multiple servers, where consolidation means that cloud providers put tenants on shared servers to improve resource utilization and thus reduce operation and maintenance costs. With replicas of each tenant on multiple servers, our objective is to minimize the total number of open servers and ensure that a particular failure will not result in overload of any remaining server. In this paper, we propose the Adaptive Tenant Placement Considering Fault Tolerance algorithm. Unlike existing consolidation algorithms, our algorithm can tolerate multiple server failures while ensuring that no server becomes overloaded. Furthermore, it does not classify replicas into different types. Through experimental evaluations, we show that the proposed algorithm performs better than existing solutions and achieves near-optimal replication allocation.

1 Introduction

Cloud computing relies on distributed computing and visualization technology. It realizes resource integration and sharing through elastic computing resource utilization. In general, client applications, called tenants, emerge dynamically over time. Each tenant has a workload that demands a certain amount of computing resources and is assigned some servers to host it. These servers may be shared by multiple tenants. When the resource utilization rate of the server is too low, the server load is far lower than the idle processing capacity of system resource allocation, resulting in wasted system resources. Server consolidation aims to reduce the number of servers by improving resource utilization and reducing the number of servers. In this way, consolidation effectively reduces energy costs on the premise of ensuring service performance [6,9].

Fault tolerance is an important concept in cloud computing that helps ensure service capability and reliability [2,4,7]. In a real-time, high-performance, large-scale cloud environment, failures may occur at any time due to complex dynamic systems [10–12]. To address this issue, a common strategy is to create multiple replicas of each tenant in the system and assign them to different servers [1,5].

© Springer Nature Switzerland AG 2021
Z. Liu et al. (Eds.): WASA 2021, LNCS 12939, pp. 566–573, 2021.
https://doi.org/10.1007/978-3-030-86137-7_60

As a result, if one or more servers fail, the affected workload can be redirected to functioning servers that share the same tenant. However, when using this method, it must be ensured that that the redirected extra workload will not lead to overload of the destination servers.

In this paper, we study the fault tolerance problem for server consolidation in an online setting. The objective is to ensure service continuity against multiple simultaneous server failures while reducing the total number of hosting servers to meet SLA. To achieve this target, any feasible algorithm should satisfy three constraints: online constraint, exclusion constraint, and space constraint. The online constraint means that the cloud provider has no priority information about future tenants' requests. The exclusion constraint dictates that at least $f+1$ replicas must be created and placed at different servers for each tenant against arbitrary f server failures. The space constraint requires that the redirected workloads are distributed to other servers associated with the same tenant and will not result in overload at the destination servers. This requires that each server reserves a certain amount of capacity for possible server failure.

Several strategies have been proposed to achieve fault tolerance targets, such as the Mirroring, Shift [3], and CubeFit [8] algorithms. The Mirroring algorithm sets f mirrored servers for each server; in other words, there are at least $f+1$ servers with the same total capacity and packed replicas. The Mirroring algorithm places the first replica of each tenant into servers by adopting the Best-Fit algorithm. The remaining replicas of the tenant are packed into the mirrored servers. To achieve valid packing, the capacity of each server is assumed to be 0.5 when each tenant has two replicas. This is because, when a server fails, its entire workload is redirected to the mirrored server and the total workload is thus doubled. Compared with the Mirroring algorithm, the Shifting algorithm can achieve a better performance. However, both of these algorithms can only deal with tenants that have two replicas.

The CubeFit algorithm extends the Shifting algorithm to tolerate multiple server failures while ensuring that no server becomes overloaded. However, the CubeFit algorithm wastes some capacity and cannot quickly reuse the open servers. As a result, it must rapidly open a large number of servers to pack the new tenants.

To decrease empty space and the number of open servers, tolerate multiple server failures, and ensure that no server becomes overloaded, we propose the Adaptive Tenant Placement Considering Fault Tolerance (ATPCFT) algorithm. Compared with the CubeFit algorithm, ATPCFT does not classify replicas into different types so that it can place replicas into empty space. As a result, ATPCFT can reuse open servers more quickly without the need to open a large number of new servers.

The rest of this paper is organized as follows. Sections 2 and 3 introduce the system model and the ATPCFT algorithm, respectively. The simulation results are shown in Sect. 4 and we conclude the paper in Sect. 5.

2   System Model

In this section, we formally define the server consolidation problem with consideration of fault tolerance. We consider an online setting in which tenants appear one by one. We assume that each server has a capacity of 1 and that the total numbers of open servers and tenants are M and I, respectively. M equals 0 when there are no tenants arriving. Each tenant is characterized by its workload, which is defined as the minimum amount of in-memory server computing resources required by the tenant to meet its SLA. The workload of tenant $i, i \in [1, 2, \ldots, I]$ is represented by θ_i. In addition, we assume that the workload of each tenant is in the range $(0, 1]$. Upon arrival of tenant $i, i \in [1, 2, \ldots, I]$, $f+1$ replicas of the tenant are created, where f is the maximum number of servers that may simultaneously fail. Typically, f is equal to 2 or 3 since more replicas require complex management and the problem becomes more constrained [8]. Each replica has a workload of $\frac{\theta_i}{f+1}$. All replicas associated with one tenant are placed on $f + 1$ different servers.

When a server fails, the workload associated with each replica hosted by that server is uniformly distributed among the servers that host the remaining replicas, thereby ensuring that the total tenant workload hosted by each server does not exceed its capacity. For a specific example, assume W_n is the total workload deployed on the nth server and $W_n \cap W_m$ denotes the total workload of tenants hosted on server n, which has a replica on server m. Let $\mathbf{S}^{-n}$ be a server set formed by any f servers except server n. To achieve the fault tolerance target, we should ensure that $\sum_{m \in \mathbf{S}^{-n}} W_n \cap W_m \leq 1 - W_n$. In other words, when all servers in $\mathbf{S}^{-n}$ fail simultaneously, the total workload directed to the nth server should not be larger than the reserved capacity.

For example, consider a sequence of tenants $\phi_1 = < a = 0.4, b = 0.2, c = 0.6, d = 0.8 >$ in which each tenant has two replicas. Two packing solutions for ϕ_1 are shown in Fig. 1: The left solution is a valid packing solution. The right solution is invalid, since servers S_1 and S_3 share the workload of tenant a and, if server S_3 fails, a workload with a size of 0.4 will be directed to S_1. Thus, the total workload hosted by server S_1 is $0.4 + 0.3 + 0.4 = 1.1$, which exceeds the unit capacity of the server.

3   Adaptive Tenant Placement Considering Fault Tolerance Algorithm

In this section, we introduce the ATPCFT algorithm. The rationale of ATPCFT is as follows: Once the last tenant i with θ_i workload appears, ATPCFT creates $f + 1$ replicas for tenant i, and each replica has $\frac{\theta_i}{f+1}$ workload. Compared with the CubeFit algorithm, ATPCFT does not classify replicas into different types. ATPCFT then identifies any server with a remaining capacity larger than the size of one replica of the last tenant plus the larger of the following: the reserved space of the server or the least reserved space of the last tenant. Any server satisfying this constraint is placed into set **B**. If **B** is not an empty set, then

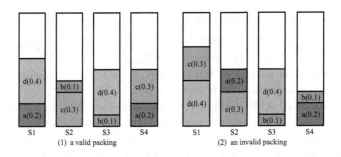

Fig. 1. The comparison between valid pack solution and invalid packing solution

ATPCFT puts the replica of tenant i into the open server with the least empty space among all servers in $\mathbf{B}$ while ensuring that no two servers share replicas of more than one tenant. If $\mathbf{B}$ is an empty set, ATPCFT opens $f + 1$ servers and places one replica of tenant i into one server.

The details of ATPCFT are as follows: When tenant i arrives, ATPCFT creates $f + 1$ replicas for tenant i, and each replicas has $\frac{\theta_i}{f+1}$ workload. It then determines the set of servers likely to be eligible to host the replicas of tenant i. To do so, for each open server n, ATPCFT maintains its occupied capacity O_n (occupied by the replicas of the tenants) and its reserved capacity R_n (reserved for load redirection from other servers during failures). If one replica of tenant i is packed at the nth server, then both O_n and R_n must be updated. O_n will update to $O_n + \theta_i/(f + 1)$. If the servers hosting the other f replicas of tenant i all simultaneously fail, the loads of these f replicas will all be redirected to server n. Thus, n must have a reserved capacity of at least $\frac{f}{f+1}\theta_i$, i.e.,

$$\frac{\theta_i}{f + 1} + O_n + f \times \frac{\theta_i}{f + 1} \leq 1.$$

Therefore, a necessary condition for server s to be eligible to host tenant i is

$$(1 - (O_n + \theta_i/(f + 1) + \Delta_n)) \geq 0 \tag{1}$$

$$\Delta_n = \max\left(R_n, f \times \frac{\theta_i}{f + 1}\right) \tag{2}$$

We define $\mathbf{B}$ as the set of open servers satisfying (1) and (2). If $\mathbf{B}$ is an empty set, ATPCFT opens $f + 1$ new servers and places a replica of tenant i in each of these servers. In this case, the occupied capacity of each new server is set to $\frac{\theta_i}{f+1}$ and the reserved capacity of each new server is set to $\frac{f}{f+1}\theta_i$.

If $\mathbf{B}$ is not an empty set, ATPCFT places one replica of tenant i into the server with the least empty space (i.e., $1 - (O_n + R_n)$) among all servers in $\mathbf{B}$. Assume server s^* is selected. It must then satisfy the following Eq. (3):

$$s^* = \underset{s \in \mathbf{B}}{\arg\min}\,(1 - (O_s + R_s)) \tag{3}$$

After placing a replica of tenant i, the reserved capacity of s^* is updated as $\max\left(R_{s^*}, \frac{f}{f+1}\theta_i\right)$ and the occupied space O_{s^*} updates to $O_s^* + \frac{\theta_i}{f+1}$. In addition, ATPCFT deletes s^* from $\mathbf{B}$. Assume set $\mathbf{X}_n$. includes the label of tenants in which one replica is packed in the nth server, and $\mathbf{Y}_i$ represents the label of servers packing the replicas of tenant i. Initially, $\mathbf{X}_n$ and $\mathbf{Y}_i$ are empty. Once server s^* is selected, ATPCFT puts number i into set $\mathbf{X}_{s^*}$ and number s^* into $\mathbf{Y}_i$. As mentioned above, any two replicas associated with one tenant must not be placed on same server and no two servers can share replicas of more than one tenant placed by ATPCFT. Therefore, ATPCFT must delete the servers sharing the same tenant with server s^* from $\mathbf{B}$. For a precise example, consider two sets $\mathbf{\Phi}$ and $\mathbf{\Psi}$, and let $\mathbf{\Phi} - \mathbf{\Psi}$ represent the elements belonging to $\mathbf{\Phi}$ but not $\mathbf{\Psi}$. The updated available server set is then $\mathbf{B} - \mathbf{Y}_j, j \in \mathbf{X}_{s^*}$. Note that the available servers list $\mathbf{B}$ might be an empty set after updating. In that case, ATPCFT opens a new server for packing a replica. The above process is repeated until all replicas associated with one tenant are packed.

Lemma 1. *No two servers can share replicas of more than one tenant placed by the ATPCFT algorithm.*

Proof. Consider any tenant j. If $\mathbf{B}$ is not an empty set, ATPCFT selects servers for packing the replis of tenant j only from $\mathbf{B}$. After replica packing into server s, ATPCFT delete the servers sharing the same tenant with server s from $\mathbf{B}$. If $\mathbf{B}$ becomes an empty set after updating, then ATPCFT opens new servers to pack the remaining replicas. Importantly, if there are no active servers packing the replicas of tenant j (in other word, $\mathbf{B}$ is an empty set), then ATPCFT opens $f+1$ new servers to accommodate the new tenant, guaranteeing that each server only packs one replica of a new tenant. Therefore, no two servers share replicas of more than one tenant placed by the ATPCFT algorithm. □

Theorem 1. *In the scenarios resulting from ATPCFT, no server is overloaded in case of failure of at most f servers.*

Proof. Consider an arbitrary server S_n in ATPCFT and server set $\mathbf{S}^{-n}$, where $\mathbf{S}^{-n}$ has any f servers but does not include S^n. In addition, let ξ_n be a replica packed in S^n characterized by its workload being the maximum one among all replicas packed in S^n, and let $|\xi_n|$ be the workload of ξ_n. We show that, in case of simultaneous failure of all servers in $\mathbf{S}^{-n}$, the extra workload redirected to S^n does not cause overload. By Lemma 1, server S^n and the severs in $\mathbf{S}^{-n}$ share at most one replica. Thus, the workload redirected to S^n from the failed servers in $\mathbf{S}^{-n}$ is at most $f \times |\xi_n|$. As previously stated, once the replica is packed into a server, the reserved space of the server is updated following (2). This implies that $R_n \leq f \times |\xi_n|$. In other words, there is no overflow for S^n when all servers in $\mathbf{S}^{-n}$ fail simultaneously. □

Theorem 2. *The competitive ratio of ATPCFT with fault tolerance $f = 2$ and $f = 3$ approaches $\max\left(4/\alpha - 2, 4\right)$ and $\max\left(4/\alpha - 3, 16/8\right)$, respectively, for any sufficiently long sequence, where $0 < \alpha \leq 1$.*

Proof. Consider a sufficiently long sequence β composed of two subsequences. The first subsequence includes replicas smaller than or equal to $\alpha/4$ and is denoted by β_1. The second subsequence is formed by replicas larger than $\alpha/4$ and is represented by β_2. In addition, let W_1 denote the total workload of β_1 and let L_2 represent the number of replicas in β_2. To prove the Theorem 2, we show that the total number of occupied servers for the optimal solution for packing sequence β is at least $W_1 + L_2\alpha/(4 - 2\alpha)$ with factor $f = 2$, and that of ATPCFT is at most $4W_1 + L_2 + c$. Thus, the competitive ratio for the ATPCFT algorithm is at most $\max(4/\alpha - 2, 4)$.

The total number of occupied servers for the optimal solution for packing sequence β is no less than the total size of all replicas in the two sequences plus the required reserved space. Let N denote the number of servers occupied by the optimal solution for packing subsequence β_2 and set an integer $i \geq 2$, so that $1/(i+3) < \alpha/4 \leq 1/(i+2)$. Therefore, one server includes at most i replicas of β_2 when $f = 2$; otherwise, overflow will happen when two servers fail. Thus, $N \geq L_2/i$. In addition, if a server packs one or more replicas with a size larger than $\alpha/4$, then the reserved space is at least $2 \times \alpha/4$. Hence, the total reserved space for the optimal packing is more than $N \times 2 \times (\alpha/4) \geq L_2\alpha/(2i)$. Furthermore, because $\alpha/4 \leq 1/(i+2)$, we have $L_2\alpha^2/(8 - 4\alpha)$. The total replica size of the two subsequences plus the reserved space required for subsequence β_2 is more than $W_1 + L_2\alpha/4 + L_2\alpha^2/(8 - 4\alpha)$. Consequently, we obtain $OPT(\beta) > W_1 + L_2\alpha/4 + L_2\alpha^2/(8 - 4\alpha) = W_1 + L_2\alpha/(4 - 2\alpha)$, where $OPT(\beta)$ denotes the number of servers occupied by the optimal solution for packing sequence β.

Recall that $|S_n|$ is the total workload deployed on server S_n and $|S_n \cap S_m|$ denotes the workload shared by one tenant, whose two replicas are placed at S_n, S_m. In addition, $\mathbf{S}^{-n}$ is a server set formed by at most f servers, except server S_n. Let $L(S_n)$ denote the remaining capacity of server S_n which is equal to the total capacity of the server minus the total workload of the server and the maximum workload redirected to the server when f servers fail. To be more precise, $L(S_n) = 1 - |S_n| - \max\left(\sum_{S_m \in \mathbf{S}^{-n}} |S_n \cap S_m|\right)$. Since the definition of the available servers is the Eqs. (1) and (2), server S_n includes a replica with a size smaller than or equal to $\alpha/4$ and will pack replicas until $L(S_n) < \alpha/4$ in the ATPCFT algorithm. Therefore, $L(S_n) < \alpha/4$ and also $\alpha \times L(S_n) < \alpha/4$. We then obtain $\alpha \times (1 - 3|S_n|) < \alpha/4$. The inequality holds because the workload redirected to server S_n is less than two-fold the workload hosted on server S_n and the definition of $L(S_n)$. Hence, we get $|S_n| \geq 1/4$. Thus, the total workload of all servers that include only replicas with a maximum size $\alpha/4$, except potentially a constant number of them, is at least $1/4$. The total size of all replicas in these servers is at most W_1. Hence, the number of these servers packing replicas with a size less than $\alpha/4$ is at most $4W_1 + c$, and that packing replicas with a size larger than $\alpha/4$ is at most L_2. Therefore, the number of servers opened by the ATPCFT algorithm is at most $4W_1 + L_2 + c$. $\square$

4   Simulation Results

In this section, we compare our proposed algorithm with the CubeFit and Mirror algorithms. In the CubeFit algorithm, we classify the replicas into nine types based on their size [8]. The size of a tenant is defined as $0.01 \times c$, where c is a positive integer varying from 1 to $\frac{1}{f+1} \times 100$. c in Fig. 2, 3 and 4 is generated from a uniform distribution. The value of f in Fig. 2, 3 and 4 varies from 1 to 3.

From Fig. 2, 3 and 4, we see that the ATPCFT algorithm achieves a better performance than the CubeFit algorithm. The reasons are as follows: the ATPCFT algorithm does not classify replicas into different types. As a result, it does not need to maintain $f + 1$ server groups for each type of replica. Hence, ATPCFT can pack replicas into servers while satisfying Eqs. (1) and (2) such that it does not need to open new servers to pack the replicas. ATPCFT further decreases the number of servers by using empty space to pack replicas.

From Fig. 2, 3 and 4, we can see that only when the replica size is less than 0.1 or $f = 1$, the Mirror algorithm can achieve a better performance than ATPCFT. In other cases, the number of servers opened by ATPCFT is lower than that opened by Mirror. This is because the Mirror algorithm requires each server to reserve $\frac{f}{f+1}$ capacity; thus, even when $f = 1$, 50% of the capacity is reserved for receiving the failed workload. As f increases, the Mirror algorithm requires more capacity to achieve the fault tolerance target.

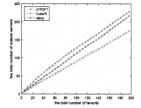 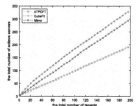 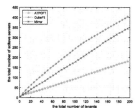

Fig. 2. Packing solutions with $f = 1$ and c following uniform distribution   **Fig. 3.** Packing solutions with $f = 2$ and c following uniform distribution   **Fig. 4.** Packing solutions with $f = 3$ and c following uniform distribution

5   Conclusion

In this paper, we proposed the ATPCFT algorithm to effectively handle multiple simultaneous server failures. The proposed algorithm ensures that the redirected workload does not overload any destination server by requiring fewer servers than the existing approaches. Through theoretical analysis and experimental evaluations, we showed that ATPCFT performs better than existing algorithms and achieves near-optimal replication allocation.

Acknowledgment. We would like to acknowledge the financial support provided by the China Scholarship Council (NO. 201806250168) during Boyu Li's visit to Nanyang Technological University.

References

1. Cheraghlou, M.N., Khadem-Zadeh, A., Haghparast, M.: A survey of fault tolerance architecture in cloud computing. J. Netw. Comput. Appl. **61**, 81–92 (2016)
2. Das, P., Khilar, P.M.: Vft: a virtualization and fault tolerance approach for cloud computing. In: 2013 IEEE Conference on Information & Communication Technologies, pp. 473–478. IEEE (2013)
3. Daudjee, K., Kamali, S., López-Ortiz, A.: On the online fault-tolerant server consolidation problem. In: Proceedings of the 26th ACM Symposium on Parallelism in Algorithms and Architectures, pp. 12–21 (2014)
4. Ganga, K., Karthik, S.: A fault tolerent approach in scientific workflow systems based on cloud computing. In: 2013 International Conference on Pattern Recognition, Informatics and Mobile Engineering, pp. 387–390. IEEE (2013)
5. Kumari, P., Kaur, P.: A survey of fault tolerance in cloud computing. J. King Saud Univ. Comput. Inf. Sci. (2018)
6. Li, H., Li, W., Wang, H., Wang, J.: An optimization of virtual machine selection and placement by using memory content similarity for server consolidation in cloud. Futur. Gener. Comput. Syst. **84**, 98–107 (2018)
7. Li, W., Sun, X., Liao, K., Xia, Y., Chen, F., He, Q.: Maximizing reliability of data-intensive workflow systems with active fault tolerance schemes in cloud. In: 2020 IEEE 13th International Conference on Cloud Computing (CLOUD), pp. 462–469. IEEE (2020)
8. Mate, J., Daudjee, K., Kamali, S.: Robust multi-tenant server consolidation in the cloud for data analytics workloads. In: 2017 IEEE 37th International Conference on Distributed Computing Systems (ICDCS), pp. 2111–2118. IEEE (2017)
9. Mazumdar, S., Pranzo, M.: Power efficient server consolidation for cloud data center. Futur. Gener. Comput. Syst. **70**, 4–16 (2017)
10. Ray, B., Saha, A., Khatua, S., Roy, S.: Proactive fault-tolerance technique to enhance reliability of cloud service in cloud federation environment. IEEE Trans. Cloud Comput. (2020)
11. Xie, X., et al.: AZ-code: an efficient availability zone level erasure code to provide high fault tolerance in cloud storage systems. In: 2019 35th Symposium on Mass Storage Systems and Technologies (MSST), pp. 230–243. IEEE (2019)
12. Xu, X., Mo, R., Dai, F., Lin, W., Wan, S., Dou, W.: Dynamic resource provisioning with fault tolerance for data-intensive meteorological workflows in cloud. IEEE Trans. Industr. Inf. **16**(9), 6172–6181 (2019)

PM2.5 and PM10 Concentration Estimation Based on the Top-of-Atmosphere Reflectance

Lei Zhang, Jie Hao$^{(\boxtimes)}$, and Wenjing Xu

Nanjing University of Aeronautics and Astronautics, Nanjing 211106, China
haojie@nuaa.edu.cn

Abstract. Estimating ground-level PM2.5/10 based on satellite aerosol optical depth (AOD) products is a research hotspot at home and abroad. It has large area and high-density coverage characteristics, making up for the lack of ground monitoring stations. The AOD products are usually retrieved from top-of-atmosphere (TOA) reflectance via an atmospheric radiative transfer model. However, the strict surface assumptions in the AOD retrieval process make it impossible to retrieve AOD effectively in specific regions or periods. Therefore, this paper proposes a method based on machine learning to estimate ground-level PM2.5/10 concentration using TOA reflectance, observation angles and meteorological data, called TOA-PM2.5/10 model, and compares it with the AOD-PM2.5/10 model, whose inputs are AOD data and meteorological data. The comparative results show that the R2, RMSE, and MAE of PM2.5/10 concentration estimated using the TOA-PM2.5/10 model can reach 0.888, 6.158, 3.580 for PM2.5 and 0.889, 13.887, 8.141 for PM10 respectively, which is superior to that of the AOD-PM2.5/10 model.

Keywords: Top-of-Atmosphere Reflectance · AOD · PM2.5/10 · Machine learning

1 Introduction

With the rapid economic development and increasing urbanization level, air pollution is becoming increasingly severe [1]. As two of the major air pollutants, PM2.5 (particulate matter with aerodynamic equivalent diameter below 2.5 um) and PM10 (particulate matter with aerodynamic equivalent diameter below 10 um), seriously affect people's living environment and health and even induce respiratory diseases, cardiovascular, cerebrovascular diseases and various bacterial diseases [2, 3]. At present, the hazy weather in most cities in China is caused by particulate matter pollution. According to the Report on the State of the Ecology and Environment in China 2019, 47.2% of cities nationwide have annual average PM2.5 concentration and 32.0% have annual average PM10 concentration exceeding secondary standards. It can be seen that the air environment management in cities still faces significant challenges. Therefore, it is urgent to monitor

This work is supported in part by the National Key R&D Program of China under Grant 2019YFB2102002, and in part by the Collaborative Innovation Center of Novel Software Technology and Industrialization.

© Springer Nature Switzerland AG 2021
Z. Liu et al. (Eds.): WASA 2021, LNCS 12939, pp. 574–581, 2021.
https://doi.org/10.1007/978-3-030-86137-7_61

the spatial and temporal distribution of atmospheric particulate matter. In China, the monitoring of particulate matter is mainly carried out by the air pollution monitoring stations. Still, the number of stations in each city is limited and unevenly distributed, making it difficult to obtain more accurate PM2.5/10 concentration information in a large area. With the advantages of large spatial coverage, data collection at different scales and less restricted conditions, satellite remote sensing technology can be used to monitor PM2.5/10 distribution in a large area. Researchers often use satellite AOD data to estimate PM2.5/10 since it had been proved that correlated.

Wang et al. [4] used MODIS AOD products and ground-level PM2.5 concentration in a city of Alabama, USA. They found good mutuality with a direct correlation coefficient R of 0.7 and monthly average correlation up to 0.9 or more. According to Gupta et al. [5], MODIS AOD products and ground-level PM2.5 have a relatively good correlation in 26 cities worldwide, where aerosol concentration, relative humidity, cloudiness, and atmospheric boundary layer height are the key influencing factors. Ghotbi S et al. [6] used MODIS 3 km AOD product and meteorological parameters from WRF model to estimate urban ground-level PM10. In addition, many different models have been developed to represent the relationship between AOD and PM2.5/10, such as linear regression [7], geographical weighted regression [8], bayesian [9], random forest [10], deep belief network [11] and a hybrid algorithm [12] and so on. Based on these models, AOD play an important role in the estimation of ground-level PM2.5/10.

In general, PM2.5/10 estimation based on satellite data is usually divided into two steps. The first step is to retrieve the AOD data from TOA reflectance via an atmospheric radiative transfer model. The second step is to establish an estimation model using AOD data and ground-level PM2.5/10 concentration data. However, AOD retrieval itself is a rather tedious and complicated process and requires some strict assumptions, so not only it is impossible to retrieve AOD data at some times or areas, but also it will incur accumulative error in this two-step process.

The purpose of this research is to establish a PM2.5/10 concentration estimation model based on machine learning, using satellite TOA reflectance instead of satellite AOD data to estimate ground-level PM2.5/10. Specifically, we will use the model to establish the relationship between the ground-level PM2.5/10 and TOA reflectance, observation angles, and meteorological factors. Through this end-to-end direct modelling, we can simplify the PM2.5/10 estimation process based on satellite remote sensing data and obtain a more refined model for PM2.5/10 concentration estimation.

2   Data Selection and Preprocessing

In this section, we will introduce the data of interst, including ground-level PM2.5/10 concentration, remote sensing satellite data and meteorological data, as well as data processing methods used in this paper.

2.1   Ground-Level PM2.5/10

The study region of this paper is a city in eastern China. The study period is from October 2020 to January 2021. The hourly ground-level PM2.5/10 concentration data for this city can be obtained from China National Environmental Monitoring Center (CNEMC) website, which has 12 pollutant monitoring stations, and more than 500 self-built pollutant monitoring stations. The distribution of these pollutant monitoring stations is shown in Fig. 1.

Fig. 1. The spatial distribution of pollution monitoring stations.

2.2 Remote Sensing Satellite Data

The satellite remote sensing data in this paper are obtained from the MODIS sensor, the main sensor launched in the NASA-EOS program, with 36 bands in the spectral range of 0.4–14.4 μm and spatial resolutions of 250 m, 500 m, and 1 km. The transit time of these two satellites in China is 10:00–12:00 and 12:00–14:00. In this paper, MYD021 km data of Aqua satellite is selected as satellite remote sensing data, where the spatial resolution of this product is 1 km at the lowest point. Although the AOD retrieval process is skipped in this paper, previous researches have shown that PM2.5/10 is correlated with AOD. The TOA reflectance on bands 1, 3, and 7 (R1, R3, and R7) and observation angles (i.e., sensor azimuth, sensor zenith, solar azimuth, and solar zenith) are usually exploited for the retrieval of AOD via a dark-target-based algorithm [13]. Therefore, the primary inputs of the model established in this paper are also the TOA reflectance and the observation angles. In the extended dark-target-based algorithm [14], the normalized difference vegetation index (NVDI) is also an important parameter for AOD retrieval. Therefore, in this paper, another TOA reflectance on band 2 (R2) is selected to calculate NVDI. The formula is as follows:

$$NVDI = (NIR - R)/(NIR + R). \qquad (1)$$

Where NIR is near infrared band reflectance, R is infrared band reflectance.

In addition, MYD04 3K data is selected as the AOD data sources for comparison in this paper.

2.3 Meteorological Data

The meteorological reanalysis information selected for this paper is the ECMWF publicly available ERA5-Land data. ERA5-Land is a reanalysis dataset with a higher spatial and temporal resolution of hour-by-hour and spatial resolution of $0.1° * 0.1°$ than ERA5. It is shown that the accuracy of the ECMWF reanalysis data is higher than that of the National Center for Environmental Prediction (NCEP) reanalysis data [15, 16]. In this paper, ERA5-Land meteorological data for this city from October 2020 to January 2021 were used, and the meteorological variables included 2 m dew point temperature (d2m), 2 m air temperature (t2m), surface pressure (SP), 10 m longitudinal wind speed (u10) and 10 m latitudinal wind speed (v10). It has been demonstrated that these parameters can influence the relationship between PM2.5/10 and AOD [9–11, 17].

2.4   Data Preprocessing and Matching

Since the model construction requires the correspondence of PM2.5/10 concentration data, satellite remote sensing data and meteorological data, all data need to be pre-processed to form a temporally and spatially consistent data set. In this paper, the TOA reflectance and angles data of MYD021km were geometrically corrected and sampled to the 1 km * 1 km level and then synthesized in the same coordinate system. The AOD data and meteorological data were also geometrically corrected and resampled. Used a cloud detection algorithm to remove cloud covered areas. Extracted satellite remote sensing data and meteorological data of the geographic location of pollutant monitoring stations. For the PM2.5/10 concentration data, selected the average value of the satellite transit time within one hour.

3   Stacking Based TOA-PM2.5/10 Modelling for PM2.5/10 Estimation

In studying the relationship between remote sensing data and PM2.5/10, this paper used TOA reflectance on bands 1, 2, 3, and 7 observation angles, NVDI, and meteorological data (u10, v10, d2m, t2m, and SP) as the independent variables of the PM2.5/10 concentration estimation model. Then the datasets were randomly separated into training dataset (80%) and test dataset (20%) to be applied to the training phase and testing phase of the model, respectively. Based on the same training and test dataset, this paper established TOA-PM2.5/10 concentration estimation models based on stacking model [18] and single ensemble model (Random Forest, XGBoost and LightGBM).

Stacking is a way to ensemble multiple classifications or regression model. In general, it is a matter of training a multi-layer (typically two-layer) learner structure, where the first layer (also called base-model) uses n different classifiers (or models with different parameters) to merge the obtained predictions into a new feature set and use it as input to the next layer (also called meta-model). First, stacking divides the training set into n datasets. Each training takes out $n−1$ copies for the training set and one copy for the validation set and inputs them into each base learner of the layer one prediction model. Each base learner outputs its prediction results on the test set. Stacking generalizes the output of multiple models to improve the overall prediction accuracy.

For the stacking model, Random Forest, XGBoost and LightGBM were selected as the base-model to model the PM2.5/10 concentration estimation, respectively. Using 10-folds and 10-times cross-validations on the training dataset, calculated the average estimation accuracy of these models and determined the model parameters according to the average accuracy maximization criterion. Choosing the SVR model as the meta-model, we feed the output result of the base-model into the meta-model for training, and obtain the final TOA-PM2.5/10 model. The stacking model training process established in this paper is shown in Fig. 2.

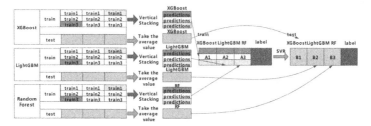

Fig. 2. The training process of TOA-PM2.5/10 model based on stacking.

The correlation coefficient (R2), root mean square error (RMSE) and mean absolute error (MAE) were used as the evaluation metrics of the model performance. Then, selected the optimal model to estimate ground-level PM2.5/10 concentration.

In order to evaluate the established TOA-PM2.5/10 model, this paper compared it with the AOD-PM2.5/10 model, whose inputs were AOD data and meteorological data.

4   Results and Analysis

4.1   Stacking Model vs. Single Ensemble Models

In this experiment, we compare the performance of TOA-PM2.5/10 model based on stacking and single ensemble models. The comparison result is shown in Table 1.

Table 1. Accuracies of the TOA-PM2.5/10 model based on stacking model and single ensemble models.

Models	Aqua-TOA-PM2.5			Aqua-TOA-PM10		
	R2	RMSE $(\mu g/m^3)$	MAE $(\mu g/m^3)$	R2	RMSE $(\mu g/m^3)$	MAE $(\mu g/m^3)$
RF	0.850	6.471	3.660	0.855	14.374	8.021
XGBoost	0.845	6.587	3.987	0.846	14.843	8.744
LightGBM	0.853	6.427	3.894	0.855	14.377	8.692
Stacking	0.860	6.283	3.652	0.862	14.083	8.239

It can be seen that the four models can achieve R2 greater than 0.85 when using satellite TOA reflectance to estimate PM2.5/10 concentration. LightGBM performs best when using a single ensemble model to predict PM2.5, with R2, RMSE and MAE of 0.853, 6.427 and 3.894. Random forest performs best when using a single ensemble model to predict PM10, with R2, RMSE and MAE of 0.855, 14.374 and 8.021. The estimation results indicate the feasibility of estimating PM2.5/10 concentration by modelling directly using TOA reflectance.

When comparing the results of the three single ensemble models and the stacking model, it can be seen that the prediction effect of stacking is significantly better than that of each single ensemble model, with R2, RMSE and MAE of 0.860, 6.283, 3.652 for PM2.5 and 0.862, 14.083, 8.239 for PM10, indicating that the effect of establishing a PM2.5/10 concentration estimation model based on the model fusion strategy (stacking) is better than that of a single ensemble model, and the stacking model is more robust.

4.2 TOA-PM2.5/10 Model vs. AOD-PM2.5/10 Model on Dark-Target Dataset

In this experiment, we compare the performance of TOA-PM2.5/10 model based on stacking and AOD-PM2.5/10 model based on stacking. Since the AOD data used in this study is retrieved based on the dark-target-based algorithm, the data for the following experiments is obtained from the dark target region in order to compare the performance of the AOD-PM2.5/10 and TOA-PM2.5/10 models. The distribution of AOD containing study region on December 21, 2020, is shown in Fig. 3.

Fig. 3. Distribution of AOD containing study region on December 21, 2020.

The AOD retrieval process cannot be performed for the bright areas (masked in black in Fig. 3) in satellite images. Therefore, we extract the TOA reflectance corresponding to the AOD data and establish the TOA-PM2.5/10 concentration estimation model of

Table 2. Accuracies of the TOA-PM2.5/10 and AOD-PM2.5/10 model based on stacking on dark-target dataset.

Models	PM2.5			PM10		
	R2	RMSE ($\mu g/m^3$)	MAE ($\mu g/m^3$)	R2	RMSE ($\mu g/m^3$)	MAE ($\mu g/m^3$)
AOD	0.871	6.536	3.627	0.879	14.640	8.438
Dark-TOA	0.888	6.158	3.580	0.889	13.887	8.141

the dark-target area. The accuracy of estimating PM2.5/10 on the dark target dataset is shown in the Table 2.

The R2, RMSE and MAE of the model for estimating PM2.5 and PM10 concentration are 0.888, 6.158, 3.580 and 0.889, 13.887, 8.141, respectively. Its performance on the dark-target dataset is superior to that of the AOD-PM2.5/10 model, further demonstrating the feasibility of using TOA reflectance and observation angles instead of AOD. Also, the performance lost using the complete TOA data including dark and bright target is limited, which testifies our method is robust, thus it is practicable to use the TOA-PM2.5/10 model for the full coverage PM2.5/10 concentration estimation.

5   Conclusions and Future Work

In this paper, an end-to-end TOA-PM2.5/10 concentration estimation model based on the stacking algorithm was established. The ground-level PM2.5/10 concentration can be estimated directly using TOA reflectance, observation angles, NVDI, and meteorological data while avoiding AOD retrieval. Using the study region as an example, the results show that the stacking model proposed in this paper has a better performance compared with the traditional AOD-PM2.5/10 model. On dark-target dataset, the R2 of the model for estimating PM2.5 and PM10 concentration can reached 0.888 and 0.889 respectively.

Although estimating PM2.5/10 directly from the TOA reflectance has achieved satisfactory performance, the spatial distribution characteristics of PM2.5/10 were not considered in this paper. Geographical factors will be added to the model in future studies to increase the accuracy of the model.

References

1. Gan, T., Liang, W., Yang, H., Liao, X.: The effect of economic development on haze pollution (pm2.5) based on a spatial perspective: urbanization as a mediating variable. J. Clean. Prod. **266**, 121880 (2020)
2. Domingo, J.L., Rovira, J.: Effects of air pollutants on the transmission and severity of respiratory viral infections. Environ. Res. **187**, 109650 (2020)
3. Fanny, W., Ko, S., David, S., Hui, C.: Air pollution and chronic obstructive pulmonary disease. Respirology **17**(3), 395--401 (2012)
4. Wang, J., Christopher, S.A.: Intercomparison between satellite-derived aerosol optical thickness and pm2.5 mass: implications for air quality studies. Geophys. Res. Lett. **30**(21) (2003)
5. Gupta, P., Christopher, S.A., Wang, J., Gehrig, R., Lee, Y., Kumar, N.: Satellite remote sensing of particulate matter and air quality assessment over global cities. Atmos. Environ. **40**(30), 5880–5892 (2006)
6. Ghotbi, S., Sotoudeheian, S., Arhami, M.: Estimating urban ground-level pm10 using modis 3km aod product and meteorological parameters from wrf model. Atmospheric Environment, pp. 333--346 (2016)
7. Yang, L., Park, R.J., Jacob, D.J., Qinbin, L.: Mapping annual mean ground-level pm2.5 concentrations using multiangle imaging spectroradiometer aerosol optical thickness over the contiguous united states. J. Geophys. Res. Atmospheres **109**(D22) (2004)
8. Hu, X., et al.: Estimating ground-level pm2.5 concentrations in the southeastern u.s. using geographically weighted regression. Environ. Res. **121**, 1–10 (2013)

9. Yu, W., Liu, Y., Ma, Z., Bi, J: Improving satellite-based PM2.5 estimates in China using Gaussian processes modeling in a Bayesian hierarchical setting.: Sci. Rep. **7**(1), 2045–2322 (2017)
10. Liu, Y., Cao, G., Zhao, N., Mulligan, K., Ye, X.: Improve ground-level pm2.5 concentration mapping using a random forests-based geostatistical approach. Environmental Pollution (2018)
11. Li, T., Shen, H., Yuan, Q., Zhang, X., Zhang, L.: Estimating ground-level pm2.5 by fusing satellite and station observations: A geo-intelligent deep learning approach. Geophys. Res. Lett. **44**(23), 11985–11993 (2017)
12. Ferrero, L., et al.: Satellite aod conversion into ground pm10, pm2.5 and pm1 over the po valley (milan, italy) exploiting information on aerosol vertical profiles, chemistry, hygroscopicity and meteorology. Atmospheric Pollution Res. **10**(6), 1895–1912 (2019)
13. Kaufman, Y.J., Tanré, D., Remer, L.A., Vermote, E.F., Chu, A., Holben, B.N.: Operational remote sensing of tropospheric aerosol over land from eos moderate resolution imaging spectroradiometer. J. Geophys. Res. Atmospheres **102**(D14), 51–17 (1997)
14. Levy, R.C., et al.: Global evaluation of the collection 5 modis dark-target aerosol products over land. Atmospheric Chemistry and Physics (2010)
15. Decker, M., Brunke, M.A., Wang, Z., Sakaguchi, K., Zeng, X., Bosilovich, M.G.: Evaluation of the reanalysis products from gsfc, ncep, and ecmwf using flux tower observations. J. Clim. **25**(6), 1916–1944 (2010)
16. Chen, Q.M., Song, S.L., Zhu, W.Y.: An analysis for the accuracy of tropospheric zenith delay calculated from ecmwf/ncep data over asia. Chin. J. Geophys. **55**(3), 275–283 (2012)
17. Fang, X., Zou, B., Liu, X., Sternberg, T., Zhai, L.: Satellite-based ground pm2.5 estimation using timely structure adaptive modeling. Remote Sens. Environ. **186**, 152--163 (2016)
18. Agarwal, S., Chowdary, C.R.: A-stacking and a-bagging: adaptive versions of ensemble learning algorithms for spoof fingerprint detection. Expert Syst. Appl. **146**, 113160 (2019)

A Secure Sensing Data Collection Mechanism Based on Perturbed Compressed Sensing

Xiaomeng Lu[1], Wenjing Xu[1], Jie Hao[1,2(✉)], and Xiaoming Yuan[3]

[1] Nanjing University of Aeronautics and Astronautics, Nanjing 211106, Jiangsu, China
haojie@nuaa.edu.cn
[2] Collaborative Innovation Center of Novel Software Technology and Industrialization, Nanjing 211106, Jiangsu, China
[3] HUAWEI Technologies CO., LTD., Nanjing 210000, Jiangsu, China

Abstract. The security mechanisms have always been a research concern in Wireless Sensor Networks (WSNs). In the last decade, compressed sensing (CS) has been introduced in the design of security mechanisms thanks to its capability of compressing and encrypting the original data simultaneously, especially in a large scale multi-hop WSN. Although there have been extensive research work in CS for privacy protection, CS for data authentication, integrity, and etc. have been neglected. This paper aims to propose a security mechanism which can jointly achieve confidentiality, authentication and integrity without introducing additional communication overhead. Specifically, we introduce perturbations for encryption and authentication to perturb the original data. Extensive experiments based on real-life datasets are conducted which verify the proposed mechanism can protect the data privacy, achieve authentication and integrity in WSNs.

Keywords: Wireless sensor networks · Compressed sensing · Perturbation · Data encryption · Data authentication

1 Introduction

In a data collection application scenario, a wireless sensor network (WSN) usually deploys a number of sensor nodes to take measurements, and wirelessly transmit them to the sink node via multiple hops. During wireless transmission, WSN faces the security problems including eavesdropping, data falsification and so on. As the original data can be captured to falsify/tamper the original data or infer the private information [1], security mechanisms in WSNs have been a research concern in recent decades. A straightforward design thought is directly following the security mechanisms in wireless networks. However, the constrained resource of WSNs calls for more lightweight mechanisms suitable for WSNs.

This work is supported in part by the National Key R&D Program of China under Grant 2019YFB2102002, and in part by the Collaborative Innovation Center of Novel Software Technology and Industrialization. The work by Xiaoming Yuan was accomplished when he was a master student in Nanjing University of Aeronautics and Astronautics.

© Springer Nature Switzerland AG 2021
Z. Liu et al. (Eds.): WASA 2021, LNCS 12939, pp. 582–593, 2021.
https://doi.org/10.1007/978-3-030-86137-7_62

Compressed sensing (CS) [2, 3] is a promising tool for data compression in WSNs as it can compress the original data with a much lower rate than Nyquist frequency. Recently, CS has drawn increasing attentions for its potential in data security. As in a WSN, when using CS the sender transmits compressed data, i.e., linearly projected data on the wireless channel. If the compression method is encrypted, the data in the wireless channel are encrypted, too. Although CS is not perfect to guarantee encryption, literature [4] has proved that it requires overwhelmingly high amount of computation to infer the original data, which is even impossible in practice. The related work mainly studies the encryption capacity achieved by CS [1, 4] against the attacks including brute force attack [4], structural attack [4], PCA analysis [5], and etc.

However, encryption is not the only security requirement in WSNs. Authentication is also a key issue to be addressed. Compared with the rich body of research work on encryption, only a few studies explore the usage of CS in data authentication [6–8]. A well-known authentication mechanism in traditional networks is Message Authentication Code (MAC) [9, 10], which adds MAC for authentication in the end of the original data. Apparently MAC based authentication incurs extra communication overhead. On the contrary, CS can achieve authentication along with encryption by its random sensing matrix in a single hop network [6–8]. What's more, CS based encryption and authentication dose not introduce any extra communication overhead.

However, this method proposed in [6–8] only considers the single-hop network topology which is not applied for the multi-hop scenarios. In a multi-hop network, all sensor nodes generally share the same sensing matrix or know the statistical characteristics of the sensing matrix. After receiving the compressed data, the receiver can reconstruct the original data or detect the statistical information through the common sensing matrix. Therefore, there may exist a risk of privacy information leakage in the multi-hop network.

To address this security risk in a multi-hop WSN, we propose a security mechanism which can jointly encrypt and authenticate the original data. We assume the nodes in the network have certain reliability, i.e., the data compression and forwarding at nodes are faithful, but the nodes are also interested in and want to detect the data characteristics of the other nodes. This scenario is also common in crowdsensing based on social networks. At the same time, there may be illegal nodes in the network to eavesdrop on private data, or to falsify or tamper data. For this application scenario, we need to design a data security mechanism suitable for multi-hop networks, which can be used for encryption, authentication and integrity guarantee without introducing additional overhead. Each receiving node cannot recover the original data or infer the privacy statistics and it also performs data authentication and integrity assurance. To this end, we introduce two perturbations in the original data, namely encryption perturbation and authentication perturbation, which are used to hide private information and data authentication, respectively. We also study the impact of perturbation parameters on security performance.

The rest of this paper is organized as follows. Section 2 introduces the related work of this paper; Sect. 3 presents the preliminaries; Sect. 4 details the proposed security mechanism; Sect. 5 presents the evaluation results of the proposed security mechanism; and Sect. 6 concludes this paper.

2 Related Work

When applying CS in a WSN, a sender usually compresses the original data before transmission. Since the data transmitted on the wireless channel are not the original data, but a small number of projections of the original data based on the random sensing matrix, it is naturally encrypted. Literature [4] verifies the confidentiality of CS and points out that CS cannot provide perfect confidentiality. But if the eavesdropper does not know the random sensing matrix used by CS, the amount of computation required to recover the original data is overwhelmingly huge. Therefore, CS can provide encryption service if the random sensing matrix is established as a shared key between the sensor and the Sink. Compared with porting traditional encryption methods in WSNs [11–13], CS is suitable for resource limited WSNs as it can simultaneously reduce the amount of data and encrypt it. Thus, CS for security become a hot topic in recent years.

Some research work theoretically studies the security performance of CS. The literature [4] proves that CS's ability to resist brute-force attacks and structured attacks is extremely high, and it can protect the privacy as well. The literature [14–16] assumes that the noise/perturbation conforms to a certain characteristic, and proves that the use of dictionary learning, PCA, frequency domain filtering and other methods can eliminate the noise/perturbation interference and recover the original signal with a high accuracy. Although these work does not clarify its relationship with security, on the other hand, their research proves that if the noise/perturbation is small enough, the eavesdropper is likely to obtain the original data. Therefore, if data encryption is to be performed by perturbation, it is necessary to increase the perturbation amplitude to reduce the possibility of recovery. Some work [6, 16] clearly states that if the perturbation is independent of the original data, adding perturbation does not guarantee data confidentiality. To enhance confidentiality, noise/perturbation is required to own the characteristics dependent on the original data [6]. This makes it impossible for the eavesdropper to separate the raw data from the noise/perturbation. But this method also allows the eavesdroppers to obtain data distribution characteristics and infer private information. Other studies have added perturbations in the random sensing matrix [17], which reduces the probability of the eavesdropper acquiring the real random sensing matrix, thereby enhancing the security of the data.

There is also some work to study CS-based encryption algorithms in different application scenarios [18–20]. Literature [18, 19] mainly studies the use of CS technology to protect user location privacy in the crowdsourcing mechanism. Literature [20] focuses on CS- based security for voice signals and image data. These efforts have proved that compressed sensing can achieve better anti-attack and anti-eavesdropping capabilities in specific practical applications. For example, the literature [18] improves the positioning error from 50 m to 9000 m by CS encryption, which protects the user's true position information. For the privacy-sensitive data in the wireless audit network, [14] pointed out that the eavesdropper can infer the user's private information and they introduce a perturbation to hide the original data characteristics [1].

Although there has been a lot of research on CS-based data confidentiality, there is few work on the other security issues, such as data authentication. Previous studies have focused on CS adding watermarks on pictures [6–8]. The receiver can perform data authentication before data reconstruction, which can effectively protect against attacks such as data tampering and forgery. However, this method is only applicable to the single-hop networks of the user-sink. In a multi-hop network, the receiver can recover the original data through a common sensing matrix, so there may be a problem of privacy information leakage.

This paper proposes a lightweight perturbation-based security mechanism for wireless multi-hop networks. It allows simultaneous data encryption and authentication without introducing additional overhead. Therefore, it can effectively prevent privacy leakage, data forgery, tampering, and so on.

3 Preliminaries

Given a WSN, n sensors are deployed to sense the environment periodically, i.e., each node takes a sample and produces one data packet in each cycle, transmit the packet to sink via multi-hop routing. As a result, in one cycle sink will collect n data packets. Thanks to the spatial correlation, in fact only $m \ll n$ compressed data packets are required to reconstruct the original n data packets according to CS. Mathematically, a signal $x_{n \times 1}$ (consisting of the n data packets generated by all sensor nodes) can be compressed to $y_{m \times 1} = \phi_{m \times n} x_{n \times 1}$, where $\phi_{m \times n}$ is referred to as sensing matrix, which is usually Gaussian random. Upon the reception of $y_{m \times 1}$, $x_{n \times 1}$ can be reconstructed by solving

$$\min_{\tilde{s} \in R^N} ||\tilde{s}||_o \quad s.t. \quad y_{m \times 1} = \phi_{m \times n} \Psi_{n \times n} \tilde{s}_{n \times 1}.$$

$$\tilde{x}_{n \times 1} = \Psi_{n \times n} \tilde{s}_{n \times 1} \tag{1}$$

where $\Psi_{n \times n}$ is a sparse basis.

Although the proposed mechanism can work with any transmission scheme, we present how it works based on a classic CS-based data transmission scheme CDG [21] to facilitate understanding. Let $d = [d_1, d_2, ..., d_n]^T$ be the data vector produced by nodes $s_1, ..., s_n$. With CS, each sensor node s_i sends out m weighted data $\phi_{subtree(i)} d_{subtree(i)}$, where $subtree(i)$ is the subtree with s_i as the root node, $d_{subtree(i)}$ is composed of the data packets from the nodes on $subtree(i)$, i.e., $d_{subtree(i)} = [d_k | k \in subtree(i)]$ and $\phi_{subtree(i)}$ is the matrix consisting of the involved columns of the sensing matrix $\phi_{m \times n}$. For example in Fig. 1, s_3 transmits $\phi_{subtree(3)} d_{subtree(3)} = [\phi_1, \phi_2, \phi_3][d_1, d_2, d_3]^T$, where ϕ_i is the i-th column of matrix $\phi_{m \times n}$. In this way, sink obtains m compressed data packets, i.e., $\phi_{m \times n} d$. As CDG only requires $O(mn)$ transmissions in total and each sensor node takes the same transmissions, it is more energy efficient and balanced than the transmission schemes without CS with roughly $O(n(n-1)/2)$ transmissions.

Now we discuss the security risks in the transmission procedure when using CDG. Firstly, the nodes in the network can recover the data of the other nodes through the shared sense matrix, which infringes on the privacy of the other sensor nodes. Secondly, it is easy for the eavesdropper to learn the statistical characteristics of the original data, especially the data at the leaf nodes. Thirdly, the forged or falsified data highly affect the data recovery quality, especially when the forgery or falsification happens near sink. Thus data authentication is in urgent need. The following section will detail how the proposed mechanism addresses these security risks without extra communication overhead.

4 Perturbed CS Based Security Mechanism

In this section, we will first briefly describe the working process of the security mechanism based on perturbed CS as shown in Fig. 1, and then introduce in detail how the mechanism is used for data confidentiality and data authentication.

4.1 Overview

To address the security issues as mentioned in Sect. 3, we introduce two types of perturbations, i.e., encryption perturbation and authentication perturbation. After receiving the data packets from its children, each node s_i compresses the sum of its own data packet and two perturbations p_i^c and p_i^a, adds the result to the received data, and finally sends it out, where p_i^c is the encryption perturbation and p_i^a is the authentication perturbation.

To achieve security, three types of keys exist as shown in the following:

- key_ϕ for producing the random sensing matrix ϕ, which is shared by all sensor nodes and sink;
- key_i^c for producing the encryption perturbation p_i^c, which is shared by node s_i and sink, i.e., each sensor node does not know the encryption perturbation key of the other nodes;
- key_i^a for generating the authentication perturbation p_i^a, shared by node s_i and its parent. For example, in Fig. 1(a), key_1^a is only known by s_1 and its parent s_3.

p_i^c is a random sequence that conforms to a uniform distribution; p_i^a is a random sequence of values $\pm\alpha$ ($\alpha > 0$), which is independent of p_i^c.

Now we briefly introduce how the security mechanism works as shown in Fig. 1(a). Compared with Eq. (1), the data packet sent by node s_i includes two perturbations as follows:

$$x_i = \left[\sum_{s_k \in subtree(s_i)} \phi_k(d_k + p_k^c) + \phi_i p_i^a \right] \tag{2}$$

$$= \phi_{subtree(i)}\left(d_{subtree(i)} + p_{subtree(i)}^c \right) + \phi_i \cdot p_i^a$$

where $p_{subtree(i)}^c = [p_k^c | s_k \in subtree(s_i)]$, operator $\bullet$ indicates that the corresponding elements of the two vectors are multiplied.

Upon the reception of x_i at the parent node, the parent node s_j firstly carries out data authentication. If the authentication succeeds at parent s_j, s_j first removes the authentication perturbation from the received data x_i and hence $\phi_{subtree(i)}\left(d_{subtree(i)} + p_{subtree(i)}^c \right)$ remains. The data generated by s_j is added to the authentication perturbation p_j^a and the encryption perturbation p_j^c and then weighted using the sensing matrix. Thus $\phi_j \cdot (d_j + p_j^c + p_j^a)$ is produced. The data that s_j should send is the aggregation of the data (in which the authentication perturbation is removed) from all children and its own weighted data. Therefore,

$$x_j = \left[\phi_{subtree(j)}\left(d_{subtree(j)} + p_{subtree(j)}^c \right) + \phi_j \cdot p_j^a \right]$$

$$= \sum_{s_k \in subtree(s_i)} \phi_k(d_k + p_k^c) + \phi_i p_i^a. \tag{3}$$

In the end, s_j transmits x_j to its parent node.

If the authentication fails at the parent node s_j, it implies that a false data attack might happen. The working procedure at each node is shown in Fig. 1(b).

Since a parent node does not know the encryption perturbation key of its child nodes, the data characteristics of the child nodes cannot be inferred. Hence, the encryption perturbation can prevent data privacy leakage. Below we will detail how encryption perturbation and authentication perturbation works, respectively.

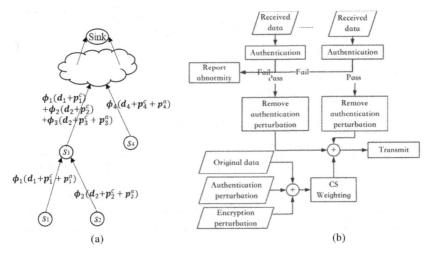

Fig. 1. Secure transmission process: (a) of the entire network; (b) at each node.

4.2 Encryption Perturbation

We first analyze the privacy leakage risk in CS when there is no perturbation. It is assumed that each element of the Gaussian sensing matrix is independently and identically distributed, with statistical properties of mean 0 and variance $\sigma^2 = \frac{1}{m}$.

For leaf nodes, the raw data can be easily obtained. Taking s_1 in Fig. 1(a) with pure CS as an example, the data packets received by s_3 is $\{\phi_{11}d_1, \phi_{21}d_1, \ldots, \phi_{m1}d_1\}$, and s_3 can easily calculate the original data according to the shared ϕ. The eavesdropper can obtain the variance as v, thus obtaining the original data $d_1 = \sqrt{v/\sigma^2}$.

For the other nodes, when a parent receives the data of its child node s_i as x_i, s_i can calculate the original data of the node on its subtree $d_{subtree(s_i)} = [d_{i_1}, d_{i_2}, \ldots, d_{i_k}]^T$ according to the shared ϕ, where $i_1, \ldots, i_k \in subtree(s_i)$. The eavesdropper can guess the mean and variance range of d based on x_i. For the j th data in x_i as:

$$x_{ij} = \phi_{ji_1}d_{i_1} + \phi_{ji_2}d_{i_2} + \cdots + \phi_{ji_k}d_{i_k}, \tag{4}$$

the eavesdropper can infer the variance of x_{ij} as

$$v(x_{ij}) = \frac{1}{m}\sum_{l=1}^{k} d_{i_l}^2, \tag{5}$$

and further

$$v(\boldsymbol{x}_i) \approx v(x_{ij}), \tag{6}$$

$$\sum_{l=1}^{k} d_{i_l}^2 = mv(\boldsymbol{x}_i), \tag{7}$$

where $v(*)$ represents the variance of $*$. Also as known as

$$\frac{1}{k}\sqrt{\sum_{l=1}^{k} d_{i_l}^2} \leq \overline{d} \leq \frac{1}{\sqrt{k}}\sqrt{\sum_{l=1}^{k} d_{i_l}^2} \tag{8}$$

the eavesdropper can get

$$\frac{1}{k}\sqrt{mv(\boldsymbol{x}_i)} \leq \overline{d} \leq \frac{1}{\sqrt{k}}\sqrt{mv(\boldsymbol{x}_i)}. \tag{9}$$

Similarly, the standard deviation of $\boldsymbol{d}$ can be obtained as:

$$\sqrt{\frac{1}{(k-1)}\sum_{l=1}^{k} \left(d_{i_l} - \overline{d}\right)^2} \approx \sqrt{\frac{1}{k}\sum_{l=1}^{k} d_{i_l}^2 - \overline{d}^2} \leq \frac{\sqrt{k-1}}{k}\sqrt{mv(\boldsymbol{x}_i)}. \tag{10}$$

Now, the eavesdropper can guess the range of the mean and variance of the original data. In particular, the eavesdropper at sink can obtain the range of the mean and standard deviation of the original data of the whole network, which is sometimes privacy relevant [1].

It can be seen from the above analysis that if the perturbation is not added, the traditional transmission mechanism based on CS has a privacy leakage risk.

To address the risk, the proposed scheme introduces encryption perturbation. Since the encryption perturbation is only known by the node itself and sink, any node in the network cannot reconstruct the data of the other nodes, and the encryption perturbation also makes it more difficult for the eavesdropper to infer the data characteristics. The effect of the encryption perturbation will be detailed further in the evaluation section.

4.3 Data Authentication

Data authentication is implemented based on the authentication perturbation shared between the parent node and its children. The basic principle is that any two different (pseudo) random sequences are ideally not correlated. Since the parent node s_t and the child node s_i share the key of the authentication perturbation, the authentication perturbation $\boldsymbol{p}_i^a$ of the child node can be repeatedly generated and the authentication watermark $\boldsymbol{w}_i^a = \phi_i \cdot \boldsymbol{p}_i^a$ can also be generated. Among all the components of received $\boldsymbol{x}_i$, $\boldsymbol{p}_i^a$ has only correlation with $\boldsymbol{p}_i^a$, and has no correlation with the original data and encryption perturbations. After receiving the data $\boldsymbol{x}_i$ of the child node s_i, the parent node will calculate $\boldsymbol{x}_i \cdot \boldsymbol{w}_i^a$ and check its operation result.

For the reader's understanding, we start with explaining the data authentication process from the leaf node. At the leaf node s_i, if there is no authentication perturbation $\boldsymbol{p}_i^a$

in the child node data x_i, then $x_i \cdot w_i^a = x_i \cdot \left(\phi_i \cdot p_i^a\right) = \left[\phi_i \cdot (d_i + p_i^c)\right] \cdot \left(\phi_i \cdot p_i^a\right)$ has a mean of 0; only when there is p_i^a in the received data x_i,

$$x_i \cdot w_i^a = x_i \cdot \left(\phi_i \cdot p_i^a\right) = \left[\phi_i \cdot (d_i + p_i^c + p_i^a)\right] \cdot \left(\phi_i \cdot p_i^a\right), \tag{11}$$

has different statistical properties. Therefore, after receiving the data x_i of s_i, the parent node s_j can perform data authentication by checking the statistical characteristics of $x_i \cdot w_i^a$, and complete data authentication by a statistical distribution testing. We adopt a statistical distribution as defined in [7, 23]

$$q_i = \frac{x_i^T w_i^a}{V \sqrt{m}} = \frac{M \sqrt{m}}{V} \tag{12}$$

where $M = \frac{\sum_{j=1}^m x_{ij} w_{ij}}{m}$, $V^2 = \frac{\sum_{j=1}^m (x_{ij} w_{ij} - M)^2}{m-1}$, x_{ij} is the j th element of x_i, $w_i^a = \phi_i \cdot p_i^a$, and w_{ij} is the jth element of w_i^a. If p_i^a is not included in x_i, q_i follows the normal distribution $N(0, 1)$, i.e., $q_i \sim N(0, 1)$ in the case of large samples exist; if p_i^a is included in x_i, then $q_i \sim N(\mu_i, 1)$ with $\mu_i > 0$. Therefore, we can judge whether the authentication perturbation is embedded in the received data packets by testing the statistical characteristics of the operation result.

Similarly, in an ideal case, if a non-leaf node s_i sends x_i as shown in Eq. (3) to its parent, $q_i \sim N(\mu_i, 1)$ with $\mu_i > 0$ only when x_i contains p_i^a; otherwise $q_i \sim N(0, 1)$. Thus authentication (i.e., statistical distribution testing) is equivalent to comparing whether q_i is close to $N(0, 1)$ or $N(\mu_i, 1)$. Therefore, we need to choose the parameters such that the two distributions have an extremely low probability of overlapping. One method is to compare the mean value of q_i with 0 and μ_i, if the mean value is closer to 0, the authentication fails; otherwise, the authentication succeeds. As we know the probability that $P(x < 3.5) = 99.98\%$ under $N(0, 1)$, we require $\mu_i > 7$ in this paper and choose a threshold 3.5 to judge whether authentication succeeds. In the evaluation section, we will describe how the parameters are set to ensure a sufficient μ_i. Another method is to use Kullback-Leibler divergence to measure the distribution distance between the distribution of q_i and the two normal distributions. In this paper, we exploit the first method since it can achieve a good enough performance.

4.4 Working Procedure Summary

Figure 1(a) summarizes the working flow. The leaf node s_1 transmits $x_1 = \phi_1 \cdot (d_1 + p_1^c + p_1^a)$ to its parent s_3. On one hand, as s_3 is not aware of p_1^c, the data characteristics of s_1 cannot be detected by s_3. On the other hand, s_1 and s_3 share the authentication key, p_1^a and further w_1^a can be re-produced at s_3. For authentication, s_3 checks the statistical characteristics of $x_1 \cdot w_1^a$. By comparing if the mean value of $x_1 \cdot w_1^a$ is larger or smaller than 3.5, s_3 decides if the received data is legal and whether it is forged. In the same way, s_3 performs authentication upon the data from s_2. After receiving the data packets from all its children, s_3 removes w_1^a from x_1 and w_2^a from x_2, and adds its own data and authentication perturbation. Finally, s_3 transmits $\sum_{s_k \in subtree(s_3)} \phi_k \cdot (d_k + p_k^c) + \phi_3 \cdot p_3^a$. All the other nodes carry out the same operation until all data packets reach sink.

5 Numeric Evaluation

In this section, we conduct experiments to assess the performance of the proposed data
security mechanism in terms of privacy protection and authentication. Compressed sensing uses a Gaussian random matrix as the random sensing matrix, Discrete Cosine Transform (DCT) as the sparse basis and Basic Pursuit (BP) algorithm as the reconstruction
algorithm. The Mersenne Twister pseudo-random number generator (PRNG) is used to
generate the encryption perturbation and authentication perturbation sequence.

5.1 Data Privacy Protection

This subsection assesses the data privacy protection performance achieved by using perturbation. Since the situation at the leaf node is relatively simple, in this experiment, we
only highlight how the encryption perturbation at sink works against the eavesdropper
inferring the data characteristics. This experiment selects the temperature data collected
by the 508 weather stations [24] for verification, i.e., n = 508. It is assumed that the
eavesdropper will accumulate a large amount of observation data and calculate the statistical characteristics (expectation and standard deviation) of the raw data according to
the method in [1]. We also vary the amplitude of the encryption perturbation to observe
its impact on the performance. We choose $p \in \{15, 25, 35, 45\}$ and $r \in \{1, 2, 3, 4, 5\}$
where p is the mean value of the encryption perturbation and r denotes the perturbation
range, respectively. Here, p and r are set depending on the normalized raw data.

Table 1. Privacy protection performance on the statistical properties of raw data

	Expectation	Standard deviation
Raw data	19.045	6.936
$p = 0$	[0.9, 20.2]	≤ 20.249
$p = 15$	[14.8, 333.8]	≤ 333.503
$p = 25$	[23.7, 533.7]	≤ 533.233
$p = 35$	[32.5, 733.7]	≤ 733.003
$p = 45$	[41.4, 933.7]	≤ 932.786

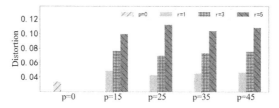

Fig. 2. Comparison of the distortion of recovered data under different encryption level

In Table 1, we fix $r = 3$. It is shown that in the absence of perturbation ($p = 0$), the
eavesdropper can accurately infer the boundary of the statistical characteristics of the

raw data. The higher p, the farther of the inference result from the ground truth. This result suggests us a high enough encryption perturbation [14–16], e.g., $p \geq 15$.

Figure 2 evaluates the trade-off between privacy protection performance and data distortion, in which data distortion is expressed as:

$$\varepsilon = \|\boldsymbol{d} - \boldsymbol{d}^r\|_2 / \|\boldsymbol{d}\|_2 \tag{13}$$

where $\boldsymbol{d}$ is the original data and $\boldsymbol{d}^r$ is the reconstructed data. It can be seen from Fig. 2 that the encryption perturbation increases the distortion slightly. However, we believe it is worthwhile compared with the improvement in terms of privacy protection. Therefore, considering the trade-off between the encryption strength and the distortion, we adopt a fixed p of 25 and r of 3 in the following experiments.

5.2 Data Authentication

According to the analysis of μ in [7] and also from Eq. (12), if x_i is authenticated, its corresponding $\mu_i \approx \alpha \|\phi_i \cdot \boldsymbol{p}_i^a\|_2 \sqrt{m} / \| \sum_{s_k \in ST(s_i)} \phi_k \cdot (\boldsymbol{d}_k + \boldsymbol{p}_k^c)\|_2$. Therefore, the larger α and m and the smaller k, where k is the subtree size, the larger μ_i, and the more likely that the authentication perturbation can be detected. The effects of α and k on performance are detailed below.

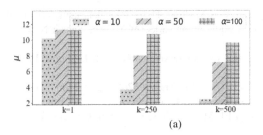 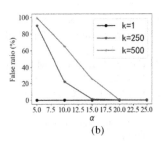

(a)   (b)

Fig. 3. The impact of k and α on the authentication results.

We first fix the sample rate as 0.5, i.e., $m = 0.5n$ and vary α and k to show their impact. To assess the performance statistically, we generate random network topologies 1000 times. In Fig. 3, the statistic of q is calculated based on the 1000 trials, which uses the raw data from [24] and randomly generated Gaussian sensing matrix. We refer to the hypnosis authentication perturbation exist as H_1 and otherwise H_0.

We collect the values of q under H_1 and H_0 of the nodes with its subtree size of k and plot the mean value μ and false ratio in Fig. 3(a) and Fig. 3(b), respectively. The false ratio is defined as the sum of False Positive ratio and True Negative ratio, i.e., the ratio of q under H_1 less than 3.5 and q under H_0 exceeding 3.5. $k = 1$ means we collect the statistics of q from leaf nodes. For $k = 250$, we divide the network into two subtrees each containing 250 sensor nodes and for $k = 500$ we collect the statistics of q from sink.

From Fig. 3(a), we can see that μ decreases with increasing k, which conforms to the analysis in Section IV-C. This implies that we need to tune the parameters to obtain a sufficiently high q under H_1 for each sensor node, in particular for the sensor nodes near the collection tree root. We simply choose a large α to achieve this. With a large α (e.g., $\alpha = 100$), the decrease of μ with increasing k is restrained. Even when $k = 500$, we still have $\mu = 9.6$ under $\alpha = 100$.

The false ratio in Fig. 3(b) shows us that the value of α can be lowered in practice. The false ratio under $k = 500$ reaches zero with α grows to 25. Considering a larger α also enhances the data confidentiality, it is highly recommended that α higher than 25 is chosen. Obviously, α should be increased along with the network size.

6 Conclusion

In this paper, we propose a data security mechanism based on perturbed CS for WSNs. By introducing encryption perturbation and authentication perturbation, privacy protection, authenticity and integrity can be achieved simultaneously without any additional overhead. The experiment results demonstrate that the proposed security mechanism has low resource consumption and low distortion and can be applied to any multi-hop wireless sensor network with data correlation.

References

1. Tan, R., Chiu, S.Y., Nguyen, H.H., Yau, D.K.Y., Jung, D.: A joint data compression and encryption approach for wireless energy auditing networks. ACM Tran. Sensor Networks, **13**(2), 1–32 (2017)
2. Candes, E.J., Wakin, M.B.: An introduction to compressive sampling. IEEE Signal Process. Mag. **25**(2), 21–30 (2008)
3. Donoho, D.L.: Compressed sensing. IEEE Trans. Inf. Theory **52**(4), 1289–1306 (2006)
4. Orsdemir, A., Altun, H.O., Sharma, G., Bocko, M.F.: On the security and robustness of encryption via compressed sensing. In: IEEE Military Communications Conference, pp.1–7 (2008)
5. Huang, Z., Du, W., Chen, B.: Deriving private information from randomized data. In: ACM SIGMOD International Conference on Management of Data, pp. 37–48 (2005)
6. Valenzise, G., Tagliasacchi, M., Tubaro, S., Cancelli, G., Barni, M.: A compressive-sensing based watermarking scheme for sparse image tampering identification. In: IEEE International Conference on Image Processing, pp. 1265–1268 (2009)
7. Hu, G., Di, X., Tao, X., Bai, S., Zhang, Y.: A compressive sensing based privacy preserving outsourcing of image storage and identity authentication service in cloud. Inf. Sci. **387**, 132–145 (2017)
8. Wang, Q., Zeng, W., Tian, J.: A compressive sensing based secure watermark detection and privacy preserving storage framework. IEEE Trans. Image Process. **23**(3), 1317–1328 (2014)
9. Wang, Y., Attebury, G., Ramamurthy, B.: A survey of security issues in wireless sensor networks. IEEE Commun. Surv. Tutorials **8**(2), 2–23 (2006)
10. Perrig, A., Szewczyk, R., Tygar, J.D., et al.: SPINS: security protocols for sensor networks. Wireless Netw. **8**(5), 521–534 (2002)
11. Elhoseny, M., Yuan, X., El-Minir, H.K., et al.: An energy efficient encryption method for secure dynamic WSN. Secur. Commun. Networks **9**(13), 2024–2031 (2016)
12. Lu, Y., Zhai, J., Zhu, R., et al.: Study of wireless authentication center with mixed encryption in WSN. J. Sensors **3**, 1–7 (2016)

13. Chu, C.K., Liu, J.K., Zhou, J., et al.: Practical ID-based encryption for wireless sensor network. ACM, pp. 337–340 (2010)
14. Yang, Z., Zhang, C., Xie, L.: Robustly stable signal recovery in compressed sensing with structured matrix perturbation. IEEE Trans. Signal Process. **60**(9), 4658–4671 (2012)
15. Herman, M.A., Strohmer, T.: General deviants: an analysis of perturbations in compressed sensing. IEEE J. Sel. Top. Signal Process. **4**(2), 342–349 (2010)
16. Kargupta, H., Datta, S., Wang, Q., et al.: On the privacy preserving properties of random data perturbation techniques. In: IEEE International Conference on Data Mining, p. 99 (2003)
17. Aldroubi, A., Chen, X., Powell, A.M.: Perturbations of measurement matrices and dictionaries in compressed sensing. Appl. Comput. Harmon. Anal. **33**(2), 282–291 (2012)
18. Kong, L., He, L., Liu, X.Y., et al.: Privacy-preserving compressive sensing for crowdsensing based trajectory recovery. In: IEEE International Conference on Distributed Computing Systems, pp. 31–40 (2015)
19. Zhang, Z., Jin, C., Li, M., Zhu, L.: A perturbed compressed sensing protocol for crowd sensing. Mobile Information Systems, pp. 1–9 (2016)
20. Cambareri, V., Mangia, M., Pareschi, F., et al.: Low-complexity multiclass encryption by compressed sensing. IEEE Trans. Signal Process. **63**(9), 2183–2195 (2015)
21. Luo, C., Wu, F., Sun, J., et al.: Compressive data gathering for large-scale wireless sensor networks. In: ACM International Conference on Mobile Computing and Networking, pp. 145–156 (2009)
22. Liu, K., Giannella, C., Kargupta, H.: A Survey of Attack Techniques on Privacy-Preserving Data Perturbation Methods. Privacy-Preserving Data Mining. Springer US, pp. 583–587 (2008)
23. Zhang, W., Liu, Y., Das, S.K., et al.: Secure data aggregation in wireless sensor networks: a watermark based authentication supportive approach. Pervasive Mob. Comput. **4**(5), 658–680 (2008)
24. https://data.gov.au/dataset/82e2ab28-5437-456f-aca2-fd23ce41cd37

Correction to: Performance Analysis of V2V-Based Vehicular Platoon with Modified CACC Scheme

Siyuan Zhou, Liangliang Xiang, and Guoping Tan

Correction to:
Chapter "Performance Analysis of V2V-Based Vehicular Platoon with Modified CACC Scheme" in: Z. Liu et al. (Eds.): *Wireless Algorithms, Systems, and Applications*, **LNCS 12939, https://doi.org/10.1007/978-3-030-86137-7_52**

In the originally published chapter 52 the Figure 3 did not present the information correctly. The Figure 3 has been corrected by adding a blue dotted line to the graph.

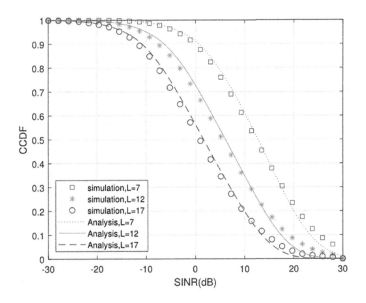

Fig. 3. The CCDF with the SINR derived in (7)

The updated version of this chapter can be found at
https://doi.org/10.1007/978-3-030-86137-7_52

Author Index

Printed in the United States
by Baker & Taylor Publisher Services